Housing Act 1988

with annotations by

Andrew Arden,
LL.B., Barrister,

Caroline Hunter,
B.A., Barrister

LONDON
SWEET & MAXWELL
1989

Published in 1989 by
Sweet & Maxwell Limited of,
11 New Fetter Lane, London,
and printed in Great Britain
by The Eastern Press Limited
of London and Reading

British Library Cataloguing in Publication Data

Great Britain
  [Housing Act 1988]. Housing Act 1988. — Current law
  statutes annotated reprints.
  1. Great Britain. Housing. Law, — Statutes
  I. [Housing Act 1988]   II. Arden, Andrew, *1948—*
  III. Hunter, Caroline   IV. Series
  344.104'63635'02633

  ISBN 0-421-40920-7

CONTENTS

Housing Act 1988

TABLE OF CASES

References are to section numbers of the Housing Act 1988

vii

HOUSING ACT 1988*

(1988 c. 50)

ARRANGEMENT OF SECTIONS

PART I

RENTED ACCOMMODATION

CHAPTER I

ASSURED TENANCIES

Meaning of assured tenancy etc.

CHAPTER II

ASSURED SHORTHOLD TENANCIES

CHAPTER III

ASSURED AGRICULTURAL OCCUPANCIES

---

* Annotations by Andrew Arden, L.L.B., Barrister and Caroline Hunter, B.A., Barrister.

An Act to make further provision with respect to dwelling-houses let on tenancies or occupied under licences; to amend the Rent Act 1977 and the Rent (Agriculture) Act 1976; to establish a body, Housing for Wales, having functions relating to housing associations; to amend the Housing Associations Act 1985 and to repeal and re-enact with amendments certain provisions of Part II of that Act; to make provision for the establishment of housing action trusts for areas designated by the Secretary of State; to confer on persons approved for the purpose the right to acquire from public sector landlords certain dwelling-houses occupied by secure tenants; to make further provision about rent officers, the administration of housing benefit and rent allowance subsidy, the right to buy, repair notices and certain disposals of land and the application of capital money arising thereon; to make provision consequential upon the Housing (Scotland) Act 1988; and for connected purposes. [15th November 1988]

PARLIAMENTARY DEBATES

Hansard, H.C. Vol. 122, col. 1234; Vol. 123, col. 619; Vol. 134, col. 993; Vol. 135, cols. 74, 271; Vol. 136, col. 22; Vol. 140, cols. 334, 671. H.L. Vol. 499, cols. 596, 1493; Vol. 500, cols. 50, 191, 387, 389, 592, 724, 1342, 1509, 1614, 1725; Vol. 501, cols. 395, 837.

The Bill was considered in Standing Committee G from December 10, 1987, until March 15, 1988.

INTRODUCTION AND GENERAL NOTE

The Housing Act 1988 received the Royal Assent on November 15, 1988; most of its provisions come into operation two months later—the commencements are noted to the end of the outline descriptions of each Part which follow.

There are five Parts. Part I may itself be considered under two headings: the introduction of what is in substance, if not in name, a new Rent Act, containing assured tenancies in place of protected tenancies, and shortholds, and applicable to private landlords and housing associations; and, significant changes in the law of eviction, strengthening provisions against illegal eviction and harassment and (by and large) increasing the circumstances when notice to quit and court order are needed. Part II establishes Housing for Wales to take over the Housing Corporation's functions in Wales, and transfers many functions from the Secretary of State to the two corporations. Part III introduces housing action trusts, broadly to take over local authority housing and housing powers and duties. Part IV introduces the right of other (approved) landlords to take over local authority housing stock on their own initiative. Part V contains a range of miscellaneous provisions, including changes to right to buy.

It may be seen, therefore, that the Act covers the gamut of housing law. With the exceptions of Parts III and IV, between which there is a degree of correlation, the Parts must all be considered separately and are "self-contained" save where duplication would follow.

Part I

The Housing Act 1980 contained two measures intended to "revive" the private rented sector. One of these was the "assured tenancy", the other was the "shorthold tenancy". Under the 1980 Act, assured tenancies were lettings of newly-built property, by authorised landlords. Rents were freely negotiable, and security derived from adaptation of Part II, Landlord and Tenant Act 1954, *i.e.* that which formerly applied only to business lettings. By the Housing and Planning Act 1986, the concept of the assured tenancy was extended to include properties not only newly-built, but also those newly-repaired (as defined). A substantial number of landlords were approved. Shorthold tenancies were protected tenancies, subject to a mandatory right of re-possession on fulfilment of the qualifying conditions.

The 1980 Act provisions co-existed with conventional protection under the Rent Act 1977, *i.e.* the protected and statutory tenancy which conferred full security of tenure, and rent control by means of rents registered by Rent Officers. After the commencement of this Act, however, no new protected tenancies can be granted, save for a small number of exceptions designed to preserve existing rights, and all private sector residential lettings by way of tenancy will be either (i) substantially free from statutory control, or (ii) assured tenancies, or (iii) assured shorthold tenancies. Existing assured tenancies are brought within the provisions of this Act.

In the public sector, the 1980 Act introduced security of tenure (and the right to buy) not only for local authority (and other public sector) landlords, but also for those in the so-called "quasi-public" sector, *i.e.* housing associations and trusts. Rents for such secure tenants nonetheless remained in Part VI of the Rent Act 1977, the fair rent system. By this Act, most housing association and trust tenants are moved into the private sector, with new lettings qualifying as assured in the same way as other private sector lettings, subject again to the exceptions designed to preserve existing rights.

Chapter One of Part I governs the conventional assured tenancy, providing security of tenure less generous but conceptually similar to that available under the Rent Act 1977, but much more limited intervention in rents, which will no longer, as the fair rent, be to the disregard of scarcity, but open market instead. Chapter Two introduces the assured shorthold tenancy, with an additional mandatory ground for possession, but a little more right to refer a rent to a Rent Assessment Committee. Chapter Three introduces assured agricultural occupancies, applicable in place of the Rent (Agriculture) Act 1976. Chapter Four makes a number of important amendments to the law governing eviction (legal and illegal) and harassment.

Chapter Five contains transitional provisions governing the inter-action of the old and new bodies of law and, particularly, changes the law of statutory succession under the 1976 and 1977 Acts. There are four circumstances in which a Rent Act protected tenancy may be granted on or after the commencement of this Act. The first is pursuant to a contract made before commencement; the second is the grant of a new tenancy to a former protected or statutory tenant of the same landlord; the third is where the grant is as suitable alternative accommodation to an existing protected or statutory tenancy; the fourth is a transitional provision affecting former new town tenants only. There are analogous circumstances when a letting by a housing association may yet be secure (and "housing association", *i.e.* within Part VI, Rent Act 1977, as regards rents), together with a particular exception referable to the provisions of the Housing Act 1985, Part XVI (system-built defective premises).

Restricted contracts—which may be tenancies or licences—are those lettings which fall, by the Rent Act 1977, s.19, within the jurisdiction of the Rent Tribunal. Best known for the (limited) protection they confer on the tenants or licensees of resident landlords, there are provisions to prevent the creation of new restricted contracts on or after the commencement date of this Act. Assured tenancies as defined and prescribed by the Housing Act 1980 will normally become assured tenants within the meaning of this Act.

So far as statutory succession under the Rent Act 1977 and Rent (Agriculture) Act 1976 is concerned, under the new provisions, if a spouse (redefined to include a cohabitant) succeeds, there will be one succession which will remain fully protected, but a second succession (which will now occur in only limited circumstances) will be assured; if the first succession is by a member of the family, it will be assured and there will be no second succession. There are special provisions governing orders for possession against such assured tenants by succession. In addition, the residential qualifications to succeed of members of the family (on either first or second succession) have been increased. The new provisions will apply to deaths after the commencement of this Act (subject to a transitional adaptation of the period of residential qualification of a member of the family).

Commencement: January 15, 1989.

Part II

Since 1974, the Housing Corporation has been the central body which, *inter alia*, registers and monitors registered housing associations in England and Wales. Under Part II, a new body is created, Housing for Wales, which is to take over the responsibilities and powers of the Housing Corporation in Wales. In addition, Part II redefines the permissible additional purposes or objects of housing associations, eligible for registration. The Housing Corporation and Housing for Wales are empowered to issue "guidance" to registered housing associations, relating to their "management", and to have regard to the extent of compliance with the management guidance when determining whether to exercise powers under Part I.

Responsibility for administering grants is, and a number of related powers are or may be, transferred from the Secretary of State for the Environment to the Housing Corporation and Housing for Wales. The Corporations' powers as to procedures, circumstances in which grant is payable or not, method of calculation of grants, manner of payment and conditions, as well as transfer of grant in whole or part to follow transfer of property to another registered housing association, are very wide indeed, and markedly less circumscribed by statute than under the current system. The Corporations themselves are brought within the provisions of the Race Relations Act 1976, s.71.

Commencement: As the Secretary of State may order by S.I.

Part III

Part III introduces the "housing action trust" (H.A.T.) and its "designated area", which—subject to a ballot of tenants (secure and as defined for the purpose) which does not produce a majority opposed to the proposal—may be established by a "designation order". In some ways, the concept resembles the urban development corporation of the Local Government, Planning and Land Act 1980, but it is significantly different in that (a) it presumes the transfer to the H.A.T. of local authority housing stock (together with housing and other powers—but some of these can also attach to an urban development corporation), and (b) the considerations which give rise to the H.A.T. are different.

In outline, leaving aside ballot, the conditions which justify H.A.T. treatment are set out in s.60. There is a precondition of consultation. The primary objects are repair or improvement of housing stock held by the H.A.T., its proper and effective management and use, to secure or facilitate the improvement of living and social conditions in the area, and its general environment, and—importantly—"to encourage diversity in the interests by virtue of which housing accommodation in the area is occupied and, in the case of accommodation which is occupied under tenancies, diversity in the identity of the landlords". The landlords who purchase from H.A.T.s have to be "approved" by the Housing Corporation or Housing for Wales, and their subsequent disposals require the consent of the Secretary of State (save in a class of "exempt disposal", of which the most important are: the grant of a secure or assured tenancy, sales to people who have the right to buy).

Once the H.A.T. has been established, it has to draw up and consult on a statement of proposals, and it may prepare and consult on further statements of proposals at its own discretion or on the direction of the Secretary of State. The designation order may confer on the H.A.T. the following housing powers or duties of local authorities, either co-extensive with those authorities or in substitution for them, and subject to possible modifications: housing powers under the Housing Act 1985, Part II, repairs notices under *ibid.*, Part VI, improvement notes under *ibid.*, Part VII, slum clearance under *ibid.*, Part IX, overcrowding responsibilities under *ibid.*, Part X, houses in multiple occupation duties under *ibid.*, Part XI, responsibilities for common lodging houses under *ibid.*, Part XII, responsibilities for dwellings of defective design or construction under *ibid.*, Part XVI, consideration of the special needs with respect to housing of the chronically sick and disabled under the Chronically Sick and Disabled Persons Act 1970, s.3(1), the financing of registered housing associations under the Housing Associations Act 1985, Part II, and related rehousing obligations under the Land Compensation Act 1973, ss.39–41.

In addition, the H.A.T. may in effect be empowered to by-pass local authority planning controls, and the Secretary of State can pass to the H.A.T. the authority's planning powers, in whole or part, and again co-extensive with or in substitution for the authority. The housing powers of local authorities under the Public Health Acts may similarly be passed, instead of or concurrently with the local authority to the H.A.T. The H.A.T. must comply with any directions, whether general or specific, from the Secretary of State. The Secretary of State has power to transfer local authority housing to the H.A.T., together with other land held or provided in connection with that housing and even non-housing land or property subject to prior consultation. The H.A.T. may enjoy compulsory purchase powers. The tenants of H.A.T.s are to be secure tenants, enjoying the right to buy. There is express power to delegate the functions of the H.A.T., subject to the approval of the Secretary of State. H.A.T.s are intended to secure their objects as soon as practicable and then to make proposals for their own dissolution and transfer of their residual functions.

Commencement: November 15, 1988.

Part IV

Part IV enables *approved* persons—would-be landlords—to seek to remove from the public sector *freehold* property, provided a majority of the existing tenants do not object. The subject-matter is the stock of local housing authorities, new town corporations, the Development Board for Rural Wales, and the new Housing Action Trusts within Part III. The Part applies to houses, or flats, provided the landlord owns the fee simple, together with property reasonably required for occupation with such houses or flats, again provided that what the landlords holds is fee simple. Detailed terms cover exclusions, inclusions (at public sector landlord's request), price or disposal cost (for the public sector landlord may have to pay the approved landlord in effect to take the stock off its hands, *i.e.* if repair cost will be greater than existing cost), and the classes of tenant who have to be consulted.

Commencement: As the Secretary of State may order by S.I.

Part V
Part V contains a range of miscellaneous provisions, as follows (with commencement date in brackets):

> *s.115*—amending the law on allowable premiums for long, Rent Act protected tenancies (January 15, 1989);
> *s.116*—amending the Landlord and Tenant Act 1985, s.11, to extend landlord's obligations to common parts of buildings and services supplied from outside individual dwellings (January 15, 1989);
> *ss.117, 118*—excluding assured, protected and secure tenancies from the definition of a bankrupt's estate, thus permitting bankrupts to retain their tenancies (January 15, 1989);
> *s.119*—amending the Landlord and Tenant Act 1987 (as the Secretary of State may order by S.I.);
> *s.120*—changes to rent officer schemes consequent upon the reduction of their duties in the light of the provisions of Part I of this Act (January 15, 1989);
> *s.121*—introducing new rent officer functions relating to housing benefits (January 15, 1989);
> *ss.122–128*—changes to right to buy, including preserved right to buy (ss.122, 124, 128, as the Secretary of State may order by S.I.; ss.123, 125–127, January 15, 1989);
> *s.129*—allowing "portable discounts" in the public sector, *i.e.* to permit a tenant to purchase in the private sector instead of exercising the right to buy (as the Secretary of State may order by S.I.);
> *s.130*—changes to repairs notices under Housing Act 1985, Part VI, including to render non-compliance a criminal offence and to extend operation so far as blocks of flats are concerned (January 15, 1989);
> *s.131*—changes to letting conditions applicable to housing improvement grants (January 15, 1989);
> *ss.132–136*—amending consent disposals under Housing Act 1985, Part II (ss.132, 133, 135, November 15,1988; s.134, as the Secretary of State may order by S.I.; s.136, January 15, 1989);
> *s.137*—amendments to Race Relations Act 1976 concerning codes of practice in the field of rented housing (January 15, 1989);
> *ss.138–141*—financial provisions, application, amendments, commencement (ss.138, 139, 141, November 15, 1988; s.140, as the Secretary of State may order by S.I.).

PART 1

RENTED ACCOMMODATION

CHAPTER I

ASSURED TENANCIES

Meaning of assured tenancy etc.

Assured tenancies

1.—(1) A tenancy under which a dwelling-house is let as a separate dwelling is for the purposes of this Act an assured tenancy if and so long as—

(a) the tenant or, as the case may be, each of the joint tenants is an individual; and
(b) the tenant or, as the case may be, at least one of the joint tenants occupies the dwelling-house as his only or principal home; and

(c) the tenancy is not one which, by virtue of subsection (2) or subsection (6) below, cannot be an assured tenancy.

(2) Subject to subsection (3) below, if and so long as a tenancy falls within any paragraph in Part I of Schedule 1 to this Act, it cannot be an assured tenancy; and in that Schedule—

(a) "tenancy" means a tenancy under which a dwelling-house is let as a separate dwelling;

(b) Part II has effect for determining the rateable value of a dwelling-house for the purposes of Part I; and

(c) Part III has effect for supplementing paragraph 10 in Part I.

(3) Except as provided in Chapter V below, at the commencement of this Act, a tenancy—

(a) under which a dwelling-house was then let as a separate dwelling, and

(b) which immediately before that commencement was an assured tenancy for the purposes of sections 56 to 58 of the Housing Act 1980 (tenancies granted by approved bodies),

shall become an assured tenancy for the purposes of this Act.

(4) In relation to an assured tenancy falling within subsection (3) above—

(a) Part I of Schedule 1 to this Act shall have effect, subject to subsection (5) below, as if it consisted only of paragraphs 11 and 12; and

(b) sections 56 to 58 of the Housing Act 1980 (and Schedule 5 to that Act) shall not apply after the commencement of this Act.

(5) In any case where—

(a) immediately before the commencement of this Act the landlord under a tenancy is a fully mutual housing association, and

(b) at the commencement of this Act the tenancy becomes an assured tenancy by virtue of subsection (3) above,

then, so long as that association remains the landlord under that tenancy (and under any statutory periodic tenancy which arises on the coming to an end of that tenancy), paragraph 12 of Schedule 1 to this Act shall have effect in relation to that tenancy with the omission of sub-paragraph (1)(h).

(6) If, in pursuance of its duty under—

(a) section 63 of the Housing Act 1985 (duty to house pending inquiries in case of apparent priority need),

(b) section 65(3) of that Act (duty to house temporarily person found to have priority need but to have become homeless intentionally), or

(c) section 68(1) of that Act (duty to house pending determination whether conditions for referral of application are satisfied),

a local housing authority have made arrangements with another person to provide accommodation, a tenancy granted by that other person in pursuance of the arrangements to a person specified by the authority cannot be an assured tenancy before the expiry of the period of twelve months beginning with the date specified in subsection (7) below unless, before the expiry of that period, the tenant is notified by the landlord (or, in the case of joint landlords, at least one of them) that the tenancy is to be regarded as an assured tenancy.

(7) The date referred to in subsection (6) above is the date on which the tenant received the notification required by section 64(1) of the Housing Act 1985 (notification of decision on question of homelessness or threatened homelessness) or, if he received a notification under section 68(3) of that Act (notification of which authority has duty to house), the date on which he received that notification.

DEFINITIONS
"dwelling-house": s.45.
"fully mutual housing association": s.45.
"let": s.45.
"tenancy": s.45.
"tenant": s.45.

GENERAL NOTE

The Housing Act 1980 contained two measures intended to "revive" the private rented sector. One of these was the "assured tenancy", the other was the "shorthold tenancy" (see, now, below, Chapter II, merging the two concepts into the "assured shorthold tenancy"). Under the 1980 Act, assured tenancies were lettings of newly-built property, by authorised landlords. Rents were freely negotiable, and security derived from adaptation of Landlord and Tenant Act 1954, Part II, *i.e.* that which formerly applied only to business lettings. By the Housing and Planning Act 1986, the concept of the assured tenancy was extended to include properties not only newly-built, but also those newly-repaired (as defined). A substantial number of landlords were approved: see Encyclopaedia of Housing Law and Practice, notes to the 1980 Act, s.56.

The 1980 Act provisions co-existed with conventional protection under the Rent Act 1977, *i.e.* the protected and statutory tenancy which conferred full security of tenure, and rent control by means of rents registered by rent officers. After the commencement of this Act, however, no new protected tenancies can be granted (see below, s.34), save for a small number of exceptions designed to preserve existing rights, and all private sector residential lettings by way of tenancy will be either (i) substantially free from statutory control, (primarily because the letting does not fulfil the requirements of this section, or falls within the exemptions in Sched. 1) or (ii) assured tenancies as defined in this Chapter, or (iii) assured shorthold tenancies as defined in the next Chapter. Existing assured tenancies are brought within the provisions of this Act: see subs. (3), below.

Security of tenure is governed by ss.5–10, below, together with Sched. 2, which contains the grounds for possession available against an assured tenant (and to which s.11 is relevant, permitting the tenant removal expenses payable by the landlord in some cases). Rent and other terms are governed by ss.13–16; restriction on distress for rent is to be found in s.19. There are provisions for compensating a tenant against whom a possession order is obtained by misrepresentation or concealment (s.12); such limited statutory succession as is available is governed by s.17.

Letting includes sub-letting (s.45), and the effect of determination of an intermediate, superior interest is dealt with by s.18.

The effect of the Act cannot be avoided by "contracting out", *i.e.* agreeing that it is not to apply: *Barton* v. *Fincham* [1921] 2 K.B. 291, C.A., *R.M.R. Housing Society Ltd.* v. *Combs* [1951] 1 K.B. 486, *A.G. Securities* v. *Vaughan, Antoniades* v. *Villiers* (1988), *The Times*, November 11, 1988, 21 H.L.R., H.L.

Subs. (1)

The Act applies to "a tenancy under which a dwelling-house is let as a separate dwelling". This definition of its subject-matter raises three immediate considerations: is it a tenancy; is the letting of a dwelling-house (see also, s.2, below); and, is the property let as a separate dwelling (see also, ss.3 and 4, below).

1. Tenancy

Tenancy includes sub-tenancy: s.45; tenant includes joint tenant, and a reference to the tenant in such a case means a reference to all of the joint tenants.

The question of whether or not a letting constitutes a tenancy or a licence is of the first importance in the law of landlord and tenant, and has been the principal issue under the Rent Acts for many years. The Rent Acts, as this Act, do not apply to licences, only to tenancies: see, *e.g.*, *Oakley* v. *Wilson* [1927] 2 K.B. 279, *Fordree* v. *Barrell* [1933] 2 K.B. 257, C.A., *Marcroft Waggons* v. *Smith* [1951] 2 K.B. 496, C.A., and *Marchant* v. *Charters* [1977] 1 W.L.R. 1181, C.A. A tenancy may be of as little as a single room (but see below under "let as a separate dwelling"): *A.G. Securities* v. *Vaughan, Antoniades* v. *Villiers* (1988) *The Times*, November 11, 1988, 21 H.L.R., H.L.

There has, however, been some case law independent of the question of licences. Tenancies of all sorts are included, whether oral, written, under seal or by implication of law, and regardless of whether periodical, fixed term, at sufferance (*Artizans, Labourers & General Dwelling Co.* v. *Whitaker* [1919] 2 K.B. 301, *Dobson* v. *Richards* (1919) 63 S.J. 663; [1919] W.N. 166, K.B., *Remon* v. *City of London Real Property Co.* [1921] 1 K.B. 49,

C.A.), or at will (*Chamberlain* v. *Farr* (1942) 112 L.J.K.B. 206, C.A.). A tenancy by estoppel is within the term (*Lewis* v. *Morelli* [1948] 2 All E.R. 1021, *Mackley* v. *Nutting* [1949] 2 K.B. 55, C.A., *Whitmore* v. *Lambert* [1955] 1 W.L.R. 495, C.A., *Stratford* v. *Syrett* [1958] 1 Q.B. 107, C.A.), although in such a case the true owner will not, in the absence of acquiescence or delegation, be bound by it: *Jessamine Investment* v. *Schwartz* [1978] Q.B. 264, C.A.

A purchaser of a dwelling-house, allowed into occupation before completion paying periodic sums, could qualify, but not if the payments are only referable to the contract of sale: compare *Chamberlain* v. *Farr*, above, *Francis Jackson Developments* v. *Stemp* [1943] 2 All E.R. 601, C.A., and *Dunthorne and Shore* v. *Wiggins* [1943] 2 All E.R. 678, C.A.; if no contract yet exists, then payments cannot be referable to it, and the criteria in *Street* v. *Mountford* [1985] A.C. 809, 17 H.L.R. 402, H.L. will apply (see further below): see *Bretherton* v. *Paton* (1986) 18 H.L.R. 257, C.A. Similar agreements may, however, constitute shams: *Martin* v. *Davies* (1952) 42 T.C. 114n, 7 H.L.R. 119, C.A., and *Sharman* v. *Taylor* (1968) 207 E.G. 1227.

If the landlord lacks the capacity to create a tenancy, and one cannot exist by estoppel, then only a licence can arise: *Southgate B.C.* v. *Watson* [1944] 1 Q.B. 541, C.A.

Equitable leases are not excluded. There is no need to draw a distinction between tenancies and tenancy agreements on the one hand and mere contracts for leases (see notes to s.34, below) on the other (*cf. City Permanent B.S.* v. *Miller* [1952] Ch. 840, C.A.), as specific performance will normally be available to support the doctrine in *Walsh* v. *Lonsdale* (1882) 21 Ch. D. 9 (*cf. Kingswood Estate Co.* v. *Anderson* [1963] 2 Q.B. 169, C.A.). S.37, and Sched. 1, para. 1, both presume that contracts for tenancies will be enforceable.

Until recently, the distinction between tenancy and licence was becoming increasingly difficult to discern. A long line of cases in the Court of Appeal had accepted as licences arrangements which on a traditional approach would seem to have constituted a tenancy, notwithstanding that the standard ingredients of tenancy were present, *i.e.* defined parties (a person cannot grant a tenancy to himself: *Rye* v. *Rye* [1962] A.C. 496, H.L.), defined subject-matter (land, but defined widely to include buildings and parts of buildings howsoever divided up: Law of Property Act 1925, s.205(1)(ix)), a reversionary interest, a certain term (see, *e.g.*, *Lace* v. *Chantler* [1944] K.B. 368, *Centaploy* v. *Matlodge* [1974] Ch. 1; the term may, however, be fixed or periodic), and, crucially, "exclusive possession" (see further below). The departure from tradition placed greater emphasis on "intention" (see further below).

The first four ingredients have not proved problematic in rented housing law. It is above all the term exclusive possession which has given rise to problems of definition, and which has been at the centre of revision by the Court of Appeal: in *Marchant* v. *Charters* (above), Lord Denning M.R. referred to the law as having been "revolutionised" over recent years. The fundamental proposition, that there can be no tenancy without exclusive possession, remains intact: see, *e.g. Thomas* v. *Sorrell* (1673) Vaugh. 330, *Addiscombe Garden Estates Ltd.* v. *Crabbe* [1958] 1 Q.B. 513, C.A., *Errington* v. *Errington and Woods* [1952] 1 K.B. 290, C.A., *Grand Junction Co.* v. *Bates* [1954] 2 Q.B. 160, *Oakley* v. *Wilson* [1927] 2 K.B. 279, *Lynes* v. *Snaith* [1899] 1 Q.B. 486, *A.G. Securities* v. *Vaughan*, *Antoniades* v. *Villiers*, above.

Exclusive possession means that the grantee has the right to exclude all others from the premises, including the grantor. Not uncommonly, a grantor will reserve certain rights to enter, *e.g.* to inspect the condition of the premises, or to carry out repairs, or to discharge obligations such as cleaning or the provision of services. Such reservation is not inconsistent with the right of exclusive possession; indeed, the express reservation of such a right is a positive indication of tenancy, for if only a licence has been granted then possession will have remained with the grantor, and the reservation would be superfluous: *Addiscombe Garden Estates Ltd.* v. *Crabbe* (above); *Street* v. *Mountford* [1985] A.C. 809, 17 H.L.R. 402, H.L.

The converse proposition is that a licence confers no right to exclusive possession, and it is this which was undermined in the cases in which the Court of Appeal upheld lettings as licences notwithstanding that the occupier enjoyed exclusive use of premises: see, *e.g. Booker* v. *Palmer* [1942] 2 All E.R. 674, *Cobb* v. *Lane* [1952] 1 T.L.R. 1037, *Murray Bull & Co.* v. *Murray* [1953] 1 Q.B. 211, *Abbeyfield (Harpenden) Society* v. *Woods* [1968] 1 W.L.R. 374, *Shell-Mex & B.P.* v. *Manchester Garages* [1971] 1 W.L.R. 612, *Barnes* v. *Barratt* [1970] 2 Q.B. 657, *Luganda* v. *Service Hotels* [1969] Ch. 209, *Heslop* v. *Burns* [1974] 1 W.L.R. 1241, *Marchant* v. *Charters* (above). Most, but not all, of these cases concerned residential lettings.

Where no exclusive use has been granted, whether it be called possession or occupation, there can be no tenancy, for there has been no letting of land, merely a right to use land.

Abandonment of exclusive possession as a key indicator of tenancy placed reliance on the remaining element of tenancy, "intention". It is well established that parties must intend there to be a tenancy: see, *e.g. Brewer* v. *Hill* (1794) 2 Anstr. 413, *Doe d. Hughes* v. *Derry* (1840) 9 C. & P. 494, *Mayhew* v. *Suttle* (1854) 4 E. & B. 347, *Taylor* v. *Jackson* (1846) 2 C. & K. 22. Thus, a friendly arrangement, or an act of kindness or charity, is evidence of want of intention to create a tenancy, for it is a golden rule that the law will not impute intention to create legal relations where none are intended: *Booker* v. *Palmer* (above).

The way in which the law developed before its reconsideration is best illustrated by a passage from the judgement of Lord Denning M.R. in *Marchant* v. *Charters* (above):

"What is the test to see whether the occupier of one room in a house is a tenant or a licensee? It does not depend on whether he or she has exclusive possession or not. It does not depend on whether the room is furnished or not. It does not depend on whether the occupation is permanent or temporary. It does not depend on the label which the parties put on it. All these are factors which may influence the decision but none of them is conclusive. All the circumstances have to be worked out. Eventually the answer depends on the nature and quality of the occupancy. Was it intended that the occupier should have a stake in the room or did he have only permission for himself personally to occupy the room, whether under a contract or not?"

The whole of the law in this area has recently been considered in the House of Lords: *Street* v. *Mountford* (above). The decision is one primarily referable to *residential* lettings, and some of its criteria would seem inappropriate to other premises: see *Dresden Estates* v. *Collinson* (1987) 281 E.G. 1321, C.A., but *cf. London & Associated Investments Trust* v. *Calow* (1986) 280 E.G. 1252, C.A. These and other business cases have displayed some differences in the application of *Street, inter alia*, as it concerns payment of rent, and whether or not there is a written letting document: see also *Dellneed* v. *Chin* (1986) 281 E.G. 531, Ch. D., *Smith* v. *Northside Developments* (1987) 283 E.G. 1211, C.A., and *Ashburn Anstalt* v. *Arnold* [1988] 2 W.L.R. 706, C.A.

The principal speech in *Street* was given by Lord Templeman, with whom all the other members of the Committee agreed. Several passages reflect the strength of the view that there should be a return to the traditional approach to the distinction. This was described as lying "in the grant of land for a term at a rent with exclusive possession" (p.816/F–G). (The necessity for a rent was questioned in *Ashburn Anstalt* v. *Arnold*, above, itself followed in the residential case of *A.G. Securities* v. *Vaughan* (above), and see further below). In the later case (see further below) of *A.G. Securities* v. *Vaughan* (above), Lord Templeman summarised exclusive possession as meaning: "either exclusive occupation or receipt of rents and profits" (Published speech, p.2). In *Street*, he said:

"In the case of residential accommodation there is no difficulty in deciding whether the grant confers exclusive possession. An occupier of residential accommodation at a rent for a term is either a lodger or a tenant. The occupier is a lodger if the landlord provides attendance or services which require the landlord or his servants to exercise unrestricted access to and use of the premises. A lodger is entitled to live in the premises but cannot call the place his own. . ." (pp.817/H–818/A, citing *Allen* v. *Liverpool Overseers* (1874) L.R. 9 Q.B. 180).

"If on the other hand residential accommodation is granted for a term at a rent with exclusive possession, the landlord providing neither attendance nor services, the grant is a tenancy; any express reservation to the landlord of limited rights to enter and view the state of the premises and to repair and maintain the premises only serves to emphasise the fact that the grantee is entitled to exclusive possession and is a tenant. . . There can be no tenancy unless the occupier enjoys exclusive possession; but an occupier who enjoys exclusive possession is not necessarily a tenant. He may be owner in fee simple, a trespasser, a mortgagee in possession, an object of charity or a service occupier. To constitute a tenancy the occupier must be granted exclusive possession for a fixed or periodic term certain in consideration of a premium or periodical payments. The grant may be express, or may be inferred where the owner accepts weekly or other periodical payments from the occupier" (at p.818/C–F).

Lord Templeman considered service occupation:

"The test is whether the servant requires the premises he occupies in order the better to perform his duties as a servant: Where the occupation is necessary for the performance of services, and the occupier is required to reside in the house in order to perform those services, the occupation being strictly ancillary to the performance of the duties which the occupier has to perform, the occupation is that of a servant; *per* Mellor J. in *Smith* v. *Seghill Overseers* (1875) L.R. 10 Q.B. 422, 428" (*Street*, p.818/G–H).

Street therefore adopts the higher standard of *Smith* v. *Seghill Overseers* rather than the lower standard to be found in *Fox* v. *Dalby* (1874) L.R. 10 C.P. 285, where it was held that a person could be a service occupier if *either* it was necessary for the purposes of the job, *or* the employer imposed the requirement in the court of the contract of employment.

Lord Templeman analysed a number of the cases in which a licence had been upheld, notwithstanding the grant of exclusive possession, describing *Booker* v. *Palmer* (above) as a case only concerned with intention to create legal relations, and *Marcroft Wagons Ltd.* v. *Smith*, *Cobb* v. *Lane* and *Heslop* v. *Burns* (above) as of similar quality; *Errington* v. *Errington and Woods* (above) was considered to be a case of "exceptional circumstances which negatived the prima facie intention to create a tenancy" (see further below); *Murray Bull & Co. Ltd.* v. *Murray* (above) was considered wrongly decided; *Addiscombe (Harpenden) Society Ltd.* v. *Woods* and *Marchant* v. *Charters* (above) were considered cases of "lodging".

While *Marchant* was accordingly not considered wrongly decided, although described only as "sustainable", the principal judgement, that of Lord Denning M.R. (set out above), was criticised:

> "But in my opinion in order to ascertain the nature and quality of the occupancy and to see whether the occupier has or has not a stake in the room or only permission for himself personally to occupy, the court must decide whether upon its true construction the agreement confers on the occupier exclusive possession. If exclusive possession at a rent for a term does not constitute a tenancy then the distinction between a contractual tenancy and a contractual licence of land becomes wholly unidentifiable" (p.825/C).

Lord Templeman considered the three elements of exclusive occupation of residential accommodation, payments and term: "Unless these three hallmarks are decisive, it really becomes impossible to distinguish a contractual tenancy from a contractual licence save by the professed intention of the parties or by the judge awarding marks for drafting. . ." (p.826/E–F).

> "The only intention which is relevant is the intention demonstrated by the agreement to grant exclusive possession for a term at a rent. Sometimes it may be difficult to discover whether, on the true construction of an agreement, exclusive possession is conferred. Sometimes it may appear from the surrounding circumstances that there was no intention to create legal relationships. Sometimes it may appear from the surrounding circumstances that the right to exclusive possession is referable to a legal relationship other than a tenancy. Legal relationships to which the grant of exclusive possession might be referable and which would or might negative the grant of an estate or interest in the land include occupancy under a contract for the sale of the land, occupancy pursuant to a contract of employment or occupancy referable to the holding of an office. But where as in the present case the only circumstances are that residential accommodation is offered and accepted with exclusive possession for a term at a rent, the result is a tenancy" (pp.826/G–H–827/B).

> "Henceforth the courts which deal with these problems will, save in exceptional circumstances, only be concerned to inquire whether as a result of an agreement relating to residential accommodation the occupier is a lodger or a tenant. . ." (p.827/F).

The speech *appears* to offer two approaches to the question of whether or not tenancy has been granted. One is dependent on finding exclusive possession, or occupation, together with rent and term, subject to the exclusion of lodgers and cases of exceptional circumstances; the other starts with lodging, so that if there is neither lodging as defined nor exceptional circumstances as illustrated, tenancy follows, from which exclusive possession will follow. Following the decision in *A.G. Securities* v. *Vaughan* (above; see further below) the former must now be taken to be correct (see also *Brooker Settled Estates Ltd.* v. *Ayres* (1987) 19 H.L.R. 246, C.A.).

Leaving aside the cases concerning multiple occupation considered below, other post-*Street* decisions to which reference may be made are *Royal Philanthropic Society* v. *County* (1985) 18 H.L.R. 83, C.A., *Postcastle Properties Ltd.* v. *Perridge* (1985) 18 H.L.R. 100, C.A., *Bretherton* v. *Paton* (1986) 18 H.L.R. 257, C.A., *Sharp* v. *McArthur* (1986) 19 H.L.R. 364, C.A., and *Crancour Ltd.* v. *Da Silvaesa* (1986) 18 H.L.R. 265, C.A.

Documentation seems to have been considered subordinate in this area of law, *cf.* Lord Templeman's reference to "marks for drafting" (above). *Street* adopts principles well-established in earlier cases: that the label parties choose to put on a relationship is not itself decisive, *e.g. Addiscombe Garden Estates Ltd.* *Crabbe*; and that in cases under the Rent Acts the courts should be astute to detect a sham, *e.g. Buchmann* v. *May* [1978] 2 All E.R. 993, 7 H.L.R. 1, C.A., and should look at the substance and reality of the matter not its form, *e.g. Samrose Properties Ltd.* v. *Gibbard* [1958] 1 W.L.R. 235, C.A., approved in *Elmdene Estates Ltd.* v. *White* [1960] A.C. 528, H.L., see also *Regor Estates Ltd.* v. *Wright* [1951] 1 K.B. 689, C.A., *Woods* v. *Wise* [1955] 1 All E.R. 767, C.A.

"...The consequences in law of the agreement, once concluded, can only be determined by consideration of the effect of the agreement. If the agreement satisfied all the requirements of a tenancy, then the agreement produced a tenancy and the parties cannot alter the effect of the agreement by insisting that they only created a licence. The manufacture of a five-pronged implement for manual digging results in a fork even if the manufacturer, unfamiliar with the English language, insists that he intended to make and has made a spade.

"It was also submitted that in deciding whether the agreement created a tenancy or a licence, the court should ignore the Rent Acts. . . I accept that the Rent Acts are irrelevant to the problem of determining the legal effect of the rights granted by the agreement. Like the professed intention of the parties, the Rent Acts cannot alter the effect of the agreement" (p.819/E–H). However:

"Although the Rent Acts must not be allowed to alter or influence the construction of an agreement, the court should, in my opinion, be astute to detect and frustrate sham devices and artificial transactions whose only object is to disguise the grant of a tenancy and to evade the Rent Acts" (p.825/H).

Nonetheless, because exclusive possession was conceded in *Street*, notwithstanding an express written declaration that the agreement was not intended to create a tenancy, the case therefore dealt only peripherally with the issue of *how* to approach written documentation conflicting with the "three hallmarks" test. A written agreement is good prima facie evidence of what is intended, and the burden will lie on the person seeking to disturb the plain statement on the face of the document: *Buchmann* v. *May*, above.

Once it is alleged that a written agreement does not accurately reflect the actual agreement, whether because it is said to be a sham (see *Snook* v. *London and West Riding Investments Ltd.* [1967] 2 Q.B. 786) or as it has been called "false label" (see *R.* v. *Rent Officer for L.B. Camden, ex p. Plant* (1981) 7 H.L.R. 15, Q.B.D.), or as it has most recently been termed by Lord Templeman in *A.G. Securities* v. *Vaughan*, "pretence", a court will be bound to investigate what the real arrangement was, according to the *Street* criteria. In so doing, then insofar as intention remains relevant post-*Street*, this means intention objectively ascertained rather than by reference to what the parties say they intended (*Reardon-Smith Line* v. *Hansen-Tangen* [1976] 1 W.L.R. 989, H.L.). While subsequent conduct is not a permissible aid to interpretation of the agreement itself, it is admissible as evidence on the question whether documents were or were not genuine, giving effect to the parties' true intentions: *A.G. Securities* v. *Vaughan* (above), see particularly the speeches of Lord Oliver of Aylmerton (p.17 of the official transcript of the case) and Lord Jauncey of Tullichettle (p.24 of the official transcript of the case).

The remaining problems have proved most acute where rather than sole tenancy, joint tenancy or occupation is involved. In *Street*, Lord Templeman considered the non-exclusive occupation agreements which had become popular following the Court of Appeal decision in *Somma* v. *Hazlehurst* [1978] 1 W.L.R. 1014, under which a landlord grants to a number of people, by separate written agreements, a right to use premises, but no particular part of them (so as to avoid a finding of tenancy of such part, *e.g.* one room in a flat or house), together with such others to whom he may grant a similar right (often including himself), each normally paying a separate rent. The purpose is to defeat exclusive possession on the part of any one of the occupiers, or, since the landlord selects other occupants, the occupants jointly.

Prior to *Street*, there had been five such cases: *Somma* v. *Hazlehurst* (above); 7 H.L.R. 30, C.A.; *Aldrington Garages* v. *Fielder* (1978) 7 H.L.R. 51, C.A.; *Sturolson & Co.* v. *Weniz* (1984) 17 H.L.R. 140, C.A.; *O'Malley* v. *Seymour* (1978) 7 H.L.R. 70, C.A.; and *Demuren* v. *Seal Estates Ltd.* (1978) 7 H.L.R. 83, C.A. The arrangements had been held effective to grant no more than licences in the first three named, and ineffective in the other two—in the case of *O'Malley* v. *Seymour*, because only one occupier was ever involved or intended to reside in the premises, and in the case of *Demuren Estates Ltd.* v. *Seal*, on the ground of prior oral agreement for tenancy, or concurrent mutual intention that the occupiers should jointly enjoy exclusive occupation in circumstances that amounted to tenancy. The three "successful" cases were all disapproved in *Street*, as sham devices or artificial transactions.

Nonetheless, in *Hadjiloucas* v. *Crean* [1988] 1 W.L.R. 1006, (1987) 20 H.L.R. 54, while allowing an appeal from a county court decision and remitting it for rehearing, the Court of Appeal appeared to consider that separate agreements for the same period of time did not necessarily amount to joint tenancy. Converseley, in *A.G. Securities Ltd.* v. *Vaughan* (1987)

20 H.L.R. 212, at the Court of Appeal it was held (by a majority) that there was a joint tenancy between four occupiers who came into premises under non-exclusive occupation agreements at different times, for different periods, and paying different rents, and therefore *not* enjoying (joint) exclusive possession for identical periods of time (unity of time normally being considered one of the four "unities" without which there can be no joint tenancy.) The want of a single, identified rent for the whole of the premises was not considered fatal, following *Ashburn Anstalt* v. *Arnold* (above.) Furthermore, in *Antoniades* v. *Villiers and Bridger* (1988) 20 H.L.R. 439, C.A., the Court of Appeal found that non-exclusive occupation agreements of a small flat granted to a cohabiting couple constituted licences, because the terms were inconsistent with any grant of exclusive possession.

The state of confusion these conflicting decisions generated has now been brought to as near a certain end as case-law can achieve by the decision of the House of Lords in *A.G. Securities* v. *Vaughan, Antoniades* v. *Villiers* (above; page references are to the official transcript of the case).

The landlord's appeal in *A.G. Securities* itself was successful: the four agreements were independent of each other, the occupiers had not been jointly entitled to exclusive occupation of the flat, there was no artificiality in the contracts, but "a sensible and realistic [arrange-ment] to provide accommodation for a shifting population of individuals who were genuinely prepared to share the flat with others introduced from time to time who would, at least initially, be strangers to them" (*per* Lord Bridge of Harwich, p.1), it would have required "the highest degree of artificiality to force the contracts into the mould of a joint tenancy" (*ibid.*, p.2), the agreements reflected "the true bargain between the parties" and "there was never a group of persons coming to the flat altogether" (*per* Lord Oliver of Aylmerton, p.18), the absence of the four unities (above) was fatal. Their lordships also noted that at no time had it been alleged that the occupiers enjoyed separate tenancies of individual rooms, although they clearly identify this as one of the options as to how premises may be let to a number of people.

But the tenants' appeal in the *Antoniades* case was also successful. Lord Templeman's speech is, again, the most significant, canvassing in depth a number of the issues arising and in terms that may be described as completing the circle and rendering the decision much more widely applicable than merely to multiple occupation: it addresses a range of points relevant also to other classes of "sham", "artificial device" or as he prefers to call it "pretence", especially where the intention is to avoid protective legislation (in that case, under the Rent Act 1977, but the principles are as applicable under this).

Lord Templeman reiterated a number of basic principles:

"Parties to an agreement cannot contract out of the Rent Acts; if they were able to do so the Acts would be a dead letter because in a state of housing shortage a person seeking residential accommodation may agree to anything to obtain shelter. The Rent Acts protect a tenant but they do not protect a licensee. Since parties to an agreement cannot contract out of the Rent Acts, a document which expresses the intention, genuine or bogus, of both parties or of one party to create a licence will nevertheless create a tenancy if the rights and obligations enjoyed and imposed satisfy the legal requirements of a tenancy. A person seeking residential accommodation may concur in any expression of intention in order to obtain shelter. Since parties to an agreement cannot contract out . . . a document must nevertheless be examined and construed by the court in order to decide whether the rights and obligations enjoyed and imposed create a licence or a tenancy. . . The grant of a tenancy to two persons jointly cannot be concealed, accidentally or by design, by the creation of two documents in the form of licences. . . In considering one or more documents for the purpose of deciding whether a tenancy has been created, the court must consider the surrounding circum-stances including any relationship between the prospective occupiers, the course of negotiations and the nature and extent of the accommodation and the intended and actual mode of occupation of the accommodation . . ." (pp.6–7).

Referring to the two agreements signed by the occupiers, he notes: they were interdepen-dent, both would have been signed or neither, the occupiers applied to rent the flat jointly, and sought and enjoyed joint and exclusive occupation of the flat as a whole, sharing the rights and obligations imposed. "They acquired joint and exclusive occupation of the flat in consideration of periodical payments and they therefore acquired a tenancy jointly" (p.9). He continues by analysing the clause (clause 16) of the agreements under which the landlord reserved a right to come into and share the premises with the occupiers, the exercise of which rights he finds "would at common law put an end to [their] exclusive occupation of the flat . . . terminate [their] tenancy and convert [them] into licensees" (*ibid.*). *However*, this had to take effect subject to the Rent Acts:

". . . The powers reserved . . . by clause 16 cannot be lawfully exercised because they are inconsistent with the provisions of the Rent Acts. . . The exclusive occupation of the tenant coupled with the payment of rent created a tenancy which at common law could be terminated and converted into a licence as soon as the landlord exercised his power to share occupation. But under the Rent Acts, if a contractual tenancy is terminated, the Acts protect the occupiers from eviction" (*ibid.*),

i.e. by statutory tenancy. The same applies under this Act, for a landlord *cannot* terminate an assured tenancy except by the means and on the grounds to be found in ss.5–9 and Sched. 1, below.

"Where a landlord creates a tenancy of a flat and reserves the right to go into exclusive occupation at any time of the whole or part of the flat with or without notice, that reservation is inconsistent with the provisions of the Rent Acts and cannot be enforced without an order of the court. . . Where a landlord creates a tenancy of a flat and reserves the right to go into occupation of the whole or part of the flat with or without notice, jointly with the existing tenants, that reservations is also inconsistent with the provisions of the Acts. Were it otherwise every tenancy agreement would be labelled a licence and would contract out of the Rent Acts by reserving power to the landlord to share possession with the tenant at any time after the commencement of the term. . . The Rent Act prevents the exercise of a power which would destroy the tenancy . . . and would deprive them of the exclusive occupation . . . which they are now enjoying. . ." (p.10).

Lord Templeman turned to an alternative basis on which clause 16 had to be ignored. It "was not a genuine reservation . . . of a power to share the flat and a power to authorise other persons to share the flat. [He] did not genuinely intend to exercise the powers save possibly to bring pressure to bear to obtain possession. Clause 16 was only intended to deprive [them] of the protection of the Rent Acts. . ." (*ibid*). After citing his own reference in *Street* to "sham devices and artificial transactions" he continues:

"It would have been more accurate and less liable to give rise to misunderstandings if I had substituted the word "pretence". . . *Street* v. *Mountford* reasserted three principles. First, parties to an agreement cannot contract out of the Rent Acts. Secondly, in the absence of special circumstances, not here relevant, the enjoyment of exclusive occupation for a term in consideration of periodic payments creates a tenancy. Thirdly, where the language of licence contradicts the reality of lease, the facts must prevail. The facts must prevail over the language in order that the parties may not contract out of the Rent Acts. In the present case clause 16 was a pretence" (p.11).

In common with most such agreements, those in the *Antoniades* case had contained declarations to the effect that the occupiers did not have exclusive possession, and indeed that the Rent Acts did not apply. On the subject of "express" declarations of intention, Lord Templeman said (p.12) that "an express statement of intention is not decisive and that the court must pay attention to the facts and surrounding circumstances and to what people do as well as to what people say."

Lord Templeman then reanalysed *Somma* (above), *Aldrington* (above) and *Sturolson* (above), as containing clauses "contrary to the provisions of the Rent Acts and in addition . . . in the circumstances, a pretence intended only to get round the Rent Acts" (pp.12–13). He also disapproved the outcome of *Hadjiloucas* v. *Crean* (above): "The Court of Appeal ordered a retrial in order that all the facts might be investigated. Since, however, the two ladies applied for and enjoyed exclusive occupation unless and until one of their agreements was terminated, the ladies acquired a tenancy protected by the Rent Acts. The reservation to the owner of the right at common law to require one of the ladies to share the flat with a stranger was a pretence" (p.13).

In summary:

(1) If exclusive occupation, for a term, at a rent, is granted under the terms of an agreement, it will, absent lodging or special circumstances, constitute tenancy: *Street*.

(2) Where questions of statutory protection arise, (a) parties cannot contract out, (b) whatever may have been expressed as the intention of the parties, the court must look at the rights and obligations actually conferred in order to determine whether or not what has been created is licence or tenancy: *Street, A.G. Securities*.

(3) In appropriate circumstances, a number of documents may have to be construed together: *A.G. Securities*.

(4) In considering documents for the purpose of deciding whether tenancy has been created and/or whether or not an agreement genuinely represents the intention of the parties, the surrounding circumstances must be considered, including relationships between the prospective occupiers, course of negotiations, nature and extent of

accommodation and intended and actual mode of occupation even although the latter is subsequent to the agreement: *ibid.*

(5) A clause which if exercised will determine tenancy is subordinate to the protective legislation and cannot be enforced if contrary to it: *ibid.*

(6) A "pretence" intended to get around the protective legislation is ineffective: *ibid.*

2. Dwelling-House

Dwelling-house includes a part of a dwelling-house: s.45. By s.2, below, it comprises not only the house or part, but also land let together with the house or part, if, but only if, and so long as "the main purpose of the letting" is to provide a home for the tenant or at least one of joint tenants; if the main purpose is not, or ceases to be, such, then the tenancy as a whole ceases to be assured. If, however, the additional land comprises agricultural land exceeding two acres, then by definition the letting cannot be assured: see Sched. 1, para. 6. (See also *ibid.*, para. 7, excluding dwelling-houses comprised in an agricultural holding). See, further, notes to s.2, below.

The term "dwelling-house" has long been in use under the Rent Acts, and housing legislation, and has accordingly generated a substantial body of caselaw. Caution must be exercised when contemplating decisions under other legislation: "As usual, though the matter is so very clear to my mind on the facts and on the Act. . ., it has been embarrassed by a reference to a number of authorities. . ." (*per* Jessel M.R., *Duke of Bedford* v. *Dawson* (1875) L.R. 20 Eq. 353, 357, cited by Browne L.J. in *Sovmots Investments Ltd.* v. *Secretary of State for the Environment* at the Court of Appeal [1976] 3 All E.R. 720, 728).

In *Quillotex Co. Ltd.* v. *Minister of Housing and Local Government* [1966] 1 Q.B. 704, Salmon L.J. adopted the view of Sir George Jessel M.R. in *Attorney-General* v. *Mutual Tontine Westminster Chambers Association* (1876) 1 Ex. D. 469, C.A., that no real help can be gained as to the meaning of a word in Statute A by reference to its meaning in Statute B, C or D. "What is the ordinary natural meaning of the word within the context of the section in which it appears?" And: "In construing the language of any statutory enactment, it is important to look at it in its context and to consider, amongst other things, the mischief at which it is aimed. . ."

In *Annicola Investments* v. *Minister of Housing and Local Government* [1968] 1 Q.B. 631, it was said "that the word has a distinct fluidity of meaning, and that it is best construed in relation to the context in which it is found, and in relation to the objects and purposes of the Act or of the section of the Act in which it is used". In *Butler, Camberwell (Wingfield Mews) No. 2 Clearance Order 1936, Re* [1939] 1 K.B. 570, C.A., Sir Wilfred Greene M.R. said that

"whether a particular building does or does not fall under that word is a mixed question of fact and law; fact in so far as it is necessary to ascertain all the relevant facts relating to the building, and law in so far as the application of the word "houses" to those facts involves the construction of the Act.

"However, as so frequently happens in dealing with Acts of Parliament, words are found used—and very often the commoner the word is, the greater doubt it may raise—the application of which to individual cases can only be settled by the application of a sense of language in the context of the Act, and if I may say so, a certain amount of common sense in using and understanding the English language in a particular context . . .".

The closest statutes are clearly the Rent Acts, and the Housing Act 1985, Part IV, governing public sector security. Under the Rent Act 1977, protection attaches to "a dwelling-house (which may be a house or part of a house)" (s.1): "It must be a question of fact whether premises are a house or not. . .", *per* Scarman L.J., *Horford Investments Ltd.* v. *Lambert* [1976] Ch. 39, 51, C.A. Under the Rent Act 1977, s.19, governing restricted security (see notes to s.36, below), protection attaches to "a dwelling", also defined to mean a house or part of a house. A purpose-built hostel has been held to be a house under what is now s.19: *Luganda* v. *Service Hotels Ltd.* [1969] 2 Ch. 209, C.A.

In *Makins* v. *Elson* [1977] 1 W.L.R. 221, it was held that a caravan can constitute a "house" for Rent Act purposes, where the wheels had been raised and permanent services connected; see also *R.* v. *Guildford Area Rent Tribunal, ex p. Grubey* (1951) (unreported), April 19, D.C.); see further *Norton* v. *Knowles* [1969] 1 Q.B. 572, as to qualification under the Protection From Eviction Act 1977, where, however, what is in issue is residential occupation of "any premises", not statutorily defined.

In *R.* v. *Rent Officer of Nottingham Registration Area, ex p. Allen* (1985) 17 H.L.R. 481, Q.B.D., it was said that just because what is let is a caravan it is not necessarily outside the Rent Acts; whether or not it qualifies depends on the circumstances of the letting; if the caravan is let as a moveable chattel, it cannot be a house; where it is rendered completely immobile, either by the removal of its wheels, or permanently blocked in, then it is more likely to be regarded as a house much as a prefabricated dwelling or bungalow would be. The difficulties arise between these extremes: it is necessary to look at those features revealing elements of permanence on site, and those features revealing mobility. If the caravan is used by the tenant as his permanent home, there is a greater likelihood of it being permanently in place than if it is being used as a temporary expedient.

Bearing in mind the danger of relying on decisions under other legislation, attention may nonetheless be drawn to some of the cases. Under provisions of the Housing Acts other than Part IV of the 1985 Act, it has been said that "house" has no very precise meaning: the word can cover many types of building (*Quillotex* v. *Minister of Housing and Local Government* [1966] 1 Q.B. 704, C.A. See also *Critchell* v. *Lambeth Borough Council* [1957] 2 Q.B. 535, C.A.—a house means what is commonly called a house, *i.e.* a separate structure, but in this Part of this Act it of course includes flats by virtue of the definition in s.44.

A house is "a building for human habitation; especially a building that is the ordinary dwelling place of a family", according to the Oxford English Dictionary as quoted by Pearson L.J. in *Reed* v. *Hastings Corporation* (1964) 62 L.G.R. 588, C.A. In *Ashbridge Investments Ltd.* v. *Ministry of Housing and Local Government* [1965] 1 W.L.R. 1320, C.A., a greengrocer's shop with a rear living room and scullery, three first floor rooms and an outside lavatory, was considered within what could properly be held a house: "It is apparent that a "house". . . means a building which is constructed or adapted for use as or for the purposes of a dwelling" (*per* Lord Denning M.R. at p.1324).

In *Butler, Camberwell (Wingfield Mews) No. 2 Clearance Order 1936, Re* [1939] 1 K.B. 570, C.A., a structure consisting of a garage or workshop with a dwelling above was held to be a house (see also *Hammersmith (Bergham Mews) Clearance Order, 1936, Re* [1937] 3 All E.R. 539). Where a building is used partly for residential purposes, and partly for other purposes, the building has to be looked at as a whole to ascertain whether, as a question of degree, it can properly be described as a house: *Annicola Investments* v. *Minister of Housing and Local Government* [1968] 1 Q.B. 631, C.A. It need not be shown that all of the rooms in a building are used for residential purposes: *Premier Garage Co.* v. *Ilkeston Corporation* (1933) 97 J.P. 786.

Although original construction of a building is an important consideration (*Butler, Camberwell (Wingfield Mews) No. 2 Clearance Order 1936, Re* [1939] 1 K.B. 570, C.A.) regard may be had to the use of a building at the time the question falls to be determined (*ibid.*; see also *Grosvenor* v. *Hampstead Junction Railway* [1857] L.J. Ch. 731), so that something not built as a house but used as such may qualify. An unfinished house may qualify as a house: *Alexander* v. *Crystal Palace Railway* (1862) 30 Beav. 556 (not a Housing Act case). A building constructed as a house but used for other purposes has been held to remain a house: *Howard* v. *Ministry of Housing and Local Government* (1967) 65 L.G.R. 257.

A hostel or a building used for multiple occupation or as a lodging-house may itself qualify as a house: see *London County Council* v. *Rowton Houses* (1897) 62 J.P. 68; *Ross and Leicester Corporation, Re* (1932) 96 J.P. 459; *R.* v. *London Borough of Southwark, ex p. Lewis Levy* (1983) 8 H.L.R. 1, Q.B.D.; *R.* v. *London Borough of Camden, ex p. Rowton (Camden Town)* (1983) 10 H.L.R. 28, Q.B.D., all Public Health or Housing Act cases. See also *R.* v. *London Borough of Hackney, ex p. Evanbray* (1987) 19 H.L.R. 557, where it was held under Part XI of the Housing Act 1985, that part of a hotel occupied by homeless families was a house since it was a building constructed and used for human habitation.

Similarly, a building subdivided into flats can remain a house, whether so constructed or not: *Annicola Investments* v. *Minister of Housing and Local Government* [1968] 1 Q.B. 631, *Quillotex Co.* v. *Minister of Housing and Local Government* [1966] 1 Q.B. 704, *Benabo* v. *Wood Green Borough Council* [1946] 1 K.B. 38, *Critchell* v. *London Borough of Lambeth* [1957] 2 Q.B. 535, C.A., *Okereke* v. *London Borough of Brent* [1967] 1 Q.B., C.A. However, a flat itself is not a house (though can be a dwelling-house under this section, by way of being part of a dwelling-house under s.44): *R.* v. *London Borough of Lambeth, ex p. Clayhope* (1987) 19 H.L.R. 426, C.A.

In *Lake* v. *Bennett* [1970] 1 Q.B. 663, C.A., under the Leasehold Reform Act 1967, Lord Denning M.R. doubted that a tower block could reasonably be called a house, but Salmon L.J. emphasised that the decision did not necessarily affect the Housing Acts, and the wording of the 1967 Act refers to a house "reasonably so called".

3. Let as a Separate Dwelling

The phrase "let as a separate dwelling" is modelled on the Rent Act 1977, s.1, and was applied in the public sector by what is now Housing Act 1985, s.79. Under the Rent Acts, the term "let" has generated considerable case-law, based on the distinction between tenancy and licence: see above.

As: The letting has to be "as" a separate dwelling. This word imports consideration of the purpose of the letting: *Horford Investments* v. *Lambert* [1976] Ch. 39, C.A. The terms of the letting, so far as they indicate purpose, are the "primary consideration" (*Wolfe* v. *Hogan* [1949] 2 K.B. 194, C.A.; *Horford*), but they are not conclusive, for a court may conclude that there has been a sufficient consensual variation to bring security into play, although something more than mere payment of rent in knowledge of changed user is probably called for, *i.e.* a positive statement or act of affirmation: see *Wolfe*, *Court* v. *Robinson* [1951] 2 K.B. 60, C.A., *Whitty* v. *Scott-Russell* [1950] 2 K.B. 32, C.A., *Williams* v. *Perry* [1924] 1 K.B. 936, D.C., *Levermore* v. *Jobey* [1956] 1 W.L.R. 697, C.A.

What is contemplated by the agreement may be a matter of construction. Thus, a letting of a shop with living accommodation above it is likely to be construed as a letting for use as a dwelling: *R.* v. *Folkestone Rent Tribunal, ex p. Webb* [1954] 1 Q.B. 454, *Rolfe* v. *Sidney McFarlane* (1957) 168 E.G. 584, C.A., *R.* v. *Brighton and Area Rent Tribunal, ex p. Slaughter* [1954] 1 Q.B. 446, D.C., *Levermore* v. *Jobey* [1956] 1 W.L.R. 697, C.A. And where no specific user is contemplated by the agreement, then *de facto* user as at the time possession is sought or the question is otherwise raised, will govern whether or not the premises are let as a separate dwelling: *Gidden* v. *Mills* [1925] 2 K.B. 713, D.C.

In *Russell* v. *Booker* (1982) 5 H.L.R. 10, C.A., a property had been let as an agricultural holding, but over the years the agricultural use had been abandoned (see further notes to s.2, below). The court did not uphold the claim to a Rent Act protected tenancy, applying the following principles:

(i) Where the terms of a tenancy agreement provide for or contemplate the use of the premises for some particular purposes, then, subject to the qualification in (ii), below, that purpose is the essential factor in deciding whether or not the property has been let "as" a dwelling;

(ii) Nevertheless, where the original tenancy agreement provided for or contemplated the use of the premises for some particular purpose, but, by the time possession proceedings are commenced, that agreement has been superseded by a subsequent contract providing for a different user, the subsequent contract may be looked at in deciding purpose;

(iii) If a tenant changes the user of the premises and the fact of the change is fully known to, and accepted by, the landlord, it may be possible for the court to infer a subsequent contract to let "as" a dwelling, although this would be a contract different in essentials from the original tenancy agreement;

(iv) However, unless such a contract can be spelled out, a mere unilateral change of user will not enable a tenant to claim protection (or security) in a case where the terms of the tenancy agreement itself provide for and contemplate the use of the premises for some particular purpose which does not attract protection;

(v) Where the tenancy agreement itself does *not* provide for or contemplate the use of the premises for any particular purpose, actual subsequent use has to be looked at in determining the purpose of the letting.

A: The purpose must be to let as "a" separate dwelling. In *St. Catherine's College* v. *Dorling* [1980] 1 W.L.R. 66, C.A., a college took the tenancy of a flat, already subdivided into separate living units, for sub-leasing to their own students. As against the college, the students could not enjoy full Rent Act protection (*cf.* 1977 Act, s.8; see Sched. 1, para. 8 for the analogous exemption under this Act). As against the landlord, the college could not avail itself of a statutory tenancy following the contractual arrangement, for a corporate body cannot as such "reside" (*c.f.* notes below on "Individual"; under this Act, it could not have protection even during the contractual period). The college sought, however, to avail itself of the provisions of Part IV of the 1977 Act, governing the registration of rents.

It was held that the letting was not as "a" separate dwelling but, indeed, as several separate dwellings: see also *Whitty* v. *Scott-Russell* [1950] 2 K.B. 32, C.A., *Horford Investments* v. *Lambert* [1976] Ch. 39, C.A., *Regalian Securities* v. *Ramsden* (1980) 254 E.G. 1191, C.A.

But two or more dwellings may be let for use as one: *Langford Property Co.* v. *Goldrich* [1949] 1 K.B. 511, C.A., *Whitty* v. *Scott-Russell* (above), *Lower* v. *Porter* [1956] 1 Q.B. 325, C.A. Similarly, several lettings at different times may add up to one letting, as one dwelling: *Verity* v. *Waring* [1953] C.P.L. 423, C.A. And while a letting of a unit already subdivided into several separate living units for use as such, will not be let as "a" dwelling, a letting of one unit subsequently subdivided into living units, *e.g.* into bedsitting rooms, does not cease to be a letting as a separate dwelling on that account: *Sissons Cafe* v. *Barber* (1929) E.G.D. 117, D.C. (see, further, notes to s.4, below).

In *Hampstead Way Investments Ltd.* v. *Lewis-Weare* [1985] 1 W.L.R. 164, 17 H.L.R. 152, H.L., it was said that where a person is a tenant of two different parts of the same house under different lettings by the same landlord, and carries on some of his living activities in one part of the house and the rest of them in the other part, neither tenancy will normally be protected (for want of a letting as a "separate" dwelling: see next sub-heading). If, however, the true view of the facts is that there is, in substance, a single composite letting of the two parts of the house as a whole, then the tenancies of both parts together will, or may, be protected: see *Wimbush* v. *Cibulia* [1949] 2 K.B. 564, C.A.

Separate: The essence of "separate" dwelling is that the premises in question must be capable of use on their own, as a dwelling, even if they comprise no more than a single room (see, *e.g. Curl* v. *Angelo* [1948] 2 All E.R. 189, C.A.), so that there is and needs be no sharing with another of "living accommodation". The term "living accommodation" is a judicial creation, and does not extend to the sharing of a bathroom or lavatory: *Cole* v. *Harris* [1945] K.B. 474, C.A. A bathroom or lavatory is accommodation not used for living in, but merely visited for occasional, specific purposes, as distinct from a room used for the primary purposes of living, or one in which a person spends a significant part of his time: see also *Curl, Goodrich* v. *Paisner* [1957] A.C. 65, H.L., *Marsh* v. *Cooper* [1969] 1 W.L.R. 803, C.A.

For these purposes, the primary living purposes may be considered as sleeping, cooking and feeding (*Wright* v. *Howell* (1947) 92 S.J. 26, C.A., *Curl* v. *Angelo* [1948] 2 All E.R. 189, C.A.), but *not*, as noted, sanitary activities.

But a kitchenette, even though too small to eat in and only available to cook or wash up in, has been held to constitute living accommodation (*Winters* v. *Dance* [1949] L.J.R. 165, C.A.), as also has a normal kitchen: *Neale* v. *Del Soto* [1945] K.B. 144, C.A., *Sharpe* v. *Nicholls* (1945) 147 E.G. 177, C.A. So if the letting comprises premises together with shared use of such living accommodation, there is, prima facie, no use as a "separate dwelling": *Winters* v. *Dance, Neale* v. *Del Soto, Goodrich* v. *Paisner* [1957] A.C. 65, H.L.

Sharing with one's own sub-tenant, or sub-licensee, does not prevent use as a separate dwelling: see s.4 below, and *Baker* v. *Turner* [1950] A.C. 401, H.L. Where a tenant has exclusive occupation of some accommodation but shares living accommodation with other tenants, then the effect of the exclusion from qualification as an assured tenancy, by reason of want of "separate" dwelling, is overriden by s.3, below.

Sharing living accommodation must be distinguished from a letting which leaves someone else, *e.g.* another occupier or even the landlord, with a defined or limited right merely to use part of the accommodation which has been let, *e.g.* the right to come in and make a morning cup of tea as in *James* v. *James* [1952] C.L.Y. 2948, C.C., a right of passage as in *James* v. *Coleman* [1949] E.G.D. 122, C.C., a right to use a bath sited in a kitchen as in *Trustees of the Waltham Abbey Baptist Church* v. *Stevens* (1950) E.G. 294, C.C., and a right to draw and boil water weekly as in *Hayward* v. *Marshall* [1952] 2 Q.B. 89, C.A.

In each case, the whole of the circumstances must be looked at in order to ascertain whether a person has the right to use a separate dwelling, or something less: *Goodrich* v. *Paisner* [1957] A.C. 65, H.L. In Rent Act law, the fact that a sharing right is not exercised does not bring the tenant back into full protection: *Stanley* v. *Compton* [1951] 1 All E.R. 859, C.A., *Kenyon* v. *Walker* [1946] 2 All E.R. 595, C.A. although it has been thought that a clear abandonment of the right might do so: *Stanley* v. *Compton*. Also under the Rent Acts, it has been held that the question is to be determined as at the date when it is relevant, rather than as at the date of letting: *Baker* v. *Turner* [1950] A.C. 401, H.L.

See, also, the note on *Hampstead Way Investments Ltd.* v. *Lewis-Weare*, under "a", above.

Dwelling: "Dwelling" itself has been defined as something in which all the major activities of life, such as sleeping, cooking and feeding, are carried out: *Wright* v. *Howell* (1947) 92 S.J. 26, C.A., *Curl* v. *Angelo* [1948] 2 All E.R. 189, C.A., *Metropolitan Properties* v. *Barder* [1968] 1 All E.R. 536. Premises not used for sleeping cannot be in use as a dwelling: *Wimbush* v. *Cibulia* [1949] 2 K.B. 564, C.A. Under the Rent Acts, use need not be by the person to whom the premises are let: *Whitty* v. *Scott-Russell* [1950] 2 K.B. 32, C.A., *Edgware Estates* v. *Coblentz* [1949] 2 K.B. 717, C.A., *Carter* v. *S.U. Carburetter Co.* [1942] 2 K.B. 288, C.A., *Watson* v. *Saunders-Roe Ltd.* [1947] K.B. 437, C.A., *Anspach* v. *Charlton Steam Shipping Co.* [1955] 2 Q.B. 21, C.A. Under this Act, however, use has to be, and to continue to be, as an only or principal home, *by* the tenant or one of joint tenants—see notes on "Only or Principal Home", below.

Presuming these three conditions are fulfilled, there will prima facie be an assured tenancy for the purposes of this Act. However, this will only be so "if and so long as" the tenant is an individual, or in the case of a joint tenancy each of the joint tenants is an individual; the tenant or at least one of joint tenants occupies the dwelling-house as his only or principal home; and, the tenancy is not precluded from being an assured tenancy by virtue of subss.

(2)–(4) of this section, and Sched. 1, Part I. There are accordingly three further conditions which have to be fulfilled, and which must continue to be fulfilled.

4. Individual

Under the Rent Acts, there was no requirement that a tenant be an individual, *during* the contractual period of tenancy; the tenant could be, *e.g.* a company or other body. However, once the contractual tenancy came to an end, reliance had to be placed on statutory protection (statutory tenancy—see under this Act, ss.5, 6, below), and this was only available to an individual (or individuals), because statutory tenancy, unlike contractual tenancy (under the Rent Acts), was dependent on residence, and an artificial person could not reside: see, *e.g. Hiller* v. *United Dairies (London) Ltd.* [1934] 1 K.B. 57 C.A., *Firstcross* v. *East West Ltd.* (1980) 7 H.L.R. 98, C.A., *Tetragon Ltd.* v. *Shidash Construction Co.* (1981) 7 H.L.R. 113, C.A., *Estavest Investments* v. *Commercial Express Travel* (1988) 21 H.L.R., C.A., *Hilton* v. *Plustitle Ltd.* (1988) 21 H.L.R., C.A.

Under this Act, as under the Housing Act 1985, Part IV (secure tenants—see notes to s.35, below), however, it is a precondition of assured tenancy that the tenant is an individual, or that if there is a joint tenancy, each of the joint tenants is an individual. This is a most important requirement, and means that reliance by landlords on "Company Lets" will be effective from the outset of the tenancy. Hitherto, company let cases where "sham" is alleged have been approached relatively narrowly, and traditionally, consistent with the pre-*A.G. Securities* (or, at least, pre-*Street*) approach to non-exclusive occupation (see notes above). In the light of *A.G. Securities*, (a) it is clear that post-agreement conduct will be admissible to determine whether or not to the terms of the agreement genuinely represent the intentions of the parties (minimising express intention), and (b) the courts may be expected to scrutinise such agreements with much greater care and caution.

Where joint tenants are concerned, note the possibility that if or once periodic (see also notes to s.5, below), one of them may determine the joint tenancy by notice to quit served *on* the landlord: *Greenwich London Borough Council* v. *McGrady* (1982) 6 H.L.R. 36, C.A.—see further notes to s.5 below (which constrains termination by the landlord, not by the tenant).

5. Only or Principal Home

This important phrase is not defined in the Act. It is the same as that used in the Housing Act 1985, s.81, governing public sector security. Under that Act, it has recently been held that there is no material difference between occupation as a "home" and occupation as a "residence", so that, following caselaw under the Rent Acts (see further below), actual physical occupation is not necessary to establish occupation as a home: it is clear that two houses can contemporaneously be occupied as a home—*Crawley Borough Council* v. *Sawyer* (1987) 20 H.L.R. 98, C.A., in which a tenant was able to maintain his security of tenure in one place, while living temporarily in another.

The expression is similar to that used in the Leasehold Reform Act 1967, s.1(2): "only or main residence". By analogy, it would accordingly include a tenant who occupies part, but sublets the remainder of his home: see *Harris* v. *Swick Securities* [1969] 1 W.L.R. 1604. In *Poland* v. *Cadogan* [1980] 3 All E.R. 544, C.A., it was held that while long absences from a house may not prevent occupation, a long absence abroad with the premises sublet may indicate a lack of intention to occupy, sufficient to defeat the meaning of occupation for the purposes of that Act. In *Fowell* v. *Radford* (1970) 21 P. & C.R. 99, C.A., a claim by a husband and wife each to be occupying a different house as the main home, although considered unusual, was upheld.

The phrase "only or main residence" also occurs in relation to taxation. In *Frost* v. *Feltham* [1981] 1 W.L.R. 452, Ch.D., it was held that a publican who lived above his public house, which was rented, and who spent two or three days a month in a house he owned in Wales—the only property he actually owned—was entitled to claim the house in Wales as his only or main residence.

What is absolutely clear is that reliance cannot be placed on case law decided under the closest equivalent Rent Act phrase—"if and so long as he occupies the dwelling-house as his residence" (Rent Act 1977, s.2)—so far as this has been interpreted (generously) by the courts, in effect to mean occupation as *a* residence: see, *e.g. Bevington* v. *Crawford* (1974) 232 E.G. 191, C.A., *Gofor Investments* v. *Roberts* (1975) 119 S.J. 320, C.A., and *Brickfield Properties Ltd.* v. *Hughes* (1987) 20 H.L.R. 108, C.A.; see also *Langford Property Co. Ltd.* v. *Tureman* [1949] 1 K.B. 29, C.A., and *Beck* v. *Scholtz* [1953] 1 Q.B. 570, C.A., for two cases which usefully illustrate where the line is drawn. See, for a similar comparison, *Regalian Securities Ltd.* v. *Scheuer* (1982) 5 H.L.R. 48, C.A., and *Richards* v. *Green* (1983) 11 H.L.R. 1, C.A. For a full and authoritative restatement of the principles under that Act, see *Hampstead Way Investments* v. *Lewis-Weare* [1985] 1 W.L.R. 164, 17 H.L.R. 152. It would quite clearly be contrary to the intention of Parliament under this Part, to permit a person an assured tenancy in more than one property (though two people could presumably have two joint assured tenancies between them).

Occupation need only be by one of the joint tenants. This embodies the effect of *Lloyd* v. *Sadler* [1978] Q.B. 774, C.A., under the Rent Acts.

See also notes to Sched. 1, para. 4, for the relationship of this requirement to a degree of business or professional use.

6. Precluded from Being Assured Tenancy
The class of letting which is precluded from being an assured tenancy is governed by subss. (2) and (6), (7) and Sched. 1, Part I, see below.

Subs. (2)
Sched. 1 contains the classes of letting which are *not* to qualify as an assured tenancy. This is, however, expressed to be subject to subs. (3), which governs assured tenancies existing at the commencement of this Act, under the provisions of the Housing Act 1980, ss.56–58 (as amended). The net effect of subs. (3) (taken together with subss. (4)–(5), below) is to leave within assured tenancies a number of lettings which under the new provisions would not so have qualified. Accordingly, subss. (3)–(5) constitute an additional class of assured tenancy.

Sched. 1 contains 14 categories of excluded letting, most of which resemble those long excluded from full Rent Act protection under (now) the Rent Act 1977. In all cases, references to tenancy mean a tenancy under which a dwelling-house is let as a separate dwelling (see notes, above): subs. (2)(a).

Para. 1
A tenancy which is entered into before, or pursuant to a contract made before, the commencement of this Act cannot be an assured tenancy (save if it was itself an assured tenancy and qualifies within the transitional provisions of subss. (3) and (4). A contract for an assured tenancy which predates the commencement of this Act does not fall within subss. (3) and (4), but although apparently excluded by this paragraph, is to be treated as a contract for an assured tenancy under this Act, and will accordingly not be excluded from being an assured tenancy, by s.37(4), below.)

Para. 2
High rateable value tenancies are excluded. The limits are £1,500 in Greater London, and £750 elsewhere. Part II of Sched. 1 prescribes how rateable value is to be determined: see notes thereto, below.

Para. 3
Low rent tenancies are excluded. A low rent tenancy is one under which either no rent is payable or the rent payable is less than two-thirds of the rateable value of the dwelling-house, disregarding sums payable in respect of rates, services, management, repairs, maintenance or insurance. See, further, notes to Sched. 1, below.

Para. 4
Business tenancies within the protection of the Landlord and Tenant Act 1954 are excluded: see notes to Sched. 1, below.

Para. 5
Licensed premises are excluded. These are tenancies under which the dwelling-house consists of or comprises premises licensed for the sale of intoxicating liquors for consumption on the premises.

Para. 6
Tenancies under which agricultural land in excess of two acres is let together with the dwelling-house cannot be assured. As regards the letting of other land, and the phrase "let together with", see s.2, below. Agricultural land is as defined in the General Rate Act 1967, s.26(3)(a).

Para. 7
Also excluded are tenancies under which the dwelling-house is comprised in an agricultural holding, within the meaning of the Agricultural Holdings Act 1986, and which is occupied

by the person responsible for the control of the farming of the holding, whether as tenant or as servant or agent of the tenant.

Para. 8

Specified student lettings are excluded. These are lettings granted *to* a person who pursues, or who is intending to pursue, a course of study provided by a specified educational institution, *by* his own institution or another specified institution or body of persons. The Secretary of State specifies institutions or body of persons by statutory instrument.

Para. 9

A tenancy the purpose of which is to confer on the tenant the right to occupy the dwelling-house for a holiday is not an assured tenancy.

Para. 10

There is no assured tenancy where the tenancy is one granted by a resident landlord, as defined. See notes to Sched. 1, para. 10, which also covers the ancillary provisions of Part III of Sched. 1 governing the position which arises when there is a death or change of the resident landlord.

Para. 11

Crown tenancies are exempt. These are tenancies under which the interest of the landlord belongs to Her Majesty in right of the Crown, or to a government department, or is held in trust for Her Majesty for the purposes of a government department. But when the property is under the management of the Crown Estate Commissioners, the exemption does not apply, and their tenants are accordingly (unless otherwise excluded) assured, as under the Rent Act 1977.

Para. 12

Tenancies granted by the following bodies are not assured:—local authorities (as defined for the purposes of the paragraph: see notes to Sched. 1, below), the Commission for the New Towns, the Development Board for Rural Wales, an urban development corporation within s.135 of the Local Government, Planning and Land Act 1980, a development corporation within the New Towns Act 1981, waste disposal authorities, a residuary body within the Local Government Act 1985, a fully mutual housing association within Part I of the Housing Associations Act 1985, and a housing action trust within Part III, below. See, further, notes to Sched. 1, below.

Para. 13

Shared ownership leases are not assured tenancies. See, further, notes to Sched. 1, below.

Para. 14

The following tenancies are not assured: protected tenancies within the Rent Act 1977; housing association tenancies within Part VI of the Rent Act 1977; secure tenancies, within Part IV of the Housing Act 1985; and, the relevant tenancy of a protected occupier within the Rent (Agriculture) Act 1976. See, further, notes to Sched. 1, below.

Subss. (3)–(5)

An existing assured tenancy—under the Housing Act 1980, ss.56–58 (as amended) will in most cases become an assured tenancy under this Act, on the commencement date. Such an assured tenancy is *not* excluded by Sched. 1, Part I, as a whole, but is normally only excluded if within its paras. 11 and 12, *i.e.* Crown tenancies and tenancies from public bodies (see notes, above). Where, however, the landlord, under a 1980 Act assured tenancy, is a fully mutual housing association, and remains such, the tenancy will not be excluded from becoming a new assured tenancy so long as the landlord remains the fully mutual housing association: this is the effect of the qualifying words in the middle of subs. (4)(a) and subs. (5). As to the meaning of "fully mutual" association, see s.45, below.

However, all 1980 Act assured tenancies will continue as such and subject to its regime, if an application has been made to the court before the commencement date of this Act for the grant of a new tenancy and, pending the resolution of that application, the former tenancy has been automatically continued (under the provisions of the Landlord and Tenant Act 1954, as applied to 1980 Act assured tenancies): see s.37, below. If the court agrees to the grant of a new tenancy on such an application, that new tenancy *will* be an assured tenancy under this Act: *ibid.*

Subss. (6) and (7)

Part III of the Housing Act 1985 is entitled "Housing the Homeless" and contains the provisions formerly found in the Housing (Homeless Persons) Act 1977. Housing duties thereunder are classified as temporary, limited or full: see *per* Lord Bridge of Harwich, *Cocks* v. *Thanet D.C.* [1983] 2 A.C. 286, 291. The temporary duty arises under the 1985 Act, s.63, when application is made by a homeless person who the authority have reason to believe may be homeless *and* in priority need of accommodation; the limited duty arises under 1985, s.65, when the authority are satisfied that the applicant is homeless and in priority need but are also satisfied became homeless intentionally; not within the classification of Lord Bridge, but also temporary, is the duty to house under the 1986 Act, s.68, pending the resolution of a dispute between authorities as to who has full housing responsibility under the local connection provisions of the Act.

Under the 1985 Act itself, a person housed under any of these provisions will not be a secure tenant (or licensee) until a year has elapsed from when a decision has been notified to the applicant under the requirements to be found in ss.64, 68, *i.e.* informing the person of the outcome of his application (and, where adverse or potentially adverse, of the reasons for the decision): see the 1985 Act, Sched. 1, para. 4. This exclusion applies whether the housing authority themselves provide the temporary or limited accommodation or whether they secure its provision through another landlord (whose tenants are, or were, secure), *e.g.* a housing association: see *Family Housing Association* v. *Miah* (1982) 5 H.L.R. 94, C.A., from which it also appears that if no notification has been given, the tenant might be able to rely on when it *ought* to have been given, but with the burden of proof lying upon him to establish what that date was.

In *Restormel B.C.* v. *Buscombe* (1982) 14 H.L.R. 91, and in *Royal Borough of Kensington and Chelsea* v. *Hayden* (1984) 17 H.L.R. 114, the Court of Appeal expressed some doubt whether temporary accommodation pending long-term resolution of the position of a homeless person constituted accommodation under tenancy or licence capable of attracting security under the 1985 Act in any event. Such doubt appeared to have been removed by the House of Lords in *Eastleigh B.C.* v. *Walsh* [1985] 1 W.L.R. 525, 17 H.L.R. 392, shortly preceding *Street* v. *Mountford* (above), in which what is now the 1985 Act, Sched. 1, para. 4 was expressly considered and in which it was held that normal principles applied. However, in *Ogwr B.C.* v. *Dykes, The Times*, November 10, 1988, 21 H.L.R., the Court of Appeal held that the grant of a right of exclusive occupation, for a fixed period of 13 weeks, under an agreement headed "Licence to Occupy", pursuant to the 1985 Act, Part III, was a licence, because the fact that the grant was pursuant to statutory obligation negatived the inference of tenancy, within Lord Templeman's "exceptions" in *Street* (above). *Ogwr* was decided shortly before the decision in *A.G. Securities* v. *Vaughan* (above), in which the House of Lords reinforced the views expressed in *Street* and while not inconsistent with the decision in *A.G. Securities*, there would certainly seem to be an inconsistency in emphasis and "direction".

The purpose of the present subsections—introduced before the decision in *Ogwr* and to that extent perhaps rendered slightly redundant—is to allow housing authorities to make arrangements for temporary or limited housing of homeless people through housing associations, whose *tenants* (but not, of course, their licensees) will now be assured rather than secure: see s.35, below, or, rather, will be unless, *inter alia*, excluded by these provisions. But the exclusion from assured security is not confined to housing association landlords but will permit such arrangements also through private landlords. The exclusion will not apply if the landlord notifies the tenant that the tenancy is to be regarded as assured before the end of that period.

Letting of a dwelling-house together with other land

2.—(1) If, under a tenancy, a dwelling-house is let together with other land, then, for the purposes of this Part of this Act,—

  (a) if and so long as the main purpose of the letting is the provision of a home for the tenant or, where there are joint tenants, at least one of them, the other land shall be treated as part of the dwelling-house; and

  (b) if and so long as the main purpose of the letting is not as mentioned in paragraph (a) above, the tenancy shall be treated as not being one under which a dwelling-house is let as a separate dwelling.

(2) Nothing in subsection (1) above affects any question whether a tenancy is precluded from being an assured tenancy by virtue of any provision of Schedule 1 to this Act.

DEFINITIONS
"dwelling-house": s.45.
"let": s.45.
"tenancy": s.45.
"tenant": s.45.

GENERAL NOTE
This section reiterates the principle to be found in both the Rent Act 1977 and the Housing Act 1985, *i.e.* that land let together with a dwelling-house is to be treated as part of the dwelling-house, *save* (subs. (2) and Sched. 1, para. 6) where the land is agricultural land within the meaning of the General Rate Act 1967, s.26(3)(a), exceeding two acres. In *Bradshaw* v. *Smith* (1980) 255 E.G. 699, C.A., under the Rent Act, it was held that a field of more than two acres was not agricultural land within the meaning of s.26 of the 1977 Act, as it was not *used* only as a meadow or pasture within the General Rate Act 1967, s.26, but was used mainly or exclusively for the purposes of recreation; therefore, the field was part of the letting and enjoyed protection. "Land" includes buildings and parts of buildings: see *Langford Property Co.* v. *Batten* [1951] A.C. 223, H.L.

Under this Act, however, there is a refinement of the principle: the "main purpose" of the letting must be the provision of a home for the tenant or, where there are joint tenants, at least one of them; if this condition is not fulfilled, then the letting as a whole cannot be an assured tenancy (subs. (1)(b)). This section, applying only to the case of a dwelling-house let together with other land, deals with "purpose", rather than the factual considerations contained in s.1. Express provision is needed to cover provision of a home for one only of joint tenants, because by s.45(3), where the word tenancy is used without qualification, and is applicable to a joint tenancy, it implies *all* of the joint tenants.

Subs. (1)
Let together with. For land to be let together with the dwelling-house, it is not necessary that land and house should be let under the one tenancy or agreement: *Mann* v. *Merrill* [1945] 1 All E.R. 705, C.A.; see also *Wimbush* v. *Cibulia* [1949] 2 K.B. 564, C.A. Nor need the land and the dwelling be contiguous, provided they are within the same vicinity: *Langford Property Co.* v. *Batten* [1951] A.C. 223, H.L. Nor, indeed, need the landlord be the same or payment be under one rent: *Jelley* v. *Buckman* [1974] 2 Q.B. 488, C.A.; but *cf.* *Cumbes* v. *Robinson* [1951] 2 K.B. 83, C.A., and *Lewis* v. *Purvis* (1947) 177 L.T. 267, C.A. But there must *be* a dwelling-house for any land to be let together with it: *Ellis & Sons Amalgamated Properties* v. *Sisman* [1948] 1 K.B. 653, C.A. The issue is to be decided at the date when it arises, not the date of letting: *Mann* v. *Merrill*.

The more difficult theoretical issue is the meaning to attach to the words "if and so long as the main purpose of the letting". "If and so long as he occupies" occurs in the Rent Act 1977, s.2, and there is no difficulty understanding that this requires a continuing state of affairs. Here, however, the words are in theory susceptible to two different interpretations. The phrase could mean "if the main purpose of the letting was and so long as it remains," or it could mean "if and provided that the main purpose of the letting was". As *use* of the premises must be as an only or principal home (s.1(1)(b)), which is clearly a continuing condition, (a) the argument as to "purpose" may be largely academic, and (b) the courts may be expected to incline in favour of the more consistent interpretation, *i.e.* "if . . . and so long as it remains".

On this basis, the main purpose of a tenancy of a dwelling-house together with other land at its commencement must be use as a home, though *not* necessarily an "only or principal home". As to "purpose", see notes to s.1, above, under "As". In particular, note the careful analysis in *Russell* v. *Booker* (1982) 5 H.L.R. 10, and the proposition that if no specific user is contemplated by the agreement, *de facto* user as at the time possession is sought or the question is otherwise raised, will govern purpose: *Gidden* v. *Mills* [1925] 2 K.B. 713, D.C.

The continuing purpose must also be as "a" home, not "only or principal home". As there is no difference between the word "home" and "residence" (see *Crawley Borough Council* v. *Sawyer* (1987) 20 H.L.R. 98, C.A.), this would seem to permit reliance on Rent Act case-law, to the effect that a person may have more than one home, may be absent for perhaps a long period of time and indeed need not show physical occupation in order to sustain the claim to be in occupation as a home, although must always maintain the intention to continue use or to resume use as a home (see, *e.g. Bevington* v. *Crawford* (1974) 232

E.G. 191, C.A., *Gofor Investments* v. *Roberts* (1975) 119 S.J. 320, C.A., and *Brickfield Properties* v. *Hughes* (1987) 20 H.L.R. 108, C.A.; see also *Langford Property Co.* v. *Tureman* [1949] 1 K.B. 29, C.A., *Beck* v. *Scholtz* [1953] 1 Q.B. 570, C.A., *Regalian Securities Ltd.* v. *Scheuer* (1982) 5 H.L.R. 48, C.A., and *Richards* v. *Green* (1983) 11 H.L.R. 1, C.A. For "two homes" cases, see further *Dixon* v. *Tommis* [1952] 1 All E.R. 725, C.A., and *Hallwood Estates* v. *Flack* (1950) 66 T.L.R. (Pt. 2) 368).

Whether premises are in use as a residence and, therefore, a home, is a question of fact: *Middleton* v. *Bull* [1951] W.N. 517; 2 T.L.R. 1040, C.A.; see also *Tomkins* v. *Rowley* (1949) E.G.D. 314, C.A., *Turnbull* v. *O'Brien* (1948) L.J.N.C.C.R. 12. Use as a residence has been defined as "a substantial degree of regular personal occupation . . . of an essentially residential nature": *Herbert* v. *Byrne* [1964] 1 W.L.R. 519, C.A. If a tenant ceases to show a regular degree of personal occupation, for a sufficiently prolonged period to raise an inference of abandonment, then a landlord will be entitled to claim that the main purpose of the letting has ceased to be used as a home, and the burden of proof will shift to the tenant to show that, notwithstanding absence, there is no such abandonment: *Roland House Gardens* v. *Cravitz* (1974) 29 P. & C.R. 432, C.A.

This will require both a demonstration of intention to return to use as a home, and some tangible or visible clothing of that intention: *Brown* v. *Brash* [1948] 2 K.B. 247, C.A. An attempt to demonstrate occupation through other people, or belongings, *without* intention to return, is insufficient to demonstrate continued use of premises as a home: *Thomson* v. *Ward* [1953] 2 Q.B. 153, C.A., *Colin Smith Music* v. *Ridge* [1975] 1 W.L.R. 463, C.A. But absence, whether or not on account of another home, with intention to return will suffice if clothed by the presence of belongings, or other people: *Turnbull* v. *O'Brien* (above), *Langford Property Co.* v. *Tureman* (above), *Gofor Investments* v. *Roberts* (above).

A tenant who sublets the whole of the premises runs the risk of losing the status of assured (leaving entirely aside the question of breach of covenant: see s.14, below.) Rent Act case law (*Haskins* v. *Lewis* [1931] 2 K.B. 1, C.A., *Skinner* v. *Geary* [1931] 2 K.B. 546, C.A., *Regalian Securities* v. *Ramsden* [1981] 1 W.L.R. 611, H.L.), renders this a likely result, although it is by no means a necessary consequence, because use as a home can be maintained by intermittent occupation and temporary breaks during which subletting occurs (see, *e.g.* *Leslie & Co.* v. *Cumming* [1926] 2 K.B. 417, *Francis Jackson Developments* v. *Hall* [1951] 2 K.B. 488, C.A., *Oak Property Co.* v. *Chapman* [1947] K.B. 886, C.A.; see also *Berkeley* v. *Papadoyannis* [1954] 2 Q.B. 149, C.A.).

However, unlike the Rent Acts, where once "statutory residence" has terminated, *e.g.* for want of residence, it cannot theoretically revive (see *Jessamine Investment Co.* v. *Schwartz* [1978] Q.B. 264, and *Leith Properties* v. *Springer* [1982] 3 All E.R. 731, C.A.), under this section, dealing only it must be recalled with the case of a dwelling-house let together with other land, such a revival appears possible because of the wording of subs. (1)(b). This, too, utilises the expression "if and so long as", which is bound to be construed in the same way as subs. (1)(a), and therefore only treats the letting as non-assured (by treating it as not being let as a separate dwelling) "if *and so long as* the main purpose of the letting is *not*" (emphases added) use as a home.

Tenant sharing accommodation with persons other than landlord

3.—(1) Where a tenant has the exclusive occupation of any accommodation (in this section referred to as "the separate accommodation") and—

(a) the terms as between the tenant and his landlord on which he holds the separate accommodation include the use of other accommodation (in this section referred to as "the shared accommodation") in common with another person or other persons, not being or including the landlord, and

(b) by reason only of the circumstances mentioned in paragraph (a) above, the separate accommodation would not, apart from this section, be a dwelling-house let on an assured tenancy,

the separate accommodation shall be deemed to be a dwelling-house let on an assured tenancy and the following provisions of this section shall have effect.

(2) For the avoidance of doubt it is hereby declared that where, for the purpose of determining the rateable value of the separate accommodation, it is necessary to make an apportionment under Part II of Schedule 1 to

this Act, regard is to be had to the circumstances mentioned in subsection (1)(a) above.

(3) While the tenant is in possession of the separate accommodation, any term of the tenancy terminating or modifying, or providing for the termination or modification of, his right to the use of any of the shared accommodation which is living accommodation shall be of no effect.

(4) Where the terms of the tenancy are such that, at any time during the tenancy, the persons in common with whom the tenant is entitled to the use of the shared accommodation could be varied or their number could be increased, nothing in subsection (3) above shall prevent those terms from having effect so far as they relate to any such variation or increase.

(5) In this section "living accommodation" means accommodation of such a nature that the fact that it constitutes or is included in the shared accommodation is sufficient, apart from this section, to prevent the tenancy from constituting an assured tenancy of a dwelling-house.

DEFINITIONS
"assured tenancy": s.1.
"dwelling-house": s.45.
"landlord": s.45.
"let": s.45.
"tenancy": s.45.
"tenant": s.45

GENERAL NOTE
This section, too, has its origins in the Rent Acts. It derives from the proposition that there is no letting as a "separate" dwelling unless it is capable of use on its own, as a dwelling, even if it comprises no more than a single room (*Curl* v. *Angelo* [1948] 2 All E.R. 189, C.A.), so that there is and needs be no sharing with another of "living accommodation". As to what is meant by "living accommodation", see notes to s.1, above, under "Separate". Without this section, therefore, many lettings of, *e.g.* single rooms, would be disqualified.

The section provides that if the terms of the letting (i) grant exclusive occupation (see also notes to s.1, above) of some accommodation—here called "the separate accommodation", and (ii) include the use by the tenant in common with other persons not including the landlord of other accommodation ("the shared accommodation"), and (iii) *only* for this reason, the letting would not otherwise be assured, it is deemed to be let on an assured tenancy. This section governs the such issues as assessment of rateable value, and terms: see also s.10, below, governing terms where an order, *e.g.* a suspended order, for possession is made.

Where a tenant *sublets* part of the premises, on such terms, then as against his own landlord, he does not lose the status of being an assured tenant: see s.4, below, incorporating the effect of *Baker* v. *Turner* [1950] A.C. 401, H.L. But the sub-tenant will not have an assured tenancy, for he shares living accommodation, and is unassisted by this section ("not being or including the landlord".) In any event, the landlord is likely to be a resident landlord within Sched. 1, para. 10, and this would defeat a claim to being an assured tenant.

Subs. (1)
It is the terms of the tenancy which are important. A tenancy which does not contemplate sharing, even though the tenant permits someone, *e.g.* nominated by the landlord, or indeed the landlord himself, to share some part of the living accommodation, is not excluded from being let as a separate dwelling and therefore does not need to rely on this section: *Rogers* v. *Hyde* [1951] 2 K.B. 923, C.A., *Bowler* v. *Williams* [1949] W.N. 180, C.A., *Baker* v. *Turner* (above). There may be difficult questions of construction, as to whether there has been a letting as a separate dwelling (perhaps subject to the reservation of a "sharing" right—see notes to s.1, "Separate", above) or no such letting, because it was dependent upon sharing living accommodation not comprised in the tenancy: see *Goodrich* v. *Paisner* [1957] A.C. 65, H.L.

The fact that a sharing right is not exercised by a landlord does not bring back an assured tenancy: *Stanley* v. *Compton* [1951] 1 All E.R. 859, C.A., *Kenyon* v. *Walker* [1946] 2 All E.R. 595, C.A. However, if a landlord who has himself hitherto shared the living accommodation puts in another tenant, it seems that this section might become operative: *Stanley* v. *Compton.*

Subs. (2)

It is unlikely to be the case that the separate accommodation could itself be disqualified from being an assured tenancy on the ground of rateable value, but against that remote eventuality, (a) the provisions of Sched. 1, Part II, will apply, and (b) in reaching a decision, regard is to be had to the use of the shared accommodation.

Subss. (3) and (4)

These subsections prevent termination or modification of the terms on which the tenant is entitled to use shared accommodation, even if such is provided for in the tenancy agreement itself, save so far as numbers of sharers is concerned. The effect is to prevent the landlord altering or dimishing the tenant's use of the shared accommodation, *e.g.* hours of such use: see *Lockwood* v. *Lowe* [1954] 2 Q.B. 267, C.A. A term modifying (but not terminating) the right to use shared living accommodation may, however, be effected notwithstanding subs. (3), by application to the court under s.10, below.

Subs. (5)

See note to s.1, "Separate", above, as to living accommodation which prevents a tenancy from being assured.

Certain sublettings not to exclude any part of sub-lessor's premises from assured tenancy

4.—(1) Where the tenant of a dwelling-house has sub-let a part but not the whole of the dwelling-house, then, as against his landlord or any superior landlord, no part of the dwelling-house shall be treated as excluded from being a dwelling-house let on an assured tenancy by reason only that the terms on which any person claiming under the tenant holds any part of the dwelling-house include the use of accommodation in common with other persons.

(2) Nothing in this section affects the rights against, and liabilities to, each other of the tenant and any person claiming under him, or of any two such persons.

DEFINITIONS
  "assured tenancy": s.1.
  "dwelling-house": s.45.
  "landlord": s.45.
  "tenancy": s.45.
  "tenant": s.45.

GENERAL NOTE

This section incorporates the effect of the decision of the House of Lords in *Baker* v. *Turner* [1950] A.C. 401, to the effect that sharing with one's own subtenants (or lodgers) does not deprive the tenant of a letting as a separate dwelling, *i.e.* the letting from landlord to tenant remains as such, notwithstanding that it may not be used as such by the tenant on account of sharing living accommodation: see notes to s.1, "Separate", and to s.3, above. The sub-tenancy will not be assured, for (a) there is sharing with the landlord (the *mesne* tenant), and (b) that landlord will in any event be resident within Sched. 1, para. 10, below. As to the extent of the right to sublet, see s.15, below.

Security of tenure

Security of tenure

5.—(1) An assured tenancy cannot be brought to an end by the landlord except by obtaining an order of the court in accordance with the following provisions of this Chapter or Chapter II below or, in the case of a fixed term tenancy which contains power for the landlord to determine the tenancy in certain circumstances, by the exercise of that power and, accordingly, the service by the landlord of a notice to quit shall be of no effect in relation to a periodic assured tenancy.

(2) If an assured tenancy which is a fixed term tenancy comes to an end otherwise than by virtue of—

(a) an order of the court, or

(b) a surrender or other action on the part of the tenant,

then, subject to section 7 and Chapter II below, the tenant shall be entitled to remain in possession of the dwelling-house let under that tenancy and, subject to subsection (4) below, his right to possession shall depend upon a periodic tenancy arising by virtue of this section.

(3) The periodic tenancy referred to in subsection (2) above is one—

    (a) taking effect in possession immediately on the coming to an end of the fixed term tenancy;

    (b) deemed to have been granted by the person who was the landlord under the fixed term tenancy immediately before it came to an end to the person who was then the tenant under that tenancy;

    (c) under which the premises which are let are the same dwelling-house as was let under the fixed term tenancy;

    (d) under which the periods of the tenancy are the same as those for which rent was last payable under the fixed term tenancy; and

    (e) under which, subject to the following provisions of this Part of this Act, the other terms are the same as those of the fixed term tenancy immediately before it came to an end, except that any term which makes provision for determination by the landlord or the tenant shall not have effect while the tenancy remains an assured tenancy.

(4) The periodic tenancy referred to in subsection (2) above shall not arise if, on the coming to an end of the fixed term tenancy, the tenant is entitled, by virtue of the grant of another tenancy, to possession of the same or substantially the same dwelling-house as was let to him under the fixed term tenancy.

(5) If, on or before the date on which a tenancy is entered into or is deemed to have been granted as mentioned in subsection (3)(b) above, the person who is to be the tenant under that tenancy—

    (a) enters into an obligation to do any act which (apart from this subsection) will cause the tenancy to come to an end at a time when it is an assured tenancy, or

    (b) executes, signs or gives any surrender, notice to quit or other document which (apart from this subsection) has the effect of bringing the tenancy to an end at a time when it is an assured tenancy,

the obligation referred to in paragraph (a) above shall not be enforceable or, as the case may be, the surrender, notice to quit or other document referred to in paragraph (b) above shall be of no effect.

(6) If, by virtue of any provision of this Part of this Act, Part I of Schedule 1 to this Act has effect in relation to a fixed term tenancy as if it consisted only of paragraphs 11 and 12, that Part shall have the like effect in relation to any periodic tenancy which arises by virtue of this section on the coming to an end of the fixed term tenancy.

(7) Any reference in this Part of this Act to a statutory periodic tenancy is a reference to a periodic tenancy arising by virtue of this section.

DEFINITIONS

  "assured tenancy": s.1.

  "dwelling-house": s.45.

  "fixed-term tenancy": s.45.

"landlord": s.45.
"let": s.45.
"tenancy": s.45.
"tenant": s.45.

GENERAL NOTE
This is the primary section which confers security of tenure on an assured tenant. It is modelled on the method of conferring security under the Housing Act 1985, Part IV (formerly, Housing Act 1980, Part I, Chapter II), rather than on the earlier, and more familiar, "statutory tenancy" arising under the Rent Acts on the termination of a contractual tenancy.

Security operates by the fundamental proposition that the tenancy cannot be brought to an end by the landlord except by his serving a notice seeking possession (see notes to s.8, below) and obtaining an order of the county court (see further, s.7, below). The notice of seeking possession replaces notice to quit, and thereby avoids the disproportionate arguments familiar under the Rent Acts over whether or not a contractual tenancy has been determined. Such notice of seeking possession may, however, be "waived" by a court, if the court considers it just and equitable so to do: see notes to s.8, below.

Where fixed-term tenancy is involved, the landlord can still exercise a contractual right to earlier termination—if such a right is contained within the contract—but save where a court makes an order for possession, following notice of seeking possession—a periodic tenancy automatically follows, as it does when a fixed-term tenancy expires by effluxion of time.

Subs. (1)
The prohibition is on termination by *the landlord*, not the tenant. A tenant may determine his tenancy in the usual way: if periodic, by notice to quit or surrender; if fixed-term, and unless the contract otherwise provides, only by surrender. See *Harrison* v. *London Borough of Hammersmith & Fulham* [1981] 1 W.L.R. 650, C.A., and *Greenwich London Borough Council* v. *McGrady* ((1982) 6 H.L.R. 36, C.A.), as to the continuation of the common law other than as specified.

If the tenancy is a joint tenancy, and periodic, then one of a number of joint tenants can give notice to quit a periodic tenancy even without the assent of the other or others: *Greenwich London Borough Council* v. *McGrady* (above,) *Doe d. Aslin* v. *Summersett* (1830) 1 B. & Ad. 135. But one of a number of joint tenants cannot surrender a fixed-term tenancy without the agreement of the other or others: *Leek & Moorlands Building Society* v. *Clark* [1952] 2 Q.B. 788, C.A. This statement of the common law position would seem to be unaffected by s.45(3), below, by which, save where the Act otherwise provides, joint tenants means *all* of them, for that is applicable only to references in the Act to "tenant" as applied to joint tenancy. The position so far as statutory periodic joint tenancy is concerned is considered in relation to subs. (7), below.

The apparent alternative of determination by the landlord by exercise of a power in a fixed-term tenancy is not as generous as it sounds: subs. (2) introduces a periodic tenancy to follow a fixed-term tenancy whether it expires by effluxion of time or by the exercise of such a power, and this will only be defeated if an order for possession is made (see notes to s.7, below), or if the tenant surrenders or takes some other action to determine (but see also notes to subs. (5), below). Furthermore, a notice of seeking possession will still be required: s.8, below.

A fixed-term tenancy is any tenancy other than a periodic tenancy: s.45, below. This avoids the argument that arises when the expression used is "term of years", that there may be a need for at least one year (*cf. Land and Premises at Liss, Hants, Re* [1971] Ch. 986, *Gladstone* v. *Bower* [1960] 2 Q.B. 384, but see, in any event, the Rent Act 1977, Sched. 15, Case 13, referring to "a term of years certain not exceeding 8 months. . .").

Unless a right to forfeit for breach of covenant is expressly reserved, there is only a right to forfeit if the breach is of an express condition in the lease, or an implied condition fundamental to the nature of the agreement: see, generally, Woodfall, *Landlord and Tenant* (28th ed., 1978), Vol. 1, paras. 1–1880 *et seq.* A right of re-entry for a forfeiture has to be exercised within 12 years after the right has accrued: Limitation Act 1980, s.15(1) and Sched. 1, para. 7. The right must also still be extant, *i.e.* it must not have been waived.

The most common form of waiver is acceptance of rent, in knowledge of the breach giving rise to the right to forfeit. While on the one hand, a mere single acceptance of rent may not suffice (especially where, as under this Part, the tenant would be entitled to remain in occupation until a court orders him out, *cf. Oak Property Co.* v. *Chapman* [1947] K.B. 886, C.A.), on the other hand a landlord cannot have the best of both worlds by continuing to accept rent and "reserving" for future use, as it best suits him, his right to forfeit: *Carter* v. *Green* [1950] 2 K.B. 76, C.A., *Oak Property Co.* v. *Chapman* (above).

To establish that there has been a waiver, it is necessary to show that the landlord knew of the breach, and has so conducted himself, by words or action, as to affirm the continuation of the term, in spite of the breach. Such knowledge may, however, be the knowledge of an employee or agent, attributed to the landlord: see, *e.g. Ace Parade Ltd.* v. *Barrow* (1957) [1957] E.G.D. 176, C.C., *Gailinski* v. *Wheatley* (1955) 165 E.G. 724, C.A., *Metropolitan Properties Co.* v. *Cordery* (1979) 251 E.G. 567, C.A. But *cf. Swallow Securities* v. *Isenberg* (1985) 274 E.G. 1028, C.A.

Although it is said that courts of law always lean against a forfeiture (*Goodright Walter* v. *Davids* (1778) 2 Cowp. 803) it is clear that mere knowledge of a breach is not enough to establish waiver, and some positive action of affirmation of tenancy is called for: *Doe d. Sheppard* v. *Allen* (1810) 3 Taunt. 78. The state of the landlord's knowledge is important: he must be (or be deemed to be) aware of the facts which give rise to the exercise of his right to forfeit, before he can be deemed to have waived those rights: *David Blackstone* v. *Burnetts (West End)* [1973] 1 W.L.R. 1487. In *Chrisdell* v. *Johnson and Tickner* (1987) 19 H.L.R. 406, C.A., a landlord, suspecting there might be a breach of covenant, received a representation from the tenant which, if true, would have meant there had been no such breach; the landlord was not confident enough of the untruth of what the tenant said and decided not to take proceedings; when later the landlord issued proceedings, it was held there had been no waiver as the landlord had not known all the necessary facts to establish the breach.

Whether or not money is tendered and accepted *as rent*, for the purposes of waiver, is a question of fact, but once decided that it was, whether or not the consequence is waiver is one of law: *Windmill Investments (London)* v. *Milano Restaurant* [1962] 2 Q.B. 373.

Even a demand for rent expressed to be "without prejudice" can operate as a waiver of forfeiture: *Segal Securities* v. *Thoseby* [1963] 1 Q.B. 887. But in the same case it was held that a demand for rent payable in advance operates only as a waiver of such breaches as are known to the landlord at the time of the demand, *i.e.* past breaches, and of those which it is known to the landlord will continue during such period as he knows they will continue for, *i.e.* it does not operate as a blanket waiver for the whole of the period paid for in advance. And an act of waiver in relation to a covenant prohibiting a particular user of premises only waives past breaches, because a breach of such a covenant is a continuing breach: *Cooper* v. *Henderson* (1982) 5 H.L.R. 1, C.A.

S.7, below, details the operation of the power of the court to make an order for possession, in relation to assured tenancies whether periodic or fixed-term. The question of forfeiture and relief therefrom, so far as either is relevant under this Act, is discussed in the notes thereto.

Subs. (2)

On the termination of a fixed-term tenancy, either by effluxion of time or because the landlord exercises a right to terminate beforehand, a periodic tenancy—known as a "statutory periodic tenancy" (subs. (7))—comes into being, *save* (a) if a new fixed-term tenancy within subs. (4) is granted, or (b) if an order for possession is made which takes effect at the same time as the fixed-term tenancy ends, or (c) unless prevented by the assured shorthold provisions of Chapter II, below, or (d) if the tenant surrenders or takes some other similar action: see further notes to subs. (5), below. It seems that this periodic tenancy will be a proper, periodical tenancy, as distinct from the personal right to remain, or "status of irremovability" (*Jessamine Investment Co.* v. *Schwartz* [1978] Q.B. 264), comprising the Rent Act "statutory tenancy". The present Act expressly refers to the right to remain in possession *depending on* a periodic tenancy *arising* by virtue of this section.

Subs. (3)

This subsection details the terms of the statutory periodic tenancy: it follows immediately on the expiry or determination of the preceding fixed-term, is deemed to have been granted by the landlord under the fixed-term immediately before expiry or determination to the then tenant, of the same property, on periods the same as those for which rent was last payable under the fixed-term and under which, save as varied under s.6, below, all other terms are the same as under the fixed-term tenancy *except that* any provision for termination by the landlord or the tenant is excluded as long as the tenancy remains assured.

This does not mean that neither can terminate. Either can do so: the landlord by obtaining an order for possession under s.7, below, the tenant by surrender, or by notice to quit. Under the Protection From Eviction Act 1977, s.5, notice to quit must be in writing and must be given not less than four weeks before the date on which it is to take effect.

The four week minimum can include day of service or of expiry: *Schabel* v. *Allard* [1967] 1 Q.B. 627, C.A. But a proper quitting date (first or last day of tenancy) must be identified, or with reasonable certainty identifiable (*Dalgleigh* v. *Jennings* June 23, 1980, C.A.T. No. 501). A notice to quit must specify the premises in question—thus, a notice to quit two rooms, where the tenant was only tenant of one, was held invalid in *Jankovitch* v. *Petrovitch* [1977] L.A.G. Bulletin 189, C.A.

See also s.15, below, as to terms governing assignment and subletting implied into periodic tenancies (not merely statutory periodic tenancies,) and s.16, access to carry out repairs (implied into all assured tenancies, not only periodic).

Subs. (4)

The statutory periodic tenancy is avoided if there is agreement for the grant of another tenancy which confers upon the tenant the right to possession of the same "or substantially the same" property. Presumably the quoted words justify a minor variation, *e.g.* attached land, or one of a number of rooms comprising a (non-self-contained) flat, but the bulk of the property under the letting must be identical. Terms may, however, be different than under the preceding fixed-term tenancy or, therefore, than would be implied under subs. (3). The new letting need not itself be fixed-term. Note that agreement to a new tenancy deprives the parties of the opportunity of referring to the rent assessment committee its terms: see s.6, below.

Although protective in intent, it is likely to prove ineffective to prevent a landlord, *e.g.* moving the tenant of a single room or flat from one room or flat to another within a house, for while this would not constitute "substantially the same dwelling-house" ("dwelling-house" includes part of a house (s.45, below)) the tenant will no longer be using the former premises as an only or principal home within s.1. It would, however, be effective if the tenant changed his mind and declined to move, perhaps after taking advice, for the presumed statutory periodic tenancy would arise to "cover" or "justify" his continued occupation of the (former) room.

Subs. (5)

This subsection is designed to prevent a landlord defeating the provision for automatic statutory periodic tenancy by persuading the tenant to surrender or give notice to quit. It only affects the period *before* the deemed new (periodic) tenancy.

Subs. (6)

By s.1(4), a former assured tenancy under the Housing Act 1980 becomes an assured tenancy under this Act, notwithstanding that Sched. 1, paras. 1–10 and 13–14 might otherwise prevent it being an assured tenancy, and similarly, under s.37(5), a new tenancy granted by a court to a former assured tenant will be assured unless precluded by Sched. 1, paras. 11–12.

Subs. (7)

For a statutory periodic tenancy to arise, there must of course still be an assured tenancy, which requires, *inter alia*, occupation of the property by the tenant as an only or principal home. If the tenancy is joint, occupation need only be by one of them (s.1(1)(b)). If at the termination of the fixed-term, only one joint tenant is in such occupation, there is a right to a statutory periodic tenancy, but "the tenant" will—by subs. 3(b) of this section, be *all* the joint tenants: see also s.45(3). That residence by one will be sufficient to maintain the statutory periodic tenancy is consistent with the Rent Act position: see *Lloyd* v. *Sadler* [1978] Q.B. 774, C.A.

However, while under the Rent Act one of a number of joint tenants cannot terminate the "status of irremoveability" (see notes above) by common law notice to quit, which is inapplicable, the opposite would seem to be true under this Act, even during a *statutory* periodic tenancy, where common law notice to quit is the principal means by which a tenant will terminate.

Fixing of terms of statutory periodic tenancy

6.—(1) In this section, in relation to a statutory periodic tenancy,—
   (a) "the former tenancy" means the fixed term tenancy on the coming to an end of which the statutory periodic tenancy arises; and
   (b) "the implied terms" means the terms of the tenancy which

have effect by virtue of section 5(3)(e) above, other than terms
as to the amount of the rent;
but nothing in the following provisions of this section applies to a statutory
periodic tenancy at a time when, by virtue of paragraph 11 or paragraph
12 in Part I of Schedule 1 to this Act, it cannot be an assured tenancy.

(2) Not later than the first anniversary of the day on which the former
tenancy came to an end, the landlord may serve on the tenant, or the
tenant may serve on the landlord, a notice in the prescribed form
proposing terms of the statutory periodic tenancy different from the
implied terms and, if the landlord or the tenant considers it appropriate,
proposing an adjustment of the amount of the rent to take account of the
proposed terms.

(3) Where a notice has been served under subsection (2) above,—

(a) within the period of three months beginning on the date on
which the notice was served on him, the landlord or the tenant,
as the case may be, may, by an application in the prescribed
form, refer the notice to a rent assessment committee under
subsection (4) below; and

(b) if the notice is not so referred, then, with effect from such
date, not falling within the period referred to in paragraph (a)
above, as may be specified in the notice, the terms proposed
in the notice shall become terms of the tenancy in substitution
for any of the implied terms dealing with the same subject
matter and the amount of the rent shall be varied in accordance
with any adjustment so proposed.

(4) Where a notice under subsection (2) above is referred to a rent
assessment committee, the committee shall consider the terms proposed
in the notice and shall determine whether those terms, or some other
terms (dealing with the same subject matter as the proposed terms), are
such as, in the committee's opinion, might reasonably be expected to be
found in an assured periodic tenancy of the dwelling-house concerned,
being a tenancy—

(a) which begins on the coming to an end of the former tenancy; and

(b) which is granted by a willing landlord on terms which, except in so
far as they relate to the subject matter of the proposed terms, are
those of the statutory periodic tenancy at the time of the committee's consideration.

(5) Whether or not a notice under subsection (2) above proposes an
adjustment of the amount of the rent under the statutory periodic tenancy,
where a rent assessment committee determine any terms under subsection
(4) above, they shall, if they consider it appropriate, specify such an
adjustment to take account of the terms so determined.

(6) In making a determination under subsection (4) above, or specifying
an adjustment of an amount of rent under subsection (5) above, there
shall be disregarded any effect on the terms or the amount of the rent
attributable to the granting of a tenancy to a sitting tenant.

(7) Where a notice under subsection (2) above is referred to a rent
assessment committee, then, unless the landlord and the tenant otherwise
agree, with effect from such date as the committee may direct—

(a) the terms determined by the committee shall become terms of the
statutory periodic tenancy in substitution for any of the implied
terms dealing with the same subject matter; and

(b) the amount of the rent under the statutory periodic tenancy shall
be altered to accord with any adjustment specified by the
committee;

but for the purposes of paragraph (b) above the committee shall not direct
a date earlier than the date specified, in accordance with subsection (3)(b)
above, in the notice referred to them.

(8) Nothing in this section requires a rent assessment committee to continue with a determination under subsection (4) above if the landlord and tenant give notice in writing that they no longer require such a determination or if the tenancy has come to an end.

<small>DEFINITIONS</small>
"fixed term tenancy": s.45.
"landlord": s.45.
"prescribed": s.45.
"statutory periodic tenancy": s.5(7).
"tenancy": s.45.
"tenant": s.45.

<small>GENERAL NOTE</small>
This section governs variation of terms, *other* than rent, as to which see ss.13 and 14, *save* insofar as a rent increase may follow a variation of the terms. The power to vary would not seem to override ss.15 (assignment, subletting) and 16 (access to execute repairs). A variation cannot be made which has the effect of removing "sharing" rights under s.3, above, *unless* a possession order in relation to the sharer's own (or in the terminology of s.3 "separate") accommodation is also made: see s.10, below.

The variation procedure is available to both landlords, and tenants, and operates only in relation to a statutory periodic tenancy arising by s.5, above; it is therefore not available under a new periodic tenancy arising by agreement (see s.5(4)). Nor is it available in respect of a period when by virtue of Sched. 1, paras. 11 or 12 (crown and public landlords) the tenancy is not assured.

The procedure is applicable exclusively to former fixed-term tenants. It refers only to terms implied by s.5(3)(e), above, *i.e.* it does not apply to premises or periods.

Subs. (2)
To initiate variation of terms implied by s.5(3)(e), above, either a landlord or a tenant can serve notice in prescribed form (see s.45) proposing alternative terms, within one year of the expiry or termination of the fixed-term tenancy. Only a landlord, however, can propose an adjustment in the rent to take account of the proposed new terms.

Subs. (3)
The proposed terms—and, if any, variation in rent—automatically become the terms of the statutory periodic tenancy unless the recipient of the notice applies in prescribed form to a rent assessment committee within three months of service. The notice has to specify a date from when it is proposed that the variation will take effect, not within the three month response period. This automatic application means that it is extremely important for the recipient to refer the notice in time, and it is to be hoped that the prescribed form will so advise.

Subss. (4)–(7)
Rent assessment committees are bodies established under the Rent Act 1977, s.65, initially designed to review rents set by rent officers; see also notes to s.41, below. Subsequently, their functions have been extended: to valuations under the Leasehold Reform Act 1967 (at which time they are known as Leasehold Valuation Tribunals), to aspects of service charge provisions under Landlord and Tenant Act 1985, and to carry out the functions in relation to restricted contract tenancies formerly performed by Rent Tribunals (at which time they are known as Rent Tribunals). Small wonder that the Housing Act 1980, s.148, introduced provision for pensions for their presidents and vice-presidents. Their historical role in relation to rents is continued by ss.13–14, below, but *ab initio*, not by way of review of a decision of a rent officer.

By this section, they are also to determine terms of tenancies. Their powers are confined. They are to consider the terms proposed in the notice, and decide *not* whether they are fair, appropriate or reasonable, *but* whether they are such as the committee consider might reasonably be expected to be found in an assured periodic tenancy of the property, beginning at the expiry or termination of the former fixed-term tenancy, granted by a willing landlord on the other, non-contentious terms applicable. The fact that there is a sitting tenant is to be disregarded: subs. (6). In effect, they have to ask whether a new grant of a periodic assured tenancy might reasonably be expected to contain the term or terms in issue.

The committee's power extends to permit them to introduce their own version of a term in issue, but—with one exception—*only* of the terms proposed for variation in the notice ("dealing with the same subject matter") not an unrelated term. The exception is that it has power of its own motion to propose a rent adjustment to take account of variation of terms: subs. (5).

The committee's decision is to specify the date from which the term they have decided is to take effect, but is not binding (in the sense that, *e.g.* a Rent Act registered rent is binding), for the landlord and the tenant are free to agree that the decision is not to lead to a term to be contained in the tenancy. This meets the problem of the compromise result which disappoints all parties.

Appeal: There is no provision within the Act for appeal against a decision of the rent assessment committee. However, appeal on a point of law is available under, Tribunals and Inquiries Act 1971, s.13, and committees are susceptible to judicial review under R.S.C. Ord. 53: see, further, notes to s.14, below.

Subs. (8)

A reference to the rent assessment committee may be withdrawn by landlord and tenant *jointly*. Under the Rent Acts, an objection to a rent officer's registration could not unilaterally be withdrawn, because the fixing of a fair rent involved a matter of public interest, though a rent assessment committee could permit withdrawal by agreement of both parties, if satisfied that it was proper to do so: *Hanson* v. *Church Commissioners* [1978] 1 Q.B. 823, C.A.; see also *R.* v. *Bristol Rent Assessment Committee, ex p. Dunworth* (1987) 19 H.L.R. 351, Q.B.D.

Under the present Act, the "public interest" is not substantial. (It is not quite non-existent, for what a rent assessment committee find to be reasonably expected by way of terms may well come to form a body of influential evidence: see s.42, below). In any event, if the person who has referred the notice to the committee wishes to withdraw his objection, the person who served it will undoubtedly agree, just as if the person who served it wishes to withdraw, the person who referred it and objected to it will himself be willing to agree. The rent assessment committee may continue with a reference, even though the tenancy has come to an end, but is not obliged to do so, and it will presumably be in rare circumstances that they will decide to do so.

Orders for possession

7.—(1) The court shall not make an order for possession of a dwelling-house let on an assured tenancy except on one or more of the grounds set out in Schedule 2 to this Act; but nothing in this Part of this Act relates to proceedings for possession of such a dwelling-house which are brought by a mortgagee, within the meaning of the Law of Property Act 1925, who has lent money on the security of the assured tenancy.

(2) The following provisions of this section have effect, subject to section 8 below, in relation to proceedings for the recovery of possession of a dwelling-house let on an assured tenancy.

(3) If the court is satisfied that any of the grounds in Part I of Schedule 2 to this Act is established then, subject to subsection (6) below, the court shall make an order for possession.

(4) If the court is satisfied that any of the grounds in Part II of Schedule 2 to this Act is established, then, subject to subsection (6) below, the court may make an order for possession if it considers it reasonable to do so.

(5) Part III of Schedule 2 to this Act shall have effect for supplementing Ground 9 in that Schedule and Part IV of that Schedule shall have effect in relation to notices given as mentioned in Grounds 1 to 5 of that Schedule.

(6) The court shall not make an order for possession of a dwelling-house to take effect at a time when it is let on an assured fixed term tenancy unless—

    (a) the ground for possession is Ground 2 or Ground 8 in Part I of Schedule 2 to this Act or any of the grounds in Part II of that Schedule, other than Ground 9 or Ground 16; and

    (b) the terms of the tenancy make provision for it to be brought to an end on the ground in question (whether that provision takes the form of a provision for re-entry, for forfeiture, for determination by notice or otherwise).

(7) Subject to the preceding provisions of this section, the court may make an order for possession of a dwelling-house on grounds relating to a fixed term tenancy which has come to an end; and where an order is made in such circumstances, any statutory periodic tenancy which has arisen on the ending of the fixed term tenancy shall end (without any notice and regardless of the period) on the day on which the order takes effect.

DEFINITIONS
"assured tenancy": s.1.
"dwelling-house": s.45.
"fixed term": s.45.
"statutory periodic tenancy": s.5.
"tenancy": s.45.

GENERAL NOTE
This is the traditional, and principal, means of conferring security of tenure, by limiting the circumstances in which a court can make an order for possession. The requirement for a court order before eviction is to be found in the Protection From Eviction Act 1977: see also notes to s.30, below. Both the Rent Act 1977, s.98, and the Housing Act 1985, s.84, adopt the same method, and much of the law decided thereunder will be of relevance here.

The section imposes a barrier on the *landlord's* right to possession: *Moses* v. *Lovegrove* [1952] 2 Q.B. 533, C.A., *Goldthorpe* v. *Bain* [1952] 2 Q.B. 455, C.A.; see most recently *Appleton* v. *Aspin* (1987) 20 H.L.R. 182, C.A. The saving clause at the end of subs. (1) applies where the *tenant* is a mortgagor; those who lend money for tenants to purchase what will presumably and normally be a long lease but one not excluded by reason of low rent (see Sched. 1, para. 3) (and even if periodic, because a premium is paid will be entitled to assign: see notes to s.15, below) will be able to secure possession under the mortgage in the normal way to enforce their security.

The landlord must prove that the preconditions for an order have been fulfilled: *Smith* v. *McGoldrich* (1976) 242 E.G. 1047, C.A., *Mann* v. *Cornella* (1976) 242 E.G. 1047, C.A. It follows that there can be no "consent order", for parties cannot give to the court a jurisdiction of which it has been deprived by Parliament: *Barton* v. *Fincham* [1921] 2 K.B. 291, C.A.; see also *R.* v. *Bloomsbury and Marylebone County Court, ex p. Blackburne* (1984) 14 H.L.R. 56, Q.B.D., *Wandsworth London Borough Council* v. *Fadayomi* (1987) 19 H.L.R. 512, C.A. See also *Appleton* v. *Aspin* (1987) 20 H.L.R. 182, C.A.

Rather, if it is not intended to dispute a claim, the tenant must *admit* the relevant ingredients of the landlord's case: *Blackburne*. In general, the term consent order is to be avoided: *Thorne* v. *Smith* [1947] 1 K.B. 307, C.A.; see also *Plashkes* v. *Jones* (1982) 9 H.L.R. 110, C.A. *Thorne* suggests that in an appropriate case an admission or concession by the tenant may be *implied;* but *Blackburne* refers to express concession. This concesssion must go so far as to amount to a plain admission that the qualifying conditions for whichever ground is relied on are met, and, in discretionary cases, that it is reasonable for the order to be made: *R.* v. *Newcastle upon Tyne County Court, ex p. Thompson* (1988) 20 H.L.R. 430, Q.B.D.

Where a possession order is wrongly made, but the tenant has gone out of possession by the time it is set aside by the Court of Appeal, that court has power under R.S.C. Ord. 59, r.10(4), to order compensation: *Pollock* v. *Kumar* (1976) 242 E.G. 371, C.A., in which the calculation was remitted to the county court.

As to the powers of the court on an application for possession, see s.9. below; see also s.10, below, where "shared accommodation" (see s.3, above) is involved; see further s.11, below, for the tenant's entitlement to "removal expenses" on specified grounds, and s.12, below, for the entitlement to compensation where an order has been obtained by misrepresentation or concealment of material facts.

Subss. (1) and (2)
The grounds for possession are those set out in Sched. 2. They fall into two grounds: those which are mandatory, and those which are discretionary, in the sense that in addition to the ground itself, it must be established that it is reasonable to make the order sought. By s.8, a notice of seeking possession must be served before the court can entertain proceedings,—save where the court waives the requirement,—and the notice must specify

the ground on which possession is sought (although these may be altered or added to with the leave of the court.) The notice must still be in force at the time the proceedings are commenced. See, further, notes to s.8, below.

Subss. (3), (5)

The first set of grounds is contained in Sched. 2, Part I, and is "mandatory", *i.e.* if the landlord proves (*Smith* v. *McGoldrich*, above) that any one of them applies, the court is bound to make the order sought. Note, however, that where the assured tenancy is fixed-term and has not yet expired or been determined, only some of these grounds are available: see further subs. (6), below.

The Part I, Sched. 2, grounds are, in outline, as follows (see, further, notes to Sched. 2, below):

Ground 1. Prior occupation by landlord, or required for occupation by landlord, in either case subject to a notice before the beginning of the tenancy that possession might be recovered on this ground (or such notice requirement is waived by a court); see also Sched. 2, Part IV, governing notices.

Ground 2. Prior mortgage and required for sale by mortgagee, subject to notice before the beginning of the tenancy or waiver of requirement of notice; see also Sched. 1, Part IV.

Ground 3. Fixed-term of not more than eight months, and prior holiday letting, of which notice was given before the beginning of the tenancy (which requirement cannot be waived by a court); see also Sched. 1, Part IV.

Ground 4. Fixed-term of not more than one year, and prior student letting, of which notice was given before the beginning of the tenancy (which requirement cannot be waived); see also Sched. 1, Part IV.

Ground 5. Required for occupation by minister of religion, and notice before beginning of tenancy (which requirement cannot be waived); see also Sched. 1, Part IV.

Ground 6. Demolition or reconstruction or major works. This ground carries an entitlement to removal expenses: see s.11, below.

Ground 7. Death of former tenant.

Ground 8. More than three months in arrears at notice of seeking possession and hearing.

Subs. (4)

The second set of grounds for possession requires the landlord to prove not only that one such ground applies, but also that it is "reasonable" for an order for possession to issue. Powers are given to the court to adjourn, stay, suspend or postpone possession when this set of grounds is applicable: s.9, below.

Even where there is an element of reasonableness in the body of the ground (as in grounds 13 and 15), the court must proceed to consider reasonableness in its own right: *Shrimpton* v. *Rabbits* (1942) 131 L.T. 478, D.C., *Hensman* v. *McIntosh* (1954) 163 E.G. 322, C.A., *Peachey Property Corporation* v. *Robinson* [1967] 2 Q.B. 543, C.A. However, if reasonableness has been considered in relation to a specific element of the ground, the Court of Appeal will, in the absence of a case to the contrary, be inclined to presume that the county court judge has both considered reasonableness overall and considered it properly: *Rhodes* v. *Cornford* [1947] 2 All E.R. 601, C.A., *Tendler* v. *Sproule* [1947] 1 All E.R. 193, C.A.

The Court of Appeal will rarely intervene in the question of reasonableness, even if it might itself have come to a different view, for it is primarily a question for the trial judge: *Cresswell* v. *Hodgson* [1951] 2 K.B. 92, C.A. There is no general restriction, save relevance, as to what the court can take into account under this general heading of reasonableness (see *Cresswell* v. *Hodgson*) which is to be considered as at the date of the hearing (*Rhodes* v. *Cornford*). Nonetheless, an order may be made even if conduct leading to an order has abated by the date of hearing: see, *e.g.*, *Florent* v. *Horez* (1983) 12 H.L.R. 1, C.A.

"Reasonable" means reasonable having regard to the interests of the parties, and also reasonable having regard to the interests of the public: *Enfield London Borough Council* v. *McKeon* (1986) 18 H.L.R. 330, C.A.; see also *Battlespring* v. *Gates* (1983) 11 H.L.R. 6, C.A. In *Gladyric Ltd.* v. *Collinson* (1983) 11 H.L.R. 12, C.A., it was considered proper to take into account when determining reasonableness that the tenant had been told at the beginning of the tenancy that it would only be for a short period, on account of the landlord's development plans.

Conduct in a general sense is relevant to reasonableness: *Yelland* v. *Taylor* [1957] 1 W.L.R. 459, C.A., *Abrahams* v. *Wilson* [1971] 2 Q.B. 88, C.A. However, where neglect of a garden led to an order in the county court, the Court of Appeal allowed the appeal on the grounds that for some part of the period of neglect the tenant did not have *legal* (as distinct from moral) responsibility for the garden *qua* tenant, *i.e.* he had become tenant by succession during the (latter part of the) period of neglect: *Holloway* v. *Povey* (1984) 15 H.L.R. 104, C.A.

In considering reasonableness in relation to arrears (grounds 10 and 11), it is an important factor to take into account that the tenant is willing to arrange for payments of rent by way of housing benefit to be paid direct to the landlord: *Second W.R.V.S. Housing Society Ltd.* v. *Blair* (1986) 19 H.L.R. 104, C.A. Under the Rent Act 1977 and the Housing Act 1985, it would not normally, *prima facie*, be reasonable to make an order for possession on the ground of arrears if arrears had been cleared by the date of hearing: *Dellenty* v. *Pellow* [1951] 2 K.B. 858, C.A., *Hayman* v. *Rowlands* [1957] 1 W.L.R. 317, C.A. It is not, however, necessarily wrong: see also *Lee-Steere* v. *Jennings* (1986) 20 H.L.R. 1, C.A.

Under this Act, however, the discretionary grounds (grounds 10 and 11) must be read against the mandatory ground (ground 8), more than three months arrears at service of notice seeking possession and hearing. This complex structure of "arrears grounds" will limit the application of earlier precedent.

The Part II, Sched. 2, grounds are, in outline, as follows (see, further, notes to Sched. 2, below):

Ground 9. Suitable alternative accommodation; see also Sched. 2, Part III, below, defining such accommodation. This ground carries an entitlement to removal expenses: see s.11, below.

Ground 10. Arrears at date of notice of seeking possession (unless such waived) and at issue of proceedings.

Ground 11. Persistent delays in paying rent.

Ground 12. Obligation of tenancy (other than rent) broken or not performed.

Ground 13. Deterioration of dwelling-house, common parts, owing to waste by, neglect or default of tenant or lodger or sub-tenant.

Ground 14. Nuisance or annoyance, or use of dwelling-house for immoral or illegal purposes, by tenant or person residing with him.

Ground 15. Deterioration of furniture, owing to ill-treatment by tenant or lodger or sub-tenant.

Ground 16. Determination of employment or service tenant.

Subs. (6)

In the case of a fixed-term tenancy, a tenancy may come to an end by effluxion of time, or to a premature end—automatically, or after service of a notice by a landlord—if there is provision for re-entry or forfeiture, *e.g.* for breach of condition: see notes to s.5, above. Some such tenancies also include a provision for earlier termination by notice, whether by the landlord or the tenant (more commonly the tenant).

This subsection is concerned only with a fixed-term assured tenancy, and refers expressly to one which is subsisting; see subs. (7), for an order where the fixed-term has already expired. It will therefore operate in conjunction with an application for forfeiture for unless the tenancy itself is forfeit, no order for possession can be made. It permits a court to make an order for possession on limited grounds (grounds 2, and 8–15), if the terms of the tenancy permit it to be brought to an end on the ground in question, *i.e.* on which possession is sought, "whether that provision takes the form of a provision for re-entry, for forfeiture, for determination by notice or otherwise".

Relief from forfeiture may still be sought, under the Law of Property Act 1925, s.146, and may well be worthwhile, *e.g.* to protect a period at a particular, advantageous rent. Save when the forfeiture is for rent arrears, the Law of Property Act 1925, s.146, requires that preliminary notice be given a tenant before a forfeiture, to give the tenant an opportunity to remedy a breach, provided the breach is remediable, and to give him an opportunity of applying to the court for relief from forfeiture. A breach of covenant against immoral user is not capable of remedy within s.146: *British Petroleum Pension Trust Ltd.* v. *Behrendt* (1985) 18 H.L.R. 42, C.A. S.146(4) permits application for relief from a sub-tenant. The s.146 notice must comply with the formal requirements of s.196 of the 1925 Act.

Where the basis of the claim to forfeit is dilapidations, the provisions of the Landlord and Tenant Act 1927, s.18(2), add to the requirements of s.146, and in some cases, the Leasehold Property (Repairs) Act 1938, as extended by s.51 of the Landlord and Tenant Act 1954, will impose additional restrictions (but the 1938 Act only applies to tenancies for a term certain of not less than seven years, of which three or more years remain unexpired).

A s.146 notice should be served on the assignee (not the assignor) of a tenancy, for he is the person concerned to avoid the forfeiture: *Old Grovebury Manor Farm* v. *W. Seymour Plant Sales* [1979] 1 W.L.R. 1397. All joint tenants must be served: *Blewett* v. *Blewett* [1936] 2 All E.R. 188. Service of the notice may be by delivery at the premises: *Newborough (Lord)* v. *Jones* [1975] Ch. 90.

Relief may be granted in respect of part only property comprised in lease: *G.M.S. Syndicate* v. *Gary Elliott* [1982] Ch. 1. In general, the courts are unwilling to specify rules or principles for the grant of relief: *Rose* v. *Hyman* [1912] A.C. 623, H.L. If a breach has been remedied, relief will commonly but not invariably be granted: see, *e.g. Bathurst (Earl)* v. *Fine* [1974] 1 W.L.R. 905. Remedy of breach is normally required as a condition of relief, although, again, not invariably: see, *e.g. Belgravia Insurance Co.* v. *Meah* [1964] 1 Q.B. 436. *Central Estates Ltd.* v. *Woolgar (No. 2)* [1972] 1 Q.B. 48, C.A., *Scala* v. *Forbes* [1974] Q.B. 575. Although the tenant will normally have to bear the costs of an application for relief (*Belgravia*), this will not be so if the landlord's claim to forfeit is wholly unmeritorious: see, *e.g. Woodtrek Ltd.* v. *Jezek* (1982) 261 E.G. 571.

While an application for relief is pending, the tenant may still enforce, or seek to enforce, the covenants in the lease: *Peninsular Maritime* v. *Padseal Ltd.* (1981) 259 E.G. 860, C.A.

Where arrears of rent are concerned, relief is governed by the Supreme Court Act 1981, s.38, and the County Courts Act 1984, s.138, under the provisions of which latter Act a tenant can acquire automatic relief in the course of proceedings issued by the landlord in the county court, by paying into court, at least five clear days before the date specified for the hearing, the whole of the arrears together with the costs of the action. A court will, in any event, invariably order payment of arrears as a condition of relief, within a time specified if not forthwith: *Barton, Thompson & Co.* v. *Stapling Machines Co.* [1966] Ch. 499.

Under s.138, however, if its terms are not complied with, the right to relief is entirely lost, and it has been held that this means relief is not otherwise available in both county court and High Court: *Di Palma* v. *Victoria Square Property Co.* [1984] Ch. 346, 17 H.L.R. 448, C.A.

Subs. (7)

This makes clear that once a fixed-term assured tenancy has expired, the full range of grounds is available, and if an order is made in relation to a tenant who has formerly enjoyed the benefit of a fixed-term, then it either prevents a statutory periodic tenancy arising (if termination will be contemporaneous with expiry of fixed-term) or terminates the statutory periodic tenancy, without the need for any additional notice under s.8, below.

Notice of proceedings for possession

8.—(1) The court shall not entertain proceedings for possession of a dwelling-house let on an assured tenancy unless—
  (a) the landlord or, in the case of joint landlords, at least one of them has served on the tenant a notice in accordance with this section and the proceedings are begun within the time limits stated in the notice in accordance with subsections (3) and (4) below; or
  (b) the court considers it just and equitable to dispense with the requirement of such a notice.

(2) The court shall not make an order for possession on any of the grounds in Schedule 2 to this Act unless that ground and particulars of it are specified in the notice under this section; but the grounds specified in such a notice may be altered or added to with the leave of the court.

(3) A notice under this section is one in the prescribed form informing the tenant that—
  (a) the landlord intends to begin proceedings for possession of the dwelling-house on one or more of the grounds specified in the notice; and
  (b) those proceedings will not begin earlier than a date specified in the notice which, without prejudice to any additional limitation under subsection (4) below, shall not be earlier than the expiry of the period of two weeks from the date of service of the notice; and
  (c) those proceedings will not begin later than twelve months from the date of service of the notice.

(4) If a notice under this section specifies, in accordance with subsection (3)(a) above, any of Grounds 1, 2, 5 to 7, 9 and 16 in Schedule 2 to this Act (whether with or without other grounds), the date specified in the notice as mentioned in subsection (3)(b) above shall not be earlier than—

(a) two months from the date of service of the notice; and
(b) if the tenancy is a periodic tenancy, the earliest date on which, apart from section 5(1) above, the tenancy could be brought to an end by a notice to quit given by the landlord on the same date as the date of service of the notice under this section.

(5) The court may not exercise the power conferred by subsection (1)(b) above if the landlord seeks to recover possession on Ground 8 in Schedule 2 to this Act.

(6) Where a notice under this section—
(a) is served at a time when the dwelling-house is let on a fixed term tenancy, or
(b) is served after a fixed term tenancy has come to an end but relates (in whole or in part) to events occurring during that tenancy,

the notice shall have effect notwithstanding that the tenant becomes or has become tenant under a statutory periodic tenancy arising on the coming to an end of the fixed term tenancy.

DEFINITIONS
"assured tenancy": s.1.
"dwelling-house": s.45.
"fixed term": s.45.
"landlord": s.45.
"prescribed form": s.45.
"tenancy": s.45.
"tenant": s.45.

GENERAL NOTE
This section introduces the "notice of proceedings for possession", or notice of seeking possession as such a form has come to be known under the legislation on which it is modelled, Housing Act 1985, s.83. Contrary to common law (cf. notes to s.1, above), and overriding the presumption in s.45(3), below, the notice may be served by one or less than all of a number of joint landlords. The notice must still be in force at the time the proceedings are issued: see notes to subs. (3), below.

The requirement to serve notice applies equally to periodic assured tenancies, and fixed term assured tenancies. The court's power to "waive" is a power to waive notice altogether. A periodic tenant could therefore find himself in court without *any* notice at all, for the provisions of s.5 and this section replace common law notice to quit. There can be no waiver if possession is sought on ground 8 (three months in arrears of rent at service of notice and hearing): see notes to Sched. 2, below.

The court can only waive notice, however, if it is "just and equitable" to do so. It is inconceivable that a court would find it just and equitable to waive notice unless *either* (a) the tenant was substantively forewarned of proceedings, *or* (b) the act of which complaint is made is *so* serious that no tenant could expect anything other than immediate proceedings. "Abandonment" is not included, because if the tenant has abandoned, he will have ceased use as an only or principal home, from which it follows that the tenancy will have ceased to be assured.

The phrase "just and equitable" has been considered in cases arising under the Rent Act 1977, where prior notice is required as part of the operation of some of the mandatory grounds for possession, but may be waived by the court if just and equitable to do so. In *Fernandes* v. *Parvardin* (1982) 5 H.L.R. 33, C.A., it was held on the facts that oral notice was enough to justify use of the power to waive the requirement for written notice where there was no suggestion of misunderstanding on the part of the tenants and no injustice or inequity resulted, which the majority considered the correct test. Stephenson L.J., in the minority, considered that there was no need to restrict the approach, holding that the words were of very wide import.

The decision in *Bradshaw* v. *Baldwin-Wiseman* (1985) 17 H.L.R. 260, C.A. concerns the need for a tenant to have known that a tenancy was subject to the mandatory ground and, as such, is not here relevant. However, in the course of the judgment, the court expressed the view that the minority approach in *Fernandes* was to be preferred. The court should look at all the circumstances of the case, affecting both landlord and tenant, and those in which the failure to give written notice arose.

Subss. (2)–(5)

The notice must be in prescribed form, and has to specify the ground on which possession is to be sought, although these may be varied or added to with the leave of the court. Not only must the ground be specified but also "particulars" of the ground: see *Torridge D.C. v. Jones* (1985) 18 H.L.R. 107, C.A., in which s.82 of the Housing Act 1985 in analogous terms was held to require sufficient particulars to show the tenant what he had to do to put matters right before proceedings commenced.

The tenant must also be informed that proceedings will begin no earlier than either two weeks, or two months, from date of service of notice, depending on the ground, and no later than 12 months from date of service. A period of two months is required if Sched. 2, grounds 1, 2, 5–7, 9 and 16, are specified: formerly occupied by landlord or required by landlord, mortgagee exercising power of sale, for occupation by minister of religion, demolition, reconstruction or major works, possession after death of former tenant, suitable alternative accommodation, former service tenant. Where the two month minimum applies, there is an alternative minimum (if, as it rarely will be, it is longer), that the tenancy is periodic and could be brought to an end by notice to quit given by the landlord, *e.g.* a quarterly tenancy which would require a quarter's notice.

Subs. (6)

A statutory periodic tenancy automatically follows a fixed term assured tenancy, unless an order for possession is made which prevents such arising. This subsection permits a ground for possession arising during a fixed term to be applied during such subsequent statutory periodic tenancy, whether it is served during the fixed term, or merely relates to events occurring during the fixed term.

Extended discretion of court in possession claims

9.—(1) Subject to subsection (6) below, the court may adjourn for such period or periods as it thinks fit proceedings for possession of a dwelling-house let on an assured tenancy.

(2) On the making of an order for possession of a dwelling-house let on an assured tenancy or at any time before the execution of such an order, the court, subject to subsection (6) below, may—

(a) stay or suspend execution of the order, or

(b) postpone the date of possession,

for such period or periods as the court thinks just.

(3) On any such adjournment as is referred to in subsection (1) above or on any such stay, suspension or postponement as is referred to in subsection (2) above, the court, unless it considers that to do so would cause exceptional hardship to the tenant or would otherwise be unreasonable, shall impose conditions with regard to payment by the tenant of arrears of rent (if any) and rent or payments in respect of occupation after the termination of the tenancy (mesne profits) and may impose such other conditions as it thinks fit.

(4) If any such conditions as are referred to in subsection (3) above are complied with, the court may, if it thinks fit, discharge or rescind any such order as is referred to in subsection (2) above.

(5) In any case where—

(a) at a time when proceedings are brought for possession of a dwelling-house let on an assured tenancy, the tenant's spouse or former spouse, having rights of occupation under the Matrimonial Homes Act 1983, is in occupation of the dwelling-house, and

(b) the assured tenancy is terminated as a result of those proceedings,

the spouse or former spouse, so long as he or she remains in occupation, shall have the same rights in relation to, or in connection with, any such adjournment as is referred to in subsection (1) above or any such stay, suspension or postponement as is referred to in subsection (2) above, as he or she would have if those rights of occupation were not affected by the termination of the tenancy.

(6) This section does not apply if the court is satisfied that the landlord is entitled to possession of the dwelling-house—

(a) on any of the grounds in Part I of Schedule 2 to this Act; or

(b) by virtue of subsection (1) or subsection (4) of section 21 below.

DEFINITIONS

"assured tenancy": s.1.
"dwelling-house": s.45.
"landlord": s.45.
"tenancy": s.45.
"tenant": s.45.

GENERAL NOTE

This section specifies the powers of the county court (see s.40, below) on a claim for possession where the ground is a discretionary ground for possession: see notes to s.7, above (subs. (6).) It is modelled on the Rent Act 1977, s.100, and the Housing Act 1985, s.85. Where no specific legislation or inherent jurisdiction (e.g. on forfeiture proceedings—cf. notes to s.7, above) of the court permits suspension or postponement of the operation of a possession order, as is the case where possession is ordered on a mandatory ground, the court's powers on an application for possession will normally be subject to the restrictions imposed by the Housing Act 1980, s.89, i.e. to make an order to take effect within 14 days or, in a case of exceptional hardship, such longer period as it considers appropriate to a maximum of six weeks. The provisions of s.89, however, restrict only the county court, not the High Court: see Bain & Co. v. Church Commissioners of England (1988) 21 H.L.R., Ch. D.

Note the s.10, limitation below, on the orders which may be made against someone who is a "sharer" within s.3, above.

The principal power is that contained in subs. (2). It is exercisable at any time before execution of the order, but this does not deprive the county court of power to set aside a judgment or order under County Court Rules 1981, Ord. 37, r.8(3) even after execution: see Governors of the Peabody Donation Fund v. Hay (1986) 19 H.L.R. 145, C.A. The powers of the subsection are available on subsequent application, i.e. prior to execution, even if the initial order was an outright or absolute order for possession: Birtwistle v. Tweedale [1954] 1 W.L.R. 190, C.A.; Yates v. Morris [1951] 1 K.B. 77, C.A.; Vandermolen v. Toma (1981) 9 H.L.R. 91, C.A. The court has power to make more than one order, but only prior to execution; a mere application for a stay or suspension does not operate as a stay in itself—Moore v. Registrar of Lambeth County Court [1969] 1 All E.R. 782, C.A.

It is likely that a tenancy will be considered to remain in force even though a suspended or conditional order has been made: Sherrin v. Brand [1965] 1 Q.B. 403, C.A. When a conditional order has been made, e.g. payment off arrears, the assured tenancy will continue until there is a failure to comply with the condition: see Thompson v. Elmbridge Borough Council (1987) 19 H.L.R. 526, C.A.; see also R. v. Croydon London Borough Council, ex p. Toth (1986) 18 H.L.R. 493, Q.B.D. However, even a failure to comply with the condition is not to be read as an order enabling the landlord to execute as soon as the condition is not complied with; accordingly, the court still has power to entertain an application by the tenant to suspend the warrant for possession when the landlord seeks to execute it: R. v. Ilkeston County Court, ex p. Kruza (1985) 17 H.L.R. 539, Q.B.D.

A court should not make an order producing an indefinite suspension: Vandermolen v. Toma (1981) 9 H.L.R. 91, C.A.; even an order likely to last for a lengthy period is not desirable,—rather, no order for possession should be made, but the tenant warned, and the landlord advised, that on further default, an outright order will follow: Mills v. Allen [1953] 2 Q.B. 341, C.A.

If Rent Act precedent is followed, then a tenant on whom the tenancy has devolved on death will—unless or until the subject of proceedings for possession under Sched. 2, ground 7,—take subject to either an absolute order if such has been made (American Economic Laundry v. Little [1951] 1 K.B. 400, C.A.) or a suspended order: Sherrin v. Brand (above).

Subs. (3)

There is a presumption that the tenant will be required to make payments of any arrears of rent, and continuing payments of rent or mesne profits, unless the court considers that it would cause exceptional hardship to the tenant or would otherwise be unreasonable (e.g.

where a tenant patently unable to pay a high rent has been accepted by the landlord without even minimal enquiries). Where arrears are continuing, and there is a likelihood that the tenant will dissipate any housing benefit unless an order is made, it may be possible for a landlord to obtain an interlocutory order to require the tenant to pay his housing benefit towards the rent: *Berg* v. *Markhill* (1985) 17 H.L.R. 455, C.A.

Subs. (4)

This might be applicable when an order had been suspended on payment of current rent plus an amount off the arrears, which arrears have now been cleared, or where the order was on terms that there be no further nuisance to neighbours, an order might be discharged after a period of "good behaviour".

Subs. (5)

This subsection extends to the spouse of an assured tenant the same rights to a stay, suspension, postponement or adjournment, as the assured tenant. There is, however, a degree of mismatch between housing law and matrimonial law so far as its value to *former* spouses is concerned.

The position is best understood historically. Under the Rent Acts, if a tenancy was a sole tenancy, and the sole tenant departed, leaving a spouse in occupation, then prima facie all that would be needed would be for the landlord to determine the contractual tenancy, and in the absence of residential occupation (see also notes to s.1, above) by the departed tenant-spouse, there could be no statutory tenancy. However, the courts held that, *so long as the marriage subsisted*, the occupation of the non-tenant-spouse would be treated as the occupation of the departed tenant-spouse, and the statutory tenancy accordingly sustained: see *Brown* v. *Draper* [1944] K.B. 309, C.A., *Robson* v. *Headland* (1948) 64 T.L.R. 596, C.A., *Old Gate Estates* v. *Alexander* [1950] 1 K.B. 311, C.A., *Middleton* v. *Baldock* [1950] 1 K.B. 657, C.A., *Wabe* v. *Taylor* [1952] 2 Q.B. 735, C.A., *Heath Estates Ltd.* v. *Burchell* (1979) 251 E.G. 1173, C.A.

The key phrase is that emphasised in the last paragraph: the "extended" meaning of occupation ended with decree absolute. Furthermore, all it served to achieve was that the occupation of the remaining spouse was treated as the occupation of the departed spouse, so that the statutory tenancy was not lost for want of residence. If a possession order was nonetheless made against the departed tenant-spouse, rights of occupation were lost, including to the non-tenant-spouse: see *Penn* v. *Dunn* [1970] 2 Q.B. 686, C.A.; see also *Grange Lane South Flats Ltd.* v. *Cook* (1979) 254 E.G. 499, C.A. In 1980, amendments to the Rent Act 1977, by the Housing Act 1980, overcame the problem posed by *Penn* v. *Dunn*, by extending to the remaining tenant-spouse the right to seek a suspension, postponement, adjournment, etc., under the equivalents in those Acts of this section.

Turning now to matrimonial legislation, the proposition that the occupation of the non-tenant-spouse was to be treated as the occupation of the departed tenant-spouse was statutorily adopted under the Matrimonial Homes Act 1973. However, again this did not extend beyond decree absolute. The 1973 Act also gave the non-tenant spouse the right to apply for a transfer of the tenancy, although this, too, ended with decree absolute. In 1981, the Matrimonial Homes and Property Act 1981 extended the right to transfer beyond divorce, although not once the spouse applying for transfer has remarried. The 1973 and 1981 Acts have now been consolidated into the Matrimonial Homes Act 1983. The Act applies these principles to protected and secure tenants, and by amendment, now also to assured tenants (see Sched. 17, paras. 33, 34).

Under this Act, occupation is as much a requirement for qualification of a tenancy as assured as it is under the Housing Act 1985 for a secure tenancy or under the Rent Act 1977 for a statutory tenancy: s.1. Such occupation will be deemed to be that of the departed tenant-spouse if maintained by a non-tenant-spouse, under the Matrimonial Homes Act 1983, and caselaw, *until decree absolute*. Afterwards, however, although there remains a right to claim the transfer of the tenancy until remarriage, and although this section is available to "former" spouses, there will be no *assured* (or secure or statutory) tenancy, for want of occupation, where the spouse who has departed is the tenant-spouse. (The less common position is where transfer is sought by a departed non-tenant-spouse against a remaining tenant-spouse; such a case benefits from the extension beyond decree absolute.)

In *Lewis* v. *Lewis* [1985] A.C. 459, 17 H.L.R. 459, the House of Lords considered the right to transfer after divorce, as introduced in 1981, and dismissed an attempt to apply it retrospectively. Part of the reasoning, however, was that the Act could not be used to revive a statutory (or, therefore, secure or assured) tenancy which had ceased to exist before application for transfer, which is exactly the position which will arise in the circumstances described in the last paragraph. In *Thompson* v. *Elmbridge Borough Council* (1987) 19

H.L.R. 526, C.A., similarly, a secure tenancy was held to have determined for failure to meet conditions of a suspended order, and there was accordingly nothing to transfer under the Matrimonial Homes Act 1983.

There are, it is submitted, only two possible resolutions. One is to conclude that the 1983 Act is only applicable where the tenant-spouse remains in occupation, under this Act as an only or principal home, and the non-tenant-spouse seeks a transfer or, under this section, the exercise of the court's discretion; this is the *less* common case. The alternative is that Parliament has intended to extend the proposition that occupation by a non-tenant-spouse is deemed occupation by a tenant-spouse beyond decree absolute. Until this point is resolved, non-tenant-spouses should not rely on the reference herein to "former" spouses, but should ensure that application for transfer is made *before* decree absolute.

Special provisions applicable to shared accommodation

10.—(1) This section applies in a case falling within subsection (1) of section 3 above and expressions used in this section have the same meaning as in that section.

(2) Without prejudice to the enforcement of any order made under subsection (3) below, while the tenant is in possession of the separate accommodation, no order shall be made for possession of any of the shared accommodation, whether on the application of the immediate landlord of the tenant or on the application of any person under whom that landlord derives title, unless a like order has been made, or is made at the same time, in respect of the separate accommodation; and the provisions of section 6 above shall have effect accordingly.

(3) On the application of the landlord, the court may make such order as it thinks just either—

(a) terminating the right of the tenant to use the whole or any part of the shared accommodation other than living accommodation; or

(b) modifying his right to use the whole or any part of the shared accommodation, whether by varying the persons or increasing the number of persons entitled to the use of that accommodation or otherwise.

(4) No order shall be made under subsection (3) above so as to effect any termination or modification of the rights of the tenant which, apart from section 3(3) above, could not be effected by or under the terms of the tenancy.

DEFINITIONS
"landlord": s.45.
"separate accommodation": s.3.
"shared accommodation": s.3.
"tenancy": s.45.
"tenant": s.45.

GENERAL NOTE
S.3 permits a tenant who shares "living accommodation" with other tenants (but not his own landlord) to be an assured tenant, notwithstanding that there is no letting as a separate dwelling: see notes thereto, above. The "separate accommodation" is that of which he has exclusive occupation; the "shared accommodation" is that which he shares with other tenants. Under this section, and subject to a "variation order" under subs. (3), no order can be made for possession of the shared accommodation, unless an order is to be made in respect of the separate accommodation. This is so whether the applicant for possession is the tenant's landlord, or indeed a superior landlord.

However, there can be a variation, though not amounting to absolute removal of the right to use shared *living* accommodation, on application to the court, *if* such variation is permitted under the terms of the tenancy, for this purpose (only) ignoring s.3(3), avoiding any term permitting (termination or) modification of shared living accommodation. The effect is to reinstate a term avoided by s.3(3), so far as modification only is concerned, by application to the court.

Payment of removal expenses in certain cases

11.—(1) Where a court makes an order for possession of a dwelling-house let on an assured tenancy on Ground 6 or Ground 9 in Schedule 2 to this Act (but not on any other ground), the landlord shall pay to the tenant a sum equal to the reasonable expenses likely to be incurred by the tenant in removing from the dwelling-house.

(2) Any question as to the amount of the sum referred in subsection (1) above shall be determined by agreement between the landlord and the tenant or, in default of agreement, by the court.

(3) Any sum payable to a tenant by virtue of this section shall be recoverable as a civil debt due from the landlord.

DEFINITIONS
  "assured tenancy": s.1.
  "dwelling-house": s.45.
  "landlord": s.45.
  "tenant": s.45.

GENERAL NOTE
  Where possession is ordered on Sched. 2, ground 6 (demolition, reconstruction or major works), or ground 9 (suitable alternative accommodation), the tenant is entitled to recover the reasonable expenses he is likely to incur moving from the property. The phrase "removing from" would not seem to confine the expenditure to "moving out" costs only, *i.e.* it would seem to extend to "removal into elsewhere".
  The same expression is to be found in the Land Compensation Act 1973, s.38, quantifying "disturbance payments" under *ibid.*, s.37. Under that Act, construed in "a common sense way", and distinguishing the term "expenses of the removal" to be found in earlier legislation, as a narrower expression, it was held that expenses in removing "may include reasonable expenses, reasonably incurred as a direct and natural consequence of, and in, the compulsory removing, in addition to the expenses strictly referable to "the removal" itself . . .", *per* Lord Cameron, Lord President, *Glasgow Corporation* v. *Anderson* (1970) S.L.T. 225 (Court of Session). Even the cost of redecorating or rewiring might be included: *ibid.*
  More obviously there are items such as reconnection of utilities, redirection of mail, actual removal costs, adapting furniture or carpetting: see *Nolan* v. *Sheffield M.D.C.* (1979) 38 P. & C.R. 741 (L.T.) for a useful analysis in some detail of a number of common items.

Compensation for misrepresentation or concealment

12. Where a landlord obtains an order for possession of a dwelling-house let on an assured tenancy on one or more of the grounds in Schedule 2 to this Act and it is subsequently made to appear to the court that the order was obtained by misrepresentation or concealment of material facts, the court may order the landlord to pay to the former tenant such sum as appears sufficient as compensation for damage or loss sustained by that tenant as a result of the order.

DEFINITIONS
  "assured tenancy": s.1.
  "dwelling-house": s.45.
  "landlord": s.45.
  "tenant": s.1.

GENERAL NOTE
  This section permits the court to compensate a tenant against whom an order for possession has been made, secured by misrepresentation or concealment of material facts: the section is modelled on the Rent Act 1977, s.102, see also *Thorne* v. *Smith* [1947] K.B. 307, C.A. Because the term "tenant" means "all the persons who jointly constitute the . . . tenant" (s.45, below), it would seem that application under this section must be made by *all* the joint tenants displaced: see also, *e.g. Jacobs* v. *Chaudhuri* [1968] 2 Q.B. 470, C.A., *T.M. Fairclough* v. *Berliner* [1931] 1 Ch. 60, *Turley* v. *Panton* (1975) 29 P. & C.R. 397, *Newman* v. *Keedwell* (1978) 35 P. & C.R. 393; but *cf. Howson* v. *Buxton* (1928) 97 L.J.K.B. 749, and *Lloyd* v. *Sadler* [1978] Q.B. 774, C.A.

In the light of s.40(2), below, action may be brought in the county court, notwithstanding that the damages sought exceed the county court limit for the time being; indeed, if action is taken in the High Court instead, costs will only be awarded on the county court scale— s.40(4).

Rent and other terms

Increase of rent under assured periodic tenancies

13.—(1) This section applies to—

   (a) a statutory periodic tenancy other than one which, by virtue of paragraph 11 or paragraph 12 in Part I of Schedule 1 to this Act, cannot for the time being be an assured tenancy; and

   (b) any other periodic tenancy which is an assured tenancy, other than one in relation to which there is a provision, for the time being binding on the tenant, under which the rent for a particular period of the tenancy will or may be greater than the rent for an earlier period.

(2) For the purpose of securing an increase in the rent under a tenancy to which this section applies, the landlord may serve on the tenant a notice in the prescribed form proposing a new rent to take effect at the beginning of a new period of the tenancy specified in the notice, being a period beginning not earlier than—

   (a) the minimum period after the date of the service of the notice; and

   (b) except in the case of a statutory periodic tenancy, the first anniversary of the date on which the first period of the tenancy began; and

   (c) if the rent under the tenancy has previously been increased by virtue of a notice under this subsection or a determination under section 14 below, the first anniversary of the date on which the increased rent took effect.

(3) The minimum period referred to in subsection (2) above is—

   (a) in the case of a yearly tenancy, six months;

   (b) in the case of a tenancy where the period is less than a month, one month; and

   (c) in any other case, a period equal to the period of the tenancy.

(4) Where a notice is served under subsection (2) above, a new rent specified in the notice shall take effect as mentioned in the notice unless, before the beginning of the new period specified in the notice,—

   (a) the tenant by an application in the prescribed form refers the notice to a rent assessment committee; or

   (b) the landlord and the tenant agree on a variation of the rent which is different from that proposed in the notice or agree that the rent should not be varied.

(5) Nothing in this section (or in section 14 below) affects the right of the landlord and the tenant under an assured tenancy to vary by agreement any term of the tenancy (including a term relating to rent).

DEFINITIONS
   "assured tenancy": s.1.
   "landlord": s.45.
   "prescribed": s.45.
   "statutory periodic tenancy": s.5(7).
   "tenancy": s.45.
   "tenant": s.45.

GENERAL NOTE
   Substantively, this and the next section are two of the most important sections of this Part of the Act, because they represent the limits of statutory intervention in rents; compared to Rent Act rent controls, that intervention is slight indeed. The next section governs the *levels* at which rents may be fixed by a rent assessment committee (see also notes to s.6, above);

this section determines *when and how* rent increases may come to be payable. It has no effect on a statutory periodic tenancy which is prevented for the time being from being assured because of the crown or public ownership restrictions in Sched. 1, paras. 11 or 12. Its application is confined to *periodic* tenancies.

The starting-point is agreement. Landlord and tenant may agree a variation in the rent, regardless of the provisions of this section, or the next: subs. (6). Similarly, if a periodic tenancy contains a term permitting a rent increase, that term will prevail *to the exclusion of this section*: subs. (1)(b). Otherwise, the procedure is similar to s.6, above: a landlord can serve notice in prescribed form proposing a new rent to take effect from a specified date, which will take effect unless before that date the tenant refers the notice to a rent assessment committee, or the landlord and tenant agree a different rent or that no increase is to be sought. There is no procedure at all for a tenant to refer a matter to the rent assessment committee; its jurisdiction arises exclusively on a landlord's attempt to secure an increase.

Subs. (1)

The procedure is that which is applicable, instead of that contained in s.6, above, to increase of rent under a statutory periodic tenancy which will normally follow a fixed-term tenancy, save where there has been a proposal for variation of terms, with consequential variation of rent, in which case s.6 will apply—see notes thereto, above.

The procedure is also applicable to an ordinary periodic tenancy, save where that tenancy contains a provision binding on the tenant, permitting the landlord to impose a rent increase, *e.g.* a rent review or inflation-linking clause.

Subss. (2) and (3)

A notice proposing a rent increase must be in prescribed form. The form will presumably advise the tenant of his right to refer the rent to a rent assessment committee under subs. (4). The notice must specify the new rent, and identify the period of the tenancy from when it is to take effect. There is no earliest date when the notice can be *served*, but the earliest date which can be specified as from when the increase will take effect is governed by three criteria: save in the case of a statutory periodic tenancy, it must be no earlier than the first anniversary of the date on which the first period of the tenancy began; it must be no earlier than the "minimum period" following service of the notice; and, it can be no earlier than one year after a former increase took effect, whether by notice or by rent assessment committee under s.14, below.

The saving for statutory periodic tenancies entitles a landlord to seek an immediate rent increase following the expiry of a fixed-term assured tenancy of less than a year.

The minimum period reflects the law governing notice to quit. If the tenancy is a yearly tenancy, it is six months; if the tenancy is less than a month, it is one month; if the tenancy is of a month or more (but less than a year), it is of one period of the tenancy.

Subs. (4)

The rent specified in the notice will take effect unless either the tenant refers the notice to a rent assessment committee before the beginning of the period to which it applies, by application in prescribed form, or before the beginning of the period to which it applies either the landlord and tenant agree a different rent, or agree that no increase is called for. There is no requirement that such an agreement should be in writing, but a tenant would be well-advised to make sure that it is, for otherwise he might find the right to refer the rent to the rent assessment committee entirely lost: there is no procedure at all for a tenant to refer a matter to the rent assessment committee of his own initiative; its jurisdiction arises exclusively on a landlord's attempt to secure an increase. Where there are joint tenants the application to the rent assessment committee will have to be by *all* the tenants, unless it is made with the full authority of all the tenants by one acting as their agent: *Turley* v. *Panton* (1975) 29 P. & C.R. 397, Q.B.D., *R.* v. *Rent Officer for Camden L.B.C., ex p. Felix* (1988) 21 H.L.R., Q.B.D., see also s.45(3).

Determination of rent by rent assessment committee

14.—(1) Where, under subsection (4)(a) of section 13 above, a tenant refers to a rent assessment committee a notice under subsection (2) of that section, the committee shall determine the rent at which, subject to subsections (2) and (4) below, the committee consider that the dwelling-house concerned might reasonably be expected to be let in the open market by a willing landlord under an assured tenancy—

(a) which is a periodic tenancy having the same periods as those of the tenancy to which the notice relates;

(b) which begins at the beginning of the new period specified in the notice;

(c) the terms of which (other than relating to the amount of the rent) are the same as those of the tenancy to which the notice relates; and

(d) in respect of which the same notices, if any, have been given under any of Grounds 1 to 5 of Schedule 2 to this Act, as have been given (or have effect as if given) in relation to the tenancy to which the notice relates.

(2) In making a determination under this section, there shall be disregarded—

(a) any effect on the rent attributable to the granting of a tenancy to a sitting tenant;

(b) any increase in the value of the dwelling-house attributable to a relevant improvement carried out by a person who at the time it was carried out was the tenant, if the improvement—

(i) was carried out otherwise than in pursuance of an obligation to his immediate landlord, or

(ii) was carried out pursuant to an obligation to his immediate landlord being an obligation which did not relate to the specific improvement concerned but arose by reference to consent given to the carrying out of that improvement; and

(c) any reduction in the value of the dwelling-house attributable to a failure by the tenant to comply with any terms of the tenancy.

(3) For the purposes of subsection (2)(b) above, in relation to a notice which is referred by a tenant as mentioned in subsection (1) above, an improvement is a relevant improvement if either it was carried out during the tenancy to which the notice relates or the following conditions are satisfied, namely—

(a) that it was carried out not more than twenty-one years before the date of service of the notice; and

(b) that, at all times during the period beginning when the improvement was carried out and ending on the date of service of the notice, the dwelling-house has been let under an assured tenancy; and

(c) that, on the coming to an end of an assured tenancy at any time during that period, the tenant (or, in the case of joint tenants, at least one of them) did not quit.

(4) In this section "rent" does not include any service charge, within the meaning of section 18 of the Landlord and Tenant Act 1985, but, subject to that, includes any sums payable by the tenant to the landlord on account of the use of furniture or for any of the matters referred to in subsection (1)(a) of that section, whether or not those sums are separate from the sums payable for the occupation of the dwelling-house concerned or are payable under separate agreements.

(5) Where any rates in respect of the dwelling-house concerned are borne by the landlord or a superior landlord, the rent assessment committee shall make their determination under this section as if the rates were not so borne.

(6) In any case where—

(a) a rent assessment committee have before them at the same time the reference of a notice under section 6(2) above relating to a tenancy (in this subsection referred to as "the section 6 reference") and the reference of a notice under section 13(2) above relating to the same tenancy (in this subsection referred to as "the section 13 reference"), and

(b) the date specified in the notice under section 6(2) above is not later than the first day of the new period specified in the notice under section 13(2) above, and

(c) the committee propose to hear the two references together,

the committee shall make a determination in relation to the section 6 reference before making their determination in relation to the section 13 reference and, accordingly, in such a case the reference in subsection (1)(c) above to the terms of the tenancy to which the notice relates shall be construed as a reference to those terms as varied by virtue of the determination made in relation to the section 6 reference.

(7) Where a notice under section 13(2) above has been referred to a rent assessment committee, then, unless the landlord and the tenant otherwise agree, the rent determined by the committee (subject, in a case where subsection (5) above applies, to the addition of the appropriate amount in respect of rates) shall be the rent under the tenancy with effect from the beginning of the new period specified in the notice or, if it appears to the rent assessment committee that that would cause undue hardship to the tenant, with effect from such later date (not being later than the date the rent is determined) as the committee may direct.

(8) Nothing in this section requires a rent assessment committee to continue with their determination of a rent for a dwelling-house if the landlord and tenant give notice in writing that they no longer require such a determination or if the tenancy has come to an end.

DEFINITIONS

"assured tenancy": s.1.
"dwelling-house": s.45.
"landlord": s.45.
"let": s.45.
"tenancy": s.45.
"tenant": s.45.

GENERAL NOTE

This section governs the level of rent to be set by the rent assessment committee (as to which, see notes to s.6, above), and from when it takes effect.

Subs. (1)

The starting-point is open market rental, of a periodic tenancy having the same periods as the tenancy in question, beginning at the period the landlord has identified in his s.13 notice, the (other) terms of which being the same as those of the tenancy in question, taking into account any notice served under Sched. 2, grounds 1–5 (prior occupation by landlord, required for landlord's occupation, required for sale by mortgagee, prior holiday letting, prior student letting, required for minister of religion).

Subss. (2), (3)

This section requires the committee to disregard: (a) the fact that the tenant is a sitting tenant, which customarily lowers value; (b) any increase in the value of the property attributable to tenant's "relevant" improvements as defined; and (c) any reduction in the value of the property attributable to the tenant's failure to comply with obligations under the tenancy, *e.g.* repairs.

There must be a failure on the part of a tenant: see *McGee* v. *London Rent Assessment Committee* (1969) 113 S.J. 384 (disrepair attributed to poltergeist). An obligation to keep premises in tenant-like repair, or the implied obligation to use premises in a tenant-like manner, has been held not to create a repairing obligation failure to comply with which in turn creates a disregardable disrepair, but the analogous wording under the Rent Act refers specifically to disrepair and defects, rather than the more general terminology of this section: see *Firstcross Ltd.* v. *Teasdale* (1982) 8 H.L.R. 112.

If a tenant *repairs* (rather than improves) voluntarily, *e.g.* where the burden is on the landlord under s.11 of the Landlord and Tenant Act 1985 (see further notes to s.107, below), the landlord will be able to avail himself of the increase in value: *Mackie* v. *Gallagher* (1967) S.C. 59. Nor is the committee bound to take into account the landlord's failure to repair in accordance with his obligations, for while *de facto* condition will undoubtedly diminish recoverable rent, the landlord's covenant will itself have a value: *Sturolson & Co. v. Mauroux* (1988) 20 H.L.R., C.A.

"Relevant improvements" are as defined in subs. (3). They include improvements during the tenancy to which the notice (of increase of rent) relates, or improvements carried out under an earlier tenancy, provided (a) that they were carried out no more than 21 years before, *and* (b) at all times since, the dwelling has been let under an assured tenancy, *and* (c) at no time since has the tenant (or one of joint tenants) quit.

Improvements which the tenant has contracted to perform will not normally be disregarded, but "voluntary" improvements will be: subs. (2)(b)(i). However, if the tenant is *obliged* (note, not merely "permitted") to carry out improvements, but subject to the landlord's consent, this is to be construed in the same way, as a "voluntary" improvement, and accordingly is also to be disregarded. In either case, the disregarded improvements can be those of the tenant, or any person who at the time of the improvement was tenant, *e.g.* a previous tenant, *cf. Trustees of Henry Smith's Charity* v. *Hemmings* (1982) 6 H.L.R. 47, C.A.

Appeal. There is no express provision for appeal against a decision of the rent assessment committee, but such is available on a point of law (only) under s.13, Tribunals and Inquiries Act 1971, s.13, and committees are susceptible to judicial review pursuant to R.S.C.Ord.53. It has recently been said that, notwithstanding the right of appeal, there are advantages to judicial review: (1) the rent assessment committee could be represented, while on appeal they are not, which may necessitate delay for the *amicus* to be appointed; (2) costs follow the event; (3) the committee could appeal against a challenge successful at first instance— see *Ellis & Sons Fourth Amalgamated Properties* v. *Southern Rent Assessment Panel* (1984) 14 H.L.R. 48, Q.B.D. This view was adopted in *R.* v. *London Rent Assessment Panel, ex p. Chelmsford Building Co.* (1986) 278 E.G. 979, Q.B.D. However, leave is required to proceed by way of judicial review, and is not so required under the 1971 Act, s.13.

It is clear that a decision will be bad if the rent assessment committee do not comply with the requirements of natural justice: *Hanson* v. *London Rent Assessment Panel* [1978] Q.B. 823; in *Metropolitan Properties Co. (F.G.C.)* v. *Lannon* [1969] 1 Q.B. 577, C.A., if a reasonable person considered that the chairman of the committee might be biased there would be grounds for intervention. See also *R.* v. *Bristol Rent Assessment Committee, ex p. Dunworth* (1986) 19 H.L.R. 351, Q.B.D., *Dundon* v. *Kenna* (1981) 261 E.G. 367, and *R.* v. *A Rent Assessment Committee for London, ex p. Ellis-Rees* (1982) 262 E.G. 1298, for cases where the operation of the requirements of natural justice have been considered.

Majority decisions are available as a matter of law: *Picea Holdings* v. *London Rent Assessment Panel* [1971] 2 All E.R. 805; however, under the current Rent Assessment Committee Regulations (Rent Assessment Committees (England and Wales) Regulations 1971 (S.I. 1971 No. 1065) as amended by S.I. 1980 No. 1699, and S.I. 1981 No. 1783), reg. 10(1), this is not to be disclosed. For further procedural provisions, see both the above-mentioned Regulations and R.S.C.Ord.55, governing appeals under the 1971 Act.

Subs. (4)

Rent has been held, under the Rent Acts, to mean "the total monetary payment to be made by the tenant to the landlord", even if, *e.g.* it includes a sum attributable to rates: *Sidney Trading Co.* v. *Finsbury B.C.* [1952] 1 All E.R. 460. See also *Wilkes* v. *Goodwin* [1923] 2 K.B. 86, C.A., *Artillery Mansions Ltd.* v. *Mabartney* [1947] K.B. 164. In *Property Holding Co. Ltd.* v. *Clark* [1948] 1 K.B. 630, all payments—whether for rates, or for board, attendance, furniture or other services or amenities—were held to be rent, whether aggregated or expressed as a global sum or identified separately.

Rent must, however, be monetary or, at the least, be quantifiable in monetary terms: *Hornsby* v. *Maynard* [1925] 1 K.B. 514, *Barnes* v. *Barratt* [1970] 2 Q.B. 657, C.A, *Montague* v. *Browning* [1954] 1 W.L.R. 1039, C.A. A residual problem is whether a premium is a genuine premium, or commuted rent, in which case it would have to be apportioned across the whole of the agreed period of the letting; to resolve this question, the court must look at the substance and reality of the matter, regardless of the terms the parties put upon it— see *Woods* v. *Wise* [1955] 2 Q.B. 29, C.A., *Samrose Properties* v. *Gibbard* [1958] 1 W.L.R. 235, C.A. and *Elmdene Estates* v. *White* [1960] A.C. 528, H.L. See, on all of these issues, notes to Sched. 1, para. 3, below, to which they are of central relevance, for if no or a low rent is payable, the tenancy cannot be assured.

Save for rates, which are dealt with below, and "service charges", as defined, this section embodies the proposition that any sums payable by the tenant to the landlord qualify as rent for the purpose of reference to the rent assessment committee, whether for the use of furniture, or "for services, repairs, maintenance, insurance or the landlord's costs of management" (Landlord and Tenant Act 1985, s.18(1)(a)), and whether identified separately from the rent or not, and whether payable under the tenancy or under separate agreements.

Not included is a service charge defined by s.18 of the Landlord and Tenant Act 1985, which is a charge for any of the items quoted in the last paragraph, "the whole or part of which varies or may vary according to the relevant costs" (s.18(1)(b)). In other words, if the tenancy agreement makes provision for a *variable* service charge, it is outwith the jurisdiction of the rent assessment committee (but within the control of the 1985 Act), but if no such provision is made, then although the items for which payment is made are the same, it classes as rent within this section.

Subs. (5)

The decision of the rent assessment committee is to be expressed exclusive of rates. Such rates will still be payable: either by the tenant direct, or if payable to the landlord (and thence to the local authority) under the terms of the tenancy, will be added to the amount of rent determined by the committee—see also the parenthesis in subs. (7).

Subs. (6)

A reference under s.6, and a reference under s.13, may relate to the same tenancy, but be lodged independently before the rent assessment committee. The committee can decide to hear them together, but in such a case must determine terms under s.6 before they turn to rent.

Subs. (7)

Unless the parties otherwise agree, the decision of the rent assessment committee will become the rent under the tenancy (plus any rates) with effect from the period specified in the landlord's notice under s.13, unless the committee considers that this would cause undue hardship to the tenant, in which case they may direct that the increase take effect from a later date, though no later than the date of the decision.

Subs. (8)

See notes to s.6(7), above.

Limited prohibition on assignment etc. without consent

15.—(1) Subject to subsection (3) below, it shall be an implied term of every assured tenancy which is a periodic tenancy that, except with the consent of the landlord, the tenant shall not—

    (a) assign the tenancy (in whole or in part); or

    (b) sub-let or part with possession of the whole or any part of the dwelling-house let on the tenancy.

(2) Section 19 of the Landlord and Tenant Act 1927 (consents to assign not to be unreasonably withheld etc.) shall not apply to a term which is implied into an assured tenancy by subsection (1) above.

(3) In the case of a periodic tenancy which is not a statutory periodic tenancy subsection (1) above does not apply if—

    (a) there is a provision (whether contained in the tenancy or not) under which the tenant is prohibited (whether absolutely or conditionally) from assigning or sub-letting or parting with possession or is permitted (whether absolutely or conditionally) to assign, sub-let or part with possession; or

    (b) a premium is required to be paid on the grant or renewal of the tenancy.

(4) In subsection (3)(b) above "premium" includes—

    (a) any fine or other like sum;

    (b) any other pecuniary consideration in addition to rent; and

    (c) any sum paid by way of deposit, other than one which does not exceed one-sixth of the annual rent payable under the tenancy immediately after the grant or renewal in question.

Definitions

"assured tenancy": s.1.

"dwelling-house": s.45.

"landlord": s.45.
"let": s.45.
"tenancy": s.45.
"tenant": s.45.

GENERAL NOTE
Save *either* where the agreement covers the issue, *or* where a premium is paid on the grant or renewal of the tenancy, into every periodic assured tenancy is to be implied a covenant against assignment, and sub-letting or parting with possession of the whole or any part of the premises, without the consent of the landlord. Breach of the term will constitute a discretionary ground for possession under Sched. 2, ground 12.

The long-standing position under the Landlord and Tenant Act 1927, s.19, that into any such clause there will be implied a proviso that such consent will not unreasonably be withheld is *not* to apply, from which it follows that the landlord can withhold consent on any grounds he wishes.

However, and save in the case of a statutory periodic tenancy, if the tenancy agreement—or a separate agreement—deals with assignment, subletting or parting with possession, then *its* terms will prevail, *i.e.* if absolutely prohibited an absolute prohibition will apply, while if conditionally prohibited (which in effect equals conditionally permitted), s.19 of the 1927 Act *will* apply in the normal way, to prevent the landlord withholding consent unreasonably. Similarly, and save in the case of a statutory periodic tenancy, if a premium was required on the grant or renewal of the tenancy, s.19 will apply.

Subs. (1)
The term is implied into every assured tenancy which is a periodic tenancy. The prohibitions are on assignment, subletting or parting with possession of the whole or any part of the premises the subject of the assured tenancy, *without the consent of the landlord*. To that extent, they may be considered to introduce the *possibility* of assignment, subletting or parting with possession; but as such consent may be withheld on any grounds, however unreasonable, and as even an absolute prohibition may of course always be waived, the terms are prohibitive not permissive.

Note that an assignment, to be effective, must be by deed, even if the tenancy under assignment did not itself require to be in writing: see the Law of Property Act 1925, s.52; *Botting* v. *Martin* (1808) 1 Camp 317. However, in some circumstances, this requirement may be avoided if the assignment is evidenced in writing, or if there is sufficient part performance of the assignment, in which case the assignment may take effect as an enforceable contract for the assignment: see Law of Property Act 1925, s.40, *Butcher* v. *Stapeley* (1685) 1 Vern. 363, *Montacute* v. *Maxwell* (1720) 1 P.Wms. 616, *Walsh* v. *Lonsdale* (1882) 21 Ch. 9. It follows that unless these requirements are fulfilled, there will have been no assignment and, therefore, no breach of the term.

This is not so, however, where the assignment is a deemed assignment arising out of a subletting of the residue of a fixed-term (*Milmo* v. *Carreras* [1946] K.B. 306, C.A.,) but as no such deemed assignment arises out of a subletting under a periodic tenancy, even if for identical periods, (*Wheeler* v. *Smith* [1926] E.G.D. 194, D.C.,) or indeed out of a fixed term subletting in excess of the periods of the tenancy (*Curteis* v. *Corcoran* (1947) 150 E.G. 44,) this will not be an applicable exception under this section.

Under the Rent Act 1977, Sched. 15, ground 6, which gives rise to a discretionary ground for possession on the assignment or subletting of the whole of the dwelling-house the subject of the tenancy, a vesting order by trustees has been held to constitute an assignment: *Pazgate* v. *McGrath* (1984) 17 H.L.R. 127, C.A. If this is correct under this Act, then without consent of the landlord, there will be two grounds for possession available against a tenant who inherits on death: the mandatory ground 8, and the discretionary ground 12. There is no assignment, however, when a vesting order is made on a change of trustee: *March* v. *Gilbert* (1980) 256 E.G. 715.

The prohibition on sub-letting is against sub-letting of the whole or part. This means that without consent, an assured periodic tenant can do no more than take in "lodgers", *i.e.* licensees to whom no possession passes. A covenant against sub-letting is not broken by letting to a lodger, nor does such constitute a parting with possession: *Edwards* v. *Barrington* [1901] 85 L.T. 650 H.L., *Segal Securities Ltd.* v. *Thoseby* [1963] 1 Q.B. 887.

As to the distinction between (sub-)tenant and lodger, see notes to s.1 above, and, specifically, the discussion of the decision of the House of Lords in *Street* v. *Mountford* [1985] A.C. 809, 17 H.L.R. 402. See also, *e.g. Douglas* v. *Smith* [1907] 2 K.B. 568, C.A., and *Appah* v. *Parncliffe Investments* [1964] 1 W.L.R. 1064). The key issue will be the degree of control retained by the tenant over the lodger's rooms. There should be no difficulty at all over taking in an elderly relative, or friend, or where the lodger shares cooking facilities: see *e.g. Booker* v. *Palmer* [1942] 2 All E.R. 674, C.A., *Marcroft Waggons* v. *Smith* [1951] 2 K.B. 496, C.A., *Abbeyfield (Harpenden) Society* v. *Woods* [1968] 1 W.L.R. 374, C.A., *Barnes* v. *Barratt* [1970] 2 Q.B. 657, C.A.

A sub-letting in contravention of the term, even though it will constitute an illegal sub-letting and, for the tenant, a breach of a term of his tenancy (*cf.* Sched. 2, ground 12) will still be valid as between tenant and sub-tenant, for the illegality will be that of the tenant, who cannot take advantage of his own wrong: *Critchley* v. *Clifford* [1962] 1 Q.B. 131, C.A. As to waiver of illegality, including illegal sub-tenancy, see notes to s.5, above.

The sub-tenant, whether legal or illegal, will usually not have an assured sub-tenancy, because his landlord (the tenant) will qualify as a resident landlord: see Sched. 1, para. 10. The fact that the *superior* landlord will not be bound will not affect the matter at all, for the position must be viewed as between sub-tenant and tenant, if only by estoppel: *Lewis* v. *Morelli* [1948] 2 All E.R. 1021, *Stratford* v. *Syrett* [1958] 1 Q.B. 107.

A *legal* sub-tenant may become the tenant of a superior landlord direct: see s.18, below. But even an illegal sub-tenant may in some circumstances come to hold a tenancy of the landlord direct. With the determination of a tenancy, normally all inferior interests also determine: thus, on determination of the mesne tenancy, the sub-tenancy will come to an end, even without notice to quit. But exceptionally, if the *mesne* tenant surrenders, or if the mesne tenant gives notice to quit to the landlord, then there is considered to be a merger of landlord and mesne tenant's interest, with the result that interests binding on the mesne tenant, come to bind the landlord, *whether legal or illegal interests*, so that in such circumstances, both an illegal, and a legal, sub-tenant will become the tenant of the landlord direct and, all other things being equal, will become an assured tenant: *Mellor* v. *Watkins* (1874) L.R. 9 (Q.B.), 400, *Parker* v. *Jones* [1910] 2 K.B. 32. Note, however, that this will not apply to lodgers who, as licensees, have no interest at law in any part of the premises.

Subss. (2), (3)

Under the Landlord and Tenant Act 1927, s.19, where there is a clause which prohibits assignment or sub-letting without the consent of the landlord, it is statutorily implied that such consent will not unreasonably be withheld. That section does *not* apply to the clause implied by subs. (1) of this section.

The case-law on unreasonable withholding is not, however, irrelevant, for s.19 will continue to imply that consent is not unreasonably to be withheld if instead of relying on subs. (1), subs. (3) is applicable. By subs. (3), and save in the case of a statutory periodic tenancy, if the tenancy or a separate agreements contains its own prohibition or permission, whether absolute or conditional, subs. (1) is inapplicable and the "normal" law applies. Where, therefore, such prohibition is itself a qualified prohibition, the 1927 Act, s.19, will also apply.

Under the remainder of this heading, the law on unreasonable withholding will be considered, for its application by virtue of subs. (3). The alternative ground on which subs. (1) may now apply—if a premium was required on grant or renewal of tenancy—will be considered under the next heading.

Where consent is not unreasonably to be withheld, but is unreasonably withheld, it is treated as given: see *Balls Brothers Ltd.* v. *Sinclair* [1931] 2 Ch. 325. But a tenant cannot rely on a withheld consent in defence to an action based upon an illegal assignment or sub-letting, unless consent has actually been sought, no matter how unreasonable *any* withholding might be, or how well-founded the anticipation of (unreasonable) withholding: see *Barrow* v. *Isaacs* [1891] 1 Q.B. 417, *Eastern Telegraph Co.* v. *Dent* [1899] 1 Q.B. 835. Where the application for consent is made in writing, the landlord owes a duty within a reasonable time to give consent unless it can reasonably be withheld, if withheld to give reasons for the withholding, and if subject to conditions, to specify the conditions: Landlord and Tenant Act 1988, s.1(3).

It is unreasonable withholding that is prohibited by s.19, not unreasonable refusal, so that a failure to reply to a request for consent amounts to unreasonable withholding, on failure to respond within a reasonable time: see *Wilson* v. *Fynn* [1948] W.N. 242; [1948] 2 All E.R. 40. It is theoretically open to a tenant from whom consent has unreasonably been withheld to carry on with the letting or assignment, and subsequently defend any proceedings on the ground that an unreasonably withheld consent is to be treated as given, but a tenant is well-advised to seek a declaration even if confident of the outcome of any such subsequent proceedings: *Mills* v. *Cannon Brewery Co.* [1920] 2 Ch. 38. But if proceedings are commenced on the mere failure to seek consent, when it could not unreasonably have been withheld, no order for possession will follow: *cf. Leeward Securities* v. *Lilyheath Properties* (1983) 17 H.L.R. 35, C.A.

Save where the application is made in writing, within the Landlord and Tenant Act 1988, the burden is on the tenant to show that consent has unreasonably been withheld: *Shanley* v. *Ward* (1913) 29 T.L.R. 714, *Pimms* v. *Tallow Chandlers Co.* [1964] 2 Q.B. 547, *Lambert* v. *F. W. Woolworth & Co. (No. 2)* [1938] Ch. 883, *Frederick Berry* v. *Royal Bank of Scotland* [1949] 1 K.B. 619, *International Drilling Fluids* v. *Louisville Investments (Uxbridge)* [1986] 1 All E.R. 321, C.A., *Rayburn* v. *Wolf* (1985) 18 H.L.R. 1, C.A. Where the application is made in writing under the Landlord and Tenant Act 1988, the burden lies on the landlord to show that withholding of consent is reasonable, or that conditions have reasonably been attached: s.1(6).

It is the reasonableness of the particular landlord that is to be taken into account: in order to establish reasonable withholding, it is sufficient to show (a) that "any" reasonable landlord could withhold consent, and (b) that the particular landlord does so; but if no reasonable landlord could withhold consent, then the withholding will be unreasonable—see *Re Town Investments Underlease* [1954] Ch. 301, *Pimms* v. *Tallow Chandlers* [1964] 2 Q.B. 547, *Lovelock* v. *Margo* [1963] 2 Q.B. 786, *International Drilling Fluids* v. *Louisville Investments (Uxbridge)* (above.)

Although prima facie it is such matters as the identity of the proposed sub-tenant or assignee, or the use to which the premises will be put, even if a particular use is not prohibited under the tenancy, which dominate the issue (*Houlder Bros. & Co.* v. *Gibbs* [1925] Ch. 575, *Swanson* v. *Forton* [1949] Ch. 143, *Bates* v. *Donaldson* [1896] 2 Q.B. 241, *International Drilling Fluids* v. *Louisville Investments (Uxbridge)* (above),) it is reasonable to take into account matters affecting other property belonging to the landlord, *e.g.* the use of facilities on an estate or in a block of flats: *Tredegar* v. *Harwood* [1929] A.C. 72, H.L. *Houlder Bros. & Co.* v. *Gibbs* (above,) *Rayburn* v. *Wolf* (above.)

Consent cannot be withheld in order to obtain for the landlord a windfall benefit wholly outside the contemplation of the agreement or simply because the landlord's policy or practice dictates a withholding: *Bromley Park Garden Estates* v. *Moss* [1982] 1 W.L.R. 1019, 4 H.L.R. 61, C.A. See also *Rayburn* v. *Wolf* (above.) A landlord cannot set out in advance, *e.g.* in a tenancy agreement, in what circumstances consent will or will not be withheld: *Creery* v. *Summersell and Flowerdew & Co. Ltd.* [1949] Ch. 751, *Smith's Lease, Re, Smith* v. *Richards* [1951] 1 T.L.R. 254. The refusal must have something to do with the relationship of landlord and tenant in regard to the subject-matter of the tenancy: *Houlder Brothers* v. *Gibbs* (above,) *Internal Drilling Fluids* v. *Louisville Investments (Uxbridge)* (above.)

It would be unreasonable to refuse consent because the would-be subtenant or assignee was the landlord's tenant elsewhere, and the property it was intended to quit would be hard to let again: *Houlder Brothers & Co. Ltd.* v. *Gibbs* (above). The authorities were considered divergent in *International Drilling Fluids* v. *Louisville Investments (Uxbridge)* (above), as to whether a court may have regard to the consequences of refusal to the tenant, but this could be reconciled by the proposition that while a landlord need usually only have regard to his own relevant interests, there may be cases where there is such a disproportion between his benefit and the detriment to the tenant that refusal might thereby become unreasonable.

If a sub-tenant's or assignee's references are taken up, and are inadequate, this may be sufficient to justify a refusal of consent: *Shanley* v. *Ward* (1913) 29 T.L.R. 714. A landlord may take into account breaches of other covenants by the tenant, although just how relevant this will be in relation to a would-be sub-letting or assignment will be a question of fact in each set of circumstances, and may be affected by the severity of the tenant's breach: *Farr* v. *Cummings* (1928) 44 T.L.R. 249, *Goldstein* v. *Sanders* [1915] 1 Ch. 549, *Cosh* v. *Fraser* (1964) 108 S.J. 116.

If the landlord has grounds for fearing that the new tenant or sub-tenant will cause breaches of covenant, refusal may be reasonable (*Granada T.V. Network* v. *Great Universal Stores* (1963) 187 E.G. 391) although this is not decisive, because the landlord will still have recourse to other remedies: *Killick* v. *Second Covent Garden Property Co.* [1973] 1 W.L.R. 658. The question will always turn on the facts of each case: see *Houlder Bros. & Co.* v. *Gibbs* (above), see also *Lee* v. *K. Carter* [1949] 1 K.B. 85 and *Bickel* v. *Duke of Westminster* [1977] Q.B. 517, C.A. This will be so even if questions of statutory protection under this, or another Act, will arise: *West Layton* v. *Joseph* [1979] Q.B. 593, C.A., *Leeward Securities* v. *Lilyheath* (1983) 17 H.L.R. 35, C.A.

A refusal based on illegal discrimination, whether sex or race, will, however, itself be illegal and, as such, inescapably unreasonable: see Sex Discrimination Act 1975, s.31, Race Relations Act 1976, s.24. Subject to these principles, each case is a question of fact depending on all its circumstances: *International Drilling Fluids* v. *Louisville Investments (Uxbridge)* (above).

A contractual covenant requiring a tenant to offer to surrender instead of exercising a right to sub-let or to assign does not offend the prohibition on unreasonable withholding of consent where it is applicable: *Adler* v. *Upper Grosvenor Street Investments* [1957] 1 W.L.R. 227, and *Bocardo S.A.* v. *S. & M. Hotels* [1980] 1 W.L.R. 17, C.A.

A breach might be considered waived by acceptance of rent with knowledge of the improvement (*cf. Metropolitan Properties Co.* v. *Cordery* (1979) 251 E.G. 576, C.A., as to knowledge of an agent or employee sufficing, but *cf. Swallow Securities* v. *Isenberg* (1985) 274 E.G. 1028, C.A.). Breach of the term may give rise to an order for possession, although it will be one subject to the overriding requirement of reasonableness in any event, under ground 12 of Sched. 2, below. See, further, notes to s.5, above.

Subs. (3), (4)

The term defined in subs. (1) will also (*cf.* subs. (2)) not be implied if a premium was required on the grant or renewal of a tenancy, other than a statutory periodic tenancy. Premium is defined in subs. (4) in terms similar to those used in the Rent Act 1977, s.128. The distinction is in subs. (4)(c): under the Rent Act, deposit is excluded from premium if (i) not more than one-sixth of annual rent *and* (ii) it is not unreasonable in relation to the liability it is intended to cover. Here, a deposit up to one-sixth of annual rent is not a premium regardless of its reasonableness relative to liability.

Actual payment of money is not essential: "The phrase 'any other pecuniary consideration' is apt to cover any other consideration that sounds in money to the tenant, either in the way of involving him in a payment of money or of foregoing a receipt of money" (*per* Lord Keith of Avonholm, *Elmdene Estates* v. *White* [1960] A.C. 528, H.L., in which an estate agent offered to buy a person's house for a price professedly lower than market value, but in addition to which he also undertook to secure that person a tenancy; thus, the price for the protected tenancy was the reduction in the price of the house, and was held to constitute a premium.)

A requirement for a new or incoming tenant to pay off the arrears of a former tenant (even a spouse) will constitute a premium, for the arrears would not be owed by the new tenant to the landlord: *Hampstead Way Investments* v. *Mawdsley* (1980) 9 C.L. 115, County Ct. A deposit is paid under a collateral agreement giving rights *in personam* not *in rem*, and so cannot be set off against rent owing to the assignee of the reversion: *Edenpark Estates* v. *Longman* (1980) New L.J. 482, C.A. The express reference to deposits follows a number of lower court decisions in which such had been held to constitute a premium, but contraverts the decision in *R.* v. *Ewing* (1976) 251 E.G. 55, C.A.(Crim.) that a returnable deposit did not constitute an illegal Rent Act premium.

In practice and theory, there can be considerable difficulty distinguishing between a premium properly so-called, and a payment of commuted rent or rent in advance: see notes to s.14(3), above.

Under the Rent Act 1977, the prohibition (constituting a criminal offence) is on "any person" requiring or receiving a payment, which was held in *Farrell* v. *Alexander* [1977] A.C. 59, H.L., to apply not only to a landlord, but also to an outgoing tenant who required a premium for arranging the grant of a tenancy on the surrender of his own. While the same words do not apply here, bearing also in mind that the decision was concerned with, *inter alia*, a criminal offence requiring more strict construction than in this case, the wording of this section is similarly not confined to "required" *by* the landlord.

Access for repairs

16. It shall be an implied term of every assured tenancy that the tenant shall afford to the landlord access to the dwelling-house let on the tenancy and all reasonable facilities for executing therein any repairs which the landlord is entitled to execute.

Definitions

"assured tenancy": s.1.
"dwelling-house": s.45.
"landlord": s.45.
"let": s.45.
"tenancy": s.45.
"tenant": s.45.

General Note

Under a periodic tenancy, or a fixed-term of less than seven years, the landlord will normally bear the principal repairing obligations: see Landlord and Tenant Act 1985, s.11; see also notes to s.115, below. Whether under that provision or otherwise, this section confers on the landlord a right to enter to repair, failure to permit which will constitute a breach of a term of the tenancy, which gives rise to a discretionary ground for possession under Sched. 2, ground 12.

Such a right in any event attaches to a right or duty to repair (*Saner* v. *Bilton* (1878) 7 Ch.D. 815), although subject to notice by the landlord (*Granada Theatres* v. *Freehold Investment (Leytonstone)* [1959] 1 W.L.R. 570). But the right to enter is limited to such entry and occupation as is strictly necessary to do the works of repair, which does not amount to an obligation to give the landlord exclusive occupation of the premises, nor to permit him access to all parts of the house at the same time, unless either is essential: *McGreal* v. *Wake* (1984) 13 H.L.R. 107, C.A.

Miscellaneous

Succession to assured periodic tenancy by spouse

17.—(1) In any case where—
    (a) the sole tenant under an assured periodic tenancy dies, and
    (b) immediately before the death, the tenant's spouse was occu-pying the dwelling-house as his or her only or principal home, and
    (c) the tenant was not himself a successor, as defined in subsection (2) or subsection (3) below,
then, on the death, the tenancy vests by virtue of this section in the spouse (and, accordingly, does not devolve under the tenant's will or intestacy).

(2) For the purposes of this section, a tenant is a successor in relation to a tenancy if—
    (a) the tenancy became vested in him either by virtue of this section or under the will or intestacy of a previous tenant; or
    (b) at some time before the tenant's death the tenancy was a joint tenancy held by himself and one or more other persons and, prior to his death, he became the sole tenant by survivorship; or
    (c) he became entitled to the tenancy as mentioned in section 39(5) below.

(3) For the purposes of this section, a tenant is also a successor in relation to a tenancy (in this subsection referred to as "the new tenancy") which was granted to him (alone or jointly with others) if—
    (a) at some time before the grant of the new tenancy, he was, by virtue of subsection (2) above, a successor in relation to an earlier tenancy of the same or substantially the same dwelling-house as is let under the new tenancy; and
    (b) at all times since he became such a successor he has been a tenant (alone or jointly with others) of the dwelling-house which is let under the new tenancy or of a dwelling-house which is substantially the same as that dwelling-house.

(4) For the purposes of this section, a person who was living with the tenant as his or her wife or husband shall be treated as the tenant's spouse.

(5) If, on the death of the tenant, there is, by virtue of subsection (4) above, more than one person who fulfils the condition in subsection (1)(b) above, such one of them as may be decided by agreement or, in default of agreement, by the county court shall be treated as the tenant's spouse for the purposes of this section.

DEFINITIONS
    "assured tenancy": s.1.
    "dwelling house": s.45.
    "tenant" s.45.

GENERAL NOTE
    This section confers a right of succession to a periodic assured tenancy, limited by comparison to that which was available under the Rent Act 1977 (*cf.* below, s.39 and Sched.

4) (a) to a surviving spouse, and (b) to a single succession. It is here expressly declared that such statutory succession pre-empts devolution under a will or on intestacy: see *Moodie* v. *Hosegood* [1952] A.C. 61, H.L. A successor will take subject to an outstanding possession order against the tenant, *i.e.* suspended or absolute, including its conditions (if any): see *Sherrin* v. *Brand* [1956] 1 Q.B. 403, C.A., *American Economic Laundry* v. *Little* [1951] 1 K.B. 400, C.A.

Subss. (1), (2), (4)

Succession has no application to joint tenancy: succession is only available if the deceased was (i) a sole tenant, *and* (ii) *not* himself a successor, which is defined (subs. (2)) to include a person who has succeeded to the joint tenancy by right of survivorship and to include a person who has succeeded to an *assured* tenancy under the amended succession provisions of the Rent Act 1977 (see notes to s.39, below). Even if there were joint tenants, not married, one of whom was married to another (who also fulfilled the residential qualification), who died contemporaneously, the older would be deemed to die before the younger, and would not therefore have been a sole tenant at time of death, and the younger would notionally have secured the status of sole tenant by right of survivorship at the instant of death, and his spouse would accordingly not succeed on that ground.

The provision only affects periodic tenancies: a fixed-term tenancy will devolve by will or on intestacy, and the person who takes under it will enjoy an assured tenancy (and right to subsequent statutory periodic tenancy), but will of course be a successor, thus precluding any further succession: subs. (2)(a). The provisions are modelled on those to be found in the Housing Act 1985, ss.87, 88.

The limitation to one succession, in the case of a periodic tenancy, is achieved by excluding someone who has already succeeded under this section: *ibid.*

The would-be successor has to be (a) a spouse, and (b) in occupation of the dwelling-house as his or her only or principal home at the time of the tenant's death: there is no requirement that he or she be living *with* the deceased. The residence must be as an "only or principal home": see notes to s.1, above.

"Spouse" is defined (subs. (4)) to include persons living together as husband and wife, thus incorporating the effect of Rent Act case-law, although under that Act, such persons were treated *not* as widow or widower, but as a "member of the family": see notes to s. 39, below. Under the Housing Act 1980, now 1985, the corresponding provisions also refer to "living together as husband and wife". In *Harrogate Borough Council* v. *Simpson* (1984) 17 H.L.R. 205, the Court of Appeal held that this expression was not apt to include a lesbian or homosexual relationship.

Subs. (3)

The limitation to one succession is reinforced by treating as a successor a tenant who became such by the grant of a new tenancy of the same or substantially the same dwelling-house, following an earlier tenancy to which he had succeeded.

Subs. (4)

There can only be one qualifying member of the family, and if there is more than one, then the two putative qualifying members of the family may agree amongst themselves, or else the matter may be determined by the county court. An agreement may be inferred from the fact of lengthy acquiescence in one party being treated as the successor: *Dealex Properties* v. *Brooks* [1966] 1 Q.B. 542, C.A., *Trayfoot* v. *Lock* [1957] 1 W.L.R. 351, C.A. For the agreement to be valid there is no need for the landlord to be a party to it or even to be notified of it, nor need it be reached within any particular time: *General Management* v. *Locke* (1980) 255 E.G. 155, C.A. The county court decision will involve consideration of all competing factors, including but not conclusively, the wishes of the deceased: *Williams* v. *Williams* [1970] 1 W.L.R. 1530, C.A.

As succession is confined to spouses (as defined), the subsection seems to imply a surprising degree of sophistication, repeated elsewhere in this Act (see s.39 and Sched. 4).

Provisions as to reversions on assured tenancies

    18.—(1) If at any time—

        (a) a dwelling-house is for the time being lawfully let on an assured tenancy, and

        (b) the landlord under the assured tenancy is himself a tenant under a superior tenancy; and

        (c) the superior tenancy comes to an end,

then, subject to subsection (2) below, the assured tenancy shall continue in existence as a tenancy held of the person whose interest would, apart from the continuance of the assured tenancy, entitle him to actual possession of the dwelling-house at that time.

(2) Subsection (1) above does not apply to an assured tenancy if the interest which, by virtue of that subsection, would become that of the landlord, is such that, by virtue of Schedule 1 to this Act, the tenancy could not be an assured tenancy.

(3) Where, by virtue of any provision of this Part of this Act, an assured tenancy which is a periodic tenancy (including a statutory periodic tenancy) continues beyond the beginning of a reversionary tenancy which was granted (whether before, on or after the commencement of this Act) so as to begin on or after—

(a) the date on which the previous contractual assured tenancy came to an end, or

(b) a date on which, apart from any provision of this Part, the periodic tenancy could have been brought to an end by the landlord by notice to quit,

the reversionary tenancy shall have effect as if it had been granted subject to the periodic tenancy.

(4) The reference in subsection (3) above to the previous contractual assured tenancy applies only where the periodic tenancy referred to in that subsection is a statutory periodic tenancy and is a reference to the fixed-term tenancy which immediately preceded the statutory periodic tenancy.

DEFINITIONS
"assured tenancy": s.1.
"dwelling-house": s.45.
"fixed term": s.45.
"landlord": s.45.
"statutory periodic tenancy": s.5.
"tenancy": s.45.
"tenant": s.45.

GENERAL NOTE
This section governs what happens to a subordinate assured tenancy on the determination of a superior tenancy. In outline, the assured tenancy will continue, with the superior landlord as direct landlord, unless Sched. 1 applies on the replacement of the mesne tenant/landlord. The superior landlord is unlikely to have an assured tenancy, because of the requirement to use the premises as an only or principal home: see s.1, above. However (see notes thereto), it is not impossible that the superior landlord is an assured tenant, but this section applies whether or not he has an assured tenancy.

Subss. (1), (2)
An assured tenancy can be a sub-tenancy: see s.45, below. If the landlord is a resident landlord, the sub-tenancy will not be assured: Sched. 1, para. 10. Unless the landlord is resident, it is unlikely that *he* will have an assured tenancy, for want of residence as an only or principal home, but this is not impossible: see notes to s.1, above. However, this section applies regardless of the qualification within this Act of the superior letting.

At common law, with the determination of a tenancy, normally all inferior interests also determine: thus, on determination of mesne tenancy, sub-tenancy will come to an end, even without notice to quit: see *Moore Properties* v. *McKeon* [1976] 1 W.L.R. 1278. But exceptionally, if the mesne tenant surrenders, or if the mesne tenant gives notice to quit to the landlord, then there is considered to be a merger of landlord and mesne tenant's interest, with the result that interests binding on the mesne tenant, come to bind the landlord, *whether legal or illegal interests*, so that in such circumstances, both an illegal, and a legal, sub-tenant will become the tenant of the landlord direct and, all other things being equal, will become an assured tenant: *Mellor* v. *Watkins* (1874) L.R. 9 (Q.B.), 400, *Parker* v. *Jones* [1910] 2 K.B. 32. Note, however, that this will not apply to lodgers who, as licensees, ̇ ̇ ̇ no interest at law in any part of the premises.

This section overrides the first of these principles (automatic determination) and makes reliance on the second (tenant's notice to quit or surrender) unnecessary, *save* where the sub-tenancy is illegal (as to which, see notes to ss.5 and 15, above). If the sub-tenancy has been legitimised by waiver, it will qualify as rights depend on the position at the determination of the landlord's tenancy: *Jessamine Investment Co.* v. *Schwartz* [1978] Q.B. 264, C.A.; see also *Oak Properties Co.* v. *Chapman* [1947] K.B. 886, C.A.

The section applies howsoever the tenancy comes to an end. The person who would otherwise resume possession—*i.e.* the mesne tenant's landlord (who could, of course, himself still be a tenant or, *e.g.* long leaseholder) becomes the assured tenant's landlord.

This will not be so if any of the exceptions to assured tenancy contained in Sched. 1, apply, *e.g.* if the superior landlord is himself a resident landlord (para. 10), or is the Crown (para. 11) or a public body within para. 12.

Subss. (3), (4)

These subsections govern the creation of a reversionary tenancy of premises which are subject to an assured tenancy which is a statutory periodic tenancy (*i.e.* has arisen on the determination of a previous fixed-term tenancy) or a periodic tenancy which has extended beyond its earliest termination date at common law, but the landlord has not been able to determine because of the provisions of this Act. In short, the reversionary interest takes subject to the continued assured tenancy. The purpose is presumably to prevent the creation of intermediate interests which would deprive the assured tenant of his protection.

Restriction on levy of distress for rent

19.—(1) Subject to subsection (2) below, no distress for the rent of any dwelling-house let on an assured tenancy shall be levied except with the leave of the county court; and, with respect to any application for such leave, the court shall have the same powers with respect to adjournment, stay, suspension, postponement and otherwise as are conferred by section 9 above in relation to proceedings for possession of such a dwelling-house.

(2) Nothing in subsection (1) above applies to distress levied under section 102 of the County Courts Act 1984.

DEFINITIONS
"assured tenancy": s.1.
"dwelling-house": s.45.
"let": s.45.

GENERAL NOTE
Notwithstanding the 1969 recommendation for the abolition of distress by the Payne Committee on the Enforcement of Judgment Debts (Cmnd. 3909), and the description by the then Master of the Rolls, Lord Denning, that distress was "an archaic remedy. . . largely fallen into disuse" (*Abingdon Rural District Council* v. *O'Gorman* [1968] 3 All E.R. 69, C.A., distress for rent has remained in use, particularly in the public sector, although it is not available under the Rent Act 1977 without the leave of the court: see the 1977 Act, s.147.

As under that Act, it may not be levied under this without the leave of the court where the property is let under an assured tenancy, and on such an application the court has the same powers to adjourn, suspend, stay or vary its order as under s.9 (see notes thereto, above.) In these circumstances, it is unlikely to be used much, when one mandatory ground and two discretionary grounds for possession relating to rent arrears are available: see Sched. 2, grounds 8, 10–11.

Subs. (2)

Where a bailiff seizes or is to seize goods in execution of a county court judgment, County Courts Act 1984, s.102, permits a landlord to ask the bailiff additionally to seize goods in respect of rent arrears, and the claim to those rent arrears will take precedence over the judgment in respect of which the goods were initially seized or to be seized. This class of distress, alone, is exempt from the requirement to seek the prior leave of the court.

CHAPTER II

ASSURED SHORTHOLD TENANCIES

Assured shorthold tenancies

20.—(1) Subject to subsection (3) below, an assured shorthold tenancy is an assured tenancy—

(a) which is a fixed term tenancy granted for a term certain of not less than six months; and

(b) in respect of which there is no power for the landlord to determine the tenancy at any time earlier than six months from the beginning of the tenancy; and

(c) in respect of which a notice is served as mentioned in subsection (2) below.

(2) The notice referred to in subsection (1)(c) above is one which—

(a) is in such form as may be prescribed;

(b) is served before the assured tenancy is entered into;

(c) is served by the person who is to be the landlord under the assured tenancy on the person who is to be the tenant under that tenancy; and

(d) states that the assured tenancy to which it relates is to be a shorthold tenancy.

(3) Notwithstanding anything in subsection (1) above, where—

(a) immediately before a tenancy (in this subsection referred to as "the new tenancy") is granted, the person to whom it is granted or, as the case may be, at least one of the persons to whom it is granted was a tenant under an assured tenancy which was not a shorthold tenancy, and

(b) the new tenancy is granted by the person who, immediately before the beginning of the tenancy, was the landlord under the assured tenancy referred to in paragraph (a) above,

the new tenancy cannot be an assured shorthold tenancy.

(4) Subject to subsection (5) below, if, on the coming to an end of an assured shorthold tenancy (including a tenancy which was an assured shorthold but ceased to be assured before it came to an end), a new tenancy of the same or substantially the same premises comes into being under which the landlord and the tenant are the same as at the coming to an end of the earlier tenancy, then, if and so long as the new tenancy is an assured tenancy, it shall be an assured shorthold tenancy, whether or not it fulfils the conditions in paragraphs (a) to (c) of subsection (1) above.

(5) Subsection (4) above does not apply if, before the new tenancy is entered into (or, in the case of a statutory periodic tenancy, takes effect in possession), the landlord serves notice on the tenant that the new tenancy is not to be a shorthold tenancy.

(6) In the case of joint landlords—

(a) the reference in subsection (2)(c) above to the person who is to be the landlord is a reference to at least one of the persons who are to be joint landlords; and

(b) the reference in subsection (5) above to the landlord is a reference to at least one of the joint landlords.

(7) Section 14 above shall apply in relation to an assured shorthold tenancy as if in subsection (1) of that section the reference to an assured tenancy were a reference to an assured shorthold tenancy.

DEFINITIONS
  "assured tenancy": s.1.
  "landlord": s.45.

"prescribed": s.45.
"tenancy": s.45.
"tenant": s.45.

GENERAL NOTE

The second limb of the 1980 Housing Act proposals for reviving the private rented sector (*cf.* the "original" assured tenancy, see notes to s.1, above) was the "shorthold" tenancy or, strictly, "protected shorthold tenancy". It operated relatively simply, by permitting the service of a notice on someone who would otherwise become a Rent Act protected tenant which would entitle the landlord to utilise a new mandatory ground for possession, in effect merely that he wanted to repossess. The "assured shorthold tenancy" operates similarly, save that the "ground" is set out in the next section.

Subs. (1)

An assured shorthold tenancy is simply an assured tenancy in respect of which a notice under subs. (2) has been served. The tenancy must, however, be for a term certain of not less than six months, not a periodic tenancy (although a subsequent tenancy, which remains shorthold in practice pursuant to subs. (4), below, may be periodic); there must be no power for the landlord to bring the tenancy to an end any earlier than six months, other than by forfeiture or a power of re-entry (*cf.* s.45(4), below; see also *Paterson* v. *Aggio* (1987) 19 H.L.R. 551, C.A.). The tenancy will be deemed to run from when it is granted, not any earlier date from which it is said to run, so that a landlord cannot evade the six month minimum term by the grant of a six month term halfway through its duration: *Roberts* v. *Church Commissioners for England* [1972] 1 Q.B. 278, C.A.

Subs. (2)

The notice must be served before the assured tenancy is "entered into", which can be before the start of the tenancy, and before the tenant has the right to take up occupation. The notice must be in the form prescribed by the Secretary of State. The notice must be served by the person who is to be the landlord (or if joint landlords, by at least one of them: subs. (6)), on the person who is to be the tenant, and must state that the assured tenancy is to be a shorthold tenancy. As there is nothing express to the contrary, "tenant" means *all* joint tenants: s.43(3).

Subs. (3)

This is an "anti-avoidance" provision, intended to prevent a landlord persuading an assured tenant to accept a new tenancy, which is shorthold. The premises need not be the same, nor indeed in a strict sense "the tenant", for if the tenant was "a" tenant (which appears apt to include one of a number of joint tenants) under an earlier joint tenancy, or if the new grant is of a joint tenancy under which one of the tenants had an earlier tenancy, the provisions will apply. The provisions only apply, however, where "the" landlord is the same under both former, and new, tenancies, and where there is no hiatus between former and new tenancies. With these qualifications, a grant of a tenancy purportedly shorthold to a former non-shorthold tenant will not be effective as a shorthold, *cf. Dibbs* v. *Campbell* (1988) 20 H.L.R. 374, C.A.

Subss. (4), (5)

Unless the landlord (or if joint landlords, at least one of them: subs. (6)) serves notice before the beginning of a *further* tenancy or before a statutory periodic tenancy takes effect in possession, that the new (or statutory periodic) tenancy is *not* to be a shorthold tenancy (which might be because, *e.g.* he seeks a higher rent, *cf.* s.22, below)—see subs. (5),—the subs. (2) notice will relate not only to the initial term certain, but also to any new or continued statutory periodic assured tenancy of the same or substantially the same (see notes to s.5, above) premises which comes into being between the same landlord and the same tenant "at" the expiry of the initial term certain, regardless of whether it is for a term certain or is periodic (and regardless of whether the prior tenancy has ceased to be *assured*, *e.g.* for want of residence).

In *Gent* v. *De La Mare* (1987) 20 H.L.R., C.A., a protected shorthold tenancy was granted for one year "subject to the provision that the landlords shall give to the tenant three months notice in writing prior to the expiration date in the event of their not wishing to renew this Agreement for a further term." The year expired without service of the notice, but at the end of the second year notice was served and possession proceedings were issued claiming possession, *inter alia*, under Case 19 of Sched. 15 to the Rent Act 1977, the "shorthold" ground. The initial "shorthold notice" was held effective to leave the tenant within Case 19.

Subs. (7)

If the landlord seeks an increased rent under s.13, above, then on their determination, under s.14, the Rent Assessment Committee are to take into account the fact that the tenancy is shorthold.

Recovery of possession on expiry or termination of assured shorthold tenancy

21.—(1) Without prejudice to any right of the landlord under an assured shorthold tenancy to recover possession of the dwelling-house let on the tenancy in accordance with Chapter I above, on or after the coming to an end of an assured shorthold tenancy which was a fixed term tenancy, a court shall make an order for possession of the dwelling-house if it is satisfied—

    (a) that the assured shorthold tenancy has come to an end and no further assured tenancy (whether shorthold or not) is for the time being in existence, other than a statutory periodic tenancy; and

    (b) the landlord or, in the case of joint landlords, at least one of them has given to the tenant not less than two months' notice stating that he requires possession of the dwelling-house.

(2) A notice under paragraph (b) of subsection (1) above may be given before or on the day on which the tenancy comes to an end; and that subsection shall have effect notwithstanding that on the coming to an end of the fixed term tenancy a statutory periodic tenancy arises.

(3) Where a court makes an order for possession of a dwelling-house by virtue of subsection (1) above, any statutory periodic tenancy which has arisen on the coming to an end of the assured shorthold tenancy shall end (without further notice and regardless of the period) on the day on which the order takes effect.

(4) Without prejudice to any such right as is referred to in subsection (1) above, a court shall make an order for possession of a dwelling-house let on an assured shorthold tenancy which is a periodic tenancy if the court is satisfied—

    (a) that the landlord or, in the case of joint landlords, at least one of them has given to the tenant a notice stating that, after a date specified in the notice, being the last day of a period of the tenancy and not earlier than two months after the date the notice was given, possession of the dwelling-house is required by virtue of this section; and

    (b) that the date specified in the notice under paragraph (a) above is not earlier than the earliest day on which, apart from section 5(1) above, the tenancy could be brought to an end by a notice to quit given by the landlord on the same date as the notice under paragraph (a) above.

DEFINITIONS

    "assured shorthold tenancy": s.18.
    "dwelling-house": s.45.
    "landlord": s.45.
    "statutory periodic tenancy": s.5.
    "tenancy": s.45.
    "tenant": s.45.

GENERAL NOTE

    In substance, this section contains an additional ground for possession. Note that the normal grounds for possession in Sched. 2 are still, and additionally, applicable. The court is to make an order for possession if satisfied (a) that the assured shorthold tenancy has come to an end, (b) that the only assured tenancy in existence is a statutory periodic tenancy, *i.e.* one following the initial fixed term, and (c) that the landlord has given not less than two months notice. In the case of a statutory periodic tenancy, the notice must be at least two months, and not less than would have been required by notice to quit, *i.e.* four weeks under the Protection From Eviction Act 1977, or one period of the tenancy whichever is greater: subs. (4).

Notice must be served even if it is intended to recover possession at the end of the fixed term. The notice can be served during the fixed term, and is adequate to cover a periodic statutory tenancy arising. There is, astonishingly, no requirement that the notice should be in writing, but the word "served" in subs. (2) would seem to imply a need for writing in a way that "given" in subs. (1)(b) does not. The court order is effective to terminate the periodic statutory tenancy on the day it is to take effect, an express provision which could usefully have been incorporated into ss.5 or 9, above.

Reference of excessive rents to rent assessment committee

22.—(1) Subject to section 23 and subsection (2) below, the tenant under an assured shorthold tenancy in respect of which a notice was served as mentioned in section 20(2) above may make an application in the prescribed form to a rent assessment committee for a determination of the rent which, in the committee's opinion, the landlord might reasonably be expected to obtain under the assured shorthold tenancy.

(2) No application may be made under this section if—

    (a) the rent payable under the tenancy is a rent previously determined under this section; or

    (b) the tenancy is an assured shorthold tenancy falling within subsection (4) of section 20 above (and, accordingly, is one in respect of which notice need not have been served as mentioned in subsection (2) of that section).

(3) Where an application is made to a rent assessment committee under subsection (1) above with respect to the rent under an assured shorthold tenancy, the committee shall not make such a determination as is referred to in that subsection unless they consider—

    (a) that there is a sufficient number of similar dwelling-houses in the locality let on assured tenancies (whether shorthold or not); and

    (b) that the rent payable under the assured shorthold tenancy in question is significantly higher than the rent which the landlord might reasonably be expected to be able to obtain under the tenancy, having regard to the level of rents payable under the tenancies referred to in paragraph (a) above.

(4) Where, on an application under this section, a rent assessment committee make a determination of a rent for an assured shorthold tenancy—

    (a) the determination shall have effect from such date as the committee may direct, not being earlier than the date of the application;

    (b) if, at any time on or after the determination takes effect, the rent which, apart from this paragraph, would be payable under the tenancy exceeds the rent so determined, the excess shall be irrecoverable from the tenant; and

    (c) no notice may be served under section 13(2) above with respect to a tenancy of the dwelling-house in question until after the first anniversary of the date on which the determination takes effect.

(5) Subsections (4), (5) and (8) of section 14 above apply in relation to a determination of rent under this section as they apply in relation to a determination under that section and, accordingly, where subsection (5) of that section applies, any reference in subsection (4)(b) above to rent is a reference to rent exclusive of the amount attributable to rates.

Definitions
"assured shorthold tenancy": s.20.
"dwelling-house": s.45.
"landlord": s.45.
"tenancy": s.45.
"tenant": s.45.

General Note
The rent reference machinery for an ordinary assured tenancy is dependent on the landlord serving notice proposing an increase: see notes to s.13, above; s.14 governs the method of determining the rent, and includes taking into account any notices given referable to mandatory grounds for possession under Sched. 2, below. The tenant cannot initiate a reference unless the landlord proposes an increase. The tenant accordingly cannot refer the rent of an agreement under a new letting, or, *e.g.* because of disrepair or other change of circumstances.

This section permits an assured *shorthold* tenant to refer a rent to the rent assessment committee. Note, however, that the tenant may only make one such reference: see subs. (2). Note, further, that such reference must be during the *initial* shorthold, and cannot be made once there has been a new tenancy agreed or a statutory periodic tenancy arising under s.20(4), above. A landlord seeking an *increase* under an assured shorthold tenancy can still use the s.13 procedure, and the tenant can respond by requiring reference to the rent assessment committee, who will then utilise the criteria contained in s.14, as adapted by s.20(7), above.

Subs. (1)
The starting-point is the tenant's application in prescribed form. Where there are joint tenants the application must be by *all* the tenants, unless it is made with the full authority of all the tenants by one acting as their agent: *Turley* v. *Panton* (1975) 29 P. & C.R. 397, Q.B.D., *R.* v. *Rent Officer for Camden London Borough Council, ex p. Felix* (1988) 21 H.L.R., Q.B.D., see also s.45(3). The tenant's application is for the committee to set the rent which "the landlord might reasonably be expected to obtain". This is a somewhat general criterion, but not dissimilar to the criterion applicable to rents under restricted contracts (*e.g.* resident landlord rents) in the Rent Act 1977, s.78. Note that in the absence of an express disregard, it can be reasonable to charge a rent which reflects tenant's improvements: *Ponsford* v. *H.M.S. Aerosols* [1979] A.C. 63, H.L.

Note that ". . . in conditions of scarcity, the open market value may be forced up to a point which does exceed all reason; and it is essential in order to make legislation of this kind effective that the tribunal which is to fix the rent should be able to discount contemporary open market values to the extent necessary in its opinion to arrive at a fair result." (*per* Jenkins L.J., *John Kay* v. *Kay* [1952] 2 Q.B. 258, under the Leasehold Property (Temporary Provisions) Act 1951).

Subs. (2)
No application can be made if the rent payable under the tenancy is one which has already been determined under this section. Nor can there be a reference if the tenancy is a new tenancy agreed, or a statutory periodic tenancy arising, following the initial shorthold, but in practice still shorthold, under s.20(4), above.

Subs. (3)
The committee is to refuse to make a determination unless "there is a sufficient number of similar tenancies in the locality let on assured tenancies (whether shorthold or not)". This imports an "adverse scarcity" test, in the sense that if there are too few tenancies for the purpose of comparison, the tenant loses the right to have the rent determined by the committee. There will also be no determination, rather than affirmation of the rent, unless the committee considers that the rent payable *is* significantly higher than reasonably to be expected on comparison: see notes to subs. (1), above.

The subsection involves a "comparability" test such as that which took precedence in relation to the registration of fair rents under the Rent Acts: see, *e.g. Mason* v. *Skilling* [1974] 1 W.L.R. 1437, H.L. But whereas the register of fair rents built up a body of levels to compare to, this Act merely refers to other rents "payable" under assured tenancies, *i.e.* whether or not themselves referred to the rent assessment committee, although there may be a register, see s.42 below.

"Similar dwelling-houses" is unproblematic: a clear question of fact, pre-eminently for the rent assessment committee. Similarly, what is "significantly higher" is likely to be treated as

50–65

a matter for them, although reliance may perhaps be placed on the Rent Act cases determining what constitutes a "substantial proportion" of rent, for various purposes: see *Woodward* v. *Docherty* [1974] 1 W.L.R. 966, C.A., *Palser* v. *Grinling* [1948] A.C. 291, H.L.

"The locality" means the same locality as that in which is situated the dwelling-house the subject of the assured shorthold tenancy, but the rent assessment committee is entitled to determine what that comprises, *i.e.* how narrowly or broadly to interpret the term: *Palmer* v. *Peabody Trust* [1975] Q.B. 604; *Metropolitan Property Holdings* v. *Finegold* [1975] 1 W.L.R. 349. The latter case suggests a fairly restricted definition.

Subs. (4)
Determination takes effect from such date as the committee direct, no earlier than the date of application. From that date, any excess is irrecoverable. The landlord may not serve a notice proposing an increase until after the first anniversary of the date the determination takes effect.

Subs. (5)
This applies to this section the definition of rent to be found in s.14(4), the requirement to reach a determination exclusive of rates in s.14(5) and the power of the committee to discontinue the process if the landlord and the tenant give notice in writing that they no longer require a determination, or if the tenancy has come to an end, contained in s.14(8).

Termination of rent assessment committee's functions

23.—(1) If the Secretary of State by order made by statutory instrument so provides, section 22 above shall not apply in such cases or to tenancies of dwelling-houses in such areas or in such other circumstances as may be specified in the order.

(2) An order under this section may contain such transitional, incidental and supplementary provisions as appear to the Secretary of State to be desirable.

(3) No order shall be made under this section unless a draft of the order has been laid before, and approved by a resolution of, each House of Parliament.

DEFINITIONS
"dwelling-house": s.45.
"tenancy": s.45.

GENERAL NOTE
The Secretary of State may by order disapply the provisions of s.22, *i.e.* the right to refer a rent to the rent assessment committee, either to areas as a whole, or to classes of tenancies, or as otherwise he may determine.

CHAPTER III

ASSURED AGRICULTURAL OCCUPANCIES

Assured agricultural occupancies

24.—(1) A tenancy or licence of a dwelling-house is for the purposes of this Part of this Act an "assured agricultural occupancy" if—
    (a) it is of a description specified in subsection (2) below; and
    (b) by virtue of any provision of Schedule 3 to this Act the agricultural worker condition is for the time being fulfilled with respect to the dwelling-house subject to the tenancy or licence.

(2) The following are the tenancies and licences referred to in subsection (1)(a) above—
    (a) an assured tenancy which is not an assured shorthold tenancy;
    (b) a tenancy which does not fall within paragraph (a) above by reason

only of paragraph 3 or paragraph 7 of Schedule 1 to this Act (or of both of those paragraphs); and

(c) a licence under which a person has the exclusive occupation of a dwelling-house as a separate dwelling and which, if it conferred a sufficient interest in land to be a tenancy, would be a tenancy falling within paragraph (a) or paragraph (b) above.

(3) For the purposes of Chapter I above and the following provisions of this Chapter, every assured agricultural occupancy which is not an assured tenancy shall be treated as if it were such a tenancy and any reference to a tenant, a landlord or any other expression appropriate to a tenancy shall be construed accordingly; but the provisions of Chapter I above shall have effect in relation to every assured agricultural occupancy subject to the provisions of this Chapter.

(4) Section 14 above shall apply in relation to an assured agricultural occupancy as if in subsection (1) of that section the reference to an assured tenancy were a reference to an assured agricultural occupancy.

DEFINITIONS

"assured shorthold tenancy": s.20.
"assured tenancy": s.1.
"dwelling-house": s.45.
"landlord": s.45.
"tenancy": s.45.
"tenant": s.45.

GENERAL NOTE

The problem of tied accommodation in agriculture was tackled in the Rent (Agriculture) Act 1976, which created a structure similar to the Rent Acts themselves, applicable notwithstanding that many if not most agricultural workers occupy their accommodation under licences, rather than tenancies, and that many—even if tenants—pay no rent (or no quantifiable rent is deducted from wages). This section and the next two deal with tied occupiers in agriculture (and forestry: see further, below), to put them on the same footing as assured tenants.

Agricultural workers are often only licensees (see notes to s.1 above), known as service occupants or service occupiers, because they are required to occupy a particular dwelling in consequence of their employment: see, *e.g. Crane* v. *Morris* [1965] 1 W.L.R. 1104, C.A.

It is not impossible, however, for them to be tenants, known as service tenants. The earliest reported attempt to draw the distinction between service tenant and service occupier appears to be in *Dobson* v. *Jones* (1844) 5 Man. & G. 112, *per* Tindal C.J., referred to in *Northern Ireland Commissioner of Valuation* v. *Fermanagh Protestant Board of Education* [1969] 1 W.L.R. 1708, H.L. The clearest definition of the distinction is to be found in *Smith* v. *Seghill Overseers* (1875) L.R. 10 Q.B. 422:

"Where the occupation is necessary for the performance of services and the occupier is required to reside in the house in order to perform those services, the occupation being strictly ancillary to the performance of the duties which the occupier has to perform, the occupation is that of the servant. Required means more than the master saying you must reside in one of my houses if you come into my service. The residence must be ancillary and necessary to the performance of the servant's duty and unless he is required for that purpose to reside in the house and not merely as an arbitrary regulation on the part of the master, I do not think he is prevented from occupying as tenant. Unless the men are required to live in the houses for the better performance of their duties, it does not convert the occupation of a tenant into that of a servant. The governing principle is that in order to constitute an occupation as a servant it must be an occupation ancillary to the performance of the duties which the occupier has engaged to perform."

A somewhat more lax test was mooted in the contemporaneous case of *Fox* v. *Dalby* (1874) L.R. 10 C.P. 285, where it was held that a person could be a service occupier if *either* it was necessary for the purposes of the job, *or* the employer imposed the requirement in the course of the contract of employment.

In *Glasgow Corporation* v. *Johnstone* [1965] A.C. 609, H.L., it was said that "if the servant is given the privilege of residing in the house of the master as part of his emoluments the occupation is that of the servant. . . If on the other hand the servant is genuinely obliged by his master for the purposes of the master's business or if it is necessary for the servant to reside in the house for the performance of his services, the occupation will be that of the master . . ."

This test was adopted in *Hirst* v. *Sargant* (1967) 65 L.G.R. 127, but qualified by the observation that "the word necessary used in that test is clearly to be applied strictly. Once it is accepted. . .that these were part of his duties under his contract of service and once it is recognised as obvious. . .that these functions could not possibly have been performed otherwise than by a man living in this hereditament or house similarly situated then it seems to me clear that the second limb of. . .(that) test is satisfied."

The more strict approach is consistent with the decision of the House of Lords in *Street* v. *Mountford* [1985] A.C. 809, 17 H.L.R. 402, H.L., where the emphasis is on "required" to occupy so far as service occupation is discussed: see notes to s.1, above. See also the *post-Street* decision in *Royal Philanthropic Society* v. *County* (1986) 18 H.L.R. 83, C.A.; see further *Postcastle Properties* v. *Perridge* (1985) 18 H.L.R. 100, C.A.

Subs. (1)

There are two pre-conditions to the existence of an "assured agricultural occupancy". The first is that it fulfils what may be called the "occupation condition"; the second, what may be called the "employment condition".

There are three ways in which the occupation condition may be fulfilled: if the occupation is under an assured tenancy, but not an assured shorthold tenancy; or a tenancy that would be assured but for either or both paras. 3 (tenancy at a low rent) and 7 (tenancies of agricultural holdings) of Sched. 1 to this Act; or a licence conferring exclusive occupation (see notes to s.1, above) and which if it were a tenancy would either be assured, or would only be excluded from assured tenancy by paras. 3 and/or 7 of Sched. 1. Accordingly, neither the fact that a letting is a licence, nor the fact that no or a low rent is paid, will exclude the worker from the protection of this Chapter. However, if a licence, it must confer exclusive occupation of a dwelling-house "as a separate dwelling": see notes to s.1, above.

The employment condition is based on the Rent (Agriculture) Act 1976. Sched. 3 to this Act applies the provisions of the 1976 Act to the questions of what is meant by "agriculture", whether a person is a "qualifying worker", including its provisions governing persons "incapable of whole-time work in agriculture, or work in agriculture as a permit worker, in consequence of a qualifying injury or disease", and "whether a dwelling-house is in qualifying ownership".

Agriculture includes dairy farming, livestock keeping and breeding, arable farming, market gardening and forestry. Gamekeepers do not qualify within this definition: *Flendyne* v. *Rapley* (1978) 245 E.G. 573, C.A., *Earl of Normanton* v. *Giles* [1980] 1 W.L.R. 28, H.L.

Qualifying Worker. A qualifying worker is a person who has worked whole-time in agriculture or has worked in agriculture as a permit-worker for not less than 91 out of the previous 104 weeks. A person works whole-time if he works not less than the standard number of hours in agriculture. A permit-worker is one who has been granted a permit under s.5 of the Agricultural Wages Act 1948. There are provisions to protect a worker against loss of qualifying time by reason of injury or disease, holiday entitlement, or if the worker is absent with the consent of his employer. In addition to those who thus qualify, a worker who has a "qualifying injury or disease" retains the same rights.

Qualifying Ownership. Premises are in qualifying ownership if *either* the occupier's employer is the owner of the dwelling, *or* the dwelling has been let by some person with whom the occupier's employer has made arrangements for the premises in question to be used as housing for persons employed by him in agriculture. It is not necessary for the employer, or the person with whom such arrangements have been made, actually to own the premises in question; it is enough to establish that he is the occupier's immediate landlord licensor. *Employer* means the person by whom the worker is employed, or one of the persons by whom he is employed.

Under Sched. 3 to this Act, the employment condition is fulfilled if:

(a) the property is or has been in qualifying ownership at any time during the subsistence of the tenancy or licence and *either* the occupier (or if there are joint occupiers, one of them) is or has been a qualifying worker at any time during the subsistence of the tenancy or licence, *or* he is incapable of whole-time work in agriculture or work in agriculture as a permit worker in consequence of a qualifying injury or disease (Sched. 3, para. 2); or

(b) the tenancy or licence was granted to the occupier in consideration of his giving up possession of another dwelling-house which qualified under the "occupation condition" (above) and immediately before he gave up occupation of it, the last paragraph or the next paragraph of these notes applied (Sched. 3, para. 4); or

(c) the conditions in the penultimate paragraph of these notes were fulfilled but the worker/occupier has died, and the occupier is either the "qualifying widow or widower" or "the qualifying member of the family of" the deceased. A widow or widower qualifies if she or he was residing in the dwelling-house immediately before the death. For these purposes, widow and widower include someone with whom the deceased was living as wife or husband immediately before his or her death.

If there is no qualifying widow or widower, then the qualifying member of the family is a member of the family who was residing with the deceased at the time of, and for a period of two years before, his death (Sched. 3, para. 3).

Residence in each case means in the subject-property: see also *Edmunds* v. *Jones* [1957] 1 W.L.R. 1118, C.A., *Collier* v. *Stoneman* [1957] 1 W.L.R. 1108, C.A., *South Northamptonshire D.C.* v. *Power* (1987) 20 H.L.R. 133, C.A.

There can only be one qualifying successor (whether spouse as defined or member of the family), and if there is more than one, then the two putative successors may agree amongst themselves, or else the matter may be determined by the county court: see notes to s.17, above.

While most relationships will be easy to define as "family" or not, one question which arises is that of children not legally adopted. *De facto* adoption has been permitted under the Rent Acts: *Brock* v. *Wollams* [1949] 2 K.B. 388, C.A., even although by the time the question arose, the child had achieved his majority. But as there can be no *de jure* adoption between adults, there can likewise be no *de facto* adoption between adults: *Carega Properties S.A.* v. *Sharratt* [1979] 1 W.L.R. 928, H.L.; *Sefton Holdings Ltd.* v. *Cairns* (1987) 20 H.L.R. 124, C.A.

In the case of a member of the family, there must be residence *with the deceased*. These words "must be given their ordinary popular significance" (*Collier* v. *Stoneman*, above; see also *Morgan* v. *Murch* [1970] 1 W.L.R. 778, C.A., but *cf. Foreman* v. *Beagley* [1969] 1 W.L.R. 1387, C.A., in which a son failed to establish that he was "residing with" his hospitalised mother—there must be more than merely residing at the same address, but a degree of community or household).

In *Swanbrae Ltd.* v. *Elliott* (1986) 19 H.L.R. 86, C.A., the appellant had been sleeping at the premises at least three to four nights a week from when her mother became ill with cancer. She still retained her own tenancy elsewhere. It was held that while it was not necessary to dwell permanently in the sense of indefinitely in the premises in question, the residence must be more than transient. It was not sufficient that the appellant was "living at" the premises; it was necessary to show she had a settled home there and had truly become part of the deceased's household. It is essentially a question of fact whether or not someone has been residing with the deceased, though the burden lies on the would-be successor: *Swanbrae, Peabody Donation Fund Governors* v. *Grant* (1982) 6 H.L.R. 41, C.A.

Where the occupier, under any of these provisions, agrees to move, then even although he may not have fulfilled one of the employment conditions in the new property, protection will continue in the same way: Sched. 3, para. 4. The provisions also apply where a new tenancy or licence of the same premises is granted to a qualifying occupier: Sched. 3, para. 5.

Subs. (3)

This Chapter operates by making all assured agricultural occupancies into assured tenancies, to whom the protection of Chapter One is afforded, but rendering that protection subject to this Chapter. The important point to note is that assured *tenants* will by reason of this provision become assured agricultural *occupancies* for this purpose, *i.e.* their protection under Chapter One will be subject to the provisions of this Chapter. This is the effect of including assured tenants in subs. (2)(a), and this subsection.

Subs. (4)

This adapts s.14 in the same way for assured agricultural occupants as for assured shorthold tenants by s.20(7), above.

Security of tenure

25.—(1) If a statutory periodic tenancy arises on the coming to an end of an assured agricultural occupancy—

    (a) it shall be an assured agricultural occupancy as long as, by virtue of any provision of Schedule 3 to this Act, the agricultural worker condition is for the time being fulfilled with respect to the dwelling-house in question; and

(b) if no rent was payable under the assured agricultural occupancy which constitutes the fixed term tenancy referred to in subsection (2) of section 5 above, subsection (3)(d) of that section shall apply as if for the words "the same as those for which rent was last payable under" there were substituted "monthly beginning on the day following the coming to an end of".

(2) In its application to an assured agricultural occupancy, Part II of Schedule 2 to this Act shall have effect with the omission of Ground 16.

(3) In its application to an assured agricultural occupancy, Part III of Schedule 2 to this Act shall have effect as if any reference in paragraph 2 to an assured tenancy included a reference to an assured agricultural occupancy.

(4) If the tenant under an assured agricultural occupancy gives notice to terminate his employment then, notwithstanding anything in any agreement or otherwise, that notice shall not constitute a notice to quit as respects the assured agricultural occupancy.

(5) Nothing in subsection (4) above affects the operation of an actual notice to quit given in respect of an assured agricultural occupancy.

DEFINITIONS
"assured agricultural occupancy": s.24.
"fixed term tenancy": s.45.
"tenant": s.45.
"statutory periodic tenancy": s.5.

GENERAL NOTE
This section governs what happens (a) on the termination of a fixed-term tenancy or licence which qualifies as an assured agricultural occupancy, and (b) on the termination of employment.

Subs. (1)
A statutory periodic tenancy only arises after a fixed-term tenancy, for a periodic tenancy cannot be brought to an end save by an order of the court: see notes to s.5, above. Provided the employment condition—see notes to s.24, above,—continues to be fulfilled, the statutory periodic tenancy is also an assured agricultural occupancy. If the employment ceases, then the statutory periodic tenancy would seem to cease to be an assured agricultural occupancy but to become instead an ordinary statutory periodic (assured) tenancy.

In the case of a normal statutory periodic tenancy, its periods are those for which rent was last payable under the former fixed-term: if no rent was payable under the fixed-term assured agricultural occupancy, then the statutory periodic tenancy is to be a monthly tenancy.

Subs. (2)
The discretionary ground for possession available against service tenants is not available against an assured agricultural occupant. This is necessary because under the qualifying conditions, the occupier may no longer be in employment (or may have been succeeded by a surviving spouse or member of the family), yet retain protection: see Sched. 3, and notes to s.24(1), (2), above.

Subs. (3)
Sched. 2, Part III defines suitable alternative accommodation, for the purposes of ground 1 of the grounds for possession. By this addition, another assured agricultural occupancy *is* suitable alternative accommodation for an assured agricultural occupant.

Subss. (4) and (5)
The Act operates by restricting the *landlord's* power to terminate a tenancy, and does not prevent the *tenant* terminating, *e.g.* by notice to quit: see notes to s.5, above; see *Greenwich London Borough Council* v. *McGrady* (1982) 6 H.L.R. 36, C.A. Commonly, an occupancy agreement will include a proviso that the right of occupation is to determine if the employee gives notice to leave his employment. While preserving the right of the occupier to give notice to quit the premises should he wish to do so (subs. (5)), subs. (4) ensures that,

regardless of anything in the agreement, notice to terminate employment is not to be treated as notice to quit the premises.

Rehousing of agricultural workers etc.

26. In section 27 of the Rent (Agriculture) Act 1976 (rehousing: applications to housing authority)—
  (a) in subsection (1)(a) after "statutory tenancy" there shall be inserted "or an assured agricultural occupancy"; and
  (b) at the end of subsection (3) there shall be added "and assured agricultural occupancy has the same meaning as in Chapter III of Part I of the Housing Act 1988".

DEFINITION
"assured agricultural occupancy": s.24.

GENERAL NOTE
Under the Rent (Agriculture) Act 1976, s.27, the occupier of agricultural land may apply to the local housing authority to rehouse an occupier "in the interests of efficient agriculture". This extends the procedure under that Act to the rehousing of assured agricultural occupants under this.

CHAPTER IV

PROTECTION FROM EVICTION

Damages for unlawful eviction

27.—(1) This section applies if, at any time after 9th June 1988, a landlord (in this section referred to as "the landlord in default") or any person acting on behalf of the landlord in default unlawfully deprives the residential occupier of any premises of his occupation of the whole or part of the premises.

(2) This section also applies if, at any time after 9th June 1988, a landlord (in this section referred to as "the landlord in default") or any person acting on behalf of the landlord in default—
  (a) attempts unlawfully to deprive the residential occupier of any premises of his occupation of the whole or part of the premises, or
  (b) knowing or having reasonable cause to believe that the conduct is likely to cause the residential occupier of any premises—
      (i) to give up his occupation of the premises or any part thereof, or
      (ii) to refrain from exercising any right or pursuing any remedy in respect of the premises or any part thereof,
    does acts likely to interfere with the peace or comfort of the residential occupier or members of his household, or persistently withdraws or withholds services reasonably required for the occupation of the premises as a residence,
and, as a result, the residential occupier gives up his occupation of the premises as a residence.

(3) Subject to the following provisions of this section, where this section applies, the landlord in default shall, by virtue of this section, be liable to pay to the former residential occupier, in respect of his loss of the right to occupy the premises in question as his residence, damages assessed on the basis set out in section 28 below.

(4) Any liability arising by virtue of subsection (3) above—
  (a) shall be in the nature of a liability in tort; and
  (b) subject to subsection (5) below, shall be in addition to any

liability arising apart from this section (whether in tort, contract or otherwise).

(5) Nothing in this section affects the right of a residential occupier to enforce any liability which arises apart from this section in respect of his loss of the right to occupy premises as his residence; but damages shall not be awarded both in respect of such a liability and in respect of a liability arising by virtue of this section on account of the same loss.

(6) No liability shall arise by virtue of subsection (3) above if—

    (a) before the date on which proceedings to enforce the liability are finally disposed of, the former residential occupier is reinstated in the premises in question in such circumstances that he becomes again the residential occupier of them; or

    (b) at the request of the former residential occupier, a court makes an order (whether in the nature of an injunction or otherwise) as a result of which he is reinstated as mentioned in paragraph (a) above;

and, for the purposes of paragraph (a) above, proceedings to enforce a liability are finally disposed of on the earliest date by which the proceedings (including any proceedings on or in consequence of an appeal) have been determined and any time for appealing or further appealing has expired, except that if any appeal is abandoned, the proceedings shall be taken to be disposed of on the date of the abandonment.

(7) If, in proceedings to enforce a liability arising by virtue of subsection (3) above, it appears to the court—

    (a) that, prior to the event which gave rise to the liability, the conduct of the former residential occupier or any person living with him in the premises concerned was such that it is reasonable to mitigate the damages for which the landlord in default would otherwise be liable, or

    (b) that, before the proceedings were begun, the landlord in default offered to reinstate the former residential occupier in the premises in question and either it was unreasonable of the former residential occupier to refuse that offer or, if he had obtained alternative accommodation before the offer was made, it would have been unreasonable of him to refuse that offer if he had not obtained that accommodation,

the court may reduce the amount of damages which would otherwise be payable by such amount as it thinks appropriate.

(8) In proceedings to enforce a liability arising by virtue of subsection (3) above, it shall be a defence for the defendant to prove that he believed, and had reasonable cause to believe—

    (a) that the residential occupier had ceased to reside in the premises in question at the time when he was deprived of occupation as mentioned in subsection (1) above or, as the case may be, when the attempt was made or the acts were done as a result of which he gave up his occupation of those premises; or

    (b) that, where the liability would otherwise arise by virtue only of the doing of acts or the withdrawal or withholding of services, he had reasonable grounds for doing the acts or withdrawing or withholding the services in question.

(9) In this section—

    (a) "residential occupier", in relation to any premises, has the same meaning as in section 1 of the 1977 Act;

    (b) "the right to occupy", in relation to a residential occupier, includes any restriction on the right of another person to recover possession of the premises in question;

    (c) "landlord", in relation to a residential occupier, means the person who, but for the occupier's right to occupy, would be entitled to occupation of the premises and any superior landlord under whom that person derives title;

(d) "former residential occupier", in relation to any premises, means the person who was the residential occupier until he was deprived of or gave up his occupation as mentioned in subsection (1) or subsection (2) above (and, in relation to a former residential occupier, "the right to occupy" and "landlord" shall be construed accordingly).

DEFINITIONS

"former residential occupier": subs. (8).
"landlord": subs. (8).
"1977 Act": s.33.
"residential occupier": subs. (8).
"right to occupy": subs. (8).

GENERAL NOTE

Illegal eviction and harassment are the subjects of the Protection from Eviction Act 1977, together with (a) the requirement for notices to quit to be of a minimum period and to be in writing and in some circumstances to contain prescribed information, and (b) special provisions to permit courts to suspend orders for possession against agricultural workers, not within the protection of the Rent (Agriculture) Act 1976. This Chapter contains provisions amending all of these aspects of the 1977 Act.

Under the 1977 Act, s.1, two offences are created. The first is illegal eviction and arises "if any person unlawfully deprives the residential occupier of any premises of his occupation of the premises or any part thereof, or attempts to do so, he shall be guilty of an offence unless he proves that he believed, and had reasonable cause to believe, that the residential occupier had ceased to reside in the premises" (the 1977 Act, s.1(2)).

The second is harassment, and arises "if any person with intent to cause the residential occupier of any premises—

"(a) to give up the occupation of the premises or any part thereof; or

"(b) to refrain from exercising any right or pursuing any remedy in respect of the premises or part thereof; does acts calculated to interfere with the peace or comfort of the residential occupier or members of his household, or persistently withdraws or withholds services reasonably required for the occupation of the premises as a residence, he shall be guilty of an offence" (the 1977 Act, s.1(3)). (With reference to offences after January 15, 1988, the word "likely" is substituted for calculated, see s.29(1), below).

A residential occupier (the 1977 Act, s.1(1)), "in relation to any premises, means a person occupying the premises as a residence, whether under a contract or by virtue of any enactment or rule of law giving him the right to remain in occupation or restricting the right of any other person to recover possession of the premises." This definition includes those under existing tenancies or licences, and former tenants within, *e.g.* the Rent Act 1977, Rent (Agriculture) Act 1976, Landlord and Tenant Act 1954, Parts I and II and, now, Chapters I-III. above.

Ss.2 and 3 of the 1977 Act impose restrictions on the recovery of possession of residential premises, by requiring a court order where otherwise none might be needed, and accordingly operate as enactments bringing additional classes of occupier within s.1.

S.2 renders it unlawful to enforce a right of re-entry or forfeiture premises let as a dwelling while any person is lawfully residing in the premises or part of them, other than by court proceedings. S.3 introduces a requirement to take court proceedings to recover possession of premises let as a dwelling under a tenancy (see notes to s.1, above) "which is not a statutorily protected tenancy", and the tenancy has come to an end but the occupier has continued to reside in the premises or part of them. In 1980, s.3 was extended to include former licensees which created restricted contracts (*i.e.* within the jurisdiction of the Rent Tribunal), entered into after the commencement of the Housing Act 1980, s.69 (November 28, 1980).

"Statutorily protected tenancies" are excluded, because as defined, the "former tenants" are protected from eviction without court proceedings by other statutory provisions: the Landlord and Tenant Act 1954, Parts I or II, Rent (Agriculture) Act 1976, Rent Act 1977, Agricultural Holdings Act 1986—see, the 1977 Act, s.8. By s.33(2), below, assured tenants and assured agricultural occupants within Chapters I and III, above, are now brought within the definition of "statutorily protected tenancy" for the purposes of the 1977 Act, so that they are *not* protected from eviction without court proceedings by s.3 of that Act, because they already require a court order by reason of the provisions of this Act.

Two problems have been perceived with the operation of the 1977 Act as described thus far. First of all, it was held in *McCall* v. *Abelesz* [1976] Q.B. 585, C.A., that s.1 did *not* create a cause of action for breach of statutory duty on the basis of which a tenant could take action, *e.g.* for damages or reinstatement. Instead, action has had to be taken under other causes, *e.g.* breach of contract, breach of covenant for quiet enjoyment, derogation from grant, nuisance, trespass—see, generally, *Quiet Enjoyment,* Arden and Partington, Legal Action Group (1985), Chapt. Two (2nd Ed.).

In *Warder* v. *Cooper* [1970] 1 All E.R. 1112, it was held, however, that breach of s.3 (and, therefore, presumably, s.2), did create a cause of action, so that the effects of the *McCall* decision were (a) to require selection of causes of action other than the more straightforward "illegal eviction" or "harassment", pursuant to what became the 1977 Act, s.1, and (b) to leave out of protection altogether those who did not qualify as "residential occupiers" within s.3, which primarily meant (i) former licencees whose licences did not qualify as restricted contracts within the jurisdiction of the Rent Tribunal at all (see notes to s.1, above), or (ii) whose such contracts commenced before November 28, 1980.

This and the next sections address this problem, by reversing the effect of *McCall* in part, by introducing a right to damages (assessed under s.28, below), for illegal eviction and harassment. Note, however, that if the occupier is reinstated before proceedings are commenced, or if a court on interlocutory application orders re-admission, there is no liability under this section (subs. (6)), from which it follows that action for damages—and indeed for an injunction for readmission—will have to remain under other causes.

The second problem perceived relates to the need to prove "intent" in connection with "harassment": this is addressed by amendment of the 1977 Act, s.1, in s.29, below, and by the way the new right to damages is defined in this section.

Subs. (1)

The section is retrospective, to June 9, 1988. The wrong is "unlawful deprivation" of occupation of the whole *or any part* of premises, *i.e.* an offence under the 1977 Act, s.1(2), but not including the offence of *attempted* unlawful eviction under the 1977 Act, s.1(2), which is incorporated instead into subs. (2).

Deprivation need not be permanent, *e.g.* exclusion for weeks or months will suffice, but what might be described as a "locking out case", where someone has been deprived of occupation for a day or two, is more appropriately dealt with as an act of harassment: *R.* v. *Yuthiwattana* (1984) 16 H.L.R. 49, C.A. (Crim.). It is a defence to a charge of illegal eviction to prove that the accused believes, *and* has reasonable cause to believe, that the occupier had ceased to reside in the premises, which matters are for a jury to decide: *R.* v. *Davidson-Acres* (1980) Crim. L.R. 50, C.A. (Crim.).

In relation to the civil action, the same defence arises by subs. (8)(a), below.

Subs. (2)

This subsection corresponds to subs. (1), but is concerned with *attempted* unlawful eviction under the 1977 Act, s.1(2), and harassment under *ibid,* s.1(2) and (3A) (the latter added by s.29, below), but only where it actually results in the residential occupier giving up occupation of the premises as a residence. The acts of harassment must be committed "knowing or having reasonable cause to believe that the conduct is likely to cause the residential occupier" to quit or to refrain from exercising a right or remedy, and where peace or comfort is concerned "likely to interfere", to which extent a minor act of harassment, even with the necessary intent, which would not lead a normal or reasonable occupier to quit, is unlikely to result in a successful claim for damages; however, if the act is sufficiently serious to qualify as "likely" then the residential occupier need not also prove that it was reasonable to quit.

Although the plural "acts" is used, a single act suffices: *R.* v. *Evangelos Polycarpou* (1978) 9 H.L.R. 129, C.A.(Crim.). "Failure to act" is not sufficient. In *R.* v. *Ahmad* (1986) 18 H.L.R. 416, C.A.(Crim.), a landlord started works to a flat (without the then necessary intention, see notes to s.29, below). The works rendered the flat uninhabitable and the landlord refused to do the works necessary to make it habitable again for the tenant. It was found that he did this *with* the necessary intention. Nonetheless, failure to take steps to complete the work was not the doing of an act or acts for the purposes of the 1977 Act, s.1(3). The different parts of the provisions did not create different offences. The act in question is the act calculated to interfere with peace or comfort: *Schon* v. *L. B. Camden* (1986) 18 H.L.R. 341, C.A.(Crim.).

Contrary to what seems to have been suggested in *McCall* by Ormrod L.J., there is no requirement that an act of harassment must be such that it gives rise to a remedy in trespass, or for breach of contract or of the covenant for quiet enjoyment, but can arise in relation to something voluntarily or gratuitously given, as in *R.* v. *Yuthiwattana* (1984) 16 H.L.R. 49, C.A.(Crim.) (landlord's refusal to supply a replacement key to the house to a tenant who had lost his).

In the criminal context, if the defendant raises a defence that he honestly believed that the person harassed was no longer a residential occupier, the prosecutor must prove that he did not honestly so believe, although a court may direct a jury that there has to be a reasonable basis for the belief: *R.* v. *Phekoo* (above). In the present context, the position is governed by subs. (8)(a), below; see also subs. (7), below.

Subss. (3)–(5)
Damages *for loss of the right of occupation* are assessed in accordance with s.28, below. The liability is in tort and is additional to any liability arising apart from this section. However, damages for loss of the right of occupation can only be awarded once, *either* under this head, *or* under another cause of action, *e.g.* breach of contract. See further notes to s.28, below.

Subs. (6)
Action cannot be brought for damages for loss of the right of action, under this section, if before proceedings are finally disposed of, the former occupier is reinstated sufficiently to qualify as a residential occupier, *i.e.* with the full rights of which he has been deprived. Similarly, if a court orders readmission, on the application of the occupier.

The first case is relatively straightforward. The second is slightly more problematic. The county court has jurisdiction to grant an injunction for re-admission, either as ancillary to another claim within its jurisdiction (County Courts Act 1984, s.38), *e.g.* for damages up to £5,000 for tort or breach of contract, or otherwise "in respect of, or relating to, and land, or the possession, occupation, use or enjoyment of land" under the County Courts Act 1984, s.22. But there must be a cause of action, in either case. If action is launched under this section, and it is *successfully* accompanied by a claim for interlocutory relief by way of an order readmitting the occupier, the action under this section falls, by reason of subs. (6)(b).

Accordingly, it would seem that the best course will be to issue proceedings under *both* (a) another cause of action, (i) for an injunction readmitting the occupier if this is wanted, and (ii) for classes of damages other than for the loss of the right of occupation, *and* (b) under this section—for damages for the loss of the right of occupation, if the claim for an injunction fails.

Subs. (7)
This subsection authorises mitigation of damages either on account of the conduct of the former residential occupier or someone living with him or if the landlord offers reinstatement and it would be, or have been, unreasonable for the occupier to refuse to accept: this necessarily accepts that sufficiently bad conduct by the landlord will justify a decision not to come back; but it seems a little harsh that an offer of reinstatement made *after* the occupier has found alternative accommodation should justify mitigation of damages, and it is submitted that courts should be chary of such offers if this provision is not to lead to abuse, *i.e.* to offers made in the knowledge that the occupier has found somewhere else and is accordingly not likely to return. The offer must, however, be made before the proceedings are begun.

Subs. (8)
This incorporates for the purposes of the action under this section the defences available in criminal proceedings: see notes to subss. (1) and (2), above. Note in particular that there must be reasonable cause for a belief that the residential occupier had ceased to reside in the premises. Note, too, the defences of "reasonable grounds for doing the acts" and "reasonable grounds . . .for withdrawing or withholding . . . services".

The measure of damages

28.—(1) The basis for the assessment of damages referred to in section 27(3) above is the difference in value, determined as at the time immediately before the residential occupier ceased to occupy the premises in question as his residence, between—

    (a) the value of the interest of the landlord in default determined on the assumption that the residential occupier continues to have the same right to occupy the premises as before that time; and

(b) the value of that interest determined on the assumption that the residential occupier has ceased to have that right.

(2) In relation to any premises, any reference in this section to the interest of the landlord in default is a reference to his interest in the building in which the premises in question are comprised (whether or not that building contains any other premises) together with its curtilage.

(3) For the purposes of the valuations referred to in subsection (1) above, it shall be assumed—

(a) that the landlord in default is selling his interest on the open market to a willing buyer;

(b) that neither the residential occupier nor any member of his family wishes to buy; and

(c) that it is unlawful to carry out any substantial development of any of the land in which the landlord's interest subsists or to demolish the whole or part of any building on that land.

(4) In this section "the landlord in default" has the same meaning as in section 27 above and subsection (9) of that section applies in relation to this section as it applies in relation to that.

(5) Section 113 of the Housing Act 1985 (meaning of "members of a person's family") applies for the purposes of subsection (3)(b) above.

(6) The reference in subsection (3)(c) above to substantial development of any of the land in which the landlord's interest subsists is a reference to any development other than—

(a) development for which planning permission is granted by a general development order for the time being in force and which is carried out so as to comply with any condition or limitation subject to which planning permission is so granted; or

(b) a change of use resulting in the building referred to in subsection (2) above or any part of it being used as, or as part of, one or more dwelling-houses;

and in this subsection "general development order" has the same meaning as in section 43(3) of the Town and Country Planning Act 1971 and other expressions have the same meaning as in that Act.

DEFINITIONS
"landlord": s.27.
"residential occupier": s.27.

GENERAL NOTE
This section defines the damages which may be obtained under the last section, subject to mitigation under s.27(7), see notes thereto above.

Note (a) that the claim is in tort, and (b) that the claim to damages assessed in accordance with this section is not exclusive of a claim for damages under some other head of action, *save* that damages for the actual loss of the right of occupation are not to be awarded twice: see above, s.27(4) and (5). Decided cases on what is in practice illegal eviction will remain relevant under two headings:

1. They will be relevant to losses *other* than for loss of the right of occupation;

2. A choice may yet be made as to under which head (the last section, or another cause of action) to claim for the loss of the right of occupation itself.

Damages awards for loss of the right of occupation have not, however, been particularly generous, and it would seem will be higher if assessed in accordance with this section: see, *e.g. Drane* v. *Evangelou* [1978] 1 W.L.R. 455, C.A., *Guppys (Bridport)* v. *Brookling* (1983) 14 H.L.R. 1, C.A. *Ashgar* v. *Ahmed* (1984) 17 H.L.R. 25, C.A., *McMillan* v. *Singh* (1984) 17 H.L.R. 120, C.A., *Millington* v. *Duffy* (1984) 17 H.L.R. 120, C.A. Recent county court awards are regularly reported in *Legal Action*. As to the law on damages under other heads of action, and for losses other than the right of occupation itself, see generally, Arden and Partington, *Quiet Enjoyment*, 2nd Ed., Legal Action Group (1985), Chapt. Three.

Subss. (1)–(3), (6)
The basis of the assessment is difference in value as at the date when the residential occupier left the premises, between the value of the landlord's interest *with* the occupier still

enjoying the right to occupy, and the value of the landlord's interest *without* such right. Thus the lower figure will be with the occupier having a right of occupation, and the higher figure without such right. Of course, the amount could be considerable, in the case of, *e.g.* a protected or assured tenant: property can be worth twice as much or even 60–40 with vacant possession. But it is the *right* which is to be valued, so that eviction of someone with a lesser right, *e.g.* a restricted contract, an assured shorthold tenant, will produce a correspondingly lower amount of damages.

However, that which is to be valued is the whole building in which the premises are comprised (subs. (2)), so that the potential gain to, *e.g.* the last protected tenant of a bedsitting room in a house with the potential for conversion into flats or resale for owner-occupation will be considerable, as in *Guppys (Bridport) Ltd.* v. *Brookling* (1983) 14 H.L.R. 1, C.A. Against that, though, must be set the assumption in subs. (3)(c), that there is no extant "substantial development" or "demolition" permission.

Development is defined in the Town and Country Planning Act 1971, s.22, as "the carrying out of building, engineering, mining or other operations in, on, over or under land, or the making of any material change in the use of any buildings or other land." This is, however, subject to a number of exclusions, including, relevantly:

(a) maintenance or improvement works, or other alterations, affecting only the interior of the building or not materially affecting exterior appearance;

(b) the use of a building within the curtilage of a dwelling-house for a purpose incidental to the enjoyment of the dwelling-house as such; and

(c) changes of use within the same use class pursuant to the use classes orders issued by the Secretary of State for the Environment.

It is expressly provided that the use as two or more separate dwelling-houses of any building previously used as a single dwelling-house constitutes a material change of use: s.22(3). A change from use as a single house to a house of bed-sitting rooms or some similar such multiple occupation may constitute a material change of use: see, *e.g. Birmingham Corporation* v. *Habib Ullah* [1964] 1 Q.B. 178, *Clarke* v. *Minister of Housing and Local Government* (1966) 18 P. & C.R. 82, *Hammersmith London Borough Council* v. *Secretary of State for the Environment* (1975) 119 S.J. 591, *Mornford Investments* v. *Minister of Housing and Local Government* [1970] 2 All E.R. 253, *Mayflower (Cambridge)* v. *Secretary of State for the Environment* (1975) 30 P. & C.R. 28, *Panayi* v. *Secretary of State for the Environment* (1985) 50 P. & C.R. 109.

In some cases, a large scale demolition may itself constitute an engineering or building operation and, as such, a development, without the benefit of the added words in subs. (3)(c): *London County Council* v. *Marks & Spencer* [1953] A.C. 535, H.L., but *cf. Iddenden* v. *Secretary of State for the Environment* [1972] 3 All E.R. 833.

It is to be assumed under subs. (3)(c) that it is unlawful to carry out substantial development or to demolish the building. For these purposes, substantial development means any development other than one within a general development order under the Town and Country Planning Act 1971, or a change of use which results in the building to dwelling-house use. *Such* "development" (including change of use) is *not* to be disregarded.

Also to be assumed on valuation are (a) that the landlord is selling on the open market to a willing buyer, and (b) that neither the residential occupier nor any member of his family wishes to buy.

Subs. (5)

The following are members of a person's family under the Housing Act 1985, s.113:

(a) a spouse, or persons living together as husband and wife;

(b) a parent, grandparent, child, grandchild, brother, sister, uncle, aunt, nephew or niece, treating relationships by marriage as if by blood, half-blood relationships as whole blood, stepchildren as children, and illegitimate children as legitimate.

Offences of harassment

29.—(1) In section 1 of the 1977 Act (unlawful eviction and harassment of occupier), with respect to acts done after the commencement of this Act, subsection (3) shall have effect with the substitution, for the word "calculated", of the word "likely".

(2) After that subsection there shall be inserted the following subsections—

"(3A) Subject to subsection (3B) below, the landlord of a residential occupier or an agent of the landlord shall be guilty of an offence if—

(a) he does acts likely to interfere with the peace or comfort of the residential occupier or members of his household, or

(b) he persistently withdraws or withholds services reasonably required for the occupation of the premises in question as a residence,

and (in either case) he knows, or has reasonable cause to believe, that that conduct is likely to cause the residential occupier to give up the occupation of the whole or part of the premises or to refrain from exercising any right or pursuing any remedy in respect of the whole or part of the premises.

(3B) A person shall not be guilty of an offence under subsection (3A) above if he proves that he had reasonable grounds for doing the acts or withdrawing or withholding the services in question.

(3C) In subsection (3A) above "landlord", in relation to a residential occupier of any premises, means the person who, but for—

(a) the residential occupier's right to remain in occupation of the premises, or

(b) a restriction on the person's right to recover possession of the premises,

would be entitled to occupation of the premises and any superior landlord under whom that person derives title."

Definition
"1977 Act": s.33.

General Note
This section introduces a new offence into the Protection From Eviction Act 1977, s.1: see, generally, notes to s.27, above. The problem which it seeks to resolve is the necessity to prove intent, and calculation, in connection with an offence of harassment under the Protection From Eviction Act 1977, s.1(3).

The essence of the amendment is that it is no longer necessary to prove *intent*. Under the 1977 Act, s.1(3), the offence is not one of strict liability, and specific intent has to be shown, *i.e.* intent to cause the occupier either to quit or to refrain from exercising a right or pursuing a remedy, *e.g.* registration of a rent, seeking repairs or using shared accommodation: *R. v. Phekoo* [1981] 1 W.L.R. 1117, C.A. (Crim.). A positive intent must be shown, not merely a "hopeful inactivity" over services: *McCall* v. *Abelesz* [1976] Q.B. 585, C.A. The element of calculated acts or persistent withdrawal of services has to be proved: *Westminster County Council* v. *Peart* (1968) 19 P. & C.R. 736, C.A., and *R. v. Abrol* [1972] Crim.L.R. 318, C.A.(Crim.). The *facts* leading to an earlier conviction may be admissible, to prove intent, although the conviction itself will not normally be: *R. v. Shepherd* (1980) C.A. (Crim.) 124 S.J. 290.

Under the new offence, a landlord (which includes a superior landlord: new subs. (3C))—or agent—is guilty if *either* he does acts likely to interfere with the peace or comfort of the residential occupier, *or* he persistently withdraws or withholds services reasonably required for the occupation of the premises as a residence, *and*—in either case—he knows or has reasonable cause to believe that the conduct is likely to cause the residential occupier *either* to quit the premises in whole or part *or* to refrain from exercising any right of pursuing any remedy, *e.g.* registration of a rent, repairs, or use of common or shared facilities.

Both acts and withdrawal or withholding of services can, however, be justified on "reasonable grounds", pursuant to the new subs. (3B). It is submitted that in view of the distinction drawn in the related s.27, above (civil action) between the same "defence" (set out in s.27(8)) and mitigation of damages in s.27(7), provocation by an occupier cannot constitute such "reasonable grounds".

The test is defined to include actual knowledge of likely effect, or "reasonable cause to believe" likely effect, which will make it considerably easier to prove a case against, *e.g.* an elderly or frail landlord.

The offence carries a fine on summary conviction of up to level 2 on the standard scale, currently £2,000, pursuant to Criminal Penalties etc. (Increase) Order 1984 (S.I. 1984 No. 447), Sched. 4, or on conviction on indictment a fine or imprisonment for a term not exceeding two years, or both: the 1977 Act, s.1(4). Conviction for an offence does not preclude civil liability: 1977, s.1(5).

Variation of scope of 1977 ss. 3 and 4

30.—(1) In section 3 of the 1977 Act (prohibition of eviction without due process of law), in subsection (1) for the words "not a statutorily protected tenancy" there shall be substituted "neither a statutorily protected tenancy nor an excluded tenancy".

(2) After subsection (2A) of that section there shall be inserted the following subsections—

"(2B) Subsections (1) and (2) above apply in relation to any premises occupied as a dwelling under a licence, other than an excluded licence, as they apply in relation to premises let as a dwelling under a tenancy, and in those subsections the expressions "let" and "tenancy" shall be construed accordingly.

(2C) References in the preceding provisions of this section and section 4(2A) below to an excluded tenancy do not apply to—

(a) a tenancy entered into before the date on which the Housing Act 1988 came into force, or

(b) a tenancy entered into on or after that date but pursuant to a contract made before that date,

but, subject to that, "excluded tenancy" and "excluded licence" shall be construed in accordance with section 3A below."

(3) In section 4 of the 1977 Act (special provisions for agricultural employees) after subsection (2) there shall be inserted the following subsection—

"(2A) In accordance with section 3(2B) above, any reference in subsections (1) and (2) above to the tenant under the former tenancy includes a reference to the licensee under a licence (other than an excluded licence) which has come to an end (being a licence to occupy premises as a dwelling); and in the following provisions of this section the expressions "tenancy" and "rent" and any other expressions referable to a tenancy shall be construed accordingly."

DEFINITION
"1977 Act": s.33.

GENERAL NOTE
S.3 of the Protection From Eviction Act 1977 restricts recovery of possession of residential premises without a court order, in cases where the former tenancy was not "statutorily protected", *i.e.* is not protected by another statutory provision: see General Note to s.27, above. It was extended in 1980 to some licencees: *ibid.*

Subs. (1)
By this amendment, the class of occupier within s.3 is *reduced*, to those who were *neither* statutorily protected (as defined in the 1977 Act, s.8: see notes to s.27, above), *nor* an "excluded tenant". Excluded tenant is defined in s.31, below: see notes thereto. However, this reduction does not apply to a tenancy entered into before the commencement of this Act, or pursuant to a contract made before this Act commenced: subs. (2).

Subs. (2)
By this amendment, the class of occupier within s.3 is *extended*, to *all* licences (not only restricted contracts commencing on or after November 28, 1980, see notes to s.27, above), save an "excluded licence", which is as defined in s.31, below: see notes thereto.

Subs. (3)
S.4 of the 1977 Act makes special provisions for agricultural employees, not protected by the Rent (Agriculture) Act 1976 (see notes to s.24, above), permitting a court to suspend an order for possession for up to six months, subject to conditions. This amendment makes the

same extension to licensees, other than under excluded licences, as is made generally by the amendment contained in subs. (2), above.

Excluded tenancies and licences

31. After section 3 of the 1977 Act there shall be inserted the following section—

> **"Excluded tenancies and licences**
>
> 3A.—(1) Any reference in this Act to an excluded tenancy or an excluded licence is a reference to a tenancy or licence which is excluded by virtue of any of the following provisions of this section.
>
> (2) A tenancy or licence is excluded if—
>> (a) under its terms the occupier shares any accommodation with the landlord or licensor; and
>> (b) immediately before the tenancy or licence was granted and also at the time it comes to an end, the landlord or licensor occupied as his only or principal home premises of which the whole or part of the shared accommodation formed part.
>
> (3) A tenancy or licence is also excluded if—
>> (a) under its terms the occupier shares any accommodation with a member of the family of the landlord or licensor;
>> (b) immediately before the tenancy or licence was granted and also at the time it comes to an end, the member of the family of the landlord or licensor occupied as his only or principal home premises of which the whole or part of the shared accommodation formed part; and
>> (c) immediately before the tenancy or licence was granted and also at the time it comes to an end, the landlord or licensor occupied as his only or principal home premises in the same building as the shared accommodation and that building is not a purpose-built block of flats.
>
> (4) For the purposes of subsections (2) and (3) above, an occupier shares accommodation with another person if he has the use of it in common with that person (whether or not also in common with others) and any reference in those subsections to shared accommodation shall be construed accordingly, and if, in relation to any tenancy or licence, there is at any time more than one person who is the landlord or licensor, any reference in those subsections to the landlord or licensor shall be construed as a reference to any one of those persons.
>
> (5) In subsections (2) to (4) above—
>> (a) "accommodation" includes neither an area used for storage nor a staircase, passage, corridor or other means of access;
>> (b) "occupier" means, in relation to a tenancy, the tenant and, in relation to a licence, the licensee; and
>> (c) "purpose-built block of flats" has the same meaning as in Part III of Schedule 1 to the Housing Act 1988;
>
> and section 113 of the Housing Act 1985 shall apply to determine whether a person is for the purposes of subsection (3) above a member of another's family as it applies for the purposes of Part IV of that Act.
>
> (6) A tenancy or licence is excluded if it was granted as a temporary expedient to a person who entered the premises in question or any other premises as a trespasser (whether or not, before the beginning of that tenancy or licence, another tenancy

or licence to occupy the premises or any other premises had been granted to him).

(7) A tenancy or licence is excluded if—

(a) it confers on the tenant or licensee the right to occupy the premises for a holiday only; or

(b) it is granted otherwise than for money or money's worth.

(8) A licence is excluded if it confers rights of occupation in a hostel, within the meaning of the Housing Act 1985, which is provided by—

(a) the council of a county, district or London Borough, the Common Council of the City of London, the Council of the Isles of Scilly, the Inner London Education Authority, a joint authority within the meaning of the Local Government Act 1985 or a residuary body within the meaning of that Act;

(b) a development corporation within the meaning of the New Towns Act 1981;

(c) the Commission for the New Towns;

(d) an urban development corporation established by an order under section 135 of the Local Government, Planning and Land Act 1980;

(e) a housing action trust established under Part III of the Housing Act 1988;

(f) the Development Board for Rural Wales;

(g) the Housing Corporation or Housing for Wales;

(h) a housing trust which is a charity or a registered housing association, within the meaning of the Housing Associations Act 1985; or

(i) any other person who is, or who belongs to a class of person which is, specified in an order made by the Secretary of State.

(9) The power to make an order under subsection (8)(i) above shall be exercisable by statutory instrument which shall be subject to annulment in pursuance of a resolution of either House of Parliament."

DEFINITION
"1977 Act": s.33.

GENERAL NOTE
This section amends the Protection From Eviction Act 1977 to define "excluded tenancy" and "excluded licence" for the purposes of the variations on the application of the 1977 Act, s.3, made under s.30, above (and for the purposes of s.32, below).

The following classes of tenancy and licence are "excluded", *i.e. not* within s.3 (see also s.31, below, for the effect of terms varying an excluded tenancy or licence):

(1) The occupier has the use in common with the landlord, and (a) immediately before the grant of the tenancy or licence, *and* (b) when it comes to an end, the landlord occupied as his only or principal home premises of which the whole or part of the shared accommodation formed part. As to occupation as an only or principal home, see notes to s.1, above. As to shared accommodation, generally, see notes to s.3, above. However, this exemption is not confined to shared *living* accommodation, but extends to a right to share the use of *any* accommodation: other than storage, staircase, passage, corridor or other means of access: new s.3A, subss. (4), (5). As to "member of the family", see notes to s.28(5), above.

(2) The occupier has the use in common with a member of the landlord's family of any accommodation, and (a) immediately before the grant of the tenancy or licence, *and* (b) when it comes to an end, the member of the landlord's family occupied as his only or principal home premises of which the whole or part of the shared accommodation formed part, *and* (c) the landlord occupies as *his* only or principal home other premises in the same building, not including a building which is a purpose-built block

of flats. As to occupation as an only or principal home, see notes to s.1, above. As to shared accommodation, generally, see notes to s.3, above; as to accommodation in this section, see new s.3A, subss. (4), (5). As to "member of the family", see notes to s.28(5), above. As to "purpose-built block of flats", see notes to Sched. 1, Part III, below.

(3) The occupier was granted a tenancy or licence as a temporary expedient, having initially entered the premises in question or some other premises, as a trespasser. This follows the terminology of Housing Act 1985, s.79 (definition of secure tenant), excluding former squatters, who may subsequently have been granted short-life licences of the properties squatted, or of other properties, perhaps eventually intended for improvement, conversion, redevelopment, etc. The phrase in new s.3A, subs. (6) "any other premises" is extremely wide, but it seems tolerably clear that there must be some nexus between original squat and current licence or tenancy, even if there has been a series of intervening licences or tenancies.

(4) Holiday lettings (see notes to Sched. 1, para. 9, below) and lettings other than for money or money's worth (see notes to Sched. 2, ground 1, below), *e.g.* family arrangements.

(5) Hostel accommodation, provided by one of the identified public bodies, or someone else within a class of person specified for this purpose by order of the Secretary of State. A hostel is defined in Housing Act 1985, s.622, as "a building in which is provided, for person generally or for a class or classes of persons:
(a) residential accommodation otherwise than in separate and self-contained sets of premises, and
(b) either board or facilities for the preparation of food adequate to the needs of those persons, or both."

Notice to quit etc.

32.—(1) In section 5 of the 1977 Act (validity of notices to quit) at the beginning of subsection (1) there shall be inserted the words "Subject to subsection (1B) below".

(2) After subsection (1) of that section there shall be inserted the following subsections—

"(1A) Subject to subsection (1B) below, no notice by a licensor or a licensee to determine a periodic licence to occupy premises as a dwelling (whether the licence was granted before or after the passing of this Act) shall be valid unless—
(a) it is in writing and contains such information as may be prescribed, and
(b) it is given not less than 4 weeks before the date on which it is to take effect.

(1B) Nothing in subsection (1) or subsection (1A) above applies to—
(a) premises let on an excluded tenancy which is entered into on or after the date on which the Housing Act 1988 came into force unless it is entered into pursuant to a contract made before that date; or
(b) premises occupied under an excluded licence."

DEFINITION
"1977 Act": s.33.

GENERAL NOTE
S.5 of the Protection From Eviction Act 1977 requires that all notices to quit by either a landlord or a tenant of premises let as a dwelling have to be in writing, and contain such information as may be prescribed, and be given not less than four weeks before the date on which it is to take effect. The prescribed information in fact governs only notices from landlords to tenants: see Notices to Quit (Prescribed Information) Regulations 1980 (S.I. 1980 No. 1624). The section applies only to tenancies.

By this amendment, licences (other than excluded licences: see notes to s.31, above)—whether granted before or after the commencement of this Act—are brought within the same requirement, although (new s.5(1B)(a)) takes "excluded tenancies" following the commencement of this Act (unless pursuant to a contract made before the commencement of this Act) out of the requirements for writing and to contain the prescribed information.

Note that while a notice to quit has to comply with common law conditions as to validity, there are no such conditions governing a notice determining a licence (unless such are within the contract). A notice determining a licence has in any event to be a "reasonable" period, but in an overwhelming majority of cases this will now be fulfilled by compliance with the four week minimum.

Interpretation of Chapter IV and the 1977 Act

33.—(1) In this Chapter "the 1977 Act" means the Protection from Eviction Act 1977.

(2) In section 8 of the 1977 Act (interpretation) at the end of subsection (1) (statutory protected tenancy) there shall be inserted—

> "(e) an assured tenancy or assured agricultural occupancy under Part I of the Housing Act 1988."

(3) At the end of that section there shall be added the following subsections—

> "(4) In this Act "excluded tenancy" and "excluded licence" have the meaning assigned by section 3A of this Act.

> (5) If, on or after the date on which the Housing Act 1988 came into force, the terms of an excluded tenancy or excluded licence entered into before that date are varied, then—
>
> (a) if the variation affects the amount of the rent which is payable under the tenancy or licence, the tenancy or licence shall be treated for the purposes of sections 3(2C) and 5(1B) above as a new tenancy or licence entered into at the time of the variation; and
>
> (b) if the variation does not affect the amount of the rent which is so payable, nothing in this Act shall affect the determination of the question whether the variation is such as to give rise to a new tenancy or licence.

> (6) Any reference in subsection (5) above to a variation affecting the amount of the rent which is payable under a tenancy or licence does not include a reference to—
>
> (a) a reduction or increase effected under Part III or Part VI of the Rent Act 1977 (rents under regulated tenancies and housing association tenancies), section 78 of that Act (power of rent tribunal in relation to restricted contracts) or sections 11 to 14 of the Rent (Agriculture) Act 1976; or
>
> (b) a variation which is made by the parties and has the effect of making the rent expressed to be payable under the tenancy or licence the same as a rent for the dwelling which is entered in the register under Part IV or section 79 of the Rent Act 1977."

GENERAL NOTE

Apart from incidental amendments to the Protection From Eviction Act 1977, already dealt with in the notes to foregoing sections of this Chapter, provision is here made to govern variation of the terms of an excluded tenancy or licence for the purposes of determining whether or not the tenancy or licence commences before or after this Act comes into force. If the variation is as to rent, then unless it is within subs. (5), the tenancy or licence *is* to be treated as a new tenancy or licence. Subs. (5) cancels this effect if the variation is pursuant to a registration of rent (of a regulated or housing association tenancy), or has the effect of making the rent for the time being the same as such a registered rent.

If the variation is as to another term of the tenancy, it retains the common law as to whether it is so fundamental as to reverse the character of the letting, albeit that there has been no new tenancy or licence agreement: see, *e.g. Stagg* v. *Brickett* [1951] 1 K.B. 648, C.A., *Welch* v. *Nagy* [1950] 1 K.B. 455, C.A., *Mitas* v. *Hyams* (1951) 2 T.L.R. 1215,

Plymouth Corporation v. *Harvey* [1971] 1 W.L.R. 549, *Smirk* v. *Lyndale Developments* [1975] 1 Ch. 317, C.A.

CHAPTER V

PHASING OUT OF RENT ACTS AND OTHER TRANSITIONAL PROVISIONS

New protected tenancies and agricultural occupancies restricted to special cases

34.—(1) A tenancy which is entered into on or after the commencement of this Act cannot be a protected tenancy, unless—

(a) it is entered into in pursuance of a contract made before the commencement of this Act; or

(b) it is granted to a person (alone or jointly with others) who, immediately before the tenancy was granted, was a protected or statutory tenant and is so granted by the person who at that time was the landlord (or one of the joint landlords) under the protected or statutory tenancy; or

(c) it is granted to a person (alone or jointly with others) in the following circumstances—

(i) prior to the grant of the tenancy, an order for possession of a dwelling-house was made against him (alone or jointly with others) on the court being satisfied as mentioned in section 98(1)(a) of, or Case 1 in Schedule 16 to, the Rent Act 1977 or Case 1 in Schedule 4 to the Rent (Agriculture) Act 1976 (suitable alternative accommodation available); and

(ii) the tenancy is of the premises which constitute the suitable alternative accommodation as to which the court was so satisfied; and

(iii) in the proceedings for possession the court considered that, in the circumstances, the grant of an assured tenancy would not afford the required security and, accordingly, directed that the tenancy would be a protected tenancy; or

(d) it is a tenancy in relation to which subsections (1) and (3) of section 38 below have effect in accordance with subsection (4) of that section.

(2) In subsection (1)(b) above "protected tenant" and "statutory tenant" do not include—

(a) a tenant under a protected shorthold tenancy;

(b) a protected or statutory tenant of a dwelling-house which was let under a protected shorthold tenancy which ended before the commencement of this Act and in respect of which at that commencement either there has been no grant of a further tenancy or any grant of a further tenancy has been to the person who, immediately before the grant, was in possession of the dwelling-house as a protected or statutory tenant;

and in this subsection "protected shorthold tenancy" includes a tenancy which, in proceedings for possession under Case 19 in Schedule 15 to the Rent Act 1977, is treated as a protected shorthold tenancy.

(3) In any case where—

(a) by virtue of subsections (1) and (2) above, a tenancy entered into on or after the commencement of this Act is an assured tenancy, but

(b) apart from subsection (2) above, the effect of subsection (1)(b) above would be that the tenancy would be a protected tenancy, and

    (c) the landlord and the tenant under the tenancy are the same as
at the coming to an end of the protected or statutory tenancy
which, apart from subsection (2) above, would fall within
subsection (1)(b) above,
the tenancy shall be an assured shorthold tenancy (whether or not it fulfils
the conditions in section 20(1) above) unless, before the tenancy is entered
into, the landlord serves notice on the tenant that it is not to be a
shorthold tenancy.

    (4) A licence or tenancy which is entered into on or after the com-
mencement of this Act cannot be a relevant licence or relevant tenancy
for the purposes of the Rent (Agriculture) Act 1976 (in this subsection
referred to as "the 1976 Act") unless—

    (a) it is entered into in pursuance of a contract made before the
commencement of this Act; or

    (b) it is granted to a person (alone or jointly with others) who,
immediately before the licence or tenancy was granted, was a
protected occupier or statutory tenant, within the meaning of the
1976 Act, and is so granted by the person who at that time was the
landlord or licensor (or one of the joint landlords or licensors)
under the protected occupancy or statutory tenancy in question.

    (5) Except as provided in subsection (4) above, expressions used in this
section have the same meaning as in the Rent Act 1977.

GENERAL NOTE

This is the first of five sections which restrict the continuity of existing provisions under
the Rent Act 1977 and the Housing Acts 1980 and 1985.

Subss. (1)–(3)

There are only four circumstances in which a Rent Act protected tenancy may be granted
on or after the commencement of this Act. The first is pursuant to a contract made before
commencement; the second is the grant of a new tenancy to a former (non-shorthold or still
subject to shorthold ground) protected or statutory tenant of the same landlord; the third is
where the grant is as suitable alternative accommodation to an existing protected or statutory
tenancy; the fourth is a transitional provision affecting former new town tenants only.

    1. *Pursuant to Contract*

This would seem to mean a legally enforceable contract. A contract for a tenancy has to
be in writing (even if the grant itself would not require to be in writing: Law of Property Act
1925, s.40; *Botting* v. *Martin* (1808) Camp. 317) or evidenced by part performance. Writing
is not needed if the grant is for a term of three years or less and is in possession: Law of
Property Act 1925, s.54. If accompanied by occupation, it takes effect as an equitable
tenancy: *Walsh* v. *Lonsdale* (1882) 21 Ch.D. 9 (C.A.).

No particular form of writing is required—what is sought is evidence to defeat fraud: *Re
Hoyle* [1893] 1 Ch. 84, *Daniels* v. *Trefusis* [1914] 1 Ch. 788, *Barkworth* v. *Young* (1856) 4
Drew. 1, *Moore* v. *Hart* (1683) 1 Vern. 110, *Welford* v. *Beezely* (1747) 1 Ves. Sen. 6. The
evidence may be constituted of more than one written document (*Jones Bros.* v. *Joyner*
(1900) 82 L.T. 768, *Timmins* v. *Moreland Street Property Co.* [1958] Ch. 110, *Elias* v. *George
Sahely (Barbados)* [1982] 3 All E.R. 801, P.C.), and oral evidence may be admitted to
identify something referred to in the body of the written evidence: *Long* v. *Millar* (1879) 4
C.P.D. 450, *Franco-British Ship Store Co.* v. *Compagnie des Chargeurs Française* (1926) 42
T.L.R. 735, *Baumann* v. *James* (1868) 3 Ch. App. 508.

There is no requirement to prove the whole contract in writing: *Shippey* v. *Derrison* (1805)
5 Esp. 190, *Re. Holland* [1902] 2 Ch. 360. But the evidence must be that there is a complete
and binding contract (*Munday* v. *Asprey* (1880) 13 Ch.D. 855, *Thirkell* v. *Cambi* [1919] 2
K.B. 590, *Tiverton Estates* v. *Wearwell* [1975] Ch. 146, C.A.), so that all of the essential
elements of the contract must be proved in the written evidence (*Peirce* v. *Corf* (1874) L.R.
9 Q.B. 210, *Beckett* v. *Nurse* [1948] 1 K.B. 535), save insofar as there may have been
subsequent, mutually agreed, oral variations: *Morris* v. *Baron & Co.* [1918] A.C. 1. Terms,
including parties, need only be identifiable, not identified: *Potter* v. *Duffield* (1874) L.R. 18
Eq. 1, *Rosser* v. *Miller* (1878) 2 App. Cas. 1124, *Sheers* v. *Thimbelby & Son* (1897) 76 L.T.
709, *Ogilvie* v. *Foljambe* (1817) 3 Mer. 53, *Bleakely* v. *Smith* (1840) 11 Sim. 150, *Wood* v.
Scarth (1855) 2 K. & J. 33, *Cowley* v. *Watts* (1853) 17 Jur. 172, *Plant* v. *Bourne* [1897] 2 Ch.
281.

"Part performance" is based on the proposition that in reliance on the contract, a party has gone ahead and undertaken action (and to an extent therefore resembles estoppel): *Mundy* v. *Joliffe* (1839) 5 My. & Cr. 167, *Buckmaster* v. *Harrop* (1802) 7 Ves. 341. The act which is said to constitute the act of part performance must be attributable to a binding contract: *Cooth* v. *Jackson* (1801) 6 Ves. 12. Parol evidence will be admitted to show, *e.g.* that a contract is not void for uncertainty, or subject to contract: *Reynolds* v. *Waring* (1831) You. 346, *Price* v. *Salusbury* (1863) 32 L.J. Ch. 441, *ex p. Foster* (1883) 22 Ch. D. 797. If terms are vague, a court will nonetheless strive to give effect to them: *Hart* v. *Hart* (1881) 18 Ch. D. 670.

The act must have been performed by the plaintiff, or by someone on his behalf (*Williams* v. *Evans* (1875) L.R. 19 Eq. 547), not the person against whom the enforcement is sought: *Buckmaster* v. *Harrop* (above). The defendant must be shown to have known that the action was undertaken in reliance on the contract: *Dann* v. *Spurrier* (1802) 7 Ves. 231. The act must be referable to the agreement, but this means no more than that it is referable to some identifiable land, rather than an identifiable interest in land: *Maddison* v. *Alderson* (1883) 8 App.Cas. 467. Even the requirement for identification of the land has been relaxed: *Steadman* v. *Steadman* [1976] A.C. 536, *Kingswood Estate Co. Ltd.* v. *Anderson* [1963] 2 Q.B. 169.

The whole of the circumstances must be taken into account when determining whether an act constitutes a good act of part performance: *Steadman* v. *Steadman* (above). Payment of money has been held part performance, when accompanied by a deed submitted for signature: *ibid.* Taking possession is probably the best part performance (*Bowers* v. *Cator* (1798) 4 Ves. 91, *Pain* v. *Coombs* (1857) 1 De G. & J. 34, *Smallwood* v. *Sheppards* [1895] 2 Q.B. 627, *Hohler* v. *Astond* [1920] 2 Ch. 420, *Brough* v. *Nettleton* [1921] 2 Ch. 25. But such possession must be authorised, not taken by force or clandestinely: *Delaney* v. *T. P. Smith Ltd.* [1946] K.B. 393. Making alterations or improvements may amount to part performance: *Lester* v. *Foxcroft* (1701) Coll. P.C. 108, *Shillibeer* v. *Jarvis* (1856) 8 De G.M. & G. 79, *Reddin* v. *Jarman* (1867) 16 L.T. 449, *Broughton* v. *Snook* [1938] A.C. 124.

Payment of taxes, or presumably therefore rates, or other such expenditure, even in the face of an explicable non-payment of rent, can also be part performance: *Gregory* v. *Mighell* (1811) 18 Ves. 328. But acts preparatory to a contract, such as surveying or valuing, are not sufficient to constitute acts of part performance: *Clerk* v. *Wright* (1737) 1 Alk. 12, *Cooth* v. *Jackson* (above), *Whitbread* v. *Brockhurst* (1784) 1 Bro. C.C. 404. A wife's consent to divorce on terms, *inter alia*, that she would not ask for maintenance if the husband conveyed a bungalow to her, was held to amount to an act of part performance, in *Sutton* v. *Sutton* [1984] 2 W.L.R. 146, Ch.D., even though the promise not to seek maintenance was not enforceable and could not be relied on as a defence (see *Price* v. *Strange* [1978] Ch. 337).

2. New Tenancy for Current Tenant

Under this provision, the grant of a new tenancy to an existing protected tenant is to remain a protected tenancy under the 1977 Act. The premises need not be the same, and for the exclusion from the operation of this section to apply, it is only necessary in the case of a joint tenancy to show that one of the tenants was the protected or statutory tenant under the former tenancy (which would seem to imply in turn one of joint protected or statutory tenants: see *Lloyd* v. *Sadler* [1978] Q.B. 774, C.A.). Similarly, and supporting the proposition in parenthesis in the last sentence, if the grantor is one of a number of former joint landlords, the exclusion from the operation of this section will apply.

For this purpose, however, a tenant under a protected shorthold tenancy which ended before the commencement of this Act, and which at commencement remained subject to the shorthold ground for possession, is to be treated as an assured shorthold tenant instead (unless the landlord serves notice that the tenancy is not to be shorthold, *i.e.* is to be fully assured), provided the landlord and the tenant are the same: subss. (2) and (3).

3. Suitable Alternative Accommodation

One of the *discretionary* grounds for possession under Rent Act 1977, s.98 and Sched. 15, (*cf.* under this Act, the *mandatory* ground 1, in Sched. 2), is the provision of suitable alternative accommodation: the equivalent provisions under the Rent (Agriculture) Act 1976 are s.6 and Sched. 4, Case 1, there is similar provision for certain agricultural workers under the 1977 Act, Sched. 16, para. 1.

The purpose of this exclusion is to permit the continued use of that ground in relation to Rent Act protected tenancies, or Rent (Agriculture) Act occupancies, for without it there would be likely to be an overwhelming argument on the part of the tenant that however physically suitable the alternative accommodation might be, and suitable and reasonable in other respects, an assured tenancy would not afford "reasonably equivalent security" (the 1977 Act, Sched. 15, Part IV, para. 3; the 1976 Act, Sched. 4, para. 2), and accordingly no order would be made: now, the court is to consider whether or not assured security affords the required security and, if it decides that it does not, can order that the new tenancy be protected. Note, however, that this extension of protected tenancies and occupancies requires an express direction by the court that the tenancy should be protected, *in the proceedings for possession* (*cf. Victoria Square Property Co. Ltd.* v. *Southwark L.B.C.* [1978] 1 W.L.R. 463, C.A.).

4. *Former New Town Tenants*
    See notes to s.38, below.

Subs. (4)
    This subsection makes the identical provision for protected or statutory occupiers under the Rent (Agriculture) Act 1976 (see Chapter III, above) as is made under subs. (1), above, save insofar as such occupiers are already within subs. (1): see notes thereto.

Removal of special regimes for tenancies of housing associations etc.

35.—(1) In this section "housing association tenancy" has the same meaning as in Part VI of the Rent Act 1977.

(2) A tenancy which is entered into on or after the commencement of this Act cannot be a housing association tenancy unless—

(a) it is entered into in pursuance of a contract made before the commencement of this Act; or

(b) it is granted to a person (alone or jointly with others) who, immediately before the tenancy was granted, was a tenant under a housing association tenancy and is so granted by the person who at that time was the landlord under that housing association tenancy; or

(c) it is granted to a person (alone or jointly with others) in the following circumstances—

    (i) prior to the grant of the tenancy, an order for possession of a dwelling-house was made against him (alone or jointly with others) on the court being satisfied as mentioned in paragraph (b) or paragraph (c) of subsection (2) of section 84 of the Housing Act 1985; and

    (ii) the tenancy is of the premises which constitute the suitable accommodation as to which the court was so satisfied; and

    (iii) in the proceedings for possession the court directed that the tenancy would be a housing association tenancy; or

(d) it is a tenancy in relation to which subsections (1) and (3) of section 38 below have effect in accordance with subsection (4) of that section.

(3) Where, on or after the commencement of this Act, a registered housing association, within the meaning of the Housing Associations Act 1985, grants a secure tenancy pursuant to an obligation under section 554(2A) of the Housing Act 1985 (as set out in Schedule 17 to this Act) then, in determining whether that tenancy is a housing association tenancy, it shall be assumed for the purposes only of section 86(2)(b) of the Rent Act 1977 (tenancy would be a protected tenancy but for section 15 or 16 of that Act) that the tenancy was granted before the commencement of this Act.

(4) A tenancy or licence which is entered into on or after the commencement of this Act cannot be a secure tenancy unless—

(a) the interest of the landlord belongs to a local authority, a new town corporation or an urban development corporation, all within the meaning of section 80 of the Housing Act 1985, a housing action trust established under Part III of this Act or the Development Board for Rural Wales; or

(b) the interest of the landlord belongs to a housing co-operative within the meaning of section 27B of the Housing Act 1985 (agreements between local housing authorities and housing co-operatives) and the tenancy or licence is of a dwelling-house comprised in a housing co-operative agreement falling within that section; or

(c) it is entered into in pursuance of a contract made before the commencement of this Act; or

(d) it is granted to a person (alone or jointly with others) who, immediately before it was entered into, was a secure tenant and is so granted by the body which at that time was the landlord or licensor under the secure tenancy; or

(e) it is granted to a person (alone or jointly with others) in the following circumstances—

(i) prior to the grant of the tenancy or licence, an order for possession of a dwelling-house was made against him (alone or jointly with others) on the court being satisfied as mentioned in paragraph (b) or paragraph (c) of subsection (2) of section 84 of the Housing Act 1985; and

(ii) the tenancy or licence is of the premises which constitute the suitable accommodation as to which the court was so satisfied; and

(iii) in the proceedings for possession the court considered that, in the circumstances, the grant of an assured tenancy would not afford the required security and, accordingly, directed that the tenancy or licence would be a secure tenancy; or

(f) it is granted pursuant to an obligation under section 554(2A) of the Housing Act 1985 (as set out in Schedule 17 to this Act).

(5) If, on or after the commencement of this Act, the interest of the landlord under a protected or statutory tenancy becomes held by a housing association, a housing trust, the Housing Corporation or Housing for Wales, nothing in the preceding provisions of this section shall prevent the tenancy from being a housing association tenancy or a secure tenancy and, accordingly, in such a case section 80 of the Housing Act 1985 (and any enactment which refers to that section) shall have effect without regard to the repeal of provisions of that section effected by this Act.

(6) In subsection (5) above "housing association" and "housing trust" have the same meaning as in the Housing Act 1985.

DEFINITIONS
"secure tenancy": s.45.
"secure tenant": s.45.

GENERAL NOTE
Housing association tenants are (a) secure tenants, within public sector security pursuant to the Housing Act 1985, Part IV, and (b) subject to a rent officer, "fair rent" regime, analogous to that applicable to protected and statutory tenants, under the Rent Act 1977. This section removes *both* classes of protection for future lettings, subject to the same exceptions as protected and statutory tenants, and protected and statutory occupiers, under s.34, above, and to a particular exception referable to the provisions of the Housing Act 1985, Part XVI (system-built defective premises).

Subs. (1)

1. *Housing Association Tenancy.* By the Rent Act 1977, a housing association tenancy is a tenancy, other than a co-ownership tenancy, where the interest of the landlord under the tenancy belongs to a housing association, housing trust or the Housing Corporation, and would be protected but for ss.15 or 16 of the 1977 Act, and is not a tenancy to which the Landlord and Tenant Act 1954, Part II applies (business tenancies: see notes to Sched. 1, para. 4, below). For these purposes:

A. *Housing Association* is defined in the Housing Associations Act 1985, s.1, (and thence into Rent Act 1977, s.86), and in the Housing Act 1985, s.4, to mean a society, body of trustees or company which is established for the purpose of, or amongst whose objects or powers are included those of, providing, constructing, improving or managing, or facilitating or encouraging the construction or improvement of, housing accommodation, and which does not trade for profit or whose constitution or rules prohibit the issue of capital with interest or dividend exceeding such rate as may be prescribed by the Treasury, with or without differentiation as between share and loan capital. The rule against trading for profit means profits which are taken out of the enterprise, and is not offended because one of its activities makes a profit which has to be kept within, or ploughed back into, the association: *Goodman* v. *Dolphin Square Trust Ltd.* (1979) 38 P. & C.R. 257, C.A.

B. *Housing Trust* is defined in the Housing Associations Act 1985, s.2, and in the Housing Act 1985, s.6, and in the Rent Act 1977, s.15 (and thence into the Rent Act 1977, s.86), as a corporation or body of persons which is required by the terms of its constituent instrument to use the whole of its funds, including any surplus which may arise from its operations, for the purpose of providing housing accommodation, or which is required by the terms of its constituent instrument to devote the whole, or substantially the whole, of its funds to charitable purposes and in fact uses the whole or substantially the whole of its funds for the purposes of providing housing accommodation.

C. *Co-ownership Tenancy* is defined in the 1977 Act, s.86(3A), as being one granted by a housing association which is a co-operative housing association, and the tenant (or his personal representative) will, under the terms of the tenancy agreement or the agreement by which he became a member of the association, be entitled on his ceasing to be a member and subject to any conditions stated in either agreement to a sum calculated by reference directly or indirectly to the value of the dwelling-house, *i.e.* as distinct from a par value association.

Co-operative housing association has the same meaning as under the Housing Associations Act 1985, s.1, which is a fully mutual housing association (as to which see notes to s.45, below) which is a society registered under the Industrial and Provident Societies Act 1965, and which restricts membership of the association to persons who are tenants or prospective tenants of the association, and which precludes the grant or assignment of tenancies to persons other than members.

D. *The 1977 Act, ss.15 and 16* prevent certain tenancies being protected or statutory tenancies. These are tenancies from housing associations registered under the Housing Associations Act 1985, s.4, or a co-operative housing association within that Act (see last paragraph), the Housing Corporation, or a housing trust (see B, above) which is a charity within the meaning of the Charities Act 1960.

2. *Secure Tenancy.* A secure tenancy is one under which a dwelling-house is let as a separate dwelling (see notes to s.1, above) at any time when both the landlord condition and the tenant condition are fulfilled: Housing Act 1985, s.79. This is, however, subject to the 1985 Act, Sched. 1, exempting certain tenancies from the definition. It is also subject to tenancies which cease to be secure on the death of the former tenant, or on assignment or subletting, under the 1985 Act, ss.89, 90, 91 and 93. Note, however, that a *licence* is treated as a secure tenancy, *unless* it is one granted as a temporary expedient to a person who entered the dwelling-house or another other land as a trespasser, whether or not there had been the grant of intervening licences: s.79(3), (4), and *cf.* notes to s.31, above.

A. *The Landlord Condition* (the 1985 Act, s.80) is that the interest of the landlord belongs to one of the following: a local authority, a new town corporation, an urban development corporation, the Development Board for Rural Wales, the Housing Corporation, a housing trust (defined by the 1985 Act, s.6, in the same terms as under 1.B. of these notes, above) which is a charity, or a housing association (defined by the 1985 Act, s.5, in the same terms as under 1.A. of these notes, above) or housing co-operative to which the section applies. The section applies to a registered housing association *other than* a co-operative housing association, an unregistered housing association which *is* a co-operative housing association, in each case co-operative housing association being defined (the 1985 Act, s.5) in the same terms as under 1.C. of these notes.

A housing co-operative, however, is something different (commonly called a "management co-operative"). This is a co-operative formed under the 1985 Act, s.27, with the consent of the Secretary of State, to take over the whole or part of a local authority's management responsibilities. Such agreements could, prior to the commencement of the Housing and Planning Act 1986, extend to an actual letting of land, and although such lettings were prohibited from that commencement date (the 1985 Act, s.27B, added by the 1986 Act, s.10) earlier such agreements remain valid. The tenants of such a co-operative are secure.

B. *The Tenant Condition* is (by the 1985 Act, s.81) that the tenant is an individual and occupies the dwelling-house as his only or principal home or, where the tenancy is a joint tenancy, that each of the joint tenants is an individual and at least one of them occupies the dwelling-house as his only or principal home: see notes to s.1, above.

Subs. (2)

This subsection prevents the grant of a housing association tenancy, and therefore the application of rent officer jurisdiction to set a fair rent for the tenancy under Rent Act 1977, Part VI, on or after the commencement of this Act, *save* in the analogous circumstances to those applicable under s.34(1), above—see notes thereto.

Subs. (3)

In certain circumstances, a person who has purchased a system-built dwelling designated as defective under Housing Act 1985, Part XVI, may be able to require the former landlord to repurchase the premises and to grant a new tenancy of them: such a tenancy granted by a registered housing association will be a housing association tenancy, notwithstanding that it is granted after the commencement of this Act.

Subs. (4)

This subsection prevents the grant of a secure tenancy on or after the commencement of this Act, by restating the landlord condition of Housing Act 1985, s.80 (see notes to subs. (1), above), so as to exclude housing associations and trusts, *except* tenants of housing co-operatives pre-dating the Housing and Planning Act 1986: see note 2.A. to subs. (1), above. Note the inclusion of Housing Action Trusts under Part III of this Act. In addition, the same circumstances which could give rise to a new housing association tenancy could give rise to a new secure tenancy from a housing association or trust, *i.e.* as under s.34, above—see notes thereto; see also Sched. 17, para. 65, below. Subs.(4)(f) contains the analogous provision to that described in the notes to subs. (3), above.

Subs. (5)

Where a housing association, a housing trust, the Housing Corporation or Housing for Wales, purchase the interest of the landlord under a protected or statutory tenancy, on or after commencement, then notwithstanding the foregoing the tenancy will become a housing association and secure tenancy, rather than assured.

Subs. (6)

See notes to subs. (1), above.

New restricted contracts limited to transitional cases

36.—(1) A tenancy or other contract entered into after the commencement of this Act cannot be a restricted contract for the purposes of the Rent Act 1977 unless it is entered into in pursuance of a contract made before the commencement of this Act.

(2) If the terms of a restricted contract are varied after this Act comes into force then, subject to subsection (3) below,—

(a) if the variation affects the amount of the rent which, under the contract, is payable for the dwelling in question, the contract shall be treated as a new contract entered into at the time of the variation (and subsection (1) above shall have effect accordingly); and

(b) if the variation does not affect the amount of the rent which, under the contract, is so payable, nothing in this section shall affect the determination of the question whether the variation is such as to give rise to a new contract.

(3) Any reference in subsection (2) above to a variation affecting the amount of the rent which, under a contract, is payable for a dwelling does not include a reference to—

(a) a reduction or increase effected under section 78 of the Rent Act 1977 (power of rent tribunal); or

(b) a variation which is made by the parties and has the effect of making the rent expressed to be payable under the contract the same as the rent for the dwelling which is entered in the register under section 79 of the Rent Act 1977.

(4) In subsection (1) of section 81A of the Rent Act 1977 (cancellation of registration of rent relating to a restricted contract) paragraph (a) (no cancellation until two years have elapsed since the date of the entry) shall cease to have effect.

(5) In this section "rent" has the same meaning as in Part V of the Rent Act 1977.

GENERAL NOTE

Restricted contracts—which may be tenancies or licences (see, *e.g. R.* v. *South Middlesex Rent Tribunal, ex p. Beswick* (1976) 32 P. & C.R. 67, D.C.)—are those lettings which fall, by the Rent Act 1977, s.19, within the jurisdiction of the Rent Tribunal (which is a Rent Assessment Committee, sitting as a Rent Tribunal—Housing Act 1980, s.72). Best known for the (limited) protection they confer on the tenants or licensees of resident landlords (defined in similar terms to Sched. 1, paras. 10 and 18–22, below), their original jurisdiction (pre-Rent Act 1974) was over furnished lettings, and they have retained jurisdiction over most licenses. This section is intended to achieve the same effect as the last two and the next, *i.e.* to prevent the creation of new restricted contracts on or after the commencement date.

Subs. (1)

The only exception to the general principle of no new restricted contracts is if the contract is granted pursuant to a contract made before the commencement of this section. Note that where the contract is alleged to be for a *licence* rather than tenancy, the requirement for writing or part performance (see notes to s.34, above) will not apply.

Subss. (2), (3)

These subsections are intended to govern the question whether or not a variation amounts to the grant of a new letting. Where the variation is of the rent payable, there will be a new contract, *unless either* it results from an exercise of the Rent Tribunal's rent-fixing jurisdiction, *or* it is by agreement to achieve a (Rent Tribunal) registered rent (subs. (3)): subs. (2)(a). Otherwise, the question is determined without regard to this section: subs. (2)(b). See, generally, notes to s.33(3), above.

Subs. (4)

This removes the restriction on cancellation within two years of an earlier registration, so that cancellation can be achieved as soon after registration as there is no restricted contract in relation to the dwelling.

Subs. (5)

Rent is exclusive of rates: the 1977 Act, s.79(3).

No further assured tenancies under Housing Act 1980

37.—(1) A tenancy which is entered into on or after the commencement of this Act cannot be an assured tenancy for the purposes of sections 56 to 58 of the Housing Act 1980 (in this section referred to as a "1980 Act tenancy").

(2) In any case where—
(a) before the commencement of this Act, a tenant under a 1980 Act tenancy made an application to the court under section 24 of the Landlord and Tenant Act 1954 (for the grant of a new tenancy), and
(b) at the commencement of this Act the 1980 Act tenancy is continuing by virtue of that section or of any provision of Part IV of the said Act of 1954,
section 1(3) of this Act shall not apply to the 1980 Act tenancy.

(3) If, in a case falling within subsection (2) above, the court makes an order for the grant of a new tenancy under section 29 of the Landlord and Tenant Act 1954, that tenancy shall be an assured tenancy for the purposes of this Act.

(4) In any case where—

(a) before the commencement of this Act a contract was entered into for the grant of a 1980 Act tenancy, but

(b) at the commencement of this Act the tenancy had not been granted,

the contract shall have effect as a contract for the grant of an assured tenancy (within the meaning of this Act).

(5) In relation to an assured tenancy falling within subsection (3) above or granted pursuant to a contract falling within subsection (4) above, Part I of Schedule 1 to this Act shall have effect as if it consisted only of paragraphs 11 and 12; and, if the landlord granting the tenancy is a fully mutual housing association, then, so long as that association remains the landlord under that tenancy (and under any statutory periodic tenancy which arises on the coming to an end of that tenancy), the said paragraph 12 shall have effect in relation to that tenancy with the omission of sub-paragraph (1)(h).

(6) Any reference in this section to a provision of the Landlord and Tenant Act 1954 is a reference only to that provision as applied by section 58 of the Housing Act 1980.

<small>GENERAL NOTE</small>

The purpose of this section, as the last three, is to prevent the creation of a new letting under a former system of protection, in this case assured tenancies as defined and prescribed by the Housing Act 1980. That Act applied an adapted version of the security available to business tenants under the Landlord and Tenant Act 1954, Part II, to its assured tenants. By s.1(3), above, subject to this section, "1980 Act assured tenants" become assured tenants within the meaning of this Act, and subject therefore to the provisions of Chapter One, above—see notes to s.1(3), (4), above.

To summarise the effect of s.1, Sched. 1, para. 1, and this section, the position is:

(a) A 1980 Act assured tenancy cannot be an assured tenancy under this Act, pursuant to Sched.1, para. 1, because it was granted before the commencement of this Act, *but*

(b) *Is* an assured tenancy under this Act by virtue of s.1(3), *unless*

(c) By s.1(4),(5) above, it is excluded by paras. 11 and 12 of Sched. 1, *only*, *i.e.* it will not be excluded by any of the other paragraphs of that Schedule, and it will not even be excluded by para. 12(1)(h) if before the commencement of this Act the landlord was a fully mutual housing association (as to the meaning of which, see notes to s.45, below), and the association has remained the landlord since, *and unless*

(d) It is continued by virtue of an application for the grant of a new tenancy under the Landlord and Tenant Act 1954, s.24, in which case, by subs. (2) of this section, s.1(3) does not apply, and the 1980 Act assured tenancy will continue until the outcome of the court proceedings, in which case either there will be no new tenancy, or by subs. (3) of this section, the new tenancy will be an assured tenancy under this Act, *unless*

(e) By subs. (5) of this section, it is excluded by paras. 11 and 12 of Sched. 1, *only*, *i.e.* it will not be excluded by any of the other paragraphs of that Schedule, nor will it even be excluded by para. 12(1)(h) if before the commencement of this Act the landlord was a fully mutual housing association (as to the meaning of which, see notes to s.45, below), and the association has remained the landlord since. *Further*

(f) An assured tenancy granted pursuant to a contract before the commencement of this Act (as to which, see notes to s.32, above) cannot be an assured tenancy, pursuant to Sched. 1, para. 1, *but*

(g) *Is* an assured tenancy under this Act by virtue of subs. (4) of this section, *unless*

(h) By subs. (5) of this section, it is excluded by paras. 11 and 12 of Sched. 1, *only*, *i.e.* it will not be excluded by any of the other paragraphs of that Schedule, nor will it even be excluded by para. 12(1)(h) if before the commencement of this Act the landlord was a fully mutual housing association (as to the meaning of which, see notes to s.45, below), and the association has remained the landlord since.

Transfer of existing tenancies from public to private sector

38.—(1) The provisions of subsection (3) below apply in relation to a tenancy which was entered into before, or pursuant to a contract made before the commencement of this Act if,—

(a) at that commencement or, if it is later, at the time it is entered into, the interest of the landlord is held by a public body (within the meaning of subsection (5) below); and

(b) at some time after that commencement, the interest of the landlord ceases to be so held.

(2) The provisions of subsection (3) below also apply in relation to a tenancy which was entered into before, or pursuant to a contract made before, the commencement of this Act if,—

(a) at the commencement of this Act or, if it is later, at the time it is entered into, it is a housing association tenancy; and

(b) at some time after that commencement, it ceases to be such a tenancy.

(3) On and after the time referred to in subsection (1)(b) or, as the case may be, subsection (2)(b) above—

(a) the tenancy shall not be capable of being a protected tenancy, a protected occupancy or a housing association tenancy;

(b) the tenancy shall not be capable of being a secure tenancy unless (and only at a time when) the interest of the landlord under the tenancy is (or is again) held by a public body; and

(c) paragraph 1 of Schedule 1 to this Act shall not apply in relation to it, and the question whether at any time thereafter it becomes (or remains) an assured tenancy shall be determined accordingly.

(4) In relation to a tenancy under which, at the commencement of this Act or, if it is later, at the time the tenancy is entered into, the interest of the landlord is held by a new town corporation, within the meaning of section 80 of the Housing Act 1985, subsections (1) and (3) above shall have effect as if any reference in subsection (1) above to the commencement of this Act were a reference to—

(a) the date on which expires the period of two years beginning on the day this Act is passed; or

(b) if the Secretary of State by order made by statutory instrument within that period so provides, such other date (whether earlier or later) as may be specified by the order for the purposes of this subsection.

(5) For the purposes of this section, the interest of a landlord under a tenancy is held by a public body at a time when—

(a) it belongs to a local authority, a new town corporation or an urban development corporation, all within the meaning of section 80 of the Housing Act 1985; or

(b) it belongs to a housing action trust established under Part III of this Act; or

(c) it belongs to the Development Board for Rural Wales; or

(d) it belongs to Her Majesty in right of the Crown or to a government department or is held in trust for Her Majesty for the purposes of a government department.

(6) In this section—

(a) "housing association tenancy" means a tenancy to which Part VI of the Rent Act 1977 applies;

(b) "protected tenancy" has the same meaning as in that Act; and

(c) "protected occupancy" has the same meaning as in the Rent (Agriculture) Act 1976.

DEFINITION

"secure tenancy": s.45.

GENERAL NOTE

The provisions of the Housing Act 1985, governing secure tenants (see notes to s.35, above) apply "at any time when" certain criteria are fulfilled (and, of course, subject to such express exceptions and qualifications as are contained in that Act). It follows that when a condition, *e.g.* the landlord condition (see notes to s.35, above) ceases to be fulfilled, there will be a pre-existing tenancy, *not* granted on or after the commencement of this Act, and accordingly not within the foregoing sections. As removal from public to private sector is at the forefront of government policy (see the Housing and Planning Act 1986, ss.6–9, and Part IV and s.111 of this Act, below), this is a subject of some contemporary significance.

Subss. (1), (5)

This applies the provisions of subs. (3) to a tenancy which fulfills the following conditions:
(a) It was entered into, or pursuant to a contract made before (see notes to s.34, above), the commencement of this Act, *and*
(b) At the commencement of the Act the interest of the landlord is held by a public body as defined in subs. (5) below, *and*
(c) At some time after the commencement of the Act, the interest of the landlord ceases to be held by a public landlord as so defined.

For "commencement" may be read a date two years after the Act is passed, or such other earlier or later date as the Secretary of State may prescribe, in the case of a new town corporation: subs. (4).

Public body is defined in subs. (5) to mean local authority, new town corporation or an urban development corporation, the Development Board for Rural Wales or Her Majesty in right of the Crown or a government department or held in trust for Her Majesty for the purposes of a government department, or a housing action trust under Part III of this Act.

Subss. (2), (6)(a)

This applies the provisions of subs. (3) to a tenancy which fulfills the following conditions:
(a) It was entered into, or pursuant to a contract made before (see notes to s.32, above), the commencement of this Act, *and*
(b) At the commencement of the Act, the tenancy is a housing association tenancy as defined in subs. (5) below, or becomes such a housing association tenancy because a housing association later acquires the landlord's interest in the tenancy, *and*
(c) At some time after the commencement of the Act, the tenancy ceases to be a housing association tenancy as so defined.

The definition of housing association tenancy is (by subs. (6)) one to which the Rent Act 1977, Part VI, applies: see notes to s.33, above.

Subss. (3), (5), (6)

Subs. (3) is the substantive subsection, preventing such a tenancy becoming a housing association tenancy (see notes to s.35, above), a protected tenancy under the Rent Act 1977 or a protected occupancy under the Rent (Agriculture) Act 1976 (see notes to Chapter III, above). Nor can such a tenancy become a secure tenancy unless the landlord comes again to be held by a public body. Instead, the tenancy will be an assured tenancy, unless excluded by any of the provisions of Sched. 1, below, *save* Sched. 1, para. 1 (which excludes tenancies commencing before the commencement of this Act, or pursuant to contracts made before the commencement of this Act: see notes to ss.1, 37, above). Note, however, that this effect may be deferred for two years from the date this Act was passed, or such earlier or later date as the Secretary of State may prescribe, in the case of a new town corporation: subs. (4).

Statutory tenants: succession

39.—(1) In section 2(1)(b) of the Rent Act 1977 (which introduces the provisions of Part I of Schedule 1 to that Act relating to statutory tenants by succession) after the words "statutory tenant of a dwelling-house" there shall be inserted "or, as the case may be, is entitled to an assured tenancy of a dwelling-house by succession".

(2) Where the person who is the original tenant, within the meaning of Part I of Schedule 1 to the Rent Act 1977, dies after the commencement of this Act, that Part shall have effect subject to the amendments in Part I of Schedule 4 to this Act.

(3) Where subsection (2) above does not apply but the person who is the first successor, within the meaning of Part I of Schedule 1 to the Rent Act 1977, dies after the commencement of this Act, that Part shall have

effect subject to the amendments in paragraphs 5 to 9 of Part I of Schedule 4 to this Act.

(4) In any case where the original occupier, within the meaning of section 4 of the Rent (Agriculture) Act 1976 (statutory tenants and tenancies) dies after the commencement of this Act, that section shall have effect subject to the amendments in Part II of Schedule 4 to this Act.

(5) In any case where, by virtue of any provision of—

    (a) Part I of Schedule 1 to the Rent Act 1977, as amended in accordance with subsection (2) or subsection (3) above, or

    (b) section 4 of the Rent (Agriculture) Act 1976, as amended in accordance with subsection (4) above,

a person (in the following provisions of this section referred to as "the successor") becomes entitled to an assured tenancy of a dwelling-house by succession, that tenancy shall be a periodic tenancy arising by virtue of this section.

(6) Where, by virtue of subsection (5) above, the successor becomes entitled to an assured periodic tenancy, that tenancy is one—

    (a) taking effect in possession immediately after the death of the protected or statutory tenant or protected occupier (in the following provisions of this section referred to as "the predecessor") on whose death the successor became so entitled;

    (b) deemed to have been granted to the successor by the person who, immediately before the death of the predecessor, was the landlord of the predecessor under his tenancy;

    (c) under which the premises which are let are the same dwelling-house as, immediately before his death, the predecessor occupied under his tenancy;

    (d) under which the periods of the tenancy are the same as those for which rent was last payable by the predecessor under his tenancy;

    (e) under which, subject to sections 13 to 15 above, the other terms are the same as those on which, under his tenancy, the predecessor occupied the dwelling-house immediately before his death; and

    (f) which, for the purposes of section 13(2) above, is treated as a statutory periodic tenancy;

and in paragraphs (b) to (e) above "under his tenancy", in relation to the predecessor, means under his protected tenancy or protected occupancy or in his capacity as a statutory tenant.

(7) If, immediately before the death of the predecessor, the landlord might have recovered possession of the dwelling-house under Case 19 in Schedule 15 to the Rent Act 1977, the assured periodic tenancy to which the successor becomes entitled shall be an assured shorthold tenancy (whether or not it fulfils the conditions in section 20(1) above).

(8) If, immediately before his death, the predecessor was a protected occupier or statutory tenant within the meaning of the Rent (Agriculture) Act 1976, the assured periodic tenancy to which the successor becomes entitled shall be an assured agricultural occupancy (whether or not it fulfils the conditions in section 24(1) above).

(9) Where, immediately before his death, the predecessor was a tenant under a fixed term tenancy, section 6 above shall apply in relation to the assured periodic tenancy to which the successor becomes entitled on the predecessor's death subject to the following modifications—

    (a) for any reference to a statutory periodic tenancy there shall be substituted a reference to the assured periodic tenancy to which the successor becomes so entitled;

    (b) in subsection (1) of that section, paragraph (a) shall be omitted and the reference in paragraph (b) to section 5(3)(e) above shall be construed as a reference to subsection (6)(e) above; and

(c) for any reference to the coming to an end of the former tenancy there shall be substituted a reference to the date of the predecessor's death.

(10) If and so long as a dwelling-house is subject to an assured tenancy to which the successor has become entitled by succession, section 7 above and Schedule 2 to this Act shall have effect subject to the modifications in Part III of Schedule 4 to this Act; and in that Part "the predecessor" and "the successor" have the same meaning as in this section.

DEFINITIONS
    "fixed term tenancy": s.45.
    "landlord": s.45.

GENERAL NOTE
    This section contains important amendments to the Rent Act 1977 and Rent (Agriculture) Act 1976, which limit the rights to succession on death of a protected or statutory tenant or protected occupier. At present, the position is that there can be two successions. Succession is by a spouse (meaning spouse in law) or, if no spouse, a member of the family (which can include a cohabitant: see notes below). Under the provisions as amended, if a spouse (redefined to include a cohabitant) succeeds, there will be one succession which will remain fully protected, but a second succession (which will now occur in only limited circumstances) will be assured; if the first succession is by a member of the family, it will be assured and there will be no second succession. There are special provisions governing possession orders for possession against such assured tenants by succession: see subs. (10) and Sched. 4, Part III.
    In addition, the residential qualifications to succeed of members of the family (on either first or second succession) have been increased. The new provisions will apply to deaths after the commencement of this Act (subject to a transitional adaptation of the period of residential qualification of a member of the family).

Subs. (1)
    This amendment does no more than recognise that rights of succession under the Rent Act 1977 may now give rise either to a statutory tenancy under that Act, or an assured tenancy under this, by reason of the amendments authorised by the next subsection, and Sched. 4, Part I of this Act, below.

Subss. (2), (3)
    These are the substantive amendments so far as the Rent Act 1977 is concerned. The amendments are themselves contained in Sched. 4, Part I.
    Para. 1. By para. 1 of Sched. 1, 1977 Act, either para. 2 or para. 3 of the same Schedule is to be applied to determine who is to become the statutory tenant of a dwelling-house by succession, after the death of "the original tenant".
    By para. 2 of Sched. 1 to the 1977 Act, as substituted by the Housing Act 1980, s.76, in relation to deaths after its commencement (November 28, 1980), the surviving spouse (if any) of the original tenant succeeds to the statutory tenancy, if and so long as he or she occupies the dwelling-house as his or her residence, *if* residing in the dwelling-house immediately before the death of the original tenant. Spouse for this purpose does not include cohabitant.
    By the 1977 Act, Sched. 1, para. 3, if there is no surviving spouse to succeed, a member of the family—which can include a cohabitant—who has been residing with the deceased at the time of and for six months before death, can instead succeed. If there is more than one such, they can agree between themselves or the county court may decide who can succeed.
    The meaning of these provisions and most of the terms are considered in the notes to s.17, above. As regards the qualification of a cohabitant as a member of the family, in *Gammans* v. *Ekins* [1950] 2 K.B. 328 C.A., following *Brock* v. *Wollams* [1949] 2 K.B. 388, C.A., the Court of Appeal had rejected cohabitation as family: the submission was said to be an abuse of the English language. By the time of *Hawes* v. *Evenden* [1953] 1 W.L.R. 1169, C.A., however, a woman who had lived with a man for 12 years without taking his name, and who had two children by him, was held to be a member of his family. In *Dyson Holdings* v. *Fox* [1976] 1 Q.B. 503, C.A., it was held that although relationships of a casual and intermittent character could not qualify as family, a stable relationship could do so, so that 20 years' cohabitation without marriage, where the woman had taken the man's name, should be regarded as a family relationship, having regard to the changing popular meaning of the word family.

In *Helby* v. *Rafferty* [1979] 1 W.L.R. 13, C.A., however, the Court of Appeal rejected the idea that the meaning of the word "family" could change with time, stated that it should have the meaning applicable when first used by Parliament, and rejected a claim to succeed by a man who had lived with the deceased tenant for approximately five years, as her lover, sharing expenses, caring for her while she was dying, but not having taken her name, nor she having taken his. In *Watson* v. *Lucas* [1980] 1 W.L.R. 1493, C.A., a man was held to be a member of the family of the deceased tenant, who was a woman with whom he had lived for nearly 20 years, even though he remained undivorced from his lawful wife. The Court of Appeal considered that they were bound by *Dyson*.

Most recently, in *Chios Property Investment Co.* v. *Lopez* (1987) 20 H.L.R. 120, C.A., a woman moved in with a man in 1983, with the intention that they would marry as soon as financial circumstances permitted. In 1985, they resolved to marry and to secure the blessings of their families, although conditional upon improved financial circumstances, which seemed imminent. The male tenant died. The county court judge posed the test that "what the claimant has to show is that a sufficient state of permanence and stability has been reached in the relationship with the deceased. . .for it to be said that in all the circumstances the occupant was a member of [his] family. . . The question is one of fact and degree." He concluded that the woman was entitled to succeed. The Court of Appeal upheld the decision, noting that there could be no rule about the necessary length of the relationship, although the longer it has lasted the easier it will be to infer permanence.

The first amendment here deletes the 1977 Act, Sched. 1, para. 3 option to reflect the fact that a succeeding "member of the family" will not now take a statutory tenancy, but instead an assured tenancy under this Act.

Para. 2. This para. adds to the existing 1977 Act, Sched. 1, para. 2, a definition of spouse to include someone who has been living as the husband or wife of the original tenant. With astonishing sophistication, it recognises that there may be more than one "spouse" (as redefined) residing in the premises immediately before the original tenant's death, and adds provision for agreement between them as to who should succeed, or reference to the county court: see notes to s.17 as to agreement and reference to court.

Para. 3. This amends the 1977 Act, Sched. 1, para. 3(a), to spell out that residence with the original tenant must be in the premises in question (but see *South Northamptonshire D.C.* v. *Power* (1987) 20 H.L.R. 133, C.A., decided under the Housing Act 1985, re-affirming Rent Act law that this is in any event to be implied: see *Edmunds* v. *Jones* [1957] 1 W.L.R. 1118, *Collier* v. *Stoneman* [1957] 1 W.L.R. 1108), (b) substituting for six months a residential requirement of two years, and (c) replacing entitlement to statutory tenancy with entitlement to assured tenancy. However, in relation to a death within 18 months of "the operative date" (defined in para. 9 as the date on which Part I of this Act comes into force), the residential period need only be continuous since six months before the operative date, *i.e.* may be less.

Para. 4. This amends the 1977 Act, Sched. 1, para. 4 to exclude a member of the family as a first successor to a statutory tenancy.

Para. 5. This makes amendments (a) analogous to para. 1 (both of Sched. 4 to this Act and of Sched. 1 to the 1977 Act), described above, referable to second succession, and (b) substituting for statutory tenancy an assured tenancy Act in all cases of second succession.

Para. 6. The former Sched. 1, paras. 6 and 7 to the 1977 Act replicated the first succession provisions on second succession, *i.e.* giving priority to a spouse (legally married) of the first successor, and if none permitting by way of alternative a member of the family (including cohabitant) to succeed. This para. deletes the former para. 6 and substitutes new conditions for second succession. The conditions are that the would-be successor (a) was a member of the original tenant's family immediately before his death, *and* (b) was a member of the first successor's family immediately before his death, *and* (c) has resided in the dwelling-house at the time of and for the two years preceding the death of the first successor (subject again to the transitional provision governing deaths within the 18 months which follow the commencement of Part I of this Act).

There is provision for agreement or reference to county court if there is more than one potential second successor: see notes to s.17, above. The entitlement is to an assured, not a statutory, tenancy.

Para. 7. This omits Sched. 1, para. 7 to the 1977 Act.

Para. 8. The 1977 Act, Sched. 1, para. 10 governs the grant of a new tenancy to a successor (whether first or second) and permits a landlord to grant a new contractual tenancy to a successor attracting a new generation of succession, *i.e.* the tenant retains the succession status. The amendment in this para. merely adapts that para. to reflect the new limited succession provisions.

Subs. (4)

This subsection introduces Sched. 4, Part II, which makes corresponding succession provisions in relation to the Rent (Agriculture) Act 1976. These are somewhat less complicated, as that Act only permits one succession in any event.

Subss. (5), (6)

These provisions govern the terms of an assured tenancy acquired by reason of succession to a statutory tenancy or protected occupancy. The assured tenancy is to be periodic, and treated as a statutory periodic tenancy for the purpose of increasing its rent, taking effect from the death of "the predecessor", granted by the predecessor's landlord, of the same dwelling-house as the predecessor occupied immediately before his death, on periods the same as those for which rent was last payable by the predecessor and under which the terms are—subject to ss.13–15, above—otherwise the same (but *cf.* subs. (9), below).

Subs. (7)

The assured succession tenancy will be an assured shorthold tenancy if the shorthold ground for possession was still available against the predecessor. See notes to ss.20 and 34, above.

Subs. (8)

If the succession is to a protected occupancy or statutory tenancy under the Rent (Agriculture) Act 1976, then the tenancy will be an assured agricultural occupancy: see notes to Chapter III of this Part, above.

Subs. (9)

If the predecessor was still occupying under a fixed-term tenancy at the time of death, this subsection applies s.6, above to fix the terms of the periodic assured tenancy acquired, but modified to take effect from the death of the predecessor.

Subs. (10)

By Sched. 4, Part III, below, where the tenant is an assured tenant by succession, there are additional grounds for possession available under s.7, above. The "mandatory" grounds contained in Cases 11, 12, 16–18 and 20, in Sched. 15 to the Rent Act 1977, remain available against an assured tenant by succession, *unless* that to which he has succeeded is an assured agricultural occupancy, in which case Cases XI and XII of Sched. 4 to the Rent (Agriculture) Act 1976, are available: Sched. 4, Part III, paras. 12 and 13, below. In addition, where notice had been given to the predecessor for the purposes of Cases 13–15, Sched. 15 to the Rent Act 1977, those notices will remain good in relation to grounds 3–5 of Sched. 2 to this Act: Sched. 4, Part III, para. 14, below.

The relevant provisions are, in outline, as follows:

1977, Sched. 15, Case 11:	Returning owner-occupier.
1977, Sched. 15, Case 12:	Retirement home.
1977, Sched. 15, Case 13:	Out-of-season letting of premises normally let on a holiday letting.
1977, Sched. 15, Case 14:	Off-year or out-of-season letting of premises normally let on a student letting.
1977, Sched. 15, Case 15:	Premises for occupation of a minister of religion.
1977, Sched. 15, Cases 16–18:	Required for occupation in connection with agriculture in a number of different circumstances.
1977, Sched. 15, Case 20:	Returning service personnel.
1976, Sched. 4, Case XI:	Returning owner occupier.
1976, Sched. 4, Case XII:	Retirement home.

However, one ground in this Act—ground 6, redevelopment or major works—is not available at all to someone who has succeeded to an assured tenancy under these amended provisions of the 1976 and 1977 Acts.

CHAPTER VI

GENERAL PROVISIONS

Jurisdiction of county courts

40.—(1) A county court shall have jurisdiction to hear and determine any question arising under any provision of—

(a) Chapters I to III and V above, or
(b) sections 27 and 28 above,
other than a question falling within the jurisdiction of a rent assessment committee by virtue of any such provision.

(2) Subsection (1) above has effect notwithstanding that the damages claimed in any proceedings may exceed the amount which, for the time being, is the county court limit for the purposes of the County Courts Act 1984.

(3) Where any proceedings under any provision mentioned in subsection (1) above are being taken in a county court, the court shall have jurisdiction to hear and determine any other proceedings joined with those proceedings, notwithstanding that, apart from this subsection, those other proceedings would be outside the court's jurisdiction.

(4) If any person takes any proceedings under any provision mentioned in subsection (1) above in the High Court, he shall not be entitled to recover any more costs of those proceedings than those to which he would have been entitled if the proceedings had been taken in a county court: and in such a case the taxing master shall have the same power of directing on what county court scale costs are to be allowed, and of allowing any item of costs, as the judge would have had if the proceedings had been taken in a county court.

(5) Subsection (4) above shall not apply where the purpose of taking the proceedings in the High Court was to enable them to be joined with any proceedings already pending before that court (not being proceedings taken under any provision mentioned in subsection (1) above).

GENERAL NOTE
    The county court is the "usual' court in which residential security issues are decided, and has a specific jurisdiction in relation to relevant issues arising under the Rent Act 1977, the Rent (Agriculture) Act 1976, and the Housing Act 1985, as well as its general jurisdiction in relation to land (see notes to s.28, above). Once a case falls within its jurisdiction by reason of subs. (1), it has jurisdiction regardless of the amount of the damages (subs. (2)), and jurisdiction to hear proceedings which would otherwise be outside its powers if joined to that case: subs. (3).
    If a case is taken in the High Court which could have been taken in the county court, costs will only be on the county court scale: subs. (4). Note that this does not apply if proceedings which could have been taken in the county court are joined with proceedings already issued in the High Court: subs. (5).

Rent assessment committees: procedure and information powers

41.—(1) In section 74 of the Rent Act 1977 (regulations made by the Secretary of State) at the end of paragraph (b) of subsection (1) (procedure of rent officers and rent assessment committees) there shall be added the words "whether under this Act or Part I of the Housing Act 1988".

(2) The rent assessment committee to whom a matter is referred under Chapter I or Chapter II above may by notice in the prescribed form served on the landlord or the tenant require him to give to the committee, within such period of not less than fourteen days from the service of the notice as may be specified in the notice, such information as they may reasonably require for the purposes of their functions.

(3) If any person fails without reasonable excuse to comply with a notice served on him under subsection (2) above, he shall be liable on summary conviction to a fine not exceeding level 3 on the standard scale.

(4) Where an offence under subsection (3) above committed by a body corporate is proved to have been committed with the consent or con- nivance of, or to be attributable to any neglect on the part of, any director, manager or secretary or other similar officer of the body corporate or any person who was purporting to act in any such capacity,

he as well as the body corporate shall be guilty of that offence and shall be liable to be proceeded against and punished accordingly.

GENERAL NOTE
This extends the power of the Secretary of State to make regulations governing procedures in connection with rent officers and rent assessment committees under the Rent Act 1977, s.74, to the requirements of this Part: subs. (1). A rent assessment committee has power to require information from landlords and tenants (subs. (2)), subject to criminal sanctions under subss. (3) and (4). Level 3 on the standard scale is, currently, £400: Criminal Penalties, etc. (Increase) Order 1984 (S.I. 1984 No. 447), Sched. 4.

Information as to determination of rents

42.—(1) The President of every rent assessment panel shall keep and make publicly available, in such manner as is specified in an order made by the Secretary of State, such information as may be so specified with respect to rents under assured tenancies and assured agricultural occupancies which have been the subject of references or applications to, or determinations by, rent assessment committees.

(2) A copy of any information certified under the hand of an officer duly authorised by the President of the rent assessment panel concerned shall be receivable in evidence in any court and in any proceedings.

(3) An order under subsection (1) above—
    (a) may prescribe the fees to be charged for the supply of a copy, including a certified copy, of any of the information kept by virtue of that subsection; and
    (b) may make different provision with respect to different cases or descriptions of case, including different provision for different areas.

(4) The power to make an order under subsection (1) above shall be exercisable by statutory instrument which shall be subject to annulment in pursuance of a resolution of either House of Parliament.

GENERAL NOTE
This section permits the Secretary of State to require the presidents of rent assessment committees to keep a public record or register of determinations of rents for assured tenancies, *i.e.* "comparables".

Powers of local authorities for purposes of giving information

43. In section 149 of the Rent Act 1977 (which, among other matters, authorises local authorities to publish information for the benefit of landlords and tenants with respect to their rights and duties under certain enactments), in subsection (1)(a) after sub-paragraph (iv) there shall be inserted—
    "(v) Chapters I to III of Part I of the Housing Act 1988".

Application to Crown Property

44.—(1) Subject to paragraph 11 of Schedule 1 to this Act and subsection (2) below, Chapters I to IV above apply in relation to premises in which there subsists, or at any material time subsisted, a Crown interest as they apply in relation to premises in relation to which no such interest subsists or ever subsisted.

(2) In Chapter IV above—
    (a) sections 27 and 28 do not bind the Crown; and
    (b) the remainder binds the Crown to the extent provided for in section 10 of the Protection from Eviction Act 1977.

(3) In this section "Crown interest" means an interest which belongs to Her Majesty in right of the Crown or of the Duchy of Lancaster or to the

Duchy of Cornwall, or to a government department, or which is held in trust for Her Majesty for the purposes of a government department.

(4) Where an interest belongs to Her Majesty in right of the Duchy of Lancaster, then, for the purposes of Chapters I to IV above, the Chancellor of the Duchy of Lancaster shall be deemed to be the owner of the interest.

Interpretation of Part I

45.—(1) In this Part of this Act, except where the context otherwise requires,—

"dwelling-house" may be a house or part of a house;

"fixed term tenancy" means any tenancy other than a periodic tenancy;

"fully mutual housing association" has the same meaning as in Part I of the Housing Associations Act 1985;

"landlord" includes any person from time to time deriving title under the original landlord and also includes, in relation to a dwelling-house, any person other than a tenant who is, or but for the existence of an assured tenancy would be, entitled to possession of the dwelling-house;

"let" includes "sub-let";

"prescribed" means prescribed by regulations made by the Secretary of State by statutory instrument;

"rates" includes water rates and charges but does not include an owner's drainage rate, as defined in section 63(2)(a) of the Land Drainage Act 1976;

"secure tenancy" has the meaning assigned by section 79 of the Housing Act 1985;

"statutory periodic tenancy" has the meaning assigned by section 5(7) above;

"tenancy" includes a sub-tenancy and an agreement for a tenancy or sub-tenancy; and

"tenant" includes a sub-tenant and any person deriving title under the original tenant or sub-tenant.

(2) Subject to paragraph 11 of Schedule 2 to this Act, any reference in this Part of this Act to the beginning of a tenancy is a reference to the day on which the tenancy is entered into or, if it is later, the day on which, under the terms of any lease, agreement or other document, the tenant is entitled to possession under the tenancy.

(3) Where two or more persons jointly constitute either the landlord or the tenant in relation to a tenancy, then, except where this Part of this Act otherwise provides, any reference to the landlord or to the tenant is a reference to all the persons who jointly constitute the landlord or the tenant, as the case may require.

(4) For the avoidance of doubt, it is hereby declared that any reference in this Part of this Act (however expressed) to a power for a landlord to determine a tenancy does not include a reference to a power of re-entry or forfeiture for breach of any term or condition of the tenancy.

(5) Regulations under subsection (1) above may make different pro-vision with respect to different cases or descriptions of case, including different provision for different areas.

GENERAL NOTE

The most important of these definitions is that contained in subs. (3), which interprets landlord and tenant to mean *all* persons comprising the landlord or tenant under a joint tenancy or jointly comprising the landlord—save where this Part otherwise provides—as distinct from the position upheld in *Lloyd* v. *Sadler* [1978] Q.B. 774, C.A., thus averting the argument which has been posed in different circumstances and under different statutes, leading to different conclusions: see notes to s.12, above.

Fully mutual housing association. A fully mutual housing association is one the rules of which restrict memberships to people who are tenants or prospective tenants of the association, and preclude the grant or assignment of tenancies to persons other than members: Housing Associations Act 1985, s.1(2).

PART II

HOUSING ASSOCIATIONS

Housing for Wales

Housing for Wales

46.—(1) There shall be a body known as Housing for Wales.

(2) Schedule 5 to this Act shall have effect with respect to the constitution and proceedings of, and other matters relating to, Housing for Wales.

(3) Housing for Wales shall have the functions conferred on it by the Housing Associations Act 1985 (in this Part referred to as "the 1985 Act") as amended in accordance with section 59 below.

(4) All property in Wales which, immediately before the day appointed for the coming into force of this section, is held by the Housing Corpor-ation shall on that day be transferred to and vest in Housing for Wales.

(5) Any question whether any property has been transferred to Housing for Wales by virtue of subsection (4) above shall be determined by the Secretary of State.

GENERAL NOTE

Since 1974, the Housing Corporation has been the central body which, *inter alia*, registers and monitors registered housing associations in England and Wales: see the Housing Associations Act 1985 and ss.48–53 of this Act below. By this section, a new body is created, Housing for Wales, which is to take over the reponsibilities and powers of the Housing Corporation in Wales.

Transfer to Housing for Wales of regulation etc. of housing associations based in Wales

47.—(1) Every registered housing association which, immediately before the appointed day,—

(a) is a society registered under the 1965 Act and has its registered office for the purposes of that Act in Wales, or

(b) is a registered charity and has its address for the purposes of registration by the Charity Commissioners in Wales,

shall on the appointed day cease to be registered in the register maintained by the Housing Corporation under section 3 of the 1985 Act and, by virtue of this subsection, be deemed to be registered in the register maintained by Housing for Wales under that section.

(2) Not later than one month before the appointed day, the Secretary of State shall notify every registered housing association which appears to

him to be one which on that day will be deemed to be registered as mentioned in subsection (1) above of that fact and of the effect of that subsection.

(3) As soon as may be after the appointed day, Housing for Wales shall give notice of any registration effected by virtue of subsection (1) above,—

(a) if the housing association is a registered charity, to the Charity Commissioners; and

(b) if the housing association is a society registered under the 1965 Act, to the Chief Registrar of friendly societies.

(4) All rights, liabilities and obligations to which, immediately before the appointed day, the Housing Corporation was entitled or subject in relation to—

(a) any registered housing association to which subsection (1) above applies, and

(b) land in Wales held by an unregistered housing association,

shall on that day become rights, liabilities and obligations of Housing for Wales.

(5) Any question whether any rights, liabilities or obligations have become rights, liabilities or obligations of Housing for Wales by virtue of subsection (4) above shall be determined by the Secretary of State.

(6) In this section—

"the 1965 Act" means the Industrial and Provident Societies Act 1965; and

"the appointed day" means the day appointed for the coming into force of this section.

GENERAL NOTE

This section is ancillary to s.46, and effectively transfers the registration of housing associations based in Wales to Housing for Wales. Their former registration by the Housing Corporation is deemed to constitute registration in the new register which Housing for Wales will maintain under the 1985 Act, s.3.

Registration and issue of guidance

Permissible purposes, objects or powers

48.—(1) For subsections (3) and (4) of section 4 (eligibility for registration) of the 1985 Act there shall be substituted the following subsections—

"(3) The permissible additional purposes or objects are—

(a) providing land, amenities or services, or providing, constructing, repairing or improving buildings, for the benefit of the association's residents, either exclusively or together with other persons;

(b) acquiring, or repairing and improving, or creating by the conversion of houses or other property, houses to be disposed of on sale, on lease or on shared ownership terms;

(c) constructing houses to be disposed of on shared ownership terms;

(d) managing houses which are held on leases or other lettings (not being houses falling within subsection (2)(a) or (b)) or blocks of flats;

(e) providing services of any description for owners or occupiers of houses in arranging or carrying out works of maintenance, repair or improvement, or encouraging or facilitating the carrying out of such works;

(f) encouraging and giving advice on the formation of other

housing associations or providing services for, and giving advice on the running of, such associations and other voluntary organisations concerned with housing, or matters connected with housing.

(4) A housing association shall not be ineligible for registration by reason only that its powers include power—

(a) to acquire commercial premises or businesses as an incidental part of a project or series of projects undertaken for purposes or objects falling within subsection (2) or (3);

(b) to repair, improve or convert any commercial premises acquired as mentioned in paragraph (a) or to carry on, for a limited period, any business so acquired;

(c) to repair or improve houses, or buildings in which houses are situated, after the tenants have exercised, or claimed to exercise, acquisition rights;

(d) to acquire houses to be disposed of at a discount to tenants to whom section 58 of the Housing Act 1988 applies (tenants of charitable housing associations etc.).

(5) In this section—

"acquisition right" means—

(a) in England and Wales, the right to buy or the right to be granted a shared ownership lease under Part V of the Housing Act 1985;

(b) in Scotland, a right to purchase under section 61 of the Housing (Scotland) Act 1987;

"block of flats" means a building—

(a) containing two or more flats which are held on leases or other lettings; and

(b) occupied or intended to be occupied wholly or mainly for residential purposes;

"disposed of on shared ownership terms" means—

(a) in England and Wales, disposed of on a shared ownership lease;

(b) in Scotland, disposed of under a shared ownership agreement;

"letting" includes the grant—

(a) in England and Wales, of a licence to occupy;

(b) in Scotland, of a right or permission to occupy;

"residents", in relation to a housing association, means the persons occupying the houses or hostels provided or managed by the association;

"voluntary organisation" means an organisation whose activities are not carried on for profit."

(2) The Secretary of State may by order made by statutory instrument amend the subsections substituted by subsection (1) above, but not so as to restrict or limit the permissible purposes, objects or powers.

(3) An order under subsection (2) above may contain such incidental, supplemental or transitional provisions as the Secretary of State thinks fit.

(4) A statutory instrument containing an order under subsection (2) above shall be subject to annulment in pursuance of a resolution of either House of Parliament.

GENERAL NOTE

By the Housing Associations Act 1985, s.1,

"(1) In this Act 'housing association' means a society, body of trustees or company—

(a) which is established for the purpose of, or amongst whose objects or powers are included those of, providing, constructing, improving or managing, or facilitating or encouraging the construction or improvement of, housing accommodation, and

    (b) which does not trade for profit or whose constitution or rules prohibit the issue of capital with interest or dividend exceeding such rate as may be prescribed by the Treasury, whether with or without differentiation as between share and loan capital.

  (2) In this Act 'fully mutual' in relation to a housing association, means that the rules of the association—

    (a) restrict membership to persons who are tenants or prospective tenants of the association, and

    (b) preclude the granting or assignment of tenancies to persons other than members; and 'co-operative housing association' means a fully mutual housing association which is a society registered under the Industrial and Provident Societies Act 1965. . ."

The generality of this definition means that a wide range of bodies may fall to be described as a housing association. The important practical question, however, will not be that designation, but whether or not an association has achieved registration with the Housing Corporation or Housing for Wales, for such registration is the "key" to acquiring financial support for activities, whether from central government, by way of grant aid, or indeed from local authorities, who cannot exercise their powers to fund associations under Housing Associations Act 1985, s.58, by grant or loan or guarantee, except to a registered housing association: *ibid.*, s.60.

S.4 of the Housing Associations Act 1985 governs eligibility for registration. By s.4(1), an association is eligible for registration if it is a registered charity, or a society registered under the Industrial and Provident Societies Act 1965, which fulfils the conditions specified in s.4(2). Those conditions are that the association does not trade for profit, and is established for the purpose of, or has amongst its objects or powers, the provision, construction, improvement or management of houses to be kept available for letting, or houses for occupation by members of the association, where the rules of the association restrict membership to persons entitled or prospectively entitled to occupy a house provided or managed by the association, or hostels, *and* that any additional purposes or objects fall within those specified in s.4(3) (as amended by Housing and Planning Act 1986, s.19, and Landlord and Tenant Act 1987, s.45, which also added an explanatory subs. (4)).

This section redefines the permissible additional purposes or objects of housing associations, eligible for registration.

New Subs. (3)

The new sub-paras. do not substantively alter the existing law, as amended by the Housing and Planning Act 1986 and the Landlord and Tenant Act 1987.

New Subss. (4), (5)

This permits additional classes of powers: (1) incidentally to acquire commercial premises or businesses and to repair, improve or convert such premises or even for a limited period to continue a business so acquired, when this is part of a project within the association's main objects; (2) to repair or improve houses or buildings, after tenants have exercised the right to buy or to a shared ownership lease under Housing Act 1985; Part V and (3) to acquire houses to be disposed of at a discount to tenants under s.53 of this Act—see notes thereto, below.

Guidance as to management of accommodation by registered housing associations

49. After section 36 of the 1985 Act there shall be inserted the following section—

"Issue of guidance by the Corporation

36A.—(1) In accordance with the provisions of this section, the Corporation may issue guidance with respect to the management of housing accommodation by registered housing associations and, in considering under the preceding provisions of this Part whether action needs to be taken to secure the proper management of an association's affairs or whether there has been mismanagement, the Corporation may have regard (among other matters) to the extent to which any such guidance is being or has been followed.

(2) Guidance issued under this section may make different provision in relation to different cases and, in particular, in relation to different areas, different descriptions of housing accommodation and different descriptions of registered housing associations.

(3) Without prejudice to the generality of subsections (1) and (2), guidance issued under this section may relate to—

(a) the housing demands for which provision should be made and the means of meeting those demands;

(b) the allocation of housing accommodation between individuals;

(c) the terms of tenancies and the principles upon which the levels of rent should be determined;

(d) standards of maintenance and repair and the means of achieving these standards; and

(e) consultation and communication with tenants.

(4) Guidance issued under this section may be revised or withdrawn but, before issuing or revising any guidance under this section, the Corporation—

(a) shall consult such bodies appearing to it to be representative of housing associations as it considers appropriate; and

(b) shall submit a draft of the proposed guidance or, as the case may be, the proposed revision to the Secretary of State for his approval.

(5) If the Secretary of State gives his approval to a draft submitted to him under subsection (4)(b), the Corporation shall issue the guidance or, as the case may be, the revision concerned in such manner as the Corporation considers appropriate for bringing it to the notice of the housing associations concerned."

GENERAL NOTE

This section introduces a new section into the Housing Associations Act 1985, empowering the Housing Corporation and Housing for Wales to issue "guidance" to registered housing associations, relating to their "management". Part I of the 1985 Act includes powers for the Corporations (*i.e.* the Housing Corporation in England, Housing for Wales in Wales) to investigate the affairs of registered housing associations, to conduct an extraordinary audit of their accounts, to remove or suspend committee members or officers, to direct the transfer of land to another association, and to appoint members to a committee; registered housing associations are also, under Part I, constrained by specified accounting requirements, and there are prohibitions on benefits for committee members and officers.

The Corporations may now have regard to the extent of compliance with the management guidance when determining whether to exercise powers under Part I. The guidance, which may be revised or withdrawn, must be put out to consultation with housing association representative bodies (*e.g.* the National Federation of Housing Associations, recognised under s.33 of the 1985 Act): as to consultation, see notes to s.61, below.

The need for some such guidance—see new subs. (3)—reflects the removal of housing association tenants (a) from the fair rent provisions of the Rent Act 1977, and (b) from status as secure tenants under the Housing Act 1985, Part IV which contains a number of provisions concerning management by which housing associations have hitherto been bound: see s.35, above. Non-compliance with guidance, while undoubtedly the basis for a complaint to the Corporations, will not be likely to avail tenants directly, *e.g.* by way of defence to proceedings for possession or the recovery of higher rents, not even by way of judicial review, for while the Corporations are susceptible to judicial review, housing associations themselves are not: see *Peabody Housing Association Ltd.* v. *Green* (1978) 122 S.J. 862, C.A.

Grants: functions of Corporation

Housing association grants

50.—(1) The Housing Corporation and Housing for Wales may make grants to registered housing associations in respect of expenditure incurred or to be incurred by them in connection with housing activities; and any reference in the following provisions of this section to "the Corporation" shall be construed accordingly.

(2) As respects grants under this section the following, namely—

    (a) the procedure to be followed in relation to applications for grant;

    (b) the circumstances in which grant is or is not to be payable;

    (c) the method for calculating, and any limitations on, the amount of grant; and

    (d) the manner in which, and time or times at which, grant is to be paid,

shall be such as may be specified by the Corporation, acting in accordance with such principles as it may from time to time determine.

(3) In making a grant under this section, the Corporation may provide that the grant is conditional on compliance by the association with such conditions as it may specify.

(4) On such terms as it may, with the appropriate approval, specify, the Corporation may appoint a local housing authority which is willing to do so to act as its agent in connection with the assessment and payment of grant under this section; and, where such an appointment is made, the local housing authority shall act as such an agent in accordance with the terms of their appointment.

(5) In subsection (4) above, "the appropriate approval" means the approval of the Secretary of State given with the consent of the Treasury.

(6) Where—

    (a) a grant under this section is payable to an association, and

    (b) at any time property to which the grant relates becomes vested in, or is leased for a term of years to, or reverts to, some other registered housing association, or trustees for some other such association,

this section (including this subsection) shall have effect after that time as if the grant, or such proportion of it as is specified or determined under subsection (7) below, were payable to that other association.

(7) The proportion referred to in subsection (6) above is that which, in the circumstances of the particular case—

    (a) the Corporation, acting in accordance with such principles as it may from time to time determine, may specify as being appropriate; or

    (b) the Corporation may determine to be appropriate.

(8) Where one of the associations mentioned in subsection (6) above is registered by the Housing Corporation and another is registered by Housing for Wales, the determination mentioned in subsection (7) above shall be such as shall be agreed between the two Corporations.

GENERAL NOTE

The current grant-aid structure applicable to registered housing associations is to be found in Part II of the Housing Associations Act 1985. The first major change is the transfer by this section of responsibility for payment of housing association grant from the Secretary of State for the Environment to the Housing Corporation and Housing for Wales. The Corporations' powers as to procedures, circumstances in which grant is payable or not, method of calculation of grants, manner of payment and conditions, as well as transfer of grant in whole or part to follow transfer of property to another registered housing association, are very wide indeed, and markedly less circumscribed by statute than under the current system, but see notes to s.53, below.

Of particular interest are subss. (4) and (5). These permit the Housing Corporation or Housing for Wales, with the consent of the Secretary of State, to appoint a local housing authority as an agent for the purpose of assessing and paying grant: this brings an element of "full circle" to housing association funding, for prior to the creation in 1974 of the Housing Corporation, local authorities were the principal bodies funding associations, and acquired and developed considerable skill at monitoring both individual scheme-work and associations as a whole.

Revenue deficit grants

51.—(1) The Housing Corporation or, as the case may be, Housing for Wales may make a grant to a registered housing association if—
  (a) in relation to all housing activities of the association,
  (b) in relation to housing activities of the association of a particular description, or
  (c) in relation to particular housing activities of the association,
the association's expenditure as calculated by the Corporation concerned for any period (including a period which is wholly or partly a future period) exceeds its income as so calculated for that period.

(2) In calculating an association's expenditure or income for the purposes of subsection (1) above, the Housing Corporation or, as the case may be, Housing for Wales—
  (a) shall act in accordance with such principles as it may from time to time determine; and
  (b) may act on such assumptions (whether or not borne out or likely to be borne out by events) as it may from time to time determine.

(3) Subsections (2) and (3) of section 50 above shall apply for the purposes of this section as they apply for the purposes of that section.

GENERAL NOTE
  The other principal grant which associations can currently receive from the Secretary of State for the Environment (*cf.* notes to s.45, above), is revenue deficit grant, and this is, like housing association grant, now to be transferred, subject to a wide general discretion, to the Housing Corporation and Housing for Wales. Again, the provisions are less prescribed by statute than the current provisions, but see notes to s.53, below.

Recovery etc. of grants

52.—(1) Where a grant to which this section applies, that is to say—
  (a) a grant under section 50 or 51 above, or
  (b) a grant under section 41 of the 1985 Act or any enactment replaced by that section, or
  (c) a grant under section 2(2) of the Housing (Scotland) Act 1988,
has been made to a registered housing association, the powers conferred by subsection (2) below are exercisable in such events (including the association not complying with any conditions) as the Corporation may from time to time determine (in this section referred to as "relevant events").

(2) The Corporation, acting in accordance with such principles as it may from time to time determine, may—
  (a) reduce the amount of, or of any payment in respect of, the grant;
  (b) suspend or cancel any instalment of the grant; or
  (c) direct the association to pay to it an amount equal to the whole, or such proportion as it may specify, of the amount of any payment made to the association in respect of the grant,
and a direction under paragraph (c) above requiring the payment of any amount may also require the payment of interest on that amount in accordance with subsections (7) to (9) below.

(3) Where, after a grant to which this section applies has been made to an association, a relevant event occurs, the association shall notify the Corporation and, if so required by written notice of the Corporation, shall furnish it with such particulars of and information relating to the event as are specified in the notice.

(4) Where a grant to which this section applies (other than one falling within subsection (1)(c) above) has been made to an association, the Chief Land Registrar may furnish the Corporation with such particulars

and information as it may reasonably require for the purpose of ascertaining whether a relevant event has occurred; but this subsection shall cease to have effect on the day appointed under section 3(2) of the Land Registration Act 1988 for the coming into force of that Act.

(5) Where—

    (a) a grant to which this section applies has been made to an association, and

    (b) at any time property to which the grant relates becomes vested in, or is leased for a term of years to, or reverts to, some other registered housing association, or trustees for some other such association,

this section (including this subsection) shall have effect after that time as if the grant, or such proportion of it as is specified or determined under subsection (6) below, had been made to that other association.

(6) The proportion referred to in subsection (5) above is that which, in the circumstances of the particular case,—

    (a) the Corporation, acting in accordance with such principles as it may from time to time determine, may specify as being appropriate; or

    (b) the Corporation may determine to be appropriate.

(7) A direction under subsection (2)(c) above requiring the payment of interest on the amount directed to be paid to the Corporation shall specify, in accordance with subsection (9) below,—

    (a) the rate or rates of interest (whether fixed or variable) which is or are applicable;

    (b) the date from which interest is payable, being not earlier than the date of the relevant event; and

    (c) any provision for suspended or reduced interest which is applicable.

(8) In subsection (7)(c) above—

    (a) the reference to a provision for suspended interest is a reference to a provision whereby, if the amount which is directed to be paid to the Corporation is paid before a date specified in the direction, no interest will be payable for any period after the date of the direction; and

    (b) the reference to a provision for reduced interest is a reference to a provision whereby, if that amount is so paid, any interest payable will be payable at a rate or rates lower than the rate or rates which would otherwise be applicable.

(9) The matters specified in a direction as mentioned in paragraphs (a) to (c) of subsection (7) above shall be either—

    (a) such as the Corporation, acting in accordance with such principles as it may from time to time determine, may specify as being appropriate, or

    (b) such as the Corporation may determine to be appropriate in the particular case.

DEFINITION
"Corporation": s.59.

GENERAL NOTE
The Housing Corporation and Housing for Wales, rather than the Secretary of State for the Environment, now enjoy the power to reduce, suspend or cancel grant, or require repayment: see, currently, Housing Associations Act 1985, s.52. In accordance with the philosophy of ss.50 and 51, the powers are generally described, in terms of the discretion of (now) the Housing Corporation and Housing for Wales, rather than the more particularised provisions which governed exercise by the Secretary of State, but see notes to s.53, below.

Determinations under Part II

53.—(1) A general determination may either—
  (a) make the same provision for all cases; or
  (b) make different provision for different cases or descriptions of cases, including different provision for different areas or for different descriptions of housing associations or housing activities;

and for the purposes of this subsection descriptions may be framed by reference to any matters whatever, including in particular, in the case of housing activities, the manner in which they are financed.

(2) The Corporation shall not make a determination under the foregoing provisions of this Part except with the approval of the Secretary of State given, in the case of a general determination, with the consent of the Treasury.

(3) Before making a general determination, the Corporation shall consult such bodies appearing to it to be representative of housing associations as it considers appropriate; and after making such a determination, the Corporation shall publish the determination in such manner as it considers appropriate for bringing the determination to the notice of the associations concerned.

(4) In this section "general determination" means a determination under any provision of sections 50 to 52 above, other than a determination relating solely to a particular case.

DEFINITION
  "Corporation": s.59.

GENERAL NOTE
  While the Housing Corporation and Housing for Wales have discretion to reach determinations under the past three foregoing sections, all such determinations require the approval of the Secretary of State for the Environment, and if a general determination (see subs. (4), *i.e.* one not relating solely to a particular case), (a) the Secretary of State must secure the consent of the Treasury, (b) the Corporations must consult with housing association representative bodies (*e.g.* National Federation of Housing Associations), and (c) the Corporations must publish the determination and bring it to the attention of the associations concerned.
  The choice of representative associations, and manner of publication, are within the discretion of the Corporations. The term "determination" includes any determinations of "principles" under ss.50(2), (5), 51(2) and 52(6). As to "consultation", see notes to s.61, below.

Grants: functions of Secretary of State

Tax relief grants

54.—(1) If a housing association makes a claim to the Secretary of State in respect of a period and satisfies him that throughout the period it was a housing association to which this section applies and its functions either—
  (a) consisted exclusively of the function of providing or maintaining housing accommodation for letting or hostels and activities incidental to that function, or
  (b) included that function and activities incidental to that function,
the Secretary of State may make grants to the association for affording relief from tax chargeable on the association.

(2) This section applies to a housing association at any time if, at that time—
  (a) it is registered;
  (b) it does not trade for profit; and

(c) it is not approved for the purposes of section 488 of the Income and Corporation Taxes Act 1988 (tax treatment of co-operative housing associations).

(3) References in this section to tax chargeable on an association are to income tax (other than income tax which the association is entitled to deduct on making any payment) and corporation tax.

(4) A grant under this section may be made—

(a) in a case falling within subsection (1)(a) above, for affording relief from any tax chargeable on the association for the period in respect of which the claim is made; and

(b) in a case falling within subsection (1)(b) above, for affording relief from such part of any tax so chargeable as the Secretary of State considers appropriate having regard to the other functions of the association;

and in any case shall be of such amount, shall be made at such times and shall be subject to such conditions as the Secretary of State thinks fit.

(5) The conditions may include conditions for securing the repayment in whole or in part of a grant made to an association—

(a) in the event of tax in respect of which it was made being found not to be chargeable; or

(b) in such other events (including the association beginning to trade for profit) as the Secretary of State may determine.

(6) A claim under this section shall be made in such manner and shall be supported by such evidence as the Secretary of State may direct.

(7) The Commissioners of Inland Revenue and their officers may disclose to the Secretary of State such particulars as he may reasonably require for determining whether a grant should be made on a claim or whether a grant should be repaid or the amount of such grant or repayment.

(8) In this section "letting" includes—

(a) in England and Wales, the grant of a shared ownership lease or a licence to occupy;

(b) in Scotland, disposal under a shared ownership agreement or the grant of a right or permission to occupy.

GENERAL NOTE

The breadth of powers and objects now permissible (see notes to s.48, above) means that housing association liability to tax is likely to be enhanced. This section introduces a "tax relief grant" available from the Secretary of State. One of the conditions is that the association does not "trade for profit". This phrase was considered in *Goodman* v. *Dolphin Square Trust* (1979) 38 P. & C.R. 257, C.A., and the limitation is not offended by the mere fact that an activity produces a profit. The term means trading for profit in the sense of profit which may be extracted from the organisation, to be used and enjoyed by its proprietors, as distinct from profits which must be kept within, or ploughed back into, the activities of the organisation.

Note that a tax relief grant may be subject to conditions, which may include repayment: subss. (4), (5). Note, too, the express authority granted to the Commissioners of the Inland Revenue to disclose such particulars as he may reasonably require to determine whether a grant should be made, or reclaimed, or how much to pay or reclaim.

Surplus rental income

55.—(1) An association to which this section applies, that is to say, a registered housing association which has at any time received a payment in respect of—

(a) a grant under section 50 above, or

(b) a grant under section 41 of the 1985 Act or any enactment replaced by that section, or

(c) a grant under section 2(2) of the Housing (Scotland) Act 1988, (in this section referred to as a "relevant grant") shall show separately in its accounts for any period ending after the coming into force of this section the surpluses arising from increased rental income during that period from such housing activities to which the grant relates as the Secretary of State may from time to time determine.

(2) The surpluses shall be shown by each association in a fund to be known as its rent surplus fund; and the method of constituting that fund and of showing it in the association's accounts shall be as required by order of the Secretary of State under section 24 of the 1985 Act (general requirements as to accounts) and, notwithstanding anything in subsection (5) of that section, such an order may make provision applying to any period to which this section applies.

(3) The surpluses in respect of a period shall be calculated in such manner as the Secretary of State may from time to time determine; and a determination under this subsection may provide that, in calculating surpluses, an association shall act on such assumptions (whether or not borne out or likely to be borne out by events) as may be specified in the determination.

(4) A determination under subsection (1) or (3) above may—

(a) make the same provision for all cases; or

(b) make different provision for different cases or descriptions of cases, including different provision for different areas or for different descriptions of housing associations or housing activities;

and for the purposes of this subsection descriptions may be framed by reference to any matters whatever, including in particular, in the case of housing activities, the manner in which they are financed.

(5) Before making a determination under subsection (1) or (3) above, the Secretary of State shall consult such bodies appearing to him to be representative of housing associations as he considers appropriate; and after making such a determination, the Secretary of State shall publish it in such manner as he considers appropriate for bringing it to the notice of the associations concerned.

(6) The Secretary of State may from time to time give notice to an association to which this section applies requiring it to pay to him, with interest if demanded, or to apply or appropriate for purposes he specifies, any sums standing in its rent surplus fund at the end of a period of account.

(7) Any interest demanded by such a notice is payable—

(a) at the rate or rates (whether fixed or variable) previously determined by the Secretary of State, with the consent of the Treasury, for housing associations generally and published by him or, if no such determination has been made, at the rate or rates (whether fixed or variable) specified with the consent of the Treasury in the notice; and

(b) either from the date of the notice or from such other date, not earlier than the end of the period of account, as may be specified in the notice.

(8) A notice under subsection (6) above demanding interest may with the consent of the Treasury provide that, if the sums required by the notice to be paid to the Secretary of State are paid before a date specified in the notice—

(a) no interest shall be payable for any period after the date of the notice; and

(b) any interest payable shall be payable at a rate or rates lower than the rate or rates given by subsection (7) above.

(9) The Secretary of State may from time to time give notice—

(a) to all associations to which this section applies,

(b) to associations to which this section applies of a particular description, or

(c) to particular associations to which this section applies,

requiring them to furnish him with such information as he may reasonably require in connection with the exercise of his functions under this section; and a notice under paragraph (a) or (b) above may be given by publication in such manner as the Secretary of State considers appropriate for bringing it to the attention of the associations concerned.

(10) Where—

(a) an association has received a payment in respect of a relevant grant, and

(b) at any time property to which the grant relates becomes vested in, or is leased for a term of years to, or reverts to, some other registered housing association, or trustees for some other such association,

this section (including this subsection) shall have effect in relation to periods after that time as if the payment, or such proportion of it as may be determined by the Secretary of State to be appropriate, had been made to that other association.

GENERAL NOTE

This section replaces s.53 of the Housing Associations Act 1985—Grant Redemption Fund. This section governs associations which have received a Housing Association Grant under s.50 of this Act, or s.41 of the 1985 Act, or earlier grant provisions, but does not include revenue deficit grant under this or the 1985 Act. The section requires the association to show separately in its accounts surpluses which arise from increases in rental income over that period, attributable to such housing activities (see Sched. 6, para. 34, below) as the Secretary of State determines. The fund is to be known as a "rent surplus fund" and the method of constituting it and showing in the accounts shall be in accordance with the requirements of the Secretary of State.

Calculation of the surpluses is as determined by the Secretary of State, who may make assumptions, e.g. as to rent increases, which may or may not be borne out: subs. (3). This reflects the withdrawal of housing associations from rent registration (see notes to s.35, above), and resembles the system for calculating local authority housing subsidy under Part XIII of the Housing Act 1985, under which the Secretary of State presumes an annual rent increase which, of course, may or may not be imposed by authorities. The Secretary of State is under like consultation and publication obligations to those of the Housing Corporation and Housing for Wales under s.53 of this Act, above, when it makes general determinations.

The important provision is subs. (6), entitling the Secretary of State to require payment to him, with interest if demanded, or to apply to purposes he specifies, any sum standing in an association's rent surplus funds at the end of a period of account. The power to require interest is at the rate or rates previously determined by the Secretary of State with the consent of the Treasury (subs. (7)), but includes power (also exercisable with the consent of the Treasury) to waive or reduce interest if payment is made before a specified date: subs. (8). The Secretary of State also enjoys power to require information from associations: subs. (9). The provisions may, in effect, transfer to another association, with a transfer of property: subs. (10).

Miscellaneous and supplemental

Duty of Housing Corporation and Housing for Wales in relation to racial discrimination

56. At the end of section 75 of the 1985 Act (general functions of the Corporation) there shall be added the following subsection—

"(5) Section 71 of the Race Relations Act 1976 (local authorities: general statutory duty) shall apply to the Corporation as it applies to a local authority."

GENERAL NOTE

The Housing Corporation and Housing for Wales are now brought within the provisions of s.71 of the Race Relations Act 1976, which provides:

". . . It shall be the duty of every local authority to make appropriate arrangements with a view to securing that their various functions are carried out with due regard to the need—

(a) to eliminate unlawful racial discrimination; and

(b) to promote equality of opportunity, and good relations, between persons of different racial groups".

Delegation of certain functions

57. The Secretary of State may delegate to the Corporation, to such extent and subject to such conditions as he may specify, any of his functions under—

(a) section 54 or 55 above;

(b) sections 53 (recoupment of surplus rental income), 54 to 57 (deficit grants) and 62 (grants for affording tax relief) of the 1985 Act, so far as continuing in force after the passing of this Act; and

(c) Parts I and II of Schedule 5 to the 1985 Act (residual subsidies);

and where he does so, references to him in those provisions shall be construed accordingly.

DEFINITION
"Corporation": s.59.

GENERAL NOTE
This gives the Secretary of State power to delegate to the Housing Corporation and Housing for Wales his functions in respect of tax relief grants and surplus rental income, both under this Act and under the Housing Associations Act 1985, as well as residual subsidies payable under Sched. 5 to the Housing Associations Act 1985.

Application of Housing Acts to certain transactions

58.—(1) This section applies to any tenant of a publicly-funded house who but for paragraph 1 of Schedule 5 to the Housing Act 1985 (no right to buy where landlord a charitable housing trust or housing association), would have the right to buy under Part V of the Housing Act 1985.

(2) A house is publicly-funded for the purposes of subsection (1) above if a grant under section 50 above, or a grant under section 41 of the 1985 Act or any enactment replaced by that section, has been paid in respect of a project which included—

(a) the acquisition of the house;

(b) the acquisition of a building and the provision of the house by means of the conversion of the building; or

(c) the acquisition of land and the construction of the house on the land.

(3) Where a registered housing association contracts for the acquisition of a house and, without taking the conveyance, grant or assignment, disposes of its interest at a discount to a tenant to whom this section applies, the provisions mentioned in subsection (4) below shall have effect as if the association first acquired the house and then disposed of it to the tenant.

(4) The said provisions are—

section 4 of the 1985 Act (eligibility for registration);

section 8 of that Act (disposal of land by registered housing associations);

section 9 of that Act (consent of Corporation to disposals);

section 79(2) of that Act (power of Corporation to lend to person acquiring interest from registered housing association);

Schedule 2 to that Act (covenants for repayments of discount on early disposal and restricting disposal of houses in National Parks etc.); and section 130 of the Housing Act 1985 (reduction of discount on exercise of right to buy where previous discount given).

DEFINITION
"Corporation": s.59.

GENERAL NOTE
Tenants of housing trusts and associations which are charities within the meaning of the Charities Act 1960 have always been excluded from the "right to buy" scheme introduced by the Housing Act 1980—see now, Housing Act 1985, Part V. The Housing and Building Control Act 1984 introduced the scheme which is now provided for by Housing Associations Act 1985, s.45, enabling a charitable housing trust or association to arrange the acquisition of an alternative dwelling for the purpose of immediate disposal to a tenant who, but for the charitable landlord exception from right to buy, would have had the right to buy the property he lived in. The scheme envisages a discount to the tenant: hence the term sometimes applied, "portable discount".

This section restates the Housing Associations Act 1985, s.45, applying the provisions set out in subs. (4) to such an exercise, whether the association acquires a property and then passes it to its tenant, or where it passes the benefit of a contract to acquire a property to one of its tenants, without itself actually completing (*i.e.* the tenant steps in to take the benefit of the contract, and himself completes), to include Housing Association Grant under s.50, above, as well as under the Housing Associations Act 1985, s.41.

Interpretation of Part II and amendments of Housing Associations Act 1985

59.—(1) In this Part of this Act—
  (a) "the 1985 Act" means the Housing Associations Act 1985; and
  (b) except as provided in section 50(1) above, "the Corporation" and other expressions used in this Part have the same meaning as in the 1985 Act.

(2) The 1985 Act shall have effect subject to the amendments in Schedule 6 to this Act, being amendments—
  (a) extending the supervisory powers conferred by Part I of the 1985 Act;
  (b) making provision incidental to and consequential upon the establishment by this Part of this Act of Housing for Wales and the establishment by the Housing (Scotland) Act 1988 of Scottish Homes;
  (c) making provision incidental to and consequential upon other provisions of this Part of this Act and the provisions of Part IV of this Act; and
  (d) varying the grounds on which the Secretary of State may remove a member of the Housing Corporation from office.

(3) In Schedule 6 to this Act,—
  (a) Part I contains amendments of Part I of the 1985 Act, including amendments which reproduce the effect of amendments made by Schedule 3 to the Housing (Scotland) Act 1988 with respect to Scottish Homes; and
  (b) Parts II and III contain amendments of Parts II and III respectively of the 1985 Act.

(4) Without prejudice to the operation of Schedule 3 to the Housing Scotland) Act 1988 in relation to anything done before the day appointed for the coming into force of this section, for the purpose of giving effect to the amendments in Part I of Schedule 6 to this Act, the said Schedule 3 shall be deemed never to have come into force.

PART III

HOUSING ACTION TRUST AREAS

Areas and trusts

Housing action trust areas

60.—(1) Subject to section 61 below, the Secretary of State may by order designate an area of land for which, in his opinion, it is expedient that a corporation, to be known as a housing action trust, having the functions specified in this Part of this Act, should be established.

(2) The area designated by an order under this section may comprise two or more parcels of land which—

(a) need not be contiguous; and

(b) need not be in the district of the same local housing authority.

(3) An order under this section shall be made by statutory instrument but no such order shall be made unless a draft of it has been laid before, and approved by a resolution of, each House of Parliament.

(4) In deciding whether to make an order under this section designating any area of land, the Secretary of State shall have regard to such matters as he thinks fit.

(5) Without prejudice to the generality of subsection (4) above, among the matters to which the Secretary of State may have regard in deciding whether to include a particular area of land in an order under this section, are—

(a) the extent to which the housing accommodation in the area as a whole is occupied by tenants or owner-occupiers and the extent to which it is local authority housing;

(b) the physical state and design of the housing accommodation in the area and any need to repair or improve it;

(c) the way in which the local authority housing in the area is being managed; and

(d) the living conditions of those who live in the area and the social conditions and general environment of the area.

(6) An area designated by an order under this section shall be known as a housing action trust area and in the following provisions of this Part of this Act—

(a) such an area is referred to as a "designated area"; and

(b) an order under this section is referred to as a "designation order".

DEFINITIONS
"housing accommodation": s.92.
"local authority housing": s.92.
"local housing authority": s.92.

GENERAL NOTE
This section introduces the "housing action trust" (H.A.T.) and its "designated area", which—subject to a ballot of tenants (secure and as prescribed for the purpose) which does not result in a majority against the proposal—may be established by a "designation order" pursuant to affirmative parliamentary procedure. In some ways, the concept resembles the urban development corporation of the Local Government, Planning and Land Act 1980, but it is significantly different in that (a) it presumes the transfer to the H.A.T. of local authority housing stock (together with housing and other powers—but some of these can also attach to an urban development corporation), and (b) the considerations which give rise to the H.A.T. are different.

In outline, and leaving aside ballot, the conditions which justify H.A.T. treatment are set out in this section. There is a precondition of consultation pursuant to s.61. The H.A.T. is a statutory corporation: s.62 and Sched. 7. The primary objects are repair or improvement of housing stock held by the H.A.T., its proper and effective management and use, to secure or facilitate the improvement of living and social conditions in the area, and its general environment, and—importantly—"to encourage diversity in the interests by virtue of which housing accommodation in the area is occupied and, in the case of accommodation which is occupied under tenancies, diversity in the identity of the landlords": s.63.

Once the H.A.T. has been established, it has to draw up and consult on a statement of proposals, and it may prepare and consult on further statements of proposals at its own discretion or on the direction of the Secretary of State: s.64.

The designation order may confer on the H.A.T. the following housing powers or duties of local authorities, either co-extensive with those authorities or in substitution for them, and subject to possible modifications (s.65): housing powers under Housing Act 1985, Part II, repairs notices under *ibid*, Part VI, improvement notices under *ibid.*, Part VII, slum clearance under *ibid.*, Part IX, overcrowding responsibilities under *ibid.*, Part X, houses in multiple occupation duties under *ibid.*, Part XI, responsibilities for common lodging houses under *ibid.*, Part XII, responsibilities for dwellings of defective design or construction under *ibid.*, Part XVI, consideration of the special needs with respect to housing of the chronically sick and disabled under the Chronically Sick and Disabled Persons Act 1970, s.3(1), the financing of registered housing associations under the Housing Associations Act 1985, Part II (see also notes to s.50, above), and related rehousing obligations under the Land Compensation Act 1973, ss.39–41.

H.A.T.s are bodies who must "co-operate" to the extent that is reasonable, with authorities who have homelessness obligations under the Housing Act 1985, Part III, though they have no such obligations themselves: s.70.

In addition, the H.A.T. may in effect be empowered to by-pass local authority planning controls, by s.66, below, and the Secretary of State can pass to the H.A.T. the authority's planning powers, in whole or part, and again co-extensive with or in substitution for the authority: s.67. The housing powers of local authorities under the Public Health Acts may similarly be passed, instead of or concurrently with the local authority to the H.A.T., by s.68. The H.A.T. may require the local authority to declare a street a public highway: s.69. The H.A.T. has power to give grants, loans, guarantees, and other financial assistance under s.71.

The H.A.T. must comply with any directions, whether general or specific, from the Secretary of State: s.72. The Secretary of State may transfer functions and stock and other assets from one H.A.T. to another: s.73. The Secretary of State has power to transfer local authority housing to the H.A.T., together with other land held or provided in connection with that housing and even non-housing land or property (s.74) subject to prior consultation: s.75. The H.A.T. may enjoy compulsory purchase powers: s.77. The tenants of H.A.T.s are to be secure tenants, enjoying the right to buy: s.83. There is express power to delegate the functions of the H.A.T., subject to the approval of the Secretary of State: s.87. H.A.T.s are intended to secure their objects as soon as practicable and then to make proposals for their own dissolution and transfer of their residual functions: s.88.

Subss. (1), (4), (5)

The power to designate an area of land for treatment by a housing action trust belongs—subject to ballot under s.61, below—to the Secretary of State, who has a generous discretion to exercise it when "in his opinion, it is expedient" that the H.A.T. should be established. It is clear that while judicially reviewable, the courts will only intervene in the "usual" but highly restricted circumstances: see most recently, *R.* v. *Secretary of State for the Environment, ex p. Nottinghamshire County Council* [1986] 1 A.C. 240, H.L.; see also *Council of Civil Service Unions* v. *Minister for Civil Service* [1985] A.C. 374, H.L., and *Puhlhofer* v. *Hillingdon L.B.C.* [1986] 1 A.C. 484, H.L. Reference may also be made to *R.* v. *Secretary of State for the Environment, ex p. Norwich County Council* [1982] Q.B. 808, 2 H.L.R. 1, C.A., concerning the Secretary of State's powers to intervene in "right to buy".

The breadth of the discretion is emphasised in subs. (4), which permits the Secretary of State to have regard to such matters as he thinks fit, which *may* include those specified in subs. (5). Those in subs. (5) are "housing" or "environmental" issues, but the addition of subs. (4) suggests that considerations which may in some circumstances not be considered housing considerations, *e.g.* general economic policy considerations, will be permissible. Indeed, while it seems unlikely that the courts would uphold a decision based purely on the political constitution of a local authority, it is clear that this discretion will permit him to utilise the H.A.T. to supplant the housing (and other) powers of a local authority of whose policies or practices he disapproves (see also subs. (5)(c)).

The specific considerations are listed in subs. (5) "without prejudice" to the generality of subs. (4). The first is the extent to which the housing accommodation in the area as a whole is occupied by tenants or owner-occupiers, and the extent to which it is local authority housing, *i.e.* housing accommodation provided by a local housing authority, whether or not in their own district (s.92, below). Local housing authority has the same meaning as in the Housing Act 1985 (s.92, below), *i.e.* a district council, London borough council, the Common Council of the City of London or the Council of the Isles of Scilly. S.2 of the 1985 Act determines what constitutes the "district" of a local housing authority.

"Housing accommodation" is defined in s.92 to include flats, lodging-houses and hostels. It does not specify "dwelling" (*cf.* Housing Act 1985, s.239) so that the decision in *R.* v. *Camden London Borough Council, ex p. Comyn Ching & Co. (London)* (1984) P. & C.R. 1417, Q.B.D., has only limited application, although may not be wholly irrelevant. In that case, the authority sought to treat as "housing accommodation" (as defined in the 1985 Act, s.239) a warehouse which, after purchase using housing action area powers they intended to convert to housing use. It was held that the correct test was to ask whether something could be considered a dwelling, in the hands of the person having control of it at the time the issue arises.

The second specific consideration is the physical state and design of the housing accommodation in the area, and any need to repair or improve it. The third is "the way" in which the local authority housing in the area is being managed. Finally, "the living conditions of those who live in the area and the social conditions and general environment of the area." Taken together, the second and the fourth considerations resemble an aggregation of those which give rise to housing action areas and general improvement areas under Part VIII of the Housing Act 1985, see its ss.239 ("the physical state of the housing accommodation in the area . . . and social conditions in the area") and 253 ("that living conditions in the area can most appropriately be improvement by the improvement of the amenities of the area or of dwellings in the area, or both . . .").

The breadth of the discretion, and indeed of the terminology, suggests that there will be little value in close, legalistic scrutiny of the wording, for even if, *e.g.* some intended effect does not qualify as "repair" or "improvement", or the mix of properties might be said to fall with difficulty into one or other branch of the (in any event inclusive) definition of "housing accommodation", it is likely that—leaving aside serious procedural error, non-comprehension of powers or absurdity or other abuse of powers—the courts will sustain a fairly broad approach to the Secretary of State's decision.

Nonetheless, at the end of the day, a fundamental misunderstanding of factual matters or refusal to consider the facts, will remain potentially reviewable: *Associated Provincial Picture Houses* v. *Wednesbury Corporation* [1948] 1 K.B. 223, C.A., *i.e.* "the *Wednesbury* test". See also *Secretary of State for Education and Science* v. *M.B. Tameside* [1977] A.C. 1014, H.L. ("If a judgment requires, before it can be made, the existence of some facts, then, although the evaluation of those facts is for the Secretary of State alone, the court must inquire whether those facts exist, and have been taken into account, whether the judgment has been made on a proper self direction as to those facts, whether the judgment has not been made on other facts which ought not to have been taken into account. If these requirements are not met, then the exercise of judgment, however bona fide it may be, becomes capable of challenge . . ." *per* Lord Wilberforce).

Subs. (2)

The area selected can comprise more than one area of land, which need not be contiguous nor need be in the district of the same local housing authority.

Consultation and publicity

61.—(1) Before making a designation order, the Secretary of State shall consult every local housing authority any part of whose district is to be included in the proposed designated area.

(2) Where the Secretary of State is considering a proposal to make a designation order, he shall use his best endeavours to secure that notice of the proposal is given to all tenants of houses in the area proposed to be designated who are either secure tenants or tenants of such description as may be prescribed by regulations.

(3) After having taken the action required by subsection (2) above, the Secretary of State shall either—

    (a) make arrangements for such independent persons as appear to him to be appropriate to conduct, in such manner as seems best to them, a ballot or poll of the tenants who have been given notice of the proposal as mentioned in that subsection with a view to establishing their opinions about the proposal to make a designation order; or

(b) if it seems appropriate to him to do so, arrange for the conduct of a ballot or poll of those tenants in such manner as appears to him best suited to establish their opinions about the proposal.

(4) If it appears from a ballot or poll conducted as mentioned in subsection (3) above that a majority of the tenants who, on that ballot or poll, express an opinion about the proposal to make the designation order are opposed to it, the Secretary of State shall not make the order proposed.

(5) The power to make regulations under subsection (2) above shall be exercisable by the Secretary of State by statutory instrument which shall be subject to annulment in pursuance of a resolution of either House of Parliament.

(6) Consultation undertaken before the passing of this Act shall constitute as effective compliance with subsection (1) above as if undertaken after that passing.

DEFINITIONS
"designation order": s.60.
"local housing authority": s.92.

GENERAL NOTE
This is a most important, indeed pivotal, section: it provides that before designating a housing action trust, there must be a ballot of the secure tenants (and any other tenants prescribed for the purposes of this section); the ballot may be independently commissioned, or carried out by the Secretary of State; if it appears from the ballot that a majority (of those who respond to it—*cf.* s.103(3) below, requiring that the majority must be of all those eligible to respond) is opposed to the proposals, the proposed H.A.T. cannot go ahead; in addition, the section requires consultation with local housing authorities in whose district the Trust is proposed (whether or not their own housing is involved).

Subss. (1), (6)
Whether or not their own housing is intended to be taken over by the H.A.T., the Secretary of State is bound to consult with *every* local housing authority any part of whose district is to be included in the proposed designation area, before making a designation order. He is also to take "such steps as appear to him best designed" to secure that the proposal to designate the area in question is brought to the notice of persons "appearing to him" to be likely to be affected by it. Consultation preceding the passing of the Act is to be treated as effective compliance.

There has been a number of cases on the meaning of consultation: see, *e.g. Rollo* v. *Minister of Town and Country Planning* [1948] L.J.R. 817, 1 All E.R. 13, *Re. Union of Benefices of Whippingham and East Cowes, St. James* [1954] A.C. 245, H.L., *Sinfield* v. *London Transport Executive* [1970] 1 Ch. 550, and *R.* v. *Sheffield City Council, ex p. Mansfield* (1978) 37 P. & C.R. 1. Most recently, the question was considered in relation to consultation on amendments to the Housing Benefits Regulations, as required by the Social Security and Housing Benefits Act 1982, s.36, in *R.* v. *Secretary of State for Social Services, ex p. Association of Metropolitan Authorities* (1985) 17 H.L.R. 487, Q.B.D. The importance of the case, and its apparent applicability to a number of instances in which consultation is required under this Act, suggest that it is worth considering the judgment in some detail.

(1) The essence of consultation is the communication of a genuine invitation to give advice and a genuine receipt of that advice; to achieve consultation, sufficient information must be supplied by the consulting to the consulted party to enable it to tender helpful advice; sufficient time must be given by the consulting to the consulted party to enable it to do so, and sufficient time must be available for such advice to be considered by the consulting party; sufficient in this context does not mean ample, but at least enough to enable the relevant purpose to be fulfilled; helpful advice in this context means sufficiently informed and considered information or advice about aspects of the form or substance of the implementation of the proposals, or their implication for the consulted party, being aspects material to the implementation of the proposals as to which the consulting party might not be fully informed or advised and as to which the party consulted might have relevant information or advice to offer.

(2) Where insufficient consultation is alleged, the challenge is to the vires of the subordinate legislation; accordingly, the correct test is whether there has been sufficient consultation, rather than whether the consultation process fails to satisfy the test known as "rationality", or the "unreasonable" test in *Association Provincial Picture Houses Ltd.* v. *Wednesbury Corporation* [1948] 1 K.B. 223, C.A.

(3) The power to make the regulations (under this section, the designation order) was conferred on the Secretary of State, and his is the duty to consult; both the form or substance of new regulations and the time allowed for consulting before making them, may well depend in whole or in part on matters of a political nature, as to the force or implications of which the Secretary of State rather than the court is the best judge; when considering whether or not consultation has in substance been carried out, the court should have regard not so much to the actual facts which preceded the making of the regulations, as to the material before the Secretary of State when he made the regulations, which material includes facts or information as it appeared or must have appeared to the Secretary of State acting in good faith, and any judgments made or opinions expressed to him before the making of the regulations about those facts which appeared or could have appeared to him to be reasonable.

(4) The urgency of the need for the regulations as seen by the Secretary of State *was* such, taking into account the nature of the amendments proposed, that the Department was entitled to require that views in response to its invitation for comments should be expressed quickly; the urgency of the need for the regulations, as seen by the Secretary of State, taking into account the nature of the amendments proposed, was *not* such that the Department was entitled to require views to be expressed within such a short period that those views would or might be insufficiently informed or insufficiently considered so that the applicants would or might be unable to tender helpful advice.

(5) Taking into account both the urgency of the matter, as seen by the Department, and the material features of the regulations, and bearing in mind that the applicants had no knowledge until after the regulations were made of one of their features, the Secretary of State had failed to fulfil his obligation to consult before making the regulations; the time allowed was so short, and the failure to provide amendments was such that, as the Department must have known even without imputing to them precise knowledge of the applicant association's internal arrangements for formulating a response, only piecemeal, and then only partial, assistance could be given.

(6) In the ordinary case, a decision made *ultra vires* is likely to be set aside; in the present case the applicants sought to strike down regulations which had become part of the public law of the land; it may be that when delegated legislation is held to be *ultra vires*, it is not necessarily to be regarded as normal practice to revoke the instrument. As a matter of pure discretion the Statutory Instrument would not be revoked for the following reasons: only one of the six associations which had been and habitually were consulted had applied for revocation, and that one applied only on the ground that it was not properly consulted; the regulations had been in force for about six months and authorities must have adapted themselves as best they could to the difficulties which had been imposed on them; if the regulations were revoked, all those who had been refused benefit because of them would be entitled to make fresh claims, and all authorities would be required to consider each such claim; the amendment regulations had been consolidated into new regulations, which had come into operation and which were not challenged.

In that case, the obligation to consult was considered mandatory, not directory: the same would seem to be true in the present case.

As regards "taking steps" to bring the proposed designation to the attention of those the Secretary of State considers "likely to be affected", the wording is such that a much greater discretion exists in practice because (a) it is for the Secretary of State to decide who is likely to be affected, and (b) for him to decide the steps "best designed" to secure that it is brought to their attention. Review, therefore, will be on normal principles (see notes to s.60(1), (4), (5), above), though clearly there must be *some* such steps, and there will be some people likely to be affected. Just who that is will depend on the proposed terms of the proposed order, *i.e.* what housing is in mind for transfer, in what area, and what other powers it is intended to confer upon the H.A.T.

Subss. (2)–(5)

It is these subsections, substituted for a successful, non-government amendment which succeeded in the House of Lords, which risk relegating this Part from one which might have proven a jewel in the government's housing policy crown (coronet?), to the backwaters of housing policy, for if there is a majority of tenants who respond to the ballot or poll who it "appears to" the Secretary of State are opposed to the H.A.T., there can be no designation order. While the Secretary of State has power to decide what classes of tenant may vote, this will be bound to include all or virtually all those who may be affected. The ballot or poll will be independently organised or conducted by the Secretary of State "if it seems appropriate to him to do so", with, therefore, a presumption in favour of independent ballot or poll.

Housing action trusts

62.—(1) Subject to subsection (2) below, where the Secretary of State makes a designation order, he shall, in that order or by a separate order, either—

(a) establish a housing action trust for the designated area; or

(b) specify as the housing action trust for the designated area a housing action trust already established for another designated area.

(2) Such a separate order as is referred to in subsection (1) above shall be made by statutory instrument but no such order shall be made unless a draft of it has been laid before, and approved by a resolution of, each House of Parliament.

(3) Subject to subsection (4) below, a housing action trust shall be a body corporate by such name as may be prescribed by the order establishing it.

(4) Where the Secretary of State makes the provision referred to in subsection (1)(b) above,—

(a) the housing action trust specified in the order shall, by virtue of the order, be treated as established for the new designated area (as well as for any designated area for which it is already established); and

(b) the order may alter the name of the trust to take account of the addition of the new designated area.

(5) Schedule 7 to this Act shall have effect with respect to the constitution of housing action trusts and Schedule 8 to this Act shall have effect with respect to their finances.

(6) It is hereby declared that a housing action trust is not to be regarded as the servant or agent of the Crown or as enjoying any status, immunity or privilege of the Crown and that the trust's property is not to be regarded as the property of, or property held on behalf of, the Crown.

(7) At the end of section 4 of the Housing Act 1985 (descriptions of authority) there shall be added—

"(f) "housing action trust" means a housing action trust established under Part III of the Housing Act 1988";

and at the end of section 14 of the Rent Act 1977 (landlord's interest belonging to local authority etc.) there shall be added—

"(h) a housing action trust established under Part III of the Housing Act 1988".

"designated area": s.60.
"designation order": s.60.
"housing action trust": s.60.

GENERAL NOTE
This section establishes the housing action trust for a particular area, which may be a new trust under the name given by the order, or an existing trust with an extended area of operation and, if needs be, a new name: subss. (1), (3), (4). The order establishing the trust may be the designation order itself, or a separate order, and in either event is by affirmative parliamentary procedure: subss. (1), (2). The H.A.T. will be a body corporate (subs. (3)), and is not to be regarded as the servant or agent of the Crown: subs. (6). By subs. (7), H.A.T.s are added as landlords whose tenants are disqualified from being protected tenants

under the Rent Act 1977. The constitution and financing of H.A.T.s is governed by Scheds. 7 and 8.

Sched. 7. There is to be a minimum of six, but a maximum of twelve, members of a housing action trust, including its chairman, and they are all appointed by the Secretary of State "from time to time". Members should include people who live in or have "special knowledge" of the H.A.T.'s designated area; the Secretary of State has to consult with the local housing authority before appointments.

The initial appointment will specify its period, though any member may resign membership, or the chairman—and, if one is appointed, deputy chairman—may similarly resign their offices. The Secretary of State has power to remove a member (including chairman or deputy chairman) for bankruptcy or making an arrangement with his creditors, absence from meetings without permission of the H.A.T. for a period of longer than three consecutive months, or otherwise for inability or unfitness to discharge functions, or unsuitability to continue as a member.

Members may be remunerated, and receive allowances, as determined by the Secretary of State with the approval of the Treasury, which may extend to pensions, gratuities and compensation on cessation of membership. The H.A.T. is to appoint a Chief Officer, but he or she requires the approval of the Secretary of State, who also has to approve the numbers of other employees. The H.A.T. is to determine the remuneration of employees, including its Chief Officer. The H.A.T. can also determine for itself what constitutes a quorum for a meeting, subject to any directions given by the Secretary of State. A member of the H.A.T. in receipt of remuneration is disqualified from becoming an M.P.

Sched. 8. The financial year of H.A.T.s runs from April 1. The financial duties of the H.A.T. are to be determined by the Secretary of State, after consultation with the trust and with the approval of the Treasury: these may be different for different trusts, and for different of the same trust's functions. Every determination is to be notified to the trust by the Secretary of State, and may be retrospective and contain incidental or supplementary provisions, and may be varied by a subsequent determination. The Secretary of State has power to make grants to the H.A.T., on terms if he so wishes, but in either case with the consent of the Treasury.

A housing action trust enjoys borrowing powers, temporary or long-term, either from the Secretary of State if in sterling, or subject to qualifications. Loans from the Secretary of State are out of the National Loans Fund. The Secretary of State in exercise of his lending responsibilities requires the approval of the Treasury. The Treasury may itself guarantee loans from persons or bodies other than the Secretary of State, but must inform Parliament if it does so: it will call on the Consolidated Fund in the event of a guarantee being called in.

If the H.A.T. acquires property hitherto held by or on behalf of the Crown, or by a company all of whose shares are held by or on behalf of the Crown or the wholly owned subsidiary of such, the Secretary of State may notify the H.A.T. of a corresponding "assumed debt", which is the aggregate of the consideration given when the property was first brought into public ownership, together with the costs and expenses of and incidental thereto, but with the approval of the Treasury, the Secretary of State may notify a higher sum if this would not reflect its true value. The assumed debt carries interest as notified.

If it appears to the Secretary of State, after consultation both with the H.A.T. and the Treasury, that the H.A.T. has a surplus—capital or revenue—he may direct the H.A.T. to pay it to him, after making allowance whether by transfer to reserves or otherwise for its future requirements. He may direct that such clawback may be treated as repayment of a debt from the H.A.T.

The Secretary of State, with the consent of the Treasury, shall specify by statutory instrument the maximum borrowing powers of a trust, defined to include not only borrowing but also sums which the Treasury has to pay in fulfilment of a guarantee to the trust. The statutory instrument requires an affirmative resolution of the House of Commons. The Secretary of State shall also prepare for each financial year an account of the sums paid to trusts, lent to trusts, received from trusts and paid into the Consolidated Fund or National Loans Fund by trusts, which accounts have to be examined, certified and reported on by the Comptroller and Auditor General, in such form as the Treasury may direct. H.A.T.s are within the National Audit Act 1983, s.6, which enables the Comptroller and Auditor General to examine their "economy, efficiency and effectiveness".

The trust has to keep proper accounts and ancillary and supporting records, which must show a true and fair view of its activities for each financial year, and must prepare a statement of accounts complying with the requirements of the Secretary of State (themselves requiring the consent of the Treasury), governing information, presentation and methods and principles on which the statement has been prepared. The Secretary of State shall appoint the trust's auditor, who shall not include a member, officer or employee of the trust or a partner or employee of a member, officer or employee of the trust, or a body corporate, and must be qualified within s.389 of the Companies Act 1985.

In addition, the trust has to make to the Secretary of State a report dealing generally with its operations, and a trust must provide the Secretary of State with such information in relation to its activities as he may require, and permit a person authorised by the Secretary of State to inspect and make copies of the accounts, books, documents or its papers, and afford such explanation of them as the appointee or the Secretary of State may reasonably require.

Objects and general powers of housing action trusts

63.—(1) The primary objects of a housing action trust in relation to the designated area for which it is established shall be—

  (a) to secure the repair or improvement of housing accommodation for the time being held by the trust;

  (b) to secure the proper and effective management and use of that housing accommodation;

  (c) to encourage diversity in the interests by virtue of which housing accommodation in the area is occupied and, in the case of accommodation which is occupied under tenancies, diversity in the identity of the landlords; and

  (d) generally to secure or facilitate the improvement of living conditions in the area and the social conditions and general environment of the area.

(2) Without prejudice to subsection (1) above, a housing action trust may—

  (a) provide and maintain housing accommodation; and

  (b) facilitate the provision of shops, advice centres and other facilities for the benefit of the community or communities who live in the designated area.

(3) For the purpose of achieving its objects and exercising the powers conferred on it by subsection (2) above, a housing action trust may—

  (a) acquire, hold, manage, reclaim and dispose of land and other property;

  (b) carry out building and other operations;

  (c) seek to ensure the provision of water, electricity, gas, sewerage and other services; and

  (d) carry on any business or undertaking;

and may generally do anything necessary or expedient for the purposes of those objects and powers or for purposes incidental thereto.

(4) For the avoidance of doubt it is hereby declared that subsection (3) above relates only to the capacity of a housing action trust as a statutory corporation; and nothing in this section authorises such a trust to disregard any enactment or rule of law.

(5) Section 71 of the Race Relations Act 1976 (local authorities: general statutory duty) shall apply to a housing action trust as it applies to a local authority.

(6) A transaction between any person and a housing action trust shall not be invalidated by reason of any failure by the trust to observe the objects in subsection (1) above or the requirement that the trust shall exercise the powers conferred by subsections (2) and (3) above for the purpose referred to in that subsection.

DEFINITIONS
  "designated area": s.60.
  "housing accommodation": s.92.
  "housing action trust": s.60.

This section sets out the primary objects and principal powers of the H.A.T., though—expressly—subs. (5) declares that a transaction is not to be treated as invalid, *i.e. ultra vires*, because of a failure to observe the objects or exercise the powers for their stated purposes. This is not to suggest that their activities will not be judicially reviewable: the H.A.T. is a creature of statute and, as such, its activities are in principle susceptible to judicial review; all that subs. (6) achieves is the integrity of *ultra vires* transactions, *i.e.* they will not be treated as void.

The primary objects are set out in subs. (1). "Proper and effective management and use" is a term also (see notes to s.60(1), (4), (5), above) derived from the Housing Act 1985, s.243 (housing action areas). The most controversial object is to encourage diversity in the identity of landlords, which can be achieved either by disposal (see subs. (3) and s.79, below) and/or by use of their grant-aid/financial assistance powers in s.71, below.

Their principal powers are to provide and maintain housing, and to facilitate the provision of shops, advice centres and other such facilities for the benefit of the community or communities in their areas, not merely those living in their accommodation. They accordingly enjoy power to acquire, hold, manage, reclaim and dispose of land and other property, carry out building and other operations, seek to ensure the provision of utilities and similar services and carry on "any" business or undertaking, together with a general ancillary power (*cf.* Local Government Act 1972, s.111) to do anything "necessary or expedient" for the purposes of the objects and powers or purposes incidental thereto: subs. (3).

Subs. (5)
See notes to s.56, above.

Subs. (6)
This subsection is effective to overturn the decision in *Rhyl U.D.C.* v. *Rhyl Amusements* [1959] 1 W.L.R. 465, in which was held that an *ultra vires* disposal of land by a local authority was void; see also *Minister of Agriculture and Fisheries* v. *Matthews* [1950] 1 K.B. 148, C.A.

The housing action trust's proposals for its area

64.—(1) As soon as practicable after a housing action trust has been established for a designated area, the trust shall prepare a statement of its proposals with regard to the exercise of its functions in the area.

(2) The trust shall consult every local housing authority or county council, any part of whose area lies within the designated area, with regard to the proposals contained in the statement prepared under subsection (1) above.

(3) A housing action trust shall take such steps as it considers appropriate to secure—

(a) that adequate publicity is given in the designated area to the proposals contained in the statement prepared under subsection (1) above;

(b) that those who live in the designated area are made aware that they have an opportunity to make, within such time as the trust may specify, representations to the trust with respect to those proposals; and

(c) that those who live in the designated area are given an adequate opportunity of making such representations;

and the trust shall consider any such representations as may be made within the time specified.

(4) As soon as may be after a housing action trust has complied with the requirements of subsections (1) to (3) above it shall send to the Secretary of State a copy of the statement prepared under subsection (1) above together with a report of—

(a) the steps the trust has taken to consult as mentioned in subsection (2) above and to secure the matters referred to in subsection (3) above; and

(b) the consideration it has given to points raised in the course of consultation and to representations received.

(5) At such times as a housing action trust considers appropriate or as it may be directed by the Secretary of State, the trust shall prepare a further statement of its proposals with regard to the exercise of its functions in its area; and subsections (2) to (4) above shall again apply as they applied in relation to the first statement.

DEFINITIONS
"designated area": s.60.
"housing action trust": s.60.
"local housing authority": s.92.

GENERAL NOTE
The first job of the H.A.T. is to prepare a statement of its proposals for the exercise of its functions (*cf.* the following sections as to what these may include) in its area, and to consult on them with every local housing authority, and county council, any part of whose area lies within its area (regardless of whether or not proposals and/or powers contemplate transfer of public stock to the H.A.T.): as to consultation, see notes to s.61, above. The H.A.T. also has to take such steps as *it* considers appropriate to give adequate publicity to the proposals in the designated area, and to enable the area's inhabitants to make proposals and to consider them: subs. (3). The duty to consider representations thus made, though spelled out here, is in any event implied: see notes to s.61, above. The trust has to report to the Secretary of State on the outcome of the consultation exercise, when it sends him the statement of proposals.

Subs. (4)
New proposals may be drawn up at the trust's discretion, or on the directions of the Secretary of State, in which case the consultation exercises must again be carried out.

Functions

Housing action trust as housing authority etc.

65.—(1) If the Secretary of State so provides by order, in a designated area or, as the case may be, in such part of the area as may be specified in the order, the housing action trust for the area shall have such of the functions described in subsection (2) below as may be so specified.

(2) The functions referred to in subsection (1) above are—

    (a) the functions conferred on a local housing authority by Parts II, VI, VII and IX to XII and XVI of the Housing Act 1985 and section 3(1) of the Chronically Sick and Disabled Persons Act 1970;

    (b) the functions conferred by Part II of the Housing Associations Act 1985 on a local authority, within the meaning of that Act; and

    (c) the functions conferred by sections 39 to 41 of the Land Compensation Act 1973 on the authority which is "the relevant authority" for the purposes of section 39 of that Act.

(3) As respects the designated area or part thereof to which an order under this section applies, on the coming into force of the order, any function conferred on a housing action trust by the order shall, according to the terms of the order, be exercisable either—

    (a) by the trust instead of by the authority by which, apart from the order, the function would be exercisable; or

    (b) by the trust concurrently with that authority.

(4) Any enactment under which a housing action trust is to exercise a function by virtue of an order under this section shall have effect—

    (a) in relation to the trust, and

(b) where the trust is to have the function concurrently with another authority, in relation to that authority,

subject to such modifications (if any) as may be specified in the order.

(5) Where a housing action trust is to exercise functions conferred on a local housing authority by any of Parts VI, VII, IX and XI of the Housing Act 1985, section 36 of the Local Government Act 1974 (recovery by local authorities of establishment charges) shall apply to the housing action trust as if it were a local authority within the meaning of that section.

(6) Such (if any) of the provisions of Parts XVII and XVIII of the Housing Act 1985 (compulsory purchase, land acquisition and general provisions) as may be specified in an order under this section shall have effect in relation to a housing action trust subject to such modifications as may be specified in the order.

(7) An order under this section—

    (a) may contain such savings and transitional and supplementary provisions as appear to the Secretary of State to be appropriate; and

    (b) shall be made by statutory instrument which shall be subject to annulment in pursuance of a resolution of either House of Parliament.

DEFINITIONS

"designated area": s.60.
"local authority": s.92.
"local housing authority": s.92.

GENERAL NOTE

This is the first of the sections which introduces the idea that, in their areas, H.A.T.s may be given the powers of the local authority of the area, either concurrently with the authority or instead of the authority, depending on the terms of the designation order (subs. (3)); the provisions thus conferred may take effect as amended by the designation order, and will be subject to such modifications concerning the trust itself as the order may specify, and—if the trust is to enjoy concurrent jurisdiction—so far as the authority are concerned: subs. (4).

The functions are:

    (a) *Housing Act 1985, Part II*: the general power to provide, manage, rent, and with consent sell, housing; it may be noted that there is no power to confer homelessness responsibilities under Part III of the 1985 Act on H.A.T.s, even if Part II power is transferred to them to the exclusion of the local authority, although H.A.T.s are now (s.70, below) added to the list of bodies who must afford authorities with homelessness responsibilities "co-operation", such as is "reasonable in the circumstances" under the Housing Act 1985, s.72;

    (b) *Housing Act 1985, Part VI*: the power to serve repairs notices on houses which are unfit for human habitation, or in serious disrepair, or in such disrepair as to interfere with the comfort of an occupying tenant, and which can be repaired at a reasonable expense; until the terms of the orders are seen, it is unclear to what extent this may render a local authority's own stock vulnerable to such notices, where they are not currently *normally* so vulnerable, *not* because the landlord is a local authority, but in effect because the landlord authority will normally be the enforcing authority and as such cannot serve a notice upon themselves—see *R.* v. *Cardiff C.C., ex p. Cross* (1982) 6 H.L.R. 6, C.A.

    Where a house is unfit, it is mandatory to order its repair if possible at a reasonable expense, or else to use slum clearance powers under the 1985 Act, Part IX: *R.* v. *Kerrier D.C., ex p. Guppys (Bridport) Ltd* (1977) 32 P. & C.R. 411, C.A. Again, this might now bring much local authority stock hitherto outwith Part IX orders on the *Cross* principle within it; though, again, how this would work if Part VI, but *not* Part IX powers are given to the trust is unclear. The *Cross* principle may also work to make H.A.T.'s immune from service of notices where the power to serve notices is completely transferred to them, rather than concurrently.

    (c) *Housing Act 1985, Part VII*: the relatively little used power to serve compulsory improvement notices;

(d) *Housing Act 1985, Part IX*: slum clearance, *i.e.* proceedings either to close or demolish (or otherwise secure the non-use or non-permanent use of) unfit individual houses not repairable at a reasonable expense, or clearance area action—see also notes to (b), above;

(e) *Housing Act 1985, Part X*: the overcrowding laws—see also notes to (b), above, but *cf.* the 1985 Act, s.339, requiring the consent of the Attorney-General before the authority itself can be prosecuted. This would seem to mean *the* enforcing authority, so that if a trust has the relevant powers to transferred to it, it could then prosecute the local housing authority;

(f) *Housing Act 1985, Part XI*: powers to regulate the use of properties as houses in multiple occupation, to enforce minimum standards in them, to impose the management regulations and also to take them over by control orders—see also notes to (b), above;

(g) *Housing Act 1985, Part XII*: the provisions regulating common lodging-houses, formerly contained in the Public Health Act 1936;

(h) *Housing Act 1985, Part XVI*: formerly the Housing Defects Act 1984, this Part imposes responsibilities to compensate, or repurchase and rehouse, the purchasers of dwellings defective in design or construction, primarily "system-built" housing;

(i) *Chronically Sick and Disabled Persons Act 1970, Section 3(1)*: When considering the housing conditions in their districts, and the need for further housing accommodation, under the Housing Act 1985, s.8 (a duty which may now pass to a trust: see (a), above), local housing authorities are bound to have regard to the special needs of chronically sick and disabled persons;

(j) *Housing Associations Act 1985, Part II*: Under ss.58–61, local housing authorities have powers to assist housing associations (in certain circumstances, only if the association is registered with the Housing Corporation or, now, Housing for Wales—see notes to s.46, above)—and to provide furniture to housing association tenants;

(k) *Land Compensation Act 1973, ss.39–41*: these are the provisions which govern the rehousing of residential occupiers who are displaced by certain classes of action which the H.A.T. may be empowered to take under one of the provisions above-mentioned; it is striking that the duty to make home loss payments under *ibid.*, s.29 and/or disturbance payments under *ibid.*, s.37, does not also pass.

In addition, some or all of the compulsory purchase provisions of Part XVII of the 1985 Act may be applied by the designation order, as may some or all of the general provisions of Part XVIII.

Planning control

66.—(1) A housing action trust may submit to the Secretary of State proposals for the development of land within its designated area and the Secretary of State, after consultation with the local planning authority within whose area the land is situated and with any other local authority which appears to him to be concerned, may approve any such proposals either with or without modification.

(2) Without prejudice to the generality of the powers conferred by section 24 of the 1971 Act, a special development order made by the Secretary of State under that section with respect to a designated area may grant permission for any development of land in accordance with proposals approved under subsection (1) above, subject to such conditions, if any (including conditions requiring details of any proposed development to be submitted to the local planning authority), as may be specified in the order.

(3) The Secretary of State shall give to a housing action trust such directions with regard to the disposal of land held by it and with respect to the development by it of such land as appear to him to be necessary or expedient for securing, so far as practicable, the preservation of any features of special architectural or historical interest and, in particular, of any buildings included in any list compiled or approved or having effect as if compiled or approved under section 54(1) of the 1971 Act (which

relates to the compilation or approval by the Secretary of State of lists of buildings of special architectural or historical interest).

(4) Any reference in this section to the local planning authority,—

    (a) in relation to land in Greater London or a metropolitan county, is a reference to the authority which is the local planning authority as ascertained in accordance with section 1 of the 1971 Act; and

    (b) in relation to other land, is a reference to the district planning authority and also (in relation to proposals for any development which is a county matter, as defined in paragraph 32 of Schedule 16 to the Local Government Act 1972) to the county planning authority.

DEFINITIONS

"designated area": s.60.
"housing action trust": s.60.
"local authority": s.92.
"local planning authority": subs. (4).

GENERAL NOTE

This is the first of two sections which concern the application of planning law to housing action trusts. The local housing authority will be a planning authority and, under the Town and Country Planning Act 1971, will accordingly enjoy power to approve or reject planning proposals by the H.A.T. which constitute "development" within s.22 of the 1971 Act (see notes to s.28, above). This will of course be subject to the possibility of appeal against refusal to the Secretary of State, or against the grant of permission to which (unacceptable) conditions have been attached: the 1971 Act, s.36. In addition, the Secretary of State defines by development orders development for which no planning consent is needed, or consent is only needed in specified circumstances. Development orders are either *general* (applicable to all land) or *special* (applicable only to land as prescribed by the order): the 1971 Act, s.24.

Under this section, the H.A.T. may submit development proposals directly to the Secretary of State who may, after consultation both with the local planning authority in whose area the land is situated and any other local authority which appears to him to be concerned, approve the proposals with or without modification: subs. (1). As to consultation, see notes to s.56, above. Additionally, the Secretary of State may grant planning permission by means of a special development order, subject to such conditions (if any) as the order may specify, which may include conditions requiring details of the development to be submitted to the local planning authority.

Subs. (3)

Special provisions apply in planning and indeed in housing law to buildings of special architectural or historic interest, commonly referred to as "listed buildings", under the Town and Country Planning Act 1971, s.54. This subsection permits the Secretary of State to give specific directions, including to dispose of land and to develop land, as appear to him necessary or expedient to secure the preservation of features of special architectural or historical interest, in particular those which are within a s.54 list, or have effect as if listed, *i.e.* a building subject to a building preservation notice imposed by a district planning authority as a temporary measure while application is made for listing (the 1971 Act, s.58).

Subs. (4)

The local planning authority under this section will be the district council in a metropolitan or non-Metropolitan area and a London borough council, but includes a non-metropolitan county council in relation to "county matters" as defined in the Local Government Act 1972, Sched. 16, para. 32 (minerals, aggregates, cement manufacture, operations in National Parks, and prescribed uses and operations). The metropolitan county councils were abolished by the Local Government Act 1985.

Housing action trust as planning authority

67.—(1) If the Secretary of State so provides by order, for such purposes of Part III of the 1971 Act and in relation to such kinds of development as may be specified in the order, a housing action trust shall be the local planning authority for the whole or such part as may be so specified of its designated area in place of any authority which would otherwise be the local planning authority.

(2) An order under subsection (1) above may provide—

(a) that any enactment relating to local planning authorities shall not apply to the trust; and

(b) that any such enactment which applies to the trust shall apply to it subject to such modifications as may be specified in the order.

(3) An order made by the Secretary of State may provide—

(a) that, subject to any modifications specified in the order, a housing action trust specified in the order shall have, in the whole or any part of its designated area and in place of any authority (except the Secretary of State) which would otherwise have them, such of the functions conferred by Parts IV, V and XV of the 1971 Act as may be so specified; and

(b) that such of the provisions of Part IX and sections 212 and 214 of the 1971 Act as are mentioned in the order shall have effect, in relation to the housing action trust specified in the order and to land in the trust's area, subject to the modifications there specified.

(4) An order under subsection (3) above may provide that, for the purposes of any of the provisions specified in the order, any enactment relating to local planning authorities shall apply to the housing action trust specified in the order subject to such modifications as may be so specified.

(5) In relation to a housing action trust which, by virtue of an order under subsection (1) above, is the local planning authority for the whole or part of its area, section 270 of the 1971 Act (application to local planning authorities of provisions as to planning control and enforcement) shall have effect for the purposes of Part III of the 1971 Act prescribed by that order, and in relation to the kinds of development so prescribed, as if—

(a) in subsection (1) the reference to the development by local authorities of land in respect of which they are the local planning authorities included a reference to the development by the trust of land in respect of which it is the local planning authority;

(b) in subsection (2),—

(i) in paragraph (a) for the words "such an authority" there were substituted "housing action trust" and for the words "local planning authority" there were substituted "housing action trust"; and

(ii) in paragraph (b) for the words "local planning authority" there were substituted "housing action trust".

(6) If, by virtue of an order under subsection (1) above, a housing action trust is the local planning authority in relation to all kinds of development for the whole or part of its area, it shall be the hazardous substances authority for that area or, as the case may be, that part for the purposes of the 1971 Act.

(7) Any power to make an order under this section shall be exercisable by statutory instrument which shall be subject to annulment in pursuance of a resolution of either House of Parliament; and any such order shall have effect subject to such savings and transitional provisions as may be specified in the order.

DEFINITIONS
"designated area": s.60.
"housing action trust": s.60.

GENERAL NOTE

This is the second section which deals specifically with planning law. Under this section, the Secretary of State may constitute the housing action trust as *the* local planning authority for specified classes of development, for the purposes of the Town and Country Planning Act 1971, so that, in substance, all applications in the area of those classes have to be made to them instead of to the district council or London borough council (subs. (1)). The order may either exempt the H.A.T. from planning obligations which are usually imposed on local planning authorities, or modify such enactments: subs. (2).

Subss. (3), (4)

In the alternative or additionally, the Secretary of State may confer on the H.A.T. specified functions contained in Parts IV, V and XV of the 1971 Act, to the exclusion of any other authority (save the Secretary of State himself), subject to such modifications as the order may specify, and may apply to the H.A.T. such provisions of Part IX and ss.212 and 214 of the 1971 Act, as may be specified, again subject to modifications: subs. (3). Modification in such an order extends to power to modify the enactments themselves so far as they relate to the H.A.T.: subs. (4).

Part IV of the 1971 Act deals with "additional controls in special cases," *i.e.* buildings of special architectural or historic interest, hazardous substances (see also subs. (6)), trees, advertisements. Part V deals with enforcement of control. Part XV is "miscellaneous and general". Part IX contains the provisions which in some circumstances enable an owner who is refused planning permission to require the planning authority to purchase his interest, including a blight notice. S.212 permits a local planning authority to close a road to traffic. S.214 permits extinction of public rights of way.

Subs. (5)

If an order is made under subs. (1) transferring to the H.A.T. the functions of the planning authority, s.270 of the Town and Country Planning Act 1971 has effect as amended by this subsection. S.270 governs "deemed planning applications", *i.e.* the effect of the Act on an authority's own developments.

Subs. (6)

If the H.A.T. is constituted the local planning authority in an area *without qualification*, *i.e.* in respect of *all* development, it *must* then be deemed the hazardous substances authority for that area.

Public health

68.—(1) The Secretary of State may by order provide that, in relation to premises comprising or consisting of housing accommodation, a housing action trust shall have in its designated area (or in such part of its designated area as may be specified in the order) the functions conferred on a local authority—

(a) by sections 83 and 84 of the Public Health Act 1936 (the "1936 Act") and section 36 of the Public Health Act 1961 (all of which relate to filthy or verminous premises or articles);

(b) by any enactment contained in Part III (nuisances and offensive trades) of the 1936 Act;

(c) by so much of Part XII of the 1936 Act as relates to any of the enactments mentioned in paragraphs (a) and (b) above; and

(d) by Part I of the Prevention of Damage by Pests Act 1949 (rats and mice).

(2) On the order coming into force, the trust shall have the functions conferred in relation to the designated area (or part) instead of or concurrently with any such authority, depending on the terms of the order.

(3) The order may provide that any enactment under which the trust is to exercise functions by virtue of the order shall have effect in relation to the trust and, where the trust is to have any function concurrently with another authority, in relation to that authority, as modified by the order.

(4) Where an order under this section provides that a housing action trust shall have the functions conferred upon a local authority by Part III

of the 1936 Act, section 36 of the Local Government Act 1974 (recovery
by local authorities of establishment charges) shall apply to the housing
action trust as if it were a local authority within the meaning of that
section.

(5) The order shall have effect subject to such savings and transitional
and supplementary provisions as may be specified in the order.

(6) The power to make an order under this section shall be exercisable
by statutory instrument which shall be subject to annulment in pursuance
of a resolution of either House of Parliament.

DEFINITIONS
"designated area": s.60.
"housing accommodation": s.92.
"housing action trust": s.60.

GENERAL NOTE
This section permits the Secretary of State to confer on a housing action trust specified
public health functions of a local authority, in their application to housing, either concurrently
with or instead of the local authority (which will normally be the district council or London
borough council: Public Health Act 1936, s.1). The order can modify provisions so far as
they affect the H.A.T. itself or, where there is to be concurrent jurisdiction with the local
authority, so far as they affect that authority.
The provisions are:
    (1) *Public Health Act 1936, ss.83, 84, and Public Health Act 1961, s.36.* The 1936
        Act provisions allow the authority to serve notice on an owner or occupier to
        take steps to remedy by cleansing and disinfecting premises (including if
        necessary by gas attack) which are in such a filthy or unwholesome condition as
        to be prejudicial to health, or are verminous, or by themselves cleansing,
        purifying, disinfecting or destroying articles in premises which are so filthy as to
        render such action necessary to prevent injury, or danger of injury, to the health
        of persons in the premises, or which is verminous, *e.g.* furniture. The H.A.T.
        cannot, however, undertake the cleansing of a verminous person or his clothing
        (by consent or with an order of the magistrates' court) under the 1936 Act, s.85.
        S.36 of the 1961 Act governs vacation of premises for the purposes of carrying
        out a gas attack.
    (2) *Public Health Act 1936, Part III.* This is the principal part of the Public Health
        Act 1936 which concerns bad housing conditions in general. It contains provisions
        for dealing with premises which are a "statutory nuisance", *i.e.* prejudicial to
        health or a nuisance. To qualify as a nuisance, rather than "merely" prejudicial
        to health, the source of the problem must be in premises (or, *e.g.* common
        parts) *other than* those where the effect is suffered: *National Coal Board* v.
        Thorne [1976] 1 W.L.R. 543, D.C.
            The provisions permit the authority to require abatement of the statutory
        nuisance, or to prevent its recurrence, and prosecution in default of compliance,
        but a person aggrieved can himself take proceedings, including against an
        authority (*R.* v. *Epping (Waltham Forest) Justices, ex p. Birlinson* [1948] 1 K.B.
        79): the 1936 Act, s.99. The Public Health Act 1961 and the Public Health
        (Recurring Nuisances) Act 1969, contain additional measures for tackling sta-
        tutory nuisance, including (1961 Act) a special "speedy" procedure, but these
        powers are not amongst those which can be conferred on the H.A.T.
    (3) *Public Health Act 1936, Part XII.* This contains general ancillary provisions,
        including as to enforcement.
    (4) *Prevention of Damage by Pests Act 1949, Part I.*
In all cases, however, the powers are confined to use in relation to housing accommodation:
see notes to s.60, above.

Highways

69.—(1) When any street works have been executed in a private street
(or part of a private street) in a designated area, the housing action trust
may serve a notice on the street works authority requiring it to declare
the street (or part) to be a highway which for the purposes of the
Highways Act 1980 is a highway maintainable at the public expense.

(2) Within the period of two months beginning on the date of the service of a notice under subsection (1) above, the street works authority may appeal against the notice to the Secretary of State on grounds relating to all or any of the following matters—
(a) the construction of the street (or part);
(b) its design;
(c) its layout; and
(d) the state of its maintenance.

(3) After considering any representations made to him by the housing action trust and the street works authority, the Secretary of State shall determine an appeal under subsection (2) above by setting aside or confirming the notice under subsection (1) above (with or without modifications).

(4) Where, under subsection (3) above, the Secretary of State confirms a notice,—
(a) he may at the same time impose conditions (including financial conditions) upon the housing action trust with which the trust must comply in order for the notice to take effect, and
(b) the highway (or part) shall become a highway maintainable at the public expense with effect from such date as the Secretary of State may specify.

(5) Where a street works authority neither complies with the notice under subsection (1) above, nor appeals under subsection (2) above, the street (or part) concerned shall become a highway maintainable at the public expense upon the expiry of the period of two months referred to in subsection (2) above.

(6) In this section "private street" and "street works authority" have the same meanings as in Part XI of the Highways Act 1980.

DEFINITIONS
"designated area": s.60.
"housing action trust": s.60.
"private street": subs. (6).
"street works authority": subs. (6).

GENERAL NOTE
This permits the H.A.T. to apply to the local authority with responsibility for highways to declare a street on which works have been executed in its area to be a public highway, maintainable at the public expense, and makes provision for appeal to the Secretary of State against a refusal, on terms should he think fit.

Co-operation on homelessness between local housing authorities and housing action trusts

70. In paragraph (a) of section 72 of the Housing Act 1985 (which provides that, on a request by a local housing authority for assistance in the discharge of certain statutory functions relating to homelessness, or threatened homelessness, a body of a description specified in the paragraph shall co-operate in rendering such assistance as is reasonable in the circumstances) after the words "a registered housing association" there shall be inserted "a housing action trust"; and in the words following paragraph (c) of that section after the word "authority" there shall be inserted "or other body".

DEFINITION
"housing action trust": s.60.

GENERAL NOTE
Responsibility for the homeless under Part III of the Housing Act 1985, remains with the local housing authority, *even although the power to provide housing may pass to an H.A.T.*

to the exclusion of that authority, under s.65, above. During passage of the Bill through Parliament, this minor concession was introduced. It means no more than that if the local housing authority ask the H.A.T. to "assist them in the discharge of their functions" under Part III, the H.A.T. shall "co-operate in rendering such assistance in the discharge of the functions to which the request relates as is reasonable in the circumstances".

Note, however, that the phraseology used is not "as the H.A.T. (or other public body within s.72) consider reasonable", but as *is* reasonable, which suggests that judicial intervention may more easily be forthcoming than in relation to a challenge to the authority's own decisions under Part III, where the language used is "are of the opinion that", "are satisfied that" or "have reason to believe that"—*cf. R.* v. *London Borough of Hillingdon, ex p. Puhlhofer* [1986] A.C. 484, 18 H.L.R. 158, H.L. and *Cocks* v. *Thanet D.C.* [1983] A.C. 286, 6 H.L.R. 15, H.L.; compare also *R.* v. *City of Westminster, ex p. Tansey* (1988) 20 H.L.R. 520, held on appeal to amount to no more than *obiter* ((1988) 21 H.L.R. forthcoming), and *R.* v. *London Borough of Camden, ex p. Gillan* (1988) 21 H.L.R.

Power to give financial assistance

71.—(1) For the purpose of achieving its objects a housing action trust may, with the consent of the Secretary of State, give financial assistance to any person.

(2) Financial assistance under subsection (1) above may be given in any form and, in particular, may be given by way of—

    (a) grants,

    (b) loans,

    (c) guarantees,

    (d) incurring expenditure for the benefit of the person assisted, or

    (e) purchasing loan or share capital in a company.

(3) Financial assistance under subsection (1) above may be given on such terms as the housing action trust, with the consent of the Secretary of State, considers appropriate.

(4) Any consent under this section—

    (a) may be given either unconditionally or subject to conditions; and

    (b) may be given in relation to a particular case or in relation to such description of cases as may be specified in the consent;

and the reference in subsection (3) above to the consent of the Secretary of State is a reference to his consent given with the approval of the Treasury.

(5) The terms referred to in subsection (3) above may, in particular, include provision as to—

    (a) the circumstances in which the assistance must be repaid or otherwise made good to the housing action trust and the manner in which that is to be done; or

    (b) the circumstances in which the housing action trust is entitled to recover the proceeds or part of the proceeds of any disposal of land or buildings in respect of which assistance was provided.

(6) Any person receiving assistance under subsection (1) above shall comply with the terms on which it is given and compliance may be enforced by the housing action trust.

DEFINITION

"housing action trust": s.60.

GENERAL NOTE

This is the first of the particular substantive provisions, describing the powers of a housing action trust. The powers to provide financial assistance are very wide indeed (subs. (2)), but in all cases the consent of the Secretary of State is required (subs. (1)), and terms can only attach with his consent (subs. (3)), which itself may be unconditional or subject to conditions, and which may be given generally or specifically (subs. (4)). Terms may include repayment or recovery in specified circumstances: subs. (5). The H.A.T. may enforce terms (subs. (6)).

Note that persons who may be assisted do not need to be within the H.A.T.'s area, nor necessarily is assistance confined to activity within its area. Of course, a grant or other assistance with no relation to activity with the area would be *ultra vires*, because it would not be in pursuit of the purposes or discharge of the general functions under s.63, above. However, assistance might, *e.g.* be to a company with an office outside the designated area, and might be of an order which enables the company to do something within the area, even although there is not a direct cash nexus between assistance and activity.

Directions as to exercise of functions

72.—(1) In the exercise of its functions, a housing action trust shall comply with any directions given by the Secretary of State.

(2) Directions given by the Secretary of State may be of a general or particular character and may be varied or revoked by subsequent directions.

(3) The Secretary of State shall publish any direction given under this section.

(4) A transaction between any person and a housing action trust acting in purported exercise of its powers under this Part of this Act shall not be void by reason only that the transaction was carried out in contravention of a direction given under this section; and a person dealing with a housing action trust shall not be concerned to see or enquire whether a direction under this section has been given or complied with.

DEFINITION
"housing action trust": s.60.

GENERAL NOTE
Housing action trusts must comply with the directions of the Secretary of State, which may be general or specific, and which may be varied or revoked by subsequent directions.

Subs. (4)
Because a housing action trust is a public body, its powers are circumscribed by statute, and activities will therefore be void if outside its powers, see *Rhyl U.D.C.* v. *Rhyl Amusements* [1959] 1 W.L.R. 465, in which was held that an *ultra vires* disposal of land by a local authority was void; see also *Minister of Agriculture and Fisheries* v. *Matthews* [1950] 1 K.B. 148, C.A. This subsection follows the convention (see, *e.g.* Local Government Act 1972, s.128, Town and Country Planning Act 1959, s.29) that persons dealing with a public body are not concerned to enquire into the validity of transactions and that transactions are not void for want of compliance with a specific provision, such as, here compliance with a direction of the Secretary of State.

Transfer of functions

73.—(1) If, in the case of any designated area, it appears to the Secretary of State that it is expedient that the functions of a housing action trust established for the area should be transferred—

(a) to the housing action trust established for another designated area, or

(b) to a new housing action trust to be established for the area, he may by order provide for the dissolution of the first-mentioned trust and for the transfer of its functions, property, rights and liabilities to the trust referred to in paragraph (a) above, or, as the case may be, to a new housing action trust established for the area by the order.

(2) Where an order under this section provides for the functions of a housing action trust established for a designated area to be transferred to the housing action trust established for another designated area—

(a) the latter trust shall, by virtue of the order, be treated as established for the first-mentioned designated area (as well as the area referred to in subsection (1)(a) above); and

(b) the order may alter the name of the latter trust in such manner as appears to the Secretary of State to be expedient.

(3) Before making an order under this section the Secretary of State shall consult the housing action trust whose functions are to be transferred and also, in a case falling within subsection (1)(a) above, the housing action trust to whom the functions are to be transferred.

(4) An order under this section shall be made by statutory instrument but no such order shall be made unless a draft of it has been laid before, and approved by a resolution of, each House of Parliament.

DEFINITIONS
  "designated area": s.60.
  "housing action trust": s.60.

GENERAL NOTE
This section permits the Secretary of State, after consultation with the H.A.T.s involved, by order to dissolve one H.A.T. and transfer its functions, property, rights and liabilities either to a new H.A.T. or to the H.A.T. for another area (possibly with a name change), if it appears expedient to him to do so.

Transfer of housing accommodation etc.

Transfer of land and other property to housing action trusts

74.—(1) The Secretary of State may by order provide for the transfer from a local housing authority to a housing action trust of—

(a) all or any of the authority's local authority housing situated in the designated area; and

(b) any other land held or provided in connection with that local authority housing.

(2) Without prejudice to the powers under subsection (1) above, if in the opinion of the Secretary of State a housing action trust requires for the purposes of its functions any land which, though not falling within that subsection, is situated in the designated area and held (for whatever purpose) by a local authority, the Secretary of State may by order provide for the transfer of that land to the trust.

(3) The Secretary of State may by order transfer from a local housing authority or other local authority to a housing action trust so much as appears to him to be appropriate of any property which is held or used by the authority in connection with any local authority housing or other land transferred to the trust under subsection (1) or subsection (2) above; and for this purpose "property" includes chattels of any description and rights and liabilities, whether arising by contract or otherwise.

(4) A transfer of any local authority housing or other land or property under the preceding provisions of this section shall be on such terms, including financial terms, as the Secretary of State thinks fit; and an order under this section may provide that, notwithstanding anything in section 141 of the Law of Property Act 1925 (rent and benefit of lessee's covenants to run with the reversion), any rent or other sum which—

(a) arises under a tenancy of any local authority housing or other land transferred to the housing action trust under subsection (1) or subsection (2) above, and

(b) falls due before the date of the transfer,

shall continue to be recoverable by the local housing authority or, as the case may be, the local authority to the exclusion of the trust and of any other person in whom the reversion on the tenancy may become vested.

(5) Without prejudice to the generality of subsection (4) above, the financial terms referred to in that subsection may include provision for payments by a local authority (as well as or instead of payments to a local

authority); and the transfer from a local housing authority or other local authority of any local authority housing or other land or property by virtue of this section shall not be taken to give rise to any right to compensation.

(6) Where an order is made under this section—

    (a) payments made by a local authority as mentioned in subsection (5) above shall be prescribed expenditure for the purposes of Part VIII of the Local Government, Planning and Land Act 1980 (capital expenditure of local authorities); and

    (b) unless the order otherwise provides, payments made to a local authority as mentioned in subsection (5) above shall be regarded for the purposes of that Part as sums received by the authority in respect of a disposal falling within section 75(2) of that Act.

(7) Any power to make an order under this section shall be exercisable by statutory instrument which shall be subject to annulment in pursuance of a resolution of either House of Parliament.

(8) In this section "local authority" means any of the following—

    (a) a local housing authority;

    (b) the council of a county;

    (c) the Inner London Education Authority;

    (d) an authority established by an order under section 10(1) of the Local Government Act 1985 (waste disposal);

    (e) a joint authority established by Part IV of that Act; and

    (f) a residuary body established by Part VII of that Act.

DEFINITIONS

"designated area": s.60.

"housing action trust": s.60.

"local authority": subs. (7).

"local housing authority": s.92.

GENERAL NOTE

Aside from s.61, above, this is possibly the most important section in this Part of the Act. It permits the Secretary of State to transfer by order—subject to negative parliamentary resolution (subs. (6))—housing or other land held or provided in connection with that housing belonging to a local housing authority (subs. (1)), and/or any other land held for any purpose by any local authority (as defined in subs. (7)) which the Secretary of State considers is required by the H.A.T. for the purposes of its functions (subs. (2)), and/or any other property (including rights and liabilities) belonging to any local authority (subs. (3)), on such financial terms as the Secretary of State thinks fit (subs. (4)), including payments *from* the authority to the H.A.T., without any automatic right of compensation (subs. (5)).

The proviso that there is no automatic right of compensation derives from the principle of statutory construction that an intention to take away the property of a subject without giving him a legal right to compensation for the loss of it is not to be imputed to the legislature unless that intention is expressed in unequivocal terms (*Attorney-General* v. *De Keyser's Royal Hotel* [1920] A.C. 508, H.L.), but in *R.* v. *Secretary of State for the Environment, ex p. London Borough of Newham* (1987) 19 H.L.R. 298, the Court of Appeal declined to extend the principle to a public authority on the grounds that no individual (whether corporate or not) was deprived of rights in property from which he could reasonably be expected to have a "return", in relation to a transfer of housing under London Government Act 1963, s.23. (Contrary to the view of the Secretary of State, however, the transfer *did* qualify as a disposal for the purposes of the Local Government, Planning and Land Act 1980 provisions defining "capital receipts" in the context of "prescribed expenditure": see subs. (6)). That decision has now been incorporated into the section.

Because of the extension in subs. (2) to *any* land, of a local authority (which includes local housing authority), and in subs. (3) to any of their property, the Secretary of State will be able to overcome any difficult questions which might arise as to whether or not land is "housing" and/or other land is held or provided in connection with that housing, although if an order purports to be made under subs. (1) alone those issues might yet be available to an authority seeking to resist transfer. Their powers to provide or hold land in connection with housing, as distinct from housing itself, are to be found in the Housing Act 1985, ss. 11, 12, 13 (and in London, s.15)—see *ibid*, s.17. Such land may be purchased (*ibid*), or appropriated to housing use (*ibid*, s.19). Housing itself is provided and held under *ibid*, s.9.

Subs. (4)

Rents or other amounts—*e.g.* service charges—falling due before the date of transfer may, if the order so provides, be reserved to the authority, instead of going with the reversion under the Law of Property Act 1925, s.141.

Supplementary provisions as to transfer orders

75.—(1) In this section a "transfer order" means an order under any of subsections (1) to (3) of section 74 above and, in relation to a transfer order, "the transferor authority" means the local housing authority or other local authority from whom local authority housing or other land or property is or is to be transferred by the order.

(2) Before making a transfer order, the Secretary of State shall consult the transferor authority with respect to—

   (a) the local authority housing or other land or property which it is proposed should be transferred by the order; and
   (b) the terms of the proposed transfer.

(3) Before making a transfer order with respect to any local authority housing or other land, the Secretary of State shall take such steps as appear to him to be appropriate to bring the proposed transfer to the attention of any secure tenant or other person (other than a local authority) having an interest in the property proposed to be transferred as lessor, lessee, mortgagor, or mortgagee.

(4) In connection with any transfer made by it, a transfer order may contain such incidental, consequential, transitional or supplementary provisions as appear to the Secretary of State to be necessary or expedient and, in particular, may—

   (a) apply, with or without modification, any provision made by or under any enactment; and
   (b) modify the operation of any provision made by or under any enactment.

DEFINITIONS
   "local authority": s.74.
   "local housing authority": s.92.
   "secure tenant": s.92.
   "transfer order": subs. (1).

GENERAL NOTE
Consultation (see notes to s.61, above) is a prerequisite of transfer under s.74, both as to what it is proposed to transfer and the terms of transfer. The Secretary of State also has to bring the proposed transfer to the attention of (a) any secure tenant (see further notes to ss.83 and 84, below) and (b) anyone else with an interest in the property, *i.e.* lessee or lessor, and/or mortgagee or mortgagor. The Secretary of State also has power in the transfer order to contain "incidental, consequential, transitional or supplementary" provisions, such as appear to him necessary or expedient, which power extends to the application with or without modification of *any* enactment, or the modification of any subordinate legislation.

Vesting and acquisition of land

Vesting by order in housing action trust

76.—(1) Subject to subsections (2) and (3) below, the Secretary of State may by order provide that land specified in the order which is vested in statutory undertakers or any other public body or in a wholly-owned subsidiary of a public body shall vest in a housing action trust established or to be established for the designated area in which the land is situated.

(2) An order under this section may not specify land vested in statutory undertakers which is used for the purpose of carrying on their statutory undertakings or which is held for that purpose.

(3) In the case of land vested in statutory undertakers, the power to make an order under this section shall be exercisable by the Secretary of State and the appropriate Minister.

(4) Part I of Schedule 9 to this Act shall have effect for supplementing the preceding provisions of this section.

(5) An order under this section shall have the same effect as a declaration under the Compulsory Purchase (Vesting Declarations) Act 1981 except that, in relation to such an order, the enactments mentioned in Part II of Schedule 9 to this Act shall have effect subject to the modifications specified in that Part.

(6) Compensation under the Land Compensation Act 1961, as applied by subsection (5) above and Part II of Schedule 9 to this Act, shall be assessed by reference to values current on the date the order under this section comes into force.

(7) An order under this section shall be made by statutory instrument but no such order shall be made unless a draft of it has been laid before, and approved by a resolution of, each House of Parliament.

DEFINITIONS
"appropriate minister": Sched. 9, para. 3.
"designated area": s.60.
"housing action trust": s.60.
"statutory undertakers": Sched. 9, para. 4.

GENERAL NOTE
This section permits the Secretary of State to vest—by vesting order (see subss. (5))—in a housing action trust any land in its area, belonging to a statutory undertaker or other public body (or wholly owned subsidiary thereof) (subs. (1)), *except* land held or used by a statutory undertaker for the purposes of its undertaking (subs. (2)). The vesting carries compensation (subs. (6)).

For this purpose, "statutory undertaker" is given a wide meaning (Sched. 9, para. 4, below). Included are the bodies with responsibility for railways (including light railways), tramways, road transport, water transport, canals, inland navigation, docks, harbours, piers or lighthouses, as well as the suppliers of electricity, hydraulic power and water, together with British Shipbuilders, British Steel, Civil Aviation Authority, British Coal, National Enterprise Board, the Post Office "and any other authority, body or undertakers which, by virtue of any enactment, are to be treated as statutory undertakers for the purposes of the Town and Country Planning Act 1971". The Secretary of State also has power to specify in an order further bodies to be treated for this purpose as statutory undertakers.

Acquisition by housing action trust

77.—(1) For the purposes of achieving its objects (and performing any of its functions), a housing action trust may acquire land within its designated area by agreement or, on being authorised to do so by the Secretary of State, compulsorily.

(2) A housing action trust may acquire (by agreement or, on being authorised to do so by the Secretary of State, compulsorily)—

(a) land adjacent to the designated area which the trust requires for purposes connected with the discharge of its functions in the area; and

(b) land outside the designated area (whether or not adjacent to it) which the trust requires for the provision of services in connection with the discharge of its functions in the area.

(3) Where a housing action trust exercises its powers under subsection (1) or subsection (2) above in relation to land which forms part of a common or open space or fuel or field garden allotment, the trust may

acquire (by agreement or, on being authorised to do so by the Secretary of State, compulsorily) land for giving in exchange for the land acquired.

(4) Subject to section 78 below, the Acquisition of Land Act 1981 shall apply in relation to the compulsory acquisition of land in pursuance of the preceding provisions of this section.

(5) A housing action trust may be authorised by the Secretary of State, by means of a compulsory purchase order, to purchase compulsorily such new rights as are specified in the order—

(a) being rights over land in the designated area and which the trust requires for the purposes of its functions;

(b) being rights over land adjacent to the designated area and which the trust requires for purposes connected with the discharge of its functions in the area; and

(c) being rights over land outside the designated area (whether or not adjacent to it) and which the trust requires for the provision of services in connection with the discharge of its functions in the area.

(6) In subsection (5) above—

(a) "new rights" means rights which are not in existence when the order specifying them is made; and

(b) "compulsory purchase order" has the same meaning as in the Acquisition of Land Act 1981;

and Schedule 3 to that Act shall apply to a compulsory purchase of a right by virtue of subsection (5) above.

(7) The provisions of Part I of the Compulsory Purchase Act 1965 (so far as applicable), other than section 31, shall apply in relation to the acquisition of land by agreement under this section; and in that Part as so applied "land" has the meaning given by the Interpretation Act 1978.

DEFINITIONS
"designated area": s.60.
"housing action trust": s.60.

GENERAL NOTE
This section contains the powers of purchase of a housing action trust, which may be exercised by agreement, or compulsorily with the consent of the Secretary of State (subs. (1)). The H.A.T. may purchase any land in its own area, or adjacent to its area which is required for purposes connected with the discharge of its functions in the area, and other land outside its area (whether or not adjacent to it) which is needed for the provision of services in connection with the discharge of its functions (subs. (2)). The H.A.T. may acquire land specifically to exchange it for land which it proposes to acquire—by agreement or compulsorily—which forms part of a common or open space, or fuel or field garden allotment, again either by agreement or, with the consent of the Secretary of State compulsorily (subs. (3)). The Acquisition of Land Act 1981 (*pre*-C.P.O. procedure) is applied to such a purchase, subject to s.78, below (subs. (4)).

Subss. (5), (6)
These subsections avoid the effect of *Sovmots Investments* v. *Secretary of State for the Environment* [1979] A.C. 144, H.L., in which it was held that a local authority's compulsory purchase powers did not extend to rights not yet in existence.

Subs. (7)
The Compulsory Purchase Act 1965 governs *post*-C.P.O. procedure and compensation. S.31 concerns the payment of compensation in respect of ecclesiastical property. By Interpretation Act 1978, Sched. 1, land "includes buildings and other structures, land covered with water, and any estate, interest, easement, servitude or right in or over land".

Supplementary provisions as to vesting, acquisition and compensation

78.—(1) The Acquisition of Land Act 1981, as applied by section 77 above, shall have effect subject to the modifications in Part I of Schedule 10 to this Act.

(2) The supplementary provisions in Parts II and III of that Schedule shall have effect, being,—

(a) as to those in Part II, provisions about land vested in or acquired by a housing action trust under this Part of this Act; and

(b) as to those in Part III, provisions about the acquisition by a housing action trust of rights over land under section 77(5) above.

(3) In Schedule 1 to the Land Compensation Act 1961 (actual or prospective development which is not to be taken into account in assessing compensation in certain cases or the effect of which is to reduce compensation in certain cases of adjacent land in the same ownership), the following paragraph shall be added after the paragraph 4A inserted by section 145 of the Local Government, Planning and Land Act 1980:

"4B. Where any of the relevant land forms part of a housing action trust area established under Part III of the Housing Act 1988. Development of any land other than the relevant land in the course of the development or re-development of the area as a housing action trust area."

(4) In section 6 of the Land Compensation Act 1961 (disregard of actual or prospective development in certain cases) in subsection (1)(b) for "4A" there shall be substituted "4B".

DEFINITION
"housing action trust": s.60.

GENERAL NOTE
This section introduces Sched. 10, below, (a) to modify the Acquisition of Land Act 1981 (*pre*-C.P.O. procedure) in relation to a purchase by a housing action trust, (b) to introduce supplementary provisions applicable to such a purchase, and (c) to add a paragraph to the Land Compensation Act 1961, designed to prevent compensation being increased on account of the H.A.T. development.

Sched. 10, Part I. The modification to the Acquisition of Land Act 1981 is designed to permit the Secretary of State to confirm *part* of a proposed C.P.O., and postpone consideration (to a specified time) of the remainder (para. 2).

Sched. 10, Part II. The supplementary provisions cover:

(a) automatic extinction (with compensation) of private rights of way and rights of laying down, erecting, continuing or maintaining apparatus on, under or over the land that has been purchased, and the vesting of such apparatus in the H.A.T., *other than* the rights of statutory undertakers for the purposes of their undertaking, and rights conferred under the telecommunications code on the operator of a system; the Secretary of State may, however, specifically exempt rights from extinction and either he or the trust may enter into a specific agreement concerning such (para. 4);

(b) power to override (with compensation for injurious affection) easements and analogous rights, provided the erection, construction or carrying out or maintenance of any building or work on land which has been acquired by the H.A.T. is in accordance with planning permission (*cf.* notes to ss.66, 67, above), *other than* the rights of statutory undertakers for the purpose of their undertakings, and the rights of system operators under the telecommunications code (para. 5);

(c) power to deal with consecrated land other than in accordance with ecclesiastical law or other provisions governing such land, *other than* land consisting of or forming part of a burial ground, subject to such restrictions as may be imposed, and power to deal with burial ground other than in accordance with enactment governing such, provided such dealing is in accordance with planning permission, and again subject to such restrictions as may be imposed (para. 6);

(d) power to use land acquired which was, or formed part of, a common, open space or fuel or field garden allotment, other than in accordance with the enactments relating thereto, provided the use is in accordance with planning permission (para. 7);

(e) removal of Rent Act protection in relation to a house acquired by the H.A.T., which the Secretary of State certifies it needs immediate possession of, for the purposes for which it was acquired (para. 8);

(f) power for the Secretary of State to extinguish public rights of way, subject to prior publicity and rights of objection (para. 9), which may extend to public local inquiry (para. 10), with provision for the operator of a telecommunications system installed under, in, on, over, along or across the land to remove or abandon apparatus and require compensation for relocation costs (para. 11);

(g) power to extinguish the rights of statutory undertakers and to require the removal of their apparatus, subject to rights of objection and compensation (paras. 12–14);

(h) power to extend or modify the powers and duties of statutory undertakers to secure the provision of services to the area of the H.A.T. or facilitate the adjustment of their services to reflect the acquisition of their land or the extinction of a right, on representation either of the statutory undertakers or the H.A.T. (para. 15), subject to duties of publication of proposals and rights of objection which may extend to special Parliamentary procedure and appeal to the High Court (paras. 16–18).

Sched. 10, Part III. This modifies the Compulsory Purchase Act 1965 (*post*-C.P.O. procedure and compensation) to apply it to rights as well as to land itself (paras. 20–23).

Subs. (3)

By the Land Compensation Act 1961, s.6, when assessing compensation no account is to be taken of the prospective public developments specified in the 1961 Act, Sched. 1, Part I, *i.e.* their development value; however, under *ibid*, s.7, an amount may be deducted from compensation if the vendor owns adjacent land which will benefit from such developments. This subsection specifies an additional public development with the 1961 Act, Schedule 1, Part I, namely development as a housing action trust area.

Disposals of land

Disposal of land by housing action trusts

79.—(1) Subject to subsection (2) below and any directions given by the Secretary of State, a housing action trust may, with the consent of the Secretary of State, dispose of any land for the time being held by it to such persons, in such manner and on such terms as it considers expedient for the purpose of achieving its objects.

(2) A housing action trust may not dispose of a house which is for the time being subject to a secure tenancy except—

(a) to a person who is for the time being approved by the Corporation either under this section or under section 94 below, or

(b) to a local housing authority or other local authority in accordance with section 84 below;

but this subsection does not apply to a disposal under Part V of the Housing Act 1985 (the right to buy).

(3) The reference in subsection (1) above to disposing of land includes a reference to granting an interest in or right over land and, in particular, the granting of an option to purchase the freehold of, or any other interest in, land is a disposal for the purposes of that subsection; and a consent under that subsection given to such a disposal extends to a disposal made in pursuance of the option.

(4) The consent of the Secretary of State referred to in subsection (1) above may be given—

(a) either generally to all housing action trusts or to a particular trust or description of trust;

(b) either in relation to particular land or in relation to land of a particular description; and

(c) subject to conditions.

(5) Without prejudice to the generality of subsection (4)(c) above, consent under subsection (1) above may, in particular, be given subject to conditions as to the price, premium or rent to be obtained by the housing action trust on the disposal, including conditions as to the amount by which, on the disposal of a house by way of sale or by the grant or

assignment of a lease at a premium, the price or premium is to be, or may be, discounted by the housing action trust.

(6) The Corporation shall not under this section approve—
   (a) a public sector landlord; or
   (b) the council of a county; or
   (c) any other body which the Corporation have reason to believe might not be independent of such a landlord or council;

and, for the purposes of paragraph (c) above, a body shall not be regarded as independent of a public sector landlord or the council of a county if the body is or appears likely to be under the control of, or subject to influence from, such a landlord or council or particular members or officers of such a landlord or council.

(7) In subsection (6) above "public sector landlord" means—
   (a) a local housing authority;
   (b) a new town corporation within the meaning of section 4(b) of the Housing Act 1985; and
   (c) the Development Board for Rural Wales.

(8) The Corporation shall establish (and may from time to time vary) criteria to be satisfied by a person seeking approval under this section and, in deciding whether to give such approval, the Corporation shall have regard to whether the person satisfies the criteria.

(9) Subject to any directions under section 76 of the Housing Associations Act 1985 (directions by the Secretary of State),—
   (a) an approval under this section shall not be given except to a person making an application accompanied by such fee as the Corporation, with the consent of the Secretary of State, may specify; and
   (b) an approval under this section may be made conditional upon the person or persons concerned entering into such undertakings as may be specified by the Corporation; and
   (c) if it appears to the Corporation appropriate to do so (whether by reason of a failure to honour an undertaking or to meet any criteria or for any other reason) the Corporation may revoke an approval given under this section by notice in writing served on the approved person, but such a revocation shall not affect any transaction completed before the service of the notice;

and different fees may be specified under paragraph (a) above for different descriptions of cases.

(10) The Housing Corporation and Housing for Wales shall each maintain a register of persons for the time being approved by it under this section; and each register so maintained shall be open to inspection at the head office of the Corporation by which it is maintained at all reasonable times.

(11) In section 45(2)(b) of the Housing Act 1985 (which defines "public sector authority" for the purposes of provisions of that Act restricting service charges payable after disposal of a house) after the entry "an urban development corporation" there shall be inserted "a housing action trust".

(12) A housing action trust shall be treated as a local authority for the purposes of sections 18 to 30 of the Landlord and Tenant Act 1985 (service charges).

(13) The provisions of Schedule 11 to this Act shall have effect in the case of certain disposals of houses by a housing action trust.

DEFINITIONS
   "Corporation": s.92.
   "house": s.92.
   "housing action trust": s.60.
   "local housing authority": s.92.

GENERAL NOTE

This section permits the H.A.T., with the consent of the Secretary of State which may be given generally or particularly, and may be conditional (subs. (4)), to dispose of any land in manner and terms such as it considers expedient for achieving its purposes (subs. (1)), including the right to grant an interest in or right over land, and the right to grant an option (subs. (3)). Consent may be conditional on price, premium or rent to be obtained by the H.A.T., including provision for discounts to be granted on the disposal of a house (subs. (6)). The principal constraints are on the disposal (other than under Part V of the Housing Act 1985, *i.e.* "right to buy") of houses let on secure tenancies: subs. (2), (6)–(9). See s.81 below, for restrictions on further disposals by those to whom the H.A.T. dispose.

Subss. (2), (6)–(10)

"Secure tenancies" are lettings by, primarily (and since the commencement of s.35, above, removing new housing association lettings from the regime) local authorities, and other public bodies: *cf.* notes to s.35, above. H.A.T. tenants are secure: see notes to s.83, below. By this section, a disposal of a house (or flat, see s.92, below), let on a secure tenancy can (right to buy apart) only be to (a) an approved person, or (b) a local housing authority or other local authority, under s.84, below, see also notes thereto. A landlord approved under s.94 is one approved to take a transfer from the public sector, under Part IV of this Act, below. Approval is by the Housing Corporation or Housing for Wales (*cf.* Part II, above), who must maintain a public register of persons currently so approved (subs. (10)). Approval under Part IV automatically qualifies as approval under this section. The Housing Corporation and Housing for Wales must charge a fee on application for approval: subs. (9)(a).

But the Corporations shall not approve a "public sector landlord" (as defined in subs. (7)), or a county council, or "any other body which the Corporation have reason to believe might not be independent of" a public sector landlord or county council, *i.e.* a body—perhaps not formally owned, established or funded by the public sector landlord or county council, but designed to fulfil a traditional public sector landlord role. As the judgment is that of the Corporations, the possibility of challenge to a refusal to approve will be limited: see notes to s.60, above. The wording—"is or appears likely to be under the control of, or subject to influence from"—is extremely wide. It is also significant that the unacceptable control or influence may not be that of the public sector landlord or county council themselves, but may even derive from "particular members or officers".

The irony is that while this is intended to prevent left-wing local authorities from setting up separate organisations to acquire their own former stock, from the H.A.T., many members of other councils are likely to be, as landlords, interested in such acquisitions, but will now be prevented from acquiring approval. "Officer", however, would seem to denote currently-serving officer. The Corporations may establish criteria for approval, by subs. (8). An approved landlord may lose that qualification, relative to future transactions, if he fails to honour any undertaking which the Corporations have sought as a condition of approval (subs. (9)), *e.g.* concerning houses kept available for letting, or discounts on sales to tenants.

Subss. (11), (12)

Service charges may be payable on the disposal, whether by freehold or leasehold, of a house: Housing Act 1985, ss.45–51, contains provisions restricting their recoverability, broadly to costs reasonably incurred in relation to works of a reasonable standard. Those provisions are applicable to H.A.T.s. The provisions are modelled on those now to be found in ss.18–30 of the Landlord and Tenant Act 1985 formerly only applicable to flats but now applicable to "dwellings", since amendment by the Landlord and Tenant Act, 1987, and which are also applicable to H.A.T.s.

For these purposes, "service charge" means "an amount . . . payable, directly or indirectly, for services, repairs, maintenance or insurance or the [vendor's or lessor's] [landlord's] costs of management, and the whole or part of which varies or may vary according to the relevant costs" (the latter defined to mean either actual or estimated costs, and to include overheads): Housing Act 1985, s.621A, added by Housing and Planning Act 1986, Sched. 5, para. 39; Landlord and Tenant Act 1985, s.18.

Subs. (13)

Sched. 11, below, makes provision for repayment of discount on "early" disposal, *i.e.* within a period of three years of purchase or grant, reduceable by one-third of the discount for each full year between purchase or grant, and disposal (para. 1). The repayment covenant is a charge on the premises taking priority immediately after any amount left outstanding by the purchaser or advanced to him by an approved lending institution to enable him to acquire the interest, or further advanced by such an institution (para. 2). The provisions are substantively identical to those contained in the Housing Act 1985, ss.155, 156.

Repayment is only required on a "relevant disposal" (para. 3), which includes an option (para. 7), which means a conveyance of the freehold or assignment of the lease, or the grant of a lease or sub-lease (other than a mortgage term) for a term of more than 21 years, other than at a rack rent (including a term of less than 21 years but with provision for renewal, if the term including renewal would exceed 21 years): see the 1985 Act, s.159.

But there is no repayment if the disposal is an "exempt disposal" (paras. 4, 5, see the 1985 Act, s.160) which means:

(a) a disposal of the whole of the house and a conveyance or assignment to a "qualifying person" (or, where there is more than one purchaser/assignee, all of whom are qualifying persons),

(b) the vesting of the whole of the house under a will or on intestacy,

(c) a disposal of the whole of the house in pursuance of an order made under Matrimonial Causes Act 1973, s.24, (property adjustment orders) or Inheritance (Provision for Family and Dependants Act 1975, s.2; (order for provision from estate) (Note in *R.* v. *Rushmoor Borough Council, ex p. Barrett* [1987] Q.B. 275, it was held that a disposal pursuant to an order under s.24A of the 1973 Act was *not* a disposal pursuant to an order under s.24),

(d) a compulsory disposal, or

(e) the property disposed of is property included with the house as a yard, garden, outhouse or appurtenance.

"Qualifying person" means the person, or one of the persons by whom the disposal is made (so that joint owners can dispose to one of their number), or the spouse or former spouse of that person or one of those persons, or he is a member of the family of that person or one of those persons and has resided with him for 12 months ending with the disposal. "Member of the family" is as defined in the Housing Act 1985, s.186.

Disposals made without consent

80.—(1) Any disposal of a house by a housing action trust which is made without the consent required by section 79(1) above is void unless—

(a) the disposal is to an individual (or to two or more individuals); and
(b) the disposal does not extend to any other house.

(2) Subject to subsection (1) above,—

(a) a disposal of any land made by a housing action trust shall not be invalid by reason only that it is made without the consent required by section 79(1) above; and
(b) a person dealing with a housing action trust or with a person claiming under such a trust shall not be concerned to see or enquire whether any consent required by section 79(1) above has been obtained.

DEFINITIONS
"house": s.92.
"housing action trust": s.60.

GENERAL NOTE
See notes to s.72, above, as to the common law invalidity of a disposal without consent, and the statutory validation which that section contains. But a disposal of a *house* (including *flat*—see s.91) without consent under s.79(1), above, will remain void, unless of one house only, and to an individual. This follows the Housing Act 1985, s.44.

Consent required for certain subsequent disposals

81.—(1) If, by a material disposal, a housing action trust disposes of a house which is for the time being subject to a secure tenancy to such a person as is mentioned in section 79(2)(a) above (in this section referred to as an "approved person"), the conveyance shall contain a statement that the requirement of this section as to consent applies to a subsequent disposal of the house by the approved person.

(2) For the purposes of this section a "material disposal" is—

(a) the transfer of the fee simple;
(b) the transfer of an existing lease; or
(c) the grant of a new lease;

and "the conveyance" means the instrument by which such a disposal is effected.

(3) An approved person who acquires a house on a material disposal falling within subsection (1) above shall not dispose of it except with the consent of the Secretary of State which may be given either unconditionally or subject to conditions; but nothing in this subsection shall apply in relation to an exempt disposal as defined in subsection (8) below.

(4) Where an estate or interest in a house acquired by an approved person as mentioned in subsection (3) above has been mortgaged or charged, the prohibition in that subsection applies also to a disposal by the mortgagee or chargee in exercise of a power of sale or leasing, whether or not the disposal is in the name of the approved person; and in any case where—

(a) by operation of law or by virtue of an order of a court, property which has been acquired by an approved person passes or is transferred to another person, and
(b) that passing or transfer does not constitute a disposal for which consent is required under subsection (3) above,

this section (including, where there is more than one such passing or transfer, this subsection) shall apply as if the other person to whom the property passes or is transferred were the approved person.

(5) Before giving consent in respect of a disposal to which subsection (3) above applies, the Secretary of State—

(a) shall satisfy himself that the person who is seeking the consent has taken appropriate steps to consult every tenant of any house proposed to be disposed of; and
(b) shall have regard to the responses of any such tenants to that consultation.

(6) If, apart from subsection (7) below, the consent of the Corporation would be required under section 9 of the Housing Associations Act 1985 (control of dispositions of land by housing associations) for a disposal to which subsection (3) above applies, the Secretary of State shall consult the Corporation before giving his consent in respect of the disposal for the purposes of this section.

(7) No consent shall be required under the said section 9 for any disposal in respect of which consent is given in accordance with subsection (6) above.

(8) In this section an "exempt disposal" means—

(a) the disposal of a dwelling-house to a person having the right to buy it under Part V of the Housing Act 1985 (whether the disposal is in fact made under that Part or otherwise);
(b) a compulsory disposal, within the meaning of Part V of the Housing Act 1985;
(c) the disposal of an easement or rentcharge;
(d) the disposal of an interest by way of security for a loan;
(e) the grant of a secure tenancy or what would be a secure tenancy but for any of paragraphs 2 to 12 of Schedule 1 to the Housing Act 1985;
(f) the grant of an assured tenancy or an assured agricultural occupancy, within the meaning of Part I of this Act, or what would be such a tenancy or occupancy but for any of paragraphs 4 to 8 of Schedule 1 to this Act; and
(g) the transfer of an interest held on trust for any person where the disposal is made in connection with the appointment of a new trustee or in connection with the discharge of any trustee.

(9) Where the title of a housing action trust to a house which is disposed of by a material disposal falling within subsection (1) above is not registered—

(a) section 123 of the Land Registration Act 1925 (compulsory registration of title) applies in relation to the conveyance whether or not the house is in an area in which an Order in Council under section 120 of that Act (areas of compulsory registration) is in force;

(b) the housing action trust shall give the approved person a certificate stating that it is entitled to make the disposal subject only to such encumbrances, rights and interests as are stated in the conveyance or summarised in the certificate; and

(c) for the purpose of registration of title, the Chief Land Registrar shall accept such a certificate as evidence of the facts stated in it, but if as a result he has to meet a claim against him under the Land Registration Acts 1925 to 1986 the housing action trust is liable to indemnify him.

(10) On an application being made for registration of a disposition of registered land or, as the case may be, of the approved person's title under a disposition of unregistered land, if the conveyance contains the statement required by subsection (1) above, the Chief Land Registrar shall enter in the register a restriction stating the requirement of this section as to consent to a subsequent disposal.

(11) In this section references to disposing of a house include references to—

(a) granting or disposing of any interest in the house;

(b) entering into a contract to dispose of the house or to grant or dispose of any such interest; and

(c) granting an option to acquire the house or any such interest,

and any reference to a statement or certificate is a reference to a statement or, as the case may be, certificate in a form approved by the Chief Land Registrar.

DEFINITIONS
"Corporation": s.92.
"dispose": subs. (11).
"house": s.92.
"housing action trust": s.60.
"material disposal": subs. (2).
"secure tenancy": s.92.

GENERAL NOTE
   This section restricts the right of an approved landlord (see notes to s.79, above) who has acquired housing from a housing action trust on the transfer of the fee simple, the transfer of an existing lease or the creation of a new lease (subs. (2)), further to dispose of the property other than on an exempt disposal (subs. (8)) without the consent of the Secretary of State (subs. (3)), by means of a statement in the conveyance (subs. (1)).

Subss. (1)–(7)
   The conveyance is to contain the statement that the requirements of this section apply to any subsequent disposal, where the interest which the H.A.T. has taken is transfer of fee simple or existing lease, or the grant of a new lease. The section restricts further disposals without consent, unless they are exempt disposals, as defined in subs. (8). Consent may be conditional or unconditional but by reason of subs. (5), clearly not "general": subs. (3). The restriction applies not only to the approved person, but also a mortgagee or chargee: subs. (4). No consent is to be given unless the Secretary of State is satisfied (*cf.* notes to s.60, above) that any tenants of the property in question have been consulted (as to which, see notes to s.61, above), and the Secretary of State has had regard to their responses: subs. (5).
   Where the approved landlord is a housing association, consent of the Housing Corporation or Housing for Wales may otherwise be needed under the Housing Associations Act 1985,

s.9: by subss. (6), (7), instead, consent under this section suffices, but before granting consent the Secretary of State is to consult the appropriate Corporation.

Subs. (8)

This subsection identifies the disposals which do not require consent. The reference to the right to buy under Part V of the 1985 Act, is wide enough to include the "preserved right to buy": see notes to s.84, below. But the disposal need not itself be pursuant to that Part, *i.e.* an agreed sale on different terms would be permissible if to a person with the right to buy.

A compulsory disposal under *ibid.*, Part V, is "a disposal of property which is acquired compulsorily, or is acquired by a person who has made or would have made, or for whom another person has made or would have made, a compulsory purchase order authorising its compulsory purchase for the purposes for which it was acquired": the 1985 Act, s.161.

Note that no consent is needed to a disposal by way of mortgage or charge, but *cf.* subs. (4): the mortgagee or chargee is in turn bound by the restrictions contained in this section, even if exercising the power of sale or leasing. Neither the grant of a secure tenancy nor of an assured tenancy (or, in either case, what would be such but for the specified grounds) requires consent. Nor is consent needed for a disposal related to the replacement or addition of a trustee.

Subs. (11)

It is now common to include the grant of an option as "a disposal" in housing law.

Power of Corporation to provide legal assistance to tenants after disposal

82.—(1) This section applies where a house has been disposed of by a disposal falling within section 79(2) above and, in relation to a house which has been so disposed of, a "transferred tenant" means a tenant of it who either—

(a) was the secure tenant of the house immediately before the disposal; or

(b) is the widow or widower of the person who was then the secure tenant of it.

(2) On an application by a transferred tenant of a house who is a party or a prospective party to proceedings or prospective proceedings to determine any dispute between himself and the person who acquired the house on the disposal referred to in subsection (1) above, the Corporation may give assistance to the transferred tenant if it thinks fit to do so—

(a) on the ground that the case raises a question of principle; or

(b) on the ground that it is unreasonable, having regard to the complexity of the case, or to any other matter, to expect the transferred tenant to deal with it without assistance; or

(c) by reason of any other special consideration.

(3) Assistance given by the Corporation under this section may include—

(a) giving advice;

(b) procuring or attempting to procure the settlement of the matter in dispute;

(c) arranging for the giving of advice or assistance by a solicitor or counsel;

(d) arranging for representation by a solicitor or counsel, including such assistance as is usually given by a solicitor or counsel in the steps preliminary or incidental to any proceedings, or in arriving at or giving effect to a compromise to avoid or bring to an end any proceedings; and

(e) any other form of assistance which the Corporation may consider appropriate;

but paragraph (d) above does not affect the law and practice regulating the descriptions of persons who may appear in, conduct, defend and address the court in any proceedings.

(4) In so far as expenses are incurred by the Corporation in providing a transferred tenant with assistance under this section, the recovery of those expenses (as taxed or assessed in such manner as may be prescribed by rules of court) shall constitute a first charge for the benefit of the Corporation—

(a) on any costs which (whether by virtue of a judgment or order of a court or an agreement or otherwise) are payable to the tenant by any other person in respect of the matter in connection with which the assistance was given, and

(b) so far as relates to any costs, on his rights under any compromise or settlement arrived at in connection with that matter to avoid or bring to an end any proceedings;

but subject to any charge under the Legal Aid Act 1988 and to any provision of that Act for payment of any sum to the Legal Aid Board.

DEFINITIONS
"Corporation": s.92.
"house": s.92.

GENERAL NOTE
This section, modelled on the Housing Act 1985, s.170, is designed to allow the Housing Corporation and Housing for Wales to provide legal assistance to the former secure tenants of H.A.T.s (and their surviving spouses), in relation to a dispute with a new landlord, who has acquired under s.79, above. It recognises, in effect, that if the Corporations err in approving a landlord, they ought to have a responsibility towards the tenants affected, though the section is not confined to "errors" on their part, but only to cases which "raise a question of principle" or "it is unreasonable", having regard to complexity or any other matter to expect the former tenant to deal with the case without assistance, or by reason of any other special consideration: see also s.107, below.

While legal aid is means-tested, there is no suggestion of means-testing here, but like legal aid, the Corporations have a charge on any costs recovered, or any rights under a settlement (but unlike legal aid, not on a sum actually recovered in the course of the proceedings). The Corporations' charges will, however, be subject to a legal aid charge: it is presumably envisaged that in some cases, the Corporations might take over a case where legal aid itself is withdrawn.

Secure tenancies and right to buy

Application of Parts IV and V of Housing Act 1985

83.—(1) Parts IV and V of the Housing Act 1985 (secure tenancies and the right to buy) shall be amended in accordance with this section.

(2) In section 80(1) (which lists the landlords whose tenancies can qualify as secure tenancies), after the entry specifying a new town corporation there shall be inserted—
"a housing action trust".

(3) In section 108 (heating charges to secure tenants), in paragraph (a) of subsection (5) (the definition of "heating authority") after the words "housing authority" there shall be inserted "or housing action trust".

(4) In section 114 (meaning of "landlord authority" for the purposes of that Part), in each of subsections (1) and (2), after the entry specifying a development corporation, there shall be inserted—
"a housing action trust".

(5) In section 171 (power to extend right to buy where certain bodies hold an interest in a dwelling-house), in subsection (2), after the entry specifying a new town corporation there shall be inserted—
"a housing action trust".

(6) In each of the following provisions (all of which relate to cases where premises are or were let to a person in consequence of employment), namely—

(a) paragraph 2(1) of Schedule 1 (tenancies which are not secure tenancies),

(b) Grounds 7 and 12 of Schedule 2 (grounds for possession of dwelling-houses let under secure tenancies),

(c) Ground 5 of Schedule 3 (grounds for withholding consent to assignment by way of exchange), and

(d) paragraph 5 of Schedule 5 (exceptions to the right to buy),

after the entry specifying a new town corporation there shall be inserted—

"a housing action trust".

(7) In Schedule 4 (qualifying period for right to buy and discount), in paragraph 7 (the landlord condition) after the entry specifying a new town corporation there shall be inserted—

"a housing action trust".

DEFINITIONS

"housing action trust": s.60.

"secure tenants": s.92.

GENERAL NOTE

The Housing Act 1985, Part IV, contains the security of tenure for public sector tenants introduced by the Housing Act 1980, Part I, Chapter II. The 1985 Act, Part V, contains the related "right to buy", introduced by the 1980 Act, Part I, Chapter I. This gives such tenants a range of rights: security of tenure itself, to exchange tenancies with other secure tenants, to take in lodgers, to improve, to buy (including on shared ownership leases), etc.

This section includes a housing action trust as a landlord whose tenants are "secure" for both purposes, and also brings them into the provisions which—though not yet in force—are intended to permit tenants to challenge levels of heating charges on district heating systems; defines H.A.T.s as landlord authorities whose tenants are to be consulted on matters of housing management (but see notes to s.84(8), below); includes them as bodies who may hold an interest (*e.g.* superior lease) which prevents a secure tenant exercising the right to buy, in respect of whom the Secretary of State may by order modify Part V to enable it to apply; includes them in the public sector as employers whose tenants may accordingly in specified circumstances be excluded from security or subject to grounds for possession, etc.; and, includes them as public sector landlords for the purposes of calculating discount and entitlement on right to buy.

Provisions applicable to disposals of dwelling-houses subject to secure tenancies

84.—(1) The provisions of this section apply in any case where a housing action trust proposes to make a disposal of one or more houses let on secure tenancies which would result in a person who, before the disposal, is a secure tenant of the trust becoming, after the disposal, the tenant of another person.

(2) Before applying to the Secretary of State for consent to the proposed disposal or serving notice under subsection (4) below, the housing action trust shall serve notice in writing—

(a) on any local housing authority in whose area any houses falling within subsection (1) above are situated, and

(b) if any such houses were transferred to the trust from another local housing authority or other local authority under section 74 above, on that authority,

informing the authority of the proposed disposal, specifying the houses concerned, and requiring the authority within such period, being not less than 28 days, as may be specified in the notice, to serve on the trust a notice under subsection (3) below.

(3) A notice by a local housing authority or other local authority under this subsection shall inform the housing action trust, with respect to each of the houses specified in the notice under subsection (2) above which is

in the authority's area or, as the case may be, which was transferred from the authority as mentioned in paragraph (b) of that subsection,—

   (a) that the authority wishes to acquire the house or is considering its acquisition; or

   (b) that the authority does not wish to acquire the house;

and where the authority serves notice as mentioned in paragraph (a) above with respect to any house, the notice shall give information as to the likely consequences for the tenant if the house were to be acquired by the authority.

(4) Before applying to the Secretary of State for consent to the proposed disposal, and after the expiry of the period specified in the notice under subsection (2) above, the housing action trust shall serve notice in writing on the secure tenant—

   (a) informing him of the proposed disposal and of the name of the person to whom the disposal is to be made;

   (b) containing such other details of the disposal as seem to the trust to be appropriate;

   (c) informing him of the likely consequences of the disposal on his position as a secure tenant and, if appropriate, of the effect of sections 171A to 171H of the Housing Act 1985 (preservation of right to buy on disposal to private sector landlord);

   (d) informing him, with respect to the house of which he is tenant, of the wishes of the local housing authority and of any other authority which has served a notice under subsection (3) above;

   (e) if an authority has served notice under paragraph (a) of subsection (3) above with respect to that house, informing him (in accordance with the information given in the notice) of the likely consequences for him if the house were to be acquired by that authority and also, if he wishes to become a tenant of that authority, of his right to make representations to that effect under paragraph (f) below; and

   (f) informing him of his right to make representations to the trust with respect to the proposed disposal within such period, being not less than 28 days, as may be specified in the notice.

(5) The housing action trust shall consider any representations made to it in accordance with subsection (4)(f) above and, if it considers it appropriate having regard to—

   (a) any representations so made, and

   (b) any further information which may be provided by an authority which served a notice under subsection (3)(a) above that it was considering the acquisition of a house,

the trust may amend its proposals with respect to the disposal and, in such a case, shall serve a further notice under subsection (4) above (in relation to which this subsection will again apply).

(6) When applying to the Secretary of State for consent to the proposed disposal (as amended, where appropriate, by virtue of subsection (5) above) the housing action trust shall furnish to him—

   (a) a copy of any notice served on it under subsection (3) above or served by it under subsection (4) above;

   (b) a copy of any representations received by the trust; and

   (c) a statement of the consideration given by the trust to those representations.

(7) Without prejudice to the generality of section 72 above, where an application is made to the Secretary of State for consent to a disposal to which this section applies, the Secretary of State may, by a direction under that section, require the housing action trust—

   (a) to carry out such further consultation with respect to the proposed disposal as may be specified in the direction; and

(b) to furnish to him such information as may be so specified with respect to the results of that consultation.

(8) Notwithstanding the application to a housing action trust of Part IV of the Housing Act 1985 (secure tenancies) a disposal falling within subsection (1) above shall be treated as not being a matter of housing management to which section 105 of that Act applies.

DEFINITIONS
"house": s.92.
"housing action trust": s.60.
"local authority": s.74.
"local housing authority": s.92.
"secure tenants": s.92.

GENERAL NOTE
It is a major purpose of this Part that H.A.T.s should "encourage . . . diversity in the identity of . . . landlords" (s.63(1)(c), above), to which end the Secretary of State may transfer local authority housing stock to the H.A.T. (s.74, above), who may then sell it (s.79, above), *i.e.* to a private sector landlord. The disposal will require the consent of the Secretary of State: s.79(1), above.

Before seeking consent, the H.A.T. has to serve notice on any local housing authority in whose area the house or houses (including flats: s.92, below) is or are situated, and any other local housing authority from whom the property was transferred, giving such authority a minimum of 28 days in which to tell the H.A.T. whether the authority would wish to (re)-acquire the property (subs. (2)); if the authority do so wish, they have to tell the H.A.T. what are the implications for the tenant or tenants, *e.g.* rents and other terms of tenancy, any redevelopment plans, etc. (subs. (3)).

Also before seeking consent from the Secretary of State, the H.A.T. has to serve notice on the secure tenant telling him about the proposed disposal, the identity of the proposed new landlord, such other details as the H.A.T. thinks appropriate, the wishes of the local housing or other authority served under subs. (2) and (if any) their statement of consequences under subs. (3), describing the likely consequences to him of the disposal, and giving him the right to make representations to it (including whether or not the tenant wishes to become the tenant of the authority) within a specified, reasonable time of not less than 28 days (subs. (4)).

Likely consequences are to include the effect, if appropriate, of the Housing Act 1985, ss.171A–171H, due to be added by the Housing and Planning Act 1986, s.8, but not yet brought into force, even though s.127, below, substitutes new subs. (4)(a), and adds new subs. (4)(aa) to s.171B, and a new subs. (5) to s.171C. The sections will take effect if the disposal is to a landlord who is not another body whose tenants are secure: s.171A(1). What the sections will do is to preserve the right to buy, notwithstanding that the tenant is no longer a secure tenant. But the sections will be inapplicable if the right to buy as against the former landlord was unavailable because of the 1985 Act, Sched. 5, paras. 1–3 (charities and certain housing associations), or in such other cases as may be excepted by order of the Secretary of State: the 1985 Act, s.171A(3).

The right to buy is only to be preserved so long as the tenant occupies the premises as his only or principal home (as to the meaning of which, see notes to s.1, above), but the right may be exercised by the tenant, or a qualifying successor, as defined, and may extend from the original premises to other premises to which the tenant has moved and which are rented from the same landlord (or if a company, from a connected company): the 1985 Act, s.171B. By s.171F, a court is not to make an order for possession against a protected tenant on the ground of suitable alternative accommodation without ensuring that the right to buy will be preserved (or that the tenant will be secure as against the new landlord).

S.171C empowers the Secretary of State by regulation to modify the 1985 Act, Part V, for the purposes of the preserved right to buy. A subsequent disposal by the landlord does not terminate the preserved right to buy, unless either the new landlord is a landlord whose tenants are secure, or the tenant has failed to register his right: s.171D. The preserved right to buy may also be determined on the termination of the landlord's interest by a superior landlord, other than by merger, but where this occurs by reason of the landlord's act or omission, there is a right to compensation: s.171E.

Subs. (5)
The H.A.T. may amend its proposals in the light of representations, but if it does so must then re-serve the subs. (4) notice on the tenant.

Subss. (6), (7)

The H.A.T. has to copy to the Secretary of State, when applying for consent, any representations received from an authority that they wish to acquire, its notice on the tenant(s), and the tenant's response, who may require further consultation and additional information derived therefrom.

Subs. (8)

A disposal would normally qualify as a matter of housing management within the Housing Act 1985, s.105, and by virtue of the definition of H.A.T. as a landlord whose tenants are secure, and as a landlord authority for the purpose of the housing management provisions (see s.82, above), it would therefore require compliance with the consultation provisions independently of the notification and representation procedure contained in this section. This section, accordingly, substitutes the 1985 Act, s.105.

Rents

Rents generally

85.—(1) A housing action trust may make such reasonable charges as it may determine for the tenancy or occupation of housing accommodation for the time being held by it.

(2) A housing action trust shall from time to time review rents and make such changes, either of rents generally or of particular rents, as circumstances may require.

DEFINITIONS

    "housing accommodation": s.92.

    "housing action trust": s.60.

GENERAL NOTE

This section confers on H.A.T.s the same broad rent-fixing discretion as that enjoyed by local authorities under the Housing Act 1985, s.24. With one, extreme exception (*Backhouse* v. *Lambeth L.B.C.* (1972) 116 S.J. 802, involving a professed device to defeat the provisions of the Housing Finance Act 1972) there has been no successful challenge to a local authority's decision as to rent: see, *e.g. Belcher* v. *Reading Corporation* [1950] 1 Ch. 380, *Luby* v. *Newcastle-under-Lyme Corporation* [1964] 2 Q.B. 64, C.A., *Evans* v. *Collins* [1965] 1 Q.B. 580, *Hemsted* v. *Lees and Norwich City Council* (1986) 18 H.L.R. 424, *London Borough of Wandsworth* v. *Winder (No. 2)* (1987) 20 H.L.R. 400, C.A. However, by s.72, above, the H.A.T. is bound to comply in the exercise of its functions with any directions given by the Secretary of State, which can clearly include rent levels.

Increase of rent where tenancy not secure

86.—(1) This section applies where a dwelling-house is let by a housing action trust on a periodic tenancy which is not a secure tenancy.

(2) The rent payable under the tenancy may, without the tenancy being terminated, be increased with effect from the beginning of a rental period by a written notice of increase given by the housing action trust to the tenant.

(3) A notice under subsection (2) above is not effective unless—

    (a) it is given at least four weeks before the first day of the rental period, or any earlier day on which the payment of rent in respect of that period falls to be made;

    (b) it tells the tenant of his right to terminate the tenancy and of the steps to be taken by him if he wishes to do so; and

    (c) it gives him the dates by which, if (by virtue of subsection (4) below) the increase is not to be effective, a notice to quit must be received by the trust and the tenancy be made to terminate.

(4) Where a notice is given under subsection (2) above specifying an increase in rent with effect from the beginning of a rental period and the tenancy continues into that period, the notice shall not have effect if—

(a) the tenancy is terminated by notice to quit given by the tenant in accordance with the provisions (express or implied) of the tenancy;

(b) the notice to quit is given before the expiry of the period of two weeks beginning on the day following the date on which the notice of increase is given, or before the expiry of such longer period as may be allowed by the notice of increase; and

(c) the date on which the tenancy is made to terminate is not later than the earliest day on which the tenancy could be terminated by a notice to quit given by the tenant on the last day of that rental period.

(5) In this section "rental period" means a period in respect of which a payment of rent falls to be made.

DEFINITIONS

"housing action trust": s.60.
"secure tenancy": s.92.

GENERAL NOTE

Most tenants of H.A.T.s will be secure tenants, but not all: see, particularly, Housing Act 1985, Sched. 1, for exceptions. A secure tenancy cannot be brought to an end save by a court order for possession, on limited grounds: *ibid.*, ss.82–85, and Sched. 2. Provision is accordingly contained in *ibid.*, Part IV, for increases of rent: *ibid.*, ss.102, 103. Where a tenancy is not secure, then unless the tenancy agreement makes provision for increase, an increase in rent would require notice to quit, and regrant, (see *Bathavon R.D.C.* v. *Carlile* [1958] 1 Q.B. 461), but for the provisions of *ibid.*, s.25, which is in substantively the same terms as this section.

Rent can only be increased by this means with effect from the beginning of a rental period (subs. (2)), *i.e.* the period for which rent payments are made (subs. (5)). The notice must be given at least four weeks before the date when payment falls to be made, *i.e.* either the beginning of the rental period or, if rent is payable in advance of the period to which it relates, before that payment day: subs. (3)(a). The notice must inform the tenant of his right to bring the tenancy to an end, and of what steps he must take to do so; subs. (3)(b).

Service of a notice to quit will not *per se* prevent the notice of increase taking effect: there will commonly be less than four weeks between *receipt* of notice of increase and service of (tenant's) notice, so that there would be one or more weeks during the currency of the notice to quit, *i.e.* before its expiry, at the new and higher rent level. Even a *tenant's* notice to quit must comply with the legal minimum period of four weeks: Protection From Eviction Act 1977, s.5.

However, this section provides a procedure for preventing the increase taking effect at all. The notice of increase must specify a date by which, if notice to quit is received by the authority, the increase will not take effect: subs. (3)(c). That date must be not less than two weeks; subs. (4)(b). The notice of increase must also specify the date by which the tenant's notice to quit must bring the tenancy to an end, *i.e.* a termination date for the tenancy: subs. (3)(c). That date must be not later than the *first* day on which the tenancy could be terminated by notice to quit given in the last day of the period during which the notice must be served: subs. (4)(c).

For example, notice of increase allows two weeks for service of notice to quit, notice to quit must be four weeks, earliest termination of tenancy will be six weeks after service of notice of increase, and *must* be for this date if the increase is not to take effect during the currency of the notice to quit. If the tenant's notice to quit goes beyond this date, it will not be effective to prevent the increase taking effect from the date it would have taken effect if no notice to quit in response is served, probably four weeks after it is served. It will, however, if otherwise valid, still be effective to determine the tenancy.

A tenant who does not have certain plans for alternative, and adequate or "settled" accommodation, and who quits in response to a notice of increase because he does not believe that he can afford the increased rent, runs the very real risk of a finding of intentional homelessness under the Housing Act 1985, Part III, should he then apply to the local housing authority for assistance, which means a refusal of an offer from them.

It should be noted that where there are joint tenants, notice to quit by just one of them will be effective to bring the tenancy to an end: *Greenwich London Borough Council* v. *McGrady* [1982] 6 H.L.R. 36, C.A.

Agency and dissolution

Agency agreements

87.—(1) With the approval of the Secretary of State, a housing action trust may enter into an agreement with another person whereby, in relation to any housing accommodation or other land held by the trust which is specified in the agreement, that other person shall exercise, as agent of the trust, such of the functions of the trust as are so specified.

(2) An agreement under subsection (1) above shall set out the terms on which the functions of the housing action trust are exercisable by the person who, under the agreement, is the agent of the trust (in this Part of this Act referred to as "the agent").

(3) Where the agent is a body or association, an agreement under subsection (1) above may provide that the functions of the agent under the agreement may be performed by a committee or sub-committee, or by an officer, of the body or association.

(4) The approval of the Secretary of State under subsection (1) above may be given unconditionally or subject to conditions.

(5) References in this section to the functions of a housing action trust in relation to housing accommodation or other land include—
 (a) functions conferred by any statutory provision, and
 (b) the powers and duties of the trust as holder of an estate or interest in the housing accommodation or land in question.

DEFINITIONS
 "housing accommodation": s.92.
 "housing action trust": s.60.

GENERAL NOTE
 This section permits the H.A.T. to enter into "management agreements", for the exercise of their functions—whether by statute, or merely deriving from their position as landlord or owner or lessee of property (subs. (5))—but only with the approval of the Secretary of State (which may be conditional or unconditional—subs. (4)): subs. (1). Local authorities, too, can enter into agreements for the exercise of their management functions, but also only with the consent of the Secretary of State: Housing Act 1985, s.27.
 Without express authority to "delegate" their powers, it must be doubted whether either an authority or a housing action trust could discharge the duties imposed on them by Parliament, other of course than through employees—see, *e.g. Parker* v. *Camden London Borough Council* (1985) 17 H.L.R. 380, C.A. Similarly, a "delegate" cannot sub-delegate without express power, hence the provision of subs. (3).

Dissolution of housing action trust

88.—(1) A housing action trust shall use its best endeavours to secure that its objects are achieved as soon as practicable.

(2) Where it appears to a trust that its objects have been substantially achieved, it shall—
 (a) so far as practicable, dispose or arrange to dispose of any remaining property, rights or liabilities of the trust in accordance with the preceding provisions of this Part of this Act; and
 (b) submit proposals to the Secretary of State for—
   (i) the dissolution of the trust;
   (ii) the disposal to any person of any remaining property, rights or liabilities of the trust which it has not been able to dispose of or arrange to dispose of under paragraph (a) above; and
   (iii) the transfer of any function exercisable by the trust to another person (including, where appropriate, a person with whom the trust has entered into an agreement under section 87 above).

(3) The Secretary of State may by order provide for the dissolution of a housing action trust and for any such disposal or transfer as is mentioned in subsection (2)(b) above, whether by way of giving effect (with or without modifications) to any proposals submitted to him under subsection (2) above or otherwise.

(4) Any order under this section—

    (a) where it provides for any such disposal or transfer as is mentioned in subsection (2)(b) above, may be on such terms, including financial terms, as the Secretary of State thinks fit and may create or impose such new rights or liabilities in respect of what is transferred as appear to him to be necessary or expedient;

    (b) may contain such supplementary and transitional provisions as the Secretary of State thinks necessary or expedient, including provisions amending any enactment or any instrument made under any enactment or establishing new bodies corporate to receive any functions, property, rights or liabilities transferred by the order; and

    (c) shall be made by statutory instrument which shall be subject to annulment in pursuance of a resolution of either House of Parliament.

DEFINITION
"housing action trust": s.60.

GENERAL NOTE
The intention is that H.A.T.s, like residuary bodies under the Local Government Act 1985, should be temporary bodies, and H.A.T.s are accordingly by this section placed under a duty to use their best endeavours to secure that their objects (see s.63) are achieved as soon as practicable: subs. (1). Once it appears to the H.A.T. that its objects have been "substantially" achieved, it has to dispose or arrange to dispose of its remaining property, rights and liabilities under the preceding provisions of this Part, so far as practicable, and submit proposals to the Secretary of State both for its dissolution, and for the disposal of any residual property, rights or liabilities, and for the transfer of its functions to another person, including possibly an agent under the last section (subs. (2)).

The Secretary of State may order dissolution, in accordance with those proposals or otherwise (subs. (3)), and his order may be on such terms as he thinks fit, including as to finance, and may create or impose new rights or liabilities as he thinks expedient, and may contain such supplementary and transitional provisions as he thinks necessary or expedient, to the extent of creating new bodies to take over functions, property, rights or liabilities and even amending legislation (primary or subordinate) (subs. (4)).

Miscellaneous and general

Supply of goods and services

89.—(1) A housing action trust and an urban development corporation established by an order under section 135 of the Local Government, Planning and Land Act 1980, may enter into any agreement with each other for all or any of the purposes set out in section 1(1) of the Local Authorities (Goods and Services) Act 1970, as if they were local authorities within the meaning of section 1 of that Act.

(2) Without prejudice to subsection (1) above, in section 1(4) of the Local Authorities (Goods and Services) Act 1970 (supply of goods and services by local authorities to public bodies), after the words " "public body" means any local authority" there shall be inserted "housing action trust established under Part III of the Housing Act 1988".

DEFINITION
"housing action trust": s.60.

GENERAL NOTE

The Local Authority (Goods and Services) Act 1970 empowers local authorities to enter into agreements with "public bodies" as specified for the purposes of that Act (including other local authorities), for the supply of goods or materials, for the provision of any administrative, professional or technical services, for the use of vehicle, plant or apparatus belonging to the authority, for placing the services of an employee at the disposal of a body in connection with the use of vehicle, plant or apparatus, and for the execution by the authority of works of maintenance in connection with land or buildings (s.1).

By this section, a housing action trust and an Urban Development Corporation established under the Local Government, Planning and Land Act 1980, may enter into agreements with each other as if local authorities for the purposes of the 1970 Act (subs. (1)), and H.A.T.s are treated as public bodies for the purposes of that Act, *i.e.* as bodies for whom a local authority can provide such services (subs. (2)).

Information

90.—(1) If required to do so by notice in writing given by the Secretary of State for any of the purposes mentioned in subsection (3) below, a local authority,—

(a) at such time and place as may be specified in the notice, shall produce any document; or

(b) within such period as may be so specified, or such longer period as the Secretary of State may allow, shall furnish a copy of any document or supply any information;

being a document, copy or information of a description specified in the notice.

(2) Where notice is given to a local authority under subsection (1) above, any officer of the authority—

(a) who has the custody or control of any document to which the notice relates, or

(b) who is in a position to give information to which the notice relates,

shall take all reasonable steps to ensure that the notice is complied with.

(3) The purposes referred to in subsection (1) above are—

(a) determining whether the Secretary of State should make a designation order in respect of any area;

(b) where a designation order is to be or has been made, determining whether, and to what extent, he should exercise any of his other powers under this Part of this Act; and

(c) enabling him to provide information to a housing action trust the better to enable it to carry out its functions.

(4) Without prejudice to the generality of subsection (1) above, among the information which may be required by a notice under that subsection is information with respect to the interests in, and the occupation of, land held by a local authority and, in particular, information with respect to any matter entered in a register kept under the Land Registration Act 1925 or the Land Charges Act 1972.

(5) To any extent to which, apart from this subsection, he would not be able to do so, the Secretary of State may use, for any of the purposes mentioned in subsection (3) above, any information obtained by him under, or in connection with his functions under, the Housing Act 1985 or any other enactment.

(6) If the Secretary of State considers it necessary or desirable to do so in order the better to enable a housing action trust to carry out its functions, he may disclose to the trust any information originally obtained by him for a purpose falling within paragraph (a) or paragraph (b) of subsection (3) above as well as information obtained for the purpose referred to in paragraph (c) of that subsection.

(7) In this section "local authority" has the same meaning as in section 74 above.

DEFINITIONS
"designation order": s.60.
"housing action trust": s.60.
"local authority": s.74.

GENERAL NOTE
This section empowers the Secretary of State to require information from a local authority (subs. (1)—and their officers (subs. (2)), who accordingly cannot "hide behind" a direction of the authority *not* to co-operate—in order to decide whether or not to make a designation order, what powers to exercise in connection with it, and in order to provide information to the H.A.T. to assist it the better to carry out its functions (subs. (3)). Such information can include information on the land registers: subs. (4). He may use such information not only by way of disclosure to the H.A.T., even if not initially sought for that purpose (subs (6)), but also for any purpose under the Housing Act 1985 or any other enactment (subs. (5)).

Service of notices

91.—(1) This section has effect in relation to any notice required or authorised by this Part of this Act to be served on any person by a housing action trust.

(2) Any such notice may be served on the person in question either by delivering it to him, or by leaving it at his proper address, or by sending it by post to him at that address.

(3) Any such notice may—
    (a) in the case of a body corporate, be given to or served on the secretary or clerk of that body; and
    (b) in the case of a partnership, be given to or served on a partner or a person having the control or management of the partnership business.

(4) For the purposes of this section and of section 7 of the Interpretation Act 1978 (service of documents by post) in its application to this section, the proper address of any person to or on whom a notice is to be given or served shall be his last known address, except that—
    (a) in the case of a body corporate or its secretary or clerk, it shall be the address of the registered or principal office of that body; and
    (b) in the case of a partnership or a person having the control or management of the partnership business, it shall be that of the principal office of the partnership;
and for the purposes of this subsection the principal office of a company registered outside the United Kingdom or of a partnership carrying on business outside the United Kingdom shall be its principal office within the United Kingdom.

(5) If the person to be given or served with any notice mentioned in subsection (1) above has specified an address within the United Kingdom other than his proper address within the meaning of subsection (4) above as the one at which he or someone on his behalf will accept documents of the same description as that notice, that address shall also be treated for the purposes of this section and section 7 of the Interpretation Act 1978 as his proper address.

(6) If the name or address of any owner, lessee or occupier of land to or on whom any notice mentioned in subsection (1) above is to be served cannot after reasonable inquiry be ascertained, the document may be served either by leaving it in the hands of a person who is or appears to be resident or employed on the land or by leaving it conspicuously affixed to some building or object on the land.

DEFINITION
"housing action trust": s.60.

This section governs the service of notices by H.A.T.s, which in the last resort can be by leaving a notice in the hands of a resident or employee on land, or conspicuously affixing it to some building or object on land (subs. (6)).

Interpretation of Part III

92.—(1) In this Part of this Act, except where the context otherwise requires,—

(a) "designated area" and "designation order" have the meaning assigned by section 60(6) above;

(b) any reference to a "house" includes a reference to a flat and to any yard, garden, outhouses and appurtenances belonging to the house or flat or usually enjoyed with it;

(c) "housing accommodation" includes flats, lodging-houses and hostels;

(d) "local housing authority" has the same meaning as in the Housing Act 1985 and section 2 of that Act (the district of a local housing authority) has effect in relation to this Part of this Act as it has effect in relation to that Act;

(e) "local authority housing" means housing accommodation provided by a local housing authority (whether in its own district or not);

(f) "secure tenancy" has the meaning assigned by section 79 of the Housing Act 1985 and "secure tenant" shall be construed accordingly; and

(g) "the 1971 Act" means the Town and Country Planning Act 1971.

(2) In this Part of this Act "the Corporation" means the Housing Corporation or Housing for Wales but—

(a) an approval given by the Housing Corporation shall not have effect in relation to buildings or other property in Wales; and

(b) an approval given by Housing for Wales shall not have effect in relation to buildings or other property in England.

GENERAL NOTE

House. Save for the inclusion of flats, this definition follows that to be found in the Housing Act 1985, s.56, and elsewhere in that Act, and which has long been applied in the Housing Acts.

PART IV

CHANGE OF LANDLORD: SECURE TENANTS

Preliminary

Right conferred by Part IV

93.—(1) This Part has effect for the purpose of conferring on any person who has been approved under section 94 below the right to acquire from a public sector landlord, subject to and in accordance with the provisions of this Part—

(a) the fee simple estate in any buildings each of which comprises or contains one or more dwelling-houses which on the relevant date are occupied by qualifying tenants of the public sector landlord; and

(b) the fee simple estate in any other property which is reasonably required for occupation with buildings falling within paragraph (a) above.

(2) The following are public sector landlords for the purposes of this Part, namely—

(a) a local housing authority within the meaning of section 1 of the Housing Act 1985 (in this Part referred to as "the 1985 Act");

(b) a new town corporation within the meaning of section 4(b) of that Act;

(c) a housing action trust within the meaning of Part III of this Act; and

(d) the Development Board for Rural Wales.

(3) Subject to subsection (4) below, a secure tenant of a public sector landlord is a qualifying tenant for the purposes of this Part if (and only if) his secure tenancy is held directly from the landlord as owner of the fee simple estate and, in relation to any acquisition or proposed acquisition under this Part, any reference in the following provisions of this Part to qualifying tenant is a reference only to a qualifying tenant of the public sector landlord from whom the acquisition is or is proposed to be made.

(4) A secure tenant is not a qualifying tenant for the purposes of this Part if—

(a) he is obliged to give up possession of the dwelling-house in pursuance of an order of the court or will be so obliged at a date specified in such an order; or

(b) the circumstances are as set out in any of paragraphs 5 to 11 of Schedule 5 to the 1985 Act (exceptions to right to buy).

(5) In this Part "the relevant date", in relation to an acquisition or proposed acquisition under this Part, means the date on which is made the application under section 96 below claiming to exercise the right conferred by this Part.

DEFINITIONS

"property": s.114.

"public sector landlord": subs. (2).

GENERAL NOTE

This section introduces this Part of the Act, and defines its application. *Approved persons*—would-be landlords—may seek to remove from the public sector *freehold* property, provided a majority of the existing tenants do not object. The subject-matter is the stock of local housing authorities, new town corporations, the Development Board for Rural Wales, and the new housing action trusts within Part III. The Part applies to houses or flats, provided the landlord owns the fee simple, together with property reasonably required for occupation with such houses or flats, again provided that what the landlords holds is fee simple.

In the case of a single house, it must be occupied at the relevant date (defined in subs. (5)) by a qualifying tenant (defined in subss. (3), (4)); in the case of a building containing flats, the wording of subs. (1)(a) on its own leaves unclear whether occupation by qualifying tenants (of the same public sector landlord who owns the fee simple estate in the building) needs to be of *all* its units. However, the specific exclusions set out in s.95(3), suggest that this is not so: see further notes to s.95, below.

Subss. (3), (4)

Secure tenancies end not on the date when a possession order is made, but when the possession order is scheduled to take effect: Housing Act 1985, s.82. Secure tenants are qualifying tenants, unless a possession order specifying a date to give up possession has already been obtained, or the secure tenancy falls within the specified paragraphs of Sched. 5 to the 1985 Act:

Para. 5. This exemption applies to property forming part of the curtilage of a building held for non-housing purposes (including a cemetery) and was let to the tenant or his predecessor in consequence of employment by the or another public sector (as defined for the purposes of the 1985 Act) landlord.

Paras. 6–8. These deal with dwelling-houses for the disabled, but only para. 7 continues in operation after s.123, below, comes into force, repealing paras. 6 and 8. See notes to s.123, below.

Para. 9. This deals with sheltered housing for those suffering from a mental disorder.

Paras. 10–11. These deal with housing for the elderly.

Persons by whom right may be exercised

94.—(1) The right conferred by this Part shall not be exercisable except by a person who is for the time being approved by the Corporation under this section; and neither a public sector landlord nor the council of a county nor any other body which the Corporation have reason to believe might not be independent of such a landlord or council may be approved under this section.

(2) For the purposes of subsection (1) above, a body shall not be regarded as independent of a public sector landlord or the council of a county if the body is or appears likely to be under the control of, or subject to influence from, such a landlord or council or particular members or officers of such a landlord or council.

(3) The Corporation shall establish (and may from time to time vary) criteria to be satisfied by a person seeking approval under this section and, without prejudice to subsections (1) and (2) above, in deciding whether to give such approval, the Corporation shall have regard to whether the person satisfies those criteria.

(4) Subject to any directions under section 76 of the Housing Associations Act 1985 (directions by the Secretary of State), an approval under this section—

(a) shall not be given except to a person making an application accompanied by such fee as the Corporation, with the consent of the Secretary of State, may specify; and

(b) may be given to a particular person or to persons of a particular description; and

(c) may apply either in relation to acquisitions generally or in relation to a particular acquisition or acquisitions or in relation to acquisitions made in a particular area or within a particular period; and

(d) may be made conditional upon the person or persons concerned entering into such undertakings as may be specified by the Corporation;

and different fees may be specified under paragraph (a) above for different descriptions of cases.

(5) Subject to any directions under section 76 of the Housing Associations Act 1985, if it appears to the Corporation appropriate to do so (whether by reason of a failure to honour an undertaking or to meet any criteria or for any other reason), the Corporation may revoke an approval given under this section by notice in writing served on the approved person; and where such a notice of revocation is served—

(a) the revocation shall be provisional until the expiry of such period, being not less than 14 days, as may be specified in the notice;

(b) if the Corporation withdraws the notice at any time during the specified period, the approval shall be treated as never having been revoked; and

(c) subject to paragraph (b) above, after the date of service of the notice, the person concerned may not take any steps in connection with a claim to exercise the right conferred by this Part;

but the service of a notice under this subsection shall not affect any transaction completed before the service of the notice.

(6) In the case of a body which has been approved under this section which does not have a registered office (at which documents can be served) and which appears to the Corporation to have ceased to exist or not to operate, notice under subsection (5) above shall be deemed to be served on the body if it is served at the address last known to the Corporation to be the principal place of business of the body.

(7) The Housing Corporation and Housing for Wales shall each maintain a register of persons for the time being approved by it under this section,

specifying the extent of the approval given in each case; and each register so maintained shall be open to inspection at the head office of the Corporation by which it is maintained at all reasonable times.

GENERAL NOTE
The function of approving prospective purchasers is conferred on the Housing Corporation and Housing for Wales, but public sector landlords for the purposes of this Part are themselves excluded, as are county councils and bodies "which the Corporation have reason to believe might not be independent of such a landlord or council". This phrase, added during the passage of the Bill through Parliament, is designed to defeat proposals—of which there were reports in the media—to establish private companies held or controlled by local authorities, to take over the stock: *cf.* notes to s.79, above. There are many other similarities to s.79, above: see notes thereto.

Property excluded from right

95.—(1) A building shall be excluded from an acquisition under this Part if on the relevant date—
  (a) any part or parts of the building is or are occupied or intended to be occupied otherwise than for residential purposes; and
  (b) the internal floor area of that part or those parts (taken together) exceeds 50 per cent. of the internal floor area of the building (taken as a whole);
and for the purposes of this subsection the internal floor area of any common parts or common facilities shall be disregarded.

(2) In the application of subsection (1) above to property falling within section 93(1)(b) above, a building or part of a building which, apart from this subsection, would not be regarded as occupied for residential purposes shall be so regarded if—
  (a) it is or is intended to be occupied together with a dwelling-house and used for purposes connected with the occupation of the dwelling-house; or
  (b) it is or is intended to be used for the provision of services to a dwelling-house which is comprised in a building falling within section 93(1)(a) above.

(3) A building shall be excluded from an acquisition under this Part if—
  (a) it contains two or more dwelling–houses which on the relevant date are occupied by secure tenants who are not qualifying tenants; and
  (b) the number of dwelling-houses which on that date are occupied by such tenants exceeds 50 per cent. of the total number of dwelling-houses in the building.

(4) A dwelling-house shall be excluded from an acquisition under this Part if it is a house and it is occupied on the relevant date by—
  (a) a secure tenant who is precluded from being a qualifying tenant by section 93(4)(b) above; or
  (b) a tenant who is not a secure tenant.

(5) A building or other property shall be excluded from an acquisition under this Part if—
  (a) it was specified in some other application made under section 96 below made before the relevant date; and
  (b) that other application has not been disposed of.

(6) Except to the extent that it comprises or is let together with a dwelling-house, property shall be excluded from an acquisition under this Part if it is land held—

(a) for the purposes of section 164 of the Public Health Act 1875 (pleasure grounds); or

(b) in accordance with section 10 of the Open Spaces Act 1906 (duty of local authority to maintain open spaces and burial grounds).

(7) The Secretary of State may by order substitute for the percentage for the time being specified in subsection (1)(b) above such other percentage as is specified in the order.

DEFINITIONS
"property": s.114.
"qualifying tenant": s.93.
"relevant date": s.93.

GENERAL NOTE
This section excludes from the procedures of this Part a number of freehold buildings (leasehold buildings are already excluded by s.93(1)). The first exclusion is of buildings which either are, or are intended to be, occupied for other than residential purposes, either entirely or in substantial part. If the building qualifies as non-residential for this purpose, it is excluded altogether. This definition is qualified where what is under consideration is property only within the prospective acquisition by reason of s.93(1)(b), *i.e.* "reasonably required for occupation with" a building comprising or containing a dwelling-house: clearly the principal exclusion cannot operate, for it is highly likely not to be directly occupied "for residential purposes". Accordingly, it is artificially treated as if so occupied if it is or is intended to be occupied together with a dwelling-house and used for purposes connected with such occupation or it is used or intended to be used for the provision of services to a dwelling-house in a building comprising or containing dwelling-houses: subs. (2).

To calculate whether the building is in substantial part non-residential (as defined), common parts and common facilities are disregarded, and the internal floor areas of the non-residential parts are added together, and compared to the internal floor areas of the building as a whole: if the non-residential floor areas are more than 50 per cent. (or such other percentage as the Secretary of State may prescribe: see subs. (7)), the building is exempt from the application of this Part.

The second exclusion (subs. (3)) applies only to buildings containing two or more dwelling-houses, *i.e.* normally, blocks of flats. In this case, the building is excluded if more than 50 per cent. of its dwelling-houses are occupied by secure tenants who are not qualifying tenants, *i.e.* who are excluded by s.93(3), above.

The third exclusion (subs. (4)) concerns houses, as defined (following s.114(2), below, applying definitions in Part V, the 1985 Act) by the 1985 Act, s.183, to mean a unit, whether or not detached, no material part of which overlaps or underlaps any other part of its structure. Houses are excluded from the operation of this Part if occupied on the relevant date by a secure tenant who is a non-qualifying tenant by (and only by) reason of s.93(4)(b), above, *i.e.* the relevant paragraphs of the 1985 Act, Sched. 5, or by a non-secure tenant. It follows that a building containing a flat in the occupation of a secure tenant against whom a possession order has been made, to give up possession on or by a specified date, may yet be the subject of this Part.

Fourthly (subs. (5)), a building is exempt so long as it is the subject of some other, as yet undetermined, application under this Part.

Fifthly (subs. (6)), other property is excluded if it is land held under the Public Health Act 1875, s.164, or the Open Spaces Act 1906, s.10, *save* to the extent that it comprises or is let together with a dwelling-house. As to the meaning of the phrase "let together with", see notes to s.2, above.

Initial procedures

Application to exercise right

96.—(1) An application claiming to exercise the right conferred by this Part—

(a) shall be made in the prescribed form to the public sector landlord concerned; and

(b) shall specify and be accompanied by a plan which shows—

(i) the buildings proposed to be acquired by virtue of paragraph (a) of subsection (1) of section 93 above; and

(ii) the property proposed to be acquired by virtue of paragraph (b) of that subsection.

(2) Where an application claiming to exercise the right conferred by this Part specifies, as a building proposed to be acquired by virtue of section 93(1)(a) above, a building containing a dwelling-house which is subject to an approved co-operative management agreement, the application—

(a) shall specify all the buildings which contain dwelling-houses subject to the agreement and in which the public sector landlord has the fee simple estate; and

(b) shall not specify (by virtue of paragraph (a) or paragraph (b) of subsection (1) of section 93 above) any building which contains dwelling-houses if none of them is subject to the agreement.

(3) For the purposes of subsection (2) above, an approved co-operative management agreement is an agreement—

(a) which is made with the approval of the Secretary of State under section 27 of the Housing Act 1985, either as originally enacted or as substituted by section 10 of the Housing and Planning Act 1986; and

(b) under which the body exercising functions of the local housing authority is a society, company or body of trustees approved by the Secretary of State for the purposes of subsection (2) above.

DEFINITIONS
"approved co-operative management agreement": subs. (3).
"prescribed": s.114.
"public sector landlord": s.93.

GENERAL NOTE
The first stage in the procedure is for the approved landlord to make application in the prescribed form to the public sector landlord, identifying (by words and plans) both the housing it is proposed to acquire, and any other property reasonably required for occupation with it.

Subss. (2), (3)
Under the Housing Act 1985, s.27, as originally enacted, local authorities (and pursuant to *ibid.*, s.30(2), a new town corporation and the Development Board for Rural Wales) could enter into a management agreement with a housing co-operative, usually comprised of their own tenants, in effect to take over and manage a group of housing. The provisions were amended by the Housing and Planning Act 1986, but such an arrangement could continue to be made (although s.30(2) itself was repealed, so limiting the powers of the other bodies to engage in such arrangements). Under these subsections, a prospective application must specify *all* the dwellings within such a co-operative management agreement, but *only* such dwellings.

97.—(1) Within four weeks of the relevant date, the landlord shall serve the applicant a notice specifying—

(a) the name and address of every tenant or licensee of a dwelling-house which the buildings proposed to be acquired by virtue of section 93(1)(a) above comprise or contain; and

(b) the general nature of his tenancy or licence.

(2) As from four weeks after that date, the applicant shall have the following rights, namely—

(a) a right of access, at any reasonable time and on giving reasonable notice, to any property proposed to be acquired which is not subject to a tenancy;

(b) a right, on giving reasonable notice, to be provided with a list of any documents to which subsection (3) below applies;

(c) a right to inspect, at any reasonable time and on giving reasonable notice, any documents to which that subsection applies; and

(d) a right, on payment of a reasonable fee, to be provided with a copy of any documents inspected under paragraph (c) above.

(3) This subsection applies to any document in the possession of the landlord—

(a) sight of which is reasonably required for the purpose of pursuing the application; and

(b) which, on a proposed sale by a willing vendor to a willing purchaser of the property proposed to be acquired, the landlord, as vendor, would be expected to make available to the purchaser (whether at or before contract or completion).

(4) In this section "document" has the same meaning as in Part I of the Civil Evidence Act 1968.

GENERAL NOTE

Within four weeks of application, the landlord has to respond with a notice specifying the name and address of every tenant *or licensee* (see notes to s.1, above) of a dwelling within the proposed acquisition, identifying "the general nature" of the tenancy or licence, a vague phrase but one that is unlikely to prove problematic in practice (*e.g.* general residential, short-life, employment-related, elderly persons, etc.). This duty arises irrespective of any claim by the landlord that the building does not qualify under this Part, as to which see s.98, below. The period may be extended by consent: s.110, below.

After service of this first response, there is then a four week break, from the date of the response, after which the applicant has the rights specified in subs. (2):

(1) access to empty properties or unlet parts, at reasonable times and on reasonable notice, and by implication, free of charge;

(2) a list of documents within subs. (3), on reasonable notice and by implication free of charge;

(3) inspection of such documents, at reasonable times, on reasonable notice and by implication free of charge; and

(4) copying of such documents, on payment of a reasonable charge.

Subs. (3) includes in the documentation any document in the possession of the authority, sight of which is reasonably required for the purpose of pursuing the application, *e.g.* plans, surveys, title, local land charges, etc., *and* which a willing vendor landlord would be expected to make available to a purchaser, *e.g.* excluding tenants' personal files.

Determination of property to be included

98.—(1) Within twelve weeks of the relevant date, the landlord shall serve on the applicant a notice stating—

(a) which (if any) of the buildings proposed to be acquired by virtue of paragraph (a) of subsection (1) of section 93 above should be excluded from the acquisition on the ground that they do not comprise or contain one or more dwelling-houses which on the relevant date were occupied by qualifying tenants;

(b) which (if any) property proposed to be acquired by virtue of paragraph (b) of that subsection should be excluded from the acquisition on the ground that it is not reasonably required for occupation with any of the buildings proposed to be acquired by virtue of paragraph (a) of that subsection or that it is reasonably required for occupation with such of those buildings as should be excluded from the acquisition on the ground mentioned in paragraph (a) above;

(c) which (if any) property proposed to be acquired by virtue of either paragraph of that subsection should be excluded from the acquisition on the ground that its inclusion is precluded by section 95 above or that it is reasonably required for occupation with property the inclusion of which is so precluded or that it is a building which is excluded from the acquisition by virtue of section 96(2)(b) above,

(d) which property (if any) the landlord desires to have included in the acquisition on the ground that it cannot otherwise be reasonably managed or maintained;

(e) which rights (if any) the landlord desires to retain over property included in the acquisition on the ground that they are necessary for the proper management or maintenance of land to be retained by the landlord;

(f) the other proposed terms of the conveyance; and

(g) such other particulars as may be prescribed.

(2) A building which is excluded from an acquisition by virtue of section 95 or section 96(2)(b) above may not be included by virtue of subsection (1)(d) above.

(3) Where a notice under subsection (1) above specifies property falling within paragraph (d) of that subsection, the applicant shall have a right of access, at any reasonable time and on giving reasonable notice, to any of that property which is not subject to a tenancy.

(4) Within four weeks of service of the notice under subsection (1) above, the applicant shall notify the landlord in writing of any matters stated in that notice which he does not accept.

(5) Any dispute as to any matters stated in a notice under subsection (1) above shall be determined—

(a) by a person agreed to by the parties or, in default of agreement, appointed by the Secretary of State; and

(b) in accordance with such provisions (including provisions as to costs) as may be prescribed.

(6) In relation to a proposed acquisition under this Part, any reference in the following provisions of this Part to the property to which the acquisition relates is a reference to the whole of the property which, in accordance with the provisions of this section, is to be acquired, disregarding the effect of any exclusion by virtue of regulations under section 100 below.

DEFINITIONS
"prescribed": s.114.
"property": s.114.
"qualifying tenant": s.93.
"relevant date": s.93.

GENERAL NOTE
Although predominantly procedural, this section contains some substantive law: see subs. (1)(d),(e).

Within 12 weeks of the relevant date (application under s.96, above), the landlord must serve notice on the prospective purchaser, covering the following matters:

(1) Which buildings do not fall within the provisions, because they neither comprise nor contain dwellings which on the relevant date were occupied by qualifying tenants;

(2) Which property sought in connection with the proposed purchase does not fall within the provisions, because it is not reasonably required for occupation with the dwellings it is proposed to buy, or is reasonably required for occupation but only with buildings which the landlord denies can be bought, under the first heading (not qualifying tenants);

(3) Which buildings (or property required for occupation with it) should be excluded by virtue of ss.95 and 96(2)(b) (property not subject to a co-operative management agreement) above;

(4) Which property—if any—*the landlord requires the purchaser to take* together with the purchaser's proposed acquisition on the ground that it cannot otherwise (*i.e.* if left untransferred) reasonably be managed or maintained;

(5) Which rights—if any—*the landlord requires to retain* over the property to be acquired, on the grounds that they are necessary for the proper management or maintenance of land to be retained by the landlord;

(6) Other proposed terms of conveyance (other than price: see s.99, below);

(7) Other particulars as prescribed.

The 12 week period may be extended by consent: s.110, below.

The prospective purchaser has only two weeks in which to respond identifying any aspect of the landlord's response which he does not agree with (subs. (2)), and disputes are to be determined either by an agreed arbitrator or an arbitrator appointed by the Secretary of State, which arbitration is to be conducted in accordance with provisions to be prescribed.

Determination of purchase price

99.—(1) Within eight weeks of—
  (a) if there is no dispute as to any of the matters stated in the notice under section 98(1) above, the service of that notice, or
  (b) if there is such a dispute, the determination of the dispute,
the landlord shall serve on the applicant a notice specifying—
  (i) the price which, disregarding sections 100(3) and 103(1) below, it considers should be payable for the property to be acquired or, as the case may be, the disposal cost which, disregarding section 100(3) below, is attributable to the property to be acquired by virtue of subsection (3) below; and
  (ii) if the property to which the acquisition relates includes dwelling-houses which are houses as well as other property, an amount which the landlord considers to be the amount attributable to houses as defined in section 100(4)(b) below.

(2) Subject to sections 100(3) and 103(1) below, the price payable for the property to be acquired shall be the price which on the relevant date the property to which the acquisition relates would realise if sold on the open market by a willing vendor on the following assumptions, namely—
  (a) that it was sold subject to any tenancies subsisting on that date but otherwise with vacant possession;
  (b) that it was to be conveyed with the same rights and subject to the same burdens as it would be in pursuance of the right of acquisition;
  (c) that the only bidders in the market were persons who on that date either were approved under section 94 above or fulfilled the criteria for approval established under subsection (3) of that section;
  (d) that the applicant would, within a reasonable period, carry out such works as are reasonably necessary to put the buildings included in the acquisition into the state of repair required by the landlord's repairing obligations; and
  (e) that the applicant would not be required to grant any leases in pursuance of regulations made under section 100 below.

(3) Subject to section 100(3) below, there is a disposal cost attributable to the property to be acquired if, having regard to the expense likely to be incurred in carrying out the works referred to in paragraph (d) of subsection (2) above, the property to which the acquisition relates would not realise any price in the circumstances specified in that subsection; and that disposal cost is the amount by which the expense likely to be so incurred exceeds what would be determined under that subsection as the price if those works had already been carried out.

(4) The notice under subsection (1) above shall contain sufficient information to enable the applicant to see how the price or, as the case may be, disposal cost and any amount referred to in sub-paragraphs (i) and (ii) of subsection (1) above were arrived at and, if the property to which the acquisition relates consists of or includes any dwelling-houses which are houses, the notice shall also contain a list of the addresses of the houses together with the number of habitable rooms in each of them.

(5) Within four weeks of service of the notice under subsection (1) above, the applicant shall notify the landlord in writing of any matters stated in that notice which he does not accept.

(6) Any dispute as to any matters stated in a notice under subsection (1) above shall be determined by the district valuer, in accordance with such provisions (including provisions as to costs) as may be prescribed.

DEFINITIONS
"habitable room": s.114.
"property": s.114.

GENERAL NOTE
This section governs the purchase price (which may be a negative amount: see notes to subs. (3), below), in which case the price is called "disposal cost"). It is for the landlord to specify the price payable or the disposal cost, by notice served within eight weeks either of the service of the "second response" or "detailed response" notice under s.98 (which will mean only one week after the prospective purchaser fails to object under s.98(2)), or of the final determination of a dispute: subs. (1). The period may be extended by consent: s.110, below. The notice has to contain enough information to permit the prospective purchaser to see how the stated price is arrived at: subs. (4). The prospective purchaser has two weeks to notify the landlord in writing as to any matters (price or cost, or basis of price or cost) with which he disagrees (subs. (5)), and a dispute is to be determined (in accordance with regulations to be prescribed) by the District Valuer: subs. (6).

The price or disposal cost stated is to disregard the possibility that some tenants of houses may "opt out", leading to the exclusion of their houses under s.100(3), below, for it might otherwise be argued as a valuation point that even the *prospect* of opting out had a diminishing effect on value (subs. (1)(b)(i)); however, the landlord has to identify the part of the price or disposal cost attributable to each *house* within the application (subs. (1)(b)(ii)), also disregarding the possibility of opting out under s.100, below (s.98(4)). The amount attributable to houses where the tenant opts out will be deducted or (if a disposal cost) added: see s.100(3), below. As to the meaning of house, see notes to s.95, above.

The key issue is the price or disposal cost. The basis is open market sale *as at the relevant date* by a willing vendor, on the following assumptions:

(1) Subject to tenancies subsisting on that date, but otherwise with vacant possession; as tenancies will, of definition, at the relevant date be secure, this will depress the price, although landlords may have regard to any prospective grounds for possession which may be available against particular tenants; as, however, only tenancies are referred to (*cf.* s.97(1), above), licences—even though usually secure (see Housing Act 1985, s.79(3))—may be disregarded;

(2) The terms (rights and burdens) are as they will actually be;

(3) That the "open market" is confined to approved purchasers, *i.e.* all purchasers approved by the Corporations, for the purposes of this Part, under s.94, above, *or fulfilling the criteria for and therefore qualifying for* such approval—this will depress the price as against the market as a whole, although less than if (as originally put forward) it was confined to purchasers *actually* so approved;

(4) That the prospective purchaser will put the property into the state of repair required by a landlord's repairing obligations (see Landlord and Tenant Act 1985, s.11; see also notes to s.116, below) within a reasonable period—this may depress the price if the property is run-down, though this would in any event normally be included in a valuation exercise; if the cost will be greater than the value of the property *after* the repairs, it produces a negative amount, *i.e.* the disposal cost—see notes to subs. (3), below.

(5) That no leases have to be granted pursuant to s.100, below—this will prevent s.100 operating further to depress the price. See notes thereto, below.

Subs. (3)
This section defines the "disposal cost", which is the negative value which property has attributable to the cost of repairs under subs. (2)(d), above. It is calculated by determining the repairs cost, and deducting therefrom the value of the properties *after* the works are carried out; it accordingly recognises that repairs may cost more than property is worth. What is—astonishingly—left unexpressed, but that nonetheless *seems* to be implied is that this amount will have to be paid by the public sector landlord to the "purchaser".

Subs. (4)
"Habitable room" is defined in s.114, below, to mean a room used, or intended for use, as a bedroom, living room, dining room or kitchen. The references to "living room" *and* "dining room" suggest this is an exhaustive definition, and would therefore exclude not only a bathroom or lavatory, but also, *e.g.* a utility room, for if all "living accommodation" within, *e.g.* Rent Act caselaw (see notes to s.3, above), were excluded, it would have been unnecessary to mention them separately.

Even if it is not yet known whether or not houses will be excluded under s.100 (because it is likely to turn on the tenant's choice which by this stage will not yet be stated), the landlord should pay careful attention to the amount attributed to houses, for unless the landlord takes issue with the amount thus stated *at this time*, the prospective purchaser's statement will prevail, for there is no provision to refer the issue to the district valuer at a later date than allowed under this section.

Special cases

Tenants continuing as tenants of landlord

100.—(1) The Secretary of State shall make regulations imposing the following requirements in relation to any acquisition under this Part, namely—
   (a) that any dwelling-house which is a house and is occupied by a tenant to whom subsection (2) below applies shall be excluded from the acquisition; and
   (b) that a lease of any dwelling-house which is a flat and is occupied by a tenant to whom subsection (2) below applies or by a tenant of a description prescribed for the purposes of this paragraph shall be granted by the applicant to the landlord immediately after the acquisition.
(2) This subsection applies—
   (a) to any qualifying tenant whose tenancy commenced before the relevant date, and
   (b) to any tenant of a description prescribed for the purposes of this subsection,
being, in either case, a tenant who, before the end of the period mentioned in section 102 below and in response to the consultation under that section, gives notice as mentioned in section 103(2) below of his wish to continue as a tenant of the landlord.
(3) If, by virtue of regulations under this section, any houses fall to be excluded from the acquisition—
   (a) there shall be determined the sum (in this subsection referred to as "the sum referable to excluded houses") which represents that proportion of the amount attributable to houses which the number of habitable rooms in the houses which fall to be so excluded bears to the number of habitable rooms in all of the houses comprised in the property to which the acquisition relates; and
   (b) if the amount attributable to houses is a price, the sum referable to excluded houses shall be applied as a deduction from any price payable for the property to be acquired, as determined under section 99 above, and as an increase in any disposal cost attributable to that property; and
   (c) if the amount attributable to houses is a disposal cost, the sum referable to excluded houses shall be applied as an increase in any price payable for the property to be acquired, as determined under section 99 above, and as a deduction from any disposal cost attributable to that property.
(4) In section 99(1)(ii) and subsection (3) above, "the amount attributable to houses," in relation to an acquisition under this Part, means,—
   (a) if the property to which the acquisition relates consists of dwelling-houses which are houses and no other property, the price or, as the case may be, disposal cost specified in accordance with section 99(1)(i) above; and
   (b) in any other case, the price or disposal cost which, under subsection (2) or subsection (3) of section 99 above, would be payable for, or attributable to, the property to which the acquisition relates if

there were excluded from that property all property other than dwelling-houses which are houses.

DEFINITIONS

"habitable room": s.114.
"prescribed": s.114.
"qualifying tenant": s.93.
"relevant date": s.93.

GENERAL NOTE

This is a most important section. By s.103, below, the process is only brought to an end if, during consultation required by s.102, *more than* 50 per cent. of the tenants who have to be consulted, object to the proposed transfer. However, individual tenants—whether of houses or of flats—may (subject to regulations) "opt out" of the transfer in any event. This section, however, only takes effect if the Secretary of State makes regulations. The regulations may prescribe that houses occupied by tenants within subs. (2), or by tenants of any prescribed description, shall be excluded from the acquisition, and that the prospective purchaser has to grant a lease of a flat occupied by (either class of) such tenants *to the landlord*, so that, in either event, the occupier remains the former landlord's tenant direct.

The tenants within subs. (2) are *qualifying* tenants whose tenancies begin *before* the relevant date, and other tenants within the regulations, who notify the prospective purchaser of their wish to remain the tenant of the (current) landlord before the end of the period allowed, *and in response to the consultation* (thus pre-empting a "general" opposition and, presumably, rendering it progressively more difficult for opponents of H.A.T.s to arrange for negative replies: see further notes to s.103, below). The notification has to be within the consultation period permitted by s.102, below, and in prescribed form. The period may be extended by consent: s.110, below.

Subss. (3), (4)

If the regulations permit exclusion of houses, then the price payable is reduced by the amount attributable to them, or the disposal cost accordingly adjusted to reflect that works will not need to be carried out on the excluded houses. The calculation is based on habitable rooms: the reduction is the proportion of habitable rooms in houses excluded compared to the habitable rooms either within the application as a whole (if it relates only to houses), or compared to the habitable rooms in the houses identified in the landlord's notice under s.99. As to the meaning of habitable rooms, see notes to s.99(3), above.

The prospective purchaser will have specified the amount attributable to houses in the notice under s.99, above, and unless the landlord takes issue with the amount thus stated *at that time* (not yet knowing whether houses may fall to be excluded), his statement will prevail, for there is no provision to refer the issue to the district valuer at a later date than allowed under s.99. However, while amount attributed to houses will not at this stage be challengeable, calculation of the numbers of habitable rooms (proportions) may yet be the subject of dispute, referable to the county court under s.105, below, *cf.* notes to s.103, below.

Tenancies granted after relevant date

101.—(1) Subject to subsection (4)(a) below, this section applies to any tenancy of or licence to occupy any part of the property proposed to be acquired, being a tenancy or licence commencing,—

(a) in the case of property falling within paragraph (d) of subsection (1) of section 98 above, after the date of the notice under that subsection;

(b) in any other case, after the relevant date.

(2) Notwithstanding anything in any enactment, a tenancy or licence to which this section applies—

(a) shall not be a secure tenancy, and

(b) shall not be capable of becoming an assured tenancy or an assured agricultural occupancy,

and neither Part II of the Landlord and Tenant Act 1954 (business tenancies) nor Parts III to VI of the Agricultural Holdings Act 1986 (tenancies of agricultural holdings, including market gardens and smallholdings) shall apply to a tenancy or licence to which this section applies.

(3) Every tenancy or licence to which this section applies shall be determinable by the landlord or licensor by giving not less than four weeks notice to quit expiring at any time during the tenancy; and this subsection has effect whether or not the tenancy or licence is periodic and, if it is periodic, regardless of the length of the period.

(4) The Secretary of State may make regulations—

(a) excluding from the tenancies and licences to which this section applies a tenancy or licence of a description specified in the regulations;

(b) requiring the public sector landlord to give notice to the applicant of the grant of any tenancy or licence to which this section applies;

(c) requiring the public sector landlord to give notice of the effect of this section to any tenant or licensee under a tenancy or licence to which this section applies;

(d) for securing that, on the transfer of the property included in the acquisition to the applicant, the public sector landlord gives vacant possession of any property subject to a tenancy or licence to which this section applies;

(e) that, in so far as vacant possession is not so given, any costs or expenses attributable to the recovery of vacant possession by the applicant and any losses consequent upon the failure of the public sector landlord to give vacant possession are recoverable by the applicant from that landlord as a simple contract debt; and

(f) making provision for and in connection with the disapplication of this section in any case where the applicant does not proceed with the acquisition.

DEFINITION
"relevant date": s.93.

GENERAL NOTE

Save so far as the Secretary of State by regulation excludes its operation (subs. (4)), this section overrides the definition of secure tenant in Part IV of the Housing Act 1985, for the purposes of this Part, in respect of two classes of (otherwise secure) tenant: tenancies beginning after the relevant date, *i.e.* the date when the prospective purchaser serves application under s.96, above; and, tenancies of property within s.98(1)(d), above, after the date of the notice under that section, *i.e.* tenants of property the landlord requires the prospective purchaser to acquire, being property that cannot be reasonably managed or maintained if retained.

Tenancies so qualifying, granted after the respective notice, *are not* secure, *nor* can they become assured, *nor* qualify for protection under the Landlord and Tenant Act 1954, Part II, nor under Parts III–VI of the Agricultural Holdings Act 1986 (subs. (2)), and regardless of the terms on which granted, *i.e.* regardless of periods of tenancy or whether fixed-term, are determinable by four weeks' notice to quit (subs. (3)), and (if regulations so provide) *must* be determined so that vacant possession can be granted on completion of the acquisition (subs. (4)(d), (e)). The regulations may also require the landlord to give notice of the grant of these "wholly unprotected" tenancies or licences to the applicant and/or to the occupier thereunder, and can provide for "damages" for failure to yield up vacant possession and for the "elevation" of the occupiers to secure tenant, etc., if the application does not proceed (subs. (4)).

The purpose of this draconian provision is, of course, to prevent landlords defeating an application to buy under this Part, by granting new arrangements on "long" tenancies, perhaps at a low rent, perhaps with a range of associated rights, *e.g.* right to buy, to transfer, to be consulted, etc., which mirror the superior security available as a secure tenancy compared to assured security under Part I of this Act. Henceforth, landlords wishing to protect themselves and/or their tenants against the effects of this Part will be obliged to do so (where lawfully possible) prior to any application being made hereunder.

Final procedures

Consultations by applicant

102.—(1) During such period as may be prescribed beginning with,—
  (a) if there is a determination by the district valuer under section 99 above, notification to the applicant of that determination,
  (b) if there is no such determination, service of the landlord's notice under that section,
the applicant shall consult, in accordance with such provisions as may be prescribed, tenants to whom this section applies.

(2) This section applies—
  (a) to any qualifying tenant, or tenant under a long tenancy, who on the relevant date occupied a dwelling-house proposed to be included in the acquisition and continued to occupy the dwelling during the period referred to in subsection (1) above; and
  (b) to any tenant of a description prescribed for the purposes of section 100(2) above; and
  (c) to any tenant of a description prescribed for the purposes of this section.

DEFINITIONS
"prescribed": s.114.
"relevant date": s.93.
"qualifying tenant": s.93.

GENERAL NOTE
This introduces the final stage of the process. Regulations are to prescribe a period during which *the prospective purchaser* must consult—in accordance with such provisions as may be prescribed—the tenants within this section. The period begins with the determination by the District Valuer of price, if a dispute has been referred to him, or otherwise service of the landlord's notice of price and basis of price, under s.99. If the prospective purchaser fails to comply with this obligation, within the time allowed (as extended by the landlord—see s.110(2)), then the application fails as a whole, and the process has to be recommenced: s.110(3). As to consultation, see notes to s.62, above.

The tenants who must be consulted are only those who—in occupation at and since the relevant date—count as qualifying tenants (not, therefore, all secure tenants, or all tenants whose tenancies may nonetheless be transferred), *plus* those prescribed for the purposes of s.100(2) above or for the purposes of this section, *plus* "long tenants", as defined (pursuant to the general application to this Part of definitions in Part V of the 1985 Act) in the 1985 Act, s.187, in turn referring to *ibid.*, s.115, to mean:

(1) A tenancy granted for a term certain exceeding 21 years, whether or not terminable by notice by the tenant before that time, or by the landlord by re-entry or forfeiture;
(2) A tenancy for a term fixed by law under a grant with a covenant or obligation for perpetual renewal, other than a tenancy by sub-demise from a tenancy which is not a long tenancy;
(3) A tenancy (of whatever length) granted pursuant to the right to buy;
(4) A tenancy determinable by notice after death *if* (but only if) granted by a registered housing association, at a premium calculated by reference to a percentage of the value of the property or the cost of providing it, and which at the time of the grant complied with regulations then in force under the Housing Act 1980, s.140(b), or (in the case of an earlier tenancy) with the first such regulations—*i.e.* certain shared ownership leases.

The consultation provisions of this Part appear to replace consultation under the Housing Act 1985, s.106A and Sched. 3A, added by the Housing and Planning Act 1986, s.6 and Sched. 1, brought into force from March 11, 1988, by S.I. 1988 No. 283. Those provisions require consultation with respect to the duties of "a local authority proposing to dispose of dwelling-houses subject to secure tenancies, and the Secretary of State in considering whether to give his consent to such a disposal".

While the initial proposal under this Part is, of course, not that of the authority, it could still be argued that it is—at this or a later stage in the process—"proposing to dispose of dwelling-houses subject to secure tenancies" in the sense of "intending" (albeit by statutory requirement). But the alternative interpretation (confining "propose" to something of their own initiative and in respect of which they have a choice—otherwise, why consult?) is supported by the relationship between their consultation obligation and the Secretary of State's duty to consider granting consent to the disposal (which he cannot do under the 1985 Act, Sched. 3A, if a majority of tenants object: see Sched. 3A, para. 5). Under this Part, *no consent is needed*: see Sched. 17, para. 38, below. The purpose of the consultation exercise under s.106A, would therefore be otiose.

Notice by applicant of intention to proceed

103.—(1) Subject to subsection (2) below, the applicant may, within two weeks of the end of the period mentioned in section 102 above, serve on the landlord notice of his intention to proceed with the acquisition; and in that notice the applicant, in such circumstances as may be prescribed, may inform the landlord—

(a) that he wishes to enter into a prescribed covenant to make payments to the landlord on the occasion of any prescribed disposal (occurring after the date of the acquisition) of a dwelling-house comprised in the property to be acquired; and

(b) that he requires the value of that covenant to be taken into account in reducing the price which would otherwise be payable for the property to be acquired.

(2) The applicant shall not be entitled to serve a notice under subsection (1) above if, in response to the consultation under section 102 above,—

(a) less than 50 per cent. of the tenants to whom that section applies have given notice of their wishes in such manner as may be prescribed; or

(b) the number of tenants to whom that section applies who have given notice in that manner of their wish to continue as tenants of the landlord exceeds 50 per cent. of the total number of tenants to whom that section applies.

(3) In any case where a tenancy is held by two or more persons jointly, those persons shall be regarded as a single tenant for the purposes of subsection (2) above and, accordingly, any notice given in response to the consultation under section 102 above shall be of no effect for the purposes of subsection (2) above unless it is given by or on behalf of all the joint tenants.

(4) A notice under subsection (1) above shall contain—

(a) a list of the names and addresses of tenants to whom section 102 above applies (if any) who have given notice as mentioned in subsection (2)(b) above;

(b) a list of the houses (if any) which are, by virtue of regulations under section 100 above, to be excluded from the acquisition;

(c) a list of flats (if any) of which the applicant is required, by virtue of such regulations, to grant leases to the landlord and a statement of the proposed terms of those leases;

(d) such information as may be necessary to show how the lists mentioned in paragraphs (a), (b) and (c) above were established; and

(e) the price payable for the property to be acquired (disregarding any reduction by virtue of such a covenant as is referred to in subsection (1) above) or, as the case may be, the disposal cost attributable to that property.

(5) Within two weeks of service of the notice under subsection (1) above, the landlord shall notify the applicant in writing of any matters stated in that notice which it does not accept.

(6) Where a notice has been served under subsection (1) above, every tenant to whom section 102 above applies and who has not given notice

as mentioned in subsection (2)(b) above shall be taken to have accepted, and to have given consideration for, any offer which—

    (a) relates to the terms on which, after the acquisition, he is to occupy the dwelling-house occupied by him on the relevant date;

    (b) was made to him by the applicant either in the course of the consultation required by subsection (1) of section 102 above or otherwise before the end of the period referred to in that subsection; and

    (c) was neither withdrawn by the applicant nor rejected by the tenant before the end of that period.

(7) Regulations prescribing any of the matters referred to in subsection (1) above shall also make provision with respect to the determination of the amounts which are to be payable on the occasion of prescribed disposals; and the amount of any reduction in the price payable for the property to be acquired which is attributable to such a covenant as is referred to in that subsection shall be determined by the district valuer.

DEFINITION
"prescribed": s.114.

GENERAL NOTE
Subject to the outcome of the consultation exercise, the prospective purchaser has two weeks from the end of the prescribed consultation period (see notes to s.102, above) in which to notify the landlord of his intention to proceed: subs. (1). Failure to comply with this time limit (unless extended by the landlord under s.110(2), below), would lead to the cancellation of the process as a whole, subject only to the right to recommence it: s.110(3), below.

The notice may also notify the landlord that the applicant wishes to enter into a "discount covenant" which will reduce the price payable: see notes to subs. (7), below; see also s.105, below.

The notice has to contain (subs. (4)):

(1) The names and addresses of all tenants who have notified the prospective purchaser of their opposition to the transfer;

(2) A list of houses excluded by s.100, above, *i.e.* tenants of houses who have stated that they wish to remain tenants of the landlord or those excluded by regulations;

(3) A list of flats in respect of which, pursuant to s.100(1)(b), above, the prospective purchaser is bound to grant the landlord a lease, *i.e.* tenants of flats who have stated that they wish to remain tenants of the landlord;

(4) A statement of the proposed terms of such leases;

(5) Such information as may be necessary to show how the foregoing information was established; and

(6) The price payable for the property to be acquired, or its disposal cost, disregarding the effect any discount covenant. By s.100(3), above, this will now mean the price payable after exclusions, notwithstanding s.98(4), above.

The landlord has two weeks from service of the notice in which to notify the applicant of any matters with which it does or they do not agree: there is no arbitration process, and accordingly such a dispute must be referred to the county court, under s.113, below (*cf.* ss.98(3) and 99(6), above). Such a dispute could be based on the identification of tenants opposed, *i.e.* could amount to a denial of the right to proceed at all.

Subss. (2), (6)
This is the most important part of this section. If *less than* 50 per cent. of the tenants consulted (qualifying tenants and long leaseholders, see notes to s.102 above) fail to respond, the applicant cannot proceed. If *more than* 50 per cent. of the tenants consulted notify the applicant, *in response to the consultation* (and in such manner as may be prescribed) of their opposition to the prospective purchase, *i.e.* that they wish to remain tenants of their current landlord, the applicant cannot proceed at all. Similarly, if more than 50 per cent. notify the applicant that they wish to remain tenants of the landlord the application cannot proceed. But if 50 per cent. or more respond, of whom *less* than 50 per cent. are opposed the applicant *can* proceed. Therefore, if less than 50 per cent. respond negatively, but those who respond positively take the total number of respondents above 50 per cent. the applicant can proceed. Thus if over 50 per cent. do not respond, no transfer; if over 50 per cent.

respond negatively, no transfer; but 49 per cent. respond negatively and 2 per cent. respond positively, the transfer can proceed (*cf.* the provisions of s.61, above, concerning H.A.T.'s).

A general notice, applicable to all applications, will be of no value, even if in accordance with the prescribed manner of response, for response must be to the consultation exercise in question. Opponents of the provisions of this Part will accordingly have to "re-campaign" on each occasion when application is made, which is likely to render their task progressively more difficult, and will be unable to secure an opposition applicable indefinitely, on which to rely.

While a local authority landlord cannot campaign *on political grounds* against a prospective purchase (Local Government Act 1986, s.2), there is nothing to stop them either informing tenants of the potential consequences of a transfer (including the potential loss of many rights), or of the practical, management or housing resource consequences to the authority, nor is there anything improper in the authority drawing their attention to what they need to do in order to register their opposition, or of their "opting out" potential under s.100, above.

As regards the status of tenants whose properties are transferred under the provisions of this Part, they will become assured tenants: the provisions of s.38, above, operate to prevent them becoming protected or housing association tenants, even although their tenancies will, or are likely to, have commenced before this Act (and are, as such, not precluded from protection by s.34 or housing association tenancy status by s.35). The protection afforded to formerly secure tenants will, accordingly be that contained in Part I of this Act, which not only amounts to a considerably lesser protection (without many ancillary rights under the 1985 Act, Part IV, such as right to exchange and consultation rights) but is also likely to lead to substantially higher rents.

In addition, unless and until the provisions of the Housing and Planning Act 1986, s.8, are brought fully into force (*cf.* notes to s.84, above), there is, of course, no right to buy. The combined effects are bound to suggest that, provided tenants are both fully aware of and exercise, their rights to object, this Part is unlikely to lead to the sort of substantial diminution of the public sector that is undoubtedly its intent.

Subs. (6) clearly contemplates that the prospective purchaser will be seeking to offset the drawbacks to the tenant, by "offers", which may relate to terms of tenancy after transfer, *e.g.* rent levels, contractual security, perhaps even—subject to s.105, below—a contractual "right to buy" option. "Non-objection" is hereby deemed to constitute consideration, and acceptance, of any such offers made during consultation or otherwise before the end of the consultation period, which was neither withdrawn by the prospective purchaser nor rejected by the tenant within that period. Tenants would, of course, be well-advised to ensure that any such offers are in writing, and if relying on such offers in deciding not to object to the transfer, would also be well-advised, notwithstanding this subsection, to confirm them in writing themselves.

Subs. (7)

Purchasers under this Part are restricted in their rights of further disposal: see s.105. But, *inter alia*, a disposal to a person enjoying the right to buy, including the preserved right to buy (*cf.* notes to s.84, above) when brought into force, will be exempt from the restriction. By this subsection, the Secretary of State has power to make regulations governing "prescribed disposals", which may or may not include right to buy disposals, the effect of which is that, if the applicant opts to enter into the covenant, the sale price to the applicant is reduced (in accordance with the regulations) but on subsequent disposals the applicant will be bound to pay the now former landlord a prescribed amount. The applicant's incentive to enter into such a covenant is that if there is no subsequent prescribed disposal, a reduced price will have been obtained, with no later payment involved.

Duty to complete and consequences of completion

104.—(1) Where the applicant has served on the landlord a notice under section 103(1) above, then, as soon as any dispute as to any matters stated in that notice has been determined and, where appropriate, any determination has been made under section 103(7) above—

(a) the landlord shall make to the applicant a grant of the property included in the acquisition for an estate in fee simple absolute, but subject to any rights to be retained by the landlord; and

(b) the applicant shall grant to the landlord leases of any flats of which he is required to grant leases by regulations under section 100 above.

(2) The terms of any grant or lease under subsection (1) above shall comply with such requirements as may be prescribed.

(3) The duties imposed by the preceding provisions of this section are enforceable by injunction.

(4) Notwithstanding anything in section 141 of the Law of Property Act 1925 (rent and benefit of lessee's covenants to run with the reversion) any rent or other sum which—

(a) arises under a tenancy of any property included in the acquisition, and

(b) falls due before the date of the grant under subsection (1) above,

shall continue to be recoverable by the landlord to the exclusion of the applicant and of any other person in whom the reversion on the tenancy may become vested.

(5) Without prejudice to the application of Part VIII of the Local Government, Planning and Land Act 1980 (capital expenditure of local authorities) to the price received by the landlord on the disposal (as mentioned in subsection (1)(a) above) of the property included in the acquisition, where there is a disposal cost attributable to that property any payments made by the landlord in respect of that cost shall be prescribed expenditure for the purposes of that Part.

DEFINITION
    "property": s.114.

GENERAL NOTE
    This section states that once all other matters have been resolved (including a determination as to "disposal reduction"), the landlord must make a grant of the property, and the now successful purchaser must grant back such leases as are required under s.100, above, each of which duties is enforceable by injunction, which may, pursuant to s.113, below, be obtained in the county court, regardless of size of transaction.

Subs. (4)
    Rents or other amounts, *e.g.* service charges, falling due before the date of transfer may, if the order so provides, be reserved to the authority, instead of going with the reversion under the Law of Property Act 1925, s.141: see also notes to s.74, above.

Subs. (5)
    See notes to s.74, above.

Subsequent disposals

Consent required for subsequent disposals

105.—(1) A person who acquires any property under this Part (in this section referred to as "the new landlord") shall not dispose of it except with the consent of the Secretary of State; but nothing in this subsection shall apply in relation to an exempt disposal, as defined in subsection (7) below.

(2) Where an estate or interest in property acquired by the new landlord has been mortgaged or charged, the prohibition in subsection (1) above on disposal of the property without consent applies also to a disposal by the mortgagee or chargee in exercise of a power of sale or leasing, whether or not the disposal is in the name of the new landlord.

(3) In any case where—

(a) by operation of law or by virtue of an order of a court property which has been acquired by the new landlord passes or is transferred to another person, and

(b) that passing or transfer does not constitute a disposal for which consent is required under subsection (1) above, this section (including, where there is more than one such passing or transfer, this subsection) shall apply as if the other person to whom the property passes or is transferred were the new landlord.

(4) Any consent for the purposes of subsection (1) above may be given either unconditionally or subject to conditions; but, before giving any such consent, the Secretary of State—

(a) shall satisfy himself that the person who is seeking the consent has taken appropriate steps to consult every tenant of the whole or any part of the property proposed to be disposed of; and

(b) shall have regard to the responses of any such tenants to that consultation.

(5) If, apart from subsection (6) below, the consent of the Housing Corporation or Housing for Wales would be required under section 9 of the Housing Associations Act 1985 (control of dispositions of land by housing associations) for a disposal to which subsection (1) above applies, the Secretary of State shall consult that body before giving his consent in respect of that disposal for the purposes of that subsection.

(6) No consent shall be required under the said section 9 for any disposal in respect of which consent is given in accordance with subsection (5) above.

(7) In this section an "exempt disposal" means—

(a) the grant of a lease pursuant to such a requirement as is referred to in section 100(1)(b) above;

(b) the disposal of a dwelling-house to a person having the right to buy it under Part V of the 1985 Act (whether the disposal is in fact made under that Part or otherwise);

(c) a compulsory disposal, within the meaning of Part V of the 1985 Act;

(d) the disposal of an easement or rentcharge;

(e) the disposal of an interest by way of security for a loan;

(f) the grant of a secure tenancy or what would be a secure tenancy but for any of paragraphs 2 to 12 of Schedule 1 to the 1985 Act;

(g) the grant of an assured tenancy, within the meaning of Part I of this Act, or what would be such a tenancy but for any paragraphs 4 to 8 of Schedule 1 to this Act; and

(h) the transfer of an interest which is held on trust where the disposal is made in connection with the appointment of a new trusteee or in connection with the discharge of any trustee.

(8) In this section references to disposing of property include references to—

(a) granting or disposing of any interest in property;

(b) entering into a contract to dispose of property or to grant or dispose of any such interest; and

(c) granting an option to acquire property or any such interest.

DEFINITIONS
"exempt disposal": subs. (7).
"property": s.114.

GENERAL NOTE
Save in the case of an "exempt disposal" (see notes to subs. (7), below), an approved landlord may not dispose of any property (which, therefore, includes not only actual dwellings but property acquired together with such under either s.93(1)(b) [reasonably required for use with] or s.98(1)(d) [former landlord required purchase as not reasonably manageable or maintainable on its own]) without the consent of the Secretary of State. Disposal is as defined in subs. (8), and includes the grant of an option, or of any interest. The restriction applies also to mortgagees or chargees of the approved landlord's property, even when exercising a power of sale or leasing. See also notes to s.81, above.

Consent may be given conditionally or unconditionally, but clearly not "general" (subs. (4)), but in so far as approved landlords may be registered housing associations, who accordingly normally require the approval of the Housing Corporation or Housing for Wales to dispose of property, under the Housing Associations Act 1985, s.9, the Secretary of State is to consult with the Corporation before granting consent (subs. (5)), although such consent then dispenses with the need for additional consent under s.9: subs. (6). The Secretary of State is not to give consent until satisfied that the applicant has consulted any tenant of the property to be disposed of, and has had regard to the tenants' responses.

Subs. (7)

See notes to s.81(8), above. In addition, the grant of a long lease within such requirements as may be prescribed within s.100 is an exempt disposal.

Supplemental

Service of information, advice and assistance

106.—(1) The Corporation may provide in connection with this Part a service of information, advice and assistance to, and for the benefit of,—

(a) persons who have been approved or are considering applying for approval under section 94 above; and

(b) persons who are tenants of public sector landlords.

(2) The Corporation may make charges for information, advice and assistance provided under this section otherwise than to persons falling within subsection (1)(b) above.

(3) The powers conferred on the Corporation by this section may be exercised by the Housing Corporation and Housing for Wales acting jointly.

DEFINITIONS

"Corporation": s.114.

"public sector landlord": s.93.

GENERAL NOTE

The Corporations (Housing Corporation and Housing for Wales) may establish an information, advice and assistance service in the interests of approved or would-be approved landlords, and for the tenants of public sector landlords, for which, however, they may charge. They may establish a joint service, if they wish.

Power of Corporation to provide legal assistance to tenants in relation to acquisitions

107.—(1) On an application by the tenant of a dwelling-house who is a party or a prospective party to proceedings or prospective proceedings falling within subsection (2) below, the Corporation may give assistance to the tenant if it thinks fit to do so—

(a) on the ground that the case raises a question of principle; or

(b) on the ground that it is unreasonable, having regard to the complexity of the case, or to any other matter, to expect the tenant to deal with it without assistance; or

(c) by reason of any other special consideration.

(2) The proceedings referred to in subsection (1) above are—

(a) proceedings to determine any question arising in relation to an acquisition or proposed acquisition under this Part; and

(b) proceedings to determine any dispute arising after an acquisition under this Part between a transferred tenant of a dwelling-house included in the acquisition and the body by which the acquisition was made;

and for the purposes of paragraph (b) above a tenant of a dwelling-house is a transferred tenant of it if he was the qualifying tenant of it at the time of the acquisition or is the widow or widower of the person who was then the qualifying tenant of it.

(3) Assistance given by the Corporation under this section may include—

(a) giving advice;

(b) procuring or attempting to procure the settlement of the matter in dispute;

(c) arranging for the giving of advice or assistance by a solicitor or counsel;

(d) arranging for representation by a solicitor or counsel, including such assistance as is usually given by a solicitor or counsel in the steps preliminary or incidental to any proceedings, or in arriving at or giving effect to a compromise to avoid or bring to an end any proceedings; and

(e) any other form of assistance which the Corporation may consider appropriate;

but paragraph (d) above does not affect the law and practice regulating the descriptions of persons who may appear in, conduct, defend and address the court in any proceedings.

(4) In so far as expenses are incurred by the Corporation in providing the tenant with assistance under this section, the recovery of those expenses (as taxed or assessed in such manner as may be prescribed by rules of court) shall constitute a first charge for the benefit of the Corporation—

(a) on any costs which (whether by virtue of a judgment or order of a court or an agreement or otherwise) are payable to the tenant by any other person in respect of the matter in connection with which the assistance was given; and

(b) so far as relates to any costs, on his rights under any compromise or settlement arrived at in connection with that matter to avoid or bring to an end any proceedings;

but subject to any charge under the Legal Aid Act 1988 and to any provision of that Act for payment of any sum to the Legal Aid Board.

DEFINITION
"Corporation": s.114.

GENERAL NOTE
On either an acquisition under this part, or on a prospective acquisition, or following the acquisition in the case of any dispute between a tenant and the new landlord, a tenant can apply to the Corporations for extensive legal assistance: see notes to s.82, above.

Registration of title and related matters

108. Schedule 12 to this Act shall have effect with respect to registration of title and related matters arising on acquisitions of property under this Part and disposals of property so acquired.

GENERAL NOTE
This section introduces Sched. 12, governing land registration on a transfer. Registration is mandatory, regardless of whether it is within a registration area or not, and is to contain a restriction reflecting the provisions of s.105, above (*i.e.* need for consent on further disposal): Sched. 12, para. 2.

Public open space etc.

109.—(1) To the extent that any land held—

(a) for the purposes of section 164 of the Public Health Act 1875 (pleasure grounds), or

(b) in accordance with section 10 of the Open Spaces Act 1906

(duty of local authority to maintain open spaces and burial grounds),
is included in an acquisition under this Part, it shall be deemed to be freed from any trust arising solely by virtue of its being land held in trust for enjoyment by the public in accordance with that section.

(2) Nothing in section 5 of the Green Belt (London and Home Counties) Act 1938 (restrictions on alienation of land by local authorities) applies in relation to a disposal of land included in an acquisition under this Part.

GENERAL NOTE

Land within this section will only be transferred if comprised in or let together with a dwelling the subject of transfer (s.95(5), above).

Subs. (2)

This overrules the effect of the decision in *R.* v. *Secretary of State for the Environment, ex p. Enfield London Borough Council* (1988) 86 L.G.R. 549, Q.B.D.

Extension etc. of relevant periods

110.—(1) In this section "relevant period" means any period within which anything is required by this Part to be done by either of the parties, that is to say, the applicant and the landlord.

(2) At any time before the end of any relevant period, or any such period as previously extended under this subsection, the other party may, by a written notice served on the party to whom the requirement relates, extend or further extend that period.

(3) Where a notice of revocation of the applicant's approval is served under subsection (5) of section 94 above and subsequently withdrawn as mentioned in paragraph (b) of that subsection, any relevant period which, apart from this subsection, would have expired before the withdrawal shall be taken to be extended by a period equal to that beginning with the date of the service of the notice of revocation and ending on the date of the withdrawal.

(4) Where—

    (a) the applicant is the party to whom the requirement relates, and

    (b) the relevant period, or that period as extended under subsection (2) above, expires without his doing what he is required by this Part to do within that period,

his application claiming to exercise the right conferred by this Part shall be deemed to be withdrawn, but without prejudice to his making a further such application.

GENERAL NOTE

This section permits parties—landlords or prospective purchasers—to extend time limits for compliance with the requirements of this Part, in writing: subs. (1). Unless extended, however, failure to comply with any time limit imposed on the prospective purchaser results in the abandonment of the application, without prejudice to the right to re-commence (albeit with a later relevant date, and therefore a potentially higher price and/or different factors governing the right): subs. (4). Note the provision in subs. (3) for extension of time if the Housing Corporation or Housing for Wales should give notice under s.94, above, of intention to revoke approval, which notice is then withdrawn.

Power to prescribe forms etc.

111. The Secretary of State may by regulations prescribe—

    (a) anything which by this Part is to be prescribed; and

    (b) the form of any notice, statement or other document which is required or authorised to be used under or for the purposes of this Part.

Orders and regulations

112.—(1) Any power of the Secretary of State to make orders or regulations under this Part shall be exercised by statutory instrument.

(2) A statutory instrument containing any order or regulations under this Part, other than regulations under section 111(b) above, shall be subject to annulment in pursuance of a resolution of either House of Parliament.

(3) Orders or regulations under this Part may make different provision for different cases or circumstances or different areas and may contain such incidental, supplemental or transitional provisions as the Secretary of State thinks fit.

Jurisdiction of county court

113.—(1) Subject to sections 98(5) and 99(6) above, a county court has jurisdiction—

(a) to entertain any proceedings brought under this Part; and

(b) to determine any question arising under this Part.

(2) The jurisdiction conferred by this section includes jurisdiction to entertain proceedings on any such question as is mentioned in subsection (1) above notwithstanding that no other relief is sought than a declaration.

(3) If a person takes in the High Court proceedings which, by virtue of this section, he could have taken in the county court, he shall not be entitled to recover any more costs of those proceedings than those to which he would have been entitled if the proceedings had been taken in a county court.

(4) In a case falling within subsection (3) above the taxing master shall have the same power of directing on what scale costs are to be allowed, and of allowing any item of costs, as the judge would have had if the proceedings had been taken in a county court.

GENERAL NOTE

See notes to s.40, above.

Interpretation of Part IV

114.—(1) In this Part—

"the 1985 Act" means the Housing Act 1985;

"the Corporation" means the Housing Corporation or Housing for Wales but—

(a) an approval given by the Housing Corporation shall not have effect in relation to buildings or other property in Wales; and

(b) an approval given by Housing for Wales shall not have effect in relation to buildings or other property in England;

"qualifying tenant" shall be construed in accordance with subsections (3) and (4) of section 93 above;

"prescribed" means prescribed by regulations made by the Secretary of State;

"property" means land with or without buildings;

"public sector landlord" has the meaning given by section 93(2) above;

"the relevant date" has the meaning given by section 93(5) above; and

"habitable room", in relation to a house, means a room used, or intended for use, as a bedroom, living room, dining room or kitchen.

(2) Subject to subsection (1) above, in this Part expressions which are also used in Part V of the 1985 Act have the same meaning as in that Part.

GENERAL NOTE
"Habitable room": see notes to s.99(3), above.

PART V

MISCELLANEOUS AND GENERAL

Leases

Premiums on long leases

115.—(1) With respect to—
(a) any premium received or required to be paid after the commencement of this Act, or
(b) any loan required to be made after that commencement,
section 127 of the Rent Act 1977 (allowable premiums in relation to certain long tenancies) shall have effect subject to the amendments in subsections (2) and (3) below.

(2) For subsections (2) and (3) there shall be substituted the following subsections—

"(2) The conditions mentioned in subsection (1)(a) above are—
(a) that the landlord has no power to determine the tenancy at any time within twenty years beginning on the date when it was granted; and
(b) that the terms of the tenancy do not inhibit both the assignment and the underletting of the whole of the premises comprised in the tenancy;
but for the purpose of paragraph (b) above there shall be disregarded any term of the tenancy which inhibits assignment and underletting only during a period which is or falls within the final seven years of the term for which the tenancy was granted.

(3) The reference in subsection (2) above to a power of the landlord to determine a tenancy does not include a reference to a power of re-entry or forfeiture for breach of any term or condition of the tenancy."

(3) Subsections (3C) and (3D) shall be omitted and in subsection (5) for "(2)(c)" there shall be substituted "(2)(b)".

(4) Expressions used in subsection (1) above have the same meaning as in Part IX of the Rent Act 1977.

GENERAL NOTE
As a general proposition, a "premium" cannot be sought—and if paid is recoverable—in respect of a Rent Act protected tenancy, whether on its creation or its continuation or on its assignment: Rent Act 1977, Part IX. To require or receive such is a criminal offence: *ibid.*, ss.119, 120. The prohibition has been held to apply where an outgoing tenant arranged to surrender his own tenancy, and for the landlord to grant a new tenancy: *Farrell* v. *Alexander* [1977] A.C. 59, H.L. "Premium" is as defined in *ibid.*, s.128, but includes an excessive price for furniture purchase: *ibid.*, s.123. A premium includes "any fine or other like sum, any other pecuniary consideration in addition to rent, and any sum paid by way of deposit, other than one which does not exceed one-sixth of the annual rent and is reasonable in relation to the potential liability in respect of which it is paid": *ibid.*, s.128. See, further, notes to s.15, above.
By the Rent Act 1977, s.127, some leases are either exempt from the prohibition altogether, or are subject to the special provisions of *ibid.*, Sched. 18, Part II (limiting the

amount which may be charged). The provisions are aimed at long leases which may not fall within the low rent exemption to protection, and other leases which although initially at a low rent (and which have accordingly been outwith the Rent Act, so that accordingly a premium could lawfully be charged) have been brought within protection by increases in amounts payable, normally in service charges. This section substitutes a number of different conditions which give rise to the exemption from Part IX.

If a tenancy is both a long tenancy within the Landlord and Tenant Act 1954, Part I, and a Rent Act protected tenancy, the prohibition on premiums will not apply at all if all of the conditions in the new subs. (2) are fulfilled; if none, or less than all, is or are fulfilled, then Sched. 18, Part II will be applicable. The tenancy must be granted for a term certain exceeding 21 years; it must contain no provision for termination by either landlord or tenant (other than re-entry or forfeiture for breach of term or condition of the tenancy: new subs. (3)); and, its terms must not inhibit *both* assignment *and* subletting of the whole of the premises.

Repairing obligations in short leases

116.—(1) In section 11 of the Landlord and Tenant Act 1985 (repairing obligations in short leases) after subsection (1) there shall be inserted the following subsections—

"(1A) If a lease to which this section applies is a lease of a dwelling-house which forms part only of a building, then, subject to subsection (1B), the covenant implied by subsection (1) shall have effect as if—

(a) the reference in paragraph (a) of that subsection to the dwelling-house included a reference to any part of the building in which the lessor has an estate or interest; and

(b) any reference in paragraphs (b) and (c) of that subsection to an installation in the dwelling-house included a reference to an installation which, directly or indirectly, serves the dwelling-house and which either—

(i) forms part of any part of a building in which the lessor has an estate or interest; or

(ii) is owned by the lessor or under his control.

(1B) Nothing in subsection (1A) shall be construed as requiring the lessor to carry out any works or repairs unless the disrepair (or failure to maintain in working order) is such as to affect the lessee's enjoyment of the dwelling-house or of any common parts, as defined in section 60(1) of the Landlord and Tenant Act 1987, which the lessee, as such, is entitled to use."

(2) After subsection (3) of that section there shall be inserted the following subsection—

"(3A) In any case where—

(a) the lessor's repairing covenant has effect as mentioned in subsection (1A), and

(b) in order to comply with the covenant the lessor needs to carry out works or repairs otherwise than in, or to an installation in, the dwelling-house, and

(c) the lessor does not have a sufficient right in the part of the building or the installation concerned to enable him to carry out the required works or repairs,

then, in any proceedings relating to a failure to comply with the lessor's repairing covenant, so far as it requires the lessor to carry out the works or repairs in question, it shall be a defence for the lessor to prove that he used all reasonable endeavours to obtain, but was unable to obtain, such rights as would be adequate to enable him to carry out the works or repairs."

(3) At the end of section 14(4) of the said Act of 1985 (which excludes from section 11 certain leases granted to various bodies) there shall be added—

"a housing action trust established under Part III of the Housing Act 1988".

(4) The amendments made by this section do not have effect with respect to—

(a) a lease entered into before the commencement of this Act; or

(b) a lease entered into pursuant to a contract made before the commencement of this Act.

GENERAL NOTE

The Landlord and Tenant Act 1985, s.11, contains what is now the principal modern repairing covenant, imposing on landlords the obligation to keep in repair "the structure and exterior of the dwelling-house (including drains, gutters and external pipes)," and "to keep in repair and proper working order the installations in the dwelling-house for the supply of water, gas and electricity and for sanitation (including basins, sinks, baths and sanitary conveniences, but not other fixtures, fittings and appliances for making use of the supply of water, gas or electricity)" and "to keep in repair and proper working order the installations in the dwelling-house for space heating and heating water".

The section applies in general to any lease or tenancy of a dwelling-house (or part of a house) granted on or after October 24, 1961, for a term of less than seven years (s.13) and accordingly includes periodic tenancies. For exceptions, see s.14, including s.14(4), disapplying the provision in the case of lease granted on or after October 3, 1980, to specified public bodies, now extended by subs. (3) of this section to include housing action trusts under Part III, above. The amendments contained in this section do not apply to lease or tenancies granted before this Act comes into force, or pursuant to a contract made before this Act comes into force: subs. (4).

The repairing obligation applies only to the dwelling-house in question. In *Campden Hill Towers* v. *Gardner* [1977] Q.B. 823; 13 H.L.R. 64, C.A., it was held in the case of a flat that the obligation was accordingly confined to the structure and exterior of the flat itself, and did not extend to the structure and exterior of the block in which the flat was situated. Similarly, in the same case, a central heating boiler situated in the common parts of the block was not an installation *in the dwelling-house*. *Campden Hill Towers* was followed in *Douglas-Scott* v. *Scorgie* [1984] 1 W.L.R. 716; 13 H.L.R. 97, C.A., in relation to the roof above a top floor flat, in which it was held, however, that the question was one not determined by reference to the demise, so that the roof of the block *could* qualify as structure and exterior of such a flat, depending on the construction.

The amendment in subs. (1) of this section overturns the effect of *Campden Hill Towers*, so that the structure and exterior of a building in which a flat or room is situated have to be kept in repair, and installations which supply water, gas, electricity and sanitary facilities, and which serve to provide space and water heating, to a particular flat or room have to be kept in repair and proper working order even although not situated within the flat or room, if either it is located in any part of any building in which the landlord has an estate or interest, or the installation is owned by the landlord or is under his control. The amendment only takes effect, however, if the defect is such as to affect the tenant's enjoyment of the demised premises or of common parts he is entitled to use as defined in the Landlord and Tenant Act 1987, s.60, to include the structure and exterior of that building or part of a building and any common facilities within it.

Furthermore, if remedial works require access to a part of a building or an installation to which the landlord does not have a sufficient right to gain access, then it is a defence to show that he made all reasonable efforts to gain such access and been unable to do so: subs. (2) adding the new subs. (3A).

Certain tenancies excluded from bankrupt's estate

117.—(1) In section 283 of the Insolvency Act 1986 (definition of bankrupt's estate) at the end of subsection (3) (property excluded from the estate) there shall be inserted the following subsection—

"(3A) Subject to section 308A in Chapter IV, subsection (1) does not apply to—

(a) a tenancy which is an assured tenancy or an assured agricultural occupancy, within the meaning of Part I of the Housing Act 1988, and the terms of which inhibit an assignment as mentioned in section 127(5) of the Rent Act 1977, or

   (b) a protected tenancy, within the meaning of the Rent Act 1977, in respect of which, by virtue of any provision of Part IX of that Act, no premium can lawfully be required as a condition of assignment, or

   (c) a tenancy of a dwelling-house by virtue of which the bankrupt is, within the meaning of the Rent (Agriculture) Act 1976, a protected occupier of the dwelling-house, and the terms of which inhibit an assignment as mentioned in section 127(5) of the Rent Act 1977, or

   (d) a secure tenancy, within the meaning of Part IV of the Housing Act 1985, which is not capable of being assigned, except in the cases mentioned in section 91(3) of that Act."

   (2) After section 308 of that Act there shall be inserted the following section—

"Vesting in trustee of certain tenancies

   308A. Upon the service on the bankrupt by the trustee of a notice in writing under this section, any tenancy—

   (a) which is excluded by virtue of section 283(3A) from the bankrupt's estate, and

   (b) to which the notice relates,

vests in the trustee as part of the bankrupt's estate; and, except against a purchaser in good faith, for value and without notice of the bankruptcy, the trustee's title to that tenancy has relation back to the commencement of the bankruptcy."

   (3) In section 309 of that Act (time-limit for certain notices) in subsection (1)(b)—

   (a) after the words "section 308" there shall be inserted "or section 308A"; and

   (b) after the words "the property" there shall be inserted "or tenancy".

   (4) In section 315 of that Act (disclaimer (general power)), in subsection (4) after the words "reasonable replacement value)" there shall be inserted "or 308A".

GENERAL NOTE

Under the Rent Acts, the Housing Act 1985 and Part I of this Act a degree (*cf.* notes to s.1, above) of occupation by "the tenant" (or one of joint tenants) is required in order to sustain the respective statutory protection. Under the Rent Acts, there is a distinction between the contractual, protected tenancy, and the statutory tenancy which follows common law determination. A statutory tenancy is a "status of irremovability" (see, *e.g. Jessamine Investments Co.* v. *Schwartz* [1978] Q.B. 264, C.A.; see also *Keaves* v. *Dean* [1924] 1 K.B. 685, C.A.). The effect of bankruptcy law is to vest the tenancy in the trustee in bankruptcy, with the effect that "the tenant" is no longer in occupation.

The consequence has been most marked in the private sector, where bankruptcy during contractual term has vested the protected tenancy in trustee, to the effect that no statutory tenancy can arise because "immediately before [the] termination" (the 1977 Act, s.2(1)) the tenant was not the person in occupation: *Smalley* v. *Quarrier* [1975] 1 W.L.R. 983, C.A. This is so whether or not the trustee has disclaimed the tenancy: *Eyre* v. *Hall* (1986) 18 H.L.R. 509, C.A. Where, however, the tenancy is already statutory at the time of bankruptcy, it does not (not being "a true tenancy") vest in the trustee, and the statutory tenancy can accordingly be sustained: *Sutton* v. *Dorf* [1932] 2 K.B. 304, C.A.

By the first of these amendments, the bankrupt's estate will not normally include the specified tenancies. In the first three cases, the class of tenancy excluded from the bankrupt's estate is that relating to the particular legislation under which no premium (*cf.* ss.17 and 115, above) can be recovered, so that, in effect, there is no "cash value" to be obtained from the vesting in the trustee; in the fourth case, secure tenancies cannot be assigned (save as permitted in the Housing Act 1985, s.91(3)), but this prohibition does not apply to a fixed-term secure tenancy granted before November 5, 1982 (*ibid*, s.91(1)), to which, again, a cash value may accordingly attach.

The second amendment, however, leaves it open to the trustee to claim such a tenancy, even if otherwise excluded from the estate. If the trustee serves such notice, however, he cannot disclaim it under the Insolvency Act 1986, s.315 (subs. (4)). The combined effect is to preserve such a tenancy for the bankrupt, but also to enable the trustee to take the benefit for the estate of any profit derivable from the tenancy, *e.g.* a subletting.

Certain tenancies excluded from debtor's estate: Scotland

118.—(1) In section 31 of the Bankruptcy (Scotland) Act 1985 (vesting of debtor's estate at date of sequestration) in subsection (8) after the word "means" there shall be inserted the words ", subject to subsection (9) below,".

(2) After the said subsection (8) there shall be added the following subsections—

"(9) Subject to subsection (10) below, the "whole estate of the debtor" does not include any interest of the debtor as tenant under any of the following tenancies—

(a) a tenancy which is an assured tenancy within the meaning of Part II of the Housing (Scotland) Act 1988, or

(b) a protected tenancy within the meaning of the Rent (Scotland) Act 1984 in respect of which, by virtue of any provision of Part VIII of that Act, no premium can lawfully be required as a condition of the assignation, or

(c) a secure tenancy within the meaning of Part III of the Housing (Scotland) Act 1987.

(10) On the date on which the permanent trustee serves notice to that effect on the debtor, the interest of this debtor as tenant under any of the tenancies referred to in subsection (9) above shall form part of his estate and vest in the permanent trustee as if it had vested in him under section 32(6) of this Act."

GENERAL NOTE
This makes a degree of provision in Scotland analogous to that described in the last section.

Amendment of Landlord and Tenant Act 1987

119. The Landlord and Tenant Act 1987 shall have effect subject to the amendments in Schedule 13 to this Act.

GENERAL NOTE
This section introduces Sched. 13, amending the Landlord and Tenant Act 1987: see notes to Sched. 13, below.

Rent officers

Appointment etc. of rent officers

120. Section 63 of the Rent Act 1977 (schemes for the appointment of rent officers) shall have effect subject to the amendments in Part I of Schedule 14 to this Act and after section 64 of that Act there shall be inserted the sections set out in Part II of that Schedule.

GENERAL NOTE
This introduces Sched. 14, containing amendments to the Rent Act 1977, governing administrative arrangements for the appointment of rent officers, *inter alia*, deleting the post of deputy rent officer, and extending the powers of the Secretary of State in relation to rent officer schemes, *e.g.* to enable him to require his consent to the appointment of rent officers. This reflects the reduced work-load of rent officers (but *cf.* the next section), resulting from the limited rent control applicable to assured tenancies under Part I of this Act, which function will be carried out by Rent Assessment Committees, not officers.

The new s.64A of the Rent Act 1977, added by Sched. 14, Part II, below, permits the Secretary of State to make "amalgamation schemes", *either* "if . . . of the opinion that there is at any time insufficient work in two or more registration areas to justify the existence of a separate service . . . for each area", or, "if . . . of the opinion . . . that it would at any time be beneficial for the efficient administration of the service provided by rent officers in two or more registration areas." The new s.64B, added by *ibid*, permits the Secretary of State to remove the function of appointing a rent officer service from the local authority, in effect to himself.

Rent officers: additional functions relating to housing benefit etc.

121.—(1) The Secretary of State may by order require rent officers to carry out such functions as may be specified in the order in connection with housing benefit and rent allowance subsidy.

(2) An order under this section—

   (a) shall be made by statutory instrument which, except in the case of the first order to be made, shall be subject to annulment in pursuance of a resolution of either House of Parliament;

   (b) may make different provision for different cases or classes of case and for different areas; and

   (c) may contain such transitional, incidental and supplementary provisions as appear to the Secretary of State to be desirable;

and the first order under this section shall not be made unless a draft of it has been laid before, and approved by a resolution of, each House of Parliament.

(3) In subsection (7) of section 63 of the Rent Act 1977 (expenditure arising in connection with rent officers etc.), in paragraph (a) after the words "this section" there shall be inserted "or an order under section 121 of the Housing Act 1988".

(4) At the end of section 21(6) of the Social Security Act 1986 (regulations prescribing maximum family credit and maximum housing benefit) there shall be added the words "and regulations prescribing the appropriate maximum housing benefit may provide for benefit to be limited by reference to determinations made by rent officers in exercise of functions conferred under section 121 of the Housing Act 1988".

(5) In section 30 of that Act (housing benefit finance) at the end of subsection (2) there shall be added the words "and, in relation to rent allowance subsidy, the Secretary of State may exercise his discretion as to what is unreasonable for the purposes of paragraph (b) above by reference to determinations made by rent officers in exercise of functions conferred under section 121 of the Housing Act 1988".

(6) In section 51(1)(h) of that Act (regulations may require information etc. needed for determination of a claim) the reference to information or evidence needed for the determination of a claim includes a reference to information or evidence required by a rent officer for the purpose of a function conferred on him under this section.

(7) In this section "housing benefit" and "rent allowance subsidy" have the same meaning as in Part II of the Social Security Act 1986.

GENERAL NOTE

In view of the substitution for Rent Act protected tenancies of assured tenancies under Part I of this Act, in which such rent control function as remains is conferred directly upon Rent Assessment Committees, the work-load of rent officers may be expected to decline: see also s.120, above.

By this section, however, they are to enjoy a new function. The purpose is to confer on them the role of limiting housing benefit payable, either directly under regulations under the Social Security Act 1986, s.21(6), or less directly under *ibid.*, s.30, by determining whether rents are unreasonably high, for the purpose of limiting the housing benefit subsidy payable by the government to local authorities. The avowed intention is to defeat collusion between landlords and tenants, but the practical effect will undoubtedly be to limit the amount available to those dependent on housing benefit and force them to move into cheaper accommodation.

Right to buy etc. and grants to obtain accommodation

Variation of cost floor for right to buy discount

122.—(1) Section 131 of the Housing Act 1985 (limits on amount of discount in relation to the right to buy) shall be amended in accordance with subsections (2) and (3) below.

(2) In subsection (1) (the cost floor provision) for paragraph (a) there shall be substituted the following paragraph—

"(a) is to be treated as incurred at or after the beginning of that period of account of the landlord in which falls the date which is eight years, or such other period of time as may be specified in an order made by the Secretary of State, earlier than the relevant time, and".

(3) After subsection (1) there shall be inserted the following subsection—

"(1A) In subsection (1)(a) above "period of account", in relation to any costs, means the period for which the landlord made up those of its accounts in which account is taken of those costs."

(4) This section has effect in relation to the determination of discount in any case where—

(a) the relevant time falls on or after the date on which this section comes into force; or

(b) paragraph (a) above does not apply but the landlord has not before that date served on the tenant a notice complying with section 125 of the Housing Act 1985; or

(c) the tenant has before that date claimed to exercise the right to be granted a shared ownership lease but the landlord has not before that date served on the tenant a notice complying with section 147 of that Act; or

(d) the tenant has before that date served a notice under paragraph 1 of Schedule 8 to that Act (claiming to exercise the right to acquire an additional share under a shared ownership lease) but the landlord has not before that date served a notice under sub-paragraph (3) of that paragraph;

and, for the purposes of this subsection, no account shall be taken of any steps taken under section 177 of that Act (amendment or withdrawal and re-service of notice to correct mistakes).

(5) Expressions used in subsection (4) above have the same meaning as in Part V of the Housing Act 1985.

GENERAL NOTE

Discount available on right to buy under Part V of the Housing Act 1985, is limited, *inter alia*, by (a) a "cost floor" provision (*i.e.* not to reduce the actual price below an amount), and (b) a maximum discount: the 1985 Act, s.131. By subss. (2), (3) of this section, rather than dating back to relevant expenditure since March 31, 1974, the cost floor is to refer back only eight years, or such other period before service of notice of application to buy ("relevant time") as the Secretary of State may specify by order. Subs. (4) limits the application of the change to the specified cases, referable to the commencement of this section.

Amendment of Schedule 5 to Housing Act 1985

123.—(1) Schedule 5 of the Housing Act 1985 (exceptions to the right to buy) shall be amended in accordance with this section.

(2) Paragraphs 6 and 8 shall be omitted.

(3) The repeal by this Act of paragraphs 6 and 8 of Schedule 5 shall not affect the operation of either of those paragraphs in any case where the

tenant's notice claiming to exercise the right to buy was served before the repeal comes into force unless, at that time, no notice in response had been served under section 124 of the Housing Act 1985 (landlord's notice admitting or denying right to buy).

(4) For the purposes of subsection (3) above, no account shall be taken of any steps taken under section 177 of the Housing Act 1985 (amendment or withdrawal and re-service of notice to correct mistakes).

GENERAL NOTE

Sched. 5 to the Housing Act 1985, identifies exceptions to the right to buy. Paras. 6–8 of it concern property for the physically disabled.

Para. 6: The dwelling-house has features substantially different from those of ordinary dwellings, designed to make it suitable for occupation by the physically disabled, and has had those features since construction or, where dwelling provided by conversion, since conversion.

Para. 7: The dwelling-house has features substantially different from those of ordinary dwellings, designed to make it suitable for occupation by the physically disabled, and is one of a group of dwellings which it is the landlord's practice to let for occupation by the physically disabled, to which group social services or special facilities are provided in close proximity, for the purpose of assisting those persons.

Para. 8: The landlord or the landlord's predecessor has carried out works to make the property suitable for occupation by the disabled, comprising one or more of specified alterations (additional floor space, additional bathroom or shower or vertical lift).

Only para. 7 survives this amendment. However, this is not so in relation to a claim to buy in relation to which the landlord has already served a notice in response denying the right before the repeal came into force (ignoring any amendment, withdrawal or re-service under the 1985 Act, s.177): subss. (3) and (4).

Right to buy: tenant's sanction for landlord's delays

124. After section 153 of the Housing Act 1985 there shall be inserted the following sections—

"Tenant's notices of delay

153A.—(1) Where a secure tenant has claimed to exercise the right to buy, he may serve on his landlord a notice (in this section referred to as an "initial notice of delay") in any of the following cases, namely,—

(a) where the landlord has failed to serve a notice under section 124 within the period appropriate under subsection (2) of that section;

(b) where the tenant's right to buy has been established and the landlord has failed to serve a notice under section 125 within the period appropriate under subsection (1) of that section;

(c) where the tenant has claimed to exercise the right to be granted a shared ownership lease and the landlord has failed to serve a notice under section 146 within the period of the four weeks required by that section;

(d) where the tenant's right to a shared ownership lease has been established and the landlord has failed to serve a notice under section 147 within the period of the eight weeks required by that section; or

(e) where the tenant considers that delays on the part of the landlord are preventing him from exercising expeditiously his right to buy or his right to be granted a shared ownership lease; and where an initial notice of delay specifies any of the cases in paragraphs (a) to (d), any reference in this section or section 153B to the default date is a reference to the end of the period referred to in the paragraph in question or, if it is later, the day appointed for the coming into force of section 124 of the Housing Act 1988.

(2) An initial notice of delay—
- (a) shall specify the most recent action of which the tenant is aware which has been taken by the landlord pursuant to this Part of this Act; and
- (b) shall specify a period (in this section referred to as "the response period"), not being less than one month, beginning on the date of service of the notice, within which the service by the landlord of a counter notice under subsection (3) will have the effect of cancelling the initial notice of delay.

(3) Within the response period specified in an initial notice of delay or at any time thereafter, the landlord may serve on the tenant a counter notice in either of the following circumstances—
- (a) if the initial notice specifies any of the cases in paragraphs (a) to (d) of subsection (1) and the landlord has served, or is serving together with the counter notice, the required notice under section 124, section 125, section 146 or section 147, as the case may be; or
- (b) if the initial notice specifies the case in subsection (1)(e) and there is no action under this Part which, at the beginning of the response period, it was for the landlord to take in order to allow the tenant expeditiously to exercise his right to buy or his right to be granted a shared ownership lease and which remains to be taken at the time of service of the counter notice.

(4) A counter notice under subsection (3) shall specify the circumstances by virtue of which it is served.

(5) At any time when—
- (a) the response period specified in an initial notice of delay has expired, and
- (b) the landlord has not served a counter notice under subsection (3),

the tenant may serve on the landlord a notice (in this section and section 153B referred to as an "operative notice of delay") which shall state that section 153B will apply to payments of rent made by the tenant on or after the default date or, if the initial notice of delay specified the case in subsection (1)(e), the date of the service of the notice.

(6) If, after a tenant has served an initial notice of delay, a counter notice has been served under subsection (3), then, whether or not the tenant has also served an operative notice of delay, if any of the cases in subsection (1) again arises, the tenant may serve a further initial notice of delay and the provisions of this section shall apply again accordingly.

Payments of rent attributable to purchase price etc.

153B.—(1) Where a secure tenant has served on his landlord an operative notice of delay, this section applies to any payment of rent which is made on or after the default date or, as the case may be, the date of the service of the notice and before the occurrence of any of the following events (and, if more than one event occurs, before the earliest to occur)—
- (a) the service by the landlord of a counter notice under section 153A(3);
- (b) the date on which the landlord makes to the tenant the grant required by section 138 or, as the case may be, section 150;
- (c) the date on which the tenant serves notice under section 142(2) (claiming to be entitled to defer completion);

(d) the date on which the tenant withdraws or is deemed to have withdrawn the notice claiming to exercise the right to buy or, as the case may be, the notice claiming to exercise the right to be granted a shared ownership lease; and

(e) the date on which the tenant ceases to be entitled to exercise the right to buy.

(2) Except where this section ceases to apply on a date determined under any of paragraphs (c) to (e) of subsection (1), so much of any payment of rent to which this section applies as does not consist of—

(a) a sum due on account of rates, or

(b) a service charge (as defined in section 621A),

shall be treated not only as a payment of rent but also as a payment on account by the tenant which is to be taken into account in accordance with subsection (3).

(3) In a case where subsection (2) applies, the amount which, apart from this section, would be the purchase price or, as the case may be, the tenant's initial contribution for the grant of a shared ownership lease shall be reduced by an amount equal to the aggregate of—

(a) the total of any payments on account treated as having been paid by the tenant by virtue of subsection (2); and

(b) if those payments on account are derived from payments of rent referable to a period of more than twelve months, a sum equal to the appropriate percentage of the total referred to in paragraph (a).

(4) In subsection (3)(b) "the appropriate percentage" means 50 per cent. or such other percentage as may be prescribed."

GENERAL NOTE

This section introduces the "notice of delay" which a tenant seeking to exercise the right to buy may serve which, subject to counter-notice and the other provisions of this section, leads to the benefit of further rent payments being treated as a payment on account of the purchase *and*, pursuant to Sched. 17, para. 41, below, to reduction of the period following completion when discount is repayable and indeed the amount that will be repayable.

Section 153A

An initial notice of delay may be served in the following circumstances:

(1) The landlord has failed to serve notice admitting or denying the right to buy within four weeks (save where reliance is placed by the tenant on time with another public landlord, in which case the landlord served with notice claiming the right to buy has eight weeks in which to respond): the 1985 Act, s.124(2).

(2) The landlord has failed to serve notice specifying terms, price and related information (including concerning service charges and improvement contributions) within a further eight weeks (freehold) or 12 weeks (leasehold): the 1985 Act, s.125(1).

(3) The landlord has failed to serve notice within four weeks admitting or denying the right to a shared ownership lease: the 1985 Act, s.146.

(4) The landlord has failed within eight weeks to serve notice identifying terms, price and related information for the tenant's initial share under a shared ownership lease: the 1985 Act, s.147(1).

(5) "Where the tenant considers that delays on the part of the landlord are preventing him from exercising expeditiously" either the right to buy or the right to a shared ownership lease. This is bound to prove the most controversial, and disputatious, element of the provisions.

The initial notice of delay has to identify the last action on the part of the landlord of which the tenant is aware, and give the landlord a minimum "response period" of not less than one month within which the landlord may serve a "counter-notice" effective to cancel the initial notice. The counter-notice can only be served if *either* one of the specified responses already has been served or is served contemporaneously with the counter-notice, *or* where the initial notice was based on the tenant's view that the landlord is delaying "generally" (*i.e.* the subs. (1)(e) ground), if there is no action on the part of the landlord awaited. The counter-notice has to identify its basis.

If the landlord does not serve a counter-notice within the time allowed, the tenant may then serve an "operative notice of delay" which applies s.153B to future payments of rent made by the tenant, applicable to all rents paid after "the default date" (*i.e.* the date by which the specified response ought to have been given) or if on the subs. (1)(e) ground, to all rents paid after service of the notice (*appearing* to mean the operative rather than the initial notice). It follows that in some cases, the effect of s.153B is retrospective. But note (s.153B(1)(a)) that the landlord's right to serve a counter-notice is a continuing right, so that the benefit of s.153B is brought to an end once the landlord complies.

A further initial notice may be served in appropriate circumstances even if the first is "cancelled" by a counter-notice.

Section 153B

This section identifies the effect of an operative notice of delay under the last section. The effect lasts until one of the specified events occurs. The first of these is service of a counter-notice, either confirming that a required response notice has now been served, or accompanied by such a required response notice, or intimating that there is no outstanding action awaited on the part of the landlord. Failure to comply with the initial notice response period for a counter-notice is accordingly not indefinitely fatal.

The other events are more predictable:

(1) Grant or conveyance, whether of "full" right to buy or shared ownership lease;

(2) Tenant claims right to defer completion under s.142(2);

(3) Tenant withdraws or is deemed to have withdrawn notice claiming or loses right to buy or to a shared ownership lease: see ss.138, 140, 141 (the latter two sections comprising the *landlord's* right to serve completion notices on a recalcitrant tenant) and ss.150, 152, 153 (analogous provisions on shared ownership).

The benefit of the section applies only to rent, not including rates or service charges: such "pure" rent is treated not only as rent but also as a payment on account of the purchase price (so that the effect of the payment on account is not to throw the tenant into arrears and accordingly lose him the right to complete under s.138(2)). But if the benefit of the section goes on for more than a year, a *further* 50 per cent. (or other prescribed sum) is added by way of increased "penalty".

By Sched. 17, para. 41, below, however, adding a new 1985, s.155(3A), there is an additional benefit when a tenant is entitled to have rent payments treated additionally as payment on account of purchase, under this section. All the periods for which this entitlement is established preceding the purchase are added together and deducted from the three-year period during which, following purchase, there can be no disposal (other than an exempt disposal) without repayment of discount. Thus, if one year of such payments accrues, repayment of discount is only applicable for two years after purchase, and furthermore will presume one year's occupation, so that (in this example) one-third of the discount is not repayable.

Restriction on letting etc. of certain houses in National Parks etc.

125.—(1) Section 37 of the Housing Act 1985 (restriction on disposals of dwelling-houses in National Parks etc.) shall be amended in accordance with this section.

(2) In subsection (2) (the covenanted limitation) after the word "his" there shall be inserted "(a)" and at the end there shall be added "and

  (b) there will be no disposal by way of tenancy or licence without the written consent of the authority unless the disposal is to a person satisfying that condition or by a person whose only or principal home is and, throughout the duration of the tenancy or licence, remains the house".

(3) In subsection (3) (disposals limited to persons employed or living locally) after the words "application for consent" there shall be inserted the words "or, in the case of a disposal by way of tenancy or licence, preceding the disposal".

(4) At the end of subsection (4) (disposals in breach of covenant to be void) there shall be added "and, so far as it relates to disposals by way of tenancy or licence, such a covenant may be enforced by the local authority as if—

(a) the authority were possessed of land adjacent to the house concerned; and

(b) the covenant were expressed to be made for the benefit of such adjacent land".

(5) After subsection (4) there shall be inserted the following subsection—

"(4A) Any reference in the preceding provisions of this section to a disposal by way of tenancy or licence does not include a reference to a relevant disposal or an exempted disposal."

(6) This section has effect where the conveyance, grant or assignment referred to in subsection (1) of section 37 is executed on or after the commencement of this Act.

GENERAL NOTE

Part II of the Housing Act 1985 governs "voluntary sales", using the term in contrast to "right to buy" under *ibid*, Part V. The general intention is to put the terms of voluntary sales on a par with right to buy: see *ibid*, ss.35–42. S.37 of the 1985 Act permits a vendor authority to include in conveyance or grant of a property in a National Park, an area designated under the National Parks and Access to the Countryside Act 1949, s.87, as an area of outstanding natural beauty, or an area designated as a rural area under the 1985 Act, s.157, itself, a covenant which limits the freedom of the purchaser to dispose of the dwelling, without the previous consent of the (previous) landlord in writing, save for disposals of a specified class, which includes family transactions and disposals to persons already working or living in such an area.

The purpose of the amendment in subs. (2) is to extend the prohibition on disposal to the grant of tenancies or licences: the purpose is to prevent people purchasing and then, pending the time when they can dispose without consent, letting the property, or using it for holiday lettings (which would normally be considered licences: see notes to s.1, above). However, such tenancies or licences *can* be granted without consent if the property has hitherto been the only or principal home of the grantor (see notes to s.1, above) and so remains throughout the duration of the tenancy or licence, *i.e.* while the grantor is absent for a period but without establishing a "home" elsewhere. By subs. (4), the prohibitions are elevated to the status of restrictive covenants for the benefit of an adjoining landowner.

Restriction on disposal of dwelling-houses in National Parks etc. acquired under the right to buy

126.—(1) In Part V of the Housing Act 1985 (the right to buy), section 157 (restriction on disposal of dwelling-houses in National Parks etc.) shall be amended in accordance with this section.

(2) In subsection (2) (the covenanted limitation) after the word "his" there shall be inserted "(a)" and at the end there shall be added "and—

(b) there will be no disposal by way of tenancy or licence without the written consent of the landlord unless the disposal is to a person satisfying that condition or by a person whose only or principal home is and, throughout the duration of the tenancy or licence, remains the dwelling-house".

(3) In subsection (3) (disposals limited to persons employed or living locally) after the words "application for consent" there shall be inserted the words "or, in the case of a disposal by way of tenancy or licence, preceding the disposal".

(4) At the end of subsection (6) (disposals in breach of covenant to be void) there shall be added "and, so far as it relates to disposals by way of tenancy or licence, such a covenant may be enforced by the landlord as if—

(a) the landlord were possessed of land adjacent to the house concerned; and

(b) the covenant were expressed to be made for the benefit of such adjacent land".

(5) After subsection (6) there shall be inserted the following subsection—

"(6A) Any reference in the preceding provisions of this section to a disposal by way of tenancy or licence does not include a reference to a relevant disposal or an exempted disposal."

(6) This section has effect where the conveyance or grant referred to in subsection (1) of section 157 is executed on or after the commencement of this Act.

GENERAL NOTE
   This section makes the same amendments where a disposal is under the right to buy in the Housing Act 1985, Part V, as the last section made relative to voluntary sales under *ibid.*, Part II.

Preserved right to buy

127.—(1) In subsection (4) of section 171B of the Housing Act 1985 for paragraph (a) there shall be substituted the following paragraphs—
   "(a) where the former secure tenancy was not a joint tenancy and, immediately before his death, the former secure tenant was tenant under an assured tenancy of a dwelling-house in relation to which he had the preserved right to buy, a member of the former secure tenant's family who acquired that assured tenancy under the will or intestacy of the former secure tenant;
   (aa) where the former secure tenancy was not a joint tenancy, a member of the former secure tenant's family to whom the former secure tenant assigned his assured tenancy of a dwelling-house in relation to which, immediately before the assignment, he had the preserved right to buy".

(2) In subsection (2)(a) of section 171C of that Act after the word "paragraphs" there shall be inserted "1, 3 and".

(3) After subsection (4) of that section there shall be added the following subsection—
   "(5) The disapplication by the regulations of paragraph 1 of Schedule 5 shall not be taken to authorise any action on the part of a charity which would conflict with the trusts of the charity."

GENERAL NOTE
   See notes to s.84, above. Subs. (1) of this section amends the definition of "qualifying person" enjoying the "preserved right to buy" following a transfer into the private sector, in the 1985 Act, s.171B, notwithstanding that the main provisions of the Housing and Planning Act 1986, s.8, introducing the new ss.171A–H of the 1985 Act, have not yet been brought into force. Included as a qualifying person is a "qualifying successor", and the amendments reflect the removal of Rent Act protection and introduction of assured tenancies under Part I of this Act, above. The 1985 Act, s.171C, adapts the right to buy provisions for the purposes of the preserved right to buy, and subss. (2) and (3) amends that section.

Preservation of right to buy on disposal to private sector landlord: Scotland

128. After section 81 of the Housing (Scotland) Act 1987 there shall be inserted the following section—

   "Preservation of right to buy on disposal to private sector landlord

Preservation of right to buy on disposal to private sector landlord

   81A.—(1) The right to buy provisions shall continue to apply where a person ceases to be a secure tenant of a house by reason of the disposal by the landlord of an interest in the house to a private sector landlord.

   (2) The right to buy provisions shall not, however, continue to apply under subsection (1) in such circumstances as may be prescribed.

(3) The continued application under subsection (1) of the right to buy provisions shall be in accordance with and subject to such provision as is prescribed which may—

(a) include—

(i) such additions and exceptions to, and adaptations and modifications of, the right to buy provisions in their continued application by virtue of this section; and

(ii) such incidental, supplementary and transitional provisions;

as the Secretary of State considers appropriate;

(b) differ as between different cases or descriptions of case and as between different areas;

(c) relate to a particular disposal.

(4) Without prejudice to the generality of subsection (3), provision may be made by virtue of it—

(a) specifying the persons entitled to the benefit of the right to buy provisions in their continued application by virtue of this section;

(b) preventing, except with the consent of the Secretary of State, the disposal by the private sector landlord of less than his whole interest in a house in relation to which the right to buy provisions continue to apply by virtue of this section;

(c) ensuring that where, under Ground 9 of Schedule 5 to the Housing (Scotland) Act 1988 (availability of suitable alternative accommodation), the sheriff makes any order for possession of a house in relation to which the right to buy provisions continue to apply by virtue of this section and the tenant would not have the right under this Part (other than this section) to buy the house which is or will be available by way of alternative accommodation, these provisions as so continued will apply in relation to the house which is or will be so available.

(5) In this section—

(a) "secure tenant" means a tenant under a secure tenancy;

(b) "private sector landlord" means a landlord other than one of those set out in sub-paragraphs (i) to (iv) and (viii) and (ix) of paragraph (a) of subsection (2) of section 61;

(c) the "right to buy provisions" means the provisions of this Act relating to the right of a tenant of a house to purchase it under this Part and to his rights in respect of a loan."

GENERAL NOTE

This section introduces a preserved right to buy in Scotland, the details of which are to be prescribed.

Schemes for payments to assist local housing authority tenants to obtain other accommodation

129.—(1) In accordance with a scheme made by a local housing authority and approved by the Secretary of State under this section, the authority may make grants to or for the benefit of qualifying tenants or licensees of the authority with a view to assisting each person to whom or for whose benefit a grant is made to obtain accommodation otherwise than as a tenant or licensee of the authority either—

(a) by acquiring an interest in a dwelling-house; or

(b) by carrying out works to a dwelling-house to provide additional accommodation; or

(c) by both of those means.

(2) A scheme under this section shall contain such provisions as the local housing authority considers appropriate together with any which the

Secretary of State may require as a condition of his approval and, withou͟
prejudice to the generality, a scheme may include provisions specifying,
or providing for the determination of—
  (a) the persons who are qualifying tenants or licensees for the purposes
      of the scheme;
  (b) the interests which qualifying tenants or licensees may be assisted
      to acquire;
  (c) the works for the carrying out of which grants may be made;
  (d) the circumstances in which a grant may be made for the benefit of
      a qualifying tenant or licensee;
  (e) the amount of the grant which may be made in any particular case
      and the terms on which it may be made;
  (f) the limits on the total number and amount of grants which may be
      made; and
  (g) the period within which the scheme is to apply.
  (3) The Secretary of State may approve a scheme made by a local
housing authority under this section with or without conditions and, where
a scheme has been approved, the authority shall take such steps as it
considers appropriate to bring the scheme to the attention of persons
likely to be able to benefit from it and shall take such other steps (if any)
as the Secretary of State may direct in any particular case to secure
publicity for the scheme.
  (4) The Secretary of State may revoke an approval of a scheme under
this section by a notice given to the local housing authority concerned;
and, where such a notice is given, the revocation shall not affect the
operation of the scheme in relation to any grants made or agreed before
the date of the notice.
  (5) Any grant made pursuant to a scheme under this section—
  (a) shall be regarded as a grant of a capital nature for the purposes
      of Part VIII of the Local Government, Planning and Land Act
      1980 (capital expenditure of local authorities); and
  (b) shall be regarded as expenditure on management for the
      purposes of Part II of Schedule 14 to the Housing Act 1985
      (debits to the Housing Revenue Account).
  (6) Where a scheme made by a local housing authority under this
section has been approved, a person dealing with the authority shall not
be concerned to see or inquire whether the terms of the scheme have
been or are being complied with; and any failure to comply with the terms
of a scheme shall not invalidate any grant purporting to be made in
accordance with the scheme unless the person to whom the grant is made
has actual notice of the failure.
  (7) In this section—
  (a) "local housing authority" has the meaning assigned by section
      1 of the Housing Act 1985;
  (b) "dwelling-house" has the meaning assigned by section 112 of
      that Act; and
  (c) "tenant" does not include a tenant under a long tenancy, as
      defined in section 115 of that Act.

DEFINITIONS
  "dwelling-house": subs. (7).
  "local housing authority": subs. (7).
  "tenant": subs. (7).

GENERAL NOTE
  By the Housing Act 1985, s.26, "where a tenant of one of the houses of a local housing
authority moves to another house (whether or not that house is also one of theirs), the
authority may—(a) pay any expenses of the removal, and (b) where the tenant is purchasing
the house, pay any expenses incurred by him in connection with the purchase, *other than the*

purchase price" (emphasis added). Directions as to amounts which may be paid may be issued by the Secretary of State, and such Directions are to be found in the Housing Subsidies and Accounting Manual (1981 Edition), App. H.

The passage emphasised has given rise to problems for those authorities who have wished to engage in what are sometimes called "portable discounts", *i.e.* allowing one of their tenants an amount of money, perhaps equal to that which the tenant would gain on exercise of the right to buy, to enable the tenant to move out into the private, owner-occupied sector, thus liberating existing stock for re-allocation, bearing in mind the difficulties of purchasing new stock, especially in the light of the Local Government, Planning and Land Act 1980, Part VIII (prescribed expenditure). Central government approval of such schemes was publicly expressed, and legal authority for such schemes was claimed to derive from the Local Government Act 1972, s.111 (subsidiary, or ancillary, powers). However, s.111 itself is expressed to be "subject to the provisions of this Act and any other enactment passed before or after this Act. . ." The alternative legal view, accordingly, was that such portable discounts would be illegal.

Apparently, the alternative legal view was not considered without merit, for this section now provides for portable discounts (*cf.* s.58, above) pursuant to an "approved scheme". The scheme is limited to qualifying tenants or licensees of the authority, but extends to the execution of works as well as to the acquisition of an interest in a property (subs. (1)). All of the details are to be contained in the scheme (subs. (2)) which, once approved, must be publicised (subs. (3)); approval may be revoked (subs. (4)). Expenditure is to rank as prescribed for the purposes of Part VIII of the Local Government, Planning and Land Act 1980, and as management expenditure to be debited to the Housing Revenue Account under Part XIII of and Sched. 14, Part II, (Item 3) to the Housing Act 1985.

Repair notices and improvement grants

Repair notices

130.—(1) Part VI of the Housing Act 1985 (repair notices) shall have effect subject to the amendments in Schedule 15 to this Act.

(2) In section 604 of that Act (fitness for human habitation) after subsection (1) there shall be inserted the following subsection—

"(1A) In the application, for the purposes of Part VI, of subsection (1) to premises consisting of a flat, within the meaning of that Part, regard shall be had not only to the condition of the flat itself but also to the condition of any other part of the building as it affects the flat and, accordingly, the flat may be deemed to be unfit by reference to the defective condition of a part of the building outside the flat (whether or not that part is itself used, or suitable for use, as a dwelling)."

(3) The amendments in subsection (2) above and Schedule 15 to this Act do not have effect in relation to any repair notice, within the meaning of the said Part VI, served before this section comes into force.

GENERAL NOTE

Part VI of the Housing Act 1985 concerns the repair of unfit housing. The 1985 Act, s.189, permits service of a repairs notice on a house which is unfit for human habitation, as defined in *ibid*, s.604; *ibid.*, s.190 permits service of a repairs notice where a house, though not unfit, requires substantial repairs to bring it up to a reasonable standard, or where (on a representation by an occupying tenant) its condition is such as materially to interfere with the personal comfort of the occupying tenant. Repairs notices may only be served where the works can be carried out at a reasonable expense, as defined in *ibid.*, s.206 and in the extensive case-law pursuant thereto (and to its predecessor provisions) to require consideration of (a) pre-works value, (b) post-works value, and (c) works cost. The local authority have power to execute works in default where there is non-compliance: *ibid.*, s.193.

Repairs notices are served on "the person having control", as defined in *ibid.*, s.207: see also *Pollway Nominees* v. *Croydon London Borough Council* [1987] A.C. 79, (1986) 18 H.L.R. 443, H.L., in which it was held that where the individual flats in a building—presumed for the purposes of the action to constitute a house—were let out on long leases at low rents, the freeholder of the building was *not* the person having control of it; rather, the "person having control" of the house was comprised of all the people having control of the individual dwellings within it (the freeholder so far as tenanted properties and common parts were concerned, and the individual leaseholders).

"House" is defined in *ibid.*, s.207, as including "any yard, garden, outhouses and appurtenances belonging to the house or usually enjoyed with it." It does not *prima facie* include a flat. However, by s.205, "the local housing authority may take the like proceedings under this Part in relation to—(a) any part of a building which is used, or is suitable for use as, a dwelling".

In *R.* v. *Lambeth London Borough Council, ex p. Clayhope Properties* (1987) 19 H.L.R. 426, C.A., also involving a block of flats, it was held that repairs notices served on the person having control of each dwelling, relating (a) to that dwelling, and (b) to a proportion of the cost of works to the building, were void. The notice had to be served relative only to that of which the person had control; the persons having control of the individual dwellings did not have control of the whole. It was also held that the individual dwellings were not in their own right "houses".

This section, and Sched. 15 which it introduces, *inter alia*, seek to overcome the practical difficulties posed by *Clayhope*, although they also tackle a range of additional problems under Part VI of the 1985 Act, including making non-compliance with a repairs notice a criminal offence.

Subs. (2)

This amendment allows unfitness of a flat to be determined by reference to the condition of the building in which it is situated and would seem to permit a finding of unfitness where the *only* causes lie outside the individual flat. Flat is defined in the 1985 Act, s.183, incorporated into Part VI by s.207(2) as added by Sched. 15, para. 12, below, to mean a dwelling-house which is not a house, and house is defined as "a structure reasonably so called; so that—(a) where a building is divided horizontally, the flats or other units into which it is divided are not houses; (b) where a building is divided vertically, the units into which it is divided may be houses; (c) where a building is not structurally detached, it is not a house if a material part of it lies above or below the remainder of the structure".

Sched. 15

Para. 1. This amends the 1985 Act, s.189, to refer to "dwelling-house" instead of "house", and where the unfitness derives from conditions outside a flat, requires service of the repairs notice on the person having control of that part of the building; reasonable expense is to be evaluated, however, with reference to the value of the flat.

In addition, however, and quite independently, so that it applies to all repairs notices under s.189, *i.e.* whether house, flat or part of a building, this paragraph amends s.189 to require the authority serving the notice to specify a *commencement* date (not less than seven days after the notice becomes operative) for the works, as well as (as now) a "reasonable time" for completion. Notices, which until now "may" also be served on "any other person having an interest in the house, whether as freeholder, mortgagee, lessee or otherwise" (s.189(3), and only have to be so served if an owner—as defined in the 1985 Act, s.207, see further below—has served notice on the authority under s.202), in future "shall" be so served. An operative repairs notice is now to be a local land charge.

Para. 2. This paragraph amends the 1985 Act, s.190, also by extending it to "dwelling-house", and by extending the power to serve a repairs notice on the ground of interference with personal comfort so that it is no longer confined to the tenant's complaint but can result from the authority's own initiative. There are like amendments to those under s.189 extending the power to serve notice in respect of a part of a building, to require the inclusion of a commencement date, to serve other persons with a copy of the notice, and to render the notice a local land charge.

Para. 3. There is a right of appeal against a repairs notice, under s.191, which does not specify grounds therefor; by this amendment, "without prejudice to the generality of subsection (1), it shall be a ground of appeal that some person other than the appellant, being a person who is an owner in relation to the dwelling-house or part of the building concerned, ought to execute the works or pay the whole or part of the costs of executing them" (and correspondingly (a) an obligation on the part of the appellant to serve such person with a copy of the notice of appeal, and (b) enabling the court to vary the notice to require the works to be executed by that other person, or to allocate costs between them, having regard to relative interests in the dwelling-house or part of the building, relative responsibility for conditions and relative benefit from the works. Where the court orders some other person to execute the works, that other person is treated as "the person having control" of the premises to which the notice relates for the remaining provisions of Part VI).

"Owner" means (the 1985 Act, s.207) "a person (other than a mortgagee not in possession) who is for the time being entitled to dispose of the fee simple in the premises, whether in possession or reversion, and . . . includes a person holding or entitled to the rents and profits of the premises under a lease of which the unexpired term exceeds three years".

Para. 4. Where an appeal results in a finding that the property cannot be rendered fit at a reasonable expense, the local authority may compulsorily purchase it and carry out the works themselves, but the order is not to be confirmed if the owner or mortgagee undertakes in any event to carry out the works within such time as the Secretary of State may permit. These amendments permit compulsory purchase of a dwelling-house, *i.e.* a flat as well as a house, but prevent compulsory purchase if the owner or mortgagee of the dwelling-house or part of the building concerned so undertakes.

Para. 5. By the 1985 Act, s.193, the local authority have power to do works in default "if a repairs notice is not complied with", and compliance is defined (s.193(2)) as completion of the works within the period specified in the notice or, if appeal is brought, 21 days or such longer period as the court may allow, from the date when the notice becomes operative (defined in s.191(4) to mean the expiry of time for appeal, or the decision of a court on appeal, or withdrawal of appeal).

These amendments redefine compliance as commencing and completing works within the time allowed in the notice in the absence of appeal, or within the time allowed by the court on appeal where an appeal issues and is not withdrawn, or if an appeal issues and is withdrawn, commencement within 21 days of the notice becoming operative and completion within the time allowed in the original notice running from the date when the notice becomes operative.

However, the authority may now exercise their power to do the works in default even within the period allowed for compliance "if . . . it appears to the local housing authority that reasonable progress is not being made towards compliance. . ." In addition, if works are carried out by the person having control after the authority give notice under s.194 of their intention to enter to do the works in default, their preparation costs and related administrative and other expenses, are recoverable as if they had actually done the works in default.

Para. 6. These amendments are technical, adapting s.194 to replace "house" with "premises", and to *require* service of the notice (on person having control "and, if they think fit, any owner") where hitherto service of the notice has been discretionary (and without notice would prevent prosecution for obstruction under the 1985 Act, s.194(2)).

Para. 7. The maximum penalty for obstruction (s.198) is increased from level 2 on the standard scale, to level 3.

Para. 8. It is this paragraph which introduces a new s.198A into the 1985 Act, making it a criminal offence "intentionally" to fail to comply (as defined above) with a repairs notice; the offence is summary, and carries a fine not exceeding level two on the standard scale. Non-compliance continues even although the period for completion of the works has expired. The new provision is without prejudice to the powers of the authority to do works in default.

Para. 9. This repeals provisions permitting a lessee who is the person having control to recover some or all of the cost from the lessor, and dealing with charging orders, which have been replaced by amendments in Sched. 15.

Para. 10. S.203 preserves private law rights and obligations between parties; the amendment merely substitutes "premises" for "house".

Para. 11. It is s.205 which applies the provisions of Part VI to parts of a building (see General Note, above) and also to "a hut, tent, caravan or other temporary or movable structure which is used for human habitation and which has been in the same enclosure for a period of two years next before action is taken". The amendment repeals the application to parts of building now redundant in the light of the earlier amendments discussed above.

Para. 12. This amends the Part VI definition section, s.207, to define dwelling-house as in the same terms as "house" above, *i.e.* extending to yard, garden, etc., "premises" as including a dwelling-house or a part of a building, and "flat" as described in the note to subs. (2), above.

Para. 13. Sched. 10 governs the recovery of expenses incurred by a local housing authority carrying out works in default and this paragraph amends it to reflect the principal amendments described above. There is a new defence available to an appeal against such a claim, where the works in default have been carried out on the ground that reasonable progress was not being made, even though the time for compliance has not expired, that reasonable progress *was* being made.

Subs. (3)

None of the amendments takes effect where the repairs notice has been served before this section comes into force.

Letting conditions applicable to improvement grants etc.

131.—(1) With respect to applications for grants approved after the commencement of this Act, Part XV of the Housing Act 1985 (grants for works of improvement, repair and conversion) shall have effect subject to the following provisions of this section.

(2) In each of the following provisions—

    (a) section 464 (preliminary condition: certificates as to future occupation) in subsection (5) (certificate of availability for letting), and

    (b) section 501 (condition as to availability for letting) in subsection (2) (the terms of the condition),

in paragraph (a) after the word "holiday" there shall be inserted "on a tenancy which is not a long tenancy and".

(3) After the words "Rent (Agriculture) Act 1976", in each place where they occur in—

    (a) section 464(5),

    (b) section 501(2), and

    (c) subsection (2)(d) of section 503 (restriction on imposition of further conditions in relation to certain grants),

there shall be inserted "or is occupied under an assured agricultural occupancy, within the meaning of Part I of the Housing Act 1988".

(4) In section 504 (further conditions as to letting of dwelling), at the beginning of subsection (1) there shall be inserted the words "Subject to subsection (1A)"; in paragraph (a) of that subsection after the word "letting" there shall be inserted "on an assured tenancy which is not a long tenancy or"; and at the end of that subsection there shall be inserted the following subsection—

"(1A) Paragraphs (d) to (f) of subsection (1) do not apply in the case of a dwelling which is or is to be let or available for letting on an assured tenancy."

(5) In subsection (2) of section 504 (definitions) after the words "subsection (1)" there shall be inserted "and subsection (1A)" and before paragraph (a) there shall be inserted the following paragraph—

"(aa) "assured tenancy" means a tenancy which is an assured tenancy within the meaning of Part I of the Housing Act 1988 or would be such a tenancy if paragraphs 3, 6, 7 and 10 of Schedule 1 to that Act were omitted".

(6) In section 526 (index of defined expressions in Part XV), after the entry relating to "local housing authority" there shall be inserted—

"long tenancy.................... section 115".

(7) Without prejudice to subsection (1) above, where an application for a grant—

    (a) was made but not approved before the commencement of this Act, and

    (b) was accompanied by a certificate of availability for letting in a form which does not take account of the amendments of section 464(5) by subsections (2) and (3) above,

the certificate shall be treated as if it were in a form which takes account of the amendments made by those subsections.

(8) Without prejudice to subsection (1) above, where a grant has been approved before the commencement of this Act and—

    (a) section 501(2) applies to impose a condition of the grant, or

    (b) conditions have been imposed in terms of section 504(1), the condition or conditions shall have effect as if it or they were in a form which takes account of the amendments made by subsection (3) or, as the case may be, subsections (4) and (5) above.

GENERAL NOTE

Part XV of the Housing Act 1985 sets out the current structure of grant-aid for the improvement, conversion and repair of dwellings, including houses in multiple occupation (here referred to generically as housing improvement grants).

Subs. (2)

All applications for housing improvement grants (save a mandatory repairs grant under the 1985 Act, s.494) have to be accompanied, *inter alia*, by either a certificate of owner-occupation or a certificate of availability for letting: the 1985 Act, s.464(1). The certificate of availability for letting is defined in s.464(5) and "is a certificate stating that the person giving the certificate intends that, throughout the period of five years beginning with the certified date—(a) the dwelling will be let or available for letting as a residence, and not for a holiday, to a person other than a member of the family of the person giving the certificate, or (b) the dwelling will be occupied or available for occupation by a member of the agricultural population in pursuance of a contract of service and otherwise than as a tenant, (disregarding any part of that period in which neither of the above paragraphs applies but the dwelling is occupied by a protected occupier under the Rent (Agriculture) Act 1976)". Corresponding in most respects to the certificate of future occupation are the conditions to be found in the 1985 Act, s.501, for breach of which the grant may be recovered under *ibid.*, s.506.

These amendments exclude "long tenancies" as defined in the 1985 Act, s.115, see notes to s.102, above) as compliance with either certificate or conditions.

Subs. (3)

The 1985 Act, s.503, empowers (and in some circumstances, requires) a local authority to attach further conditions to the award of a grant, as set out in *ibid.*, s.504, even when the certificate of future occupation is not required (*R.* v. *Camden London Borough Council, ex p. Christey* (1987) 19 H.L.R. 420), detailing, *inter alia*, the sort of tenancy on which a property must be let; no conditions *other than* those in ss.501–504 may be attached. No further conditions can be attached in a number of circumstances, one of which is that the grant relates to a dwelling which is occupied by a protected occupier or statutory tenant under the Rent (Agriculture) Act 1976.

These amendments permit occupation under an assured agricultural occupancy within Part I, Chapter III, above, for the purposes of the provisions described in the notes to the last subsection, and prevent further conditions being attached when the dwelling to which the grant relates is so occupied.

Subs. (4)

These amendments include assured tenancies but exclude long tenancies (see notes to s.102, above) as compliance with a s.504 further condition, but preclude attaching the last three permitted further conditions where the dwelling is let or is available for letting on an assured tenancy, which prohibit premiums and require registration of rents. These amendments reflect Part I, Chapter I, above.

Disposals of housing stock

Consents to disposals of housing stock and application of receipts

132.—(1) At the end of subsection (4) of section 34 of the Housing Act 1985 (consent to disposals of land held for the purposes of Part II—provision of housing accommodation) and at the end of subsection (4) of section 43 of that Act (consent for certain disposals of other houses) there shall be inserted the subsections set out in subsection (2) below.

(2) The subsections referred to in subsection (1) above and subsection (3) below are as follows—

"(4A) The matters to which the Secretary of State may have regard in determining whether to give consent and, if so, to what conditions consent should be subject shall include—

(a) the extent (if any) to which the person to whom the proposed disposal is to be made (in this subsection referred to as "the intending purchaser") is, or is likely to be, dependent upon, controlled by or subject to influence from the local authority making the disposal or any members or officers of that authority;

(b) the extent (if any) to which the proposed disposal would result in the intending purchaser becoming the predominant or a substantial owner in any area of housing accommodation let on tenancies or subject to licences;

(c) the terms of the proposed disposal; and

(d) any other matters whatsoever which he considers relevant.

(4B) Where the Secretary of State gives consent to a disposal by a local authority, he may give directions as to the purpose for which any capital money received by the authority in respect of the disposal is to be applied and, where any such directions are given, nothing in any enactment shall require his consent to be given for the application of the capital money concerned in accordance with the directions."

(3) Section 13 of the Housing (Scotland) Act 1987 (power of Secretary of State to impose conditions in sale of local authority houses) shall be renumbered as subsection (1) of that section and after that subsection there shall be inserted as subsections (2) and (3) the subsections which are set out in subsection (2) above and there numbered (4A) and (4B).

(4) In section 153 of the Local Government Act 1972 (application of capital money on disposal of land), in subsection (1) after the words "127(4) above" there shall be inserted "to any directions given in respect of the disposal under section 43(4B) of the Housing Act 1985".

(5) In section 430 of the Housing Act 1985 (application of capital money received on disposal of land), in subsection (1) after the word "applied", in the first place where it occurs, there shall be inserted "in accordance with any directions given in respect of the disposal under section 34(4B) or section 43(4B) and, subject thereto".

(6) In section 208 of the Housing (Scotland) Act 1987 (application of receipts from disposal of certain land), in subsection (2) there shall be inserted at the end the words "or has made directions under section 13(3)".

(7) In section 26 of the Local Government Act 1988 (provisions as to consents under section 25 for provision of financial assistance etc.), in subsection (5) (which excludes consent under various enactments where consent is given to a disposal of land under section 25) after the words "such a consent" there shall be inserted "then, if the consent given for the purposes of section 25 above so provides".

(8) This section shall be deemed to have come into force on 9th June 1988.

GENERAL NOTE

With effect from June 9, 1988 (subs. (8)), there is a new consideration to which the Secretary of State may have regard when consenting to the disposal of Part II of the 1985 Act land by a local authority, under s.34 thereof, or to the disposal of other housing held by the authority on a secure tenancy, or in respect of which a long lease has been granted under the right to buy, under s.43 thereof: see also notes to s.133, below.

The new consideration mirrors that which will influence the approval of a landlord by the Housing Corporation and Housing for Wales in relation to Part IV of this Act (see s.93, above) or of a prospective purchaser from a housing action trust under Part III (see s.79, above). The purpose is to prevent authorities setting up "related" but independent organisations to take over their stock, although in the case of this section also included is "the extent (if any) to which the proposed disposal would result in the intending purchase becoming the predominant or a substantial owner in any area", *i.e.* "wholesale disposal" such as has been suggested, and in some areas reportedly effected.

The consent may include directions as to the application of capital received.

Consent required for certain subsequent disposals

133.—(1) Where consent is required for a disposal (in this section referred to as "the original disposal") by virtue of section 32 or section 43 of the Housing Act 1985 and that consent does not provide otherwise, the person who acquires the land or house on the disposal shall not dispose of it except with the consent of the Secretary of State; but nothing in this section shall apply in relation to an exempt disposal as defined in section 81(7) above.

(2) Where an estate or interest of the person who acquired the land or house on the original disposal has been mortgaged or charged, the prohibition in subsection (1) above applies also to a disposal by the mortgagee or chargee in exercise of a power of sale or leasing, whether or not the disposal is in the name of the person who so acquired the land or house; and in any case where—

(a) by operation of law or by virtue of an order of a court, the land or house which has been acquired passes or is transferred from the person who so acquired it to another person, and

(b) that passing or transfer does not constitute a disposal for which consent is required under this section,

this section (including, where there is more than one such passing or transfer, this subsection) shall apply as if the other person to whom the land or house passes or is transferred were the person who acquired it on the original disposal.

(3) Where subsection (1) above applies—

(a) if section 34 of the Housing Act 1985 applies to the consent given to the original disposal, subsections (2)(b) and (3) to (4A) of that section shall also apply to any consent required by virtue of this section;

(b) if the consent to the original disposal was given under section 43 of that Act, subsections (2)(b) and (3) to (4A) of that section shall also apply to any consent required by virtue of this section;

(c) in the application of subsection (4A) of section 34 or section 43 to any consent required by virtue of this section, any reference to the local authority making the disposal shall be construed as a reference to the local authority making the original disposal; and

(d) the instrument by which the original disposal is effected shall contain a statement in a form approved by the Chief Land Registrar that the requirement of this section as to consent applies to a subsequent disposal of the land or house by the person to whom the original disposal was made.

(4) Subsection (4) of section 32 of the Housing Act 1985 or, as the case may be, subsection (5) of section 43 of that Act (options to purchase as disposals) applies for the purposes of this section.

(5) Before giving any consent required by virtue of this section, the Secretary of State—

(a) shall satisfy himself that the person who is seeking the consent has taken appropriate steps to consult every tenant of any land or house proposed to be disposed of; and

(b) shall have regard to the responses of any such tenants to that consultation.

(6) If, apart from subsection (7) below, the consent of the Housing Corporation or Housing for Wales would be required under section 9 of the Housing Associations Act 1985 (control of dispositions of land by

housing associations) for a disposal in respect of which, by virtue of subsection (1) above, the consent of the Secretary of State is required, the Secretary of State shall consult that body before giving his consent for the purposes of this section.

(7) No consent shall be required under the said section 9 for any disposal in respect of which consent is given in accordance with subsection (6) above.

(8) Where the title of the authority to the land or house which is disposed of by the original disposal is not registered, and the original disposal is a conveyance, grant or assignment of a description mentioned in section 123 of the Land Registration Act 1925 (compulsory registration of title)—

(a) that section applies in relation to the instrument by which the original disposal is effected whether or not the land or house is in an area in which an Order in Council under section 120 of that Act (areas of compulsory registration) is in force;

(b) the authority shall give to the person to whom the original disposal is made a certificate in a form approved by the Chief Land Registrar stating that the authority is entitled to make the disposal subject only to such encumbrances, rights and interests as are stated in the instrument by which the original disposal is effected or summarised in the certificate; and

(c) for the purpose of registration of title, the Chief Land Registrar shall accept such a certificate as evidence of the facts stated in it, but if as a result he has to meet a claim against him under the Land Registration Acts 1925 to 1986 the authority by whom the original disposal was made is liable to indemnify him.

(9) On an application being made for registration of a disposition of registered land or, as the case may be, of the title under a disposition of unregistered land, if the instrument by which the original disposal is effected contains the statement required by subsection (3)(d) above, the Chief Land Registrar shall enter in the register a restriction stating the requirement of this section as to consent to a subsequent disposal.

(10) In every case where the consent of the Secretary of State is required for the original disposal by virtue of section 32 or section 43 of the Housing Act 1985 (whether or not consent is required under this section to a subsequent disposal), the authority by which the original disposal is made shall furnish to the person to whom it is made a copy of that consent.

GENERAL NOTE

Other than under the 1985 Act, Part V (right to buy), Part IV of this Act (see Sched. 17, para. 38, below) or where there is a letting on a secure tenancy (or what would be a secure tenancy but for the 1985 Act, Sched. 1, paras. 2–12), local authorities need consent to any disposal of Part II housing (provision of housing): the 1985 Act, s.32. Similarly, where housing is held by an authority *other than* under Part II, consent is required for a disposal (other than under the 1985 Act, Part V or Part IV of this Act—see Sched. 17, para. 39, below) of a house let on a secure tenancy or of which a lease has been granted under Part V: the 1985 Act, s.43.

This section provides that unless the disposal consent otherwise specifies, the *purchaser's* right further to dispose of the property (other than on an exempt disposal) also requires consent. Save for the following observations, the provisions are substantively the same as under ss.81 and 105, above, including their application to a disposal by a mortgagee:

(1) Where the 1985 Act, s.34 applies (*i.e.* on a s.32 disposal), the further disposal consent falls within its subs. (2)(b) (consent may apply to particular land or land of a particular description), (3), (4) (consent may be subject to conditions, including in particular as to price, premium or rent, and discount) and (4A) (see notes to s.132, above);

(2) Where the 1985 Act, s.43 applies, subs. (2)(b) (general consent or in relation to any particular house or description of house—but note that subs. (5) of this section requiring consultation with tenants affected), (3), (4), (4A) (as under s.34);

(3) Ss.34(4A) and 43(4A) (see notes to s.132 above) are adapted to refer to the local authority making the disposal which required original consent;

(4) The local authority have to provide a copy of the original consent to the person to whom they dispose of the property (subs. (10)).

Consent required for certain subsequent disposals: Scotland

134. In Part I of the Housing (Scotland) Act 1987 (provision of housing) after section 12 there shall be inserted the following section—

"Consent of Secretary of State required for certain subsequent disposals

12A.—(1) Where a person acquires any land or house from a local authority under section 12(1)(c) or (d) above and the consent of the Secretary of State is required under section 12(7) above to the local authority's disposal of the land or house to that person, that person shall not dispose of the land or house without the consent in writing of the Secretary of State.

(2) Any consent for the purposes of subsection (1) above may be given either in respect of a particular disposal or in respect of disposals of any class or description (including disposals in particular areas) and either unconditionally or subject to conditions.

(3) Before giving any consent for the purposes of subsection (1) above, the Secretary of State—

(a) shall satisfy himself that the person who is seeking the consent has taken appropriate steps to consult every tenant of any land or house proposed to be disposed of; and

(b) shall have regard to the responses of any such tenants to that consultation.

(4) The consent of Scottish Homes under section 9 of the Housing Associations Act 1985 (control of dispositions) is not required for any disposal, or disposals of any class or description, in respect of which consent is given under subsection (1) above.

(5) In this section references to disposing of property include references to—

(a) granting or disposing of any interest in property;

(b) entering into a contract to dispose of property or to grant or dispose of any such interest; and

(c) granting an option to acquire property or any such interest."

General Note

This section concerns consent requirement in Scotland.

Consultation before disposal: Scotland

135.—(1) In Part III of the Housing (Scotland) Act 1987 (rights of public sector tenants) after section 81 there shall be inserted the following section—

"Consultation before disposal to private sector landlord

Consultation before disposal to private sector landlord

81B. The provisions of Schedule 6A have effect with respect to the duties of—

(a) a local authority proposing to dispose of houses let on secure tenancies;

(b) the Secretary of State in considering whether to give his consent under section 12(7) to such a disposal, to have regard to the views of tenants liable as a result of the disposal to cease to be secure tenants (that is to say, tenants under secure tenancies)."

(2) After Schedule 6 to the Housing (Scotland) Act 1987 there shall be inserted, as Schedule 6A, the Schedule set out in Schedule 16 to this Act.

(3) The amendments made by this section apply to disposals after the coming into force of this section.

GENERAL NOTE

This section concerns consultation before disposal to a private sector landlord in Scotland, and introduces the provisions of Sched. 16 to this Act as Sched. 6A to the Housing (Scotland) Act 1987.

Application of capital money to meet costs of disposals of land

136.—(1) At the end of section 430 of the Housing Act 1985 (application of capital money received on disposal of land) there shall be inserted the following subsection—

"(3) In the case of capital money received by a local authority in respect of—

    (a) disposals of land held for the purposes of Part II (provision of housing), and

    (b) any other disposals of land made by virtue of Part V (the right to buy) which do not fall within paragraph (a),

the reference in subsection (1) to any other purpose for which capital money may properly be applied includes a reference to the purpose of meeting the administrative costs of and incidental to such disposals; and, accordingly, the reference in subsection (2) to subsection (1) includes a reference to that subsection as extended by virtue of this subsection."

(2) In section 72 of the Local Government, Planning and Land Act 1980 (expenditure which authorities may make), in subsection (7) (net capital receipts for any year defined as the receipts which are capital receipts for the purposes of Part VIII of that Act, reduced by certain payments) after the words "reduced by" there shall be inserted—

"(a) any amount of capital money which in that year is applied for the purpose specified in section 430(3) of the Housing Act 1985 (meeting administrative costs of and incidental to certain disposals of land); and

    (b)".

GENERAL NOTE

These amendments govern the application of capital received on a disposal of the 1985 Act, Part II land or under Part V (right to buy), allowing its application to related administrative costs of disposal, and disregarding such for the purposes of calculating receipts under Part VIII of the Local Government, Planning and Land Act 1980 (prescribed expenditure).

Codes of practice

Codes of practice in field of rented housing

137.—(1) Section 47 of the Race Relations Act 1976 (codes of practice) shall be amended in accordance with the following provisions of this section.

(2) In subsection (1) for the words "either or both" there shall be substituted the words "all or any" and at the end there shall be added the following paragraphs—

"(c) the elimination of discrimination in the field of housing let on tenancies or occupied under licences ("the field of rented housing");

(d) the promotion of equality of opportunity in the field of rented housing between persons of different racial groups".

(3) In subsection (3), after the words "code of practice" there shall be inserted "relating to the field of employment" and after that subsection there shall be inserted the following subsection—

"(3A) In the course of preparing any draft code of practice relating to the field of rented housing for eventual publication under subsection (2) the Commission shall consult with such organisations or bodies as appear to the Commission to be appropriate having regard to the content of the draft code".

(4) In subsection (4) for the words "the draft" there shall be substituted "a draft code of practice".

(5) In subsection (10) after the words "industrial tribunal" there shall be inserted "a county court or, in Scotland, a sheriff court" and after the words "the tribunal" there shall be inserted "or the court".

GENERAL NOTE

By the Race Relations Act 1976, s.47, the Commission for Racial Equality may draw up and issue codes of practice containing practical guidance to eliminate discrimination in the field of employment, and promote equality of opportunity in the field of employment, subject to consultation requirements in s.47(3) and approval by the Secretary of State and both Houses of Parliament (subs. (4)). By s.47(10), while failure to observe the code of practice does not render a person liable to proceedings, in proceedings before an industrial tribunal the code is admissible in evidence and potentially relevant to a determination.

By this section, the code of practice duties are applied to the elimination of discrimination in the field of rented houses and the promotion of equality of opportunity in the field of rented housing, subject to consultation under the new s.47(3A) (subs. (3), above), and with appropriate adaptation of the related provisions described in the foregoing paragraph.

Supplementary

Financial provisions

138.—(1) There shall be paid out of money provided by Parliament—
(a) any sums required for the payment by the Secretary of State of grants under this Act;
(b) any sums required to enable the Secretary of State to make payments to housing action trusts established under Part III of this Act;
(c) any other expenses of the Secretary of State under this Act; and
(d) any increase attributable to this Act in the sums so payable under any other enactment.

(2) Any sums received by the Secretary of State under this Act, other than those required to be paid into the National Loans Fund, shall be paid into the Consolidated Fund.

Application to Isles of Scilly

139.—(1) This Act applies to the Isles of Scilly subject to such exceptions, adaptations and modifications as the Secretary of State may by order direct.

(2) The power to make an order under this section shall be exercisable by statutory instrument which shall be subject to annulment in pursuance of a resolution of either House of Parliament.

Amendments and repeals

140.—(1) Schedule 17 to this Act, which contains minor amendments and amendments consequential on the provisions of this Act and the Housing (Scotland) Act 1988, shall have effect and in that Schedule Part

I contains general amendments and Part II contains amendments consequential on the establishment of Housing for Wales.

(2) The enactments specified in Schedule 18 to this Act, which include
some that are spent, are hereby repealed to the extent specified in the
third column of that Schedule, but subject to any provision at the end of
that Schedule and to any saving in Chapter V of Part I of or Schedule 17
to this Act.

Short title, commencement and extent

141.—(1) This Act may be cited as the Housing Act 1988.

(2) The provisions of Parts II and IV of this Act and sections 119, 122,
124, 128, 129, 135 and 140 above shall come into force on such day as the
Secretary of State may by order made by statutory instrument appoint,
and different days may be so appointed for different provisions or for
different purposes.

(3) Part I and this Part of this Act, other than sections 119, 122, 124,
128, 129, 132, 133, 134, 135 and 138 onwards, shall come into force at the
expiry of the period of two months beginning on the day it is passed; and
any reference in those provisions to the commencement of this Act shall
be construed accordingly.

(4) An order under subsection (2) above may make such transitional
provisions as appear to the Secretary of State necessary or expedient in
connection with the provisions brought into force by the order.

(5) Parts I, III and IV of this Act and this Part, except sections 118,
128, 132, 134, 135 and 137 onwards, extend to England and Wales only.

(6) This Act does not extend to Northern Ireland.

SCHEDULES

Section 1   SCHEDULE 1

TENANCIES WHICH CANNOT BE ASSURED TENANCIES

PART I

THE TENANCIES

Tenancies entered into before commencement

1. A tenancy which is entered into before, or pursuant to a contract made before, the
commencement of this Act.

Tenancies of dwelling-houses with high rateable values

2. A tenancy under which the dwelling-house has for the time being a rateable value
which,—
   (a) if it is in Greater London, exceeds £1,500; and
   (b) if it is elsewhere, exceeds £750.

Tenancies at a low rent

3.—(1) A tenancy under which either no rent is payable or the rent payable less than
two-thirds of the rateable value of the dwelling-house for the time being.

(2) In determining whether the rent under a tenancy falls within sub-paragraph (1) above,
there shall be disregarded such part (if any) of the sums payable by the tenant as is expressed
(in whatever terms) to be payable in respect of rates, services, management, repairs,
maintenance or insurance, unless it could not have been regarded by the parties to the
tenancy as a part so payable.

Business tenancies

4. A tenancy to which Part II of the Landlord and Tenant Act 1954 applies (business tenancies).

Licensed premises

5. A tenancy under which the dwelling-house consists of or comprises premises licensed for the sale of intoxicating liquors for consumption on the premises.

Tenancies of agricultural land

6.—(1) A tenancy under which agricultural land, exceeding two acres, is let together with the dwelling-house.

(2) In this paragraph "agricultural land" has the meaning set out in section 26(3)(a) of the General Rate Act 1967 (exclusion of agricultural land and premises from liability for rating).

Tenancies of agricultural holdings

7. A tenancy under which the dwelling-house—
   (a) is comprised in an agricultural holding (within the meaning of the Agricultural Holdings Act 1986); and
   (b) is occupied by the person responsible for the control (whether as tenant or as servant or agent of the tenant) of the farming of the holding.

Lettings to students

8.—(1) A tenancy which is granted to a person who is pursuing, or intends to pursue, a course of study provided by a specified educational institution and is so granted either by that institution or by another specified institution or body of persons.

(2) In sub-paragraph (1) above "specified" means specified, or of a class specified, for the purposes of this paragraph by regulations made by the Secretary of State by statutory instrument.

(3) A statutory instrument made in the exercise of the power conferred by sub-paragraph (2) above shall be subject to annulment in pursuance of a resolution of either House of Parliament.

Holiday lettings

9. A tenancy the purpose of which is to confer on the tenant the right to occupy the dwelling-house for a holiday.

Resident landlords

10.—(1) A tenancy in respect of which the following conditions are fulfilled—
   (a) that the dwelling-house forms part only of a building and, except in a case where the dwelling-house also forms part of a flat, the building is not a purpose-built block of flats; and
   (b) that, subject to Part III of this Schedule, the tenancy was granted by an individual who, at the time when the tenancy was granted, occupied as his only or principal home another dwelling-house which,—
      (i) in the case mentioned in paragraph (a) above, also forms part of the flat; or
      (ii) in any other case, also forms part of the building; and
   (c) that, subject to Part III of this Schedule, at all times since the tenancy was granted the interest of the landlord under the tenancy has belonged to an individual who, at the time he owned that interest, occupied as his only or principal home another dwelling-house which,—
      (i) in the case mentioned in paragraph (a) above, also formed part of the flat; or
      (ii) in any other case, also formed part of the building; and
   (d) that the tenancy is not one which is excluded from this sub-paragraph by sub-paragraph (3) below.

(2) If a tenancy was granted by two or more persons jointly, the reference in sub-paragraph (1)(b) above to an individual is a reference to any one of those persons and if the interest of the landlord is for the time being held by two or more persons jointly, the reference in sub-paragraph (1)(c) above to an individual is a reference to any one of those persons.

(3) A tenancy (in this sub-paragraph referred to as "the new tenancy") is excluded from sub-paragraph (1) above if—

(a) it is granted to a person (alone, or jointly with others) who, immediately before it was granted, was a tenant under an assured tenancy (in this sub-paragraph referred to as "the former tenancy") of the same dwelling-house or of another dwelling-house which forms part of the building in question; and

(b) the landlord under the new tenancy and under the former tenancy is the same person or, if either of those tenancies is or was granted by two or more persons jointly, the same person is the landlord or one of the landlords under each tenancy.

Crown tenancies

11.—(1) A tenancy under which the interest of the landlord belongs to Her Majesty in right of the Crown or to a government department or is held in trust for Her Majesty for the purpose of a government department.

(2) The reference in sub-paragraph (1) above to the case where the interest of the landlord belongs to Her Majesty in right of the Crown does not include the case where that interest is under the management of the Crown Estate Commissioners.

Local authority tenancies etc.

12.—(1) A tenancy under which the interest of the landlord belongs to—

(a) a local authority, as defined in sub-paragraph (2) below;

(b) the Commission for the New Towns;

(c) the Development Board for Rural Wales;

(d) an urban development corporation established by an order under section 135 of the Local Government, Planning and Land Act 1980;

(e) a development corporation, within the meaning of the New Towns Act 1981;

(f) an authority established under section 10 of the Local Government Act 1985 (waste disposal authorities);

(g) a residuary body, within the meaning of the Local Government Act 1985; or

(h) a fully mutual housing association; or

(i) a housing action trust established under Part III of this Act.

(2) The following are local authorities for the purposes of sub-paragraph (1)(a) above—

(a) the council of a county, district or London borough;

(b) the Common Council of the City of London;

(c) the Council of the Isles of Scilly;

(d) the Broads Authority;

(e) the Inner London Education Authority; and

(f) a joint authority, within the meaning of the Local Government Act 1985.

Transitional cases

13.—(1) A protected tenancy, within the meaning of the Rent Act 1977.

(2) A housing association tenancy, within the meaning of Part VI of that Act.

(3) A secure tenancy.

(4) Where a person is a protected occupier of a dwelling-house, within the meaning of the Rent (Agriculture) Act 1976, the relevant tenancy, within the meaning of that Act, by virtue of which he occupies the dwelling-house.

Part II

Rateable Values

14.—(1) The rateable value of a dwelling-house at any time shall be ascertained for the purposes of Part I of this Schedule as follows—

(a) if the dwelling-house is a hereditament for which a rateable value is then shown in the valuation list, it shall be that rateable value;

(b) if the dwelling-house forms part only of such a hereditament or consists of or forms

.rt of more than one such hereditament, its rateable value shall be taken to be such alue as is found by a proper apportionment or aggregation of the rateable value or values so shown.

Any question arising under this Part of this Schedule as to the proper apportionment aggregation of any value or values shall be determined by the county court and the cision of that court shall be final.

15. Where, after the time at which the rateable value of a dwelling-house is material for the purposes of any provision of Part I of this Schedule, the valuation list is altered so as to vary the rateable value of the hereditament of which the dwelling-house consists (in whole or in part) or forms part and the alteration has effect from that time or from an earlier time, the rateable value of the dwelling-house at the material time shall be ascertained as if the value shown in the valuation list at the material time had been the value shown in the list as altered.

16. Paragraphs 14 and 15 above apply in relation to any other land which, under section 2 of this Act, is treated as part of a dwelling-house as they apply in relation to the dwelling-house itself.

PART III

PROVISIONS FOR DETERMINING APPLICATION OF PARAGRAPH 10 (RESIDENT LANDLORDS)

17.—(1) In determining whether the condition in paragraph 10(1)(c) above is at any time fulfilled with respect to a tenancy, there shall be disregarded—

(a) any period of not more than twenty-eight days, beginning with the date on which the interest of the landlord under the tenancy becomes vested at law and in equity in an individual who, during that period, does not occupy as his only or principal home another dwelling-house which forms part of the building or, as the case may be, flat concerned;

(b) if, within a period falling within paragraph (a) above, the individual concerned notifies the tenant in writing of his intention to occupy as his only or principal home another dwelling-house in the building or, as the case may be, flat concerned, the period beginning with the date on which the interest of the landlord under the tenancy becomes vested in that individual as mentioned in that paragraph and ending—

(i) at the expiry of the period of six months beginning on that date, or
(ii) on the date on which that interest ceases to be so vested, or
(iii) on the date on which that interest becomes again vested in such an individual as is mentioned in paragraph 10(1)(c) or the condition in that paragraph becomes deemed to be fulfilled by virtue of paragraph 18(1) or paragraph 20 below, whichever is the earlier; and

(c) any period of not more than two years beginning with the date on which the interest of the landlord under the tenancy becomes, and during which it remains, vested—

(i) in trustees as such; or
(ii) by virtue of section 9 of the Administration of Estates Act 1925, in the Probate Judge, within the meaning of that Act.

(2) Where the interest of the landlord under a tenancy becomes vested at law and in equity in two or more persons jointly, of whom at least one was an individual, sub-paragraph (1) above shall have effect subject to the following modifications—

(a) in paragraph (a) for the words from "an individual" to "occupy" there shall be substituted "the joint landlords if, during that period none of them occupies"; and

(b) in paragraph (b) for the words "the individual concerned" there shall be substituted "any of the joint landlords who is an individual" and for the words "that individual" there shall be substituted "the joint landlords".

18.—(1) During any period when—

(a) the interest of the landlord under the tenancy referred to in paragraph 10 above is vested in trustees as such, and

(b) that interest is or, if it is held on trust for sale, the proceeds of its sale are held on trust for any person who or for two or more persons of whom at least one occupies as his only or principal home a dwelling-house which forms part of the building or, as the case may be, flat referred to in paragraph 10(1)(a),

the condition in paragraph 10(1)(c) shall be deemed to be fulfilled and accordingly, no part of that period shall be disregarded by virtue of paragraph 17 above.

(2) If a period during which the condition in paragraph 10(1)(c) is deemed to be fulfilled by virtue of sub-paragraph (1) above comes to an end on the death of a person who was in

50–210

occupation of a dwelling-house as mentioned in paragraph (b) of that sub-paragraph, then, in determining whether that condition is at any time thereafter fulfilled, there shall be disregarded any period—
(a) which begins on the date of the death;
(b) during which the interest of the landlord remains vested as mentioned in sub-paragraph (1)(a) above; and
(c) which ends at the expiry of the period of two years beginning on the date of the death or on any earlier date on which the condition in paragraph 10(1)(c) becomes again deemed to be fulfilled by virtue of sub-paragraph (1) above.
19. In any case where—
(a) immediately before a tenancy comes to an end the condition in paragraph 10(1)(c) is deemed to be fulfilled by virtue of paragraph 18(1) above, and
(b) on the coming to an end of that tenancy the trustees in whom the interest of the landlord is vested grant a new tenancy of the same or substantially the same dwelling-house to a person (alone or jointly with others) who was the tenant or one of the tenants under the previous tenancy,
the condition in paragraph 10(1)(b) above shall be deemed to be fulfilled with respect to the new tenancy.
20.—(1) The tenancy referred to in paragraph 10 above falls within this paragraph if the interest of the landlord under the tenancy becomes vested in the personal representatives of a deceased person acting in that capacity.
(2) If the tenancy falls within this paragraph, the condition in paragraph 10(1)(c) shall be deemed to be fulfilled for any period, beginning with the date on which the interest becomes vested in the personal representatives and not exceeding two years, during which the interest of the landlord remains so vested.
21. Throughout any period which, by virtue of paragraph 17 or paragraph 18(2) above, falls to be disregarded for the purpose of determining whether the condition in paragraph 10(1)(c) is fulfilled with respect to a tenancy, no order shall be made for possession of the dwelling-house subject to that tenancy, other than an order which might be made if that tenancy were or, as the case may be, had been an assured tenancy.
22. For the purposes of paragraph 10 above, a building is a purpose-built block of flats if as constructed it contained, and it contains, two or more flats; and for this purpose "flat" means a dwelling-house which—
(a) forms part only of a building; and
(b) is separated horizontally from another dwelling-house which forms part of the same building.

GENERAL NOTE
Part I of this Schedule lists the exemptions from "assured tenancy": see, generally, notes to s.1, above. Part II governs the determination of rateable value for the purposes of ss.1 and 3, above, and of paras. 2 and 3 of this Schedule. Part III contains provisions governing the "resident landlord" exemption of para. 10 of this Schedule. Note that a tenancy is only not assured "if and so long as" an exemption applies: s.1, above.

Part 1
Para. 1
A tenancy entered into before the commencement date (see s.127, above), is not an assured tenancy; nor is a tenancy pursuant to a contract made before that date. However, by s.37(4), (5), a contract for a 1980 Act assured tenancy which has not commenced by the time this Act comes into force, the tenancy is to be an assured tenancy under this Act, as if only paras. 11 and 12 of this Schedule functioned as exemptions, *i.e.* it will not be exempt on account of any of the other paragraphs in this Schedule. A binding contract for a tenancy is enforceable, and takes effect as an equitable tenancy in any event: *Walsh* v. *Lonsdale* (1882) 21 Ch. 9.

Para. 2
Lettings of high rateable value premises are not assured. Ascertainment of rateable value is prescribed by Part II of this Schedule: see notes thereto, below.

Para. 3
No and low rent tenancies are not assured. A low rent is one that is less than two-thirds of the rateable value: see notes to Part II of this Schedule, below.
When determining what is the rent payable, to be disregarded is any part of the rent which is *expressed to be* payable in respect of rates, services, management, repairs,

maintenance or insurance, unless, even although so expressed, the rent could not have been regarded as so payable, *i.e.* the description is misleading, whether or not deliberately so. See, generally, the notes to s.14, above, as to the presumption that all sums payable to the landlord by the tenant will be rent, which this provision is designed to rebut. Its principal object is to leave out of assured tenancies long leases under which low rents are paid, but levels of service charge may well take the sum above the two-thirds limit.

The date for determining whether a tenancy is a tenancy at a low rent is the date when the relevant issue arises: *Woozley* v. *Woodall Smith* [1950] 1 K.B. 325, C.A. The words "if and so long as" in s.1 serve to emphasise this: see also *J. F. Stone Lighting & Radio* v. *Levitt* [1947] A.C. 209, H.L. In effect, a tenancy may drift in and out of being an assured tenancy, subject to fluctuating costs.

Rent means rent payable or at least quantified in money. A tenancy in exchange for services will be a no rent tenancy: see *Hornsby* v. *Maynard* [1925] 1 K.B. 514, *Barnes* v. *Barratt* [1970] 2 Q.B. 657, C.A. But where a quantified rent was deducted from an employee's pay, this was held to qualify as rent: *Montague* v. *Browning* [1954] 1 W.L.R. 1039, C.A. Even a quantifiable rent *may* qualify: see *Barnes* v. *Barratt* (above).

Para. 4

A tenancy to which Part II of the Landlord and Tenant Act 1954 applies is not an assured tenancy. The 1954 Act applies to business tenancies. If the *whole* of the premises are used for business purposes, then irrespective of whether the 1954 Act applies, there will in any event be no assured tenancy for want of use as an only or principal home: *McMillan & Co.* v. *Rees* [1946] 1 All E.R. 675, C.A. Prima facie, however, a degree of business use will not pre-empt use as an only or principal home, and will accordingly therefore not lose the status of assured tenancy: *Green* v. *Coggins* [1949] 2 All E.R. 815, C.A.; *Court* v. *Robinson* [1951] 2 K.B. 60, C.A. It is when the degree of business use is sufficient to attract the protection of the 1954 Act that the tenancy ceases to be assured.

Under s.23(1) of the 1954 Act, Part II applies "to any tenancy where the property comprised in the tenancy is or includes premises which are occupied by the tenant and are so occupied for the purposes of a business carried on by him or for those and other purposes." "Business" includes "a trade, profession or employment and includes any activity carried on by a body of persons, whether corporate or unincorporate" (s.23(2) of the 1954 Act). Part II does not apply to a tenancy for a fixed period of not more than six months, unless the tenancy contains provisions for renewal beyond that time, or the tenant or his predecessor in the business has been in occupation for more than 12 months: s.43 of the 1954 Act.

Of particular relevance are the cases determining when sub-letting and keeping lodgers or engaging in other activities amounts to such a business user as to take the letting into Part II. Where the whole of the premises are sub-let, the letting clearly cannot be an assured tenancy, for the tenant will not normally still qualify as using the premises for an only or principal home: *Ebner* v. *Lascelles* [1928] 2 K.B. 486, D.C., *Carter* v. *S.U. Carburetter Co.* [1942] 2 K.B. 288, C.A.

In order to attract the provisions of Part II the business user must be of some significance, and where there is insignificant business or professional user, the present Act may still continue to apply: compare *Cheryl Investments* v. *Saldanha* and *Royal Life Saving Society* v. *Page* reported together at [1978] 1 W.L.R. 1329, C.A. Whether the degree of business user is significant enough is a question of fact for the court: *Pulleng* v. *Curran* (1980) 44 P. & C.R. 58, C.A., in which it was also held that a lease extended under Part II of the 1954 Act cannot subsequently become residential. See also *Durman* v. *Bell* (1988) 20 H.L.R., C.A.

Keeping lodgers does not necessarily imply business user: all of the circumstances must be looked at, *e.g.* commercial advantage, number of lodgers, size of house, money charged. Spare-time activities, even if there is a minor financial element involved, do not necessarily change the character of the user from residential to business: *Lewis* v. *Weldcrest* [1978] 1 W.L.R. 1107, C.A., *Abernethie* v. *Kleiman* [1970] 1 Q.B. 10, C.A.

Four of the previously cited cases provide a useful study of the principles. Thus, in *Cheryl Investments*, a businessman rented residential premises, but almost immediately began to use them for the purposes of his business. The business had no other offices, and both stationery and telephone user were based at the premises. It was held that this user was business user within the 1954 Act, rather than residential within the Rent Act 1977. On the other hand, in *Royal Life Saving Society*, a doctor took an assignment of a lease of residential premises and, with the landlord's consent, installed a consulting room, in which he saw the occasional patient, although his principal consulting rooms and practice were elsewhere. It was held that the degree of business user was insufficient to attract the 1954 Act, the principal purpose of his occupation being residential.

In *Lewis*, an elderly lady took in lodgers, for whom she provided breakfast and Sunday lunch. Having regard to the income she derived from this alleged "business" and to all of the circumstances of the case a patently sympathetic Court of Appeal, remarking that she no doubt took in lodgers because she liked it and was good at it, held that this was not a business user within the 1954 Act. In *Abernethie*, a man used a loft in his premises to conduct Sunday School classes for about 30 children. He made no charge, but kept a subscription box for donations to a scripture mission. Again, such a spare-time activity was held not to amount to a "trade, profession or employment" within s.23 of the 1954 Act, and so the letting remained residential.

A letting of premises for sub-occupation by students may be a letting within the provisions of Part II: *Groveside Properties* v. *Westminster Medical School* (1983) 9 H.L.R. 118, C.A. In contrast, in *Chapman* v. *Freeman* [1978] 1 W.L.R. 1298, C.A., use by a hotelier of a cottage near his hotel for housing staff, when it was not essential for them to live there (*cf.* below, notes to Sched. 2, Ground 16,) was held not to constitute a business user within Part II of the 1954 Act.

Para. 5

This provision is derived from s.11 of the Rent Act 1977 and governs only on-licensed premises, *e.g.* a pub or club.

Para. 6

See notes to s.2, above. See also *Bradshaw* v. *Smith* (1980) 225 E.G. 699, C.A., in which it was held that a field of more than two acres was not agricultural land within the meaning of s.26 of the 1967 Act, because it was not *used* only as a meadow or pasture, but used mainly or exclusively for the purposes of recreation. But bear in mind that there must be a letting *as* a dwelling under s.1, so that terms of the letting may exclude an assured tenancy: see also *Russell* v. *Booker* (1982) 5 H.L.R. 10, C.A., notes to s.1, above.

Para. 7

This paragraph is derived from s.10 of the Rent Act 1977. It is designed to exclude from security farm-managers, whether they work for the landlord, or for a tenant of the land.

Para. 8

This governs lettings to students, by their own or another "specified" educational institution. The student must either already be pursuing or be intending to pursue a course of study provided by a specified education institution. The Secretary of State enjoys the power to specify educational institutions for this purpose, by statutory instrument. A letting *to* an educational institution, for onward letting to their students, will not be assured (a) because the tenant will not be an individual (see s.1, above), (b) on account of the exemption for business lettings (see para. 4, above), and (c) because there will be no letting as "a" separate dwelling: *St. Catherine's College* v. *Dorling* [1980] 1 W.L.R. 66, C.A.

Para. 9

The "holiday letting" exemption from Rent Act protection gave rise to their use as a means of avoiding its protection: see *R.* v. *Rent Officer for London Borough of Camden, ex p. Plant* (1980) 7 H.L.R. 15, Q.B.D., in which the description of the agreement as a holiday letting was considered to constitute a "false label", and as such to be ignored by the court. In *Buchmann* v. *May* [1978] 2 All E.R. 993, 7 H.L.R. 1, C.A., it was held that the express provision of the agreement was to be taken as prima facie evidence of purpose, and could only be displaced by evidence that the express purpose did not represent the true purpose, whether or not the express purpose amounted to a sham or merely a false label in the sense of a mistake in expression of intention; although in such cases the court would be astute to detect a sham, the burden lay on the tenant to show that the provision did not correspond to the true purpose of the agreement.

The cases on sham must now be considered in the light of the robust attitude of the House of Lords to agreements within protective legislation, aimed primarily at the distinction between tenancy and licence, but not without some application to the question of sham, in *Street* v. *Mountford* [1985] A.C. 809, H.L. and *A-G Securities* v. *Vaughan* (1988) *The Times*, November 11, 1988, 21 H.L.R.; see notes to s.1, above.

A "working holiday" appears to have been accepted by the county court as within the meaning of holiday in *McHale* v. *Daneham* (1979) 249 E.G. 969, and dicta in *Buchmann* v. *May* supports this proposition.

Para. 10

This exemption is modelled on, and substantively very similar to, the principal exemption from Rent Act protection—the "resident landlord," introduced in 1974, when Rent Act protection was extended to furnished lettings. Cumbersomely worded, its effect is to operate only where the would-be assured letting is of premises which form part only of a building, which is not a purpose-built block of flats (unless the letting is of premises which form part only of a flat.) Flat is defined in Part III, para. 22, of this Schedule.

With one exception (see notes to Part III, below), the landlord under the letting must occupy another part of the building or flat as his only or principal home (see notes to s.1, above). In a flat, it will commonly be the case that the landlord and the tenant share living accommodation, in which case there will be no letting as a separate dwelling (s.1, above; see also, s.3, above).

The provisions of sub-para.(1)(c) permit sale or transfer of landlord's interest to another resident landlord, without the necessity to evict the tenant, and the provisions of Part III of the Schedule govern "allowable breaks" in occupation designed to encourage such sale or transfer without eviction, *i.e.* periods during which, notwithstanding the want of occupation, an assured tenancy will not come into being.

Sub-para. (1)(d) is an "anti-evasion" measure, disapplying the exemption as a whole if the grant of the tenancy is to a person who (alone or jointly with others) had an assured tenancy of the same premises, or of other premises in the same building: the purpose is to prevent a landlord purchasing, moving in so as to qualify as a resident landlord, and then persuading a sitting, assured tenant to enter into a new tenancy which would, by the operation of para. 10, otherwise not be assured. The measure applies whether the landlord under the earlier and new tenancies is the same, or whether he was or is but one of a number of joint landlords.

By sub-para. (2), occupation as an only or principal home may be by one of two or more joint landlords. This incorporates the decision of the Court of Appeal in *Cooper* v. *Tait* (1984) 15 H.L.R. 98, C.A. In *Lyons* v. *Caffery* (1982) 5 H.L.R. 63, C.A., occupation by the landlord's mother of a room the landlord had never himself lived in, being a sun-room or conservatory that was the only part of the premises which he had formerly occupied which he had not otherwise let out, was insufficient to found a claim to residence for the analogous Rent Act provision, but the position is even clearer under this Act, requiring occupation as an only or principal home. Occupation will usually be a matter of fact: *Chetwynd* v. *Boughey* (unreported) December 14, 1979, C.A.

There is no statutory definition of the term "building". The term, in the Rent Act context, was considered in *Bardrick* v. *Haycock* (1976) 2 H.L.R. 118, C.A., where a house was entirely let off in flats, and the landlord lived in an extension of later construction tied structurally to the main house but without any internal communication and with its own front door. The Court of Appeal upheld the county court decision that this was not one building. Scarman L.J. said that the provision aimed at the mischief of "social embarrassment arising out of close proximity—close proximity which the landlord had accepted in the belief that he could bring it to an end at any time allowed by the contract of tenancy."

Reference was made to *Humphrey* v. *Young* [1903] 1 K.B. 4, under other statutory provisions, where a pair of semi-detached houses had been found to constitute two separate buildings, but *cf. Hedley* v. *Webb* [1901] 2 Ch. 126, *Cook* v. *Minion* (1979) 37 P. & C.R. 58, Ch.D. In *Guppy* v. *O'Donnell* (1979) 129 New L.J. 930, adjoining premises between which substantial connections had been made by the demolition of walls were treated as one building.

In *Griffiths* v. *English* (1981) 2 H.L.R. 126, C.A., the original house had later extensions on either side without internal connections. The landlord lived in one extension, the tenant in another, and the main house had been subdivided into flats (not purpose-built). The Court of Appeal concluded that as a matter of fact the property as a whole could constitute one building, taking into account the absence of separate gardens and the presence of a greenhouse and shed serving the garden at the back of the tenant's portion of the dwelling.

"Purpose-built" is to be determined at the time of construction: *Barnes* v. *Gorsuch* (1981) 2 H.L.R. 134, C.A.

As regards the "allowable breaks" in occupation, see notes to Part III, below.

Para. 11

In the 1980 Act, Rent Act protection was extended to tenants of the Crown, where the property was under the management of the Crown Estates Commissioners. This extension has been continued under this Act.

Para. 12
"Public" sector landlords are similarly excluded from the Act. Housing associations in general are not, however, excluded: see also s.35, above. However, a fully mutual housing association is excluded: sub-para. (1)(h) (save where the assured tenancy is one which comes into being under s.1, following a 1980 Act assured tenancy granted by the fully mutual housing association; as to the definition of such, see s.45, above). Housing action trusts, created by Part III of this Act are excluded.

Para. 13
For the avoidance of doubt, tenancies which still qualify—having been granted before the commencement of this Act—as protected under the Rent Act 1977 (see notes to s.34, above), as a housing association tenancy which qualifies under Part VI of that Act and/or as a secure tenancy under the Housing Act 1985 (see notes to s.35, above), or a protected occupier under the Rent (Agriculture) Act 1976 (see notes to s.24, above), are not assured tenancies. Unless otherwise stated, there is no necessary mutual exclusivity between protective Acts: see *e.g. London Borough of Lambeth* v. *Udechuka, The Times,* April 30, 1980; [1980] C.L.Y. 1640, C.A.

Part II
This Part of the Schedule governs the determination of rateable value for the purposes of Part I of the Act: see, particularly, ss.1 and 3, above, and paras. 2 and 3 of this Schedule, above. Unlike under both the Rent Act 1977 and the Leasehold Reform Act 1967, there is no relationship back of rateable value to "the appropriate day", which accordingly omits a substantial body of case-law.
The starting-point is the rateable value specified in the valuation list, apportioned where the dwelling-house forms part only of the hereditament as it so appears. The county court has final jurisdiction (see *Field* v. *Gover* [1944] K.B. 200) on such an apportionment. As to the factors on an apportionment, see *Bainbridge* v. *Congdon* [1925] 2 K.B. 261, *Beck* v. *Newbold* [1952] 2 All E.R. 412, C.A. If there is a back-dated variation of the valuation list, the back-dating is effective to cover issues arising under Part I of this Act, but a mere refund of rates without such alteration has no effect on determination of rateable value (*Rodwell* v. *Gwynne Trusts* [1970] 1 W.L.R. 327, H.L.) The same principles apply to land treated as part of the dwelling-house under s.2 of this Act.

Part III
This Part of the Schedule governs allowable periods of non-occupation as an only or principal home by a resident landlord, for the purposes of para. 10 of this Schedule. The first such period is a period of 28 days during which the landlord's interest vests both in law and equity (therefore, completion on sale or assignment rather than exchange) in another person, who does not occupy as his only or principal home another part of the same building (or flat): para. 17(1)(a). The second such period derives from the first, and permits an incoming resident landlord to notify the tenant in writing, within those 28 days, of his intention to take up such occupation, and allows an extension to six months: para. 17(1)(b).
If, during that time, however, the in-coming landlord changes his mind and the interest passes to another, the extension ends, but it seems that another period of 28 days (extendable to six months) arises: see also *Williams* v. *Mate* (1982) 4 H.L.R. 15, C.A. If the in-coming landlord moves in sooner, the extension period ends. The same is true if the landlord is deemed to be in occupation (again) under paras. 18(1) or 20, below, *i.e.* occupation under trust or while the landlord's interest is vested in personal representatives.
The third period is a period of up to two years in which the landlord's interest vests either in trustees as such, or in the Probate Judge by virtue of the Administration of Estates Act 1925, s.9, *i.e.* on death: para. 17(1)(c). During a period when the interest is vested in trustees, if the interest is held on trust for someone who occupies the property as an only or principal home, occupation by a resident landlord is deemed to occur, so that the two years do not run: para. 18. The same is true if it is held on trust for sale, and the proceeds are held for anyone who occupies the property as an only or principal home, which will be the case if there is joint ownership by joint landlords: *ibid.* The two-year periods available under this paragraph appear to be capable of being added together: see *Williams* v. *Mate* (above). There is provision for a break of up to two years between occupation by different beneficiaries.
As an exception to the normal rule that the *grant* must be by a resident landlord (see notes to para. 10, above), trustees may grant a second tenancy to someone treated as having a resident landlord by virtue of their trust for a "resident beneficiary", *i.e.* under para.

18(1), provided the dwelling-house is the same or substantially the same as that occupied under the earlier tenancy, without loss of the protection afforded by para. 18, para. 19.

The fourth period is also of two years, and arises when the interest of the landlord becomes vested in the personal representatives of the deceased, acting as such, *i.e.* it follows a period during which non-occupation may be disregarded under para. 18(1)(c): para. 20.

During a period disregarded by paras. 17 and 18(2)—no order for possession is to be made against the tenant other than one which might be made if the tenancy were assured: para. 21.

The effect of this is *not*, as it might seem, that if no new resident landlord moves in the tenant will *necessarily* become assured. This is true if no notice to quit (not notice of seeking possession under s.8, above) is or can be served during the disregarded period. But if such is served, and is effective to terminate the tenancy during it, once the period of disregard has ended, there is no tenancy to qualify as assured, even although no order for possession can be made (other than as permitted, which presumably *does* require notice of seeking possession under s.8, above): see *Landau* v. *Sloane* [1982] A.C. 490, H.L. The period constitutes only a "period of grace": *ibid.* See also *Caldwell* v. *McAteer* (1983) 14 H.L.R. 98, C.A.

Section 7   SCHEDULE 2

GROUNDS FOR POSSESSION OF DWELLING-HOUSES LET ON ASSURED TENANCIES

PART I

GROUNDS ON WHICH COURT MUST ORDER POSSESSION

Ground 1

Not later than the beginning of the tenancy the landlord gave notice in writing to the tenant that possession might be recovered on this ground or the court is of the opinion that it is just and equitable to dispense with the requirement of notice and (in either case)—
- (a) at some time before the beginning of the tenancy, the landlord who is seeking possession or, in the case of joint landlords seeking possession, at least one of them occupied the dwelling-house as his only or principal home; or
- (b) the landlord who is seeking possession or, in the case of joint landlords seeking possession, at least one of them requires the dwelling-house as his or his spouse's only or principal home and neither the landlord (or, in the case of joint landlords, any one of them) nor any other person who, as landlord, derived title under the landlord who gave the notice mentioned above acquired the reversion on the tenancy for money or money's worth.

Ground 2

The dwelling-house is subject to a mortgage granted before the beginning of the tenancy and—
- (a) the mortgagee is entitled to exercise a power of sale conferred on him by the mortgage or by section 101 of the Law of Property Act 1925; and
- (b) the mortgagee requires possession of the dwelling-house for the purpose of disposing of it with vacant possession in exercise of that power; and
- (c) either notice was given as mentioned in Ground 1 above or the court is satisfied that it is just and equitable to dispense with the requirement of notice;

and for the purposes of this ground "mortgage" includes a charge and "mortgagee" shall be construed accordingly.

Ground 3

The tenancy is a fixed term tenancy for a term not exceeding eight months and—
- (a) not later than the beginning of the tenancy the landlord gave notice in writing to the tenant that possession might be recovered on this ground; and
- (b) at some time within the period of twelve months ending with the beginning of the tenancy, the dwelling-house was occupied under a right to occupy it for a holiday.

Ground 4

The tenancy is a fixed term tenancy for a term not exceeding twelve months and—
- (a) not later than the beginning of the tenancy the landlord gave notice in writing to the tenant that possession might be recovered on this ground; and
- (b) at some time within the period of twelve months ending with the beginning of the tenancy, the dwelling-house was let on a tenancy falling within paragraph 8 of Schedule 1 to this Act.

Ground 5

The dwelling-house is held for the purpose of being available for occupation by a minister of religion as a residence from which to perform the duties of his office and—
- (a) not later than the beginning of the tenancy the landlord gave notice in writing to the tenant that possession might be recovered on this ground; and
- (b) the court is satisfied that the dwelling-house is required for occupation by a minister of religion as such a residence.

Ground 6

The landlord who is seeking possession or, if that landlord is a registered housing association or charitable housing trust, a superior landlord intends to demolish or reconstruct the whole or a substantial part of the dwelling-house or to carry out substantial works on the dwelling-house or any part thereof or any building of which it forms part and the following conditions are fulfilled—
- (a) the intended work cannot reasonably be carried out without the tenant giving up possession of the dwelling-house because—
  - (i) the tenant is not willing to agree to such a variation of the terms of the tenancy as would give such access and other facilities as would permit the intended work to be carried out, or
  - (ii) the nature of the intended work is such that no such variation is practicable, or
  - (iii) the tenant is not willing to accept an assured tenancy of such part only of the dwelling-house (in this sub-paragraph referred to as "the reduced part") as would leave in the possession of his landlord so much of the dwelling-house as would be reasonable to enable the intended work to be carried out and, where appropriate, as would give such access and other facilities over the reduced part as would permit the intended work to be carried out, or
  - (iv) the nature of the intended work is such that such a tenancy is not practicable; and
- (b) either the landlord seeking possession acquired his interest in the dwelling-house before the grant of the tenancy or that interest was in existence at the time of that grant and neither that landlord (or, in the case of joint landlords, any of them) nor any other person who, alone or jointly with others, has acquired that interest since that time acquired it for money or money's worth; and
- (c) the assured tenancy on which the dwelling-house is let did not come into being by virtue of any provision of Schedule 1 to the Rent Act 1977, as amended by Part I of Schedule 4 to this Act or, as the case may be, section 4 of the Rent (Agriculture) Act 1976, as amended by Part II of that Schedule.

For the purposes of this ground, if, immediately before the grant of the tenancy, the tenant to whom it was granted or, if it was granted to joint tenants, any of them was the tenant or one of the joint tenants under an earlier assured tenancy of the dwelling-house concerned, any reference in paragraph (b) above to the grant of the tenancy is a reference to the grant of that earlier assured tenancy.

For the purposes of this ground "registered housing association" has the same meaning as in the Housing Associations Act 1985 and "charitable housing trust" means a housing trust, within the meaning of that Act, which is a charity, within the meaning of the Charities Act 1960.

Ground 7

The tenancy is a periodic tenancy (including a statutory periodic tenancy) which has devolved under the will or intestacy of the former tenant and the proceedings for the recovery of possession are begun not later than twelve months after the death of the former tenant or, if the court so directs, after the date on which, in the opinion of the court, the landlord or, in the case of joint landlords, any one of them became aware of the former tenant's death.

For the purposes of this ground, the acceptance by the landlord of rent from a new tenant after the death of the former tenant shall not be regarded as creating a new periodic tenancy, unless the landlord agrees in writing to a change (as compared with the tenancy before the death) in the amount of the rent, the period of the tenancy, the premises which are let or any other term of the tenancy.

Ground 8

Both at the date of the service of the notice under section 8 of this Act relating to the proceedings for possession and at the date of the hearing—
  (a) if rent is payable weekly or fortnightly, at least thirteen weeks' rent is unpaid;
  (b) if rent is payable monthly, at least three months' rent is unpaid;
  (c) if rent is payable quarterly, at least one quarter's rent is more than three months in arrears; and
  (d) if rent is payable yearly, at least three months' rent is more than three months in arrears;
and for the purpose of this ground "rent" means rent lawfully due from the tenant.

PART II

GROUNDS ON WHICH COURT MAY ORDER POSSESSION

Ground 9

Suitable alternative accommodation is available for the tenant or will be available for him when the order for possession takes effect.

Ground 10

Some rent lawfully due from the tenant—
  (a) is unpaid on the date on which the proceedings for possession are begun; and
  (b) except where subsection (1)(b) of section 8 of this Act applies, was in arrears at the date of the service of the notice under that section relating to those proceedings.

Ground 11

Whether or not any rent is in arrears on the date on which proceedings for possession are begun, the tenant has persistently delayed paying rent which has become lawfully due.

Ground 12

Any obligation of the tenancy (other than one related to the payment of rent) has been broken or not performed.

Ground 13

The condition of the dwelling-house or any of the common parts has deteriorated owing to acts of waste by, or the neglect or default of, the tenant or any other person residing in the dwelling-house and, in the case of an act of waste by, or the neglect or default of, a person lodging with the tenant or a sub-tenant of his, the tenant has not taken such steps as he ought reasonably to have taken for the removal of the lodger or sub-tenant.

For the purposes of this ground, "common parts" means any part of a building comprising the dwelling-house and any other premises which the tenant is entitled under the terms of the tenancy to use in common with the occupiers of other dwelling-houses in which the landlord has an estate or interest.

Ground 14

The tenant or any other person residing in the dwelling-house has been guilty of conduct which is a nuisance or annoyance to adjoining occupiers, or has been convicted of using the dwelling-house or allowing the dwelling-house to be used for immoral or illegal purposes.

Ground 15

The condition of any furniture provided for use under the tenancy has, in the opinion of the court, deteriorated owing to ill-treatment by the tenant or any other person residing in the dwelling-house and, in the case of ill-treatment by a person lodging with the tenant or by a sub-tenant of his, the tenant has not taken such steps as he ought reasonably to have taken for the removal of the lodger or sub-tenant.

Ground 16

The dwelling-house was let to the tenant in consequence of his employment by the landlord seeking possession or a previous landlord under the tenancy and the tenant has ceased to be in that employment.

PART III

SUITABLE ALTERNATIVE ACCOMMODATION

1. For the purposes of Ground 9 above, a certificate of the local housing authority for the district in which the dwelling-house in question is situated, certifying that the authority will provide suitable alternative accommodation for the tenant by a date specified in the certificate, shall be conclusive evidence that suitable alternative accommodation will be available for him by that date.

2. Where no such certificate as is mentioned in paragraph 1 above is produced to the court, accommodation shall be deemed to be suitable for the purposes of Ground 9 above if it consists of either—

    (a) premises which are to be let as a separate dwelling such that they will then be let on an assured tenancy, other than—

        (i) a tenancy in respect of which notice is given not later than the beginning of the tenancy that possession might be recovered on any of Grounds 1 to 5 above, or

        (ii) an assured shorthold tenancy, within the meaning of Chapter II of Part I of this Act, or

    (b) premises to be let as a separate dwelling on terms which will, in the opinion of the court, afford to the tenant security of tenure reasonably equivalent to the security afforded by Chapter I of Part I of this Act in the case of an assured tenancy of a kind mentioned in sub-paragraph (a) above,

and, in the opinion of the court, the accommodation fulfils the relevant conditions as defined in paragraph 3 below.

3.—(1) For the purposes of paragraph 2 above, the relevant conditions are that the accommodation is reasonably suitable to the needs of the tenant and his family as regards proximity to place of work, and either—

    (a) similar as regards rental and extent to the accommodation afforded by dwelling-houses provided in the neighbourhood by any local housing authority for persons whose needs as regards extent are, in the opinion of the court, similar to those of the tenant and of his family; or

    (b) reasonably suitable to the means of the tenant and to the needs of the tenant and his family as regards extent and character; and

that if any furniture was provided for use under the assured tenancy in question, furniture is provided for use in the accommodation which is either similar to that so provided or is reasonably suitable to the needs of the tenant and his family.

(2) For the purposes of sub-paragraph (1)(a) above, a certificate of a local housing authority stating—

    (a) the extent of the accommodation afforded by dwelling-houses provided by the authority to meet the needs of tenants with families of such number as may be specified in the certificate, and

    (b) the amount of the rent charged by the authority for dwelling-houses affording accommodation of that extent,

shall be conclusive evidence of the facts so stated.

4. Accommodation shall not be deemed to be suitable to the needs of the tenant and his family if the result of their occupation of the accommodation would be that it would be an overcrowded dwelling-house for the purposes of Part X of the Housing Act 1985.

5. Any document purporting to be a certificate of a local housing authority named therein issued for the purposes of this Part of this Schedule and to be signed by the proper officer of that authority shall be received in evidence and, unless the contrary is shown, shall be deemed to be such a certificate without further proof.

6. In this Part of this Schedule "local housing authority" and "district", in relation to such an authority, have the same meaning as in the Housing Act 1985.

Part IV

Notices Relating to Recovery of Possession

7. Any reference in Grounds 1 to 5 in Part I of this Schedule or in the following provisions of this Part to the landlord giving a notice in writing to the tenant is, in the case of joint landlords, a reference to at least one of the joint landlords giving such a notice.

8.—(1) If, not later than the beginning of a tenancy (in this paragraph referred to as "the earlier tenancy"), the landlord gives such a notice in writing to the tenant as is mentioned in any of Grounds 1 to 5 in Part I of this Schedule, then, for the purposes of the ground in question and any further application of this paragraph, that notice shall also have effect as if it had been given immediately before the beginning of any later tenancy falling within sub-paragraph (2) below.

(2) Subject to sub-paragraph (3) below, sub-paragraph (1) above applies to a later tenancy—

(a) which takes effect immediately on the coming to an end of the earlier tenancy; and

(b) which is granted (or deemed to be granted) to the person who was the tenant under the earlier tenancy immediately before it came to an end; and

(c) which is of substantially the same dwelling-house as the earlier tenancy.

(3) Sub-paragraph (1) above does not apply in relation to a later tenancy if, not later than the beginning of the tenancy, the landlord gave notice in writing to the tenant that the tenancy is not one in respect of which possession can be recovered on the ground in question.

9. Where paragraph 8(1) above has effect in relation to a notice given as mentioned in Ground 1 in Part I of this Schedule, the reference in paragraph (b) of that ground to the reversion on the tenancy is a reference to the reversion on the earlier tenancy and on any later tenancy falling within paragraph 8(2) above.

10. Where paragraph 8(1) above has effect in relation to a notice given as mentioned in Ground 3 or Ground 4 in Part I of this Schedule, any second or subsequent tenancy in relation to which the notice has effect shall be treated for the purpose of that ground as beginning at the beginning of the tenancy in respect of which the notice was actually given.

11. Any reference in Grounds 1 to 5 in Part I of this Schedule to a notice being given not later than the beginning of the tenancy is a reference to its being given not later than the day on which the tenancy is entered into and, accordingly, section 45(2) of this Act shall not apply to any such reference.

GENERAL NOTE

This Schedule is divided into four Parts. Part I contains the "mandatory" grounds for possession, and Part II the discretionary grounds: see notes to s.9, above. Part III governs the meaning of suitable alternative accommodation under Part II. Part IV governs notices under Grounds 1 to 5 in Part I.

Part I
Ground 1

Prior Occupation. The first alternative arises where at some time before the beginning of the tenancy, the landlord—or if joint landlords, one of them—has occupied the dwelling-house as his only or principal home. There is no requirement that the landlord or one of them should now wish to return to occupation. There is no requirement that the previous residence should be *immediately* before the grant of the tenancy, *cf. Pocock* v. *Steel* [1984] 1 W.L.R. 229, 17 H.L.R. 181, C.A. There is no requirement that prior occupation should have been under any particular "title", *e.g.* the landlord may formerly have occupied as *tenant.* There is no requirement that the prior occupation should have been permanent or prolonged: see *Naish* v. *Curzon* (1984) 17 H.L.R. 220, C.A.

These are only the requirements specified: (a) that notice was served no later than the beginning of the tenancy that possession might be recovered under this ground, or the court considers it just and equitable to waive the requirement of notice, and (b) prior occupation as an only or principal home, as to the meaning of which see notes to s.1, above.

It must, of course, be the same premises which the landlord or one of them has formerly occupied as an only or principal home: the mere fact that the landlord has formerly lived in *another part* of the same building will not suffice unless it includes the part let; while the landlord may well be able to recover possession of the part formerly occupied, in such circumstances, he will not then be able to claim exemption from assured tenancy in relation to other parts by reason of Sched. 1, para. 10 and Part III—see notes thereto, above.

While on its face it might seem arguable that where a landlord has formerly lived in a dwelling-house as a whole, but let it off in separate dwellings, he cannot recover under this ground against any of the tenants, because he did not occupy any or each of the single lettings "as an only or principal home", this is unlikely to succeed: (a) see *Hampstead Way Investments* v. *Lewis-Weare* [1985] 1 W.L.R. 164, 17 H.L.R. 152, H.L.; (b) because of the policy of the provisions.

Required for Occupation. Either the landlord—or if joint landlords, one of them (incorporating the decision of the House of Lords in *Tilling* v. *Whiteman* [1980] A.C. 1)—requires the dwelling-house as an only or principal home (see notes to s.1, above) for his own occupation, or that of his spouse. Two joint landlords may accordingly generate four prospective occupiers. But in the absence of express extension (or the use of the phrase "member of the family" defined or undefined), spouse means lawfully married, not merely living together as husband and wife.

There is no reference to a "reasonable" requirement for occupation: see *Kenneally* v. *Dunne* [1977] 1 Q.B. 837, C.A. There is no defence of "greater hardship": cf. Rent Act 1977, Sched. 15, Case 9 and Part III. The requirement must be as at the date of hearing: *Alexander* v. *Mohamadzadeh* (1985) 18 H.L.R. 90, C.A. The ground is available to a landlord by estoppel: *Stratford* v. *Syrett* [1958] 1 Q.B. 107, C.A. A corporate landlord cannot use this ground, for it cannot reside, though *cf. Evans* v. *Engelson* (1979) 253 E.G. 577, C.A. for what may be an applicable but highly limited exemption where the landlord was a mere nominee company.

Requirement for residence for children under 18 (*i.e.* not yet adult) might also render the ground available, even though the landlord lives elsewhere (*Smith* v. *Penny* [1947] 1 K.B. 230, *Harte* v. *Frampton* [1948] 1 K.B. 73) for it has been held that "normal emanations" may be treated within the word "himself" in the analogous Rent Act legislation: *Richter* v. *Wilson* [1963] 2 Q.B. 426, C.A. The requirement is for use as an only or principal home "for some reasonable period, definite or indefinite" (not, *e.g.* if the real reason is to sell the property): *Rowe* v. *Truelove* (1976) 241 E.G. 533, C.A. The requirement for use as an only or principal home relates to the part of the premises let.

Of crucial importance, however, is that this second limb of this ground is *not* available if the landlord, or if there are joint landlords one of them, acquired his interest in the reversion on the tenancy for money or money's worth. This is the equivalent to the Rent Act prohibition on use of Case 9 by a "landlord by purchase". The essential point is clear: the value of a notice served under this ground is not for sale. But it is only ordinary commercial transactions which are precluded: *cf. Littlechild* v. *Holt* [1956] 1 K.B. 1; acquisition of the reversion under a will, or by a family re-arrangement without "payment", will not prevent the landlord using the ground, *cf. Baker* v. *Lewis* [1947] K.B. 186, C.A., *Thomas* v. *Fryer* [1970] 1 W.L.R. 845, C.A., *Powell* v. *Cleland* [1948] 1 K.B. 262, C.A.

Clearly, a landlord who buys with vacant possession and later grants the tenancy is unaffected by the restriction, for he did not acquire the reversion for money or money's worth: *Epps* v. *Rothnie* [1945] K.B. 562, *Newton* v. *Biggs* [1953] 2 Q.B. 211, C.A.; see also *Cairns* v. *Piper* [1954] 2 Q.B. 210. "Acquisition" (of reversionary interest) may, however, date from contract for sale, rather than completion: *Emberson* v. *Robinson* [1953] 1 W.L.R. 1129, C.A. If a qualifying landlord obtains an order under this ground but dies before execution, his successors will be able to proceed: *Goldthorpe* v. *Bain* [1952] 2 Q.B. 455, C.A.

Notice. Under Part IV, below, notice is given not later than the beginning of the tenancy if it is given not later than the day the tenancy is entered into, so that the general interpretation of "beginning of tenancy" to be found in s.43(2), above, treating it as the *later* date (if any) when the tenant becomes entitled to possession, is inapplicable. This endorses the principle effective in *Bradshaw* v. *Baldwin-Wiseman* (1985) 17 H.L.R. 260, C.A., a case on "just and equitable" to waive notice (see further below) that it is of the utmost importance for a tenant to appreciate when taking rented property whether or not he is obtaining security of tenure.

Under Part IV, below, however, if a notice is properly given at or before the beginning of one tenancy, it will apply to a subsequent tenancy of the same or substantially the same (see notes to s.5, above) dwelling-house, which commences immediately on the expiry of the earlier tenancy, and which is granted or deemed to be granted to the person who was the tenant under the earlier tenancy at the time of its expiry. This will not apply, if, however, the landlord gives notice in writing before the beginning of the later tenancy that it is *not* subject to a notice that possession might be recovered under this ground (if, *e.g.* seeking a higher rent—see notes to s.13, above). Notice may be given by one or less than all of a number of joint landlords: Part IV, para. 7, below.

Other than that notice must be in writing, there are no other formal, or prescribed, requirements of it. However, it must make clear that possession might be recovered under the ground, howsoever informal the phraseology: see *Fowler* v. *Minchin* (1987) 19 H.L.R. 224, C.A.

Just and Equitable Waiver of Notice. In *Fernandes* v. *Parvardin* (1982) 5 H.L.R. 33, C.A., it was held on the facts that oral notice was enough to justify use of the power to waive the requirement for written notice where there was no suggestion of misunderstanding on the part of the tenants and no injustice or inequity resulting. In *Bradshaw* v. *Baldwin-Wiseman* (above), it was said that as the original letting had not been intended to be in some way temporary, *i.e.* subject to notice, it was "inconceivable" that there would have been a waiver in that case.

In *Fernandes* v. *Parvardin*, the majority had expressed the view that the correct test was to ask what injustice or inequity followed from the failure to give notice. In *Bradshaw* v. *Baldwin-Wiseman*, however, the approach of Stephenson L.J. in *Fernandes* was preferred. There was no reason to restrict the meaning of the words "just and equitable" and they are of very wide import. The court should look at all the circumstances of the case, affecting both landlord and tenant, and those in which the failure to give written notice arose; it is only if, having considered all those circumstances, the court considers that it would be just and equitable to give possession that it should do so, because it must be borne in mind that, by failing to give the written notice, the tenant may well have been led into a wholly false position.

Under this Act, furthermore, the tenant may well have been paying a much higher rent than he would otherwise have been, for notice under this ground (and others) is a feature to be taken into account by a Rent Assessment Committee under s.14, above. This would not be applicable where there has been no reference to the committee (or none contemplated—it might be enough to show that the tenant had thought of doing so but had been advised or discovered that the committee would be unlikely to set a rent lower than proposed by the landlord under s.12, above). But where such reference has been made, or at least contemplated, there is a strong argument against waiver of requirement to serve notice.

Ground 2

Most mortgages contain a prohibition on letting, and in such circumstances should the mortgagee foreclose, the tenancy will be "illegal" and the mortgagee will not be bound by the provisions of this Act in any event: *Dudley and District Building Society* v. *Emerson* [1949] Ch. 707, C.A. It has, however, been suggested that this might not be so if the mortgagee is not selling in order to recover the security, but this was in a case in which foreclosure was "set up" in order to defeat the Rent Acts: *Quennel* v. *Maltby* [1979] 1 W.L.R. 318, C.A. This ground is accordingly directed at "legal" tenancies. It is only applicable to mortgages granted before the tenancy, and contains the same requirement of notice, subject to "just and equitable waiver" as under ground 1: see notes thereto.

The mortgagee must have acquired the power of sale conferred either by the mortgage deed, or by s.101 of the Law of Property Act 1925, and must "require" (see notes to ground 1, above) possession to sell with vacant possession in exercise of that power.

Ground 3

This is based on the Rent Act 1977, Sched. 15 and Case 13: the idea is to enable the successful alternation of out-of-season and holiday lettings. While there is no reference to a holiday "letting", the landlord's own "holiday occupation" is unlikely to suffice, for the occupation must be "under a right to occupy it for a holiday", rather than a broader or general entitlement to occupy, whether for holiday or any other use to which an owner might put the premises. The requirement for written notice (as to which, see notes to ground 1, above) cannot be waived. The letting must be for a term certain, which excludes a periodic tenancy: *cf. Centaploy* v. *Matlodge* [1974] Ch. 1.

Ground 4
This is based on Rent Act 1977, Sched. 15, Case 14, and is analogous to ground 3, above, save that what is in mind is an "off" year for someone who customarily lets to students—see notes to Sched. 1, para. 8, above. The requirement for written notice (as to which, see notes to ground 1, above) cannot be waived. The letting must be for a term certain, which excludes a periodic tenancy: *cf. Centaploy* v. *Matlodge* [1974] Ch. 1.

Ground 5
This is based on the Rent Act 1977, Sched. 15, Case 15. There is no definition of "minister of religion". The premises must be "required": see notes to ground 1, above. The requirement for written notice (as to which, see notes to ground 1, above) cannot be waived.

Ground 6
This is a new ground in the private residential sector (*cf.* Landlord and Tenant Act 1954, s.30(1)(g) and Housing Act 1985, Sched. 2, ground 10.) It applies where the landlord intends to demolish or reconstruct (*i.e.* rebuild, involving substantial interference with the property: *Percy E. Cadle & Co.* v. *Jacmarch Properties* [1957] 1 Q.B. 323) the whole or a substantial part of the dwelling-house, or to carry out substantial works on the dwelling-house or any part of it, or of any building of which it forms part, and the conditions of the ground are fulfilled. The ground is also available if the demolition, reconstruction or major works are to be carried out by a superior landlord, if, but only if, the landlord is a registered housing association or a housing trust which is a charitable housing trust (as to the meaning of which, see notes to s.35, above). It has no application at all where the assured tenancy in question is one which has arisen by succession, under the Rent Act 1977 or the Rent (Agriculture) Act 1976, as amended by this Act.
It is unavailable to a landlord who acquired his interest on the reversion of the tenancy for money or money's worth: see notes to ground 1, above, so that it remains available if the landlord's interest preceded the grant of the tenancy, or was acquired in another way. For this purpose, tenancy includes an earlier assured tenancy of the same dwelling-house, granted to the tenant, or to one of the joint tenants, or to joint tenants of whom the tenant is one: accordingly, the inhibition cannot be defeated by a purchase for money or money's worth, followed by the grant of a new (related) tenancy.
The ground is also unavailable if the works can reasonably be carried out without the tenant giving up possession, because the tenant agrees to a variation of the terms of the tenancy sufficient to give the landlord access and facilities for the work to be carried out, unless no such variation is practicable. It is unavailable if the tenant is willing to accept an assured tenancy of part of the premises, so as to leave the landlord in possession of that which is needed for the intended works, unless no such severance is practicable. It is unavailable if the landlord could reasonably do the works without recovering possession.
The relevant time to consider the landlord's intention is the date of hearing: *Wansbeck District Council* v. *Marley* (1987) 20 H.L.R. 247, C.A. The intention must be clearly defined and settled: *ibid.* The construction of a doorway linking demised to other premises was not considered works that reasonably required the tenant to give up possession: *ibid.*
Where only "works" are involved, if a tenant is keen to remain, he may wish to consider offering a licence to the landlord to enter and carry out the works, which would obviate the need for *possession* to pass (*cf.* notes to s.1, above) and will generate the problem of temporary accommodation during works. The tenant will want the landlord to provide somewhere temporarily. The landlord may then seek to say: that is too difficult, administratively. But could the landlord maintain that response in the light of the wording of this ground?

Ground 7
Provided that there has been no statutory succession under s.17, above, a periodic tenancy, including (expressly) a statutory periodic tenancy, can pass under a will or on intestacy: unless there is express provision to the contrary, it does not automatically determine on death—*Mackay* v. *Mackreth* (1785) 4 Doug. 213, *Youngmin* v. *Heath* [1974] 1 W.L.R. 135.
If testate, the tenancy devolves on the executors: *Collis* v. *Flower* [1921] 1 K.B. 409, *Abbey* v. *Barnstyn* [1930] 1 K.B. 660. If intestate, then in the first instance the property devolves on the President of the Family Division: Administration of Estates Act 1925, ss.9, 55(1), and Administration of Justice Act 1970, s.1 and Sched. 2, replaced by Supreme Court Act 1981, Sched. 7. It passes on the grant of letters of administration to the administrators (*Whitehead* v. *Palmer* [1908] 1 K.B. 151) and only thence to the beneficiary.

If an order for possession has been made, the beneficiary will take subject thereto, whether conditional (*Sherrin* v. *Brand* [1956] 1 Q.B. 403, C.A.), or absolute (*American Economic Laundry* v. *Little* [1951] 1 K.B. 400, C.A.). If notice to quit is served—for want of residence by the beneficiary—it must be served on the tenant, *cf. Wirral B.C.* v. *Smith* (1982) 4 H.L.R. 81, C.A., in which proceedings for possession against relatives of the deceased, intestate tenant were dismissed because no notice to quit determining the tenancy had been served on the President of the Family Division.

This ground is applicable only to periodic tenancies, and the proceedings must be commenced no later than *either* (a) 12 months after the death of the former tenant, *or* (b), on the court's direction, 12 months after the date on which the court considers the landlord (or one of joint landlords) became aware of the former tenant's death. The ground spells out that acceptance of rent from a new tenant after the death of the former tenant does not create a new periodic tenancy (*cf. Marcroft Waggons Ltd.* v. *Smith* [1951] 2 K.B. 496, C.A.) unless there is agreement in writing with the landlord as to amount of rent, period of tenancy, premises let or any other term.

Ground 8

This is the first of three grounds governing arrears of rent; this ground is "mandatory", while the next two are "discretionary". Under this ground, rent lawfully due from the tenant is more than three months in arrears. The court has no power to waive the requirement for notice of seeking possession, under s.8, above, even if considered "just and equitable" to do so, under this ground.

Arguably, if there is an arrangement for payment of rent direct by the local authority, under the Housing Benefit Regulations, it might be said that rent is not due "from the tenant", *cf. Wandsworth London Borough* v. *Sparling* (1987) 20 H.L.R., C.A.(Crim.), where it was held that a landlord was not in receipt of rents, because the local authority had reached agreement with him to deduct from housing benefit payments otherwise payable to him sums of money which he owed to the authority. Of course, at common law, the rent remains due from the tenant, but there are very good reasons indeed why a less strict approach should be taken where such arrears arise attributable to the failure of a local authority.

For an order to be based on arrears, the arrears must be those of the tenant himself, not those of a predecessor in title: *Tickner* v. *Clifton* [1929] 1 K.B. 207. However, it should be noted that the obligation to pay rent remains, notwithstanding the failure of the landlord to provide a rent book, under the provisions of the Landlord and Tenant Act 1985, s.4: *Shaw* v. *Groom* [1970] 2 Q.B. 504, C.A.

Arrears must exist as at the date of service of notice seeking possession under s.8, above (see also *Bird* v. *Hildage* [1948] 1 K.B. 91, C.A.) *and* at the date of hearing, and must *in both cases* be more than three months in arrears. If rent has been tendered, but refused, then there will be no arrears for the purposes of this ground: *ibid.* If rent is tendered between commencement and hearing, the court may still have power to make an order for possession: see grounds 10 and 11, below. No rent arrears may exist if the tenant is exercising a common law right of set-off, referable to the landlord's failure to repair pursuant to his obligations.

Once the landlord's repairing liability has arisen (*cf.* the requirement of notice, *O'Brien* v. *Robinson* [1973] A.C. 912, H.L.) a tenant may expend moneys on the discharge of his landlord's repairing obligations (*Lee-Parker* v. *Izzett* [1971] 1 W.L.R. 1688), whether future rents or rent arrears (*Asco Developments* v. *Lowes, Lewis & Gordon* (1978) 248 E.G. 683), and may also be able to set-off an amount by way of claim to general damages (*British Anzani (Felixstowe)* v. *International Marine Management (U.K.)* [1980] 1 Q.B. 137, C.A.).

The same principles apply on a landlord's undertaking (rather than covenant) to repair: *Melville* v. *Grapelodge Developments* (1978) 254 E.G. 1193. As a set-off, such moneys would not actually be due as rent. It is thought, however, and especially as the developments in this area are so recent (*cf.* earlier authorities to the contrary, such as *Taylor* v. *Beal* (1591) Cro.Eliz. 222; *Waters* v. *Weigall* (1795) 2 Anst. 575), that a tenant may be obliged, and is certainly well-advised, to give a landlord plenty of opportunity to repair, to consider an estimate before the tenant commissions a repair, and to agree a claim for general damages, before exercising this right (see, especially, *Lee-Parker* v. *Izzett*, above, on this point). See further, by way of comparison *Woodtrek* v. *Jezek* (1981) 261 E.G. 571, where non-payment of an irrecoverable service charge could not found a forfeiture.

Part II

These grounds *also* require the landlord to establish that it is reasonable to make the order sought: see notes to s.9, above.

Ground 9
See notes to Part III, below.

Ground 10
This is the second ground based on rent arrears. There must be arrears on the date when the proceedings for possession are commenced, *and* on the date of service of notice of seeking possession under s.8 (save where the court considers it just and equitable to waive the requirement). In *Woodspring District Council* v. *Taylor* (1982) 4 H.L.R. 95, C.A., the court dismissed an appeal against the refusal of the court below to make an outright order against tenants with a long history of good payment, who had only recently fallen into arrears on account of unemployment and illness, even though the arrears had amounted to more than £550 by the date of hearing.

No order should be made if the reason for the arrears is that there has been a genuine dispute as to the amount owing (*Dun Laoghaire Urban District Council* v. *Moran* (1921) 2 I.R. 404), and it may be inappropriate or even impossible if the reason the rent has been withheld is because of a genuine complaint of disrepair attributable to the landlord's default: see *Lal* v. *Nakum* (1981) 1 H.L.R. 50, C.A.

Where the tenant is still in occupation, and arrears are continuing, and there is a likelihood that the tenant will dissipate any housing benefit unless an order is made, it may be possible for a landlord to obtain an interlocutory order to require the tenant to pay the housing benefit towards the rent: *Berg* v. *Markhill* (1985) 17 H.L.R. 455, C.A.

Ground 11
If the tenant clears all or part of the arrears before the hearing, so that ground 10 is unavailable, or if the arrears were not in excess of three months, so that ground 8 is unavailable, this ground is available if the tenant has "persistently delayed" paying rent which has become lawfully due, even if not in arrears on the date on which proceedings are commenced.

What is not spelled out is whether or not there have to be arrears *at the date of hearing*. Under the Rent Acts, the courts have power to make an order even if there are no arrears at date of hearing (*Brewer* v. *Jacobs* [1923] 1 K.B. 528, D.C.; *Dellenty* v. *Pellow* [1951] 2 K.B. 858), though it is extremely unusual for them to do so if arrears have in fact been cleared, unless there has been a long history of arrears, or unless the landlord has repeatedly had to issue proceedings in order to get paid: *Heyman* v. *Rowlands* [1957] 1 W.L.R. 317, C.A.; *Dellenty* v. *Pellow; Grimshaw* v. *Dunbar* [1953] 1 Q.B. 408, C.A.; *Lee-Steere* v. *Jennings* (1986) 20 H.L.R. 1, C.A.

Clearly, rent delays attributable to local authority failure to housing benefit direct to the landlord cannot give rise to a claim to possession under this ground, and if housing benefit payable to the tenant for transmission to the landlord has been delayed, it is hard to see that the court could find that "the tenant has persistently delayed", as this implies a degree of positive intent or inaction on the tenant's part.

Ground 12
This is a most common ground, because not uncommonly it will be pleaded in the alternative to one of the specific "default" grounds, below (though cannot be used if the only breach is a clause requiring payment of rent): see, for example, *Heglibiston Establishment* v. *Heyman* (1977) 76 P. & C.R. 351, C.A. In the case of a breach of a term which does *not* also amount to a further ground, the courts will be less inclined to make an order, for these grounds may be considered to constitute a form of "code of eviction" in their own right. It should be noted that even where a breach is to continue, the court is entitled to decline to make the order sought: *Tideway Investments & Property Holdings* v. *Wellwood* [1952] Ch. 791.

An obligation of the tenancy does not include a personal undertaking by the tenant (*R.M.R. Housing Society* v. *Combs* [1951] 1 K.B. 486, C.A.), although it does extend to implied, as well as express, obligations: see *William Deacons Bank* v. *Catlow* [1928] E.G.D. 286; *Chapman* v. *Hughes* (1923) 129 L.T. 223. Covenants are not, of course, easily implied into a tenancy, even if they seem reasonable and desirable: *Liverpool City Council* v. *Irwin* [1977] A.C. 239, H.L. However, some terms are implied by statute, breach of which will qualify under this ground: see ss.15, 16.

A tenant must use premises in a tenant-like manner (*Warren* v. *Keen* [1954] 1 Q.B. 15, C.A.), failure to do which will, in any event, usually qualify under ground 13, below. Breach of a covenant in a term certain incompatible with Part 1, *e.g.* to yield up possession at expiry of the term, would not, of course, constitute a breach of obligation for these purposes:

Artizans Dwellings Co. v. *Whittaker* [1919] 2 K.B. 301; *R.M.R. Housing Society* v. *Combs* (above).

In *Heglibiston Establishment* v. *Heyman* (above), cohabitation by a couple was held not to constitute a breach of a covenant against immoral user, the purpose of which class of covenant is considered to be to prevent use as a brothel. In *Florent* v. *Horez* (1983) 12 H.L.R. 1, C.A., a covenant not to carry on any business on the premises was held to have been breached by the use of the premises as the headquarters of an organisation called the "Britain Turkish Cyprus Committee", as a question of fact and degree in all the circumstances: frequent visitors, committee meetings, headed notepaper and Christmas cards sent out from the premises.

It may be a defence to show that a breach has been waived, by acceptance of rent in knowledge of the breach: see notes to s.5, above. The knowledge of a porter/caretaker will be imputed to a landlord where the duties included passing on information about matters occurring at the premises: *Metropolitan Properties Co.* v. *Cordery* (1979) 251 E.G. 567, C.A. But a breach of a prohibition on a particular user of premises is a continuing breach and accordingly waiver does not operate in relation to the continuation beyond the waiver: *Cooper* v. *Henderson* (1982) 5 H.L.R. 3, C.A.

Ground 13

This ground follows the extension of the traditional Rent Act ground (Sched. 15, Case 3) from premises to premises *and* common parts, which was adopted in 1980 in relation to secure tenants: see, now, Housing Act 1985, Scheds. 2 and 3. Given the difficulty of proving by whose act deterioration in the common parts (as defined) has occurred, and the potential for abuse by unfriendly neighbours, this extended limb should clearly be applied with care. The ground may, however, apply even although there is no actual breach of obligation by the tenant: *Lowe* v. *Lendrun* (1950) 159 E.G. 423, C.A.

Deterioration of the dwelling-house can include that of a garden treated as part of it by s.2, above, so that a failure to tend a garden, allowing it to grow wholly uncontrolled throughout the growing season, can be deterioration owing to an act by the tenant: *Holloway* v. *Povey* (1984) 15 H.L.R. 104, C.A. Waste includes pulling down part of the premises, making unauthorised alterations, and the like: *Marsden* v. *Heyes* [1927] 2 K.B. 1. Not every waste will, however, qualify: there must be deterioration by waste (neglect or default).

Where the act is of a sub-tenant or lodger, it must also be shown that the tenant has not taken such steps as he ought reasonably to have taken to evict the sub-tenant or lodger.

Ground 14

This is based on a Rent Act ground, Sched. 15, Case 2, *without* the extension in 1980 to substitute "neighbours" for "adjoining occupiers": see, now, Housing Act 1985, Sched. 2, Ground 2. In *Cobstone Investments* v. *Maxim* (1984) 15 H.L.R. 113, C.A., it was, however, in any event held under the Rent Act that "adjoining" was wider than contiguous, as one meaning of the word is "neighbouring" and all that the context requires is that the premises of the adjoining occupiers should be near enough to be affected by the tenant's conduct in his premises. There may, accordingly, now be no practical difference between the different provisions.

Nuisance is not here used in a technical sense, but is given a natural meaning: indeed, even if a nuisance under statute is established, it does not follow that there is necessarily a nuisance for these purposes: *Timmis* v. *Pearson* (1934) 1 L.J.N.C.C.R. 115. Annoyance is wider than nuisance, although it must be annoyance such as would annoy a reasonable occupier, not one who is ultra-sensitive: *Todd-Heatly* v. *Benham* (1888) 40 Ch.D. 80, C.A.

Use of the premises for prostitution is a common example of nuisance and annoyance (*Frederick Platts Co.* v. *Grigor* (1950) 66 T.L.R. (Pt. 1) 859, C.A.; *Yates* v. *Morris* [1950] 2 All E.R. 577, C.A.), as is private immorality (*Benton* v. *Chapman* [1953] C.L.Y. 3099, Cty.Ct.), although cohabitation by an unmarried couple is no longer to be considered immoral for these purposes: *Heglibiston Establishment* v. *Heyman* (1977) 76 P. & C.R. 351, C.A. A tenant will not be within the ground where the conduct is of a third party, unless it can be shown that the tenant has not taken reasonable steps to abate the nuisance: *Commercial General Administration* v. *Thomsett* (1979) 250 E.G. 547, C.A.

The use of the word "guilty" of such conduct, and the express provision for persons convicted of immoral user, suggest that a court should rarely use immorality as a basis for an order for possession, where there is no such conviction. A single act of annoyance or nuisance may, strictly, qualify, but is unlikely to prove sufficient under the ground, and where the last act complained of had taken place some nine months before the hearing, with no more recent acts, a court refused to make an order, although costs were awarded against the defendant: *Ottway* v. *Jones* [1955] 1 W.L.R. 706, C.A.

The second limb, obviously, requires an actual conviction of a criminal court. It is not enough that a person has been convicted of committing a crime in the premises, although it need not be shown that user was a specific element of the criminal offence, it is a question of showing sufficient nexus between crime and user of the premises: *Abrahams* v. *Wilson* [1971] 2 Q.B. 88, C.A. In that case, the tenant was convicted of possessing a small amount of cannabis found in one of the rooms she occupied. The Court of Appeal held that conviction for such an offence could fall within the ground, but, as the county court judge had held, considering reasonableness, "the chairman of the quarter sessions, having considered the evidence, could not have been more lenient. The suggestion now is that the additional very severe penalty of eviction should be imposed."

The tenant had been convicted, and punished, once, and the court should think very carefully before imposing a further penalty, especially, *e.g.* where the offence has not, as it were, brought the premises themselves into disrepute: see also *Schneiders & Sons* v. *Abrahams* [1925] 1 K.B. 301, C.A.; *Hodson* v. *Jones* [1951] W.N. 127, C.A.; *Waller* v. *Thomas* [1921] 1 K.B. 541.

The nuisance, annoyance, or act leading to conviction for immoral or illegal user, need not be committed by the tenant, but may be committed by a person residing with him. A man living away from home, but visiting at the weekends, has, for these purposes, been held to be residing with his wife: *Green* v. *Lewis* [1951] C.L.Y. 2860.

Ground 15
This is based on the Rent Act 1977, Sched. 15, Case 4. Where the act is of a sub-tenant or lodger, it must also be shown that the tenant has not taken such steps as he ought reasonably to have taken to evict the sub-tenant or lodger.

Ground 16
Under the Rent Acts, the ground for possession against a service tenant required not only cessation of employment, but use for a new employee (Rent Act 1977, Sched. 15, Case 8): the latter is not required under this Act, although as a discretionary ground the fact that there is no new employee is of course relevant, and may have an influence, under the heading of reasonableness. The ground is available whether the tenant was the employee of the current, or a former, landlord.

The letting must, however, have been "in consequence of his employment". This would not seem to permit a landlord who has available property to offer it to an employee and add the potential of using the ground. The occupier need not, however, have known the landlord's motive in granting the right of occupation: *Royal Crown Derby Porcelain Co.* v. *Russell* [1949] 2 K.B. 417, C.A.

Part III
This Part defines "suitable alternative accommodation" for the purposes of ground 9, above. Note the provisions of para. 1, that a certificate of the local housing authority for the area in which the dwelling-house of which possession is sought that they will provide suitable alternative accommodation is to be taken as conclusive evidence that such will be available by the date specified in the certificate, to the exclusion of the considerations specified in paras. 2 and 4. The accommodation must be in that authority's district: *Sills* v. *Watkins* [1956] 1 Q.B. 250, C.A. Note, too, that in all other cases, overcrowded accommodation is not to be considered suitable: para. 4.

The accommodation has to be available by the time the order for possession takes effect: ground 9, see also *Selwyn* v. *Hamill* [1948] 1 All E.R. 70, C.A., *Kimpson* v. *Markham* [1921] 2 K.B. 157, *Nevile* v. *Hardy* [1921] 1 Ch. 404. The landlord must show that the premises will be available for the tenant against whom possession is sought, rather than general availability: *Topping* v. *Hughes* [1925] N.I. 90, C.A.

Para. 2. To qualify as suitable alternative accommodation the premises have to be let as a separate dwelling: see notes to s.1, above. They must *either* be let on an assured tenancy—not including a tenancy in respect of which a notice is served under grounds 1–5, above, or an assured shorthold tenancy—*or* on terms which the court considers will afford reasonably equivalent security thereto, *e.g.* a secure tenancy under the Housing Act 1985 (*cf. Sills* v. *Watkins* (above), decided before the introduction of statutory security to the public sector.) Shared accommodation does not qualify: *Selwyn* v. *Hamill* (above), *Barnard* v. *Towers* [1953] 1 W.L.R. 1203, C.A., *Cookson* v. *Walsh* (1954) 163 E.G. 486, C.A.

Para. 3. The alternative accommodation must *also* be "reasonably suitable to the needs of the tenant and his family" as regards the matters specified. The inclusion of family means that members of the tenant's family have an "interest" sufficient to require them to be joined if they wish in possession proceedings: see *Wandsworth London Borough Council* v.

Fadayomi [1987] 1 W.L.R. 1473, C.A. A lodger or friend is not a member of the tenant's family: *Kavanagh* v. *Lyroudias* (1983) 10 H.L.R. 20, C.A., but this would be relevant to reasonableness. See also *Darnell* v. *Millwood* [1951] 1 All E.R. 88, C.A. There must also be a degree of permanent residence by the member of the family to be taken into account: *Standingford* v. *Probert* [1950] 1 K.B. 377, C.A.

The accommodation must be reasonably suitable in respect of proximity to work. "Place of work" can include voluntary work (*Dakyns* v. *Pace* [1948] 1 K.B. 22) and a person may work in several places, *e.g.* a salesman, in which case no one place forms the place of work for these purposes, but the whole area to which the tenant must travel is to be taken into account: *Yewbright Properties* v. *Stone* (1980) 254 E.G. 863, C.A., in which it was also held that distance incorporated questions of travelling facilities and times.

The accommodation may be considered suitable by reference to local authority accommodation: see *Quick* v. *Fifield* (1981) 131 New L.J. 140, C.A. The landlord can rely on accommodation owned by the tenant: *Fennbend* v. *Millar* (1987) 20 H.L.R., C.A. However, the landlord in that case was not entitled to an interlocutory injunction to prevent the tenant disposing of the property before the hearing, since they did not have a vested right to protect, but only the prospect of a right (to possession). Suitable alternative accommodation may be comprised of part only of the tenant's current premises: *Mykolyshyn* v. *Noah* [1970] 1 W.L.R. 1271, C.A., see also *Yoland* v. *Reddington* (1982) 5 H.L.R. 41, C.A.

Under the Rent Act 1977 it is not clear whether "extent and character" (and place of work) constitute an exhaustive schedule of consideration, or indicative only: *cf. Barnard* v. *Towers* (above), and *Standingford* v. *Probert* (above). Under the Housing Act 1985, it has been held not to be exhaustive: *Enfield London Borough Council* v. *French* (1984) 17 H.L.R. 211, C.A.

In *Redspring* v. *Francis* [1973] 1 W.L.R. 134, C.A., it was held that environmental factors fell within the meaning of the word "character", and the court allowed an appeal against a possession order which would have moved the tenant from a quiet residential street to a noisy main road with a fish and chip shop next door. However, friends and/or a need to attend a religious institution do not fall within the meaning of the word "character": *Siddiqui* v. *Rashid* [1980] 1 W.L.R. 1018, C.A. (This might nonetheless be relevant to overall reasonableness.)

Needs means "housing needs", to which considerations of character may be relevant: *Hill* v. *Rochard* [1983] 1 W.L.R. 478, 8 H.L.R. 140, C.A. A garden can constitute a need: *Enfield London Borough Council* v. *French* (above); see also *De Markozoff* v. *Craig* (1949) 93 S.J. 693, C.A. In *Gladyric* v. *Collinson* (1983) 11 H.L.R. 12, C.A., an objection to moving from a cottage to a flat in a house in multiple occupation was described as an idiosyncratic peculiarity of the tenant, but this would seem to have turned (a) on the particular facts of the case, and (b) on the absence of evidence of sensitivity to, *e.g.* noise, that might have been assumed on the part of another tenant, such as an elderly person. It does not seem to have been advanced by the court as a general proposition.

Personal needs are included, so that accommodation shared with the tenant's estranged wife was unsuitable in *Heglibiston Establishment* v. *Heyman* (1978) 246 E.G. 567, C.A.; see also *Little* v. *Chatterley* (1946) 147 E.G. 269, C.A., *Cresswell* v. *Hodgson* [1951] 2 K.B. 92, C.A. But merely because accommodation is inferior is not decisive as to suitability: *Quick* v. *Fifield* (above). But a bathroom should always be available: *Esposito* v. *Ware* (1950) 155 E.G. 383.

Although there is authority for the proposition that new premises insufficient for the tenant's furniture may yet be suitable, this must surely be of dubious weight if the tenant reasonably requires all of the furniture, and would seem not to apply when what is in issue is suitability as regards *extent: cf. Mykolyshyn* v. *Noah* (above); see also *Gladyric* v. *Collinson* (above). There is authority for the proposition that premises without a garage are a suitable alternative to premises with a garage (*Briddon* v. *George* [1946] 1 All E.R. 609, C.A.), which authority has, however, been doubted by the Court of Appeal (in *MacDonnell* v. *Daly* [1969] 1 W.L.R. 1482, C.A.).

The last-mentioned decision is also authority for the proposition that where what is to be given up is for mixed residential and professional user (but not such as to take the letting out of security altogether, see notes to Sched. 1, para. 4, above), in that case an artist's studio, the alternative accommodation must also be sufficient for the professional user.

Part IV
See notes to Ground 1, above.

SCHEDULE 3

AGRICULTURAL WORKER CONDITIONS

Interpretation

1.—(1) In this Schedule—
　　"the 1976 Act" means the Rent (Agriculture) Act 1976;
　　"agriculture" has the same meaning as in the 1976 Act; and
　　"relevant tenancy or licence" means a tenancy or licence of a description specified in
　　　section 24(2) of this Act.
　(2) In relation to a relevant tenancy or licence—
　　　(a) "the occupier" means the tenant or licensee; and
　　　(b) "the dwelling-house" means the dwelling-house which is let under the tenancy
　　　　or, as the case may be, is occupied under the licence.
　(3) Schedule 3 to the 1976 Act applies for the purposes of this Schedule as it applies for
the purposes of that Act and, accordingly, shall have effect to determine—
　　(a) whether a person is a qualifying worker;
　　(b) whether a person is incapable of whole-time work in agriculture, or work in agriculture
　　　as a permit worker, in consequence of a qualifying injury or disease; and
　　(c) whether a dwelling-house is in qualifying ownership.

The conditions

2. The agricultural worker condition is fulfilled with respect to a dwelling-house subject
to a relevant tenancy or licence if—
　　(a) the dwelling-house is or has been in qualifying ownership at any time during the
　　　subsistence of the tenancy or licence (whether or not it was at that time a relevant
　　　tenancy or licence); and
　　(b) the occupier or, where there are joint occupiers, at least one of them—
　　　　(i) is a qualifying worker or has been a qualifying worker at any time during the
　　　　subsistence of the tenancy or licence (whether or not it was at that time a relevant
　　　　tenancy or licence); or
　　　　(ii) is incapable of whole-time work in agriculture or work in agriculture as a
　　　　permit worker in consequence of a qualifying injury or disease.
　3.—(1) The agricultural worker condition is also fulfilled with respect to a dwelling-house
subject to a relevant tenancy or licence if—
　　(a) that condition was previously fulfilled with respect to the dwelling-house but the
　　　person who was then the occupier or, as the case may be, a person who was one of
　　　the joint occupiers (whether or not under the same relevant tenancy or licence) has
　　　died; and
　　(b) that condition ceased to be fulfilled on the death of the occupier referred to in
　　　paragraph (a) above (hereinafter referred to as "the previous qualifying occupier");
　　　and
　　(c) the occupier is either—
　　　　(i) the qualifying widow or widower of the previous qualifying occupier; or
　　　　(ii) the qualifying member of the previous qualifying occupier's family.
　(2) For the purposes of sub-paragraph (1)(c)(i) above and sub-paragraph (3) below a
widow or widower of the previous qualifying occupier of the dwelling-house is a qualifying
widow or widower if she or he was residing in the dwelling-house immediately before the
previous qualifying occupier's death.
　(3) Subject to sub-paragraph (4) below, for the purposes of sub-paragraph (1)(c)(ii)
above, a member of the family of the previous qualifying occupier of the dwelling-house is
the qualifying member of the family if—
　　(a) on the death of the previous qualifying occupier there was no qualifying widow or
　　　widower; and
　　(b) the member of the family was residing in the dwelling-house with the previous
　　　qualifying occupier at the time of, and for the period of two years before, his death.
　(4) Not more than one member of the previous qualifying occupier's family may be taken
into account in determining whether the agricultural worker condition is fulfilled by virtue
of this paragraph and, accordingly, if there is more than one member of the family—
　　(a) who is the occupier in relation to the relevant tenancy or licence, and
　　(b) who, apart from this sub-paragraph, would be the qualifying member of the family by
　　　virtue of sub-paragraph (3) above,

only that one of those members of the family who may be decided by agreement or, in default of agreement by the county court shall be the qualifying member.

(5) For the purposes of the preceding provisions of this paragraph a person who, immediately before the previous qualifying occupier's death, was living with the previous occupier as his or her wife or husband shall be treated as the widow or widower of the previous occupier.

(6) If, immediately before the death of the previous qualifying occupier, there is, by virtue of sub-paragraph (5) above, more than one person who falls within sub-paragraph (1)(c)(i) above, such one of them as may be decided by agreement or, in default of agreement, by the county court shall be treated as the qualifying widow or widower for the purposes of this paragraph.

4. The agricultural worker condition is also fulfilled with respect to a dwelling-house subject to a relevant tenancy or licence if—

   (a) the tenancy or licence was granted to the occupier or, where there are joint occupiers, at least one of them in consideration of his giving up possession of another dwelling-house of which he was then occupier (or one of joint occupiers) under another relevant tenancy or licence; and

   (b) immediately before he gave up possession of that dwelling-house, as a result of his occupation the agricultural worker condition was fulfilled with respect to it (whether by virtue of paragraph 2 or paragraph 3 above or this paragraph);

and the reference in paragraph (a) above to a tenancy or licence granted to the occupier or at least one of joint occupiers includes a reference to the case where the grant is to him together with one or more other persons.

5.—(1) This paragraph applies where—

   (a) by virtue of any of paragraphs 2 to 4 above, the agricultural worker condition is fulfilled with respect to a dwelling-house subject to a relevant tenancy or licence (in this paragraph referred to as "the earlier tenancy or licence"); and

   (b) another relevant tenancy or licence of the same dwelling-house (in this paragraph referred to as "the later tenancy or licence") is granted to the person who, immediately before the grant, was the occupier or one of the joint occupiers under the earlier tenancy or licence and as a result of whose occupation the agricultural worker condition was fulfilled as mentioned in paragraph (a) above;

and the reference in paragraph (b) above to the grant of the later tenancy or licence to the person mentioned in that paragraph includes a reference to the case where the grant is to that person together with one or more other persons.

(2) So long as a person as a result of whose occupation of the dwelling-house the agricultural worker condition was fulfilled with respect to the earlier tenancy or licence continues to be the occupier, or one of the joint occupiers, under the later tenancy or licence, the agricultural worker condition shall be fulfilled with respect to the dwelling-house.

(3) For the purposes of paragraphs 3 and 4 above and any further application of this paragraph, where sub-paragraph (2) above has effect, the agricultural worker condition shall be treated as fulfilled so far as concerns the later tenancy or licence by virtue of the same paragraph of this Schedule as was applicable (or, as the case may be, last applicable) in the case of the earlier tenancy or licence.

GENERAL NOTE
See notes to s.24, above.

Section 39   SCHEDULE 4

STATUTORY TENANTS: SUCCESSION

PART I

AMENDMENTS OF SCHEDULE 1 TO RENT ACT 1977

1. In paragraph 1 the words "or, as the case may be, paragraph 3" shall be omitted.

2. At the end of paragraph 2 there shall be inserted the following sub-paragraphs—

   "(2) For the purposes of this paragraph, a person who was living with the original tenant as his or her wife or husband shall be treated as the spouse of the original tenant.

   (3) If, immediately after the death of the original tenant, there is, by virtue of sub-paragraph (2) above, more than one person who fulfils the conditions in sub-

paragraph (1) above, such one of them as may be decided by agreement or, in default of agreement, by the county court shall be treated as the surviving spouse for the purposes of this paragraph."
3. In paragraph 3—
   (a) after the words "residing with him" there shall be inserted "in the dwelling-house";
   (b) for the words "period of 6 months" there shall be substituted "period of 2 years"; and
   (c) for the words from "the statutory tenant" onwards there shall be substituted "entitled to an assured tenancy of the dwelling-house by succession"; and
   (d) at the end there shall be added the following sub-paragraph—
      "(2) If the original tenant died within the period of 18 months beginning on the operative date, then, for the purposes of this paragraph, a person who was residing in the dwelling-house with the original tenant at the time of his death and for the period which began 6 months before the operative date and ended at the time of his death shall be taken to have been residing with the original tenant for the period of 2 years immediately before his death."
4. In paragraph 4 the words "or 3" shall be omitted.
5. In paragraph 5—
   (a) for the words from "or, as the case may be" to "of this Act" there shall be substituted "below shall have effect"; and
   (b) for the words "the statutory tenant" there shall be substituted "entitled to an assured tenancy of the dwelling-house by succession".
6. For paragraph 6 there shall be substituted the following paragraph—
   "6.—(1) Where a person who—
      (a) was a member of the original tenant's family immediately before that tenant's death, and
      (b) was a member of the first successor's family immediately before the first successor's death,
was residing in the dwelling-house with the first successor at the time of, and for the period of 2 years immediately before, the first successor's death, that person or, if there is more than one such person, such one of them as may be decided by agreement or, in default of agreement, by the county court shall be entitled to an assured tenancy of the dwelling-house by succession.
   (2) If the first successor died within the period of 18 months beginning on the operative date, then, for the purposes of this paragraph, a person who was residing in the dwelling-house with the first successor at the time of his death and for the period which began 6 months before the operative date and ended at the time of his death shall be taken to have been residing with the first successor for the period of 2 years immediately before his death."
7. Paragraph 7 shall be omitted.
8. In paragraph 10(1)(a) for the words "paragraphs 6 or 7" there shall be substituted "paragraph 6".
9. At the end of paragraph 11 there shall be inserted the following paragraph—
   "11A. In this Part of this Schedule "the operative date" means the date on which Part I of the Housing Act 1988 came into force."

PART II

AMENDMENTS OF SECTION 4 OF RENT (AGRICULTURE) ACT 1976

10. In subsection (2) the words "or, as the case may be, subsection (4)" shall be omitted.
11. In subsection (4)—
   (a) in paragraph (b) after the words "residing with him" there shall be inserted "in the dwelling-house" and for the words "period of six months" there shall be substituted "period of 2 years"; and
   (b) for the words from "the statutory tenant" onwards there shall be substituted "entitled to an assured tenancy of the dwelling-house by succession".
12. In subsection (5) for the words "subsections (1), (3) and (4)" there shall be substituted "subsections (1) and (3)" and after that subsection there shall be inserted the following subsections—
   "(5A) For the purposes of subsection (3) above, a person who was living with the original occupier as his or her wife or husband shall be treated as the spouse of the original occupier and, subject to subsection (5B) below, the references in subsection

(3) above to a widow and in subsection (4) above to a surviving spouse shall be construed accordingly.

(5B) If, immediately after the death of the original occupier, there is, by virtue of subsection (5A) above, more than one person who fulfils the conditions in subsection (3) above, such one of them as may be decided by agreement or, in default of agreement by the county court, shall be the statutory tenant by virtue of that subsection.

(5C) If the original occupier died within the period of 18 months beginning on the operative date, then, for the purposes of subsection (3) above, a person who was residing in the dwelling-house with the original occupier at the time of his death and for the period which began 6 months before the operative date and ended at the time of his death shall be taken to have been residing with the origial occupier for the period of 2 years immediately before his death; and in this subsection "the operative date" means the date on which Part I of the Housing Act 1988 came into force."

PART III

MODIFICATIONS OF SECTION 7 AND SCHEDULE 2

13.—(1) Subject to sub-paragraph (2) below, in relation to the assured tenancy to which the successor becomes entitled by succession, section 7 of this Act shall have effect as if in subsection (3) after the word "established" there were inserted the words "or that the circumstances are as specified in any of Cases 11, 12, 16, 17, 18 and 20 in Schedule 15 to the Rent Act 1977".

(2) Sub-paragraph (1) above does not apply if, by virtue of section 39(8) of this Act, the assured tenancy to which the successor becomes entitled is an assured agricultural occupancy.

14. If by virtue of section 39(8) of this Act, the assured tenancy to which the successor becomes entitled is an assured agricultural occupancy, section 7 of this Act shall have effect in relation to that tenancy as if in subsection (3) after the word "established" there were inserted the words "or that the circumstances are as specified in Case XI or Case XII of the Rent (Agriculture) Act 1976".

15.—(1) In relation to the assured tenancy to which the successor becomes entitled by succession, any notice given to the predecessor for the purposes of Case 13, Case 14 or Case 15 in Schedule 15 to the Rent Act 1977 shall be treated as having been given for the purposes of whichever of Grounds 3 to 5 in Schedule 2 to this Act corresponds to the Case in question.

(2) Where sub-paragraph (1) above applies, the regulated tenancy of the predecessor shall be treated, in relation to the assured tenancy of the successor, as "the earlier tenancy" for the purposes of Part IV of Schedule 2 to this Act.

GENERAL NOTE
    See notes to s.39, above.

Section 46   SCHEDULE 5

HOUSING FOR WALES

Status

1.—(1) Housing for Wales is a body corporate and is in this Schedule referred to as "the Corporation".

(2) The Corporation is a public body for the purposes of the Prevention of Corruption Acts 1889 to 1916.

(3) The Corporation shall not be regarded—
    (a) as the servant or agent of the Crown; or
    (b) as enjoying any status, immunity or privilege of the Crown; or
    (c) as exempt from any tax, duty, rate, levy or other charge whatsoever, whether general or local;
and its property shall not be regarded as property of, or held on behalf of, the Crown.

Membership

2.—(1) The members of the Corporation shall be—
    (a) not less than six nor more than eight persons appointed by the Secretary of State; and

50–232

(b) the chief executive of the Corporation appointed under paragraph 7 below;
and the members appointed under paragraph (a) above are in this Schedule referred to as the "appointed members".

(2) Before appointing a person to be a member of the Corporation the Secretary of State shall satisfy himself that he will have no financial or other interest likely to affect prejudicially the exercise of his functions as a member; and the Secretary of State may require a person whom he proposes to appoint to give him such information as he considers necessary for that purpose.

3.—(1) The appointed members shall hold and vacate office in accordance with the terms of their appointment, subject to the following provisions.

(2) A member may resign his membership by notice in writing addressed to the Secretary of State.

(3) The Secretary of State may remove a member from office if he is satisfied that—

    (a) he has been adjudged bankrupt or made an arrangement with his creditors;

    (b) he has been absent from meetings of the Corporation for a period longer than three consecutive months without the permission of the Corporation; or

    (c) he is otherwise unable or unfit to discharge the functions of a member, or is unsuitable to continue as a member.

(4) The Secretary of State shall satisfy himself from time to time with respect to every appointed member that he has no financial or other interest likely to affect prejudicially the exercise of his functions as a member; and he may require an appointed member to give him such information as he considers necessary for that purpose.

Chairman and Deputy Chairman

4.—(1) The Secretary of State shall appoint one of the appointed members to be Chairman and may appoint one to be Deputy Chairman; and the members so appointed shall hold and vacate those offices in accordance with the terms of their appointment, subject to the following provisions.

(2) The Chairman or Deputy Chairman may resign by notice in writing addressed to the Secretary of State.

(3) If the Chairman or Deputy Chairman ceases to be a member of the Corporation, he also ceases to be Chairman or Deputy Chairman.

Remuneration and allowances

5.—(1) The Secretary of State may pay the Chairman, Deputy Chairman and appointed members such remuneration as he may, with the consent of the Treasury, determine.

(2) The Corporation may pay them such reasonable allowances as may be so determined in respect of expenses properly incurred by them in the performance of their duties.

Pensions

6.—(1) The Secretary of State may, with the consent of the Treasury, determine to pay in respect of a person's office as Chairman, Deputy Chairman or appointed member—

    (a) such pension, allowance or gratuity to or in respect of that person on his retirement or death as may be so determined; or

    (b) such contributions or other payments towards provision for such pension, allowance or gratuity as may be so determined.

(2) As soon as may be after the making of such a determination the Secretary of State shall lay before each House of Parliament a statement of the amount payable in pursuance of the determination.

(3) Sub-paragraph (1) above does not apply in the case of a member who has been admitted in pursuance of regulations under section 7 of the Superannuation Act 1972 to participate in the benefits of a superannuation fund maintained by a local authority.

(4) In such a case the Secretary of State shall make any payments required to be made to the fund in respect of the member by the employing authority and may make such deductions from his remuneration as the employing authority might make in respect of his contributions to the fund.

7.—(1) There shall be a chief executive of the Corporation.

(2) After consultation with the Chairman or person designated to be chairman of the Corporation, the Secretary of State shall make the first appointment of the chief executive on such terms and conditions as he may, with the consent of the Treasury, determine.

(3) The Corporation, with the approval of the Secretary of State, may make subsequent appointments to the office of chief executive on such terms and conditions as the Corporation may, with the approval of the Secretary of State given with the consent of the Treasury, determine.

8.—(1) The Corporation may appoint, on such terms and conditions as it may, with the approval of the Secretary of State, determine, such other employees as it thinks fit.

(2) In respect of such of its employees as it may, with the approval of the Secretary of State, determine, the Corporation shall make such arrangements for providing pensions, allowances or gratuities as it may determine; and such arrangements may include the establishment and administration, by the Corporation or otherwise, of one or more pension schemes.

(3) The reference in sub-paragraph (2) above to pensions, allowances or gratuities to or in respect of employees of the Corporation includes a reference to pensions, allowances or gratuities by way of compensation to or in respect of any of the Corporation's employees who suffer loss of office or employment or loss or diminution of emoluments.

(4) The Secretary of State with the consent of the Treasury may, by statutory instrument subject to annulment in pursuance of a resolution of either House of Parliament, make regulations providing for—

(a) the transfer to, and administration by, Housing for Wales of any superannuation fund maintained by the Housing Corporation in terms of the provisions of any scheme made under section 7 of the Superannuation Act 1972; and

(b) the modification, for the purposes of the regulations, of that section or any scheme thereunder.

(5) If an employee of the Corporation becomes a member of the Corporation and was by reference to his employment by the Corporation a participant in a pension scheme administered by it for the benefit of its employees—

(a) the Corporation may determine that his service as a member shall be treated for the purposes of the scheme as service as an employee of the Corporation whether or not any benefits are to be payable to or in respect of him by virtue of paragraph 6 above; but

(b) if the Corporation does so determine, any discretion as to the benefits payable to or in respect of him which the scheme confers on the Corporation shall be exercised only with the approval of the Secretary of State.

(6) Any reference in the preceding provisions of this paragraph to the approval of the Secretary of State is a reference to that approval given with the consent of the Treasury.

9.—(1) Not later than such date as the Secretary of State may determine, the Corporation shall make an offer of employment by it to each person employed immediately before that date by the Housing Corporation in connection with functions in Wales; and any question as to the persons to whom an offer of employment is to be made under this paragraph shall be determined by the Secretary of State.

(2) The terms of the offer shall be such that they are, taken as a whole, not less favourable to the person to whom the offer is made than the terms on which he is employed on the date on which the offer is made.

(3) An offer made in pursuance of this paragraph shall not be revocable during the period of 3 months commencing with the date on which it is made.

10.—(1) Where a person becomes an employee of the Corporation in consequence of an offer made under paragraph 9 above, then, for the purposes of the Employment Protection (Consolidation) Act 1978, his period of employment with the Housing Corporation shall count as a period of employment by the Corporation, and the change of employment shall not break the continuity of the period of employment.

(2) Where an offer is made in pursuance of paragraph 9 above to any person employed as mentioned in that paragraph, none of the agreed redundancy procedures applicable to such a person shall apply to him; and where that person ceases to be so employed—

(a) on becoming a member of the staff of the Corporation in consequence of that paragraph, or

(b) having unreasonably refused the offer,

Part VI of the Employment Protection (Consolidation) Act 1978 shall not apply to him and he shall not be treated for the purposes of any scheme under section 24 of the Superannuation Act 1972 or any other scheme as having been retired on redundancy.

(3) Without prejudice to sub-paragraph (2) above, where a person has unreasonably refused an offer made to him in pursuance of paragraph 9 above, the Housing Corporation shall not terminate that person's employment unless it has first had regard to the feasibility of employing him in a suitable alternative position with it.

(4) Where a person continues in employment in the Housing Corporation either—

   (a) not having unreasonably refused an offer made to him in pursuance of this paragraph, or

   (b) not having been placed in a suitable alternative position as mentioned in sub-paragraph (3) above,

he shall be treated for all purposes as if the offer mentioned in paragraph 9 above had not been made.

11.—(1) Any dispute as to whether an offer of employment complies with sub-paragraph (2) of paragraph 9 above shall be referred to and be determined by an industrial tribunal.

(2) An industrial tribunal shall not consider a complaint referred to it under sub-paragraph (1) above unless the complaint is presented to the tribunal before the end of the period of 3 months beginning with the date of the offer of employment or, in a case where the tribunal is satisfied that it was not reasonably practicable for the complaint to be presented before the end of the period of 3 months, within such further period as the tribunal considers reasonable.

(3) Subject to sub-paragraph (4) below, there shall be no appeal from the decision of an industrial tribunal under this paragraph.

(4) An appeal to the Employment Appeal Tribunal may be made only on a question of law arising from the decision of, or in proceedings before, an industrial tribunal under this paragraph.

Proceedings

12.—(1) The quorum of the Corporation and the arrangements relating to its meetings shall, subject to any directions given by the Secretary of State, be such as the Corporation may determine.

(2) The validity of proceedings of the Corporation is not affected by any defect in the appointment of any of its members.

13.—(1) Where a member of the Corporation is in any way directly or indirectly interested in a contract made or proposed to be made by the Corporation—

   (a) he shall disclose the nature of his interest at a meeting of the Corporation, and the disclosure shall be recorded in the minutes of the Corporation; and

   (b) he shall not take any part in any decision of the Corporation with respect to the contract.

(2) A general notice given by a member at a meeting of the Corporation to the effect that he is a member of a specified company or firm and is to be regarded as interested in any contract which may be made with the company or firm is a sufficient disclosure of his interest for the purposes of this paragraph in relation to a contract made after the date of the notice.

(3) A member need not attend in person at a meeting of the Corporation in order to make any disclosure which he is required to make under this paragraph provided he takes reasonable steps to secure that the disclosure is brought up and read at the meeting.

14.—(1) The fixing of the Corporation's seal may be authenticated by the signature of the Chairman or of any other person authorised for the purpose.

(2) A document purporting to be duly executed under the seal of the Corporation shall be received in evidence and be deemed to be so executed unless the contrary is proved.

GENERAL NOTE

This Schedule sets out the constitution of Housing for Wales and provides for the appointment of its members, Chairman and Deputy Chairman, the payment of remuneration, allowances and pensions, and regulates its proceedings, in terms very similar to those to be found in the Housing Associations Act 1985, Sched. 6, governing the Housing Corporation itself, save that this Schedule also governs the appointment of staff, and the transfer of Housing Corporation staff concerned with Wales to Housing for Wales.

SCHEDULE 6

AMENDMENTS OF HOUSING ASSOCIATIONS ACT 1985

PART I

AMENDMENTS OF PART I WITH RESPECT TO THE HOUSING CORPORATION, HOUSING FOR WALES
AND SCOTTISH HOMES

1. After section 2 there shall be inserted the following section—
"The Corporation
2A.—(1) In relation to a housing association which has its registered office for the purposes of the 1965 Act in Scotland, "the Corporation" means Scottish Homes.
    (2) In relation to a housing association—
            (a) which is a society registered under the 1965 Act and has its registered office for the purposes of that Act in Wales, or
            (b) which is a registered charity and has its address for the purposes of registration by the Charity Commissioners in Wales,
"the Corporation" means Housing for Wales.
    (3) In relation to any other housing association which is a society registered under the 1965 Act or a registered charity, "the Corporation" means the Housing Corporation.
    (4) Subject to subsections (1) to (3), in this Act, except where the context otherwise requires, "the Corporation" means the Housing Corporation, Scottish Homes or Housing for Wales and "the Corporations" means those three bodies."
2. Except as provided below, for the words "Housing Corporation", in each place where they occur in Part I, there shall be substituted "Corporation".
3.—(1) In section 3 (the register), in subsection (1)—
        (a) for the words "the Housing Corporation" there shall be substituted "each of the Corporations"; and
        (b) after the word "Corporation", in the second place where it occurs, there shall be inserted "by which it is maintained".
    (2) After subsection (1) of that section there shall be inserted the following subsection—
        "(1A) In this Act "register", in relation to the Corporation, means the register maintained by the Corporation under this section."
    (3) In subsection (2) of that section the words "of housing associations maintained under this section" shall be omitted.
4.—(1) In section 5 (registration) for subsection (2) there shall be substituted the following subsection—
        "(2) Nothing in subsection (1) shall require the Corporations to establish the same criteria; and each of them may vary any criteria established by it under that subsection."
    (2) For subsection (4) of that section there shall be substituted the following subsection—
        "(4) Where at any time a body is, or was, on a register maintained under section 3, then, for all purposes other than rectification of that register, the body shall be conclusively presumed to be, or to have been, at that time a housing association eligible for registration in that register."
5. In section 6(4) (removal from register) for paragraphs (a) to (c) there shall be substituted the following paragraphs—
"(a) a grant under section 41 (housing association grants),
 (b) a grant under section 54 (revenue deficit grants),
 (c) any such payment or loan as is mentioned in paragraph 2 or paragraph 3 of Schedule 1 (grant-aided land),
 (d) a grant or a loan under section 2(2) of the Housing (Scotland) Act 1988,
 (e) a grant under section 50 of the Housing Act 1988 (housing association grants), or
 (f) a grant under section 51 of that Act (revenue deficit grants)".
6. In section 7 (appeals against removal from the register), in subsection (1) for the words from "to the High Court" onwards there shall be substituted,—
"(a) where it is a decision of Scottish Homes, to the Court of Session; and
 (b) in any other case, to the High Court".
7.—(1) In section 9 (control by Corporation of disposition of land by housing associations) for subsection (1) there shall be substituted the following subsections—

"(1) Subject to section 10 and sections 81(6), 105(6) and 133(6) of the Housing Act 1988, the consent of the Corporation is required for any disposition of land by a registered housing association.

(1A) Subject to section 10, the consent of the relevant Corporation is required for any disposition of grant-aided land (as defined in Schedule 1) by an unregistered housing association; and for this purpose "the relevant Corporation" means,—

(a) if the land is in England, the Housing Corporation;

(b) if the land is in Scotland, Scottish Homes, and

(c) if the land is in Wales, Housing for Wales."

(2) In subsection (3) of that section—

(a) for the words "the consent of the Corporation", in the first place where they occur, there shall be substituted "consent"; and

(b) for the words "the consent of the Corporation", in the second place where they occur, there shall be substituted "that consent".

(3) After subsection (5) of that section there shall be added—

"(6) References in this section to consent are references,—

(a) in the case of the Housing Corporation or Housing for Wales, to consent given by order under the seal of the Corporation; and

(b) in the case of Scottish Homes, to consent in writing."

8.—(1) In section 10 (dispositions excepted from section 9), in subsection (1) for the words from "the Charity Commissioners", in the second place where they occur, onwards there shall be substituted "before making an order in such a case the Charity Commissioners shall consult,—

(a) in the case of dispositions of land in England, the Housing Corporation;

(b) in the case of dispositions of land in Scotland, Scottish Homes; and

(c) in the case of dispositions of land in Wales, Housing for Wales."

(2) In subsection (2) of that section at the end of paragraph (b) there shall be inserted "or

(c) a letting of land under an assured tenancy or an assured agricultural occupancy, or

(d) a letting of land in England or Wales under what would be an assured tenancy or an assured agricultural occupancy but for any of paragraphs 4 to 8 of Schedule 1 to the Housing Act 1988, or

(e) a letting of land in Scotland under what would be an assured tenancy but for any of paragraphs 3 to 8 and 12 of Schedule 4 to the Housing (Scotland) Act 1988."

9.—(1) In section 15 (payments and benefits to committee members, etc.) at the end of subsection (2) there shall be inserted the following paragraphs—

"(f) except in the case of housing associations registered in the register maintained by Scottish Homes, payments made or benefits granted by an association in such class or classes of case as may be specified in a determination made by the Corporation with the approval of the Secretary of State;

(g) in the case of housing associations registered in the register maintained by Scottish Homes, payments made or benefits granted by such an association with the approval of Scottish Homes (which approval may be given only in relation to a class or classes of case)."

(2) After subsection (2) there shall be inserted the following subsection—

"(3) The Housing Corporation and Housing for Wales may make different determinations for the purposes of subsection (2)(f) above and, before making such a determination, the Corporation shall consult such bodies appearing to it to be representative of housing associations as it considers appropriate; and after making such a determination the Corporation shall publish the determination in such manner as it considers appropriate for bringing it to the notice of the associations concerned."

10. For section 15A (which was inserted by section 14 of the Housing (Scotland) Act 1986) there shall be substituted the following section—

"Payments etc. in community-based housing associations in Scotland

15A.—(1) In relation to a community-based housing association in Scotland the following are also permitted, notwithstanding section 15(1)—

(a) payments made by the association in respect of the purchase of a dwelling, or part of a dwelling, owned and occupied by a person described in subsection (2) who is not an employee of the association; but only if—

(i) such payments constitute expenditure in connection with housing projects undertaken for the purpose of improving or repairing dwellings; and

(ii) the purchase price does not exceed such value as may be placed on the dwelling, or as the case may be part, by the district valuer;

    (b) the granting of the tenancy of a dwelling, or part of a dwelling, to such a person; but only if the person—

        (i) lives in the dwelling or in another dwelling owned by the association; or

        (ii) has at any time within the period of twelve months immediately preceding the granting of the tenancy lived in the dwelling (or such other dwelling) whether or not it belonged to the housing association when he lived there.

    (2) The persons mentioned in subsection (1) are—

        (a) a committee member or voluntary officer of the association; or

        (b) a person who at any time in the twelve months preceding the payment (or as the case may be the granting of the tenancy) has been such a member or officer; or

        (c) a close relative of a person described in paragraph (a), or (b).

    (3) For the purposes of subsection (1), a housing association is "community-based" if—

   (a) prior to the specified date, it was designated as such by the Housing Corporation; or

   (b) on or after that date, it is designated as such by Scottish Homes;

and, in this subsection, "specified date" has the same meaning as in section 3 of the Housing (Scotland) Act 1988.

    (4) Scottish Homes—

        (a) shall make a designation under subsection (3) only if it considers that the activities of the housing association relate wholly or mainly to the improvement of dwellings, or the management of improved dwellings, within a particular community (whether or not identified by reference to a geographical area entirely within any one administrative area); and

        (b) may revoke such a designation (including a designation made by the Housing Corporation under subsection (3) above as originally enacted) if it considers, after giving the association an opportunity to make representations to it as regards such revocation, that the association's activities have ceased so to relate."

11. In section 16 (general power to remove committee member), in subsection (4) for the words from "order to the High Court" onwards there shall be substituted "order,—

   (a) if it is an order of the Housing Corporation or Housing for Wales, to the High Court, and

   (b) if it is an order of Scottish Homes, to the Court of Session."

12. In section 17 (power to appoint new committee members) at the end of subsection (1) there shall be added the words "and the power conferred by paragraph (c) may be exercised notwithstanding that it will cause the maximum number of committee members permissible under the association's constitution to be exceeded".

13.—(1) In section 18 (exercise of powers in relation to registered charities), in subsection (1) immediately before the entry relating to section 41 of the 1985 Act there shall be inserted the following entries—

      "section 50 of the Housing Act 1988 (housing association grants),

        section 51 of that Act (revenue deficit grants)".

    (2) In subsection (3) of that section (appointment by Corporation of trustees of associations which are registered charities: appointments not to exceed maximum number of trustees) the words from "and the Corporation" onwards shall be omitted.

14. In section 19 (change of rules under the 1965 Act), in subsection (3) for the words "given by order under the seal of the Corporation" there shall be substituted "given,—

   (a) in the case of the Housing Corporation or Housing for Wales, by order under the seal of the Corporation; and

   (b) in the case of Scottish Homes, by notice in writing."

15. In section 21 (amalgamation and dissolution under the 1965 Act), in subsection (6) for the words from "are to an order" onwards there shall be substituted "are,—

   (a) in the case of the Housing Corporation or Housing for Wales, to consent given by order under the seal of the Corporation; and

   (b) in the case of Scottish Homes, to consent given in writing."

16. In section 22 (Corporation's power to petition for winding up), in subsection (1) after the word "applies" there shall be inserted "(a)" and at the end there shall be added "or

   (b) on the ground that the association is unable to pay its debts within the meaning of section 518 of the Companies Act 1985."

17.—(1) In section 24 (general requirements as to accounts and audit), in subsection (2) after the word "association" there shall be inserted "which is a registered charity".

(2) In subsection (5) of that section after the words "different areas" there shall be inserted "or for different descriptions of housing associations or housing activities".

(3) After subsection (5) of that section there shall be inserted the following subsection—

"(6) For the purposes of subsection (5)(a), descriptions may be framed by reference to any matters whatever, including in particular, in the case of housing activities, the manner in which they are financed."

18. In section 27 (responsibility for securing compliance with accounting requirements), in subsection (2) at the end of paragraph (c) there shall be added "or

(d) section 55(9) of the Housing Act 1988 is not complied with".

19.—(1) In section 28 (Corporation may appoint a person to inquire into the affairs of a registered housing association), in subsection (1) for the words "the Corporation's staff" there shall be substituted "staff of any of the Corporations" and at the end of that subsection there shall be added "and, if the appointed person considers it necessary for the purposes of the inquiry, he may also inquire into the business of any other body which, at a time which the appointed person considers material, is or was a subsidiary or associate of the association concerned".

(2) In subsection (2) of that section at the end of paragraph (b) there shall be added "or

(c) any person who is, or has been, an officer, agent or member of a subsidiary or associate of the association; or

(d) any other person whom the appointed person has reason to believe is or may be in possession of information of relevance to the inquiry";

and in the words following paragraph (b) for the words "the association's business" there shall be substituted "the business of the association or any other such body as is referred to in subsection (1)".

(3) After subsection (3) of that section there shall be inserted the following subsections—

"(3A) Where, by virtue of subsection (2), any books, accounts or other documents are produced to the appointed person, he may take copies of or make extracts from them.

(3B) The appointed person may, if he thinks fit during the course of the inquiry, make one or more interim reports to the Corporation on such matters as appear to him to be appropriate."

(4) After subsection (5) of that section there shall be added the following subsections—

"(6) In this section, in relation to a housing association, "subsidiary" means a company with respect to which one of the following conditions is fulfilled,—

(a) the association is a member of the company and controls the composition of the board of directors; or

(b) the association holds more than half in nominal value of the company's equity share capital; or

(c) the company is a subsidiary, within the meaning of the Companies Act 1985 or the Friendly and Industrial and Provident Societies Act 1968, of another company which, by virtue of paragraph (a) or paragraph (b), is itself a subsidiary of the housing association;

and, in the case of a housing association which is a body of trustees, the reference in paragraph (a) or paragraph (b) to the association is a reference to the trustees acting as such and any reference in subsection (7) to the association shall be construed accordingly.

(7) For the purposes of subsection (6)(a), the composition of a company's board of directors shall be deemed to be controlled by a housing association if, but only if, the association, by the exercise of some power exercisable by the association without the consent or concurrence of any other person, can appoint or remove the holders of all or a majority of the directorships.

(8) In this section, in relation to a housing association, "associate" means—

(a) any body of which the association is a subsidiary, and

(b) any other subsidiary of such a body,

and in this subsection "subsidiary" has the same meaning as in the Companies Act 1985 or the Friendly and Industrial and Provident Societies Act 1968 or, in the case of a body which is itself a housing association, has the meaning assigned by subsection (6).

(9) In relation to a company which is an industrial and provident society,—

(a) any reference in subsection (6)(a) or subsection (7) to the board of directors is a reference to the committee of management of the society; and

(b) the reference in subsection (7) to the holders of all or a majority of the directorships is a reference to all or a majority of the members of the committee or, if the housing association is itself a member of the committee, such number as together with the association would constitute a majority."

20. In section 29(1) (extraordinary audit) after the words "section 28" there shall be inserted "into the affairs of a registered housing association".

21.—(1) In section 30 (general powers of Corporation as a result of an inquiry or audit) after subsection (1) there shall be inserted the following subsection—

"(1A) If at any time the appointed person makes an interim report under section 28(3B) and, as a result of that interim report, the Corporation is satisfied that there has been misconduct or mismanagement as mentioned in subsection (1),—

(a) the Corporation may at that time exercise any of the powers conferred by paragraphs (b) to (d) of that subsection; and

(b) in relation to the exercise at that time of the power conferred by subsection (1)(b), the reference therein to a period of six months shall be construed as a reference to a period beginning at that time and ending six months after the date of the report under section 28(4)."

(2) In subsection (4) of that section (appeal against certain orders) for the words from "order to the High Court" onwards there shall be substituted "order,—

(a) if it is an order of the Housing Corporation or Housing for Wales, to the High Court; and

(b) if it is an order of Scottish Homes, to the Court of Session."

22.—(1) In section 31 (exercise of powers in relation to registered charities), in subsection (1) immediately before the entry relating to section 41 of the 1985 Act there shall be inserted the following entries—

"section 50 of the Housing Act 1988 (housing association grants),

section 51 of that Act (revenue deficit grants)".

(2) At the end of subsection (2)(b) of that section there shall be added the words "and such other activities (if any) of the association as are incidental to or connected with its housing activities".

23. In section 33 (recognition of central association), in subsection (1) after "housing associations" there shall be inserted "in Great Britain or in any part of Great Britain".

24. After section 33 there shall be inserted the following section—

"Provision of services between the Corporations

33A. Any of the Corporations may enter into an agreement with the others or either of them for the provision of services of any description by the one to the other or others on such terms, as to payment or otherwise, as the parties to the agreement consider appropriate."

25. In section 39 (minor definitions) before the definition of "mental disorder" there shall be inserted—

" "assured tenancy" has, in England and Wales, the same meaning as in Part I of the Housing Act 1988 and, in Scotland, the same meaning as in Part II of the Housing (Scotland) Act 1988;

"assured agricultural occupancy" has the same meaning as in Part I of the Housing Act 1988."

26. In section 40 (index of defined expressions in Part I)—

(a) after the entry relating to "appropriate registrar" there shall be inserted—
" "assured agricultural occupancy" .... section 39
"assured tenancy .... section 39";

(b) after the entry relating to "the Companies Act" there shall be inserted—
" "the Corporation" .... section 2A"; and

(c) in the entry beginning "register", in the second column for "3(2)" there shall be substituted "3".

PART II

AMENDMENTS OF PART II WITH RESPECT TO THE HOUSING CORPORATION AND HOUSING FOR WALES

27.—(1) In section 63 (building society advances) for the words "the Housing Corporation", in each place where they occur in subsections (1) and (2), there shall be substituted "one of the Corporations" and in subsection (1)(b) for the words "the Corporation" there shall be substituted "that one of the Corporations which is concerned".

(2) After subsection (2) of that section there shall be inserted the following subsection—

"(2A) In this section "the Corporations" means the Housing Corporation and Housing for Wales".

28.—(1) In section 69 (power to vary or terminate certain agreements) at the end of subsection (1)(a) there shall be added "(including such an agreement under which rights and obligations have been transferred to Housing for Wales)".

(2) After subsection (2) of that section there shall be inserted the following subsection—

"(2A) In the case of an agreement under which rights and obligations have been transferred to Housing for Wales, the reference to a party to the agreement includes a reference to Housing for Wales."

29. In section 69A (land subject to housing management agreement) for the words "housing association grant, revenue deficit grant or hostel deficit grant" there shall be substituted "grant under section 50 (housing association grant) or section 51 (revenue deficit grant) of the Housing Act 1988".

30.—(1) In Part I of Schedule 5 (residual subsidies)—

(a) in paragraph 5(3) the words "at such times and in such places as the Treasury may direct" and "with the approval of the Treasury" shall be omitted; and

(b) at the end of paragraph 6(2)(b) there shall be added "or Housing for Wales".

(2) In Part II of that Schedule, in paragraph 5(3) the words "at such times and in such places as the Treasury may direct" and "with the approval of the Treasury" shall be omitted.

PART III

AMENDMENTS OF PART III WITH RESPECT TO THE HOUSING CORPORATION AND HOUSING FOR WALES

31.—(1) In section 74 (constitution of Housing Corporation etc.), in subsection (1) after the words "Housing Corporation" there shall be inserted "and Housing for Wales, each of".

(2) In subsection (2) of that section for the words "the Corporation" there shall be substituted "the Housing Corporation".

(3) At the end of that section there shall be inserted the following subsections—

"(3) In this Part "registered housing association" in relation to the Corporation, means a housing association registered in the register maintained by the Corporation.

(4) In this Part,—

(a) in relation to land in Wales held by an unregistered housing association, "the Corporation" means Housing for Wales; and

(b) in relation to land outside Wales held by such an association, "the Corporation" means the Housing Corporation."

32. In section 75 (general functions), in subsection (1)(c) for the words "a register of housing associations" there shall be substituted "the register of housing associations referred to in section 3".

33. At the end of section 77 (advisory service) there shall be added the following subsection—

"(3) The powers conferred on the Corporation by subsections (1) and (2) may be exercised by the Housing Corporation and Housing for Wales acting jointly".

34.—(1) In section 83 (power to guarantee loans), in subsection (3) (maximum amount outstanding in respect of loans etc.) for the words "the Corporation", in each place where they occur, there shall be substituted "the Housing Corporation".

(2) After subsection (3) of that section there shall be inserted the following subsection—

"(3A) The aggregate amount outstanding in respect of—

(a) loans for which Housing for Wales has given a guarantee under this section, and

(b) payments made by Housing for Wales in meeting an obligation arising by virtue of such a guarantee and not repaid to Housing for Wales,

shall not exceed £30 million or such greater sum not exceeding £50 million as the Secretary of State may specify by order made with the approval of the Treasury".

(3) In subsection (4) of that section (procedure for orders of Secretary of State) after the words "subsection (3)" there shall be inserted "or subsection (3A)".

35.—(1) In section 93 (limit on borrowing), in subsection (2) for the words from "shall not exceed" onwards there shall be substituted "shall not exceed the limit appropriate to the Corporation under subsection (2A)".

(2) At the end of subsection (2) of that section there shall be inserted the following subsection—

"(2A) The limit referred to in subsection (2) is,—

(a) in the case of the Housing Corporation, £2,000 million or such greater sum not exceeding £3,000 million as the Secretary of State may specify by order made with the consent of the Treasury; and

(b) in the case of Housing for Wales, £250 million or such greater sum not exceeding £300 million as the Secretary of State may specify by order made with the consent of the Treasury."

(3) In subsections (3) to (5) of that section for "(2)", in each place where it occurs, there shall be substituted "(2A)".

36. In section 106(1) (minor definitions: general) for the definition of "housing activities" there shall be substituted the following—

" "housing activities", in relation to a registered housing association, means all its activities in pursuance of such of its purposes, objects or powers as are of a description mentioned in section 1(1)(a) or subsections (2) to (4) of section 4."

37. In Schedule 6, paragraph 3(3)(b) shall be omitted.

GENERAL NOTE

Most of these provisions reflect the sub-division of the Housing Corporation into the Housing Corporation and Housing for Wales; others are consequential upon the various changes contained in this Act, and in particular Part II, though note the extended control powers in paras. 19 and 21.

Section 62(5) SCHEDULE 7

HOUSING ACTION TRUSTS: CONSTITUTION

Members

1. A housing action trust (in this Schedule referred to as a "trust") shall consist of a chairman and such number of other members (not less than five but not exceeding eleven) as the Secretary of State may from time to time appoint.

2.—(1) In appointing members of a trust the Secretary of State shall have regard to the desirability of securing the services of persons who live in or have special knowledge of the locality in which the designated area is situated and before appointing any such person as a member he shall consult every local housing authority any part of whose district is included in the designated area.

(2) Before appointing a person to be a member of a trust the Secretary of State shall satisfy himself that that person will have no financial or other interest likely to affect prejudicially the exercise of his functions as a member; and the Secretary of State may require a person whom he proposes to appoint to give him such information as he considers necessary for that purpose.

(3) For the purposes of sub-paragraph (2) above, the fact that a person is or may become a tenant of a trust shall not be regarded as giving to that person an interest likely to affect prejudicially the exercise of his functions as a member.

(4) The Secretary of State shall appoint one of the members to be chairman and, if he thinks fit, another to be deputy chairman of the trust.

3. Subject to the following provisions of this Schedule, each member of the trust as such and the chairman and deputy chairman as such shall hold and vacate office in accordance with his appointment.

4. If the chairman or deputy chairman ceases to be a member of the trust, he shall also cease to be chairman or deputy chairman, as the case may be.

5. Any member of the trust may, by notice in writing addressed to the Secretary of State, resign his membership; and the chairman or deputy chairman may, by like notice, resign his office as such.

6. If the Secretary of State is satisfied that a member of the trust (including the chairman or deputy chairman)—

(a) has become bankrupt or made an arrangement with his creditors, or

(b) has been absent from meetings of the trust for a period longer than three consecutive months without the permission of the trust, or

(c) is otherwise unable or unfit to discharge the functions of a member, or is unsuitable to continue as a member,

the Secretary of State may remove him from his office.

7. A member of the trust who ceases to be a member or ceases to be chairman or deputy chairman shall be eligible for reappointment.

Remuneration

8. The trust may pay to each member such remuneration and allowances as the Secretary of State may with the approval of the Treasury determine.

9. The trust may pay or make provision for paying, to or in respect of any member, such sums by way of pensions, allowances and gratuities as the Secretary of State may with the approval of the Treasury determine and, with that approval, the Secretary of State may undertake to meet any liabilities arising in respect of such pensions, allowances or gratuities after the dissolution of the trust.

10. Where a person ceases to be a member of a trust and it appears to the Secretary of State that there are special circumstances which make it right for him to receive compensation, the trust may make to him payment of such amount as the Secretary of State may with the approval of the Treasury determine.

Staff

11.—(1) There shall be a chief officer of the trust who shall be appointed by the trust with the approval of the Secretary of State.

(2) The chief officer shall be responsible to the trust for the general exercise of the trust's functions.

(3) The trust may appoint such number of other employees as may be approved by the Secretary of State.

(4) References in paragraph 12 below to employees of the trust include references to the chief officer as well as other employees.

12.—(1) Employees of the trust shall be appointed at such remuneration and on such other terms and conditions as the trust may determine.

(2) The trust may pay such pensions, allowances or gratuities as it may determine to or in respect of any of its employees, make such payments as it may determine towards the provision of pensions, allowances or gratuities to or in respect of any of its employees or provide and maintain such schemes as it may determine (whether contributory or not) for the payment of pensions, allowances or gratuities to or in respect of any of its employees; and with the approval of the Treasury the Secretary of State may undertake to meet any liabilities arising in respect of such pensions, allowances or gratuities after the dissolution of the trust.

(3) The reference in sub-paragraph (2) above to pensions, allowances or gratuities to or in respect of any of the trust's employees includes a reference to pensions, allowances or gratuities by way of compensation to or in respect of any of the trust's employees who suffer loss of office or employment or loss or diminution of emoluments.

(4) If an employee of the trust becomes a member and was by reference to his employment by the trust a participant in a pension scheme maintained by the trust for the benefit of any of its employees, the trust may determine that his service as a member shall be treated for the purposes of the scheme as service as an employee of the trust whether or not any benefits are to be payable to or in respect of him by virtue of paragraph 9 above.

(5) A determination of the trust for the purposes of this paragraph is ineffective unless made with the approval of the Secretary of State given with the consent of the Treasury.

Meetings and proceedings

13. The quorum of the trust and the arrangements relating to its meetings shall, subject to any directions given by the Secretary of State, be such as the trust may determine.

14. The validity of any proceedings of the trust shall not be affected by any vacancy among its members or by any defect in the appointment of any of its members.

Instruments, etc.

15. The fixing of the seal of the trust shall be authenticated by the signature of the chairman or of some other member authorised either generally or specially by the trust to act for that purpose.

16. Any document purporting to be a document duly executed under the seal of the trust shall be received in evidence and shall, unless the contrary is proved, be deemed to be so executed.

17. A document purporting to be signed on behalf of a trust shall be received in evidence and shall, unless the contrary is proved, be deemed to be so signed.

18. In Part III of Schedule 1 to the House of Commons Disqualification Act 1975 (disqualifying offices), there shall be inserted at the appropriate place the following entry—

"Any member, in receipt of remuneration, of a housing action trust (within the meaning of Part III of the Housing Act 1988)."

GENERAL NOTE
See notes to s.62, above.

Section 62(5)   SCHEDULE 8

HOUSING ACTION TRUSTS: FINANCE ETC.

PART I

PRELIMINARY

1.—(1) References in this Schedule to a trust are to a housing action trust.
(2) The financial year of a trust shall begin with 1 April and references to a financial year in relation to a trust shall be construed accordingly.

PART II

FINANCE

Financial duties

2.—(1) After consultation with a trust, the Secretary of State may, with the Treasury's approval, determine the financial duties of the trust, and different determinations may be made in relation to different trusts or for different functions and activities of the same trust.
(2) The Secretary of State shall give the trust notice of every determination, and a determination may—
(a) relate to a period beginning before the date on which it is made;
(b) contain incidental or supplementary provisions; and
(c) be varied by a subsequent determination.

Government grants

3.—(1) The Secretary of State may (out of moneys provided by Parliament and with the consent of the Treasury) pay to a trust, in respect of the exercise of its functions and in respect of its administrative expenses, such sums as he may (with the approval of the Treasury) determine.
(2) The payment may be made on such terms as the Secretary of State (with the approval of the Treasury) provides.

Borrowing

4.—(1) A trust may borrow temporarily, by way of overdraft or otherwise, such sums as it may require for meeting its obligations and discharging its functions—
(a) in sterling from the Secretary of State; or
(b) with the consent of the Secretary of State, or in accordance with any general authority given by the Secretary of State, either in sterling or in currency other than sterling from a person other than the Secretary of State.
(2) A trust may borrow otherwise than by way of temporary loan such sums as the trust may require—
(a) in sterling from the Secretary of State; or
(b) with the consent of the Secretary of State, in a currency other than sterling from a person other than the Secretary of State.
(3) The Secretary of State may lend to a trust any sums it has power to borrow from him under sub-paragraph (1) or sub-paragraph (2) above.

(4) The Treasury may issue to the Secretary of State out of the National Loans Fund any sums necessary to enable him to make loans under sub-paragraph (3) above.

(5) Loans made under sub-paragraph (3) above shall be repaid to the Secretary of State at such times and by such methods, and interest on the loans shall be paid to him at such times and at such rates, as he may determine.

(6) All sums received by the Secretary of State under sub-paragraph (5) above shall be paid into the National Loans Fund.

(7) References in this paragraph to the Secretary of State are references to him acting with the approval of the Treasury.

Guarantees

5.—(1) The Treasury may guarantee, in such manner and on such conditions as they think fit, the repayment of the principal of and the payment of interest on any sums which a trust borrows from a person or body other than the Secretary of State.

(2) Immediately after a guarantee is given under this paragraph, the Treasury shall lay a statement of the guarantee before each House of Parliament; and, where any sum is issued for fulfilling a guarantee so given, the Treasury shall lay before each House of Parliament a statement relating to that sum, as soon as possible after the end of each financial year, beginning with that in which the sum is issued and ending with that in which all liability in respect of the principal of the sum and in respect of interest on it is finally discharged.

(3) Any sums required by the Treasury for fulfilling a guarantee under this paragraph shall be charged on and issued out of the Consolidated Fund.

(4) If any sums are issued in fulfilment of a guarantee given under this paragraph, the trust shall make to the Treasury, at such times and in such manner as the Treasury may from time to time direct, payments of such amounts as the Treasury so direct in or towards repayment of the sums so issued and payments of interest, at such rates as the Treasury so direct, on what is outstanding for the time being in respect of sums so issued.

(5) Any sums received by the Treasury in pursuance of sub-paragraph (4) above shall be paid into the Consolidated Fund.

Assumed debt

6.—(1) On any acquisition to which this paragraph applies, a trust shall assume a debt to the Secretary of State of such amount as may be notified to the trust in writing by him, with the approval of the Treasury.

(2) This paragraph applies to any acquisition by the trust of property held—
    (a) by or on behalf of the Crown; or
    (b) by a company all of whose shares are held by or on behalf of the Crown or by a wholly owned subsidiary of such a company.

(3) Subject to sub-paragraph (4) below, the amount to be notified is the aggregate of the following—
    (a) the consideration given when the property was first brought into public ownership; and
    (b) the costs and expenses of and incidental to its being brought into public ownership.

(4) If it appears to the Secretary of State that there has been such a change in circumstances since the property was first brought into public ownership that its true value would not be reflected by reference to the consideration mentioned in sub-paragraph (3) above, the Secretary of State, with the approval of the Treasury, shall determine the amount to be notified.

(5) The rate of interest payable on the debt assumed by a trust under this paragraph, and the date from which interest is to begin to accrue, the arrangements for paying off the principal, and the other terms of the debt shall be such as the Secretary of State, with the approval of the Treasury, may from time to time determine.

(6) Different rates and dates may be determined under sub-paragraph (5) above with respect to different portions of the debt.

(7) Any sums received by the Secretary of State under sub-paragraph (5) above shall be paid into the National Loans Fund.

Surplus funds

7.—(1) Where it apppears to the Secretary of State, after consultation with the Treasury and the trust, that a trust has a surplus, whether on capital or on revenue account, after making allowance by way of transfer to reserve or otherwise for its future requirements, the trust shall, if the Secretary of State with the approval of the Treasury and after consultation with the trust so directs, pay to the Secretary of State such sum not exceeding the amount of that surplus as may be specified in the direction.

(2) Any sum received by the Secretary of State under this paragraph shall, subject to sub-paragraph (4) below, be paid into the Consolidated Fund.

(3) The whole or part of any payment made to the Secretary of State by a trust under sub-paragraph (1) above shall, if the Secretary of State with the approval of the Treasury so determines, be treated as made by way of repayment of such part of the principal of loans under paragraph 4(3) above, and as made in respect of the repayments due at such times, as may be so determined.

(4) Any sum treated under sub-paragraph (3) above as a repayment of a loan shall be paid by the Secretary of State into the National Loans fund.

Financial limits

8.—(1) The aggregate amount of the sums mentioned in sub-paragraph (2) below shall not exceed such sum as the Secretary of State, with the consent of the Treasury, may by order made by statutory instrument specify.

(2) The sums are—

    (a) sums borrowed by all trusts under paragraph 4 above minus repayments made in respect of the sums; and

    (b) sums issued by the Treasury in fulfilment of guarantees under paragraph 5 above of debts of all trusts.

(3) No order shall be made under sub-paragraph (1) above unless a draft of it has been laid before, and approved by a resolution of, the House of Commons.

Grants and loans: accounts

9.—(1) The Secretary of State shall prepare in respect of each financial year an account—

    (a) of the sums paid to trusts under paragraph 3 above;

    (b) of the sums issued to him under paragraph 4(4) above and the sums received by him under paragraph 4(5) above and of the disposal by him of those sums; and

    (c) of the sums paid into the Consolidated Fund or National Loans Fund under paragraph 7 above.

(2) The Secretary of State shall send the account to the Comptroller and Auditor General before the end of the month of November next following the end of that year.

(3) The Comptroller and Auditor General shall examine, certify and report on the account and lay copies of it and of his report before each House or Parliament.

(4) The form of the account and the manner of preparing it shall be such as the Treasury may direct.

PART III

GENERAL ACCOUNTS ETC.

Accounts

10.—(1) A trust shall keep proper accounts and other records in relation to them.

(2) The accounts and records shall show, in respect of the financial year to which they relate, a true and fair view of the trust's activities.

(3) A trust shall prepare in respect of each financial year a statement of accounts complying with any requirement which the Secretary of State has (with the consent of the Treasury) notified in writing to the trust relating to—

    (a) the information to be contained in the statement;

    (b) the manner in which the information is to be presented; and

    (c) the methods and principles according to which the statement is to be prepared.

(4) Subject to any requirement notified to the trust under sub-paragraph (3) above, in preparing any statement of accounts in accordance with that sub-paragraph the trust shall follow, with respect to each of the matters specified in paragraphs (a) to (c) of that sub-paragraph, such course as may for the time being be approved by the Secretary of State with the consent of the Treasury.

(5) Section 6 of the National Audit Act 1983 (which enables the Comptroller and Auditor General to conduct examinations into the economy, efficiency and effectiveness with which certain departments, authorities and bodies have used their resources) shall apply to a trust.

Audit

11.—(1) The trust's accounts and statements of accounts shall be audited by an auditor to be appointed annually by the Secretary of State in relation to the trust.

(2) A person shall not be qualified for appointment under sub-paragraph (1) above unless he is qualified for appointment as auditor of a company under section 389 of the Companies Act 1985.

(3) A person shall not be qualified for appointment under sub-paragraph (1) above if the person is—

(a) a member, officer or servant of the trust,

(b) a partner of, or employed by, a member, officer or servant of the trust, or

(c) a body corporate.

Transmission to Secretary of State

12. As soon as the accounts and statement of accounts of the trust for any financial year have been audited, the trust shall send to the Secretary of State a copy of the statement, together with a copy of any report made by the auditor on the statement or on the accounts.

Reports

13.—(1) As soon as possible after the end of each financial year, a trust shall make to the Secretary of State a report dealing generally with the trust's operations during the year, and shall include in the report a copy of its audited statement of accounts for that year.

(2) Without prejudice to the generality of sub-paragraph (1) above, a report shall give particulars of the name and address of every person who, in the financial year to which the report relates, has received financial assistance from the trust under section 71(1) of this Act, together with particulars of the form of the assistance, the amount involved and the purpose for which the assistance was given.

(3) The Secretary of State shall lay a copy of the report before each House of Parliament.

Information

14. Without prejudice to paragraph 13 above, a trust shall provide the Secretary of State with such information relating to its activities as he may require, and for that purpose shall permit any person authorised by the Secretary of State to inspect and make copies of the accounts, books, documents or papers of the trust and shall afford such explanation of them as that person or the Secretary of State may reasonably require.

GENERAL NOTE
See notes to s.62, above.

Section 76   SCHEDULE 9

ORDERS VESTING LAND IN HOUSING ACTION TRUSTS

PART I

PROVISIONS SUPPLEMENTING SECTION 76(1) TO (3)

1. In this Part of this Schedule "the principal section" means section 76 of this Act.

2.—(1) In the principal section and paragraph 3 below, "statutory undertakers" and "statutory undertaking" shall be construed in accordance with paragraph 4 below.

(2) In the principal section and the following provisions of this Part of this Schedule, "wholly-owned subsidiary" has the meaning given by section 736 of the Companies Act 1985.

3.—(1) In subsection (3) of the principal section the reference to the Secretary of State and the appropriate Minister—

(a) in relation to statutory undertakers who are also statutory undertakers for the purposes of any provision of Part XI of the Town and Country Planning Act 1971, shall be construed as if contained in that Part; and

(b) in relation to any other statutory undertakers shall be construed in accordance with an order made by the Secretary of State.

(2) If, for the purposes of subsection (3) of the principal section, any question arises as to which Minister is the appropriate Minister in relation to any statutory undertakers, that question shall be determined by the Treasury.

4. In the principal section and, except where the context otherwise requires, in paragraph 3 above "statutory undertakers" means—

(a) persons authorised by any enactment to carry on any railway, light railway, tramway, road transport, water transport, canal, inland navigation, dock, harbour, pier or lighthouse undertaking, or any undertaking for the supply of electricity, hydraulic power or water;

(b) British Shipbuilders, the British Steel Corporation, the Civil Aviation Authority, the British Coal Corporation, the National Enterprise Board, the Post Office and any other authority, body or undertakers which, by virtue of any enactment, are to be treated as statutory undertakers for any of the purposes of the Town and Country Planning Act 1971;

(c) any other authority, body or undertakers specified in an order made by the Secretary of State; and

(d) any wholly-owned subsidiary of any person, authority, body or undertakers mentioned in sub-paragraphs (a) and (b) above or specified in an order made under paragraph (c) above;

and "statutory undertaking" shall be construed accordingly.

5. An order under any provision of this Part of this Schedule shall be made by statutory instrument which shall be subject to annulment in pursuance of a resolution of either House of Parliament.

PART II

MODIFICATIONS OF ENACTMENTS

Land Compensation Act 1961

6. The Land Compensation Act 1961 shall have effect in relation to orders under section 76 of this Act subject to the modifications in paragraphs 7 to 11 below.

7. References to the date of service of a notice to treat shall be treated as references to the date on which an order under section 76 of this Act comes into force.

8. Section 17(2) shall be treated as if for the words "the authority proposing to acquire it have served a notice to treat in respect thereof, or an agreement has been made for the sale thereof to that authority" there were substituted the words "an order under section 76 of the Housing Act 1988 vesting the land in which the interest subsists in a housing action trust has come into force, or an agreement has been made for the sale of the interest to such a trust".

9. In section 22—

(a) subsection (2) shall be treated as if at the end of paragraph (c) there were added the words "or

(cc) where an order has been made under section 76 of the Housing Act 1988 vesting the land in which the interest subsists in a housing action trust"; and

(b) subsection (3) shall be treated as if, in paragraph (a), after the words "paragraph (b)" there were inserted "or paragraph (cc)".

10. Any reference to a notice to treat in section 39(2) shall be treated as a reference to an order under section 76 of this Act.

11. In Schedule 2 paragraph 1(2) shall be treated as if at the end there were added the following paragraph—

"(k) an acquisition by means of an order under section 76 of the Housing Act 1988 vesting land in a housing action trust."

Compulsory Purchase (Vesting Declarations) Act 1981

12.—(1) In Schedule 2 to the Compulsory Purchase (Vesting Declarations) Act 1981 (vesting of land in urban development corporation), in paragraph 1 after the word "declaration)" there shall be inserted "or under section 76 of the Housing Act 1988 (subsection (5) of which contains similar provision)".

50–248

(2) At the end of sub-paragraph (a) of paragraph 3 of that Schedule there shall be added "or, as the case may be, the housing action trust".

GENERAL NOTE

This Schedule contains the definition of "statutory undertaker" for the purposes of s.76, above, and amends the relevant procedural and compensation statutes when applied by s.76.

Section 78   SCHEDULE 10

HOUSING ACTION TRUSTS: LAND

PART I

MODIFICATIONS OF ACQUISITION OF LAND ACT 1981

1. The Acquisition of Land Act 1981 (in this Part referred to as "the 1981 Act") shall apply in relation to the compulsory acquisition of land under section 77 of this Act with the modifications made by this Part of this Schedule.

2.—(1) Where a compulsory purchase order authorising the acquisition of any land is submitted to the Secretary of State in accordance with section 2(2) of the 1981 Act then, if the Secretary of State—
   (a) is satisfied that the order ought to be confirmed so far as it relates to part of the land comprised in it, but
   (b) has not for the time being determined whether it ought to be confirmed so far as it relates to any other such land,

he may confirm the order so far as it relates to the land mentioned in paragraph (a) above, and give directions postponing the consideration of the order, so far as it relates to any other land specified in the directions, until such time as may be so specified.

(2) Where the Secretary of State gives directions under sub-paragraph (1) above, the notices required by section 15 of the 1981 Act to be published and served shall include a statement of the effect of the directions.

3. The reference in section 17(3) of the 1981 Act to statutory undertakers includes a reference to a housing action trust.

PART II

LAND: SUPPLEMENTARY

Extinguishment of rights over land

4.—(1) Subject to this paragraph, on an order under section 76 of this Act coming into force or the completion by a housing action trust of a compulsory acquisition of land under Part III of this Act, all private rights of way and rights of laying down, erecting, continuing or maintaining any apparatus on, under or over the land shall be extinguished, and any such apparatus shall vest in the trust.

(2) Sub-paragraph (1) above does not apply—
   (a) to any right vested in, or apparatus belonging to, statutory undertakers for the purpose of carrying on their undertaking; or
   (b) to any right conferred by or in accordance with the telecommunications code on the operator of a telecommunications code system or to any telecommunications apparatus kept installed for the purposes of any such system.

(3) In respect of any right or apparatus not falling within sub-paragraph (2) above, sub-paragraph (1) above shall have effect subject—
   (a) to any direction given by the Secretary of State before the coming into force of the order (or, as the case may be, by the trust before the completion of the acquisition) that sub-paragraph (1) above shall not apply to any right or apparatus specified in the direction, and
   (b) to any agreement which may be made (whether before or after the coming into force of the order or completion of the acquisition) between the Secretary of State (or trust) and the person in or to whom the right or apparatus in question is vested or belongs.

(4) Any person who suffers loss by the extinguishment of a right or the vesting of any apparatus under this paragraph shall be entitled to compensation from the trust.

(5) Any compensation payable under this paragraph shall be determined in accordance with the Land Compensation Act 1961.

Power to override easements

5.—(1) The erection, construction or carrying out, or maintenance of any building or work on land which has been vested in or acquired by a housing action trust for the purposes of Part III of this Act, whether done by the trust or by any other person, is authorised by virtue of this paragraph if it is done in accordance with planning permission, notwithstanding that it involves interference with an interest or right to which this paragraph applies, or involves a breach of a restriction as to the user of land arising by virtue of a contract.

(2) Nothing in sub-paragraph (1) above shall authorise interference with any right of way or right of laying down, erecting, continuing or maintaining apparatus on, under or over land, being a right vested in or belonging to statutory undertakers for the purpose of the carrying on of their undertaking or a right conferred by or in accordance with the telecommunications code on the operator of a telecommunications code system.

(3) This paragraph applies to the following interests and rights, that is to say, any easement, liberty, privilege, right or advantage annexed to land and adversely affecting other land, including any natural right to support.

(4) In respect of any interference or breach in pursuance of sub-paragraph (1) above, compensation shall be payable under section 7 or section 10 of the Compulsory Purchase Act 1965, to be assessed in the same manner and subject to the same rules as in the case of other compensation under those sections in respect of injurious affection where the compensation is to be estimated in connection with a purchase by a housing action trust or the injury arises from the execution of works on land acquired by such a trust.

(5) Where a person other than the housing action trust by or in whom the land in question was acquired or vested is liable to pay compensation by virtue of sub-paragraph (4) above and fails to discharge that liability, the liability shall (subject to sub-paragraph (6) below) be enforceable against the trust.

(6) Nothing in sub-paragraph (5) above shall be construed as affecting any agreement between the trust and any other person for indemnifying the trust against any liability under that sub-paragraph.

(7) Nothing in this paragraph shall be construed as authorising any act or omission on the part of any person which is actionable at the suit of any person on any grounds other than such an interference or breach as is mentioned in sub-paragraph (1) above.

(8) Nothing in this paragraph shall be construed as authorising any act or omission on the part of a housing action trust, or of any body corporate, in contravention of any limitation imposed by law on its capacity by virtue of the constitution of the trust or body.

Consecrated land and burial grounds

6.—(1) Any consecrated land, whether including a building or not, which has been vested in or acquired by a housing action trust for the purposes of Part III of this Act may (subject to the following provisions of this paragraph) be used by the trust, or by any other person, in any manner in accordance with planning permission, notwithstanding any obligation or restriction imposed under ecclesiastical law or otherwise in respect of consecrated land.

(2) Sub-paragraph (1) above does not apply to land which consists or forms part of a burial ground.

(3) Any use of consecrated land authorised by sub-paragraph (1) above, and the use of any land, not being consecrated land, vested or acquired as mentioned in that sub-paragraph which at the time of acquisition included a church or other building used or formerly used for religious worship or the site thereof, shall be subject to compliance with the prescribed requirements with respect to the removal and reinterment of any human remains, and the disposal of monuments and fixtures and furnishings; and, in the case of consecrated land, shall be subject to such provisions as may be prescribed for prohibiting or restricting the use of the land, either absolutely or until the prescribed consent has been obtained, so long as any church or other building used or formerly used for religious worship, or any part thereof, remains on the land.

(4) Any regulations made for the purposes of sub-paragraph (3) above—

    (a) shall contain such provisions as appear to the Secretary of State to be requisite for securing that any use of land which is subject to compliance with the regulations shall, as nearly as may be, be subject to the like control as is imposed by law in the case of a similar use authorised by an enactment not contained in this Act or by a Measure, or as it would be proper to impose on a disposal of the land in question otherwise than in pursuance of an enactment or Measure;

    (b) shall contain requirements relating to the disposal of any such land as is mentioned in sub-paragraph (3) above such as appear to the Secretary of State requisite for securing that the provisions of that sub-paragraph shall be complied with in relation to the use of the land; and

    (c) may contain such incidental and consequential provisions (including provision as to the closing of registers) as appear to the Secretary of State to be expedient for the purposes of the regulations.

(5) Any land consisting of a burial ground or part of a burial ground which has been vested in or acquired by a housing action trust for the purposes of Part III of this Act may be used by the trust in any manner in accordance with planning permission, notwithstanding anything in any enactment relating to burial grounds or any obligation or restriction imposed under ecclesiastical law or otherwise in respect of burial grounds.

(6) Sub-paragraph (5) above shall not have effect in respect of any land which has been used for the burial of the dead until the prescribed requirements with respect to the removal and reinterment of human remains and the disposal of monuments in or upon the land have been complied with.

(7) Provision shall be made by any regulations made for the purposes of sub-paragraphs (3) and (6) above—

    (a) for requiring the persons in whom the land is vested to publish notice of their intention to carry out the removal and reinterment of any human remains or the disposal of any monuments; and

    (b) for enabling the personal representatives or relatives of any deceased person themselves to undertake the removal and reinterment of the remains of the deceased and the disposal of any monument commemorating the deceased, and for requiring the persons in whom the land is vested to defray the expenses of such removal, reinterment and disposal, not exceeding such amount as may be prescribed; and

    (c) for requiring compliance with such reasonable conditions (if any) as may be imposed, in the case of consecrated land, by the bishop of the diocese, with respect to the manner of removal and the place and manner of reinterment of any human remains and the disposal of any monuments; and

    (d) for requiring compliance with any directions given in any case by the Secretary of State with respect to the removal and reinterment of any human remains.

(8) Subject to the provisions of any such regulations as are referred to in sub-paragraph (7) above, no faculty shall be required for the removal and reinterment in accordance with the regulations of any human remains or for the removal or disposal of any monuments, and the provisions of section 25 of the Burial Act 1857 (which prohibits the removal of human remains without the licence of the Secretary of State except in certain cases) shall not apply to a removal carried out in accordance with the regulations.

(9) Any power conferred by this paragraph to use land in a manner therein mentioned shall be construed as a power so to use the land, whether it involves the erection, construction or carrying out of any building or work, or the maintenance of any building or work, or not.

(10) Nothing in this paragraph shall be construed as authorising any act or omission on the part of any person which is actionable at the suit of any person on any grounds other than contravention of any such obligation, restriction or enactment as is mentioned in sub-paragraph (1) or sub-paragraph (5) above.

(11) Sub-paragraph (8) of paragraph 5 above shall apply in relation to this paragraph as it applies in relation to that.

(12) In this paragraph "burial ground" includes any churchyard, cemetery or other ground, whether consecrated or not, which has at any time been set apart for the purposes of interment, and "monument" includes a tombstone or other memorial.

(13) In this paragraph "prescribed" means prescribed by regulations made by the Secretary of State.

(14) The power to make regulations under this paragraph shall be exercisable by statutory instrument which shall be subject to annulment in pursuance of a resolution of either House of Parliament.

Open spaces

7.—(1) Any land being, or forming part of, a common, open space or fuel or field garden allotment, which has been vested in or acquired by a housing action trust for the purposes of Part III of this Act may be used by the trust, or by any other person, in any manner in accordance with planning permission, notwithstanding anything in any enactment relating to land of that kind, or in any enactment by which the land is specially regulated.

(2) Nothing in this paragraph shall be construed as authorising any act or omission on the part of any person which is actionable at the suit of any person on any grounds other than contravention of any such enactment as is mentioned in sub-paragraph (1) above.

(3) Sub-paragraph (8) of paragraph 5 above shall apply in relation to this paragraph as it applies in relation to that.

Displacement of persons

8. If the Secretary of State certifies that possession of a house which has been vested in or acquired by a housing action trust for the purposes of Part III of this Act and is for the time being held by that trust for the purposes for which it was acquired, is immediately required for those purposes, nothing in the Rent (Agriculture) Act 1976 or the Rent Act 1977 or this Act shall prevent that trust from obtaining possession of the house.

Extinguishment of public rights of way

9.—(1) Where any land has beeen vested in or acquired by a housing action trust for the purposes of Part III of this Act and is for the time being held by that trust for those purposes, the Secretary of State may by order extinguish any public right of way over the land.

(2) Where the Secretary of State proposes to make an order under this paragraph, he shall publish in such manner as appears to him to be requisite a notice—

(a) stating the effect of the order, and

(b) specifying the time (not being less than 28 days from the publication of the notice) within which, and the manner in which, objections to the proposal may be made,

and shall serve a like notice—

(i) on the local planning authority in whose area the land is situated; and

(ii) on the relevant highway authority.

(3) In sub-paragraph (2) above "the relevant highway authority" means any authority which is a highway authority in relation to the right of way proposed to be extinguished by the order under this paragraph.

(4) Where an objection to a proposal to make an order under this paragraph is duly made and is not withdrawn, the provisions of paragraph 10 below shall have effect in relation to the proposal.

(5) For the purposes of this paragraph an objection to such a proposal shall not be treated as duly made unless—

(a) it is made within the time and in the manner specified in the notice required by this paragraph; and

(b) a statement in writing of the grounds of the objection is comprised in or submitted with the objection.

(6) Where it is proposed to make an order under this paragraph extinguising a public right of way over a road on land acquired for the purposes of this Act by a housing action trust and compensation in respect of restrictions imposed under section 1 or section 2 of the Restriction of Ribbon Development Act 1935 in respect of that road has been paid by the highway authority (or, in the case of a trunk road, by the authority which, when the compensation was paid, was the authority for the purposes of section 4 of the Trunk Roads Act 1936), the order may provide for the payment by the housing action trust to that authority, in respect of the compensation so paid, of such sums as the Secretary of State, with the consent of the Treasury may determine.

(7) Where the Secretary of State makes an order under this paragraph on the application of a housing action trust, he shall send a copy of it to the Post Office.

10.—(1) In this paragraph any reference to making a final decision, in relation to an order, is a reference to deciding whether to make the order or what modification, if any, ought to be made.

(2) Unless the Secretary of State decides apart from the objection not to make the order, or decides to make a modification which is agreed to by the objector as meeting the objection, the Secretary of State shall, before making a final decision, consider the grounds of the objection as set out in the statement comprised in or submitted with the objection, and may, if he thinks fit, require the objector to submit within a specified period a further statement in writing as to any of the matters to which the objection relates.

(3) In so far as the Secretary of State, after considering the grounds of the objection as set out in the original statement and in any such further statement, is satisfied that the objection

relates to a matter which can be dealt with in the assessment of compensation, the Secretary of State may treat the objection as irrelevant for the purpose of making a final decision.

(4) If, after considering the grounds of the objection as set out in the original statement and in any such further statement, the Secretary of State is satisfied that, for the purpose of making a final decision, he is sufficiently informed as to the matters to which the objection relates, or if, where a further statement has been required, it is not submitted within the specified period, the Secretary of State may make a final decision without further investigation as to those matters.

(5) Subject to sub-paragraphs (3) and (4) above, the Secretary of State, before making a final decision, shall afford to the objector an opportunity of appearing before, and being heard by, a person appointed for the purpose by the Secretary of State; and if the objector avails himself of that opportunity, the Secretary of State shall afford an opportunity of appearing and being heard on the same occasion to the housing action trust on whose representation the order is proposed to be made, and to any other persons to whom it appears to the Secretary of State to be expedient to afford such an opportunity.

(6) Notwithstanding anything in the preceding provisions of this paragraph, if it appears to the Secretary of State that the matters to which the objection relates are such as to require investigation by public local inquiry before he makes a final decision, he shall cause such an inquiry to be held; and where he determines to cause such an inquiry to be held, any of the requirements of those provisions to which effect has not been given at the time of that determination shall be dispensed with.

Telegraphic lines

11.—(1) Where an order under paragraph 9 above extinguishes a public right of way is made on the application of a housing action trust and at the time of the publication of the notice required by sub-paragraph (2) of that paragraph any telecommunication apparatus was kept installed for the purposes of a telecommunications code system under, in, on, over, along or across the land over which the right of way subsisted—

(a) the power of the operator of the system to remove the apparatus shall, notwithstanding the making of the Order, be exercisable at any time not later than the end of the period of three months from the date on which the right of way is extinguished and shall be exercisable in respect of the whole or any part of the apparatus after the end of that period if before the end of that period the operator of the system has given notice to the trust of his intention to remove the apparatus or that part of it, as the case may be;

(b) the operator of the system may by notice given in that behalf to the trust not later than the end of the said period of three months abandon the telecommunication apparatus or any part of it;

(c) subject to paragraph (b) above, the operator of the system shall be deemed at the end of that period to have abandoned any part of the apparatus which he has then neither removed nor given notice of his intention to remove;

(d) the operator of the system shall be entitled to recover from the trust the expense of providing, in substitution for the apparatus and any other telecommunication apparatus connected with it which is rendered useless in consequence of the removal or abandonment of the first-mentioned apparatus, any telecommunication apparatus in such other place as the operator may require; and

(e) where under the preceding provisions of this sub-paragraph the operator of the system has abandoned the whole or any part of any telecommunication apparatus, that apparatus or that part of it shall vest in the trust and shall be deemed, with its abandonment, to cease to be kept installed for the purposes of a telecommunications code system.

(2) As soon as practicable after the making of an order under paragraph 9 above extinguishing a public right of way in circumstances in which sub-paragraph (1) above applies in relation to the operator of any telecommunications code system, the Secretary of State shall give notice to the operator of the making of the order.

Statutory undertakers

12.—(1) Where any land has been acquired by a housing action trust under section 77 of his Act and—

(a) there subsists over that land a right vested in or belonging to statutory undertakers for the purpose of the carrying on of their undertaking, being a right of way or a right of laying down, erecting, continuing or maintaining apparatus on, under or over that land, or

(b) there is on, under or over the land apparatus vested in or belonging to statutory undertakers for the purpose of the carrying on of their undertaking,

the trust, if satisfied that the extinguishment of the right or, as the case may be, the removal of the apparatus, is necessary for the purpose of carrying out any development, may serve on the statutory undertakers a notice stating that, at the end of the period of 28 days from the date of service of the notice or such longer period as may be specified therein, the right will be extinguished or requiring that, before the end of that period, the apparatus shall be removed.

(2) The statutory undertakers on whom a notice is served under sub-paragraph (1) above may, before the end of the period of 28 days from the service of the notice, serve a counter-notice on the trust stating that they object to all or any provisions of the notice and specifying the grounds of their objection.

(3) If no counter-notice is served under sub-paragraph (2) above—

(a) any right to which the notice relates shall be extinguished at the end of the period specified in that behalf in the notice; and

(b) if, at the end of the period so specified in relation to any apparatus, any requirement of the notice as to the removal of the apparatus has not been complied with, the trust may remove the apparatus and dispose of it in any way it may think fit.

(4) If a counter-notice is served under sub-paragraph (2) above on a trust, the trust may either withdraw the notice (without prejudice to the service of a further notice) or may apply to the Secretary of State and the appropriate Minister for an order under this paragraph embodying the provisions of the notice with or without modification.

(5) Where by virtue of this paragraph any right vested in or belonging to statutory undertakers is extinguished, or any requirement is imposed on statutory undertakers, those undertakers shall be entitled to compensation from the trust.

(6) Sections 238 and 240 of the Town and Country Planning Act 1971 (measure of compensation to statutory undertakers) shall apply to compensation under sub-paragraph (5) above as they apply to compensation under section 237(2) of that Act.

(7) Except in a case in which paragraph 11 above has effect—

(a) the reference in paragraph (a) of sub-paragraph (1) above to a right vested in or belonging to statutory undertakers for the purpose of the carrying on of their undertaking shall include a reference to a right conferred by or in accordance with the telecommunications code on the operator of a telecommunications code system; and

(b) the reference in paragraph (b) of that sub-paragraph to apparatus vested in or belonging to statutory undertakers for the purpose of the carrying on of their undertaking shall include a reference to telecommunication apparatus kept installed for the purposes of any such system.

(8) Where paragraph (a) or paragraph (b) of sub-paragraph (1) above has effect as mentioned in sub-paragraph (7) above, in the rest of this paragraph and in paragraph 17 below—

(a) any reference to statutory undertakers shall have effect as a reference to the operator of any such system as is referred to in sub-paragraph (7) above; and

(b) any reference to the appropriate Minister shall have effect as a reference to the Secretary of State for Trade and Industry.

13.—(1) Before making an order under paragraph 12(4) above the Ministers proposing to make the order—

(a) shall afford to the statutory undertakers on whom notice was served under paragraph 12(1) above an opportunity of objecting to the application for the order; and

(b) if any objection is made, shall consider the objection and afford to those statutory undertakers and to the trust on whom the counter-notice was served, an opportunity of appearing before and being heard by a person appointed by the Seretary of State and the appropriate Minister for the purpose;

and the Ministers may then, if they think fit, make the order in accordance with the application either with or without modification.

(2) Where an order is made under paragraph 12(4) above—

(a) any right to which the order relates shall be extinguished at the end of the period specified in that behalf in the order; and

(b) if, at the end of the period so specified in relation to any apparatus, any requirement of the order as to the removal of the apparatus has not been complied with, the trust may remove the apparatus and dispose of it in any way it may think fit.

14.—(1) Subject to this paragraph, where any land has been acquired by a housing action trust under section 77 of this Act and—

(a) there is on, under or over the land apparatus vested in or belonging to statutory undertakers, and

(b) the undertakers claim that development to be carried out on the land is such as to require, on technical or other grounds connected with the carrying on of their undertaking, the removal or re-siting of the apparatus affected by the development,

the undertakers may serve on the trust a notice claiming the right to enter on the land and carry out such works for the removal or re-siting of the apparatus or any part of it as may be specified in the notice.

(2) Where, after the land has been acquired as mentioned in sub-paragraph (1) above, development of the land is begun to be carried out, no notice under this paragraph shall be served later than 21 days after the beginning of the development.

(3) Where a notice is served under this paragraph the trust on which it is served may, before the end of the period of 28 days from the date of service, serve on the statutory undertakers a counter-notice stating that it objects to all or any of the provisions of the notice and specifying the grounds of its objection.

(4) If no counter-notice is served under sub-paragaph (3) above, the statutory undertakers shall, after the end of the said period of 28 days, have the rights claimed in their notice.

(5) If a counter-notice is served under sub-paragraph (3) above, the statutory undertakers who served the notice under this paragraph may either withdraw it or may apply to the Secretary of State and the appropriate Minister for an order under this paragraph conferring on the undertakers the rights claimed in the notice or such modified rights as the Secretary of State and the appropriate Minister think it expedient to confer on them.

(6) Where by virtue of this paragraph or an order of Ministers made under it, statutory undertakers have the right to execute works for the removal or re-siting of apparatus, they may arrange with the trust for the works to be carried out by the trust, under the superintendence of the undertakers, instead of by the undertakers themselves.

(7) Where works are carried out for the removal or re-siting of statutory undertakers' apparatus, being works which the undertakers have the right to carry out by virtue of this paragraph or an order of Ministers made under it, the undertakers shall be entitled to compensation from the trust.

(8) Sections 238 and 240 of the Town and Country Planning Act 1971 (measure of compensation to statutory undertakers) shall apply to compensation under sub-paragraph (7) above as they apply to compensation under section 237(3) of that Act.

(9) In sub-paragraph (1)(a) above, the reference to apparatus vested in or belonging to statutory undertakers shall include a reference to telecommunication apparatus kept installed for the purposes of a telecommunications code system.

(10) Where sub-paragraph (1)(a) above has effect as mentioned in sub-paragraph (9) above, in the rest of this paragraph—

(a) any reference to statutory undertakers shall have effect as a reference to the operator of any such system as is referred to in sub-paragraph (9) above; and

(b) any reference to the appropriate Minister shall have effect as a reference to the Secretary of State for Trade and Industry.

15.—(1) The powers conferred by this paragraph shall be exercisable where, on a representation made by statutory undertakers, it appears to the Secretary of State and the appropriate Minister to be expedient that the powers and duties of those undertakers should be extended or modified, in order—

(a) to secure the provision for a designated area of services which would not otherwise be provided, or which would not otherwise be satisfactorily provided; or

(b) to facilitate an adjustment of the carrying on of the undertaking necessitated by any of the acts and events mentioned in sub-paragraph (2) below.

(2) The said acts and events are—

(a) the acquisition under Part III of this Act of any land in which an interest was held, or which was used, for the purpose of the carrying on of the undertaking of the statutory undertakers in question; and

(b) the extinguishment of a right or the imposition of any requirements by virtue of paragraph 12 above.

(3) The powers conferred by this paragraph shall also be exercisable where, on a representation made by a housing action trust, it appears to the Secretary of State and the appropriate Minister to be expedient that the powers and duties of statutory undertakers should be extended or modified, in order to secure the provision of new services, or the

extension of existing services, for the purposes of a designated area under Part III of this Act.

(4) Where the powers conferred by this paragraph are exercisable, the Secretary of State and the appropriate Minister may, if they think fit, by order provide for such extension or modification of the powers and duties of the statutory undertakers as appears to them to be requisite in order to secure the provision of the services in question, as mentioned in sub-paragraph (1)(a) or sub-paragraph (3) above, or to secure the adjustment in question, as mentioned in sub-paragraph (1)(b) above, as the case may be.

(5) Without prejudice to the generality of sub-paragraph (4) above, an order under this paragraph may make provision—

(a) for empowering the statutory undertakers to acquire (whether compulsorily or by agreement) any land specified in the order, and to erect or construct any buildings or works so specified;

(b) for applying, in relation to the acquisition of any land or the construction of any such works, enactments relating to the acquisition of land and the construction of works;

(c) where it has been represented that the making of the order is expedient for the purposes mentioned in sub-paragraph (1)(a) or sub-paragraph (3) above, for giving effect to such financial arrangements between the housing action trust and the statutory undertakers as they may agree, or as, in default of agreement, may be determined to be equitable in such manner and by such tribunal as may be specified in the order; and

(d) for such incidental and supplemental matters as appear to the Secretary of State and the appropriate Minister to be expedient for the purposes of the order.

16.—(1) As soon as may be after making such a representation as is mentioned in sub-paragraph (1) or sub-paragraph (3) of paragraph 15 above—

(a) the statutory undertakers, in a case falling within sub-paragraph (1), or

(b) the housing action trust, in a case falling within sub-paragraph (3),

shall publish, in such form and manner as may be directed by the Secretary of State and the appropriate Minister, a notice giving such particulars as may be so directed of the matters to which representation relates, and specifying the time within which, and the manner in which, objections to the making of an order on the representation may be made, and shall also, if it is so directed by the Secretary of State and the appropriate Minister, serve a like notice on such persons, or persons of such classes, as may be so directed.

(2) Orders under paragraph 15 above shall be subject to special parliamentary procedure.

17.—(1) Where, on a representation made by statutory undertakers the appropriate Minister is satisfied that the fulfilment of any obligations incurred by those undertakers in connection with the carrying on of their undertaking has been rendered impracticable by an act or event to which this sub-paragraph applies, the appropriate Minister may, if he thinks fit, by order direct that the statutory undertakers shall be relieved of the fulfilment of that obligation, either absolutely or to such extent as may be specified in the order.

(2) Sub-paragraph (1) above applies to the following acts and events—

(a) the compulsory acquisition under this Part of this Act of any land in which an interest was held, or which was used, for the purpose of the carrying on of the undertaking of the statutory undertakers; and

(b) the extinguishment of a right or the imposition of any requirement by virtue of paragraph 12 above.

(3) As soon as may be after making a representation to the appropriate Minister under sub-paragraph (1) above, the appropriate statutory undertakers shall, as may be directed by the appropriate Minister, either publish (in such form and manner as may be so directed) a notice giving such particulars as may be so directed of the matters to which the representation relates, and specifying the time within which, and the manner in which, objections to the making of an order on the representation may be made, or serve such a notice on such persons, or persons of such classes, as may be so directed, or both publish and serve such notices.

(4) If any objection to the making of an order under this paragraph is duly made and is not withdrawn before the order is made, the order shall be subject to special parliamentary procedure.

(5) Immediately after an order is made under this paragraph by the appropriate Minister, he shall publish a notice stating that the order has been made and naming a place where a copy of it may be seen at all reasonable hours, and shall serve a like notice—

(a) on any person who duly made an objection to the order and has sent to the appropriate Minister a request in writing to serve him with the notice required by this sub-paragraph, specifying an address for service; and

(b) on such other persons (if any) as the appropriate Minister thinks fit.

(6) Subject to the following provisions of this paragraph, an order under this paragraph shall become operative on the date on which the notice required by sub-paragraph (5) above is first published.

(7) Where in accordance with sub-paragraph (4) above the order is subject to special parliamentary procedure, sub-paragraph (6) above shall not apply.

(8) If any person aggrieved by an order under this paragraph wishes to question the validity of the order on the ground that it is not within the powers conferred by this paragraph, or that any requirement of this paragraph has not been complied with in relation to the order, he may, within six weeks from the date on which the notice required by sub-paragraph (5) above is first published, make an application to the High Court under this paragraph.

(9) On any application under sub-paragraph (8) above the High Court—

  (a) may by interim order wholly or in part suspend the operation of the order, either generally or in so far as it affects any property of the applicant, until the final determination of the proceedings; and

  (b) if satisfied that the order is wholly or to any extent outside the powers conferred by this paragraph, or that the interests of the applicant have been substantially prejudiced by the failure to comply with any requirement of this paragraph, may wholly or in part quash the order, either generally or in so far as it affects any property of the applicant.

(10) Subject to sub-paragraph (8) above, the validity of an order under this paragraph shall not be questioned in any legal proceedings whatsoever, either before or after the order has been made.

18.—(1) For the purposes of paragraphs 15 and 17 above, an objection to the making of an order thereunder shall not be treated as duly made unless—

  (a) the objection is made within the time and in the manner specified in the notice required by paragraph 16 or (as the case may be) paragraph 17 above; and

  (b) a statement in writing of the grounds of the objection is comprised in or submitted with the objection.

(2) Where an objection to the making of such an order is duly made in accordance with sub-paragraph (1) above and is not withdrawn, the following provisions of this paragraph shall have effect in relation thereto; but, in the application of those provisions to an order under paragraph 15 above, any reference to the appropriate Minister shall be construed as a reference to the Secretary of State and the appropriate Minister.

(3) Unless the appropriate Minister decides apart from the objection not to make the order, or decides to make a modification which is agreed to by the objector as meeting the objection, the appropriate Minister, before making a final decision, shall consider the grounds of the objection as set out in the statement, and may, if he thinks fit, require the objector to submit within a specified period a further statement in writing as to any of the matters to which the objection relates.

(4) In so far as the appropriate Minister after considering the grounds of the objection as set out in the original statement and in any such further statement, is satisfied that the objection relates to a matter which can be dealt with in the assessment of compensation, the appropriate Minister may treat the objection as irrelevant for the purpose of making a final decision.

(5) If, after considering the grounds of the objection as set out in the original statement and in any such further statement, the appropriate Minister is satisfied that, for the purpose of making a final decision, he is sufficiently informed as to the matters to which the objection relates, or if, where a further statement has been required it is not submitted within the specified period, the appropriate Minister may make a final decision without further investigation as to those matters.

(6) Subject to sub-paragraphs (4) and (5) above, the appropriate Minister, before making a final decision, shall afford to the objector an opportunity of appearing before, and being heard by, a person appointed for the purpose by the appropriate Minister; and if the objector avails himself of that opportunity, the appropriate Minister shall afford an opportunity of appearing and being heard on the same occasion to the statutory undertakers, local authority or Minister on whose representation the order is proposed to be made, and to any other persons to whom it appears to the appropriate Minister to be expedient to afford such an opportunity.

(7) Notwithstanding anything in the preceding provisions of this paragraph, if it appears to the appropriate Minister that the matters to which the objection relates are such as to require investigation by public local inquiry before he makes a final decision, he shall cause such an inquiry to be held; and where he determines to cause such an inquiry to be held,

any of the requirements of those provisions to which effect has not been given at the time of that determination shall be dispensed with.

(8) In this paragraph any reference to making a final decision, in relation to an order, is a reference to deciding whether to make the order or what modification (if any) ought to be made.

Interpretation

19. Any expression used in this Part of the Schedule to which a meaning is assigned by paragraph 1 of Schedule 4 to the Telecommunications Act 1984 has that meaning in this part.

PART III

ACQUISITION OF RIGHTS

20.—(1) The Compulsory Purchase Act 1965 (in this Part of the Schedule referred to as "the 1965 Act") shall have effect with the modifications necessary to make it apply to the compulsory purchase of rights by virtue of section 77(5) of this Act as it applies to the compulsory purchase of land so that, in appropriate contexts, references in the 1965 Act to land are read as referring, or as including references, to the rights or to land over which the rights are or are to be exercisable, according to the requirements of the particular context.

(2) Without prejudice to the generality of sub-paragraph (1) above, in relation to the purchase of rights in pursuance of section 77(5) of this Act—

(a) Part I of the 1965 Act (which relates to compulsory purchases under the Acquisition of Land Act 1981) shall have effect with the modifications specified in paragraphs 21 to 23 below; and

(b) the enactments relating to compensation for the compulsory purchase of land shall apply with the necessary modifications as they apply to such compensation.

21.—(1) For section 7 of the 1965 Act (which relates to compensation) there shall be substituted the following—

"7.—(1) In assesssing the compensation to be paid by the acquiring authority under this Act regard shall be had not only to the extent, if any, to which the value of the land over which the right is purchased is depreciated by the purchase but also to the damage, if any, to be sustained by the owner of the land by reason of injurious affection of other land of the owner by the exercise of the right.

(2) The modifications subject to which subsection (1) of section 44 of the Land Compensation Act 1973 is to have effect, as applied by subsection (2) of that section to compensation for injurious affection under this section, are for the words "land is acquired or taken" there shall be substituted the words "a right over land is purchased" and for the words "acquired or taken from him" there shall be substituted the words "over which the right is excercisable"."

22. For section 8 of the 1965 Act (which relates to cases in which a vendor cannot be required to sell part only of a building or garden) there shall be substituted the following—

"8.—(1) Where in consequence of the service on a person in pursuance of section 5 of this Act of a notice to treat in respect of a right over land consisting of a house, building or manufactory or of a park or garden belonging to a house (hereafter in this subsection referred to as "the relevant land")—

(a) a question of disputed compensation in respect of the purchase of the right would apart from this section fall to be determined by the Lands Tribunal (hereafter in this section referred to as "the Tribunal"); and

(b) before the Tribunal has determined that question the person satisfies the Tribunal that he has an interest which he is able and willing to sell in the whole of the relevant land and—

(i) where that land consists of a house, building or manufactory, that the right cannot be purchased without material detriment to that land, or

(ii) where that land consists of such a park or garden, that the right cannot be purchased without seriously affecting the amenity or convenience of the house to which that land belongs,

the compulsory purchase order to which the notice to treat relates shall, in relation to that person, cease to authorise the purchase of the right and be deemed to authorise the purchase of that person's interest in the whole of the relevant land including, where the land consists of such a park or garden, the house to which it belongs, and the notice shall be deemed to have been served in respect of that interest on such date as the Tribunal directs.

(2) Any question as to the extent of the land in which a compulsory purchase order is deemed to authorise the purchase of an interest by virtue of the preceding subsection shall be determined by the Tribunal.

(3) Where in consequence of a determination of the Tribunal that it is satisfied as mentioned in subsection (1) of this section a compulsory purchase order is deemed by virtue of that subsection to authorise the purchase of an interest in land, the acquiring authority may, at any time within the period of six weeks beginning with the date of the determination, withdraw the notice to treat in consequence of which the determination was made; but nothing in this subsection prejudices any other power of the authority to withdraw the notice.

(4) The modifications subject to which subsection (1) of section 58 of the Land Compensation Act 1973 is to have effect, as applied by subsection (2) of that section to the duty of the Tribunal in determining whether it is satisfied as mentioned in subsection (1) of this section, are that at the beginning of paragraphs (a) and (b) there shall be inserted the words "a right over", for the word "severance" there shall be substituted the words "right on the whole of the house, building or manufactory or of the house and the park or garden" and for the words "part proposed" and "part is" there shall be substituted respectively the words "right proposed" and "right is"."

23.—(1)The following provisions of the 1965 Act (which state the effect of a deed poll executed in various circumstances where there is no conveyance by persons with interests in the land), namely—

    section 9(4) (failure of owners to convey),
    paragraph 10(3) of Schedule 1 (owners under incapacity),
    paragraph 2(3) of Schedule 2 (absent and untraced owners), and
    paragraphs 2(3) and 7(2) of Schedule 4 (common land),

shall be so modified as to secure that, as against persons with interests in the land which are expressed to be overridden by the deed, the right which is to be purchased compulsorily is vested absolutely in the acquiring authority.

(2) Section 11 of the 1965 Act (powers of entry) shall be so modified as to secure that, as from the date on which the acquiring authority has served notice to treat in respect of any right, it has power, exercisable in the like circumstances and subject to the like conditions, to enter for the purpose of exercising that right (which shall be deemed for this purpose to have been created on the date of service of the notice); and sections 12 (penalty for unauthorised entry) and 13 (entry on sheriff's warrant in the event of obstruction) of the Act shall be modified correspondingly.

(3) Section 20 of the 1965 Act (compensation for short-term tenants) shall apply with the modifications necessary to secure that persons with such interests as are mentioned in that section are compensated in a manner corresponding to that in which they would be compensated on a compulsory acquisition of the interests but taking into account only the extent (if any) of such interference with such interests as is actually caused, or likely to be caused, by the exercise of the right in question.

(4) Section 22 of the 1965 Act (protection of acquiring authority's possession of land where by inadvertence an interest in the land has not been purchased) shall be so modified as to enable the acquiring authority, in circumstances corresponding to those referred to in that section, to continue to be entitled to exercise the right in question, subject to compliance with that section as respects compensation.

GENERAL NOTE
    See notes to s.78, above.

Section 79(13)   SCHEDULE 11

PROVISIONS APPLICABLE TO CERTAIN DISPOSALS OF HOUSES

Repayment of discount on early disposal

1.—(1) This paragraph applies where, on the disposal of a house under section 79 of this Act, a discount is given to the purchaser by the housing action trust in accordance with a consent given by the Secretary of State under subsection (1) of that section and that consent does not exclude the application of this paragraph.

(2) On the disposal, the conveyance, grant or assignment shall contain a covenant binding on the purchaser and his successors in title to pay to the housing action trust on demand, if

within a period of three years there is a relevant disposal which is not an exempted disposal (but if there is more than one such disposal then only on the first of them), an amount equal to the discount, reduced by one-third for each complete year which has elapsed after the conveyance, grant or assignment and before the further disposal.

Obligation to repay a charge on the house

2.—(1) The liability that may arise under the covenant required by paragraph 1 above is a charge on the house, taking effect as if it had been created by deed expressed to be by way of legal mortgage.

(2) The charge has priority immediately after any legal charge securing an amount—

    (a) left outstanding by the purchaser; or

    (b) advanced to him by an approved lending institution for the purpose of enabling him to acquire the interest disposed of on the first disposal; or

    (c) further advanced to him by that institution;

but the housing action trust may at any time by written notice served on an approved lending institution postpone the charge taking effect by virtue of this paragraph to a legal charge securing an amount advanced or further advanced to the purchaser by that institution.

(3) A charge taking effect by virtue of this paragraph is a land charge for the purposes of section 59 of the Land Registration Act 1925 notwithstanding subsection (5) of that section (exclusion of mortgages), and subsection (2) of that section applies accordingly with respect to its protection and realisation.

(4) The covenant required by paragraph 1 above does not, by virtue of its binding successors in title of the purchaser, bind a person exercising rights under a charge having priority over the charge taking effect by virtue of this paragraph, or a person deriving title under him; and a provision of the conveyance, grant or assignment, or of a collateral agreement, is void in so far as it purports to authorise a forfeiture, or to impose a penalty or disability, in the event of any such person failing to comply with the covenant.

(5) The approved lending institutions for the purposes of this paragraph are—

    (a) a building society;

    (b) a bank;

    (c) an insurance company;

    (d) a friendly society; and

    (e) any body specified, or of a class or description specified, in an order made under section 156 of the Housing Act 1985 (which makes provision in relation to disposals in pursuance of the right to buy corresponding to that made by this paragraph).

Relevant disposals

3.—(1) A disposal, whether of the whole or part of the house, is a relevant disposal for the purpose of this Schedule if it is—

    (a) a conveyance of the freehold or an assignment of the lease; or

    (b) the grant of a lease or sub-lease (other than a mortgage term) for a term of more than 21 years otherwise than at a rack rent.

(2) For the purposes of sub-paragraph (1)(b) above it shall be assumed—

    (a) that any option to renew or extend a lease or sub-lease, whether or not forming part of a series of options, is exercised; and

    (b) that any option to terminate a lease or sub-lease is not exercised.

Exempted disposals

4.—(1) A disposal is an exempted disposal for the purposes of this Schedule if—

    (a) it is a disposal of the whole of the house and a conveyance of the freehold or an assignment of the lease and the person or each of the persons to whom it is made is a qualifying person (as defined in sub-paragraph (2) below);

    (b) it is a vesting of the whole of the house in a person taking under a will or on an intestacy;

    (c) it is a disposal of the whole of the house in pursuance of an order made under section 24 of the Matrimonial Causes Act 1973 (property adjustment orders in connection with matrimonial proceedings) or section 2 of the Inheritance (Provision for Family and Dependants) Act 1975 (orders as to financial provision to be made from estate);

    (d) it is a compulsory disposal; or

(e) the property disposed of is property included with the house as being such a yard, garden, outhouse or appurtenance as is referred to in section 92(1)(b) of this Act.

(2) For the purposes of sub-paragraph (1)(a) above, a person is a qualifying person in relation to a disposal if—

(a) he is the person or one of the persons by whom the disposal is made;

(b) he is the spouse or a former spouse of that person or one of those persons; or

(c) he is a member of the family of that person or one of those persons and has resided with him throughout the period of twelve months ending with the disposal.

(3) Section 186 of the Housing Act 1985 applies to determine whether a person is a member of another person's family for the purposes of sub-paragraph (2)(c) above.

Compulsory disposal

5. In this Schedule a "compulsory disposal" means a disposal of property which is acquired compulsorily, or is acquired by a person who has made or would have made, or for whom another person has made or would have made, a compulsory purchase order authorising its compulsory purchase for the purposes for which it is acquired.

Exempted disposals ending obligation under covenants

6. Where there is a relevant disposal which is an exempted disposal by virtue of paragraph 4(1)(d) or paragraph 4(1)(e) above—

(a) the covenant required by paragraph 1 above is not binding on the person to whom the disposal is made or any successor in title of his; and

(b) that covenant and the charge taking effect by virtue of paragraph 2 above cease to apply in relation to the property disposed of.

Treatment of options

7. For the purpose of this Schedule, the grant of an option enabling a person to call for a relevant disposal which is not an exempted disposal shall be treated as such a disposal made to him.

GENERAL NOTE
See notes to s.79, above.

Section 108   SCHEDULE 12

REGISTRATION OF TITLE AND RELATED MATTERS

Interpretation

1. In this Schedule—

"transferred property" means property which is the subject of a grant under section 104(1)(a) of this Act;

"transferee", in relation to any transferred property, means the person to whom the grant is made;

"conveyance" means the instrument by which the grant is effected; and

other expressions have the same meaning as in section 104 of this Act.

Acquisitions under section 104(1)(a)

2.—(1) Where, a landlord makes a grant of transferred property, it shall ensure—

(a) that the conveyance contains a statement that the grant is made under section 104(1)(a) of this Act; and

(b) that all deeds and other documents relating to land (including, in the case of registered land, the land certificate) which are in its possession or under its control and which the transferee reasonably requires on or in connection with the grant of the transferred property are made available to him for this purpose.

(2) Where the landlord's title to the whole or any part of the transferred property is not registered—

(a) section 123 of the Land Registration Act 1925 (compulsory registration of title) applies in relation to the conveyance whether or not the transferred property is in an area in which an Order in Council under section 120 of that Act (areas of compulsory registration) is in force; and

(b) the landlord shall give the transferee a certificate stating that it is entitled to convey the freehold subject only to such incumbrances, rights and interests as are stated in the conveyance or summarised in the certificate.

(3) The Chief Land Registrar shall, for the purpose of the registration of title, accept such a certificate as is referred to in sub-paragraph (2)(b) above as sufficient evidence of the facts stated in it; but if as a result he has to meet a claim under the Land Registration Acts 1925 to 1986 the landlord is liable to indemnify him.

(4) On an application being made for registration of a disposition of registered land or, as the case may be, of the transferee's title under a disposition of unregistered land, the Chief Land Registrar shall, if the conveyance contains the statement required by sub-paragraph (1)(a) above, enter in the register a restriction stating the requirement under section 105 of this Act of consent to subsequent disposals.

(5) Any reference in the preceding provisions of this paragraph to a statement or a certificate is a reference to a statement or, as the case may be, certificate in a form approved by the Chief Land Registrar.

Procedures on termination of leases granted under section 104(1)(b)

3.—(1) If a lease granted under section 104(1)(b) of this Act comes to an end in such circumstances as may be prescribed, the public sector landlord which was the lessee under the lease shall, at such time as may be prescribed, furnish to the Chief Land Registrar such statement as may be prescribed.

(2) In any case where—

(a) under section 104(1)(b) of this Act the applicant has granted a lease of a flat (in this sub-paragraph referred to as "the landlord's lease"), and

(b) under Part V of the Housing Act 1985 (the right to buy) a lease of the flat (in this sub-paragraph referred to as "the right to buy lease") has been granted to a qualifying tenant, and

(c) by virtue of requirements prescribed under section 104(2) of this Act and related to the grant of the right to buy lease, the landlord's lease comes to an end,

then, notwithstanding anything in section 64 of the Land Registration Act 1925 (production of land certificate), notice of the grant of the right to buy lease may be entered in the register without production of the applicant's land certificate, but without prejudice to the power of the Chief Land Registrar to compel production of the certificate.

GENERAL NOTE

This Schedule contains provisions governing registration, ancillary to transfers under Part IV, above.

Section 119   SCHEDULE 13

AMENDMENTS OF LANDLORD AND TENANT ACT 1987

1. In Part I of the Landlord and Tenant Act 1987 (tenants' rights of first refusal), in section 2 (landlords for the purposes of Part I), in subsection (1) after "(2)" there shall be inserted "and section 4(1A)".

2.—(1) In section 3 of that Act (qualifying tenants), in subsection (1) (paragraphs (a) to (c) of which exclude certain tenants) the word "or" immediately preceding paragraph (c) shall be omitted and at the end of that paragraph there shall be added "or

(d) an assured tenancy or assured agricultural occupancy within the meaning of Part I of the Housing Act 1988".

(2) In subsection (2) of that section (which excludes persons having interests going beyond a particular flat), for paragraphs (a) and (b) there shall be substituted the words "by virtue of one or more tenancies none of which falls within paragraphs (a) to (d) of subsection (1), he is the tenant not only of the flat in question but also of at least two other flats contained in those premises"; and in subsection (3) of that section for "(2)(b)" there shall be substituted "(2)".

3.—(1) In section 4 of that Act (relevant disposals) after subsection (1) there shall be inserted the following subsection—

"(1A) Where an estate or interest of the landlord has been mortgaged, the reference in subsection (1) above to the disposal of an estate or interest by the

landlord includes a reference to its disposal by the mortgagee in exercise of a power
of sale or leasing, whether or not the disposal is made in the name of the landlord;
and, in relation to such a proposed disposal by the mortgagee, any reference in the
following provisions of this Part to the landlord shall be construed as a reference to
the mortgagee."

(2) In subsection (2) of that section, in paragraph (a), at the end of sub-paragraph (i)
there shall be inserted "or", sub-paragraph (ii) shall be omitted and at the end of that
paragraph there shall be inserted—

"(aa) a disposal consisting of the creation of an estate or interest by way of security
for a loan".

4.—(1) In Part III of that Act (compulsory acquisition by tenants of their landlord's
interest), in section 26 (qualifying tenants), in subsection (2) (which excludes persons having
interests going beyond a particular flat) for the words following "if" there shall be substituted
"by virtue of one or more long leases none of which constitutes a tenancy to which Part II
of the Landlord and Tenant Act 1954 applies, he is the tenant not only of the flat in question
but also of at least two other flats contained in those premises".

(2) At the end of the said section 26 there shall be added the following subsection—

"(4) For the purposes of subsection (2) any tenant of a flat contained in the premises
in question who is a body corporate shall be treated as the tenant of any other flat so
contained and let to an associated company, as defined in section 20(1)."

5. In Part IV of that Act (variation of leases), for subsections (6) and (7) of section 35
(which make provision about long leases) there shall be substituted the following
subsections—

"(6) For the purposes of this Part a long lease shall not be regarded as a long lease
of a flat if—

(a) the demised premises consist of or include three or more flats contained in the
same building; or

(b) the lease constitutes a tenancy to which Part II of the Landlord and Tenant Act
1954 applies."

6. In section 40 (application for variation of insurance provisions of lease of dwelling
other than a flat) for subsection (4) (which makes provision about long leases) there shall be
substituted the following subsections—

"(4) For the purpose of this section, a long lease shall not be regarded as a long lease
of a dwelling if—

(a) the demised premises consist of three or more dwellings; or

(b) the lease constitutes a tenancy to which Part II of the Landlord and Tenant Act
1954 applies.

(4A) Without prejudice to subsection (4), an application under subsection (1) may
not be made by a person who is a tenant under a long lease of a dwelling if, by virtue
of that lease and one or more other long leases of dwellings, he is also a tenant from
the same landlord of at least two other dwellings.

(4B) For the purposes of subsection (4A), any tenant of a dwelling who is a body
corporate shall be treated as a tenant of any other dwelling held from the same
landlord which is let under a long lease to an associated company, as defined in
section 20(1)."

7. In Part VII of that Act (general) in section 58 (exempt landlords), in subsection (1)
after paragraph (c) there shall be inserted the following paragraph—

"(ca) a housing action trust established under Part III of the Housing Act 1988."

GENERAL NOTE

The Landlord and Tenant Act 1987 introduced a number of provisions: Part I created a
"right of first refusal" whereby a landlord proposing to dispose of a building containing at
least two flats is bound to offer it to defined classes of tenant; Part II codified the power of
the court to appoint a manager where the landlord is in default of his obligations, as defined;
Part III creates a right on the part of "qualifying tenants" to purchase the landlord's interest,
notwithstanding that the landlord is not offering the premises for sale, essentially contingent
upon the same circumstances that permit the tenants to apply to the court for the
appointment of a manager. Part IV provides for application for variation of leases; Part V
makes a number of amendments to service charge and other management provisions; Part
VI governs "information to be furnished to tenants".

By *paras. 1 and 3*, the right of first refusal is extended to the case where the landlord's
interest has been mortgaged, where the mortgagee is exercising a power of sale or leasing,
even in its own name: the mortgagee is, accordingly, bound by Part I of the 1987 Act. But

a disposal in connection with the creation of a mortgage or charge is not itself a disposal giving rise to the right of first refusal.

By *para. 2,* however, assured tenants and agricultural occupants under Part I of this Act are excluded from the right of first refusal.

By *para. 4,* a tenant of at least three flats under a long lease is disqualified from the provisions of Part III enabling "compulsory purchase" to be initiated by the tenants.

By *paras. 5 and 6,* such tenants cannot apply to the court for a variation of the terms of the lease under Part IV. Leases which qualify under the Landlord and Tenant Act 1954, Part II (business tenancies—*cf.* notes to Sched. 1, para. 4, above) are similarly excluded from both Parts III and 1V, to an extent by the Act as unamended, and in part consequent upon these amendments.

By *para. 7,* housing action trusts are, like other public bodies, wholly exempt from a number of provisions in the Act, including the right of first refusal, application for appointment of manager and "compulsory purchase" initiated by tenants.

Section 120   SCHEDULE 14

Appointment etc. of Rent Officers

Part I

Amendments of Section 63 of Rent Act 1977

1. In subsection (1), paragraph (b) and the word "and" immediately preceding it shall be omitted.
2. In subsection (2)—
    (a) in paragraph (a) the words "and deputy rent officers" shall be omitted;
    (b) in paragraph (b) the words "or deputy rent officer" shall be omitted;
    (c) in paragraph (d) the words "and deputy rent officers" and the word "and" at the end of the paragraph shall be omitted; and
    (d) paragraph (e) shall be omitted.
3. After subsection (2) there shall be inserted the following subsection—
    "(2A) A scheme under this section may make all or any of the following provisions—
    (a) provision requiring the consent of the Secretary of State to the appointment of rent officers;
    (b) provision with respect to the appointment of rent officers for fixed periods;
    (c) provision for the proper officer of the local authority, in such circumstances and subject to such conditions (as to consent or otherwise) as may be specified in the scheme,—
        (i) to designate a person appointed or to be appointed a rent officer as chief rent officer and to designate one or more such persons as senior rent officers;
        (ii) to delegate to a person so designated as chief rent officer such functions as may be specified in the scheme; and
        (iii) to revoke a designation under sub-paragraph (i) above and to revoke or vary a delegation under sub-paragraph (ii) above;
    (d) provision with respect to the delegation of functions by a chief rent officer to other rent officers (whether designated as senior rent officers or not);
    (e) provision as to the circumstances in which and the terms on which a rent officer appointed by the scheme may undertake functions outside the area to which the scheme relates in accordance with paragraph (f) below;
    (f) provision under which a rent officer appointed for an area other than that to which the scheme relates may undertake functions in the area to which the scheme relates and for such a rent officer to be treated for such purposes as may be specified in the scheme (which may include the purposes of paragraphs (c) and (d) above and paragraph (c) and (d) of subsection (2) above) as if he were a rent officer appointed under the scheme; and
    (g) provision conferring functions on the proper officer of a local authority with respect to the matters referred to in paragraphs (d) to (f) above."
4. In subsection (3) the words "and deputy rent officers" shall be omitted.
5. In subsection (7)—
    (a) in paragraph (b) the words "and deputy rent officers" shall be omitted, after the words "section 7" there shall be inserted "or section 24" and for the words following "1972" there shall be substituted "or"; and

(b) at the end of paragraph (b) there shall be inserted the following paragraph—
    "(c) incurred in respect of increases of pensions payable to or in respect of rent officers (so appointed) by virtue of the Pensions (Increase) Act 1971".

PART II

SECTIONS TO BE INSERTED IN RENT ACT 1977 AFTER SECTION 64

"Amalgamation schemes

64A.—(1) If the Secretary of State is of the opinion—
    (a) that there is at any time insufficient work in two or more registration areas to justify the existence of a separate service of rent officers for each area, or
    (b) that it would at any time be beneficial for the efficient administration of the service provided by rent officers in two or more registration areas,
he may, after consultation with the local authorities concerned, make a scheme under section 63 above designating as an amalgamated registration area the areas of those authorities and making provision accordingly for that amalgamated area.

(2) Any reference in the following provisions of this Chapter to a registration area includes a reference to an amalgamated registration area and, in relation to such an area, "the constituent authorities" means the local authorities whose areas make up the amalgamated area.

(3) A scheme under section 63 above made for an amalgamated registration area—
    (a) shall confer on the proper officer of one of the constituent authorities all or any of the functions which, in accordance with section 63 above, fall to be exercisable by the proper officer of the local authority for the registration area;
    (b) may provide that any rent officer previously appointed for the area of any one of the constituent authorities shall be treated for such purposes as may be specified in the scheme as a rent officer appointed for the amalgamated registration area; and
    (c) shall make such provision as appears to the Secretary of State to be appropriate for the payment by one or more of the constituent authorities of the remunerations, allowances and other expenditure which under section 63 above is to be paid by the local authority for the area.

(4) A scheme under section 63 above made for an amalgamated registration area may contain such incidental, transitional and supplementary provisions as appear to the Secretary of State to be necessary or expedient.

New basis for administration of rent officer service

64B.—(1) If, with respect to registration areas generally or any particular registration area or areas, it appears to the Secretary of State that it is no longer appropriate for the appointment, remuneration and administration of rent officers to be a function of local authorities, he may by order—
    (a) provide that no scheme under section 63 above shall be made for the area or areas specified in the order; and
    (b) make, with respect to the area or areas so specified, such provision as appears to him to be appropriate with respect to the appointment, remuneration and administration of rent officers and the payment of pensions, allowances or gratuities to or in respect of them.

(2) An order under this section shall make provision for any expenditure attributable to the provisions of the order to be met by the Secretary of State in such manner as may be specified in the order (whether by way of grant, reimbursement or otherwise); and any expenditure incurred by the Secretary of State by virtue of this subsection shall be paid out of money provided by Parliament.

(3) An order under this section—
    (a) may contain such incidental, transitional and supplementary provisions as appear to the Secretary of State to be appropriate, including provisions amending this Part of this Act; and
    (b) shall be made by statutory instrument which shall be subject to annulment in pursuance of a resolution of either House of Parliament."

Housing Act 1988

Section 130   SCHEDULE 15

REPAIR NOTICES: AMENDMENTS OF HOUSING ACT 1985, PART VI

1.—(1) In section 189 (repair notice in respect of unfit house), in subsection (1)—
  (a) at the beginning there shall be inserted the words "Subject to subsection (1A)"; and
  (b) for the word "house", in each place where it occurs, there shall be substituted "dwelling-house".

(2) At the end of subsection (1) of that section there shall be inserted the following subsection—
  "(1A) Where the local housing authority are satisfied that a dwelling-house which is a flat is unfit for human habitation by reason of the defective condition of a part of the building outside the flat, they shall serve a repair notice on the person having control of that part of the building, unless they are satisfied that the works which would be required to that part are such that the flat is not capable of being rendered so fit at reasonable expense."

(3) In subsection (2) of that section—
  (a) in paragraph (a) for the words from "within such reasonable time" onwards there shall be substituted the words "and to begin those works not later than such reasonable date, being not earlier than the seventh day after the notice becomes operative, as is specified in the notice and to complete those works within such reasonable time as is so specified, and"; and
  (b) in paragraph (b) for the word "house" there shall be substituted "dwelling-house".

(4) In subsection (3) of that section for the words "the house", in each place where they occur, there shall be substituted "the dwelling-house or part of the building concerned", for the word "may" there shall be substituted "shall" and for the words "lessee or otherwise" there shall be substituted "or lessee".

(5) At the end of that section there shall be added the following subsection—
  "(5) A repair notice under this section which has become operative is a local land charge."

2.—(1) In section 190 (repair notice in respect of house in state of disrepair, but not unfit), in subsection (1),—
  (a) for the word "house", in each place where it occurs, there shall be substituted "dwelling-house";
  (b) in paragraph (b), after the word "satisfied" there shall be inserted "whether" and after the word "tenant", in the first place where it occurs, there shall be inserted "or otherwise".

(2) At the end of subsection (1) of that section there shall be inserted the following subsection—
  "(1A) Where the local housing authority—
    (a) are satisfied that a building containing a flat is in such a state of disrepair that, although the flat is not unfit for human habitation, substantial repairs are necessary to a part of the building outside the flat to bring the flat up to a reasonable standard, having regard to its age, character and locality, or
    (b) are satisfied, whether on a representation made by an occupying tenant or otherwise, that a building containing a flat is in such a state of disrepair that, although the flat is not unfit for human habitation, the condition of a part of the building outside the flat is such as to interfere materially with the personal comfort of the occupying tenant,
  they may serve a repair notice on the person having control of the part of the building concerned."

(3) In subsection (2) of that section for the words from "within such reasonable time" onwards there shall be substituted "to execute the works specified in the notice, not being works of internal decorative repair, and—
  (a) to begin those works not later than such reasonable date, being not earlier than the seventh day after the notice becomes operative, as is specified in the notice; and
  (b) to complete those works within such reasonable time as is so specified."

(4) In subsection (3) of that section for the words "the house", in each place where they occur, there shall be substituted "the dwelling-house or part of the building concerned", for the word "may" there shall be substituted "shall" and for the words "lessee or otherwise" there shall be substituted "or lessee".

(5) At the end of that section there shall be added the following subsection—

"(5) A repair notice under this section which has become operative is a local land charge."

3.—(1) In section 191 (appeals against repair notices), after subsection (1) there shall be inserted the following subsection—

"(1A) Without prejudice to the generality of subsection (1), it shall be a ground of appeal that some person other than the appellant, being a person who is an owner in relation to the dwelling-house or part of the building concerned, ought to execute the works or pay the whole or part of the cost of executing them."

(2) In subsection (3) of that section for the words "the house" there shall be substituted "the dwelling-house".

(3) After subsection (3) of that section there shall be inserted the following subsections—

"(3A) Where the grounds on which an appeal is brought are or include that specified in subsection (1A), the appellant shall serve a copy of his notice of appeal on each other person referred to; and on the hearing of the appeal the court may—

(a) vary the repair notice so as to require the works to be executed by any such other person; or

(b) make such order as it thinks fit with respect to the payment to be made by any such other person to the appellant or, where the works are executed by the local housing authority, to the authority.

(3B) In the exercise of its powers under subsection (3A), the court shall take into account, as between the appellant and any such other person as is referred to in that subsection,—

(a) their relative interests in the dwelling-house or part of the building concerned (considering both the nature of the interests and the rights and obligations arising under or by virtue of them);

(b) their relative responsibility for the state of the dwelling-house or building which gives rise to the need for the execution of the works; and

(c) the relative degree of benefit to be derived from the execution of the works.

(3C) If, by virtue of the exercise of the court's powers under subsection (3A), a person other than the appellant is required to execute the works specified in a repair notice, then, so long as that other person continues to be an owner in relation to the premises to which the notice relates, he shall be regarded as the person having control of those premises for the purposes of the following provisions of this Part."

4.—(1) In section 192 (power to purchase houses found on appeal to be unfit etc.), in subsections (1) and (2) for the words "the house", in each place where they occur, there shall be substituted "the dwelling-house".

(2) In subsection (3) of that section for the words "the house" there shall be substituted "the dwelling-house or part of the building in question".

(3) In subsection (4) of that section for the words "the house" there shall be substituted "the dwelling-house".

5.—(1) In section 193 (power of local housing authority to execute works) for subsection (2) there shall be substituted the following subsections—

"(2) For the purpose of this Part compliance with the notice means beginning and completing the works specified in the notice,—

(a) if no appeal is brought against the notice, not later than such date and within such period as is specified in the notice;

(b) if an appeal is brought against the notice and is not withdrawn, not later than such date and within such period as may be fixed by the court determining the appeal; and

(c) if an appeal brought against the notice is withdrawn, not later than the twenty-first day after the date on which the notice becomes operative and within such period (beginning on that twenty-first day) as is specified in the notice.

(2A) If, before the expiry of the period which under subsection (2) is appropriate for completion of the works specified in the notice, it appears to the local housing authority that reasonable progress is not being made towards compliance with the notice, the authority may themselves do the work required to be done by the notice."

(2) At the end of that section there shall be added the following subsection—

"(4) If, after the local housing authority have given notice under section 194 of their intention to enter and do any works, the works are in fact carried out by the person having control of the dwelling-house or part of the building in question, any administrative and other expenses incurred by the authority with a view to doing the works themselves shall be treated for the purposes of Schedule 10 as expenses incurred by them under this section in carrying out works in default of the person on whom the repair notice was served."

6.—(1) In section 194 (notice of authority's intention to execute works), in subsection (1)—

(a) for the words "a house" there shall be substituted "any premises";

(b) for the word "may" there shall be substituted "shall"; and

(c) for the words "the house", in each place where they occur, there shall be substituted "the premises".

(2) In subsection (2) of that section for the words "the house", in each place where they occur, there shall be substituted "the premises".

7. In section 198 (penalty for obstruction), in subsection (2) for the words "level 2" there shall be substituted "level 3".

8. After section 198 there shall be inserted the following section—

"Penalty for failure to execute works

198A.—(1) A person having control of premises to which a repair notice relates who intentionally fails to comply with the notice commits a summary offence and is liable on conviction to a fine not exceeding level 4 on the standard scale.

(2) The obligation to execute the works specified in the notice continues notwithstanding that the period for completion of the works has expired.

(3) Section 193(2) shall have effect to determine whether a person has failed to comply with a notice and what is the period for completion of any works.

(4) The provisions of this section are without prejudice to the exercise by the local housing authority of the powers conferred by the preceding provisions of this Part."

9. Sections 199 to 201 (recovery by lessee of proportion of works and provisions as to charging orders) shall cease to have effect.

10. In section 203 (saving for rights arising from breach of covenant, etc.), in subsection (3) for the words "a house" there shall be substituted "any premises".

11. In section 205 (application of provisions to parts of buildings and temporary or movable structures) paragraph (a) shall be omitted and for the word "house" there shall be substituted "dwelling-house".

12.—(1) In section 207 (definitions)—

(a) for the definition beginning "house" there shall be substituted—

" "dwelling-house" and "flat" shall be construed in accordance with subsection (2) and "the building", in relation to a flat, means the building containing the flat";

(b) in the definition of "person having control" for the words "in relation to premises" there shall be substituted "subject to section 191(3A),—

(a) in relation to a dwelling-house";

(c) at the end of that definition there shall be added "and

(b) in relation to a part of a building to which relates a repair notice served under subsection (1A) of section 189 or section 190, means a person who is an owner in relation to that part of the building (or the building as a whole) and who, in the opinion of the authority by whom the notice is served, ought to execute the works specified in the notice"; and

(d) after the definition of "person having control" there shall be inserted—

" "premises" includes a dwelling-house or part of a building and, in relation to any premises, any reference to a person having control shall be construed accordingly".

(2) At the end of that section there shall be inserted the following subsection—

"(2) For the purposes of this Part a "dwelling-house" includes any yard, garden, outhouses and appurtenances belonging to it or usually enjoyed with it and section 183 shall have effect to determine whether a dwelling-house is a flat."

13.—(1) In Schedule 10 (recovery of expenses incurred by local housing authority), in paragraph 2, in sub-paragraph (1) for the words following "authority" there shall be substituted—

"(a) where the works were required by a notice under section 189 or section 190 (repair notices), from the person having control of the dwelling-house or part of the building to which the notice relates; and

(b) in any other case, from the person on whom the notice was served;

and in the following provisions of this paragraph the person from whom expenses are recoverable by virtue of this sub-paragraph is referred to as "the person primarily liable"."

(2) In sub-paragraphs (2) and (3) of paragraph 2 of that Schedule for the words "on whom the notice was served", in each place where they occur, there shall be substituted "primarily liable".

(3) In paragraph 6 of that Schedule (appeals) after sub-paragraph (1) there shall be inserted the following sub-paragraph—

"(1A) Where the demand for recovery of expenses relates to works carried out by virtue of section 193(2A), it shall be a ground of appeal that, at the time the local housing authority gave notice under section 194 of their intention to enter and do the works, reasonable progress was being made towards compliance with the repair notice."

GENERAL NOTE
See notes to s.130, above.

Section 135   SCHEDULE 16

SCHEDULE TO BE INSERTED IN THE HOUSING (SCOTLAND) ACT 1987

"SCHEDULE 6A

CONSULTATION BEFORE DISPOSAL TO PRIVATE SECTOR LANDLORD

Disposals to which this Schedule applies

1.—(1) This Schedule applies to the disposal by a local authority of an interest in land as a result of which a secure tenant of the local authority will become the tenant of a private sector landlord.

(2) For the purposes of this Schedule the grant of an option which if exercised would result in a secure tenant of a local authority becoming the tenant of a private sector landlord shall be treated as a disposal of the interest which is the subject of the option.

(3) Where a disposal of land by a local authority is in part a disposal to which this Schedule applies, the provisions of this Schedule apply to that part as to a separate disposal.

(4) In this paragraph "private sector landlord" means a person other than one of those set out in sub-paragraphs (i) to (iv) and (viii) and (ix) of paragraph (a) of subsection (2) of section 61.

Application for Secretary of State's consent

2.—(1) The Secretary of State shall not entertain an application for his consent under section 12(7) to a disposal to which this Schedule applies unless the local authority certify either—

  (a) that the requirements of paragraph 3 as to consultation have been complied with, or

  (b) that the requirements of that paragraph as to consultation have been complied with except in relation to tenants expected to have vacated the house in question before the disposal;

and the certificate shall be accompanied by a copy of the notices given by the local authority in accordance with that paragraph.

(2) Where the certificate is in the latter form, the Secretary of State shall not determine the application until the local authority certify as regards the tenants not originally consulted—

  (a) that they have vacated the house in question, or

  (b) that the requirements of paragraph 3 as to consultation have been complied with;

and a certificate under sub-paragraph (b) shall be accompanied by a copy of the notices given by the local authority in accordance with paragraph 3.

Requirements as to consultation

3.—(1) The requirements as to consultation referred to above are as follows.

(2) The local authority shall serve notice in writing on the tenant informing him of—

  (a) such details of their proposal as the local authority consider appropriate, but including the identity of the person to whom the disposal is to be made,

  (b) the likely consequences of the disposal for the tenant, and

(c) the effect of section 81A and the provision made under it (preservation of right to buy on disposal to private sector landlord) and of this Schedule,

and informing him that he may, within such reasonable period as may be specified in the notice, which must be at least 28 days after the service of the notice, make representations to the local authority.

(3) The local authority shall consider any representations made to them within that period and shall serve a further written notice on the tenant informing him—

(a) of any significant changes in their proposal, and

(b) that he may within such period as is specified (which must be at least 28 days after the service of the notice) communicate to the Secretary of State his objection to the proposal,

and informing him of the effect of paragraph 5 (consent to be withheld if majority of tenants are opposed).

Power to require further consultation

4. The Secretary of State may require the local authority to carry out such further consultation with their tenants, and to give him such information as to the results of that consultation, as he may direct.

Consent to be withheld if majority of tenants are opposed

5.—(1) The Secretary of State shall not give his consent if it appears to him that a majority of the tenants of the houses to which the application relates do not wish the disposal to proceed; but this does not affect his general discretion to refuse consent on grounds relating to whether a disposal has the support of the tenants or on any other ground.

(2) In making his decision the Secretary of State may have regard to any information available to him; and the local authority shall give him such information as to the representations made to them by tenants and others, and other relevant matters, as he may require.

Protection of purchasers

6. The Secretary of State's consent to a disposal is not invalidated by a failure on his part or that of the local authority to comply with the requirements of this Schedule."

Section 140 SCHEDULE 17

Minor and Consequential Amendments

Part I

General Amendments

The Reserve and Auxiliary Forces (Protection of Civil Interests) Act 1951

1. In section 4 of the Reserve and Auxiliary Forces (Protection of Civil Interests) Act 1951 (recovery of possession of dwelling-houses in default of payment of rent precluded in certain cases) after subsection (2) there shall be inserted the following subsection—

"(2A) For the purposes of the foregoing provisions of this Act, a judgment or order for the recovery of possession of a dwelling-house let on an assured tenancy within the meaning of Part I of the Housing Act 1988 shall be regarded as a judgment or order for the recovery of possession in default of payment of rent if the judgment or order was made on any of Grounds 8, 10 and 11 in Schedule 2 to that Act and not on any other ground."

2. For section 16 of that Act (protection of tenure of rented premises by extension of Rent Acts), as it applies otherwise than to Scotland, there shall be substituted the following section—

"Protection of tenure of certain rented premises by extension of Housing Act 1988

16.—(1) Subject to subsection (2) of section 14 of this Act and subsection (3) below, if at any time during a service man's period of residence protection—

(a) a tenancy qualifying for protection which is a fixed term tenancy ends without being continued or renewed by agreement (whether on the same or different terms and conditions), and

(b) by reason only of such circumstances as are mentioned in subsection (4) below, on the ending of that tenancy no statutory periodic tenancy of the rented family residence would arise, apart from the provisions of this section,

Chapter I of Part I of the Housing Act 1988 shall, during the remainder of the period of protection, apply in relation to the rented family residence as if those circumstances did not exist and had not existed immediately before the ending of that tenancy and, accordingly, as if on the ending of that tenancy there arose a statutory periodic tenancy which is an assured tenancy during the remainder of that period.

(2) Subject to subsection (2) of section 14 of this Act and subsection (3) below, if at any time during a service man's period of residence protection—

(a) a tenancy qualifying for protection which is a periodic tenancy would come to an end, apart from the provisions of this section, and

(b) by reason only of such circumstances as are mentioned in subsection (4) below that tenancy is not an assured tenancy, and

(c) if that tenancy had been an assured tenancy, it would not have come to an end at that time,

Chapter I of Part I of the Housing Act 1988 shall, during the remainder of the period of protection, apply in relation to the rented family residence as if those circumstances did not exist and, accordingly, as if the tenancy had become an assured tenancy immediately before it would otherwise have come to an end.

(3) Neither subsection (1) nor subsection (2) above applies if, on the ending of the tenancy qualifying for protection, a statutory tenancy arises.

(4) The circumstances referred to in subsections (1) and (2) above are any one or more of the following, that is to say,—

(a) that the tenancy was entered into before, or pursuant to a contract made before, Part I of the Housing Act 1988 came into force;

(b) that the rateable value (as defined for the purposes of that Act) of the premises which are the rented family residence, or of a property of which those premises form part, exceeded the relevant limit specified in paragraph 2 of Schedule 1 to that Act;

(c) that the circumstances mentioned in paragraph 3 or paragraph 6 of that Schedule applied with respect to the tenancy qualifying for protection; and

(d) that the reversion immediately expectant on the tenancy qualifying for protection belongs to any of the bodies specified in paragraph 12 of that Schedule."

3. For the said section 16, as it applies to Scotland, there shall be substituted the following section—

"Protection of tenure of certain rented premises by extension of Housing (Scotland) Act 1988

16.—(1) Subject to subsection (2) of section 14 of this Act and subsection (3) below, if at any time during a service man's period of residence protection—

(a) a tenancy qualifying for protection ends without being continued or renewed by agreement (whether on the same or different terms and conditions), and

(b) by reason only of such circumstances as are mentioned in subsection (4) below, on the ending of that tenancy no statutory tenancy of the rented family residence would arise, apart from the provisions of this section,

sections 12 to 31 of the Housing (Scotland) Act 1988 shall, during the remainder of the period of protection, apply in relation to the rented family residence as if those circumstances did not exist and had not existed immediately before the ending of that tenancy and, accordingly, as if on the ending of that tenancy there arose a statutory assured tenancy during the remainder of that period.

(2) Subject to subsection (2) of section 14 of this Act and subsection (3) below, if at any time during a service man's period of residence protection—

(a) a tenancy qualifying for protection would come to an end, apart from the provisions of this section,

(b) by reason only of such circumstances as are mentioned in subsection (4) below that tenancy is not an assured tenancy, and

(c) if that tenancy had been an assured tenancy, it would not have come to an end at that time,

sections 12 to 31 of the Housing (Scotland) Act 1988 shall, during the remainder of the period of protection, apply in relation to the rented family residence as if those circumstances did not exist and, accordingly, as if the tenancy had become an assured tenancy immediately before it would otherwise have come to an end.

(3) Neither subsection (1) nor subsection (2) above applies if, on the ending of the tenancy qualifying for protection, a statutory tenancy arises.

(4) The circumstances referred to in subsections (1) and (2) above are one or more of the following, that is to say—

    (a) that the circumstances mentioned in paragraph 2 of Schedule 4 to the Housing (Scotland) Act 1988 applied with respect to the tenancy qualifying for protection;

    (b) that the circumstances mentioned in paragraph 5 of that Schedule applied with respect to the tenancy qualifying for protection; and

    (c) that the reversion immediately expectant on the tenancy qualifying for protection belongs to any of the bodies specified in paragraph 11 of that Schedule."

4.—(1) Section 17 of that Act (provisions in case of rented premises which include accommodation shared otherwise than with landlord), as it applies otherwise than to Scotland, shall be amended in accordance with this paragraph.

(2) In subsection (1)—

    (a) after the words "qualifying for protection" there shall be inserted "which is a fixed term tenancy";

    (b) in paragraph (b) for the words from "subsection (2)" to "1977" there shall be substituted "section 16(4) above, subsection (1) of section 3 of the Housing Act 1988";

    (c) for the words "said section 22" there shall be substituted "said section 3"; and

    (d) at the end there shall be added "and, accordingly, as if on the ending of the tenancy there arose a statutory periodic tenancy which is an assured tenancy during the remainder of that period".

(3) For subsection (2) there shall be substituted the following subsections—

"(2) Where, at any time during a service man's period of residence protection—

    (a) a tenancy qualifying for protection which is a periodic tenancy would come to an end, apart from the provisions of this section and section 16 above, and

    (b) paragraphs (a) and (b) of subsection (1) above apply,

section 3 of the Housing Act 1988 shall, during the remainder of the period of protection, apply in relation to the separate accommodation as if the circumstances referred to in subsection (1)(b) above did not exist and, accordingly, as if the tenancy had become an assured tenancy immediately before it would otherwise have come to an end.

(3) Neither subsection (1) nor subsection (2) above applies if, on the ending of the tenancy qualifying for protection, a statutory tenancy arises."

5.—(1) The said section 17, as it applies to Scotland, shall be amended in accordance with this paragraph.

(2) In subsection (1)—

    (a) in paragraph (b) for the words from "subsection (2)" to "1977" there shall be substituted the words "section 16(4) above, subsection (1) of section 14 of the Housing (Scotland) Act 1988";

    (b) for the words "said section 97" there shall be substituted the words "said section 14"; and

    (c) at the end there shall be added the words "and, accordingly, as if on the ending of the tenancy there arose a statutory assured tenancy during the remainder of that period".

(3) For subsection (2) there shall be substituted the following subsections—

"(2) Where, at any time during a service man's period of residence protection—

    (a) a tenancy qualifying for protection would come to an end, apart from the provisions of this section and section 16 above, and

    (b) paragraphs (a) and (b) of subsection (1) above apply,

section 14 of the Housing (Scotland) Act 1988 shall, during the remainder of the period of protection, apply in relation to the separate accommodation as if the circumstances in subsection (1)(b) above did not exist and, accordingly, as if the tenancy had become an assured tenancy immediately before it would otherwise come to an end.

(3) Neither subsection (1) nor subsection (2) above applies if, on the ending of the tenancy qualifying for protection, a statutory tenancy arises."

6.—(1) In section 18 of that Act (protection of tenure, in connection with employment, under a licence or rent-free letting), in subsection (1), as it applies otherwise than to Scotland,—

    (a) for the words "Part VII of the Rent Act 1977" there shall be substituted "Chapter I of Part I of the Housing Act 1988"; and

    (b) for the words "subject to a statutory tenancy within the meaning of the Rent Act

1977" there shall be substituted "let on a statutory periodic tenancy which is an assured tenancy".

(2) In that subsection, as it applies to Scotland,—

    (a) for the words "the Rent (Scotland) Act 1971" there shall be substituted the words "sections 12 to 31 of the Housing (Scotland) Act 1988", and

    (b) for the words "subject to a statutory tenancy within the meaning of the Rent (Scotland) Act 1971" there shall be substituted the words "let on a statutory assured tenancy".

(3) Subsection (2) of that section shall be omitted.

(4) In subsection (3) of that section, as it applies otherwise than to Scotland, at the end of paragraph (c) there shall be added "or

    (d) is a dwelling-house which is let on or subject to an assured agricultural occupancy within the meaning of Part I of the Housing Act 1988 which is not an assured tenancy."

7. For section 19 of that Act (limitation on application of Rent Acts by virtue of sections 16 to 18), as it applies otherwise than to Scotland, there shall be substituted the following section—

"Limitation on application of Housing Act 1988 by virtue of sections 16 to 18

19. Where by virtue of sections 16 to 18 above, the operation of Chapter I of Part I of the Housing Act 1988 in relation to any premises is extended or modified, the extension or modification shall not affect—

    (a) any tenancy of those premises other than the statutory periodic tenancy which is deemed to arise or, as the case may be, the tenancy which is for any period deemed to be an assured tenancy by virtue of any of those provisions; or

    (b) any rent payable in respect of a period beginning before the time when that statutory periodic tenancy was deemed to arise or, as the case may be, before that tenancy became deemed to be an assured tenancy; or

    (c) anything done or omitted to be done before the time referred to in paragraph (b) above."

8. For the said section 19, as it applies to Scotland, there shall be substituted the following section—

"Limitation on application of Housing (Scotland) Act 1988 by virtue of sections 16 to 18

19. Where by virtue of sections 16 to 18 above, the operation of sections 12 to 31 of the Housing (Scotland) Act 1988 in relation to any premises is extended or modified, the extension or modification shall not affect—

    (a) any tenancy of those premises other than the statutory assured tenancy which is deemed to arise or, as the case may be, the tenancy which is for any period deemed to be an assured tenancy by virtue of any of those provisions; or

    (b) any rent payable in respect of a period beginning before the time when that statutory assured tenancy was deemed to arise or, as the case may be, before that tenancy became deemed to be an assured tenancy; or

    (c) anything done or omitted to be done before the time referred to in paragraph (b) above."

9.—(1) Section 20 of that Act (modification of Rent Acts as respects occupation by employees), as it applies otherwise than to Scotland, shall be amended in accordance with this paragraph.

(2) In subsection (1) after the words "Case I in Schedule 15 to the Rent Act 1977" there shall be inserted "or Ground 12 in Schedule 2 to the Housing Act 1988".

(3) In subsection (2) after the words "Case 8 in the said Schedule 15" there shall be inserted "or, as the case may be, Ground 16 in the said Schedule 2" and for paragraph (b) there shall be substituted the following paragraph—

    "(b) Chapter I of Part I of the Housing Act 1988 applies in relation to the premises as mentioned in section 18(1) of this Act and a dependant or dependants of the service man is or are living in the premises or in part thereof in right of the statutory periodic tenancy or assured tenancy referred to in section 19(a) of this Act".

(4) In subsection (3)—

    (a) after the words "the Cases in Part I of the said Schedule 15" there shall be inserted "or, as the case may be, Grounds 10 to 16 in Part II of the said Schedule 2"; and

    (b) after the words "section 98(1) of the Rent Act 1977" there shall be inserted "or, as the case may be, section 7(4) of the Housing Act 1988".

10.—(1) The said section 20, as it applies to Scotland, shall be amended in accordance with this paragraph.

(2) In subsection (1) after the words "Case 1 in Schedule 2 to the Rent (Scotland) Act 1984" there shall be inserted the words "or Ground 13 in Schedule 5 to the Housing (Scotland) Act 1988".

(3) In subsection (2) after the words "Case 7 in the said Schedule 2" there shall be inserted the words "or, as the case may be, Ground 17 in the said Schedule 5" and for paragraph (b) there shall be substituted the following paragraph—

"(b) sections 12 to 31 of the Housing (Scotland) Act 1988 apply in relation to the premises as mentioned in section 18(1) of this Act and a dependant or dependants of the service man is or are living in the premises or in part thereof in right of the statutory assured tenancy or assured tenancy referred to in paragraph (a) of section 19 of this Act".

(4) In subsection (3)—

(a) after the words "the Cases in Part I of the said Schedule 2" there shall be inserted the words "or, as the case may be, Grounds 10 to 17 in Part II of the said Schedule 5"; and

(b) after the words "section 11 of the Rent (Scotland) Act 1984" there shall be inserted the words "or, as the case may be, section 18(4) of the Housing (Scotland) Act 1988".

11. In section 22 of that Act (facilities for action on behalf of men serving abroad in proceedings as to tenancies), as it applies otherwise than to Scotland, in subsection (1)—

(a) after the words "Rent Act 1977" there shall be inserted "or under Part I of the Housing Act 1988";

(b) for the words "Part V of that Act" there shall be substituted "Part V of the Rent Act 1977 or Part I of the Housing Act 1988; and

(c) in paragraph (a) after the word "tenancy" there shall be inserted "or licence".

12. In the said section 22, as it applies to Scotland, in subsection (1),—

(a) for the words "Part III of the Rent Act 1965 or under the Rent (Scotland) Act 1971" there shall be substituted the words "the Rent (Scotland) Act 1984 or under Part II of the Housing (Scotland) Act 1988";

(b) for the words "rent tribunal" there shall be substituted the words "rent assessment committee" and for the words "or tribunal" there shall be substituted the words "or committee";

(c) for the words "Part VII of that Act" there shall be substituted the words "Part VII of the said Act of 1984 or under Part II of the Housing (Scotland) Act 1988"; and

(d) in paragraph (a) after the word "tenancy" there shall be inserted the words "or licence".

13.—(1) Section 23 of that Act (interpretation of Part II), as it applies otherwise than to Scotland, shall be amended in accordance with this paragraph.

(2) In subsection (1)—

(a) after the definition of "agricultural land" there shall be inserted—

" "assured tenancy" has the same meaning as in Part I of the Housing Act 1988";

(b) after the definition of "dependant" there shall be inserted—

" "fixed term tenancy" means any tenancy other than a periodic tenancy";

(c) for the definition of "landlord" and "tenant" there shall be substituted—

"in relation to a statutory tenancy or to a provision of the Rent Act 1977 "landlord" and "tenant" have the same meaning as in that Act but, subject to that, those expressions have the same meaning as in Part I of the Housing Act 1988"; and

(d) after the definition of "relevant police authority" there shall be inserted—

" "statutory periodic tenancy" has the same meaning as in Part I of the Housing Act 1988".

(3) At the end of subsection (1) there shall be inserted the following subsection—

"(1A) Any reference in this Part of this Act to Chapter I of Part I of the Housing Act 1988 includes a reference to the General Provisions of Chapter VI of that Part, so far as applicable to Chapter I."

(4) In subsection (3) after the words "Rent Act 1977" there shall be inserted "or Chapter I of Part I of the Housing Act 1988".

14.—(1) The said section 23, as it applies to Scotland, shall be amended in accordance with this paragraph.

(2) In subsection (1)—

(a) after the definition of "agricultural land" there shall be inserted—

" "assured tenancy" and "statutory assured tenancy" have the same meaning
as in Part II of the Housing (Scotland) Act 1988";
(b) for the definition of "landlord" and "tenant" there shall be substituted—
"in relation to a statutory tenancy or to a provision of the Rent (Scotland)
Act 1984 "landlord" and "tenant" have the same meaning as in that Act but,
subject to that, those expressions have the same meaning as in Part II of the
Housing (Scotland) Act 1988".
(3) At the end of subsection (1) there shall be inserted the following subsection—
"(1A) Any reference in this Part of this Act to sections 12 to 31 of the Housing
(Scotland) Act 1988 includes a reference to sections 47 to 55 of that Act so far as
applicable to those sections."
(4) In subsection (3) after the words "Rent (Scotland) Act 1984" there shall be inserted
the words "or sections 12 to 31 of the Housing (Scotland) Act 1988".

The Leasehold Reform Act 1967

15. In section 28 of the Leasehold Reform Act 1967 (retention or resumption of land
required for public purposes) at the end of subsection (5) (bodies to whom that section
applies) there shall be added "and
(g) a housing action trust established under Part III of the Housing Act 1988."
16. In section 29 of that Act (reservation of future right to develop) after subsection (6B)
there shall be inserted the following subsection—
"(6C) Subsections (1) to (4) above shall have effect in relation to a housing action
trust as if any reference in those subsections or in Part I of Schedule 4 to this Act to
a local authority were a reference to the trust."
17.—(1) In Schedule 4A to that Act (which is set out in Schedule 4 to the Housing and
Planning Act 1986 and excludes certain shared ownership leases from Part I of the 1967 Act)
at the end of paragraph 2(1) there shall be added "or to a person who acquired that interest
in exercise of the right conferred by Part IV of the Housing Act 1988".
(2) In paragraph 2(2) of that Schedule, at the end of paragraph (e) there shall be added
the following paragraph—
"(f) a housing action trust established under Part III of the Housing Act 1988".

The Town and Country Planning Act 1971

18. In section 215 of the Town and Country Planning Act 1971 (procedure for making
certain orders), in subsection (8) (definitions of "relevant area" and "local authority") after
the words "Part IV of the Local Government Act 1985" there shall be inserted "a housing
action trust established under Part III of the Housing Act 1988".

The Local Government Act 1974

19. In section 25 of the Local Government Act 1974 (local government administration:
authorities subject to investigation), in subsection (1) after paragraph (bd) there shall be
inserted the following paragraph—
"(be) any housing action trust established under Part III of the Housing Act 1988".

The Consumer Credit Act 1974

20. In section 16 of the Consumer Credit Act 1974 (exempt agreements), in subsection
(6B), in paragraph (a) after the words "England and Wales," there shall be inserted "the
Housing Corporation, Housing for Wales and".

The Rent (Agriculture) Act 1976

21. In section 28 of the Rent (Agriculture) Act 1976 (rehousing: duty of housing authority
concerned), the following subsection shall be inserted after subsection (14) of that
section—
"(14A) Notwithstanding anything in section 127(1) of the Magistrates' Courts Act
1980, an information relating to an offence under this section may be tried if it is laid
at any time within two years after the commission of the offence and within six
months after the date on which evidence sufficient in the opinion of the housing
authority concerned to justify the proceedings comes to its knowledge."

The Rent Act 1977

22. In the Rent Act 1977, sections 68 and 69, Part II of Schedule 11 and Schedule 12 (which provide for applications by a local authority for the determination of a fair rent and make provision about certificates of fair rent) shall cease to have effect except as respects applications made before the commencement of this Act.

23. In section 77 of that Act (which provides for the reference of restricted contracts to rent tribunals by the lessor, the lessee or the local authority) the words "or the local authority" shall be omitted.

24. Section 89 of the Rent Act 1977 (which provides for the phasing of progression to a registered rent in the case of housing association tenancies) and Schedule 8 to that Act (phasing of rent increases: general provisions) shall cease to have effect except with respect to an increase in rent up to, or towards, a registered rent in relation to which the relevant date for the purposes of the said Schedule 8 falls before this Act comes into force.

25. In section 137 of the Rent Act 1977 (effect on sub-tenancy of determination of superior tenancy), in subsection (1) the words "this Part of" shall be omitted.

The Protection from Eviction Act 1977

26. In section 7 of the Protection from Eviction Act 1977 (service of notices), in subsection (3)(c) (certain licensors treated as landlords for the purposes of the section) the words "under a restricted contract (within the meaning of the Rent Act 1977)" shall be omitted.

The Justices of the Peace Act 1979

27. In section 64 of the Justices of the Peace Act 1979 (disqualification in certain cases of justices who are members of local authorities) at the end of subsection (6) there shall be added the words "and a housing action trust established under Part III of the Housing Act 1988."

The Local Government, Planning and Land Act 1980

28. In Schedule 16 to the Local Government, Planning and Land Act 1980 (bodies to whom Part X applies) after paragraph 8 there shall be inserted the following paragraph—
  "8A. A housing action trust established under Part III of the Housing Act 1988."

29. In Schedule 28 to the Local Government, Planning and Land Act 1980, in paragraph 10 after the words "Rent Act 1977" there shall be inserted "or the Housing Act 1988."

The Highways Act 1980

30. In Schedule 6 to the Highways Act 1980, in Part I, in paragraph 1(3)(b)(i) after the words "Rent Act 1977" there shall be inserted "and licensees under an assured agricultural occupancy within the meaning of Part I of the Housing Act 1988".

The New Towns Act 1981

31. In section 22 of the New Towns Act 1981 (possession of houses) after the words "Rent Act 1977" there shall be inserted "or Part I of the Housing Act 1988".

The Acquisition of Land Act 1981

32.—(1) In section 12(2) of the Acquisition of Land Act 1981 after the words "Rent (Agriculture) Act 1976" there shall be inserted "or a licensee under an assured agricultural occupancy within the meaning of Part I of the Housing Act 1988".

(2) In Schedule 1 to that Act, in paragraph 3(2) after the words "Rent (Agriculture) Act 1976" there shall be inserted "or a licensee under an assured agricultural occupancy within the meaning of Part I of the Housing Act 1988".

The Matrimonial Homes Act 1983

33. In section 1(6) of the Matrimonial Homes Act 1983 (occupation of one spouse by virtue of that section treated as occupation by the other for the purposes of certain

enactments) after the words "Housing Act 1985" there shall be inserted "and Part I of the Housing Act 1988".

34.—(1) In Schedule 1 to that Act (transfer of certain tenancies on divorce, etc.), in paragraph 1—
   (a) at the end of paragraph (c) of sub-paragraph (1) there shall be inserted "or
        (d) an assured tenancy or assured agricultural occupancy, within the meaning of Part I of the Housing Act 1988"; and
   (b) in sub-paragraph (2) after the words "secure tenancy" there shall be inserted "or an assured tenancy or assured agricultural occupancy".

(2) In paragraph 2 of that Schedule (orders transferring tenancies etc. from one spouse to another)—
   (a) in sub-paragraph (1) after the words "Housing Act 1985" there shall be inserted "or an assured tenancy or assured agricultural occupancy within the meaning of Part I of the Housing Act 1988"; and
   (b) at the end of sub-paragraph (3) there shall be inserted—
      "(4) Where the spouse so entitled is for the purposes of section 17 of the Housing Act 1988 a successor in relation to the tenancy or occupancy, his or her former spouse (or, in the case of judicial separation, his or her spouse) shall be deemed to be a successor in relation to the tenancy or occupancy for the purposes of that section.
      (5) If the transfer under sub-paragraph (1) above is of an assured agricultural occupancy, then, for the purposes of Chapter III of Part I of the Housing Act 1988,—
        (a) the agricultural worker condition shall be fulfilled with respect to the dwelling-house while the spouse to whom the assured agricultural occupancy is transferred continues to be the occupier under that occupancy; and
        (b) that condition shall be treated as so fulfilled by virtue of the same paragraph of Schedule 3 to the Housing Act 1988 as was applicable before the transfer."

The County Courts Act 1984

35.—(1) In section 66 of the County Courts Act 1984 (trial by jury: exceptions), in subsection (1) at the end of paragraph (b)(iii) there shall be inserted "or
      (iv) under Part I of the Housing Act 1988".

(2) In section 77(6) of that Act (appeals: possession proceedings) after paragraph (e) there shall be inserted the following paragraph—
   "(ee) section 7 of the Housing Act 1988, as it applies to the grounds in Part II of Schedule 2 to that Act; or".

The Matrimonial and Family Proceedings Act 1984

36. In section 22 of the Matrimonial and Family Proceedings Act 1984 (powers of the court in relation to certain tenancies of dwelling-houses), in paragraph (a) after the word "tenancy" there shall be inserted "or assured agricultural occupancy".

The Local Government Act 1985

37. In section 101 of the Local Government Act 1985 (power by order to make incidental, consequential, etc. provisions) in subsection (1)(b) after second "Act" insert "or the Housing Act 1988".

The Housing Act 1985

38. In section 32(1) of the Housing Act 1985 (power to dispose of land) after "(the right to buy)" there shall be inserted "and Part IV of the Housing Act 1988 (change of landlord: secure tenants)".

39. In section 43(1) of that Act (consent required for certain disposals) after "(the right to buy)" there shall be inserted "or Part IV of the Housing Act 1988 (change of landlord: secure tenants)".

40. In section 115 of that Act (meaning of "long tenancy"), in subsection (2)(c) after "1980" there shall be inserted "or paragraph 4(2)(b) of Schedule 4A to the Leasehold Reform Act 1967".

41. In section 155 of that Act (repayment of discount on early disposal) after subsection (3) there shall be inserted the following subsection—

"(3A) Where a secure tenant has served on his landlord an operative notice of delay, as defined in section 153A,—

(a) the three years referred to in subsection (2) shall begin from a date which precedes the date of the conveyance of the freehold or grant of the lease by a period equal to the time (or, if there is more than one such notice, the aggregate of the times) during which, by virtue of section 153B, any payment of rent falls to be taken into account in accordance with subsection (3) of that section; and

(b) any reference in subsection (3) (other than paragraph (a) thereof) to the acquisition of the tenant's initial share shall be construed as a reference to a date which precedes that acquisition by the period referred to in paragraph (a) of this subsection."

42. In section 171F of that Act (subsequent dealings after disposal of dwelling-house to private sector landlord: possession on grounds of suitable alternative accommodation) after "Rent Act 1977" there shall be inserted "or on Ground 9 in Schedule 2 to the Housing Act 1988".

43. In section 236 of that Act at the end of subsection (2) (meaning of "occupying tenant") there shall be added the words "or

(e) is a licensee under an assured agricultural occupancy."

44. In section 238 of that Act (index of defined expressions in Part VII) before the entry relating to "clearance area" there shall be inserted—

"assured agricultural occupancy ... ... section 622".

45. In section 247 of that Act (notification of certain disposals of land to the local housing authority), in subsection (5) (provision not to apply to certain disposals) after paragraph (c) there shall be inserted the following paragraph—

"(ca) the grant of an assured tenancy or assured agricultural occupancy, or of a tenancy which is not such a tenancy or occupancy by reason only of paragraph 10 of Schedule 1 to the Housing Act 1988 (resident landlords) or of that paragraph and the fact that the accommodation which is let is not let as a separate dwelling".

46. In section 263 of that Act (index of defined expressions in Part VIII) before the entry relating to "clearance area" there shall be inserted—

"assured agricultural occupancy .... section 622
assured tenancy .... section 622".

47. In Part IX of that Act (slum clearance) in the following provisions relating to the recovery of possession, namely, sections 264(5), 270(3), 276 and 286(3), after the words "Rent Acts" there shall be inserted "or Part I of the Housing Act 1988".

48. In section 309 of that Act (recovery of possession of premises for purposes of approved redevelopment), in paragraph (a) of subsection (1) after the words "the Rent Act 1977)" the following words shall be inserted "or let on or subject to an assured tenancy or assured agricultural occupancy"; and in the words following paragraph (b) of that subsection after the words "section 98(1)(a) of the Rent Act 1977" there shall be inserted "or section 7 of the Housing Act 1988".

49. In section 323 of that Act (index of defined expressions in Part IX) before the entry relating to "clearance area" there shall be inserted—

"assured agricultural occupancy .... section 622
assured tenancy .... section 622".

50. In section 368 of that Act (means of escape from fire: power to secure that part of house not used for human habitation), in subsection (6) after the words "Rent Acts" there shall be inserted "or Part I of the Housing Act 1988".

51. In section 381 of that Act (general effect of control order), in subsection (3) after the words "Rent Acts" there shall be inserted "and Part I of the Housing Act 1988".

52.—(1) In section 382 of that Act (effect of control order on persons occupying house) after subsection (3) there shall be inserted the following subsection—

"(3A) Section 1(2) of and paragraph 12 of Part I of Schedule 1 to the Housing Act 1988 (which exclude local authority lettings from Part I of that Act) do not apply to a lease or agreement under which a person to whom this section applies is occupying part of the house."

(2) In subsection (4) of that section after paragraph (b) there shall be inserted or

(c) an assured tenancy or assured agricultural occupancy within the meaning of Part I of the Housing Act 1988";

and for the words "either of those Acts" there shall be substituted "any of those Acts".

53. In section 400 of that Act (index of defined expressions for Part XI) after the entry relating to "appropriate multiplier" there shall be inserted—

"assured tenancy .... section 622
assured agricultural occupancy .... section 622".

54. In section 429A of that Act (housing management: financial assistance etc.) in subsection (2), in paragraph (a) after the words "secure tenancies)" there shall be inserted "or subsection (2A)" and at the end of that subsection there shall be inserted the following subsection—

"(2A) Subsection (2)(a) applies to the following bodies—
    (a) the Housing Corporation;
    (b) Housing for Wales;
    (c) a housing trust which is a charity;
    (d) a registered housing association other than a co-operative housing   30
        association; and
    (e) an unregistered housing association which is a co-operative housing
        association."

55. In section 434 of that Act (index of defined expressions for Part XIII) there shall be inserted, in the appropriate places in alphabetical order, the following entries—

"charity .... section 622"
"co-operative housing association .... section 5(2)"
"housing association .... section 5(1)"
"housing trust" .... section 6".

56. In section 450A of that Act (right to a loan in certain cases after exercise of right to buy) in subsection (6), in the definition of "housing authority" for the words from "housing association" onwards there shall be substituted "registered housing association other than a co-operative housing association and any unregistered housing association which is a co-operative housing association; and".

57. In section 450B of that Act (power to make loans in other cases) in subsection (4), in the definition of "housing authority" for the words from "housing association" onwards there shall be substituted "registered housing association other than a co-operative housing association and any unregistered housing association which is a co-operative housing association; and".

58. In section 459 of that Act (index of defined expressions for Part XIV) after the entry relating to "building society" there shall be inserted—

"co-operative housing association ... ... section 5(2)".

59. In section 533 of that Act (assistance for owners of defective housing; exceptions to eligibility) after the words "Rent (Agriculture) Act 1976" there shall be inserted "or who occupies the dwelling under an assured agricultural occupancy which is not an assured tenancy".

60.—(1) In section 553 of that Act (effect of repurchase of defective dwellings on certain existing tenancies) in subsection (2)—

    (a) in paragraph (a) after the words "protected tenancy" there shall be inserted "or an assured tenancy";
    (b) at the end of paragraph (b) there shall be added the words "or in accordance with any of Grounds 1, 3, 4 and 5 in Schedule 2 to the Housing Act 1988 (notice that possession might be recovered under that ground) or under section 20(1)(c) of that Act (notice served in respect of assured shorthold tenancies); and"; and
    (c) after paragraph (b) there shall be added—
        "(c) the tenancy is not an assured periodic tenancy which, by virtue of section 39(7) of the Housing Act 1988 (successors under the Rent Act 1977), is an assured shorthold tenancy".

61.—(1) In section 554 of that Act (grant of tenancy of defective dwelling to former owner-occupier) at the end of subsection (2) there shall be inserted the following subsection—

    "(2A) If the authority is a registered housing association, other than a housing co-operative, within the meaning of section 27B, their obligation is to grant a secure tenancy if the individual to whom a tenancy is to be granted—
        (a) is a person who, immediately before he acquired his interest in the dwelling-house, was a secure tenant of it; or
        (b) is the spouse or former spouse or widow or widower of a person falling within paragraph (a); or
        (c) is a member of the family, within the meaning of section 186, of a person falling within paragraph (a) who has died, and was residing with that person in the

dwelling-house at the time of and for the period of twelve months before his death."

(2) In subsection (3) of that section, at the end of paragraph (b) there shall be inserted "or

(c) an assured tenancy which is neither an assured shorthold tenancy, within the meaning of Part I of the Housing Act 1988, nor a tenancy under which the landlord might recover possession on any of Grounds 1 to 5 in Schedule 2 to that Act."

62. In section 577 of that Act (index of defined expressions for Part XVI) after the entry relating to "associated arrangement" there shall be inserted—

"assured agricultural occupancy .... section 622
assured tenancy .... section 622".

63. In section 612 of that Act (exclusion of Rent Act protection) after the words "the Rent Acts" there shall be inserted "or Part I of the Housing Act 1988".

64. In section 622 of that Act (definitions: general) before the definition of "bank" there shall be inserted—

" "assured tenancy" has the same meaning as in Part I of the Housing Act 1988;
"assured agricultural occupancy" has the same meaning as in Part I of the Housing Act 1988.

65. In Schedule 2 to that Act, in Part IV (grounds for possession: suitability of alternative accommodation) in paragraph 1, at the end of sub-paragraph (b) there shall be added "or

(c) which are to be let as a separate dwelling under an assured tenancy which is neither an assured shorthold tenancy, within the meaning of Part I of the Housing Act 1988, nor a tenancy under which the landlord might recover possession under any of Grounds 1 to 5 in Schedule 2 to that Act".

66. In Schedule 5 to that Act, in paragraph 3, after the entry for section 58(2) of the Housing Associations Act 1985 there shall be inserted the following entries—

"section 50 of the Housing Act 1988 (housing association grants), or
section 51 of that Act (revenue deficit grants)."

The Landlord and Tenant Act 1985

67.—(1) In section 5 of the Landlord and Tenant Act 1985 (information to be contained in rent books), in subsection (1)(b) after the word "tenancy" there shall be inserted "or let on an assured tenancy within the meaning of Part I of the Housing Act 1988".

(2) In subsection (2) of that section after the word "tenancy" there shall be added "or let on an assured tenancy within the meaning of Part I of the Housing Act 1988".

68. In section 26 of that Act (tenants of certain public authorities excepted from provisions about service charges etc.) in subsection (3)(c) after the words "Housing Act 1980" there shall be inserted "or paragraph 4(2)(b) of Schedule 4A to the Leasehold Reform Act 1967.

The Agricultural Holdings Act 1986

69.—(1) In Schedule 3 to the Agricultural Holdings Act 1986 (cases where consent of Tribunal to operation of notice to quit is not required), in Part II (provisions applicable to Case A: suitable alternative accommodation), in paragraph 3 after paragraph (b) there shall be inserted "or

(c) premises which are to be let as a separate dwelling such that they will then be let on an assured tenancy which is not an assured shorthold tenancy (construing those terms in accordance with Part I of the Housing Act 1988), or

(d) premises to be let as a separate dwelling on terms which will afford to the tenant security of tenure reasonably equivalent to the security afforded by Chapter I of Part I of that Act in the case of an assured tenancy which is not an assured shorthold tenancy."

(2) At the end of the said paragraph 3 there shall be added the following sub-paragraph—

"(2) Any reference in sub-paragraph (1) above to an assured tenancy does not include a reference to a tenancy in respect of which possession might be recovered on any of Grounds 1 to 5 in Schedule 2 to the Housing Act 1988."

70. In Schedule 5 to that Act (notice to quit where tenant is a service man), in paragraph 2(2)(a) after the words "Rent Act 1977" there shall be inserted "or paragraph 7 of Schedule 1 to the Housing Act 1988".

The Drug Trafficking Offences Act 1986

71. In section 15 of the Drug Trafficking Offences Act 1986 (bankruptcy of defendant etc.), in subsection (2)(b) for the words "or 308" there shall be substituted "308 or 308A" and after the word "replacement" there shall be inserted "and certain tenancies".

72. In section 16 of that Act (sequestration in Scotland of defendant), in subsection (2)(b) for the words "under subsection (6) of that section" there shall be substituted the words "under subsection (10) of section 31 of that Act or subsection (6) of the said section 32 of that Act".

The Insolvency Act 1986

73. In section 308 of the Insolvency Act 1986 (vesting in trustee of certain items of excess value), in subsection (1), for the words "the next section" there shall be substituted "section 309".

74. In section 335 of that Act (adjustment between earlier and later bankruptcy estates), in subsection (4) after the words "replacement value)" there shall be inserted the words "or section 308A (vesting in trustee of certain tenancies)".

75. In section 351 of that Act (definitions), in paragraph (a) for the words "or 308" there shall be substituted", section 308" and after the words "replacement value)" there shall be inserted "or section 308A (vesting in trustee of certain tenancies)".

The Social Security Act 1986

76. In section 31 of the Social Security Act 1986 (information relating to housing benefit), in subsection (5) (information as to registered rents), after the words "housing benefit scheme" there shall be inserted "(a)", and at the end there shall be added "and

(b) where a rent is determined under section 14 or section 22 of the Housing Act 1988 or section 25 or section 34 of the Housing (Scotland) Act 1988 (determination of rents by rent assessment committee), the committee shall note in their determination the amount (if any) of the rent which, in the opinion of the committee, is fairly attributable to the provision of services, except where that amount is in their opinion negligible; and the amounts so noted may be included in the information specified in an order under section 42 of the Housing Act 1988 or, as the case may be, section 49 of the Housing (Scotland) Act 1988 (information to be publicly available)".

The Housing (Scotland) Act 1987

77. In section 12 of the Housing (Scotland) Act 1987 (which relates, amongst other things, to the disposal by local authorities of land acquired or appropriated for housing purposes and of houses)—

(a) in subsection (1)(c), for the words "subsection (5)" there shall be substituted the words "subsections (5) and (7)";

(b) in subsection (7)—
    (i) for "(1)(d)" there shall be substituted "(1)(c) or (d)";
    (ii) for the words "house or any part share thereof" there shall be substituted the words "land, house or part share thereof";
    (iii) for the words "it is a house" there shall be substituted the words ", in the case of a house, it is one";

(c) in subsection (8) after the word "apply" there shall be inserted the words ", in the case of a house,".

78. In section 13 of that Act (power of Secretary of State in certain cases to impose conditions on sale of local authority's houses etc.) for the words "land or dwelling" there shall be substituted the words "or land".

79. In section 61(4)(b) of the Housing (Scotland) Act 1987 after sub-paragraph (vi) there shall be inserted the following sub-paragraphs—
    "(vii) section 50 of the Housing Act 1988 (housing association grants); or
    (viii) section 51 of that Act (revenue deficit grants); or".

The Access to Personal Files Act 1987

80. In Schedule 1 of the Access to Personal Files Act 1987 (accessible personal information: England and Wales), in paragraph 2 at the end of sub-paragraph (2) there shall be added "and any housing action trust established under Part III of the Housing Act 1988".

The Criminal Justice (Scotland) Act 1987

81. In section 33 of the Criminal Justice (Scotland) Act 1987 (sequestration of person holding realisable property), in subsection (2)(b) for the words "under subsection (6) of that section" there shall be substituted the words "under subsection (10) of section 31 of that Act or subsection (6) of the said section 32 of that Act".

82. In section 34 of that Act (bankruptcy in England and Wales of person holding realisable property), in subsection (2)(b) for the words "or 308" there shall be substituted "308 or 308A" and after the word "replacement" there shall be inserted "and certain tenancies".

The Criminal Justice Act 1988

83. In section 84 of the Criminal Justice Act 1988 (bankruptcy of defendant etc.), in subsection (2)(b) for the words "or 308" there shall be substituted "308 or 308A" and after the word "replacement" there shall be inserted "and certain tenancies."

84. In section 85 of that Act (sequestration in Scotland of defendant), in subsection 2(b) for the words "under subsection (6) of that section" there shall be substituted the words "under subsection (10) of section 31 of that Act or subsection (6) of the said section 32 of that Act".

The Housing (Scotland) Act 1988

85. In section 19 of the Housing (Scotland) Act 1988 (notice of proceedings for possession)—
  (a) in subsection (2) for the word "is" there shall be substituted the words "and particulars of it are";
  (b) in subsection (3) after the word "one" where it first occurs there shall be inserted the words "in the prescribed form".

86. In section 36 of that Act (damages for unlawful eviction)—
  (a) in subsection (2) for the word "calculated" there shall be substituted the word "likely";
  (b) in subsection (7)(b)—
      (i) after the word "of" where it first occurs there shall be inserted the words "the doing of acts or";
      (ii) after the word "for" there shall be inserted the words "doing the acts or".

87. In section 38 of that Act (further offence of harassment)—
  (a) for the words from "In section 22" to "after subsection (2)" there shall be substituted the words—
      "(1) Subsection (2) of section 22 of the Rent (Scotland) Act 1984 (unlawful eviction and harassment of occupier) shall, as respects acts done after the commencement of this section, have effect with the substitution of the word "likely" for the word "calculated".
      (2) After that subsection";
  (b) after "(2A)" there shall be inserted the words "Subject to subsection (2B) below";
  (c) for the word "calculated" there shall be substituted the word "likely";
  (d) the words "subject to subsection (2B) below" and "by reason only of conduct falling within paragraph (b) of that subsection" shall cease to have effect;
  (e) after the word "for" where it second occurs there shall be inserted the words "doing the acts or".

88. In section 36 of that Act (damages for unlawful eviction)—
  (a) in subsection (6), for the words "proceedings are begun to enforce the liability" there shall be substituted the words "the date on which the proceedings to enforce the liability are finally decided"; and
  (b) after subsection (6) there shall be inserted the following subsections—
      "(6A) For the purposes of subsection (6)(a) above, proceedings to enforce a liability are finally decided—
      (a) if no appeal may be made against the decision in these proceedings;
      (b) if an appeal may be made against the decision with leave and the time limit for applications for leave expires and either no application has been made or leave has been refused;

(c) if leave to appeal against the decision is granted or is not required and no appeal is made within the time limit for appeals; or

(d) if an appeal is made but is abandoned before it is determined.

(6B) If, in proceedings to enforce a liability arising by virtue of subsection (3) above, it appears to the court—

(a) that, prior to the event which gave rise to the liability, the conduct of the former residential occupier or any person living with him in the premises concerned was such that it is reasonable to mitigate the damages for which the landlord would otherwise be liable, or

(b) that, before the proceedings were begun, the landlord offered to reinstate the former residential occupier in the premises in question and either it was unreasonable of the former residential occupier to refuse that offer or, if he had obtained alternative accommodation before the offer was made, it would have been unreasonable of him to refuse that offer if he had not obtained that accommodation,

the court may reduce the amount of damages which would otherwise be payable by such amount as it thinks appropriate.".

89. In section 63 of that Act (consent for subsequent disposals) after subsection (2) there shall be inserted the following subsection—

"(2A) Before giving any consent for the purposes of subsection (1) above, Scottish Homes—

(a) shall satisfy itself that the person who is seeking the consent has taken appropriate steps to consult the tenant of the house (or, as the case may be, each house) of which the property proposed to be disposed of consists; and

(b) shall have regard to the response of such tenant to that consultation."

90. In Schedule 4 to that Act (tenancies which cannot be assured tenancies) after paragraph 11 there shall be inserted the following paragraph—

"Accommodation for homeless persons

11A. A tenancy granted expressly on a temporary basis in the fulfilment of a duty imposed on a local authority by Part II of the Housing (Scotland) Act 1987."

PART II

AMENDMENTS CONSEQUENTIAL ON THE ESTABLISHMENT OF HOUSING FOR WALES

The Land Commission Act 1967

91. In section 56(4) of the Land Commission Act 1967 (bodies exempted from betterment levy) after paragraph (e) there shall be inserted the following paragraph—

"(ea) Housing for Wales".

The Parliamentary Commissioner Act 1967

92. In Schedule 2 to the Parliamentary Commissioner Act 1967 (departments etc. subject to investigation) after the entry "Housing Corporation" there shall be inserted—

"Housing for Wales".

The Income and Corporation Taxes Act 1970

93. In section 342 of the Income and Corporation Taxes Act 1970 (disposals of land between Housing Corporation and housing societies) and in section 342A of that Act (disposals by certain housing associations) after the words "Housing Corporation" in each place where they occur there shall be inserted "or Housing for Wales".

The Land Compensation Act 1973

94. In section 32(7B)(b) of the Land Compensation Act 1973 (supplementary provisions about home loss payments) after the words "Housing Corporation" there shall be inserted "or Housing for Wales".

95. In Schedule 1 to the House of Commons Disqualification Act 1975, in Part II (bodies of which all members are disqualified) there shall be inserted at the appropriate place the following entry—
      "Housing for Wales".

The Statutory Corporations (Financial Provisions) Act 1975

96. In Schedule 2 to the Statutory Corporations (Financial Provisions) Act 1975 (bodies corporate affected by section 5 of that Act as to their power to borrow in currencies other than sterling) after the entry "The Housing Corporation" there shall be inserted—
      "Housing for Wales".

The Development of Rural Wales Act 1976

97. In section 8(2) of the Development of Rural Wales Act 1976 (assistance to the Development Board for Rural Wales from public authorities and others) for the words "the Housing Corporation" there shall be substituted "Housing for Wales".

The Rent (Agriculture) Act 1976

98. In section 5(3) of the Rent (Agriculture) Act 1976 (no statutory tenancy where landlord's interest belongs to Crown or to local authority etc.) after paragraph (d) there shall be inserted the following paragraph—
      "(da) Housing for Wales".

The Rent Act 1977

99. In section 15(2)(a) of the Rent Act 1977 (landlord's interest belonging to housing association etc.) after the words "Housing Corporation" there shall be inserted—
      "(aa) Housing for Wales".
100. In each of the following provisions of that Act, that is to say, sections 86(2)(a) (tenancies to which Part VI applies), 93(1) (increase of rent without notice to quit) and Schedule 12 (certificates of fair rent), in paragraph 12 (meaning of "secure tenancy"), after the words "Housing Corporation" there shall be inserted "or Housing for Wales".

The Criminal Law Act 1977

101. In section 7(5) of the Criminal Law Act 1977 (authorities who may authorise occupation by protected intending occupier for purposes of offence of adverse occupation of residential premises) after the words "Housing Corporation" there shall be inserted—
      "(ba) Housing for Wales".

The National Health Service Act 1977

102. In section 28A(2)(e) of the National Health Service Act 1977 (power to make payments towards expenditure on community services) at the end there shall be added the following sub-paragraph "and
      (vii) Housing for Wales."
103. In section 28B(1)(b)(v) of that Act (power of Secretary of State to make payments towards expenditure on community services in Wales) for the words "the Housing Corporation" there shall be substituted "Housing for Wales".

The Local Government, Planning and Land Act 1980

104. In Schedule 16 to the Local Government, Planning and Land Act 1980 (bodies to whom Part X of that Act applies) after paragraph 9 there shall be inserted the following paragraph—
      "9a. Housing for Wales."

The Finance Act 1981

105. In section 107(3) of the Finance Act 1981 (exemption from stamp duty in case of sale of houses at discount by local authorities etc.) after paragraph (c) there shall be inserted the following paragraph—
"(ca) Housing for Wales."

The Housing Act 1985

106. In the Housing Act 1985 for the words "Housing Corporation" in each place where they occur there shall be substituted "Corporation".

107. In Part I of that Act (introductory provisions—authorities and bodies other than local housing authorities) after section 6 there shall be inserted the following section—
"6A. In this Act "the Corporation" has the meaning assigned by section 2A of the Housing Associations Act 1985."

108. In section 57 of that Act (index of defined expressions: Part II) after the entry relating to "compulsory disposal" there shall be inserted—
"the Corporation   section 6A".

109. In section 117 of that Act (index of defined expressions: Part IV) after the entry relating to "co-operative housing association" there shall be inserted—
"the Corporation   section 6A".

110. In section 188 of that Act (index of defined expressions: Part V) after the entry relating to "co-operative housing association" there shall be inserted—
"the Corporation   section 6A".

111. In section 238 of that Act (index of defined expressions: Part VII) after the entry relating to "clearance area" there shall be inserted—
"the Corporation   section 6A".

112. In section 459 of that Act (index of defined expressions: Part XIV) after the entry relating to "building society" there shall be inserted—
"the Corporation   section 6A".

113. In section 577 of that Act (index of defined expressions: Part XVI) after the entry relating to "co-operative housing association" there shall be inserted—
"the Corporation   section 6A".

The Landlord and Tenant Act 1987

114. In section 58(1) of the Landlord and Tenant Act 1987 (exempt landlords) after paragraph (e) there shall be inserted the following paragraph—
"(ea) Housing for Wales".

The Income and Corporation Taxes Act 1988

115. In section 376(4) of the Income and Corporation Taxes Act 1988 (qualifying borrowers and lenders) after paragraph (k) there shall be inserted the following paragraph—
"(ka) Housing for Wales."

116. In section 560(2)(e) of that Act (persons who are sub-contractors or contractors for the purposes of Chapter IV of Part XIII of that Act) after the words "Housing Corporation" there shall be inserted "Housing for Wales".

GENERAL NOTE
Paras. 1–14. These adapt the Reserve and Auxiliary Forces (Protection of Civil Interests) Act 1951 to reflect the private sector changes in Part I of this Act.

Paras. 15, 16. These add housing action trusts under Part III to those landlords who can resist the exercise of rights under the Leasehold Reform Act 1967 in certain circumstances and who can reserve a right of future development.

Para. 17. "Shared ownership leases" granted by specified public bodies are excluded from the operation of the enfranchisement and extension provisions of the Leasehold Reform Act 1967 by Sched. 4A, added by s.18 of and Sched. 4 to the Housing and Planning Act 1986. These amendments add housing action trusts under Part III of this Act to those bodies and landlords who purchased under Part IV of this Act.

Para. 18. Various orders can be made by the Secretary of State, pursuant to ss.209–212 and 214 of the Town and Country Planning Act 1971, relating to works or, or the extinction of rights over, highways and other land, and *ibid,* s.215 governs the procedure the Secretary of State must follow before making such an order, to bring the proposal to the attention of persons in a relevant area, now defined to include the area of a housing action trust under Part III of this Act, who are also defined as a local authority for the purposes of objecting to such proposal.

Para. 19. Housing action trusts are to come within the jurisdiction of the Commissioner for Local Administration, *i.e.* the Local Government Ombudsman.

Paras. 22, 23. Hitherto, local authorities have enjoyed the right of their own motion to refer rents under protected or statutory tenancies, or under restricted contracts, to the rent officer or rent tribunal, either in order to keep rents down for the purpose of housing benefit, or to avoid the increased friction that can flow from a tenant's own reference. In the event, the powers go entirely.

Para. 24. Rent increases under Part VI of the Rent Act 1977, governing housing association rents, are "phased" over two years. Save where the phasing is referable to a registration pre-dating this Act, phasing now ceases.

Para. 25. The Rent Act 1977, s.137, preserves the protection of a protected sub-tenant where the protected mesne tenancy is determined by an order of a court, and effects a direct tenancy between a sub-tenant and a mesne tenant's landlord. This is a minor, technical amendment.

Para. 27. By s.64 of the Justices of the Peace Act 1979, members of local authorities are disqualified from sitting in the magistrates' court or in the Crown Court in relation to cases and appeals brought by or against their own authority; the disqualification now extends to members of housing action trusts under Part III of this Act. This would in any event be the position following *R.* v. *Smethwick Justices, ex p. Hands, The Times,* December 3, 1980.

Para. 28. Housing action trusts are public bodies in relation to whom the Secretary of State has power to direct the disposal of "underused' land, under Part X of the Local Government Planning and Land Act 1980.

Para. 29. Sched. 28 to the Local Government, Planning and Land Act 1980, governs land acquisition by urban development corporations and its para. 10 permits the Secretary of State by certification to override the security of tenure afforded by the Rent Acts and, now, Part I of this Act.

Para. 30. Tenants for a period of less than one month, or periodic tenants with tenancies less than monthly, are not entitled to notice under Sched. 6 to the Highways Act 1980, and statutory tenants under both the Rent Act 1977 and the Rent (Agriculture) Act 1976, are treated as such, as, now, are licensees under assured agricultural occupancies under Part I of this Act.

Para. 31. The Secretary of State may certify that possession of a house which has been acquired for the purposes of the New Towns Act 1981 by either a development corporation or a local highway authority, and is for the time being held by it for the purposes for which acquired, is immediately required for those purposes, in which case possession may be recovered notwithstanding anything in the Rent Act 1977, the Rent (Agriculture) Act 1976 or, now, Part I of this Act.

Para. 32. This makes the same provision as para. 24, above, in relation to s.12 of the Acquisition of Land Act 1981, where an acquisition is by a local or other public authority; Sched. 1 makes the same provision where a Minister is the acquiring authority.

Para. 33. The occupation of one spouse is treated as the occupation of the other, pursuant to s.1 of the Matrimonial Homes Act 1983, for the purposes of the statutes conferring protection on tenants, which require personal occupation by the tenant: Rent Act 1977, Rent (Agriculture) Act 1976, Part IV, Housing Act 1985. This is to ensure that a tenancy is not lost by the departure (and therefore non-occupation) of a tenant-spouse: see notes to s.9(5), above. It is essential that the property has been the matrimonial home, if the protection of s.1(6) is to apply: *Hall* v. *King* (1987) 19 H.L.R. 440, C.A. In the event, s.1(6) is now extended to Part I of this Act, so that the occupation of an assured tenant's spouse will count as his: see, further, notes to s.1, above.

Paras. 34, 36. These permit transfer of an assured tenancy or assured agricultural occupancy on, and in certain circumstances (see notes to s.9(5), above) after, divorce, from one spouse to another, under the Matrimonial Homes Act 1983, and provide that if the transferor spouse is a successor (see s.17, above), so also will be the transferee, and make analogous provisions under the Matrimonial and Family Proceedings Act 1984.

Para. 38. Local authorities require the consent of the Secretary of State to dispose of land held under Part II of the Housing Act 1985, other than where the disposal is pursuant to Part V, *i.e.* the right to buy, and, now, pursuant to Part IV of this Act. See notes to s.133, above.

Para. 39. The Housing Act 1985, s.43, introduces a consent requirement referable to property held other than under Part II, where there is occupation by a secure tenant, or a long lease granted under Part V, but not if the disposal is pursuant to Part V itself or, now, Part IV of this Act. See notes to s.133, above.

Para. 40. This defines long tenancy for the purposes of Parts IV and V of the Housing Act 1985, but excludes certain "shared ownership" leases: *cf.* notes to para. 17, above.

Para. 41. This is an important amendment, hardly "consequential". Where a tenant is entitled to have rent payments treated additionally as payment on account of purchase, under s.124, above, all the periods for which this is so which precede the purchase are added together and deducted from the three-year period during which, following purchase, there can be no disposal (other than an exempt disposal) without repayment of discount. Thus, if one year of such payments accrues, repayment of discount is only applicable for two years after purchase, and furthermore will presume one year's occupation, so that (in this example) one-third of the discount is not repayable.

Para. 42. The 1985 Act, s.171F (part of the "preserved right to buy"—see notes to s.81, above) restricts possession against a Rent Act protected tenant on the ground of suitable alternative accommodation, unless the court is satisfied that the preserved right to buy will continue to be exercisable (in relation to the new dwelling), save where the new tenancy will itself be (again) secure; this amendment makes the same provision where suitable alternative accommodation is offered under Part I of this Act.

Para. 43. This amendment adds licensees under an assured agricultural occupancy to the class of occupying tenant whose actions may result in an improvement notice under the Housing Act 1985, Part VII.

Para. 45. Owners of property in housing action areas under Part VIII of the Housing Act 1985, have to notify the local authority of "disposals", but *not* of certain classes of disposal, which already includes protected tenancies and occupancies and now includes assured tenancies or assured agricultural occupancies or what would be such but for Sched. 1, para. 10, above, or of that para. *and* the fact that the letting is not as a separate dwelling (see notes to s.1, above).

Para. 47. In relation to slum clearance action under Part IX of the 1985 Act (whether individual house or area), in certain circumstances Rent Act protection is automatically "lifted" (*i.e.* where continued occupation would conflict with the slum clearance action), and, now, protection under Part I of this Act.

Para. 48. Some classes of Part IX action can be avoided by an owner voluntarily undertaking an approved redevelopment scheme under the 1985 Act, s.108, which can entitle the owner to recover possession against a protected tenant and, now, an assured tenancy or assured agricultural occupancy.

Para. 50. This is similar to the amendments in para. 47, above, relating to the closure of a part of a house in order to render its means of escape from fire adequate.

Paras. 51 and 52. When a control order is made under Part XI of the 1985 Act (houses in multiple occupation), the local authority take over and manage the property, but without prejudice to the Rent Act protection of existing occupiers or, now, their protection under Part I of this Act.

Para. 54. Grants may be made available to those managing public sector housing; these amendments reflect that some public sector housing will now not be on secure tenancies.

Paras. 55–64. These are all truly incidental provisions.

Para. 65. Without this amendment, it would be very difficult for a housing association to continue to bring any proceedings for possession under the Housing Act 1985 which are dependent on the provision of suitable alternative accommodation, for whether or not the "new" tenancy will be assured or secure is essentially a matter for the court's discretion (see notes to s.34(5), above). This amendment permits an assured tenancy to be "offered" as suitable alternative accommodation (even if the court directs that it shall be secure), provided it is neither an assured shorthold, nor one subject to the specified, mandatory grounds under this Act.

Para. 66. Sched. 5 exempts certain lettings from the right to buy including, by para. 3, housing association property which has not been publicly funded. This amendment reflects the replacement of grants under Part II of this Act.

Para. 67. By s.4 of the Landlord and Tenant Act 1985, a "rent book or other similar document" must be provided to a tenant with a right to occupy premises as a residence in consideration of a rent payable weekly (*cf. R.* v. *Ewing* (1977) 65 Cr.App.R. 4; the basis is how the rent is *paid*, not calculated, so that a rent calculated on a weekly basis but payable fortnightly or monthly would not qualify, while a rent calculated per annum, or, *e.g.* per month, but payable weekly would do so). By *ibid.*, s.5, information may be prescribed for inclusion in the rent book (or similar document), where the tenancy is let on a restricted contract, or a protected or statutory tenancy or, now, an assured tenancy. Similarly, such information must be in prescribed form.

Para. 68. This *includes* long tenancies within service charge provisions where the landlord is a public authority, where shorter tenancies are exempt. This amendment concerns the disqualification of certain shared ownership leases from the definition of long tenancy for this purpose: see also notes to paras. 17 and 40, above.

Section 140   SCHEDULE 18

ENACTMENTS REPEALED

Chapter	Short title	Extent of repeal
14 & 15 Geo. VI c.65.	The Reserve and Auxilliary Forces (Protection of Civil Interests) Act 1951.	Section 18(2).
1976 c.80.	The Rent (Agriculture) Act 1976.	In section 4(2) the words "or, as the case may be, subsection (4)."
		In section 13(3) the words "68, 69" and "or Part II of Schedule 11 or Schedule 12 to that Act."
1977 c.42.	The Rent Act 1977.	In Schedule 4, in Part I, paragraph 2(2).
		Section 16A.
		Sections 19 to 21.
		In section 63, in subsection (1), paragraph (b) and the word "and" immediately preceding it; in subsection (2) in paragraph (a), the words "and deputy rent officers", in paragraph (b), the words "or deputy rent officer", in paragraph (d) the words "and deputy rent officers" and the word "and" at the end of the paragraph, and paragraph (e); in subsection (3), the words "and deputy rent officers"; and in subsection (7)(b), the words "and deputy rent officers".
		In section 67, in subsection (5), the words "and sections 68 and 69 of this Act" and in subsection (7), the words "Subject to section 69(4) of this Act."
		Sections 68 and 69.
		In section 74, in subsection (2), in paragraph (a) "69", in paragraph (b) the words "or II" and paragraph (c).
		In section 77(1) the words "or the local authority".
		In section 80(1) the words "or the local authority".
		Section 81A(1)(a).
		In section 87, in subsection (2), in paragraph (a) "69" and in paragraph (c) the words "and 12".
		In section 88(2) the words "then, subject to section 89 of this Act".
		Section 89.
		In section 103(1) the words "or the local authority".
		In section 137 the words "this Part of".
		In Schedule 1, in paragraph 1 the words "or, as the case may be, paragraph 3", in paragraph 4, the words "or 3", and paragraph 7.
		In Schedule 2, paragraph 6(3).
		Schedule 8.
		In Schedule 11, Part II.

Chapter	Short title	Extent of repeal
1977 c.42— cont.	The Rent Act 1977—*cont.*	Schedule 12. In Schedule 14, paragraph 4. In Schedule 15, in Part IV, paragraph 4(2). In Schedule 20, paragraph 2(2). In Schedule 24, paragraph 8(3).
1977 c.43.	The Protection from Eviction Act 1977.	In section 7(3)(c) the words from "under" to "1977)".
1980 c.51.	The Housing Act 1980.	Section 52. Sections 56 to 58. Section 59(1). Section 60. Section 73(2). Section 76(2). In Schedule 9, paragraph 2. In Schedule 10, paragraph 2. In Schedule 25, paragraph 36, in paragraph 40 "68(4)" and paragraphs 46 and 63.
1985 c.51.	The Local Government Act 1985.	In Schedule 13, in paragraph 21, the words from "and section 19(5)(aa)" onwards.
1985 c.68.	The Housing Act 1985.	In section 80, in subsection (1) the words from "the Housing Corporation" to "charity or", the words "housing association or" and subsection (2). Sections 199 to 201. In Schedule 5, in paragraph 3 the words "or" immediately following the entry for section 55 of the Housing Associations Act 1985; paragraphs 6 and 8.
1985 c.69.	The Housing Associations Act 1985.	In section 3(2) the words "of housing associations maintained under this section". In section 18(3) the words from "and the Corporation" onwards. In section 40, the entries relating to housing association grant and revenue deficit grant. Sections 41 to 57. Section 62. In section 73, the entries relating to approved development programme, hostel deficit grant, housing association grant, housing project, revenue deficit grant, shared ownership agreement and shared ownership lease. Section 75(1)(d). In section 87(1) the words "registered housing associations and other". In section 107, in subsection (3) the entries relating to sections 4, 44 and 45 and 52, and in subsection (4) the words "section 4(3)(h)". In Schedule 5, in paragraph 5(3) of Part I and in paragraph 5(3) of Part II, the words "at such times and in such places as the Treasury may direct, and" and the words "with the approval of the Treasury". In Schedule 6, paragraph 3(3)(b).

Chapter	Short title	Extent of repeal
1986 c.63.	The Housing and Planning Act 1986.	Section 7. Section 12. In section 13, subsections (1) to (3) and (5). Section 19. In Schedule 4, paragraphs 1(3) and 10. In Schedule 5, paragraph 8.
1986 c.65.	The Housing (Scotland) Act 1986.	Section 13(1). Sections 14 to 16. In Schedule 2, in paragraph 4(8), sub-paragraph (a) and, in sub-paragraph (b), the words "section 4(3)(h)".
1987 c.26.	The Housing (Scotland) Act 1987.	In section 61(4)(b) the word "or" at the end of sub-paragraph (v) and at the end of sub-paragraph (vi).
1987 c.31.	The Landlord and Tenant Act 1987.	In section 3(1)(b) the word "or". Section 4(2)(a)(ii). Section 45. Section 60(2). In Schedule 4, paragraph 7.
1988 c.9.	The Local Government Act 1988.	Section 24(5)(b).
1988 c.43.	The Housing (Scotland) Act 1988.	Section 4(4). In section 38, the words "subject to sub-section (2B) below" and "by reason only of conduct falling within paragraph (b) of that subsection". Schedule 3. In Schedule 9, paragraphs 6(b) and 7. In Schedule 10, the entry relating to the Housing Associations Act 1985.

1. The repeal of sections 19 to 21 of the Rent Act 1977 does not apply with respect to any tenancy or contract entered into before the coming into force of Part I of this Act nor to any other tenancy or contract which, having regard to section 36 of this Act, can be a restricted contract.

2. The repeal of section 52 of the Housing Act 1980 (protected shorthold tenancies) does not apply with respect to any tenancy entered into before the coming into force of Part I of this Act nor to any other tenancy which, having regard to section 34 of this Act, can be a protected shorthold tenancy.

3. The repeal of sections 56 to 58 of the Housing Act 1980 does not have effect in relation to any tenancy to which, by virtue of section 37(2) of this Act, section 1(3) of this Act does not apply.

4. The repeals in section 80 of the Housing Act 1985—

    (a) have effect (subject to section 35(5) of this Act) in relation to any tenancy or licence entered into before the coming into force of Part I of this Act unless, immediately before that time, the landlord or, as the case may be, the licensor is a body which, in accordance with the repeals, would cease to be within the said section 80; and

    (b) do not have effect in relation to a tenancy or licence entered into on or after the coming into force of Part I of this Act if the tenancy or licence falls within any of paragraphs (c) to (f) of subection (4) of section 35 of this Act.

INDEX

References are to section and Schedule number

ACCESS,
  repairs, for, 16
ACCOMMODATION,
  local housing authority tenant, assistance
    in obtaining, 129
  rented. *See* RENTED ACCOMMMODATION.
  right to buy. *See* RIGHT TO BUY.
  shared, 10
  suitable alternative, provision of, Sched.
    2
ACCOUNTS,
  housing action trust, Sched. 8
AGENCY,
  housing action trust, agreement with, 87
AGRICULTURAL OCCUPANCY,
  assured. *See* ASSURED AGRICULTURAL
    OCCUPANCY.
  new, restriction to special cases, 34
AGRICULTURAL WORKER,
  conditions, Sched. 3
  eviction, 30
AGRICULTURE,
  meaning, 24
ASSIGNMENT,
  without consent, limited prohibition on,
    15
ASSURED AGRICULTURAL OCCUPANCY,
  eviction, 33
  meaning, 24
  security of tenure, 25
ASSURED SHORTHOLD TENANCY,
  expiry, recovery of possession on, 21
  meaning, 20
  possession, recovery of, 21
  rent assessment committee,
    excessive rent, reference of, 22
    termination of functions, 23
  termination, recovery of possession on, 21
ASSURED TENANCY,
  assignment without consent, limited pro-
    hibition on, 15
  compensation,
    concealment, for, 12
    misrepresentation, for, 12
  dwelling-house let with other land, 2
  eviction, 33
  landlord, tenant sharing with person other
    than, 3
  meaning, 1
  possession,
    claim, extended discretion of court, 9
    notice of proceedings for, 8
    orders for, 7
  precluded from being, 1
  prevention of creation, 37
  removal expenses, payment of, 11
  rent,
    assured periodic tenancy, increase
      under, 13

ASSURED TENANCY—*cont.*
  rent—*cont.*
    distress for, restriction on levy of, 19
    rent assessment committee, determina-
      tion by, 14
  repairs, access for, 16
  reversion on, 18
  security of tenure, 5
  shared accommodation, 10
  spouse, succession by, 17
  statutory periodic tenancy, fixing of terms,
    6
  sub-lessor's premises, exclusion of, 4
  tenancy which cannot be,
    agricultural holdings, Sched. 1
    agricultural land, Sched. 1
    business tenancy, Sched. 1
    commencement, tenancy entered into
      before, Sched. 1
    crown tenancy, Sched. 1
    high rateable value, dwelling-house
      with, Sched. 1
    holiday lettings, Sched. 1
    licensed premises, Sched. 1
    local authority tenancy, Sched. 1
    low rent, tenancy at, Sched. 1
    rateable values, Sched. 1
    resident landlords, Sched. 1
    student lettings, Sched. 1

BANKRUPT'S ESTATE,
  certain tenancies excluded from, 117
BUY, RIGHT TO. *See* RIGHT TO BUY.

CAPITAL MONEY,
  disposal of land, application to meet costs
    of, 136
CHANGE OF LANDLORD. *See* LANDLORD.
CODES OF PRACTICE,
  rented housing, 137
COMPENSATION,
  concealment, for, 12
  misrepresentation, for, 12
COMPLETION,
  change of landlord, 104
CONCEALMENT,
  compensation for, 12
CONSENT TO CHANGE OF LANDLORD. *See*
    LANDLORD.
CONSULTATION,
  change of landlord, 102
  housing action trust, 61
  housing stock, disposal of, 135, Sched. 1
CONTRACT,
  new restricted, limit to transitional cases
    36
CORPORATION. *See* HOUSING CORPORATION.
COSTS,
  land, disposal of, 136

Index

HOUSING ACTION TRUST—*cont.*
  House of Commons disqualification, Sched. 7
  housing authority, as, 65
  information, 90
  instruments, Sched. 7
  land,
    acquisition of, 77, 78, Sched. 10
    compensation, 78
    disposal of, 79
    extinguishment of rights, Sched. 10
    transfer of, 74, 75
    vesting by order in, 76, 78, Sched. 9
  meetings, Sched. 7
  members, Sched. 7
  objects, 63
  planning authority, as, 67
  planning control, 66
  proceedings, Sched. 7
  property, transfer of, 74, 75
  proposals for area, 64
  public health functions, 68
  publicity, 61
  remuneration, Sched. 7
  rent,
    generally, 85
    increase where tenancy not secure, 86
  right to buy, 83
  secure tenancy, 83, 84
  service of notices, 91
  services, supply of, 89
  staff, Sched. 7
  transfer orders, 74, 75
  vesting by order in, 76, 78
HOUSING ASSOCIATION,
  grants. *See* GRANTS.
  Housing Acts, application of, 58
  meaning, 48
  permissible purposes, objects or powers, 48
  registered, management by, 49
  surplus rental income, 55
  tenancy, removal of special regimes, 35
  Wales. *See* HOUSING FOR WALES.
HOUSING AUTHORITY,
  housing action trust as, 65
  See also LOCAL HOUSING AUTHORITY.
HOUSING BENEFIT,
  rent officer, additional functions of, 121
HOUSING CORPORATION,
  change of landlord. *See* LANDLORD.
  determinations, 53
  grants,
    housing association, 50
    recovery of, 52
    revenue deficit, 51
  Housing Associations Act 1985, amendments of, Sched. 6
  legal assistance, 82
  racial discrimination, duty relating to, 56
  Secretary of State, delegation of functions by, 57
HOUSING FOR WALES,
  allowances, Sched. 5
  chairman, Sched. 5
  creation of, 46
  deputy chairman, Sched. 5
  determinations, 53

HOUSING FOR WALES—*cont.*
  grants, 50
  Housing Associations Act 1985, amendments of, Sched. 6
  legal assistance, 82
  membership, Sched. 5
  pensions, Sched. 5
  proceedings, Sched. 5
  racial discrimination, duty relating to, 56
  registration, transfer of, 47
  remuneration, Sched. 5
  revenue deficit grants, 51
  staff, Sched. 5
  status, Sched. 5
HOUSING STOCK,
  disposal,
    charge on house, obligation to repay, Sched. 11
    compulsory, Sched. 11
    consent to, 132
    consultation before, 135, Sched. 16
    early, repayment of discount on, Sched. 11
    exempted, Sched. 11
    options, treatment of, Sched. 11
    receipts, application of, 132
    relevant, Sched. 11
    subsequent, consent required for, 133, 134
  See also RIGHT TO BUY.

IMPROVEMENT GRANTS,
  letting conditions applicable to, 131
INCOME,
  surplus rental, 55
INDIVIDUAL,
  assured tenancy, 1
INFORMATION,
  housing action trust, 90
  local authorities, powers of, 43
  rent assessment committee, powers of, 4?
  rent, as to determination of, 42
ISLES OF SCILLY,
  application to, 139

LAND,
  disposal of, application of capital money to meet costs, housing action trust 136
  acquisition by, 77, 78, Sched. 10
  compensation, 78
  disposal by, 79
  extinguishment of rights, Sched. 10
  transfer to, 74, 75
  vesting by order in, 76, 78, Sched. 9
  other, dwelling-house let with, 2
LANDLORD,
  change of,
    advice, 106
    application to exercise right, 96
    assistance, 106
    completion,
      consequences of, 104
      duty to complete, 104
    consultation, 102
    county court, jurisdiction of, 113

[3]